HISTORIES

THE NEW PRESS POSTWAR FRENCH
THOUGHT SERIES

RAMONA NADDAFF
SERIES EDITOR

Histories, edited by Jacques Revel and Lynn Hunt

Histories

FRENCH CONSTRUCTIONS
OF THE PAST

EDITED BY

JACQUES REVEL

AND

LYNN HUNT

TRANSLATED BY

ARTHUR GOLDHAMMER AND OTHERS

POSTWAR FRENCH THOUGHT, VOLUME I

RAMONA NADDAFF, SERIES EDITOR

THE NEW PRESS

NEW YORK

Library of Congress Catalog Card Number 95-71802
ISBN 1-56584-195-6

Published in the United States by The New Press, New York
Distributed by W. W. Norton & Company, Inc., New York

Established in 1990 as a major alternative to the large, commercial
publishing houses, The New Press is the first full-scale nonprofit
American book publisher outside of the university presses. The Press
is operated editorially in the public interest, rather than for private
gain; it is committed to publishing in innovative ways works of educational, cultural, and community value that, despite their intellectual
merits, might not normally be commercially viable. The New Press's
editorial offices are located at the City University of New York.

Book design by Charles Nix

Production management by Kim Waymer
Printed in the United States of America

95 96 97 98   9 8 7 6 5 4 3 2 1

Contents

PART II

THE STRUCTURALIST MOMENT (MID-1960s TO MID-1970s)

PART IV

CRITICISMS AND REFORMULATIONS

Series Preface

Histories: French Reconstructions of the Past, edited by Jacques Revel and
Lynn Hunt, inaugurates The New Press's Postwar French Thought
series, with future volumes on Classical Studies (Nicole Loraux, Gregory
Nagy, and Laura Slatkin), Literary Criticism (Denis Holier and Jeffrey
Mehlman), and Philosophy (Etienne Balibar and John Rajchman). The
aim of this series is to produce a multi-volume anthology of seminal
writings since 1945 that reflects the theoretical innovations and richness
of French thought. Rather than reproduce excerpts of the canon of
French authors, articles, and books already known to an English-speaking audience, the editors intend to generate, from the unique perspective
of the Franco-American teams selecting texts, a new history of ideas
proper to each discipline. Moreover, the collaboration of French and
American editors has set in motion a productive dialectic which engaged
them in the rethinking of their own disciplines. The resulting history
will necessarily include texts and authors with whom specialists and
non-specialists alike are familiar. But the context and problematics
within which editors situate them will allow for the inclusion of other
forgotten and unknown writings and thinkers whose dynamic influence
has been ignored by previous critics.

This series began in conversation with André Schiffrin in 1990. Two
"events" on the international political and cultural scene particularly
motivated our thinking about the need to publish these volumes: the end
of the Cold War and the Culture Wars in America. The revolutions of
1989 not only reshaped the ways in which both Eastern and Western
European countries reflected on their intellectual and cultural legacies,
they also created the very real need for programs that secured the publication of texts hitherto unavailable in most of Eastern Europe. To collect
disparate texts from different disciplines, first in English translation and
ultimately in Eastern European languages, will form part of a timely
intellectual and political project.

Across the Atlantic, the beginning of the 1990s in America witnessed
both the rise and fall of the Canon and Culture Wars. Old canons had
been broken down while new ones emerged in their place. Vehement
and vigilant voices dismissed the interventions from France as confusing
and obfuscating the venerable tradition of Western humanism, while

others understood "French" thought to be the means by which the Western canon could be both subverted and rejuvenated. In short, each group had constructed their own canon of quintessentially French thought. While the volumes in this series will together construct a history that is only one of many possible histories, it is our hope that the plurality of voices and trends evident throughout the series will make such monolithic characterizations of French thought less plausible.

In the tradition of interdisciplinary collaboration and collective research discussed by Jacques Revel in his introduction to *Histories,* many people from different fields have been supportive and influential in helping me to think about this series as a whole: Caroline Bynum, François Dosse, Eric Fassin, Michel Feher, Arthur Goldhammer, Patrick Geary, J.-P. Gorin, Leigh Hafrey, Steven Kaplan, Nicole Loraux, Peter Sahlins, and Eric Vigne. Invaluable editorial support on this first volume came from Jessica Blatt, Ted Byfield, Denise Clegg, Tanya Erzen, Grace Farrell, Meighan Gale, Jean Poderos, Matthew Weiland, and Lara Young. André Schiffrin has been a constant advisor, interlocutor and innovator for whom I am most grateful and appreciative. Finally, I thank Lynn Hunt and Jacques Revel who in their very composition of this first volume gave shape to the volumes to come.

RAMONA NADDAFF

Acknowledgments

This book grew out of a proposal by publisher André Schiffrin, who for thirty years has played a key role in intellectual exchanges between France and the United States. He thus had no trouble persuading us to participate in his project: a series of books which would present to an American readership, without oversimplification or intellectual sloth, certain aspects of French intellectual history since World War II. We were convinced of the need for such a series by our own personal experience. (It may be worth mentioning in passing, that we are also convinced of the need for comparable works to inform French and other European readers about the complexity and subtlety of American intellectual trajectories.)

Having begun her career as a specialist in the French Revolution, Lynn Hunt has for the past twenty years had to deal with one of the most distinctive, and controversial, features of French experience (although the exceptionality of that experience has recently been subjected to serious scrutiny). And as a frequent visitor to American universities and a scholar with a professional interest in questions of historiography, Jacques Revel has had ample opportunity to measure, in his contacts with students and colleagues, the difficulties and ambiguities of what might appear to be a relatively uncomplicated cultural transference. In the 1970s and 1980s, when the *Annales* model was constantly invoked on the American side of the Atlantic, exchanges were rich and misunderstandings were numerous. Both of us, along with many others, participated in these genuine, if sometimes frustrating, dialogues. From Berkeley to the East Coast to Paris our personal relationship can attest to this: much of it involved translating, explaining, and clarifying what made sense in one of our cultures while threatening to generate a specious kind of sense in the other. We were therefore prepared to take seriously the task that was proposed to us, and we have worked together with the pleasure not only of friendship but also of learning, because we began with different interpretations and have tried to take advantage of what separated us.

Although we undertook this project jointly and the resulting book presents our shared understanding of the issues, we did not divide all the tasks equally. At Lynn Hunt's urging, Jacques Revel wrote the introduction; he was already in the midst of writing a book about the *Annales*, and it seemed sensible to present as consistent an argument as possible about this very large and often controversial subject. Although one or the other of us wrote the preliminary drafts to introduce each selection, we consulted extensively on the final versions and have not therefore identified each one by a single name.

Various colleagues helped us with their reactions to a preliminary outline: Natalie Davis, Bernard Lepetit, and Patricia O'Brien offered suggestions that proved very useful in refining our concept of the whole. Ramona Naddaff first approached us with the general idea for this book and consulted with us on many occasions about its direction; at key moments, she helped push things forward, especially on the production end, and we are very grateful to her for what she has done. Editing a disparate assortment of documents always raises a multitude of questions; Jeff Horn, Denise Davidson, and Caroline Kaufmann provided invaluable help in tracking down references, citations, and translations.

We hope that this collection will give readers some sense of why French historical writing since World War II has attracted so much interest, not only in France among a very wide public, not only in the West, but all over the world. This is the story of a great intellectual adventure, and we hope that we have captured some of that indomitable, enthusiastic, and inspired spirit.

JACQUES REVEL AND LYNN HUNT

Permissions

Roland Mousnier, Albert Soboul, and Ernest Labrousse's "Description and Measurement in Social History: A Discussion" used by permission of Presses Universitaires de France.

Roland Mousnier, J.-P. Labatut, and Y. Durand's "Problems of Social Stratification" used by permission of Presses Universitaires de France.

Denis Richet's "The Ideological Origins of the French Revolution" used by permission of Editions de l'Ecole des Hautes Etudes en Sciences Sociales.

Albert Soboul's "Classical Revolutionary Historiography and Revisionist Endeavors" used by permission of Betty Smith, International Publishers.

Alphonse Dupront's "Pilgrimage and Sacred Places" from *Pèlerinages et lieux sacrés* © Editions Gallimard 1987.

Pierre Chaunu's "Long-term Factors in Seventeenth-century Society and Civilization: Demographics" from Pierre Chaunu, *Histoire quantitative, histoire sérielle, Cahier des Annales* (Armand Colin S.A., 1978). Used by permission of Armand Colin S.A, Paris.

Claude Lévi-Strauss's "Scientific Criteria in the Social and Human Disciplines" from Claude Lévi-Strauss, "Critères scientifiques dans les disciplines sociales et humaines," *Revue internationale des sciences sociales* 16 (1964). Used by permission of International Social Science Journal.

Louis Althusser's "Reply to John Lewis." Copyright © 1972 by NLB/ Verso. Reprinted by permission of Monthly Review Foundation.

Michel Foucault's "The Archaeology of Knowledge: Introduction" from Michel Foucault, *The Archaeology of Knowledge* trans. by Alan Sheridan Smith. Copyright © 1969 by Editions Gallimard. Reprinted by permission of Georges Borchardt, Inc. and Routledge.

François Furet's "French Intellectuals: From Marxism to Structuralism" from Furet, *In the Workshop of History,* trans. by Jonathan Mandelbaum (The University of Chicago Press) © 1984 by The University of Chicago. All rights reserved. Originally published as *L'atelier de l'histoire* © 1982 Flammarion, Paris.

JACQUES REVEL

Introduction

1. The purpose of this volume is to present a selection of texts illustrating the main tendencies in French historiography since the end of World War II. We aim to cover not only the evolution of the discipline but also the debates that enlivened and at times divided it. Such an undertaking calls for a few preliminary remarks.

This book is a selection, not an honors list. The texts chosen are quite diverse. Some are classics whose absence would have been baffling, and Anglophone readers will find many of the better-known French historians. However, many of the authors and texts are less well known, and we chose them because we felt that they exhibit points of view, analyses, or critiques useful for our purposes. We do not seek to establish any hierarchy among the texts; nor do we claim that the importance of a particular historical work or the influence of a particular historian bears any relation to the presence of a text or author in these pages. Such literal calculation would be meaningless; more important, it would ignore the fact that a collective evolution, such as we are attempting to describe, is the work of more than just a small number of great historians. It is indeed collective: it reflects the convictions, choices, habits, allegiances, and strategies of a community of scholars. Beyond the professional circle, moreover, it reflects the expectations of a public (whose nature and size also vary). It relies as well on institutions, journals, and other means of circulation, and it must compete with rival or alternative offerings. Hence, there is no point in listing historians not represented in these pages or those to whom we might have given more space. As long as this volume already is, it draws on a far broader range of propositions, works, and accomplishments than we were able to include here. Anyone who wishes to form an accurate image of historical work in France during this period must remember the hundreds of thousands of unnamed contributions that nourished the work represented here and thus constitute its substance.

Over the past twenty-five years, moreover, historical debate in the West has become broadly international. Ideas, books, and scholars circulate freely, and this has dramatically altered the "terms of trade" within the discipline. In this expanded "polylogue," French historians have played a significant part. What the French provided, though, was not so much an influential model as a voice, or series of voices, in a range of discussions now under way among historians everywhere. This is not to say that all historians nowadays say the same things or speak the same language; a glance at what is being published in the leading historical journals will show that this is not the case. Confining our attention for the moment to social history (whose goals are broadly similar from country to country), any reader of the *Annales* in France, *Past and Present* in Great Britain, *Quaderni Storici* in Italy, and *Comparatives Studies in Society and History* or the *Journal of Interdisciplinary History* in the United States can attest to the existence of what for want of a better term might be called "national" styles of doing history. The term is convenient but unsatisfactory unless we are willing to accept "national character" as an explanation. However, even if such characters exist, they hardly provide the kind of answer we are looking for—indeed, they themselves are a problem that calls for an explicit formulation and solution. This is what we will attempt to do here for the French case. Although a comparative analysis would surely be profitable, space unfortunately does not allow us to pursue that line here.

Accordingly, we want to set the half century we have chosen as the chronological focus of this book in the context of a longer time frame, which, as we shall argue, can help us to understand the *caractères originaux,* the distinctive features, of contemporary French historiography. These features were not immutable; on the contrary, as we will attempt to show, they were shaped by research programs that were constantly reformulated or revised as conditions changed. Nevertheless, a certain French historiographic identity can be discerned, despite the diversity of individual works and choices. The sources of that identity are hardly self-evident, however. The purpose of this introduction is to explain what we think they are.

In doing so, we will ascribe a preponderant role to a particular historiographic movement, that associated with the journal *Annales*. If the *Annales* occupies such a central place in this collection, it is not only because the journal has become a sort of trademark of French history (even more so abroad, perhaps, than in France). Nor is it, as some have alleged without proof, because *Annales* historians monopolize French historical institutions and publications. The author of these lines would also like to think that it has nothing to do with his own history, with the fact that for some twenty-odd years he has been associated with the editorial board of *Annales* (the *Annales* movement is of course not limited to the journal proper). If *Annales* historians are overly represented here, it is primarily because the movement has been the principal source of innovation in French historiography for more than six decades. Whether one identifies with the *Annales* or prefers to keep one's distance, whether one admires the work it has produced, whether one is convinced or exasperated by it (and a single individual may at one time or another exhibit all of these attitudes), it has been a central reference for decades.[1] The history that we propose to reconstruct here is therefore only one possible history. One can imagine a quite different history of this period, not totally without foundation: one could, for example, emphasize what changed least, what was repeated—in history as in any scientific discipline, this probably accounts for the bulk of what was produced. But since our purpose is to sketch the main lines of development, we feel justified in insisting on what, for fifty years, has been an essential source of French historiography's unity and energy.[2]

2. The chronological limits we have imposed on this volume can also be justified. The years following the end of World War II coincided with a change of generations: they witnessed the birth of new institutions and, more important, of novel ways of organizing research and teaching. The intellectual climate also changed profoundly, and with it the historical agenda. History was not the only discipline affected by the change, nor was France the only country—but in France the mutation was particularly dramatic and highly visible. There were many reasons for this: the long interruption due to the war, the defeat, the Occupation, and the hard-to-endure but even harder-to-assimilate experience of Vichy, together with the widely shared sense that the Third Republic had failed, gave rise to a sense that much of French social, political, and intellectual life would have to be profoundly different after the Liberation.[3]

In reality, however, nothing actually began in 1945. The historiographic movement that had the greatest impact on French debate began well before the war.[4] It was in January 1929 that Marc Bloch and Lucien Febvre founded the *Annales d'histoire économique et sociale*, the fruit of years of planning. However, even that date, which is frequently celebrated as a new beginning (or a "historical revolution"[5]), was not really a fresh start. Whatever novelty the new journal may have seemed to possess in its early years, its birth can be understood only in a broader context, extending back to the last quarter of the nineteenth century and the reform of French academic institutions, curricula, and research. To assert this is not to succumb to the mirage that if only one goes back far enough, the sources of innovation can be found. It can, however, help us to gain a better understanding of the significance and scope as well as the limits of innovation by setting it against the context that made it possible.

In 1994, moreover, the *Annales* were sixty-five years old. This was by no means unusual for a scholarly journal; but still, this age, abetted by success, transformed what had begun as a movement into something of an institution, with not insignificant effects on the *Annales* itself, perhaps, and surely on people's perceptions of what the journal stood for. This was true not only in France but probably even more outside France, as Peter Burke recently noted, not without a certain irony: *"La nouvelle histoire*, as it is sometimes called, is at least as famous, as French, and as controversial as *la nouvelle cuisine."*[6] In fact, the story goes back a long way. Almost from the beginning two legends have attached themselves to the *Annales*, one dark, the other golden. The dark legend has it that the journal, especially in its early years, was aggressive, irritating, cocksure, and determined to overturn all the established rules and customs of the profession. This feeling has diminished somewhat, but it has by no means vanished; it even reappears in new guises. Meanwhile, the golden legend, which has been sustained by the movement's intellectual and institutional success, consecrates the work of the founding fathers and asserts the continuity of the tradition they began. Year after year, in an endless stream of editorials, anniversary lectures, portraits, citations, review essays, and the like, commentators have evoked the existence of an *"Annales* project," a common set of goals ostensibly shared by a scientific community. There is no better expression of this theme than Fernand Braudel's presentation of the "new *Annales*" that he passed on to his successors in 1969: "The *Annales,* once again, have taken on a new guise. In doing so they remain faithful to the spirit of Lucien Febvre and Marc Bloch, who founded the journal forty years ago. Their goal was always to serve history and the sciences of man, but to do so by braving all the risks, by venturing as close as they dared to the very frontiers of innovation. Other journals also serve the profession by steadfastly occupying conquered terrain. Their role is important, crucial, and irreplaceable. They thereby enable us to play a different part in the intellectual *conjoncture* of our time."[7] This text, which makes shrewd use of the rhetoric of old and new, says it all: the journal's fidelity to its past is best confirmed, Braudel maintains, by its embrace of innovation, while the movement, implicitly described as coherent and continuous, is proclaimed to be exceptional.

These two legends (to which one must add a third, which for the past twenty years or so has repeatedly announced either that the *Annales* school is finished or dead, or that it never existed) are of little importance in themselves; in the end, though, they distort our view of the *Annales* by asserting, whether in praise or blame, the continuous existence of an unvarying project across more than six decades of the twentieth century. What can the small group of professors who took the risk of founding a scholarly journal in 1929 have in common with the powerful network that formed after the war around that journal and its institutional supports? And what can that professional network have to do with the ramifications and offshoots it has produced over the past twenty-five years, many of which, if they even so much as invoke the name of the *Annales,* are beyond the journal's control? We mention these simple facts not to deny the existence and identity of a movement that over the years has proven its ability to gather support and produce results but, rather, to point out that this "identity" is a question, not an answer. Most of what has been written about the *Annales* starts with what is most accessible, namely, the journal's continuous commentary on itself. The writers take for granted the movement's continuity and coherence, which in fact it was the function of the discourse of self-commentary to guarantee. Hence they also take for granted the existence of a "school."[8] This assumption is convenient and easy, but it remains unsubstantiated. Furthermore, even if such a school did exist (which is not our view), one would still have to explain how it managed to survive over such a long period of profound change, repeated restructurings of the discipline and its subspecialties, and new developments in research methods and techniques as well as in scholarly circulation and exchange. The question becomes even more insistent when one recalls that, from the beginning, one of the proclaimed purposes of the *Annales* was to attend to the ways in which contemporary issues raised problems of interest to historians. Historiographical movements have histories of their own.

3. After 1870, the French systematically and deliberately reconstructed their university system in what amounted, in fact, to the foundation of an entirely new system. In the previous decade, the universities had been denounced for superficial curricula and other inadequacies. France's defeat by the new German Reich in 1870 triggered an unprecedented moral crisis. Contemporaries such as Ernest Renan saw the defeat as a symptom of civic, moral, and intellectual laxity. If France was to take its revenge, as it must, the country would therefore have to "rearm"—militarily, to be sure, but also morally and scientifically. There was broad agreement that the country must work to outstrip the Germans in the very areas in which Germany excelled: warfare, science, and the education of its citizens.[9] Designing a new university was thus a task for the nation. A group of determined men, including historians such as Renan, Hippolyte Taine, and above all Ernest Lavisse and Gabriel Monod, played a decisive role in redefining higher education. Curricula were revised to emphasize disciplinary and professional training. The German use of the seminar, of training for research through research, was promoted alongside the traditional public lecture. The disciplines were professionalized and organized, creating professional associations with their own organs of expression, most notably journals.[10] The Republic needed scholars and professors, and it knew how to get them. To finance

these reforms and innovations, academic budgets through the turn of the century were vastly increased, and the number of academic positions was expanded. (This led, of course, to a sharp rise in the number of students, especially in literature and science.)

In this reform effort the discipline of history played a notable role, and not just because historians were prominent in developing the new higher education policy.[11] The discipline had played an essential ideological role throughout the nineteenth century, feeding the period's diverse and contradictory passions—nostalgia, prophecy, scientism. In France, however, the trauma of defeat bestowed special importance on history. It became the repository of a humiliated nation's pride, and its instruction was to contribute to the civic rearming of the nation. Ernest Lavisse can be taken as the embodiment of history's crucial marriage with the credo of the Third Republic: he was not only one of the instigators of the "New Sorbonne" but also the author of a celebrated series of primary school textbooks and the inspiration behind the great *Histoire de France*, the period's quasi-official national history. History was in charge of the nation's teaching at a time when the country doubted itself and was obliged to seek reassurance in its past. It also enjoyed a more academic prestige whose ideological influence was no less significant. In the positivist climate of the last quarter of the nineteenth century, was not history a model of the kind of science and rigor the country needed? Since Germany stood foremost in philology, a national obsession, France must surpass it on its own terrain. History, then, must part company with literature and eschew the freedom of the belletristic essay. It must become scholarly, or better still, in the land of Descartes, it must become methodical. Method was the ubiquitous slogan of the late nineteenth century. Charles-Victor Langlois and Charles Seignobos codified historical method for the use of students in their celebrated *Introduction aux études historiques* of 1898. What did they teach? Mainly how to read texts critically—in the conviction that this necessary activity enabled researchers themselves to gather the facts from their documentary trace, thus yielding an image of the past as close as possible to what one might have seen had one been able to observe it directly. Once the "precious ore" of facts had been separated from the documentary "tailings" and "refined" by criticism, the "facts" took on an independent existence and could be arranged in sequence, generally that of chronological narrative. Clearly, such a method can fairly be characterized as positivist; it was explicitly positivist in its conception of scientific work and of the object of research, and implicitly so in its rejection of interpretation, which was henceforth regarded as useless and dangerous.[12]

Meanwhile, other new disciplines found their place in the academy and gained approval of their curricula. Among these was geography, which in France had traditionally been associated with history but in a subordinate, technical role; it also had various practical applications, but these brought it no academic legitimacy. For various reasons—including pressure from economic liberals and the colonial lobby, as well as nationalist passion—the discipline was redefined under the aegis of Paul Vidal de La Blache, the founder of the French geographical school, who codified its project, method, and lexicon, and institutionalized it as a distinct academic discipline.[13] The circumstances were less favorable to psychology, despite its contemporary scientific and ideological importance. It continued to be split between the *facultés des lettres*, where it was seen as a subspecialty of philosophy, and the *facultés de médecine*, as clinical psychology. Economics also remained a minor discipline within the law schools, where it had always had its place, although the curriculum was revised. But the most spectacular as well as the most controversial innovation was sociology. It was spectacular because Emile Durkheim managed to codify an ill-defined set of methods in a rigorous, not to say authoritarian, manner (*Les Règles de la méthode sociologique* was published in 1895), thereby achieving unquestioned intellectual legitimacy. This was also controversial, though, because the new discipline did not really succeed in finding a place in the university system, where it often went camouflaged as *pédagogie* and, later, philosophy. The troubled career of Durkheim, who, though he was one of the Third Republic's leading intellectual lights and the center of an elite group of students, won appointment to the Sorbonne only in 1902, may be taken as emblematic of sociology's difficulties.[14] What prospects of employment could the new discipline offer its recruits? Nevertheless, as a model of scientific rigor, Durkheimian sociology enjoyed unparalleled prestige. With considerable justice it could also claim to be the very embodiment of "method."

Indeed, it was the very issue of method that became a source of conflict with neighboring disciplines, history in particular. The rivalry between "social" disciplines can be interpreted on two levels. It reflected, in part, an epistemological disagreement, but it also corresponded to a battle for control of scientific legitimacy within the academy. In a series of resounding polemics, François Simiand, one of Durkheim's most brilliant disciples, attacked the methods of the geographers and especially those of the historians. These attacks were hardly unprecedented: from its inception *L'Année sociologique*, the organ of the Durkheimians, saw uncompromising critical scrutiny of publications in the emerging social sciences as part of its mission. What was new in Simiand's attacks, however, was the bitterness of the confrontation. A vast international debate over the scientific nature of the historical discipline had begun around the turn of the century, and it was this debate in which Simiand intervened. In a justly celebrated article, "Méthode historique et science sociale," he offered a systematic, detailed critique of the historians' "discourse on method" as recently codified by Langlois and Seignobos.[15] The article was nothing less than a manifesto, with the drawbacks as well as the advantages of the genre: it sharpened contrasts and simplified positions so as to make clear-cut distinctions, the better to denounce the adversary. The issues at stake consequently emerge with particular clarity. Simiand's target was what he called "historicizing" history, which we have become accustomed to calling "positivist"—that is, history that claims to develop reliable knowledge of the past on the basis of philological criticism alone. In the view of the sociologist, the scholarly techniques of philology defined not a positive science but at best an "investigative procedure" (*procédé de connaissance*). Furthermore, the empiricism on which historians prided themselves actually involved a series of implicit choices. If history wanted to become a full-fledged science, it would have to adopt genuine epistemological standards. To begin with, it would have to formulate hypotheses suitable for eventual verification. In this perspective, the singular fact, which "positivist" historians had all but apotheosized, became totally irrelevant; indeed, it was impossible to accept facts as "given." They would have to be constructed in such a way as to permit arranging them in "series" suitable for identifying the existence of patterns, on the basis of which it would then be possible to establish relations, or laws. In Simiand's view, history, in the sense of knowledge of things that happened only once, was not a science, nor could it be. It could achieve scientific status only by accepting epistemological norms comparable to those of other sciences. Historians must stop regarding time in the constraining sense of linear chronology and, instead, look upon it as a laboratory in which it should be possible to demonstrate and study the existence of variations and recurrences. In this laboratory, scholars could begin to develop a truly scientific approach to social facts, an approach that would require synchronic as well as diachronic comparison and lead ultimately, it was hoped, to the identification of systems.[16] In short, Simiand challenged the positivism of the historians in the name of a nomothetic conception of the "science of social facts." Yet because the opposing view in Simiand's account appears naive (having been oversimplified for polemical purposes), it is generally overlooked that what he proposed in its place was also a form of positivism—certainly a more subtle, more elaborate form of positivism but, in the work of the young Simiand, definitely a positivism.

Apart from his insistence on proper rules of method, Simiand also proposed a hierarchy of social scientific disciplines. What, indeed, was the provenance of this text, which so imperiously reformulated the historians' agenda? It was the work of a young proponent of a discipline that was also new as well as aggressive but that remained, as we have seen, marginal within the French academic system. Yet it exhorted colleagues to work deliberately toward a unified social science under the aegis of sociology. It was from the sociologist's point of view, in fact, that disciplinary boundaries were deemed most unacceptable: they were judged to have no epistemological validity. Institutionally as well as intellectually they played a constraining, reactionary role, preventing any thorough reexamination of fundamental scientific premises. Geography, economics, and psychology were thus exhorted to become subspecialties of a new, unified social science. In this conception of interdisciplinarity—or, perhaps more accurately, in this case, "adisciplinarity"—history was to occupy a distinctive but not central place. Although its methods were in theory to be those of all the social sciences, it would provide a terrain for exploration, an empirical test bench, as it were, for examining hypotheses formulated elsewhere. This was as it must be, since the temporal dimension was the only possible area for "experimentation" open to sciences, which, unlike the natural sciences, studied nonreproducible facts.

There is no need to underscore what the original *Annales* project owed to the program that Simiand laid out so forcefully in 1903 and, more generally, to the positions and indeed the manner—the intellectual style, one might say—of the Durkheimian movement. As students at the Ecole Normale Supérieure in Paris, Febvre (born in 1878) and Bloch (born in 1886) encountered this cauldron of ideas in their formative years: "When, in our twenties, with mixed emotions of admiration and instinctive rebellion, we read *L'Année sociologique,* one of the things that most attracted our attention was the continual effort to revise and adapt the conceptual framework, which was reshaped and altered from volume to volume but always for reasons that Durkheim and his collaborators openly stated, discussed, and formulated."[17] It is easy to see what the *Annales* preserved of the Durkheimian position at its inception a quarter of a century later: the primacy of problem-oriented history, the concern with constructing the object of research, the insistence on measurement and comparison, the use of models, and above all the determination to unify the sciences of man. First Bloch and Febvre and then, in the following generation, Braudel had no trouble at all adopting the main points of a program that has demonstrated astonishing longevity through the intellectual vicissitudes of the twentieth century.[18]

We must take care, however, not to be misled by this intellectual success. For the institutional strategy that was the other side, so to speak, of Simiand's lesson in method—a strategy that sought to take a marginal discipline and grant it epistemological authority over its neighbors—failed. At the turn of the century, sociology lacked the means to carry out its policy, and it would continue to lack them for a long time to come. It was further weakened by World War I, which decimated the ranks of the young Durkheimians. Simiand set the terms of the debate but failed to bring about the desired solution.

4. Twenty-five years later, the *Annales* would also try to unify the social sciences, but this time with the discipline of history at the center. Yet if the formal terms of the project remained the same, conditions had changed radically. Sociology had pulled in its horns, and history now found itself in a position of strength vis-à-vis the other social disciplines. Its institutional position had long been powerful: it possessed numerous academic chairs and could offer its recruits the prospect of a secure career, and it also enjoyed considerable and venerable cultural legitimacy. With these resources, it was in a position to reorganize the social sciences. In this respect it is useful to approach the *Annales* enterprise as we did the Durkheimian, that is, as both a set of scientific propositions and the expression of a strategy (at first implicit, then, with its success, increasingly explicit) that was at once scientific, disciplinary, and institutional. The point is important, and its consequences were considerable. This bears emphasizing, because it is one of the distinctive features of the French case: not only was history regarded as a social science in France, but it was to a large extent the pivotal discipline around which the social sciences were organized, at least until the 1960s.

When Marc Bloch and Lucien Febvre, then professors at the University of Strasbourg, founded their new journal, it was a modest affair; we must be careful not to overestimate its importance by dint of retrospective prophecy. To be sure, the journal enjoyed a considerable *succès d'estime*, and from the beginning it drew collaborators as well as recognition from abroad. Nevertheless, for the first ten years of its existence, it had only a few hundred readers, certainly less than the quasi-official *Revue historique,* the *Vierteljahrschrift für Sozial-und Wirtschaftsgeschichte,* or the *Historische Zeitung.* Exalted after the fact by those who participated (as well as by some who would have liked to have participated) in its early years, the journal's break with custom aroused little enthusiasm. Its marginality was only part of the reason, for in fact the journal was not all that marginal. In 1929, Febvre and Bloch were mature, well-respected historians. The University of Strasbourg where they taught was the leading university in France after the Sorbonne, and both men enjoyed brilliant careers, which took the first to the Collège de France (to which he was elected in 1932) and the second, with somewhat greater difficulty, to a chair at the Sorbonne in 1936. The network of patronage and collaborators that they cultivated around the journal skillfully mingled nonconformism with an appeal to the academic establishment.[19] If the *Annales'* debut must be painted in half-tones, surely it was because the times were scarcely favorable to innovation.[20]

If the journal's innovativeness went largely unnoticed, it was not because its editors failed to proclaim it from the rooftops. The preface to the first issue, addressed "to our readers," is a case in point. The editors denounced the disciplinary barriers that continued to separate historians from other scholars dedicated "to the study of contemporary societies and economies." They also proposed to unify empirically ("by example and deed") not just the field of historical research, which suffered from an overabundance of compartmentalized subspecialties, but the social sciences generally. This program was soon spelled out in concrete decisions. The choice of the journal's title to begin with: in the formula "histoire économique et sociale," lifted from the *Vierteljahrschrift,* the "social" soon took precedence. It was not long before Febvre was reminding readers that "there is no such thing as economic and social history. There is only history, in its unity." More than that, perhaps, it was "the social" that corresponded best to the ecumenical, unifying ambitions of the journal's program. Once again, Febvre stated this explicitly: "A word as vague as 'social' . . . seemed ideal as the trademark of a journal whose aim was not to build walls around itself." The scientific decisions of the *Annales* were also significant. The journal recruited contributors from outside the historical profession and even outside the academic community. It published a surprising amount of information and reflection on very contemporary realities, particularly on societies undergoing rapid, deliberate transformation. Following the model of *L'Année sociologique,* a good deal of space was devoted to reviews and critical essays dealing with works in sociology, economics, geography, and psychology in addition to history. Indeed, the space devoted to reviews was exceptional, as one can see by comparing the tables of contents of the early years to those of other historical reviews of the period (and of our own day as well). Another novel feature was the program of collective investigations posted and commented on by the journal editors, with the aim of attracting scholars with different specialties and interests to new research programs. At the heart of the transformation of the discipline of history in those years was the multiplicity of approaches to the social, generally inspired by the issues of the moment.

The early years of the *Annales* were thus a time of discovery and adventure. Both were permissible because they fell within the unifying vision of a science of human society. The relations that were fostered between history and the social sciences can be seen as the fruition of the ideas Simiand had put forward at the beginning of the century. Yet was the program really the same? The institutional and intellectual context was profoundly different, and so, therefore, was the program. The Durkheimians had conceived of the unity of the social sciences in terms of method, thus the problem of interdisciplinarity did not arise as such. Simiand took it for granted that sociology would provide the standard model on which the other social sciences would pattern themselves: "Indeed, I believe that in the work of present-day historians, in their choice of subject and careful construction of their work, and in their clear desire to profit from progress in adjacent disciplines, one already sees a tendency to replace traditional practices with a more positive, objective approach to human phenomena susceptible of scientific explanation, a tendency to focus the heart of the effort on the conscious elaboration of a social science." When history replaced sociology at the center of this project, however, changes were necessary, changes whose importance we need to measure.

Bloch and Febvre were initially interested in empirical comparisons, as we have seen. Clearly, they kept aspects of the Durkheimian model while rejecting others. They kept, among other things, the emphasis on interdisciplinary comparison as a way of promoting scientific progress, along with the determination to probe existing concepts and disciplinary boundaries with a critical eye. They rejected, broadly speaking, the whole theoretical and epistemological construct on which the sociological project was based. For them, the unity of the social was not so much an epistemological position as a practical conviction. Just as the historical profession was preparing itself to become the repository of the social (much as it had been the repository of "the national" in the nineteenth century), it symptomatically took on the accents and imagery of romanticism: for the founders of *Annales,* as for Jules Michelet before them and Braudel after them, the unity of history was "that of life" itself. One can find countless variations on this basic organicist theme in the pages of the journal; it was surely more an act of faith than a justification for history's new ambitions. As such, however, it proved to be a formidable source of energy or, to use the kind of carnal metaphor of which both Febvre and Bloch were fond, of an insatiable appetite—an appetite for interpretations, initiatives, experiences, and confrontations. It was an energy that drew people together and soon placed history at the center of the sciences of man.

The historians' program advertised itself as favoring the concrete over the "schematic" and the temptation of "abstraction": "History lives on realities, not abstractions." The terms of the debate now seem old-fashioned, but for several decades they characterized history as it was done under the journal's banner. They partly explain the attractiveness of a movement that, quite apart from its intellectual choices and even within those choices, remained profoundly open, even eclectic. For all the journal's constant vigilance over the historical discipline and for all its combative rhetoric, it was largely open to outsiders. Earlier, at the turn of the century, geography, as redefined largely by Vidal de la Blache, had set an example of a discipline ready to embrace new questions and to expand its diverse but integrated research program. It was also an example of multidisciplinary research dealing with concrete, almost tangible realities: a region, "human groups," a landscape. Febvre and Bloch claimed this legacy often enough that there is no need to dwell on it here.[21] If social facts were to be understood in a global perspective, no approach should be ruled out or granted priority over others. The more numerous the angles of approach, the more powerful the analysis. The (relative) predominance of the "economic and social" in the early years of the *Annales* is somehow misleading. The economic was emphasized because, in part, its study had been unduly neglected by historians but even more because the social relations that developed around the economic were especially dense and visible; yet it was never held to "determine" the whole range of social functions in the Marxist sense. Bloch (who had read Marx) and Febvre were skeptical of Marxist analysis and at times overtly critical.

The reasons for their skepticism were spelled out several times but never in a systematic way. Both men were instinctively wary of any theoretical construction that might prove constraining. More than that, their approach to history was global in principle but essentially empirical by design. The social was never treated to an elaborate, systematic conceptualization: it was, rather, a loosely defined inventory of relationships that constituted the "interdependence of phenomena." Bloch described his masterpiece, *La Société féodale*, as the "analysis and explanation of a social structure *with its associations.*" Febvre echoed this sentiment: "The task of the historian is not to exhibit an uninterrupted chain of connections linking the patterns of the past ... but rather to understand *the infinite variety and richness of the past in all its combinations*" (emphasis added). History and the social sciences were thus supposed to explain not through simplification or abstraction but rather through "complexification" of their object, by bringing out the wealth of meaning in the endless tangle of social relations (the celebrated concept *Zusammenhang*). Of course, one had to distinguish and classify, but the best approach was the one that made it possible to connect the largest number of apparently heterogeneous phenomena.

Geography provided a model and, along with sociology—sometimes in concert with it, sometimes in opposition—helped to shape the new history. Taking a broader view, however, one can see the move away from Durkheim as the reflection of a more general phenomenon: growing doubts about the positivist project and the scientistic faith that accompanied it—a critique of determinism that began in the "hard" sciences, particularly physics, at the turn of the century and gradually spread to the sciences of society (and philosophy), leading to a reconsideration of prevailing epistemological views. Thirty years before the launching of the *Annales*, the *Revue de synthèse historique*, founded in 1900 by Henri Berr, took note of the ongoing mutation in its own fashion. Febvre, Bloch, and many of the contributors to the *Annales* were also frequent contributors to the *Revue*, and many of them, especially Febvre, maintained close relations with Berr's journal after 1929. It is no exaggeration to say that the *Revue* was a prototype of the *Annales*, a preliminary experiment whose lessons were not forgotten. It was intended to be, and was, resolutely interdisciplinary and open to contributions of all kinds. It was attentive to contemporary developments. It, too, ascribed a central role to history in the evolving "synthesis" of knowledge, which Berr, a philosopher by training, persistently if at times rather mystifyingly promoted. It rejected deterministic models as scientistic and rigid, favoring instead a more flexible and pragmatic empiricism.[22] Make no mistake: compared with the *Revue*, the *Annales* were more rigorous, professional, and diligent. In the later journal one finds no trace of Berr's frequently rather sketchy eclecticism or prophetic bent. One does, however, find an alertness to the transformations of the present as well as a determination to organize the comparison of different scientific approaches and results in a carefully thought out but not prescriptive way. The difference from the Durkheimian model is clear: the Durkheimians, as we have seen, based the unity of the social sciences on the method of *the* social science, sociology, whereas Berr proposed to think of the unity of the social sciences in terms of the object they all shared. Since that object was common to all of them, it was reasonable to assume that eventually all of their diverse approaches would converge on that object, hence that all could benefit in the short run from comparison. The resulting conception of methodology was voluntarist and deeply empirical. The persistent French habit of referring to the *sciences de l'homme* rather than the *sciences sociales* might be symptomatic here. Another consequence was an open system of interdisciplinary circulation and exchange, governed by the innovativeness and effectiveness of research and not generally encumbered by *a priori* theoretical concerns.[23] This has sometimes led to what can only be called *bricolage* (tinkering), which for many years was another characteristic feature of French interdisciplinarity, but it has been a source of empirical richness as well.

5. We come at last to the end of World War II. The moment, it has been said, marks a caesura in French experience, the end of the Occupation

and Vichy and, more profound perhaps, a mutation of sensibility. The dark, anxious, nervous climate of the 1930s gave way to the voluntaristic optimism that drove the postwar reconstruction, in a spirit of broad consensus. Of course, the country needed to mobilize all its energies: it had been laid low and largely destroyed by the war and had lost much of its elite, which was compromised in the collapse of the Third Republic and the Vichy regime, to say nothing of collaboration. Yet it made a spectacular recovery, propelled—for a time, at least—by the very spirit of unity that had been forged in the Resistance, the euphoria of the Liberation, and the urgency of what needed to be done. It was the beginning of a long period of growth and modernization, the so-called *Trentes glorieuses* (1945–1975), which would transform a society that in many respects had remained firmly in the nineteenth century. Nevertheless, the war revealed a geopolitical realignment so hard for the French to accept that it took them a long time to admit their country was no longer an international power of the first rank. To acknowledge this in 1945 was out of the question. But from that date on, a country that had long thought of itself as the center of the world, and of the intellectual world in particular, became increasingly open to outside influences, and one can interpret this as an indirect recognition of France's changed status. This openness took more than one form: progressive internationalism was more commonly embraced than was the United States or the "North Atlantic community." In any case, France clearly wanted to rejoin history and to make up for lost time. Politically, this was the message both of communists and of Gaullists, whose positions were less contradictory than they might appear. Socially, this was the era of mass politics and social progress, buoyed by an economic progress whose prospects seemed endless. Culturally, existentialists, Marxists, and, more generally, intellectuals who invoked the legacy of the Resistance (such as André Malraux and Albert Camus) shared a strong conviction that France must embrace modernity and adjust its outlook to the historical realities of the time.[24] This was the age of "commitment," though difficulties and dramas lay just ahead, with the outbreak of anticolonialism and the Cold War. Nevertheless, the mood remained optimistic. In the aftermath of World War II we find none of the anguished tension or sense of guilt which had accompanied the beginnings of "intellectual and moral reform" after the defeat of 1870.

The postwar situation, which made the French feel both a part of history and a need to maintain their place, was also favorable to history in the professional sense. Indeed, the discipline proved very attractive to students who began their studies in the years immediately after the war. In their eyes history enjoyed the combined prestige of both intellectual commitment and ideological engagement. Many of the men and women who would come to prominence over the next twenty years began their work at this time: Maurice Agulhon, Pierre Chaunu, François Furet, Annie Kriegel, Jacques Le Goff, Emmanuel Le Roy Ladurie, Jacques Ozouf, Jean-Claude Perrot, Michelle Perrot, Denis Richet, and Pierre Vidal-Naquet, to name a few.[25] Many also chose to join the communist movement. They were young, committed, determined, and had a highly developed sense of their responsibilities. What were they offered?

Examples? Some older historians had participated in the Resistance (among them, Marc Bloch, murdered by the Germans in 1944, the medievalist Edouard Perroy, or the Hellenist Jean-Pierre Vernant), but others had served Vichy or collaborated with the Germans. Intellectual references? Obviously, Marxism comes to mind, because many young historians, including some of the most brilliant, became communist militants. Yet how many of them really read Marx, and how many of those incorporated their reading into their work as historians? Reading their accounts today one is struck by the fact that, for most of them, political commitment mattered more than Marxist theory, of which their knowledge remained superficial (in part because of the traditional weakness of the Marxist tradition in France[26]). Jean-Paul Sartre's existentialism and Emmanuel Mounier's Christian personalism partook of a diffuse intellectual *ambiance* yet were never invoked by historians as scientific ideologies; they carried conviction but offered no substantive conceptual apparatus. To be sure, young historians turned eagerly to social and economic subjects because they were attracted to what was supposed to be the history of the many rather than of the few, the history of the masses whom the historians wished to join. Looking back, Maurice Agulhon has told how, in the early 1950s, his choice of a thesis topic was guided by "militant inspiration"; but he also points out that he failed to find in Marx the analytical tools he needed for his research. Michelle Perrot's version is not very different, and their cases are by no means unusual.[27] It was as if personal and professional commitments were related yet distinct.

Young historians were not left to their own devices; they had scientific models and examples to guide them. However, we must warn the reader that this summary of interwar historiographic debate may be misleading. We have emphasized, perhaps overemphasized, what changed in the writing of history, matters that were truly open to debate; yet innovative work accounted for only a small portion of what the historians of the day produced. Both before and after World War II, the bulk of academic output was what the *Annales* (like Simiand twenty-five years earlier) denounced as traditional—mostly political history and the history of international relations.[28] In the late 1920s, those most drawn to the new history often chose to work in geography to circumvent academic teaching restrictions, as Pierre Vilar has noted: "It was surely no accident that between 1925 and 1930 a key group of students of my generation who had chosen to study history ultimately opted, when it came time to begin work of their own, for geography. . . . The big questions, the ones we felt would dominate our century, were not really broached anywhere except in the lectures of our geography instructors." [29] Twenty years later, things had not changed significantly. At the Sorbonne and even more in the provincial universities, the old themes were still paramount, though it is true that Pierre Renouvin at the Sorbonne had done much to give them a more modern look. But economic and social history had made an impressive academic debut thanks to two men whose names would dominate the years to come—Ernest Labrousse and Fernand Braudel.

Clearly, one generation was giving way to another. Bloch was dead; Febvre lived until 1956, but his influence was exercised mainly through his books, lectures, and, most important of all, the scientific policy he had established. Simiand had died in 1935. Labrousse (born in 1895) succeeded Bloch in the chair of economic and social history at the Sorbonne. Braudel (born in 1902) was elected to the Collège de France when Febvre retired in 1950. Though at first vastly outnumbered by traditionalists, Labrousse and Braudel would prove highly influential in the organization of research, the training and recruitment of young historians, and the formulation of research programs. The two men, whose work left its mark on the postwar period, acquired extraordinary power in the discipline, over which they would reign for the next twenty years. Labrousse came from the *faculté de droit* (economics then fell within the purview of the schools of law) and always saw himself as the intellectual heir of François Simiand. He had been associated with the *Annales* group since the mid-1930s. He made a name for himself with two great books that transformed the conception and methodology of economic and social history: *Esquisse du mouvement des prix et des revenus en France au XVIIIᵉ siècle* (1933) and *La Crise de l'économie française à la fin de l'Ancien Régime et au début de la Révolution* (1944). A great teacher, he drew many of the most brilliant young history students to the Sorbonne to do their theses under him. Braudel, seven years younger, had his career delayed by the war. It was not until 1947 that he defended his thesis, which after its publication in 1949 became the flagship of the new history: *La Méditerranée et le monde méditerranéen à l'époque de Philippe II*, an ambitious exploration of the global history of a region.[30] After Febvre met him while traveling in Brazil in 1936, Braudel became his right-hand man and designated heir. Braudel would replace Febvre not only in most of his official academic positions but also at the *Annales*, and he would soon prove himself to be politically adept.[31]

Braudel and Labrousse were great entrepreneurs, and they were also fortunate to have new resources at their disposal. The Centre National de la Recherche Scientifique, a Popular Front project, was formally established in 1939, but it did not really begin to play an important role until after the war, when scientific research was reorganized in keeping with the voluntaristic spirit of the times. It not only financed research but offered salaried posts to an elite of young *chercheurs,* thus allowing a genuine professionalization of research. Late in 1947, moreover, Febvre, Braudel, and Charles Morazé won approval for the establishment of what would become the institutional mainstay of the *Annales* movement, the so-called Sixth Section (for the economic and social sciences) of the Ecole Pratique des Hautes Etudes (EPHE).[32] At first the dimensions of the new section were modest—a handful of teachers and a very small budget, fortunately supplemented by grants from American foundations. Yet the ambition, broadly speaking, was the same as that which had inspired the foundation of the *Annales* in 1929: to create the conditions for systematic, open comparison of work in the various social sciences under the aegis of history. Febvre was the first chairman of the Sixth Section; Braudel would succeed him and remain in the chair until 1972. The dynamism of the new institution soon gave it a central position in the structure of research. It was noted, however, not for the number of its students (very small compared with the universities) but for the prestige of its teachers and the ubiquity of its influence. A collaborative research policy was soon established: research programs were formulated, goals set, and budgets allocated. Here we see another distinctive feature of the postwar scientific scene, the creation of research centers.

Previously, historical research had essentially been a solitary activity. Just before the war, however, France witnessed the first attempts to organize "laboratory research" in the humanities and social sciences on the model of the "hard" sciences. These changes primarily affected areas auxiliary to history, such as archival publication and various peripheral specialties. Lucien Febvre had issued a vigorous call for the organization of research "teams." He hoped not only to improve efficiency but to reap epistemological benefits as well: collaborative research would help to make history "at last a 'problem-oriented science' in which researchers investigated problems that could be stated explicitly if not unambiguously resolved at first sight."[33] Various examples of collaborative research did exist, for instance, the broad network of scholars associated with the International Committee for Price History and the collective *enquêtes* launched by the *Annales* in the 1930s. Professors in a small number of universities had begun to organize their own "institutes" for the study of specific topics, moreover: one or more tenured professors attempted to assemble documentary resources to improve the training of young scholars.[34] After the war, however, the scale and significance of such projects changed. The "research laboratory" became a part of the spirit of the times: the optimistic, can-do, bureaucratic outlook of the period sought to mobilize energies by making resources available and assigning production goals. Achievements, of course, often fell short of ambitions, as always, but a certain tone was set. An early illustration of the new direction was the Centre de Recherches Historiques of the Sixth Section of the EPHE, established in 1949 in the conviction that the new historical agenda called for new working methods.[35] Even the universities were won over to the new viewpoint sufficiently to give up their exclusive insistence on individual research. They, too, opened research centers, and some very eminent professors were soon voicing agreement with Labrousse and Braudel that "the nature and objectives of present-day research frequently call for teamwork, and even the most individualistic of historians cannot fail to recognize the urgency and potential usefulness of such efforts."[36]

Of course, the proliferation of research centers and collaborative research programs hardly eliminated individual work. The French-style doctoral thesis remained (and still remains today) the primary form of knowledge production and the primary means of obtaining professional recognition. Indeed, theses became increasingly massive after World War II, at times reaching monstrous proportions—yet they were no longer the only way of doing history. Besides producing solitary masterworks, historians, especially younger historians, could now "do research" in places that were also forums for debate and schools of methodology.

Take, for example, the teaching of Ernest Labrousse, who dominated the scene from 1950 to 1970. His first great book was published well before the war but did not really attract much attention before 1939. The second, *La Crise de l'économie française*, appeared during the Occupation. In the postwar *conjoncture*, however, both books took on new importance and significance: not only because their author now held a chair at the Sorbonne, at the center of what was still an extraordinarily centralized academic system, but also because they set a "standard," establishing a reproducible model of economic and social history. Labrousse's own work had focused on France. The work that he would inspire sometimes extended beyond the nation's borders: witness the program for a "history of the Western bourgeoisie in the eighteenth and nineteenth centuries" that he presented to the International Congress of Historical Sciences at Rome in 1955.[37] More frequently, however, the results of that work took the form of dozens of detailed monographs, conceived as pieces of a vast puzzle that would eventually reveal a complete image of the economic and social history of early modern and modern France. Limited to a province, department, or city, or perhaps to a sector of the economy or a profession, this work, generally carried out in the form of a doctoral thesis, was parceled out by the master in keeping with an overall plan.[38]

Braudel was influential in a very different way. As a professor at the Collège de France, he had no students in the ordinary sense but, rather, an audience. Nor did he have many students at the Ecole des Hautes Etudes, which remained a peripheral institution and in those days could not grant university degrees. But readers of *La Méditerranée* and of the *Annales* (such as Pierre Chaunu, Frédéric Mauro, Jean Delumeau, and Emmanuel Le Roy Ladurie) came to him in search of a thesis topic and decided to specialize in the Mediterranean region; some of them would later work with Braudel. He had far fewer students than Labrousse, though, in part because his position in the system was less central, but also because his book, unlike Labrousse's, set a model that was not easy to duplicate.

6. For the next quarter of a century economic and social history would reign unchallenged. In 1946, however, the *Annales d'histoire économique et sociale* changed its name to *Annales: Économies, sociétés, civilisations*. The new title needs to be interpreted correctly; the celebrated trinity of the subtitle was of course a reminder of the ambition to do "global history," but for the time being there was a serious imbalance among the three terms. The order in which they were stated was, Labrousse insisted, "logical." And Braudel, though Febvre's heir in many things, never exhibited much interest in cultural history. Economics was paramount as it never had been before the war.

There were several reasons for this. Ambient Marxism has often been invoked to explain the change. Earlier I expressed doubt about this interpretation, which I regard as superficial. It is true, on the other hand, that in those days it was easy to convince oneself of the decisive influence of economic factors on historical development: Was not that the daily experience, after all, of a country in the midst of reconstruction, a country compelled by economic planning and American aid to enter the modern world with considerable haste? At the same time, the appearance of new concepts, which though they might eventually prove contradictory were ready for use, encouraged rethinking the foundations of economic history: I am thinking not only of the concepts developed by Labrousse (and, to a lesser extent, Braudel) but also of those figuring in the economists' heated debates on the subject of growth, a topical issue if ever there was one. Some of these ideas came from John Maynard Keynes, of course, but others were the work of Simon Kuznets, François Perroux, Joseph Schumpeter (as well as other theorists of the business cycle), and, later, of Wassily Leontieff, Walt Rostow, and Jean Marczewski. The priority was thus to investigate what was perceived as the basis of all social organization as well as the primary cause of historical change. Labrousse made the point explicitly a few years later in a lecture summing up a generation of work: "Change is principally—but not always—economic. The economic retards the social when the impulse comes from the economic. Conversely, the social retards the economic when it has the initiative. In other words, structure offers resistance. But then the mental also retards the social. And the braking action of the mental is the most powerful of all. The *mentalité* of a milieu changes more slowly than the milieu itself."[39] Economy, society, culture: the idea, which would gain wide acceptance in years to come, suggests an edifice consisting of three "stories" of unequal importance, the study of which would obviously require setting priorities.[40]

One result of this was the at times rather obsessive interest in defining and interpreting economic indicators. This was not absolutely new, nor was it exclusively French. As early as the 1920s, when price history was still in its early stages, various international and comparative research projects had been launched. Now, however, scholars sought to collect a whole range of measures of economic activity and its evolution—wages, incomes, trade flows, productive output, and so on. The word that summed it all up was *conjoncture* (usually translated, somewhat misleadingly, by the cognate English term "conjuncture"), a quasi-personified concept that designated both an evolutionary trend and the factors that explained it. How can we measure the influence of this approach without an extensive survey of the literature? One way is to compare the two successive editions of Braudel's *La Méditerranée*. The original 1949 edition offered only limited statistical corroboration for its hypotheses; sixteen years later, the 1965 edition was completely revised to reflect the abundance of data generated in the interim by a whole generation of historians.

Still, the primacy of economics never resulted in "economism." The formula "economic and social history" went unchallenged in France during this period. Much earlier, in Simiand's empirical work, the goal was already to develop "a comprehensive theory of economic activity in society."[41] Labrousse had tried to extrapolate Simiand's methodology and conceptual framework to the global phenomenon of the "conjuncture." Neither man studied economic facts in and for themselves, however; those facts were always imbued with social significance. For Simiand the fluctuations of economic activity (which some commentators mistakenly regard as his sole area of interest) were a composite of long-term cycles and shorter-term fluctuations of various kinds, which, through the medium of money, shaped social behavior. For Labrousse the social interpretation of the *conjoncture* (especially in the *Esquisse du mouvement des prix*) is reflected in the differential positions of actors identified by type of income and place in the processes of production and exchange. The concern with social interpretation became increasingly important to both men, so much so that Pierre Vilar could discern a transition from "conjunctural economism" to "structural conjuncturalism."[42] Labrousse put the point in his own way: "An economy has the conjuncture of its structure." This explains the emphasis on crises in this generation's work. Crises were thought to be important in two ways: first, they marked major conjunctural turning points, and second, they reflected the resistance of the social to the effects of the economy, thus pointing up the decisive influence of structures.[43]

Interestingly, although analysis of economic change was the most visible aspect of historiographic production in the period 1945–1965, this analysis was always directed toward the identification of stable patterns or systems. Not enough attention has been paid to this fact. Behind the so-called *conjoncture*, one sought above all to understand the recurrent cyclical phenomena whose complex interrelations defined a model: this was true of Labrousse's *économie d'ancien type*, or "preindustrial economic model," which Jean Meuvret and Pierre Goubert would extend in the period in question by introducing demographic variables.[44] The point should not be overstated, however. From Simiand to Labrousse and Vilar, conjunctural analysis also focused on, in Vilar's terms, "economic time as a creative force, creative owing to its very rhythms." These concerns were expressed in a variety of reflections on growth which drew on many sources of inspiration. Generally, however, it is probably fair to say that French thought about economic growth took the form of studying the conditions under which growth was possible within a given system. Emmanuel Le Roy Ladurie's masterful *Les Paysans de Languedoc* (1966), which in some ways capped as well as concluded a generation of work, is almost a paradigmatic illustration of this. The work reconstructs a long agrarian cycle, spanning from the fourteenth to the eighteenth century, in which phases of growth and recession alternated within a model whose variables (ultimately demographic, according to Le Roy Ladurie) precluded any radical transformation.

Was this history "static" (*immobile*), as Le Roy Ladurie was to put it rather provocatively a few years later? Surely not—but its historians, convinced that they had discovered what was truly important, were certainly mesmerized by the encumbrances and inertia of the past, by long periods of time and imperceptible evolutions. Braudel was, of course, the most stalwart champion of this view of things. His first and greatest book, *La Méditerranée* (1949), was divided into three parts. The first was devoted to the almost static time of the geographic milieu (the region bordering the Mediterranean) and the quasi-permanent conditions it imposed on human effort; the second dealt with social time, especially the economic fluctuations that oriented that human effort over the course of a century, but with attention as well to states and societies; and the third considered events and conscious human actions and attempted to understand them in terms of the previously constructed system. There is no doubt, however, that what really counted for Braudel was the long time span:

> I believe in the reality of a very slow history of civilizations in their abyssal depths, in their structural and geographic features. To be sure, civilizations are mortal in their most precious excrescences; they glow brilliantly and then die out, only to flourish again in other forms. However, such dramatic changes are rare, less frequent than many people think. And they do not destroy everything indifferently. In any region of civilization, the social content can change almost entirely two or three times without affecting certain deep structural features, which will continue to distinguish that civilization sharply from its neighbors. What is more, there is something even slower than the history of civilizations: the almost static history of men in their intimate relation to the earth that sustains and nourishes them. This dialogue is repeated endlessly, repeated so as to endure. It may change, it does change superficially, yet it continues, tenaciously, as if impervious to the ravages of time.[45]

This idea would later be reformulated in more systematic fashion in the celebrated text on the *longue durée* (1958), which Braudel describes as "a change of style . . . of attitude . . . a reversal in the direction of thought . . . a new conception of the social. . . . Everything revolves around it."[46]

Few historians have ventured to follow Braudel's ambitious and intimidating lead. Surely his ideas proved influential because they formalized, in radical terms, a variety of what we have seen to be deep-seated tendencies, tendencies at work since the early *Annales* first stressed the importance of analyzing systems and systemic changes rather than mere social change. Marc Bloch's *Feudal Society* and Lucien Febvre's concept of a history of *mentalités* (see below) are excellent examples of the new approach. For a quarter century after the end of World War II, the slow history of deep structures would dominate the scene. Surely it was no accident that in these years most French historians were interested in the medieval and early modern periods, the *longue durée* of societies that preceded the Industrial Revolution. We can also see why rural history took on such importance, following the lead of Bloch's *Caractères originaux,* in the work of Meuvret, Goubert, and Le Roy Ladurie, as well as Georges Duby, René Baehrel, Pierre Toubert, and many others.[47] The countryside was where slow evolution took place, and historians analyzed it in terms of systems and structures (agrarian and social), emphasizing man's relation to the environment, in virtually every case studied within the limits of a province or region. This limited focus made it possible to refine the analysis by demonstrating the interactions between many types of phenomena over an extended period of time.

Another feature of this approach to economic and social history was the systematic use of measurement—which might seem paradoxical at first sight, since these historians were chiefly interested in periods that left few documents with numbers of any kind, let alone statistical records. However, much of the scientific effort of the time went toward developing new documentary resources and methods for exploiting them.[48] The history of money and especially of prices served as a kind of test bench that many research teams in both Europe and the United States used to perfect their techniques. Between 1930 and 1950 those techniques were then applied to the history of incomes, trade volumes, and production. After that came the systematic exploitation of demographic archives, especially parish registers, using methods perfected by the statistician Louis Henry and the historian Michel Fleury in 1956— methods that eventually led to a whole new generation of studies using notarial archives, land deeds, and industrial records. Historians had to learn how to count and compare. The program, clearly implicit in Simiand's 1903 recommendations, had been passed on through Labrousse's work and teaching; its implementation was both individual and collective. As an example of an individual approach, admittedly exceptional, one has Pierre Chaunu's ambitious study, in collaboration with Huguette Chaunu, of Spanish-American trade in the sixteenth century, based on the archives of the *Casa de la Contratacion de Indias* in Seville: twelve volumes, seven thousand pages, including five thousand pages of statistics taking the measure of an entire world during a century and a half that was crucial for European economic development in the early modern period.[49] As for the collective approach, the Centre de Recherches Historiques of the Ecole des Hautes Etudes en Sciences Sociales initiated a number of studies focusing on Braudel's Mediterranean region, looking at port movements, maritime trade, and cyclical economic changes. One also saw the first studies of social structures,[50] and the vast study, sponsored by the Institut National d'Etudes Démographiques, that produced hundreds of monographs on individual parishes in an effort to investigate the demography of the Ancien Régime.[51]

Despite the ambition to explore economic and social realities as exhaustively as possible, the investigators were not after exact measurements—which the sources, in any case, usually could not provide. What they wanted was an evaluation, or, to use an expression that Pierre Chaunu favored, a *pesée globale,* or overall summing-up. Yet this gives a poor idea of what the real aim was. Weighing the pluses and minuses of the whole long experiment in 1971, François Furet put his finger on the main issues: Quantitative history involved a change in the very concept of historical work. Obedient to Simiand's injunction, historians were at last able to "overcome the extraordinary vagueness of the object of historical knowledge." They firmly established a "constructivist" approach, a way of developing their own sources in light of an explicit objective, a working hypothesis. They learned to criticize those sources and to process them in a consistent, controllable way that could be reproduced and validated experimentally. Instead of traditional source criticism, the new techniques emphasized formalization of the data and tests for consistency. In short, historians formulated a generalizable experimental protocol. Thus, "today's historians are obliged to overcome their methodological naiveté and reflect on how they establish what they know. . . . Like all the social sciences though perhaps a little belatedly, history today is moving from the implicit to the explicit."[52] Sixty years after the fact, François Simiand was thus proven right.

7. As is often the case in the success of a scientific discipline, the definition of a standard of research played an essential role. Certainly, one reason for the attractiveness of the *Annales*, broadly understood, after the war was the existence of repeatable models: precedents, validated approaches, a repertoire of tried and true techniques, a format. The dynamic quality of economic and social history stemmed in part from the caliber of those who taught the subject and organized research, and in part from the range of hypotheses considered. However, two other important factors were surely the fact that young historians beginning their research had examples to follow, and the fact that they could be sure of reaching their goal (usually a doctorate) within a reasonable period of time and of working in a supportive scientific community. The point can be corroborated by a counterexample: the history of *mentalités*, a centerpiece of the early *Annales* exemplified by remarkable works of Bloch, Febvre, and Georges Lefebvre, vanished almost entirely for twenty years after 1945. One could argue, of course, that this was because all the emphasis had shifted to the factors that seemed to provide the key to understanding historical processes. Yet it is nonetheless true that the examples set by the founding fathers were hard to imitate—not only because they were great works, but also because they failed to define a standard of research that could be converted into academic research projects. It was not until the late 1960s, with the first quantitative (or "serial," as it was called) research in cultural history, that this too began to attract a large number of students, owing both to the novelty of the field and to the formulation of a repeatable methodology.[53]

All of these things—innovation, a can-do spirit, support (material and otherwise) for research, and a certain inevitable conformism as well—

help to explain the success of what became the central approach to history in France and, before long, elsewhere as well. Other reasons for the movement's attractiveness include its openness and eclecticism. It was open intellectually, welcoming historians of many stripes, some with real theoretical differences. Though not a Marxist, Labrousse (who had socialist leanings) knew Marx's work well and always saw himself as Simiand's heir. Braudel avoided any open declaration of theoretical allegiances (except, perhaps, to Werner Sombart); Vilar, who explicitly placed his work within the Marxist theoretical perspective, was the exception that proves the rule.[54] In the next generation, Le Roy Ladurie found his first theoretical model in Thomas Malthus, while Furet soon made theoretical references to Alexis de Tocqueville and Raymond Aron. These names are among the few who made their preferences known; most of those who joined the *Annales* movement felt no need to proclaim an orthodoxy, which in any case was not required. All the emphasis was on methodology, and theoretical debate was rare. According to the new empiricism—or, if you will, critical positivism—methodological efficacy took absolute priority over theory;[55] and it was not only over the philosophy of history, which had been banished from French historiography since the late nineteenth century, but also over any consideration of the conditions of historical production, including its underlying ideological representations.[56] One can deplore this or approve it, but there can be no doubt that the effectiveness of the movement and its power to attract new adherents were increased by the absence of any preconditions.

In contrast to the way it seemed from the outside and perhaps even to the image that the *Annales* gave of itself, the movement was never closed, much less exclusive, even in these years of militancy. The Sixth Section of the Ecole des Hautes Etudes remained until the 1960s a relatively small institution on the periphery of the academic system, and in any case it never exercised a monopoly on the new way of doing history. Labrousse was affiliated with the Sixth Section, but most of his activity was concentrated in the Sorbonne, and he was never really close to the journal, which came under the direction of Braudel. Methodological positions had been staked out, of course, but they never created unbreachable barriers between historians. For example, at the time Pierre Renouvin was Labrousse's alter ego at the Sorbonne and the champion of a new approach to the history of international relations, one that would move beyond diplomatic history as such to take account of geographic and geopolitical realities, economic and demographic considerations, and mental habits.[57] To all appearances this kind of history was a long way from what the *Annales* stood for; in particular, it was interested in political matters, which were largely absent from the journal. Moreover, it benefited primarily from the audience and resources of the Institut d'Etudes Politiques. Nevertheless, among the *grands barons* who dominated French academic politics, in history at any rate, collaboration was more common than exclusion.[58] At the time, of course, the French university was still a small world, and those who made their mark as innovators remained, whatever differences may have divided them from their colleagues, part of a tradition-bound minority. It would be a mistake, however, to conclude that the changes enjoyed a consensus of approval. What structured positions in those years of strong political tensions was ideological rather than theoretical or methodological disagreement. Two examples may help to make this point clear.

First, consider Roland Mousnier and the school of historians who gathered under his energetic authority. Mousnier dominated early modern history at the Sorbonne, having made a name for himself with an important thesis on the sale of offices under the absolute monarchy, in which he proposed a social approach to a key social institution.[59] The history that Mousnier championed was not fundamentally opposed to that for which the *Annales* movement stood; it was less concerned with measurement, but it nevertheless worked with the same archives and sought to understand how old societies function. Still, in the late 1950s, a huge debate erupted between Labrousse with his disciples and Mousnier with his school. At the heart of the controversy was a highly ideologized conflict of interpretations. The Mousnierists accused the Labroussians of being too "economistic" or, at any rate, too quick to believe that material forces determine history. Were Ancien Régime societies class societies or, as Mousnier maintained, societies of orders? Mousnier stressed social hierarchies based on esteem, honor, and loyalty rather than those based on wealth, occupation, or place in the process of production. Mousnier, who defined himself politically as a conservative, attacked the hidden "Marxism" he thought he saw everywhere in the French universities. A generation later, the terms of the debate may seem rather remote from our current preoccupations—not as to the question of social stratification, which remains as important as ever, but rather as to the scarcely concealed ideological overdetermination. For ten years, in book after book and colloquium after colloquium, in countless prefaces and thesis defenses, trench warfare raged among the historians, leaving wounds that are still evident today. From the conflict over the interpretation of seventeenth-century "popular" revolts to the Saint-Cloud colloquium (1965) that marked the triumph of social history, this debate absorbed a great deal of manpower and energy, without necessarily adding a proportional amount to the depth of the discussion.[60]

The second example is the polemic over the interpretation of the French Revolution that erupted in the mid-1960s. It began when two young historians, François Furet and Denis Richet, proposed to view the revolutionary event in the context of the *longue durée* of eighteenth-century economic growth. Furet had trained under Labrousse, and his approach at the time was still broadly within the Labroussian perspective (though the master likely did not approve of all of his disciple's propositions). Furet and Richet also stressed the contingent character of certain aspects of the revolutionary process, in particular in the notorious *dérapage* hypothesis; the word literally means "skidding," and it was intended to suggest that the Revolution at a certain point "veered out of control." [61] In France, however, the history of the Revolution is a matter of the utmost importance, a protected domain not open to all comers. Furet and Richet thus incurred a vehement rebuke from Albert Soboul, the last in a long line of great historians in the Jacobin historiographic tradition and the guardian of the temple. He too was a student of Labrousse as well as of Georges Lefebvre; he too advocated a social historical approach, which is exemplified not only in his thesis on *sans-culotterie* but also in a series of articles he published in *Annales*. [62] The conflict was internal to the social history camp, thus, yet it was also political: Soboul was an active member of the communist party, which Furet and Richet had quit in 1956 and where they were easily taken for renegades. More profoundly, it was ideological: an interpretive orthodoxy had grown up around the Revolution, and this no doubt counted more than any methodological differences, which could probably have been resolved without too much difficulty. [63]

8. During this whole period, the program remained one of creating an empirical interdisciplinarity with history at its center. Because the social sciences were slow to gain recognition in French universities, history retained the privileges of seniority and visibility for a long time. The institutions designed to bring the different disciplines together for the purpose of comparing methods and results were often conceived with history at the center. An official 1957 report on French research needs, clearly written though not signed by Fernand Braudel, envisioned an organization of flexible, adaptable networks:

> However venerable (or successful) they may be, all the human sciences have points of intersection, or, to put it another way, all offer different points of view on the same set of social and human realities. Depending on the intellectual climate, therefore, there have been and will be phases of convergence and phases of segregation among the disciplines. When new sciences (that is, new methods or new points of view) are born, each discipline delves into its own domain while defending its turf against its neighbors: these are the phases of segregation. Examples of this can be seen in the recent development of demography, sociology, and ethnography. Can the established disciplines assimilate the new results during

phases of convergence? Economic and social history developed in this way, as did social psychology. Today, after a period that saw the rather chaotic development of several new sciences, a global convergence is needed, by which I mean a sharing of what has been learned and a systematic effort to move beyond outdated positions.[64]

The goal of the envisioned institution was thus to follow the transformations that were already taking place in actual scientific work.

Until the late 1950s, however, those transformations proceeded fairly slowly. Some fields remained curiously behind the times, while others surged ahead at different rates. Although anthropology had played a central role in the social sciences for thirty years, the discipline was not really welcomed into the universities until the 1960s. The work of Claude Lévi-Strauss was slow to attract readers beyond a small group of specialists: it was neither his thesis on the Nambikwara (1948) nor even *Les Structures élémentaires de la parenté* (1949) but, rather, *Tristes tropiques* (1955) and above all *Anthropologie structurale* (1958) that brought Lévi-Strauss's name into the limelight. The work of other scholars took even longer to gain recognition. Aside from problems of reception, there were also problems stemming from slow and often inadequate institutionalization of these reformulated disciplines. It was not until 1964, for example, that the old *facultés des lettres* were rebaptized *facultés des lettres et des sciences humaines*; and it was not until the 1960s that sociology, ethnology, and linguistics offered complete, autonomous university-level curricula.

This unduly prolonged "minority" of the social sciences explains in part at least the extraordinary vehemence of the structuralist offensive in France in the 1960s. At times the antihistoricist rhetoric of the structuralists was all but intolerant of opposing views. Several factors contributed to this: the structuralists were proposing new methods that were fairly similar across disciplines that had previously been separated, they developed novel theories, and—this point deserves greater emphasis than it usually receives—they wanted to break free of intellectual and institutional domination by the discipline of history.

Braudel summed up the issues of the debate before it had really even gotten under way in his celebrated article, "La Longue durée," in which he reflected on the state of the social sciences at the time of publication, 1958.[65] His diagnosis was bleak: the social sciences were in a "general crisis," "overwhelmed by their own progress" and tempted to withdraw into themselves "on the grounds that each has its own specific area of competence." His argument proceeds on two levels. Braudel insisted on the central importance of the temporal dimension in the analysis of social facts, which was of course equivalent to insisting on history's indispensable place among the social sciences. On a more strategic level, however,

and quite presciently anticipating the impending crisis, he also argued
for a minimalist, "ecumenical" conception of interdisciplinary practice,
in pursuit of which "history—perhaps the least structured of all the human sciences—is open to all the lessons learned by its many various
neighbors, and is then at pains to reflect them back again."[66] This was a
modest vision, especially given Braudel's—and the discipline's—exceptionally powerful position at the time. Braudel saw the human sciences
as sharing a common ground and history as a kind of lingua franca. In
the short run the modesty of his proposal was not enough to stem the
structuralist offensive, but it probably did help to limit the damage. More
than that, it became the inspiration for the strategy of reconquest that
the historians later implemented (empirically and probably with no clear
notion of what they were doing) on the social sciences' own turf.

This is not the place to dwell on the structuralist episode, which still
awaits its historians.[67] Structuralism, despite its proclaimed unity, embraced a number of rather heterogeneous realities. It all started with an
attempt to borrow from and adapt the rigorous work of Lévi-Strauss
on kinship systems and Roman Jakobson on phonological contrasts in
linguistics, but from there it became many things to many people—
from a model approach to the social sciences (exemplified by Georges
Dumézil's work on the history of religion, which was belatedly recognized during the 1960s) to various claims of a generalized formalism,
whether as an "activity" capable of revolutionizing all kinds of analysis
or even an all-consuming intellectual fashion. Structuralism was all of
these things, but first of all it was a new scientism: Lévi-Strauss tirelessly
reminded his readers that his work should be classed among the hard
sciences as opposed to the human sciences with their traditional techniques.[68] Ultimately it also became an invasive scientific ideology that
attracted scholars from many fields, all eager to invoke a reassuring
model of what they took to be scientific certitude. Marxism, as revisited
by Louis Althusser in this period, is a good example: Althusser believed
he had identified a *coupure* separating science from ideology. There
were, of course, many reasons for the success of this model, and surely
the proclaimed rigor of the approach was one of them; but so was the
fascination with formalism on the part of intellectuals disappointed in
actual history, in which so many had earlier placed their hopes.[69] It was
as if the old project of unifying the social sciences around a unique,
prescriptive method—the very project that Durkheim and the Durkheimians had conceived at the turn of the century—had been revived.
The flexible, basically empirical interdisciplinarity that the first two *Annales* generations had advocated and exemplified was now opposed by a
(self-styled) unitary epistemology, which dismissed any scholarly practice that seemed to put up even passive resistance. Surely it is no accident

that this new epistemology was proposed more often than not by disciplines on the fringes of the academy or, at any rate, relatively unimportant within the system (such as anthropology, linguistics, semiotics, and to a lesser extent sociology) or else not represented at all (psychoanalysis). The pattern is exactly the same as the one we encountered a half-century earlier;[70] and once again history found itself in the place of the accused, although this time the charges were different. For Lévi-Strauss, history's function was essentially chronological, preliminary work to be performed prior to scientific analysis in the proper sense of the word: "Its originality and distinctiveness lie entirely in the apprehension of the relation of before and after."[71] More generally, structuralist analysis was concerned with defining a grammar of énoncés and relations through which social realities could be identified with subjectless processes, and in this respect it seemed totally at odds with the historical approach.

Nevertheless, the historiography that developed around the *Annales* withstood this imperious offensive. Two things made this possible. The first has to do with the conception of the movement itself: it was less concerned with explaining the forms and modalities of social change than with identifying stable systems. This was true, at any rate, of the work in economic history done under the leadership of Labrousse and Braudel. An even more striking example can be found in the concept of a history of *mentalités,* which Febvre was one of the first to propose. The project grew out of a systematic critique of the history of ideas as practiced by historians of literature and philosophy. Febvre criticized them for getting bogged down in abstract, timeless debates and for interpreting the past in an anachronistic way, especially when they insisted on "distorting the psychological reality of the past" by invoking overly general categories. He persistently attacked "those who, in seeking to rethink centuries-old systems with no concern for how those systems related to other manifestations of the age in which they were born, do exactly the opposite of what historical method requires—and who, faced with concepts engendered by disembodied intelligences and living a life of their own outside time and space, forge strange chains out of imaginary and internally seamless links."[72] Instead of a history that, in Febvre's view, focused exclusively on ideas, accepted cultural works at face value, and was satisfied to think in terms of creation, filiation, and influence, he proposed a different approach, one that would situate ideas, works, and behaviors in the social context out of which they emerged. Yet Febvre was never in the slightest tempted by a determinism that would reduce the cultural to the social—indeed, he explicitly denied this. His goals were, rather, to understand the totality of cultural phenomena as one component of a "complex and changing network of social facts" in constant interaction with one another, and to describe culture as a coherent system of instruments and signs to be understood not in terms of its proximity to us but in terms of its distance: "In fact, a man of the sixteenth century should be intelligible not as he relates to us but as he related to his contemporaries." By working from the manifestations of a culture to the conditions that made them possible, one could hope to understand both the culture's unity (or "structure," as Febvre put it in his *Rabelais et le problème de l'incroyance* of 1942) and its specificity. My point is not that the *Annales* were structuralist *avant la lettre*, a case that would be hard to argue, but, rather, that the type of analysis that they proposed was certainly better prepared than some others to confront structuralism and withstand its onslaught.[73]

The second reason has to do with the strategy that the historians spontaneously developed to deal with their now-troublesome former partners; recognizing what they had accomplished, and attempting to form novel alliances and in some cases even hybrids, that strategy called for occupying the terrain of the other social sciences.[74] Take for example historical anthropology, which flourished in these years and in many respects took up where the old history of *mentalités* left off, albeit after a long hiatus. Anthropological history focused on subjects familiar to anthropologists—family systems and, later, mythologies and symbolic products. As ever, historians borrowed anthropological concepts and methods. Old work could now be seen in a new light: in addition to Georges Dumézil's work on Indo-European mythology, there was also Jean-Pierre Vernant's work on ancient Greek mythology and thought.[75] A generation of younger historians followed their lead, among them Pierre Vidal-Naquet, Marcel Detienne, and, in the medieval realm, Jacques Le Goff.[76] The convergence of history and anthropology was the most noticeable development along these lines, as well as the most fruitful and durable, but it was not the only one. There were also efforts at this time to reformulate the relationship between history and linguistics (Régine Robin) as well as psychoanalysis (Alain Besançon and Michel de Certeau, whose styles were very different), which did not proceed in the same way. Even Althusserian Marxism, made more intransigent by the philosopher's disciples, struck a chord among historians, although it was surely the most antihistorical of structuralist teachings: Was not Althusser's definition of ideology taken up by some leading historians, including the medievalist Georges Duby? One has to allow, of course, for the effects of fashion, especially in vocabulary; one also has to allow for the prestige attached to the work of the leading structuralists, from Barthes to Lévi-Strauss to Foucault. Further, one has to pay attention to the diversity, not to say heterogeneity, of what went by the name of structuralism and contributed to its influence. Nevertheless, the historians' fascination with structuralism gave rise to a series of reformulations that enabled history to continue to participate in the social science dialogue from which it seemed for a time to have been excluded.

The historians' strategy was at first spontaneous and anything but deliberate—and all the more effective as a result. In any case, it allowed history to survive a difficult decade and even to garner new support. In this debate the work of Michel Foucault played a key role. Of all the structuralists, Foucault was in many respects the closest to historians, and he used that proximity for a time to affirm his distance from his original discipline, philosophy, even at the cost of accepting the misunderstandings and ambiguities inherent in the historians' reading of his work. Indeed, in *L'Archéologie du savoir* (1969), and especially its first few chapters, Foucault proposed a parallel between his approach and that of the *Annales* by emphasizing the importance of series, systems, and discontinuities in discursive formations. (He would return to these themes the following year in his inaugural lecture at the Collège de France, *L'Ordre du discours*.) He thus not only lent support to history but bestowed his recognition upon it. In 1971, the *Annales* felt ready to sum up the state of the debate, or rather the state of the battlefield after the cease-fire, in a special issue entitled "Histoire et structure," to which a number of leading structuralists contributed. It began by declaring an end to hostilities: "The war between history and structuralism will not take place." Taking advantage of a "calm conjuncture," André Burguière proposed a reformulation of the issues:

> If the rejection of history seemed to crystallize this diverse movement and afford it a certain cohesiveness, it was because these disciplines needed first of all to break the historicist mold in which they were all originally cast: by "historicism" I mean a constant tendency to shift the analysis from study of the phenomenon to study of its origin (genetic explanation), as well as a tendency for various approaches to toss the ball back and forth among themselves through endless recourse to dialectical reasoning (explanation in terms of external causes).

Ultimately, however, the conclusion was that the tide was already turning back toward history. All the main participants in the debate were summoned to gather on the terrain that the *Annales* had claimed from the beginning: "If structural analysis consists in uncovering permanent features, in revealing 'a system of transformations governed by certain systematic laws,' then historians must recognize that they have long been familiar with the approach, even at the risk of seeming to be asserting yet again certain rights of priority."[77] Clearly, the war was over.

9. The time had come, it seemed, for a new order of things, and as it happens the moment also coincided with a change of generation. In 1965, Labrousse resigned from the Sorbonne, where Pierre Vilar succeeded

him but only for a few years. Braudel resigned from the Collège de France and the chairmanship of the Ecole des Hautes Etudes in 1972. In 1969, he had given up the editorship of the *Annales* to a triumvirate of much younger historians, the medievalist Jacques Le Goff (who also assumed the chairmanship of the Ecole), the early modernist Emmanuel Le Roy Ladurie (who replaced Braudel at the Collège), and the contemporary historian Marc Ferro (who had been the journal's secretary under Braudel since 1964). Of course, the change was far broader and more profound: the generation of historians who had trained in the immediate postwar period now assumed the principal chairs of history in Paris as well as the provinces. This change at the top was all the more apparent in that it coincided with a spectacular increase in the number of academic positions in the wake of the crisis that had erupted in the universities in 1968: between 1967 and 1983, the number of full professors, *assistants*, and *maîtres-assistants* doubled.[78] The historical discipline was thus as important a presence as ever, especially in the universities, where it attracted many students (whose numbers were growing more rapidly than the number of teachers). There was a corresponding increase in the number of academic papers, articles, and theses generated.

These changes in the profession proceeded in a favorable climate that, while not peculiar to France, was singularly propitious there. In the 1970s, the broader public, well beyond academic circles, proved to be avid for history. The eruption of May '68 may be taken as a convenient if ambivalent marker. The social movement (which began in the universities) had its sights set on a utopian future conceived in terms of liberation from social constraints. Indeed, the movement can be understood as a rejection of contemporary society, which was seen as the source of ever-more restrictive constraints on individuals and groups. A few years later came a worldwide economic recession. In France, this marked the end of the *Trente glorieuses* and the beginnings of an economic contraction that has lasted, with certain fluctuations, to this day. The optimism of the postwar years gave way to uncertainty about the significance of a history that had seemed comprehensible only a short while before. Progress, the rallying cry in a time of rapid transformation, no longer seemed assured. The present was uncertain, the future opaque; the past became a safe place in which to invest. The result was a broad change in social attitudes toward the past, a transformation of what might be called the "regime of historicity." What people now wanted from history was no longer lessons, precedents, or ways of understanding the present but, rather, a refuge against the uncertainties of the moment. History became an exotic realm, a retrospective utopia that planted its flag in the soil of an absolute elsewhere, just as ethnological literature was doing at the same time.

Along with this transformation went a very profound change in the nature of the audience for history. Since the end of the nineteenth century essentially two types of history readers had existed in France. For the "general public," a term with just a hint of contempt, there was *la petite histoire* anecdotal, belletristic history that enjoyed little respect in the academy. For specialists and educated amateurs—that is, broadly speaking, for those who were the actual or potential producers of history—there were the works of scholars. Now, though, this simplistic division was called into question. For the first time since Michelet, Taine, Renan, and Jaurès, the work of professional historians found a very large readership indeed. The success of Le Roy Ladurie's *Montaillou* (1975) may be taken as emblematic, even though it remained exceptional—there is no certainty that the two hundred thousand people who bought this austere study of a Pyrenean community in the Middle Ages read all or even some of the work's six hundred densely written pages. Yet it hardly matters: when it comes to cultural goods, possession is often tantamount to title, and the important point is that so many people were convinced that this book and others like it were written for them. Historians had acquired a new intellectual and moral authority, as any number of signs attested: the proliferation of historical best-sellers[79] and historical lists in publishers' catalogs; the diversification of historians' contributions, other than books and articles, in the press, on television, and in the movies; the constant presence of historians in public debates largely outside their professional competence. All these signs point to an almost miraculous convergence of scholarly history with a society ready to appropriate the works of the scholars. Although this marriage will probably not last, it has nonetheless proven a powerful boost to the discipline.

Moreover, the history that fascinated all these new readers was precisely the "static history" that Le Roy Ladurie alluded to in the title of his 1973 inaugural lecture at the Collège de France.[80] People discovered, in this new past, social forms and values that previously had been neglected or underestimated. Nothing reveals this more clearly than the career of a historian like Philippe Ariès.[81] A self-described "Sunday historian," Ariès did most of his work outside the academic setting and did not receive the recognition of the universities until late in life. He was also marginal in a second way: he came out of the extreme political right, which after World War II was largely excluded from academic life. This perhaps accounts for the fact that his early work, for all its novelty, attracted little notice outside the narrow circle of those who shared his views. His acclaim came not with the publication in 1960 of his great work, *L'Enfant et la vie familiale sous l'Ancien Régime,* but ten years later, when the left (and even more the extreme left) rediscovered in everyday life and historical experience realities that it had traditionally regarded as unimportant: the family, organic solidarities, social relationships, society without the state. Ariès's lonely career can thus be read as a sign of the times, one that tells us a great deal about the extent to which the success of the "new history" was the expression of a deeply rooted collective sensibility. It is by no means clear that all the historians who reaped the benefits understood this at the time, but they were certainly surprised by the warm welcome they received.

Another external factor that contributed to the growth of French history was the acclaim it received internationally. To be sure, this was not entirely new. At international meetings, the French had long been well represented and highly respected. In the 1950s, moreover, Braudel's reputation grew in the countries bordering the Mediterranean, especially Spain and Italy. The reason is obvious: his great book cast their history in a new light. However, the reputation of French history grew exponentially when the *Annales* gained recognition in Britain and especially the United States, which until then had remained dubious if not downright skeptical about this foreign import.[82] The English translation of *La Méditerranée* in 1973 and the success that greeted its publication can serve as a convenient benchmark. Subsequent translations of other French work influenced many American historians.[83] The *Annales* were in fashion and would remain so for the next decade or so—all in all, not a bad run for a fashion. Yet fashion by itself will not do as an explanation, or, rather, fashions often reveal broader and deeper transformations. In the United States, the favor enjoyed by the *Annales* helped to bring recognition to the work of historians just coming to prominence at the time but with longstanding ties to France. Among them was Natalie Zemon Davis, whose first book, *Society and Culture in Early Modern France* (1975), was immediately hailed on both sides of the Atlantic. A few years later, in 1979, Robert Darnton published his *Business of the Enlightenment*, which was closely related to French work on the "culture of the book" in the eighteenth century. Many others would follow. But the influence did not flow in one direction only: foreign works in turn exerted a considerable influence on the interests and methods of French historians. Indeed, what began in the 1970s was an internationalization of historical debate and communication. Ideas, books, and—last but not least—people circulated as never before. Debates, problems, proposed solutions, references, and concepts were shared to an unprecedented degree. This does not mean that national traits altogether vanished from the work that was produced—far from it—but communication and comparison did become the rule. It was clearly a new order of things, and in the short run this benefited the *Annales,* which became an obligatory reference.

their objects of research by combining anthropological with historical approaches: I am thinking in particular of Nathan Wachtel's extensive exploration of the history of Andean societies.[93] In a few cases, the influence of anthropology led to the development of a comparative perspective, something that, since Marc Bloch, has been more often proclaimed than practiced.[94] One has to concede, however, that the label "historical anthropology" often served as a spiffy new facade for more traditional—and of course perfectly respectable—practices in the areas of rural history, culture, and *mentalités*. Yet even where the graft was merely superficial, the "anthropologization" of research objects points up an important change in outlook.

The period also witnessed the emergence of powerful new approaches to cultural history. In the postwar years, there was a more or less tacit consensus that economic and social realities were paramount in the understanding of historical processes. Now, however, there was an equally tacit turn toward the sociocultural on the part of many historians, including a good number of those who had already tried their hands at "weightier" topics.[95] The new expectation was that societies could be made intelligible by studying the imagination, dreams, festivals, and social representations, even if doubts persisted about how to relate the various levels of historical analysis. In any case, the shift was massive. Over the previous twenty-five years, fewer than 10 percent of the articles published in the *Annales* dealt with cultural history (including the history of *mentalités*), but by the mid-1970s this percentage tripled. The change did not end there.

Finally, the dynamism of the 1970s would be incomprehensible if we did not take into account a certain methodological optimism, which might almost be characterized as "technological," and which contrasted with the generally depressed climate of the times. We have seen how important the measurement of social facts had been in the previous period; the introduction of computers into the historian's panoply, though, generated new resources, slowly, to be sure, and somewhat chaotically. The advance was dramatic compared with the resources available to Labrousse (in the early days, nothing more than a pencil and paper) or even the postwar research teams (which had had to make do with adding machines). Now one could record, preserve, and process bodies of data previously inaccessible because of their size and complexity. Today, such operations have become routine and almost trivial, but they were still new not so very long ago. A number of major undertakings were launched, and some succeeded brilliantly, among them the vast study of the Florentine *Catasto* of 1427 conducted jointly by Christiane Klapisch and David Herlihy.[96] For the time being, the primacy of the cultural did not lead to any abandonment of quantification or the use of serial data—

indeed, it was widely felt that one could now "measure" behaviors, representations, and objects as one had long since learned to "measure" prices and outputs. Following the lead of Michel Vovelle, some historians overcame their scruples about plunging into the vast notarial archives, while others tackled the mountains of statistics left behind by the Ancien Régime and the nineteenth century. The prophet of the new order, Le Roy Ladurie, felt confident enough to predict that by the year 2000 "historians will either be programmers or they will no longer exist."[97] This may have been an exaggeration, but it did set the tone of the times.

10. All signs thus indicate that the growth of the historical profession after 1970 was spectacular. It proved difficult to control, however; more than that, it brought with it a kind of malaise and raised a series of questions about the discipline and its methods—questions that have become increasingly urgent over the past ten or fifteen years.

Consider first the malaise. The primary reasons for it were obviously related to the very progress of historical research. History had advanced steadily through annexation and accumulation. It had multiplied its objects, borrowed ideas and approaches from the other social sciences, and spun off a series of subdisciplines (whose status and even relevance varied widely). It was now in charge of a vast, ever-expanding territory—in charge, but not in control. Such was the price of conquest. Many felt intuitively that this policy of unlimited conquest threatened history with the loss if not of its soul then at least of its project and unity. Amassing riches it could not organize, it risked disintegrating into a multitude of specialized histories that could no longer be related to one another. This state of affairs was sometimes described, in self-congratulatory terms, as an "explosion of history," but later, in a more pessimistic mood, it was also denounced as "history in pieces."[98] The polemical aspect of this terminological dispute need not detain us. In my view, both formulas suffer from confusing two distinct realities: on the one hand, the vitality of historical research, which was constantly moving into new areas and absorbing suggestions from the outside (whether this was good or bad is another matter), and, on the other, the epistemological norms that governed this research and the status of the historian's work. What was in the process of changing was the relation between these two poles. In general, the historians involved were mostly unaware that the transformation was taking place. That is probably why they found it so difficult. They had allowed themselves to be swept up by the prospect of unlimited expansion. In the end, they found themselves in a fragmented, patchwork landscape. Fifteen years ago, the temporary suspension of the goal of achieving a global history may have seemed iconoclastic (and, to be perfectly frank, it may have been greeted by most historians with indifference),[99] yet today it is taken for granted. The change still elicits a certain nostalgia, though, a certain remorse at having renounced a noble ambition, even though nothing has yet emerged that might give substance to the evanescent dream.

Was this evolution accidental, or was it implicit in the very program of the *Annales*? In 1966, when Le Roy Ladurie declared in the preface to *Les Paysans de Languedoc* that he had "tried the adventure of total history," he may have seemed presumptuous, but the ambition itself was seen as legitimate, as it was for Braudel in *La Méditerranée* or Vilar in *La Catalogne*. These projects were driven by the conviction that it was possible to compile and compare the results of historical investigation. But the very dynamic of research imposed epistemological requirements that tended in the opposite direction. François Furet was one of the first to suggest this in his 1971 remarks on the generalization of quantification and its implications for historians: "It atomizes historical reality into fragments so distinct that history's classic claim to comprehend the global is compromised. Must this claim be withdrawn? My answer is that it should probably be preserved as a long-term goal but, if there is to be progress, not as a premise of research, unless we are willing to risk succumbing once again to the teleological fallacy. . . . Global analysis of the 'system of systems' is probably beyond our means."[100]

Meanwhile, as programmatic pronouncements gave way to practice, research was reorganized in novel ways. As avenues were explored in the hope of achieving a deeper general understanding of the past, new specialties gradually developed. Take the case of historical demography, which flourished in these years: the demographic factor was at first a simple variable in economic models of preindustrial society, but later it became an object of research in its own right, giving rise to a quasi-autonomous discipline within social history. Other, similar developments were less spectacular. Nevertheless, the result was that disciplinary boundaries once thought to have been banished resurrected themselves in the form of new boundaries between subspecialties.

These developments explain, no doubt, why long-neglected problems have reasserted themselves insistently over the past two decades. Epistemological criticism, once dismissed by historians as pointless, has come back into vogue. In 1971, Paul Veyne stirred passions when he published a long polemic inspired by German historicism and fortified by British and American epistemological reflections, which seriously undermined the scientific pretensions of the new history and instead proposed looking at historical writing as the construction of narrative plots. Historians were shocked but not convinced. The year before, Michel de Certeau, writing in a very different vein, had published a lengthy study of what he called the "historiographical operation." His book, though probably more influential than Veyne's, still did not really alter the historical agenda: historians were ready to acknowledge the pertinence of the questions it raised, but their energies were still largely absorbed by the practical work at hand.[101] Although these works, different in their approaches as well as their conclusions, elicited relatively little response at the time, they suggested that the moment was perhaps ripe for a reassessment of the situation. Indeed, though none of the multivolume surveys being published at the time mentioned the need for such critical evaluation, the issue was repeatedly raised in a series of less visible publications.[102]

So there was malaise, along with some preliminary critical reflections—but was the situation serious enough to warrant calling it a crisis?[103] Even those most centrally involved were not certain of the diagnosis. What is certain, however, is that the apparent unanimity of the previous period was beginning to collapse. The superficial signs of change need not detain us: after years of respectful silence, the "*Annales* system" and its offspring came in for some extremely ideological attacks.[104] More significant, some of the promoters (and beneficiaries) of the "new history" began to take their distance.[105] In 1979, Lawrence Stone stirred a great deal of discussion with a radical critique of social history's overweening and, in his view, futile and ultimately unrealized ambitions; Stone's critique ended with a call for a "revival of narrative." The attack was particularly noteworthy in that Stone was himself a leading social historian, the author of important books on English society in the seventeenth, eighteenth, and nineteenth centuries, and an editor of *Past and Present*.[106] In the same year, the Italian historian Carlo Ginzburg published a text less vehement than Stone's but even more penetratingly critical. For Ginzburg, the nascent crisis of confidence reflected history's need for a model based on something other than the exact sciences. He proposed a new paradigm, which he called the "paradigm of the clue" as opposed to the reigning "Galilean paradigm." Social history, he argued, had gone astray by searching for regular patterns when its true vocation was rather to search for significant "clues," from which one could obtain "indirect," "conjectural" knowledge in a manner that Ginzburg likened to psychoanalytic interpretation or police work.[107] These two papers, by Stone and Ginzburg, were probably the most widely commented examples of the kind of criticism being leveled at the prevailing historiographic model, but they were not the only ones: it would be easy to give a long list of others. To be sure, the issues were not always clearly formulated. Nevertheless, the most telling critiques were sharp enough and consistent enough that we may take them as symptoms of dissatisfaction and doubt. Once again, the phenomenon was not peculiar to France: similar doubts were raised in the 1980s in most of the provinces of Western historiography. They probably attracted greater attention in France, however, because social history was so closely identified with the *Annales*. It is worth taking a moment to look a little more closely at the reasons for this historical turn.

Again, those reasons were numerous and complex. To start with the most general, the social sciences were in a period of profound change—indeed, the spontaneous and ideological representations that societies produce of themselves were probably also in flux. The second half of the nineteenth century and the first three quarters of the twentieth century were dominated by powerful integrative paradigms—positivism, Marxism, and structuralism. All may be classed, without undue distortion, as functionalisms. Over the past two decades, however, the functionalist paradigm seems, despite the absence of any overt crisis, to have collapsed, and with it the scientific ideologies that had unified the social sciences (or served as a common frame of reference). Meanwhile, society itself was overcome by doubts in the face of new, seemingly inexplicable forms of crisis, and these doubts inevitably fostered skepticism about the very ambition to achieve a global understanding of the social. This had been the credo, explicit or implicit, of the previous generations; fulfillment of the goal was now postponed.

The consequences of this development were considerable, and we are just beginning to take their measure. The project of "global" history was based, as we have seen, on an optimistic belief that the human sciences would ultimately converge. As new specialties emerged within the disciplines, the intellectual architecture defining the overall shape of the edifice was shaken. Meanwhile, interdisciplinarity, or pluridisciplinarity, whose legitimacy had seemed established (however one formulated it or proposed to bring it about), again became problematic. Within the social sciences, the disciplines are less self-confident than they once were: the last few years have seen a spate of critical assessments and reflections. Nor is it as clear as it once was how the disciplines should relate. In some cases, formerly separate disciplines have come together to such an extent that it is no longer clear that they have anything left to exchange (as in certain areas of history and anthropology). More generally, the "regime of scientificity" that the social sciences seemed to share has come into question, along with the overall project. Of course, this does not mean that interdisciplinary dialogue is a thing of the past. Yet it is no longer seen as an answer: it is, rather, a problem (and should probably never have ceased to be one).[108]

Criticism also focused on the approaches with which historians were most familiar and the beliefs on which those approaches were based. Measurement had become one of history's basic techniques and had proved remarkably fruitful. However, as statistical techniques became more powerful and research programs grew more ambitious, even quantitative historians succumbed to doubt. The four decades after 1950 witnessed an unprecedented outpouring of statistical data, which advanced our understanding in many areas.[109] There were limits to what could be learned, though, for two reasons. At the most basic level, it was difficult to compare or combine different quantitative findings, despite the optimistic pronouncements of proponents. Quantification itself was not at fault, but the way it was used was: many statistics had been compiled in a chaotic manner, and there was also a great deal of redundancy, leading to a sense of diminishing returns. The second reason is more complex. For Simiand and Labrousse early in his career, the use of numbers was not an end in itself but a way of subjecting a hypothesis to empirical verification using explicit procedures. Increasingly, however, the dynamics of research turned the production of data itself into a goal, indeed a priority.[110] This was a perverse effect of the positivist attitude so prevalent in France (and elsewhere). To be sure, the history of research over the past half century has been one of constructing increasingly sophisticated objects—historical methods have become more complex and more tightly controlled—but we have meanwhile lost sight of the experimental, hypothetical nature of the objects we construct, at times succumbing to the temptation to mistake them for "things."

A good example of this tendency to reify the categories of historical analysis can be seen in the evolution of price history from Labrousse's early work (1933) to the 1960s. Other examples from the next generation include the use of geographical regions as frameworks of research as well as the use of socioprofessional categories. The priority seems to have been to amass as much data as possible, using categories defined by convention rather than by critical thinking, described more often than analyzed; the result has been the creation of vast electronic databases filled with lifeless information that, one day, is supposed to provide answers to all the questions that no one has bothered to ask. The conventionality of such research also suggests why so little thinking was done about the internal structure of the historical realities reconstituted in this way. For a long time, it was enough simply to juxtapose different aspects of the story. In France, social history was thus shaped by the preexisting mold of economic history; the first attempts to do the social history of culture in the 1960s were naturally guided by socioeconomic principles of interpretation. Serious difficulties were sometimes encountered. Things proceeded as they did not because historians accepted economic determinism in one form or another but because their epistemological reflexes had been dulled by earlier successes: this was the price to be paid for a hyperactive research effort, one that had, over a period of four or five decades, explored countless new areas and conquered vast new terrain.

The foregoing portrait is unjust, of course. It highlights the difficulties and dead ends of what has been an extraordinarily fruitful enterprise; it fails as well to acknowledge individual as well as collective efforts to rethink the project and methods of social history in ways that ultimately proved unsatisfactory.[111] Recurrent doubts were voiced even in the pages of the *Annales,* although one has the impression that they were not always heeded. In any case, my point here is not to issue a judgment as to what could or should have been done (a judgment all too easy to make after the fact) but, rather, to understand how the practice of social history gave rise to questions that have led in the past few years to a revision of our thinking. The diagnosis that I have just outlined was, after all, formulated by the *Annales,* which called upon the community of historians to reflect on these issues and, in two successive editorials, pointed to the need for a "critical turn."[112]

11. French historians were not alone in raising such doubts about the established methods and certainties of social history. Similar questions were raised more or less everywhere, though their style, content, and implicit intellectual strategies varied significantly. To appreciate the differences, one has only to compare the developments that followed the "linguistic turn" in the United States with the Italian debates around "microhistory" and the continuing French reflection on historiography. Yet French revisionist thinking did not proceed in isolation, if only because the circulation of ideas from country to country is today the rule rather than the exception.

One way to gauge the extent of that circulation is to name the authors and works mentioned by revisionist thinkers. The point is not to single out the "most important" references or to argue in terms of "influences" but, rather, to pinpoint the key elements of an ongoing debate. Some of the key references were fairly old but took on belated relevance in a new context. Take, for example, E. P. Thompson's *The Making of the English Working Class,* first published in 1963. Its French reception was delayed, though not because anyone objected to the work: Thompson's project did not fit in well with French-style social history.[113] It was only when the limits of a sociohistorical analysis based essentially on distributions became apparent that Thompson's approach, attentive to the dynamic process of constructing social identities, could be seen as an alternative. An even more telling example is the work of the sociologist Norbert Elias, whose importance for historians of all nationalities has grown steadily over the past twenty years. Elias's work was even earlier than Thompson's and very slow to find an audience.[114] Part of the explanation for the warm reception it ultimately received lies in the fact that its themes were in many ways close to the controversial issues of the moment, such as power and social control and the history of physical discipline and bodily self-restraint—the same topics that found favor in the work of Michel Foucault. Beyond these sometimes surprising coincidences, however, Elias played an important part in crystallizing growing dissatisfactions with the prevailing analytic categories and showing how they might be reformulated. Classically, quantitative approaches to history were based essentially on aggregates and distributions. Elias, however, conceived of the social in terms of individual and group interdependencies: he used the notion of "figuration" to refer to the complex, reciprocal bonds that constitute the matrix of social interaction and are constantly being redefined by the principal social actors. Clearly, these ideas became relevant because they encouraged taking a serious look at realities that had previously been largely ignored.[115]

The same can be said of ideas that came from microhistory. The term refers, as is well known, not so much to a school of historians as to a set of works that appeared in Italy in the 1970s and after, including books by Carlo Ginzburg, Giovanni Levi, Edoardo Grendi, Carlo Poni, and others. Here was yet another approach to social history. Instead of the macrohistorical approach exemplified by the *Annales* tradition, the Italian microhistorians proposed a new approach based on intensive but limited samples of social reality: communities, social networks, individual careers, and so on. Their work has had a profound impact in France in recent years for two reasons. First, the change in the scale of observation revealed not just familiar objects in miniature but different configurations of the social; and second, because microhistorical analysis reveals novel configurations, it encourages critical thinking about even the most familiar concepts.[116]

Much the same thing can also be said about other major works in the social sciences and philosophy which have recently posed challenges to historians. One name that comes immediately to mind is of course Michel Foucault, whose intellectual stature has grown steadily over the past twenty years. His influence is complex, however, if only because the focus of his work shifted progressively from *Histoire de la folie* (1961) to the two volumes of the *Histoire de la sexualité* (1984), whose sequel was cut short by Foucault's death. There has also been some confusion about the nature of that work, confusion contributed to at times by Foucault himself. Although this history remains to be written,[117] there can be no doubt that Foucault exerted a powerful influence on the reorientation of historical thinking—in part, of course, through the subjects he chose to study, but even more through his emphasis on discourse as one place where reality is produced. Between the sixteenth and eighteenth centu-

ries, the history of madness was not only a matter of the gradual marginalization and confinement of lunatics, or of the birth of psychiatry; it was
also the history of the construction, in the West and for a period of
several centuries, of the two antagonistic figures of madness and reason
(in the classical sense). Behind these pregnant words, Foucault points to
hidden divisions. By the same token, he attacks the positivism of which
history, he argues, continues to partake, as do the other social sciences.
As he put it:

> We must demystify the global instance of the real as a totality to be recon-
> stituted. . . . And perhaps we should also question a principle that is often
> implicitly taken for granted, namely, that the only reality that history
> should attempt to know is society itself. A type of rationality, a way of
> thinking, a program, a technique, a rational, coordinated set of actions,
> of goals formulated and pursued, of instruments for achieving those
> goals—all these things are the very stuff of the real, even if that real does
> not claim to be "reality" itself or the whole of "society." [118]

The sharpness of the critique threw the reasons for a prolonged misunderstanding into sharp relief. It also called upon historians to revise their
agenda, and that call was largely heeded.

Philosophical questioning, traditionally a matter for wariness if not
suspicion on the part of French historians, also made its effects felt in
other branches of thought from which history had generally kept its
distance. In general, these were associated with problems of interpretation and its construction. Hermeneutics, of course, had been at the heart
of German thought since the nineteenth century; yet it was virtually
absent from French experience, especially in the social sciences, which
were deeply imbued with the spirit of a positivism that had undergone
several revisions over the course of more than a century. Recently,
though, hermeneutics has made a strong comeback, not only in Foucault's late work but as a problem of historiography and of the social
sciences generally. The contemporary influence of Michel de Certeau, a
historian and philosopher, and of Paul Ricoeur, which came late in a
lengthy philosophical career, are two examples. [119] They and others insisted on the "effects of meaning" inextricably bound up with any intellectual operation, as well as on the importance of the reconfigurations
that result when the same utterance occurs in multiple contexts. The
reevaluation of the role of narrative, which for Ricoeur is intimately
associated with the human experience of time, is all the more noteworthy
in that French historiography from Simiand to Braudel viewed narrative
with suspicion. True, the narrative that concerns historians today has
little in common with the "chronicle" whose fundamental inadequacies
Simiand attacked at the turn of the century—or, for that matter, with

the "plot" that Paul Veyne saw in 1971 as the historian's central task. It has become instead the focal point of a complex interrogation concerning the coherence of actions and actors, the rationality of historical processes, and the possibility of explaining them. In any case, historians thus discovered a whole range of new concerns.

More generally, perhaps, the continuing critique of the positivist program (usually implicit in the social sciences, but at times openly proclaimed) has led to a rethinking of our fundamental concepts. That effort is far from complete. After a period of lawlike certitude, the social sciences entered a phase of epistemological anarchy (not unlike the "first crisis of reason" at the turn of the century). In its more extreme forms, deconstructionism threatened to make interpretation the undisputed sovereign of social science, particularly in the United States. Other recent signs suggest that old landmarks have vanished, yet nothing new has emerged to take their place. In my view, however, recent French experience points the way toward a reconstruction of sorts—the reconstruction of a feasible rational space for the social sciences to work in. It is interesting to note that history retains an essential role in this project, even if it is a very different kind of role from those it played in the past. The sociologist Jean-Claude Passeron has followed Karl Dilthey and Max Weber in invoking the historicity common to all the social sciences as grounds for rejecting the "nomological illusion," that is, the misguided belief of the social sciences in their ability to enunciate covering laws similar to the laws of natural science. Against Karl Popper, Passeron asserts that "there is not and cannot be any unified protocol language for the historical description of the empirical world." [120] The social sciences should, rather, assert their own distinctive "scientific regime": sociological (or historical) reasoning does not seek to establish laws of the type produced by experimental reasoning. Historical observation imposes certain conditions that prevent the social sciences from producing general formalizations. However, one can recognize these limits and renounce the ambition to enunciate laws without giving up on "science" or ceasing to formulate rules. The assertion is modest, to be sure; more important is the emphasis on procedures, conditions, and validations. Are we finally, after a century of positivism, freeing ourselves from its coils?

A brief look at some of the ways in which historians have responded to these recent concerns and begun to revise their approach will help to make the foregoing remarks more concrete. A word of caution is in order, however: because research is a long-term enterprise and acquired habits are hard to break, things do not change overnight. Work already in progress continues, though not necessarily as in the past. Take, for example, the quantitative "history of the book" and of literacy, two active (and curiously disjointed) areas of research in France in the 1960s and 1970s. Within these areas, the outlook changed profoundly in the 1980s after Roger Chartier changed the emphasis to the history of "reading" and the use of printed materials generally.[121] Urban history underwent a similar transformation in the wake of Jean-Claude Perrot's work in the 1970s. Although urban history was a traditional specialty, very different ideas of the subject coexisted under a single rubric. Often the distinctive character of urban history was lost: the city had simply become a neutral analytic framework for the usual brand of social history. In the new approach, the city itself—its identity, its forms, and the classifications it engenders—becomes an object of investigation. The goal is to work toward a historical definition of the urban by "recognizing the diversity of human forms obscured by the deceptive changelessness of locale and language. Rather than minimize the complexity of urban phenomena, some historians have used that complexity to understand how social actors wittingly and unwittingly redefine the organization of the social (broadly understood)."[122] History, in other words, may be finding new sources of energy not by appropriating new objects but by redefining old ones (and changing the questions put to them).

Of course, new areas are also being explored. Some of the new themes are truly international: this is obviously the case with the history of women, although there is more than one version of that history, each shaped by its own distinctive cultural, social, and experiental context.[123] Other areas are more idiosyncratic to France, however. Take, for example, the "return" to political history, a kind of history to which the *Annales* tradition had left little place, of course. What has occurred is not so much a return to politics in any traditional sense as an effort by various historians to incorporate political analysis into their work. Maurice Agulhon had given a brilliant example of this more than twenty years ago when he investigated the role of social forms in phenomena of political acculturation, looking at both the reuse of traditional forms of "sociability" and the invention of new structures. Thus for Agulhon the political remained profoundly embedded in the social. François Furet, in his efforts over the past fifteen years to demonstrate a certain autonomy of the political, has taken a much more radical approach. His early work on the Revolution remained well within the Labroussian tradition; starting with *Penser la révolution française* (1978), however, he began to explore the history of political theory and philosophy out of a conviction that the way to explain the dynamics of the Revolution was to analyze not social forces but the intrinsic logic of political action itself.[124] Furet's break with the social historical tradition, attended by its share of emotion and controversy, was thus both unequivocal and openly avowed. It was, of course, connected with the conflict of interpretations that has always marked the historiography of the French Revolution, but it was also motivated in part by a desire to construct distinctive categories of objects.

Over the past few years, another new theme has claimed a growing, at times rather obsessive place in French historical production, namely, the theme of historical memory. To understand this, one must no doubt allow for changes in a society's relation to time and to its own past; in the case of France I discussed a number of such changes earlier. Memory became a focal point of considerable investment because it offered a kind of alternative to history (that is, to actual history, not the history one finds in books). Yet that alone probably cannot account for a complex phenomenon that reflects a variety of interests and concerns. Memory can reveal hidden or repressed historical processes, particularly when misfortune or shame is involved.[125] It can also be an instrument for exploring collective identity (or identities).[126] *Lieux de mémoire*, a vast collective project in which Pierre Nora enlisted the aid of dozens of French historians over more than a decade (1984–1993), can be understood as an attempt to meet concerns of this sort through an exhaustive inventory of the national memory, which, in a society uncertain of its future yet jealous of its identity, has become fragmented. Another sign of concerns about national identity has been the revival of a previously rather neglected genre—the "history of France." Several of these have come out of the *Annales* camp, which one might have thought lukewarm to history of this sort. True, *L'Identité de la France*, the great work that Braudel left unfinished at his death, is unlike any other history of France—and so, for that matter, is the *Histoire de la France* that André Burguière and I conceived and edited a few years later—if only because both works deliberately reject the tradition of teleological narrative that had been virtually consubstantial with the genre.[127] What is striking about these projects, however, is that the specificity of France, or French identity, is taken not as an answer, much less an explanation, but as a problem in need of analysis, a reality that one must try to account for. So while it is more than likely true that a skittish France has retreated into the promise of its past, the mirror held up to it by today's historians is not the reassuring one of tradition and continuity. This shift is, logically enough, inseparable from a reevaluation of the contemporary, which is one of the most striking features of present-day historiography. What is even more remarkable is that it impinges on a tradition that long ascribed priority to the slow changes that occurred in preindustrial societies.

Any mere listing of the themes and subjects of current historiography runs the risk of giving a distorted view of the course of development, however. If there is anything consistently new about the direction things are going, it is not that history is conquering new territory but, rather, that the historian's outlook has changed in ways that, by way of conclusion, I would like briefly to explore. History, it is safe to say, is not expanding into new territory as rapidly in these waning years of the twentieth century as it was fifteen or twenty years ago. This change is noticeable, moreover, in most Western countries. The search for the "new" is no longer an absolute imperative. The slowdown is misleading, however. Although it surely reflects the critical scrutiny that historians have brought to bear on their methods and beliefs, it attests, I think, not to disenchantment within the profession—the discipline is sound, after all, and still attracting students and readers and producing no less regularly than in the past—but to a demand for greater depth.

Much has been made in recent years of the relative eclipse of the ambition to do global history which was a part of the *Annales* program from the beginning. However, that program did not stand unchanged for three quarters of a century. Bloch and Febvre conceived it as a way of bringing together various kinds of research traditionally separated by disciplinary boundaries. Braudel had a more cumulative vision, driven by his belief that if enough data were collected, the facts could ultimately be fitted together, and he accordingly encouraged research on many different fronts. This methodological optimism has certainly dissipated, and today the methods for constructing "globality" have become problematic along with the ambition of achieving a global understanding of the social. Yet has that ambition really been given up? Perhaps not. When optimism prevailed, interdisciplinary collaboration was seen as playing an essential role: it symbolized, beyond the variety of research methods, the unity of the social. Collaborative research today is a rocky road, because both history and the social sciences are less confident than they once were, and because the old system of inter- or pluridisciplinary exchange is showing signs of fatigue. Nevertheless, to say as much is not to give up on the possibility of interdisciplinarity. No longer a solution, interdisciplinarity has once again become a problem: "Rather than conceive, as many would have us do, of the relation between disciplines in terms of homology or convergence, it may be useful today to insist on their specificity and indeed irreducibility. The paradox is merely apparent. Every scientific practice constructs reality on the basis of a series of hypotheses open to verification. Because customs and concepts differ in each case, however, the objects elaborated in this way do not overlap. There are several advantages to this." [128] When the *Annales* proposed this diagnosis in 1989, the intention was to advocate research based not on an assumed proximity of the disciplines but, rather, on comparison of their differences. Since a multiplicity of possible points of view exist, why not take advantage of that fact to achieve a "critical distancing from any particular way of representing the real." Ultimately, a global (but not "total") approach remains conceivable, but in terms profoundly different from those of the past.[129]

More generally, the emphasis in recent years has been on the experimental character of historical work. The term "experimental" may seem surprising. Historians, after all, work with "what actually happened" and happened only once. "Experimental" is also an ambiguous term: on the one hand, it suggests the kind of experimentation that goes on in the natural sciences (and from which historians today seem to be distancing themselves[130]), while on the other, it conjures up the very different idea of a generalized relativism in which historians may allow their subjectivity free rein.[131] In reality, neither connotation is correct. The talk of experimentation is simply a way of reminding historians that they have to be explicit about their hypotheses, test them for consistency, and then subject them to empirical validation based on the sources. The observation is trivial, yet too often it is lost from sight. For twenty or twenty-five years now, the "new economic history" developed in the United States has come in for much debate, some admiration, and a great deal of criticism. In particular, the use of counterfactual analysis has been sharply attacked. Of course, the method as such cannot be generalized, even if one wished to do so. It is useful only when dealing with sources (and therefore areas or periods) for which certain kinds of formalization make sense. Yet the method has the advantage of throwing into sharp relief procedures that generally remain implicit yet might gain a great deal if made explicit. There have been numerous encouraging signs in this regard in recent years. Ideas and methods once taken for granted have been subjected to critical scrutiny: this is true of global and national history, as we have seen, and it also true of biography, events, and narrative.[132] In many cases, the themes and objects subjected to scrutiny go back a long way and may even have been considered old-fashioned or obsolete. The fact that historians are again thinking about them does not mean that in the end they will do exactly what was done in the past, nor is it evidence of a disillusionment that will result in rehabilitation of the old guard. In my view, the new mood reflects a conscious choice—to reexamine the basic concepts that all historians use and to evaluate the ways in which those concepts shape our thinking. A good example can be seen in recent reflections on the construction of social identities, both group and individual, and on the interpretation of trajectories and strategies.[133] The emphasis today is on critical deconstruction of traditional analytic categories. This has led not to skeptical relativism but to fresh thinking about classifications that began as hypothetical but came to be accepted as truths a priori. There is nothing abstract or theoretical about such revision, nothing that precedes actual "experimental" work. It is inextricably associated with the research itself, from the formulation of questions to the pursuit of investigative strategies. In this respect, the current movement remains faithful to the empiricism that has been a hallmark of the *Annales* from the beginning, though today that empiricism is more resolutely critical than in the past.

What has changed over the past half century (and indeed over the half century before that) should now be clear: almost everything, from relations among the disciplines to the goals of social history to the methods of historical research. Yet the fundamental choices behind the whole enterprise and the debates defining those choices have remained substantially the same: to confront work in history and the social sciences and to construct, in a conscious, deliberate manner, categories in terms of which the social can be conceptualized.[134]

TRANSLATED BY ARTHUR GOLDHAMMER

NOTES

[1] See Krzyzstof Pomian, "L'Heure des *Annales*," in Pierre Nora, ed., *Les Lieux de mémoire,* vol. 2, pt. 1: *La Nation* (Paris: Gallimard, 1986), pp. 377–429.

[2] Some of the material in this essay is taken from my forthcoming book, *Les* Annales *en mouvement* (Paris: Seuil, forthcoming).

[3] In this respect, the postwar period was merely a particularly striking example of the kind of construction of the past that has characterized the relation of the French to their history since the Revolution, something that seems to happen after every major crisis.

[4] It is misleading to identify this movement with French history in general, as is sometimes done.

[5] See, most recently, Peter Burke, *The French Historical Revolution: The* Annales *School, 1929–1989* (Stanford, Calif.: Stanford University Press, 1990).

[6] Ibid., p. 1.

[7] Fernand Braudel, *Annales ESC* 24 (1969), p. 571.

[8] The expression "*Annales* school" is common, especially outside the circles most closely connected with the journal. It lends itself to ambivalent uses: claims of membership, broad-gauged denunciations, and of course accusations of infidelity. To mention three examples, none of them new: Josep Fontana, "Ascens I decadencia de l'Escuela dels *Annales*," *Recerques* (Barcelona, 1974), pp. 283–98; Tony Judt, "A Clown in Regal Purple: Social History and the Historians," *History Workshop* 7 (1979), pp. 66–94; and, from a very different point of view, Furio Diaz, "Le stanchezze di Clio," in M. Cedronio et al., *Storiografia francese di ieri e di oggi* (Naples, 1977). The same angle can be found, however, in the very pro-*Annales* book of T. Stoianovich, *French Historical Method: The* Annales *Paradigm* (Ithaca: Cornell University Press, 1976), which contains a preface by Fernand Braudel.

[9] See the excellent book by Claude Digeon, *La Crise allemande de la pensée française* (Paris, 1959).

[10] The fundamental text remains G. Weisz, *The Emergence of Modern Universities in France, 1863–1914* (Princeton, N.J.: Princeton University Press, 1983). An interesting comparative dimension is introduced by Fritz Ringer, *Fields of Knowledge:*

French Academic Culture in Comparative Perspective, 1890–1920 (Cambridge, Eng., and New York: Cambridge University Press, 1992). Christophe Charles, *La République des universitaires, 1870–1940* (Paris, 1994).

[11] See William Keylor, *Academy and Community: The Foundation of the Historical Profession* (Cambridge, Mass.: Harvard University Press, 1975), and C.-O. Carbonell, *Histoire et historiens, une mutation idéologique des historiens français, 1865–1885* (Toulouse, 1976).

[12] In one form or another, positivism has been a durable feature of contemporary French historiography, as we shall see. For interesting reflections on this point, drawing a fundamental contrast between French and German academic culture, see Ringer, *Fields of Knowledge,* ch. 5.

[13] V. Berdoulay, *La Formation de l'école française de géographie* (Paris, 1981); C. Rhein, "La Géographie, discipline scolaire et/ou science sociale? (1860–1920)," *Revue française de sociologie* (1982), pp. 223–51. As was the case with several other new disciplines (or subspecialties) in the same period, the institutionalization of geography was marked by the creation of a major journal, the *Annales de géographie,* founded in 1891.

[14] In a series of important articles, Victor Karady has given a remarkable analysis of the combination of intellectual prestige with institutional quasi-marginality that characterized French academic sociology in its early days. See, in particular, "Durkheim, les sciences sociales et l'université: bilan d'un semi-échec," *Revue française de sociologie,* 2 (1976), pp. 267–311, as well as Philippe Besnard, ed., *The Sociological Domain: The Durkheimians and the Founding of French Sociology* (New York: Cambridge University Press, and Paris: Maison des Sciences de l'Homme, 1983), especially the contributions by Karady. Here again, the creation of a journal, *L'Année sociologique,* marked the consolidation of the new discipline in 1898.

[15] Simiand's article appeared in the new *Revue de synthèse historique,* launched in 1900 by Henri Berr (6 [1903], pp. 1–22, 129–57). It has been reprinted in a very useful anthology edited by M. Cedronio: François Simiand, *Méthode historique et sciences sociales* (Paris, 1987).

[16] "If the study of human facts seeks to provide explanations in the scientific sense of the term . . . its primary task must be to identify stable, well-defined relations . . . such as may exist among phenomena." Simiand's article also contains a very interesting critique of the ways in which historians use the concept of causality.

[17] Lucien Febvre, in his review of François Simiand's *Cours d'économie politique*: "Histoire, économie et statistique," *Annales d'histoire économique et sociale* 2 (1930), p. 583.

[18] In corroboration of this judgment, note that an abridged version of Simiand's text was reprinted in the *Annales* in 1960 at the behest of Fernand Braudel.

[19] The subtlety of the strategy can now be more readily appreciated after the publication of the first volume of the Bloch-Febvre correspondence: Bertrand Müller, ed., *Marc Bloch, Lucien Febvre, et les* Annales d'histoire, economique, et sociale, vol. 1: *Correspondance I (1928–1933),* (Paris: Fayard, 1994).

[20] The gloomy academic climate of the time is well analyzed in the unpublished thesis of O. Dumoulin, "Profession historien: Un métier en crise? (1919–1939)," Ecole des Hautes Etudes en Sciences Sociales, 1983.

[21] Febvre's thesis, *Philippe II et la Franche-Comté: Etude d'histoire politique, religieuse, et sociale* (1911), clearly fell within the Vidalian tradition, as did *La Terre et l'évolution humaine* (1922), in which Febvre defended the geographers against the attacks that Simiand had made against them before the war. As for Bloch, his interest in agrarian history culminated in *Les Caractères originaux de l'histoire rurale française* (1931).

[22] Berr was the inventor (or at any rate one of the inventors) of the phrase "new history." He was also a tireless promoter of scientific and publishing ventures that at-

tracted little notice and received no academic recognition (Berr was not a professor): among them were the Centre International de Synthèse, the Semaines de Synthèse, the Fondation "Pour la science," and the well-known historical collection "L'Evolution de l'humanité," all of which played an important role in French culture from the 1920s to the early 1950s. Berr has yet to find his historian.

[23] In a laudatory review of Simiand's *Cours d'économie politique* in 1930, Febvre asked: "Historians, what is there in this for us? Results that can be directly appropriated? Methods that can be transported with little or no modification from the present into the past? Obviously not." Of course, this text should no doubt be read as a confirmation of Simiand's view that historical experimentation would serve a heuristic function within a unified social science. Yet is it overinterpreting to see it as an expression of impatience on the part of a historian who insists on the distinctiveness of his approach and the need for a historical dimension in all reflection on social facts?

[24] This was the significance of the title of the journal *Les Temps modernes*, which Sartre founded along with other leading intellectuals of his generation in 1945.

[25] Corroborating testimony can be found in the autobiographical essays collected by Pierre Nora, *Essais d'égo-histoire* (Paris, 1987), especially those of Michelle Perrot and Maurice Agulhon. Prefaces to doctoral theses, some of them quite long, also provided an opportunity for historians to explain how their interest in history began: the most remarkable is probably Pierre Vilar's preface to his monumental *Catalogne dans l'Espagne moderne: recherches sur les fondements économiques des structures nationales* (Paris, 1962), 3 vols. Several historians of this generation have written memoirs of their experiences, among them E. Le Roy Ladurie, A. Kriegel, A. Besançon and Vidal-Naquet.

[26] The history of this weakness remains to be written. Meanwhile, see the stimulating but rather hasty essay by Daniel Lindenberg, *Le Marxisme introuvable* (Paris, 1975). The poverty of French Marxism is striking compared with the richness of Marxist debate in Germany, Italy, and Great Britain.

[27] Maurice Agulhon, "Vu des coulisses," in Nora, ed., *Essais d'ego-histoire*, pp. 9–59; Michelle Perrot, "L'Air du temps," ibid., pp. 241–92.

[28] See the convincing data presented in Dumoulin, "Profession historien."

[29] Vilar, *La Catalogne*, vol. 1, p. 12.

[30] Fernand Braudel, *La Méditerranée et le monde méditerranéen à l'époque de Philippe II* (Paris, 1949).

[31] For example, he became chairman of the jury for the *agrégation* in history in 1950 and served for twenty years, allowing him to identify talented young candidates, many of whom would join him in later years at the Ecole des Hautes Etudes.

[32] The Ecole Pratique had been in existence for a long time: it was established by minister Victor Duruy in 1868 for the purpose of bringing the seminar-oriented German model of education and research to France. As has often been the case in France, the Ecole Pratique was thus an adjunct to rather than a part of the regular university system. The Ecole included a history and philology section from its inception (it would play a key role in the Third Republic's program of academic reform). This was followed in 1885 by a section for religious science (the Fifth Section, which would serve as a refuge for several of Durkheim's disciples). A section in economic and social sciences was proposed at the beginning, but for various reasons it was delayed: see B. Mazon, *Aux Origines de l'Ecole des Hautes Études en Sciences Sociales* (Paris, 1988).

[33] Lucien Febvre, "Les Recherches collectives et l'avenir de l'histoire" (1936), reprinted in *Combats pour l'histoire* (Paris, 1956), p. 60.

[34] At the University of Strasbourg, for example, the Faculty of Letters was one of the first to experiment with this type of organization at the time that Febvre and Bloch

were teaching there. When Bloch moved to the Sorbonne, he joined with Maurice Halbwachs in 1938 to establish an Institut d'Histoire Economique et Sociale, which Labrousse would head after the war.

[35] Lutz Raphael, "Le Centre de recherches historiques de 1949 à 1975," *Cahiers du Centre de Recherches Historiques* 10 (April 1993); and, more generally, Comité français des sciences historiques, *Vingt-cinq ans de recherches historiques en France (1940–1965)* (Paris, 1965).

[36] J. Schneider, F. Braudel, E. Labrousse, P. Renouvin, "Les orientations de la recherche historique," *Revue historique* 22 (1959), p. 46.

[37] Ernest Labrousse, "Voies nouvelles vers une histoire de la bourgeoisie occidentale aux XVIIIe et XIXe siècles (1700–1850)," in Comitato Internazionale di Scienze Storiche, X Congresso Internazionale di Scienze Storiche, Rome, 4–11 Settembre 1955, *Relazioni,* vol. 4: *Storia moderna* (Florence, 1955), pp. 365–96: The work is excerpted here as "New Paths Toward a History of the Western Bourgeoisie," pp. 67–74.

[38] See, for example, Agulhon, "Vu des Coulisses," p. 25ff. Agulhon reveals his skepticism about the grand design: "I daresay that our teacher's boldness was rather naive in hoping that by piecing together a series of excellent theses, each devoted to a particular department, we would one day arrive at a true economic and social portrait of France" (ibid., p. 42).

[39] Ernest Laboursse, Introduction, *L'Histoire sociale, sources et méthodes,* Ecole Normale Supérieure de Saint-Cloud, Colloquium, May 1965 (Paris, 1967).

[40] This formulation can be seen as a simplification of the more complex interdependency model proposed by Marc Bloch (and, more generally, the early *Annales*), which allowed for reciprocal determinations of the economic and cultural, for example. For a good illustration, see Bloch, *La Société féodale* (Paris: A. Michel, 1939).

[41] See especially François Simiand, *Le Salaire, l'évolution sociale et la monnaie* (Paris, 1924); also, *Recherches anciennes et nouvelles sur le mouvement général des prix du XVIe au XIXe siècle* (Paris, 1932).

[42] Pierre Vilar, "Réflexions sur la 'crise de l'ancien type': 'Inégalité des récoltes' et 'sous-développement,' " in *Conjoncture économique, structures sociales: hommage à E. Labrousse* (Paris, 1974).

[43] Labrousse, *La Crise de l'économie française*, is perhaps the most complete example of this type of analysis, a model that over the next twenty years would be duplicated and extended in the work of Jean Meuvret, Pierre Goubert, and Emmanuel Le Roy Ladurie.

[44] Labrousse, *Esquisse* and *La Crise de l'économie française*; Jean Meuvret, "Les Crises de subsistances et la démographie d'Ancien Régime," *Population* 4 (1946), pp. 643–50; Pierre Goubert, *Beauvais et le Beauvaisis de 1600 à 1730* (Paris, 1960). Meuvret discreetly served as master to two generations of Ancien Régime historians; his chief methodological articles were collected shortly before his death in *Etudes d'histoire économique* (Paris, 1971).

[45] Fernand Braudel, "Position de l'histoire en 1950," inaugural lecture at the Collège de France, 1950, reprinted in *Ecrits sur l'histoire* (Paris, 1969), pp. 15–38; the quoted passage is on p. 24.

[46] Fernand Braudel, "Histoire et sciences sociales: la longue durée," *Annales ESC,* 13 (1958), pp. 725–53, reprinted in *Ecrits sur l'histoire,* pp. 41–83, excerpted here as "History and the Social Sciences," pp. 115–145.

[47] Meuvret, *Etudes d'histoire économique*; Georges Duby, *La Société aux Xe et XIIe siècles dans la région mâconnaise* (Paris, 1952); *L'Economie rurale et la vie des campagnes de l'Occident médiéval* (Paris, 1962), 2 vols.; Goubert, *Beauvais et le Beauvaisis*; R. Baehrel, *Une Croissance: La Basse-Provence rurale au XVIIe siècle* (Paris, 1960), 2 vols. Emmanuel Le Roy Ladurie, *Les Paysans de Languedoc* (Paris, 1966), 2 vols.;

Pierre Toubert, *Les Structures du Latium médiéval* (Paris, 1973). In addition to these, hundreds if not thousands of works on rural history in the broad sense were published in this period.

48 See Labrousse, "Voies nouvelles pour l'histoire de la bourgeoisie," and *L'Histoire sociale, sources et méthodes*, pp. 67–74.

49 Huguette and Pierre Chaunu, *Séville et l'Atlantique (1504–1650)* (Paris, 1955–1960), 12 vols.

50 Adeline Daumard and François Furet, *Structures et relations sociales à Paris au XVIIIᵉ siècle* (Paris, 1961).

51 François Furet, "L'Histoire quantitative et la construction du fait historique," *Annales ESC* 26 (1971), pp. 63–75, reprinted as "Le Quantitatif en histoire" in *L'Atelier de l'histoire* (Paris, 1982), pp. 53–72, and excerpted here as "Quantitative History," pp. 333–348.

52 Furet, "L'Histoire quantitative" (see note 51, above).

53 The first models were the theses of L. Perouas, *Le Diocèse de La Rochelle de 1648 à 1724: Sociologie et pastorale* (Paris, 1964), and Michel Vovelle, *Piété baroque et déchristianisation en Provence au XVIIIᵉ siècle* (Paris, 1971). Pierre Chaunu commented at length on both books and predicted that they would lead to what he called "the third level of the quantitative."

54 Vilar, *La Catalogne*. Vilar's principal theoretical texts are collected in *Une histoire en construction: Approche marxiste et problématiques conjoncturelles* (Paris, 1982), excerpted here as "History After Marx," pp. 75–81.

55 In the realm of methodology, debate has been particularly bitter. For example, the heterodox historian René Baehrel was shouldered aside by the Labroussian establishment in the 1960s. An aggressive but profoundly innovative thinker, Baehrel was shut out of historical discussion for twenty years. See his *Une Croissance: La Basse-Provence rurale de la fin du seizième siècle à 1789* (Paris, 1960), 2 vols., the importance of which has usefully been emphasized by Maurice Aymard in his preface to the 1988 edition.

56 The only critical reflection widely cited in those years (and until now, for that matter) was Marc Bloch's posthumously published book, *Apologie pour l'histoire* (Paris, 1946). The absence in France (until recently) of anything like the British and American epistemological and philosophical debate is striking. Even attempts to reflect on the discipline such as Henri-Irénée Marrou's *De la connaissance historique* (Paris, 1954) stirred little debate among professional historians, and Paul Ricoeur's *Histoire et vérité* (Paris, 1955) was, if anything, even less influential.

57 Renouvin's work began in the 1930s with reflections on World War I and really came into its own in the 1950s. See the introduction to his *Histoire des relations internationales* (Paris, 1954), and Pierre Renouvin and Jean-Baptiste Duroselle, *Introduction à l'histoire des relations internationales* (Paris, 1964).

58 On the relative openness of the university, see René Rémond's interesting comments in "Le Contemporain du contemporain," in Nora, ed., *Essais d'égo-histoire*, pp. 293–349, esp. pp. 317–18.

59 Roland Mousnier, *La Vénalité des offices sous Henri IV et Louis XIII* (Paris, 1945). Significantly, the book was dedicated to the memory of Fustel de Coulanges. Later, Mousnier would be strongly influenced by American sociology: See his introduction to R. Mousnier, Y. Durand, and J.-P. Labatut, *Problèmes de stratification sociale: Deux cahiers de la noblesse (1649–1651)* (Paris, 1965), excerpted here as "Problems of Social Stratification," pp. 154–158.

60 The polemic over popular uprisings was triggered by the French translation (sponsored by the Ecole des Hautes Etudes) of Boris Porchnev's *Les Soulèvements populaires en France de 1632 à 1648* (Paris, 1963), a book originally published in Russian in 1948 but known in France from his German translation, published in 1954. The

proceedings of the Saint-Cloud colloqium (1965) were published under the title
L'Histoire sociale, sources et méthodes (see note 39, above).

[61] François Furet and Denis Richet, *La Révolution française* (Paris, 1965–66), 2 vols.

[62] Albert Soboul, *Les Sans-culottes parisiens en l'an II* (Paris, 1958).

[63] Furet would give a brilliant analysis of that interpretive orthodoxy in "Le Caté-chisme révolutionnaire," *Annales* 26 (1971), reprinted in his *Penser la Révolution française* (Paris, 1978), pp. 113–72. Furet's own interpretation of the Revolution evolved profoundly in the 1970s and then again in the 1980s.

[64] Braudel was chosen to draft the section of the report on the human and social sciences by H. Longchambon, the chairman of the Conseil Supérieur de la Recherche Scientifique et du Progrès Technique, who submitted the work of his committee to the French government in June 1957. This section of the report was published, however, under Longchambon's name in *Annales ESC* 13 (1958), pp. 94–109, with the title "The Social Sciences in France: An Assessment and a Program" (the quote is from p. 96).

[65] The piece is excerpted here as "History and the Social Sciences: The *Longue Durée*," pp. 115–145.

[66] Braudel, "Histoire et sciences sociales: La longue durée," p. 42 (see note 65, above). See also "Unité et diversité des sciences de l'homme," *Revue de l'enseignement supérieur* 1 (1960), pp. 17–22, reprinted in *Ecrits sur l'histoire,* pp. 85–96.

[67] There is useful information in François Dosse, *Histoire du structuralisme* (Paris, 1991–92), 2 vols.

[68] See, for example, Claude Lévi-Strauss, "Critères scientifiques dans les disciplines sociales et humaines," *Revue internationale des sciences sociales* 16 (1964), pp. 579–97, excerpted here as "Scientific Criteria in the Social and Human Disciplines," pp. 191–194.

[69] See François Furet, "Les Intellectuels français et le structuralisme," *Preuves,* 92 (1967), pp. 3–12, reprinted in *L'Atelier de l'histoire,* pp. 37–52, and excerpted here as "French Intellectuals: From Marxism to Structuralism," pp. 217–230.

[70] Nor was it an accident, surely, that structuralism was embraced mainly by scholars trained as philosophers who had gone on to practice sociology or ethnology, as was once common in France.

[71] Claude Lévi-Strauss, *La Pensée sauvage* (Paris, 1962), ch. 9.

[72] Lucien Febvre, "Les Historiens et la philosophie: leur histoire et la nôtre," *Revue de synthèse* 1 (1932), pp. 97–103, reprinted in his *Combats pour l'histoire* (see note 33, above), pp. 276–83 (the quote is from p. 278).

[73] For one concrete illustration among others, witness the warm reception that Robert Mandrou and Fernand Braudel, writing in the *Annales*, accorded to Michel Foucault's *Histoire de la folie* (1961), even if it came at the cost of a rather problematic interpretation of the book: "Trois Clefs pour comprendre la folie à l'âge classique," *Annales ESC,* 17 (1962), pp. 761–72. On the ambiguous character of this reception, see Jacques Revel, "Le Moment historiographique," in Luce Giard, ed., *Lire Foucault* (Paris, 1992), pp. 83–96.

[74] See the interesting analysis in Roger Chartier, "Intellectual History or Sociocultural History? The French Trajectories," in Dominick LaCapra and Steven L. Kaplan, eds., *Modern European Intellectual History: Reappraisals and New Perspectives* (Ithaca, N.Y.: Cornell University Press, 1982), pp. 13–46, excerpted here as "Intellectual History or Sociocultural History?" pp. 287–297.

[75] See, for example, the excerpt here from *Myth and Thought Among the Greeks,* pp. 247–253.

[76] See, for example, the excerpt here from Jacques Le Goff and Pierre Vidal-Naquet, "Lévi-Strauss in Brocéliande," pp. 254–286.

[77] André Burguière, introduction to special issue on "Histoire et structure," *Annales ESC* 26 (1971), excerpted here as "History and Structure," pp. 231–239.

[78] This increase actually began in the mid-1960s: see Daniel Roche, "Les Historiens aujourd'hui: Remarques pour un débat," *Vingtième Siècle: Revue d'histoire* 4 (1986), pp. 3–20.

[79] Consider the success of such publishing ventures as the *Histoire de la France rurale* (Paris, 1973–76); *Histoire de la France urbaine* (Paris, 1980–85); *Histoire de la vie privée* (Paris, 1984–86); Fernand Braudel's *Civilisation matérielle, économie et capitalisme* (Paris, 1979); or Georges Duby's *Le Chevalier, la femme et le prêtre* (Paris, 1981).

[80] Emmanuel Le Roy Ladurie, "L'Histoire immobile," *Annales ESC* 29 (1974), pp. 673–92, reprinted in his *Le Territoire de l'historien* (Paris, 1973), pp. 7–34.

[81] Among the major works by Ariès (1914–1984) are *Les Traditions sociales dans les pays de France* (Paris, 1943); *Histoire des populations françaises et de leurs attitudes devant la vie* (Paris, 1946); *Le Temps de l'histoire* (Paris, 1954); *L'Enfant et la vie familiale sous l'Ancien Régime* (Paris, 1960), excerpted here as "Centuries of Childhood," pp. 371–376; and *L'Homme devant la mort* (Paris, 1977).

[82] See, for example, Bernard Bailyn's harsh review, "Braudel's Geohistory—A Reconsideration," *Journal of Economic History* 11 (1951), pp. 277–82, excerpted here, pp. 350–354.

[83] Two historians of France, Robert Forster and Orest Ranum, played an important role by publishing a collection of articles taken from the *Annales*. An ironic but rather indulgent and, in any case, well-informed and subtle interpretation appeared just before the publication of the American translation of *La Méditerranée*: J. H. Hexter, "Fernand Braudel and the *Monde Braudellien . . .*" *Journal of Modern History* 44 (1972), pp. 480–539, excerpted here, pp. 355–366.

[84] Jacques Le Goff and Pierre Nora, introduction to *Faire de l'histoire* (Paris, 1974), 3 vols., p. ix, excerpted here as "Constructing the Past," pp. 319–327.

[85] The essay is excerpted here as "The Return of the Event," pp. 427–436.

[86] This may be why there is a need periodically, and indeed with increasing frequency, to publish encyclopedic overviews of the discipline such as the collaborative *Aujourd'hui l'histoire* (Paris, 1974); Jacques Le Goff, Roger Chartier, and Jacques Revel, eds., *La Nouvelle histoire* (Paris, 1978); André Burguière, ed., *Dictionnaire des sciences historiques* (Paris, 1986). Moreover, many of these volumes included many of the same contributors.

[87] See, for example, the work by Le Goff excerpted here as "Mentalities: A History of Ambiguities," pp. 241–246.

[88] See the work by Burguière excerpted here as "Family and Society," pp. 377–380.

[89] See the works by Ariès excerpted as *Centuries of Childhood,* pp. 371–376, and by Vovelle excerpted here as "Death and the West," pp. 381–385.

[90] See the following works, as excerpted here: Duby, "The Three Orders," pp. 387–397; Agulhon, "The Circle in Bourgeois France," pp. 398–407; and Perrot, "Workers on Strike, 1871–1890," pp. 413–422.

[91] See the work by de Certeau excerpted here as "History and Mysticism," pp. 437–447.

[92] See especially Maurice Agulhon, *Pénitents et frans-maçons de l'ancienne Provence* (Paris, 1968); *La République au village* (Paris, 1970); *Le Cercle dans la France bourgeoise, 1810–1848: Étude d'une mutation de sociabilité* (Paris, 1977). The latter is excerpted here as "The Circle in Bourgeois France" pp. 398–407.

[93] Wachtel's research has evolved over a long period of time, beginning with *La Vision des vaincus* (Paris, 1971); "Anthropologie historique des sociétés andines," special issue of *Annales ESC* 33 (1978), with John Murra as coeditor; and *Le Retour*

des ancêtres (Paris, 1991). The second work is excerpted here as "Anthropological History of Andean Politics," pp. 449–457.

[94] See, for example, M. Cartier, ed., *Le Travail et ses représentations* (Paris, 1984).

[95] The career of Emmanuel Le Roy Ladurie is a case in point, moving from *Les Paysans de Languedoc* (1966) to *Montaillou* (1975) and *Le Carnaval de Romans* (1979). He was by no means alone.

[96] David Herlihy and Christiane Klapisch, *Les Toscans et leurs familles: Une étude du Catasto florentin de 1427* (Paris, 1978).

[97] The work in which he makes this remark is excerpted here as "The Historian and the Computer," pp. 329–332.

[98] The phrase "explosion of history" appeared in the triumphal announcement of the "Bibliothèque des histoires" collection that Pierre Nora launched at Gallimard in 1971. It was taken up in a polemical fashion in the 1970s, at first in the *Annales* milieu (by Braudel in particular). "History in pieces" (a more literal translation would be "history in *crumbs*") was a more negative way of saying the same thing. The phrase was later taken up by François Dosse and used as a title for his diatribe, *L'Histoire en miettes: Des* Annales *à la "nouvelle histoire"* (Paris, 1987) excerpted here as "History in Pieces."

[99] Jacques Revel, "Histoire et sciences sociales: Les paradigmes des *Annales*," *Annales ESC* 34 (1979), pp. 1360–76, excerpted here as "The Paradigms of *Annales*," pp. 471–475.

[100] Furet, "Quantitative History," excerpted here, pp. 333–348.

[101] Paul Veyne, *Comment on écrit l'histoire* (Paris, 1971), excerpted here as "Writing History," pp. 000–000; Michel de Certeau, "Faire de l'histoire: Problèmes de méthode et problèmes de sens," *Revue de science religieuse* 58 (1970), pp. 481–520, reprinted in *L'Ecriture de l'histoire* (Paris, 1975), pp. 27–62; "L'Opération historiographique," ibid., pp. 63–120.

[102] Among them: Michel de Certeau, *L'Absent de l'histoire* (Tours, 1973); G. Mairet, *Le Discours de l'historique* (Tours, 1974); the two contributions by André Burguière and Jacques Revel to the fiftieth anniversary issue of the *Annales* in 1979; the essays of Pierre Vilar, *Une Histoire en construction*, and François Furet, *L'Atelier de l'histoire* (1982), and Krzyzstof Pomian, *L'Ordre du temps* (Paris, 1984). Additional analyses of this type appeared in the 1980s, but there was little unity to these epistemological reflections.

[103] For a contemporary consideration of the crisis diagnosis, see Jacques Revel, "Sur la 'crise' de l'histoire aujourd'hui," *Bulletin de la Société française de philosophie* 79 (April 27, 1985), pp. 97–128.

[104] From different parts of the political spectrum: the right, with Hervé Coutau-Bégarie, *Le Phénomène "nouvelle histoire"* (Paris, 1983), and the extreme left, with François Dosse's *Histoire en miettes*.

[105] See the interesting debate that Pierre Nora initiated but unfortunately did not follow up in *Le Débat* 17 (1982), and 23 (1983).

[106] Lawrence Stone, "The Revival of Narrative: Reflections on a New Old History," *Past and Present* 85 (1979), pp. 3–24. Note, however, that after this article was published, widely translated, and extensively commented on, Stone returned to social history.

[107] Carlo Ginzburg, "Spie: radici di un paradigma indiziario," in A. Gargani, ed., *Crisi della ragione: nuovi modelli nel rapporto tra sapere e attività umana* (Turin, 1979), pp. 56–106.

[108] See the commonsensical remarks of Bernard Lepetit, "Propositions pour une pratique restreinte de l'interdisciplinarité," *Revue de synthèse* 3 (1990), pp. 331–38.

[109]For Ancien Régime France, see the useful catalogue in J.-Y. Grenier, *Séries économiques françaises (XVIe-XVIIIe siècles)*, (Paris, 1985).

[110]See J.-Y. Grenier and Bernard Lepetit, "L'expérience historique: A propos de C. E. Labrousse," *Annales ESC* 44 (1989), pp. 1337–60.

[111]To take just one example, consider the important work of Jean-Claude Perrot, *Genèse d'une ville moderne: Caen au XVIIIe siècle* (Paris, 1975), 2 vols., which has slowly gained influence. Beyond urban history proper, Perrot's work contributed to new thinking about the presuppositions of French social history.

[112]"Histoire et sciences sociales: Un tournant critique?" *Annales ESC* 43 (1988), pp. 291–93; "Tentons l'expérience," introduction to a special issue on "Histoire et sciences sociales: Un tournant critique," *Annales ESC* 44 (1989), pp. 1317–23. Both texts were signed jointly by the journal's editorial board. The works are excerpted here as "A Critical Turning Point" and "Let's Try the Experiment," pp. 480–491.

[113]The French translation was not published until 1988. The Ecole des Hautes Etudes was in fact instrumental in commissioning it.

[114]His book on *Court Society,* defended as a *Habilitazionsschrift* in 1933, was not published until 1969. The two volumes of *The Civilizing Process,* which came out in 1939, were not widely read until a new edition appeared in 1969, at which time Elias, born in 1897, was over seventy. It was only after his work was translated into French and hailed by French historians in the early 1970s that he gained wide recognition.

[115]A similar remark can help to explain the extremely important role that Pierre Bourdieu played, especially for cultural historians (see the excerpt of his work here, "In Other Words," pp. 514–520). Apart from the prestige and power of his own work (especially *La Distinction* [Paris, 1979] and *Le Sens pratique* [Paris, 1981]), Bourdieu helped to discredit traditional analytic distinction, in particular the three-stage construct implicitly accepted by post-Labroussian social history: economy, society, civilization. He did this by showing, for instance, that social classifications do not necessarily shape cultural distributions but may in fact be constituted in the context of cultural practices.

[116]No theoretical manifesto spells out the definition of *"micro-storia,"* a term that in fact covers a number of quite different positions. See, however, Giovanni Levi, "On Microhistory," in Peter Burke, ed., *New Perspectives on Historical Writing* (University Park: Pennsylvania State University Press, 1991), pp. 93–113; Jacques Revel, "L'Histoire au ras du sol," introduction to Giovanni Levi, *Le Pouvoir au village* (Paris, 1989), pp. i–xxxii, and "Micro-analyse et construction du social," in Jacques Revel, ed., *La Construction du social* (forthcoming 1996) excerpted here as "Micro-Analysis and the Construction of the Social," pp. 492–502.

[117]One would want to show, in particular, how a kind of orthodoxy developed around certain of Foucault's positions. Usually this was an implicit orthodoxy, a facile consensus, but its effect was to block debate. For example, the powerful alternative interpretation of the origins of psychiatry that Marcel Gauchet and Gladys Swain proposed in *La Pratique de l'esprit humain: L'institution asilaire et la révolution démocratique* (Paris: Gallimard, 1980) challenged Foucault's *Histoire de la folie,* yet it received little notice or discussion.

[118]Michel Foucault, "La Poussière et le nuage," in Michelle Perrot, ed., *L'Impossible prison* (Paris, 1980), pp. 34–35. This work also contains the outlines of a debate between Foucault and a group of historians, the terms of which were largely rewritten by the philosopher.

[119]It was essentially after the publication of Ricoeur's three-volume *Temps et récit* (Paris, 1983–85) that his work began to gain influence with French historians (the work is excerpted here as "Time and Narrative," pp. 526–537). Along with Ricoeur and de Certeau, other names deserve mention, some of them quite well known:

Hans-Georg Gadamer in hermeneutics, Clifford Geertz in interpretive anthropology, and in France, the fairly unusual example of a philosopher turned historian, Jacques Rancière, *La Nuit des prolétaires* (Paris, 1981) and *Les Noms de l'histoire* (Paris, 1992).

[120]Jean-Claude Passeron, *Le Raisonnement sociologique: L'espace non-popperien du raisonnement naturel* (Paris, 1991), excerpted here as "Sociological Reasoning," pp. 521–525. Passeron's is probably the most successful effort to date to move beyond the stage of transitional or opportunistic epistemologies.

[121]Roger Chartier, *Lecteurs et lectures dans la France d'Ancien Régime* (Paris, 1987); Roger Chartier, ed., *Les Usages de l'imprimé* (Paris, 1987); Roger Chartier and Henri-Jean Martin, eds., *Histoire de l'édition française* (Paris, 1981–86), 4 vols.

[122]Bernard Lepetit, "Urban History in France: Twenty Years of Research," in Richard Rodger, ed., *European Urban History: Prospect and Retrospect* (Leicester and London, 1993), pp. 84–93, excerpted here as "Urban History in France," pp. 559–569. Lepetit states, p. 567: Urban institutions at the end of the *Ancien Régime* were part of a secular history, and violent disputes about public order in towns need to be considered not only as indicative of behavior, relationships, and values, but also an opportunity to reconstruct a sociopolitical context that gives the town meaning and contributes to its unique identity."

[123]C. Dauphin, A. Farge, G. Fraisse, et al., "Culture et pouvoir des femmes: Essai d'historiographie," *Annales ESC* 41 (1986), pp. 271–94, excerpted here as "Women's Culture and Power," pp. 618–630. See also Georges Duby and Michelle Perrot, eds., *Histoire des femmes en occident*, 5 vols., (Paris, 1991–92).

[124]Furet, *Penser la Révolution française (Paris, 1978); La Révolution, 1770–1881* (Paris, 1988); with Mona Ozouf, eds., *Dictionnaire critique de la Révolution française* (Paris, 1988). See also Marcel Gauchet, *La Révolution des droits de l'homme* (Paris, 1989), which takes a similar line.

[125]Memory of misfortune: Wachtel, *Le Retour des ancêtres*; L. Valensi and Nathan Wachtel, *Mémoires juives* (Paris, 1986). Memory of shame: Henry Rousso, *Le Syndrome de Vichy de 1944 à nos jours*, (Paris, 1987), excerpted here as "The Vichy Syndrome," pp. 644–650. Recall that the first serious historical work on the Vichy regime was done by Americans, especially Robert O. Paxton.

[126]Pierre Nora, "Entre Mémoire et histoire," introduction to Pierre Nora, ed., *Les Lieux de mémoire*, vol. 1: *La République* (Paris, 1984), pp. xvii–xlii. This first volume was followed by three more on "the nation" and three others on the diversity of France (1993).

[127]Fernand Braudel, *L'Identité de la France*, 3 vols. (Paris, 1986); André Burguière and Jacques Revel, eds., *Histoire de la France*, 4 vols. (Paris, 1989–1993). Obviously, *Les Lieux de mémoire* should be regarded as a history of France as well, but one that is sui generis. See also Pierre Nora, "Comment écrire l'histoire de France," in Pierre Nora, ed., *Les Lieux de mémoire*, vol. 3: *Les France* (Paris, 1993), pp. 11–32.

[128]"Tentons l'expérience," editorial in a special issue on "Histoire et sciences sociales: Un tournant critique," *Annales ESC* 44 (1989), p. 1323. This issue contains several examples of attempts to reformulate the terms of collaboration between disciplines; the work is excerpted here as "Let's Try the Experiment," pp. 484–491.

[129]Current thinking about the effects of choosing different scales of observation in the social sciences exemplifies the kinds of reformulations that are possible.

[130]Passeron, *Le Raisonnement sociologique*, p. 367ff., excerpted here as "Sociological Reasoning," pp. 521–525.

[131]The risks of such relativism are stressed by the Russian historian Yuri Bessmertny, "Les *Annales* vues de Moscou," *Annales ESC* 47 (1992), pp. 245–59. See the response by Bernard Lepetit and Jacques Revel, "L'Expérimentation contre l'arbitraire," ibid., pp. 261–65.

[132]On biography, see, for example, the methodological remarks in Giovanni Levi, "Les Usages de la biographie," *Annales ESC* 44 (1989), pp. 1325–35; Passeron, *Le Raisonnement sociologique,* pp. 185–206; and, for an application, S. Loriga, *Soldats, un laboratoire disciplinaire: L'Armée piémontaise au XVIIIe siècle* (Paris, 1991).

[133]Two fine examples that also show the influence of Italian microhistory on French social history are Simona Cerrutti, *La Ville et les métiers: Naissance d'un langage corporatif (Turin, XVIIe–XVIIIe siècles)* (Paris, 1990), excerpted here as "The City and the Trades" and M. Gribaudi, *Itinéraires ouvriers: Espaces et groupes sociaux à Turin au début du XXe siècle* (Paris, 1987). On this and much other recent work the influence of E. P. Thompson is apparent.

[134]Significantly, the *Annales* changed its subtitle in 1994 from *Economies, sociétés, civilisation* to *Histoire, Sciences Sociales.*

PART I

The Time of Certainties: Social History and Global History (1945–1960s)

Competing Models and Research Agendas

———

ERNEST LABROUSSE

New Paths Toward a History of the Western Bourgeoisie (1700–1850)

1955

*By virtue of both his work and his institutional role, Ernest Labrousse (1895–1988) shared dominance of the French historiographic scene equally with his near contemporary, Fernand Braudel. With two great books (*Esquisse du mouvement des prix et des revenus en France au XVIIIe siècle *[1933] and* La Crise de l'économie française à la fin de l'Ancien Régime et au début de la Révolution *[1944]), he not only established economic and social history as accepted areas of academic research but also set a scientific "standard" in both fields. As directeur d'études at the Ecole des Hautes Etudes and even more as Marc Bloch's successor at the Sorbonne from 1945 to 1965, Labrousse, far more than Braudel, exerted his influence primarily through teaching and his supervision of numerous doctoral dissertations. Many prominent figures of the French historical school, from Maurice Agulhon to François Furet, Pierre Goubert to Emmanuel Le Roy Ladurie, Jacques Ozouf to Michelle and Jean-Claude Perrot, have worked in areas in which Labrousse was a pioneer.*

After World War II Labrousse produced no more great works, but he devoted much of his effort to a series of programmatic articles

From Ernest Labrousse, "Voies nouvelles vers une histoire de la bourgeoisie occidentale," *Relazioni del X congresso internazionale di scienze storiche,* Storia Moderna, vol. 4 (Florence, 1955), pp. 367–96.

that profoundly influenced subsequent research both in France and elsewhere. Having founded a school, he moved on to become the captain of a team, tirelessly proposing projects and offering suggestions to colleagues and students alike in the conviction that together they would one day arrive at virtually exhaustive knowledge of economies and societies from the sixteenth to the twentieth century. His dynamism reflected the legacy of Durkheim and his followers (Labrousse always saw himself as the heir of François Simiand), of the early Annales of Bloch and Febvre (in which he participated), and his own personal activism, sustained by extraordinary energy.

The following text is a good example of that dynamism. It is a proposal for a general survey of the eighteenth- and early nineteenth-century bourgeoisies, which Labrousse, at the height of his influence, presented to the International Congress of Historical Sciences at Rome in 1955. The text bears all the main hallmarks of his thinking: attention to archival sources (mainly French, it must be said, despite the somewhat formalistic call for international cooperation); concern with a statistical approach to the measurement of social realities; insistence on empirical description aimed at apprehending the variety of bourgeoisies in the plural ("First, study. First, observation. We will see about the definition later"); and the choice of chronology, which as it happens places the French Revolution at the heart of the proposed investigation.

Define the bourgeois? We are of a different opinion. Let us go instead and find this urban species where it lives, *in situ*, and subject it to observation. This would be only a preliminary operation, something provisional, a matter of conservation. The danger is lack of ambition, setting one's sights too low; therefore our imperative should be to include as many cases as possible in the study, starting with brief descriptions based on occupation and social status. Presumptions will suffice, as if we were policemen investigating possible suspects. My method is to round up anyone I suspect of being a bourgeois and sort them all out afterward, especially since there can be no doubt about the primary categories. First, study. First, observation. We will see about the definition later.

In 1939 Georges Lefebvre proposed a similar approach in connection with a study of the French bourgeoisie from the end of the Ancien Régime to the Restoration: postpone the overall definition, study "the principal social elements that are generally agreed to belong to this segment of the Third Estate," which he rapidly enumerated in terms of ranks and occupations, and "limit the study to the elements most readily available," which eliminated the special case of the "peasant bourgeoisie."

A proposal of that kind maintains the intentions of this report, which aims, prior to setting a vast international research operation in motion, to fashion certain implements that may prove useful in the effort.

Under the heading "bourgeoisie" we find the major traditional categories, whose infinite variety of nuances and degrees we would do well to keep in mind.

Prime "suspects" in the case must include the *officiers*, or holders of venal offices, found in only a few countries; and the *commis*, or functionaries with supervisory tasks—who are found everywhere—and of whom we shall keep only those not confounded with the "nobility." Other leading suspects will include the owners of property and rentiers living "*bourgeoisement*," not to be confused with the "*bourgeois*" of the "*livres de bourgeoisie*" who may owe that quality to nothing more than having resided for a certain time in the city and may in fact be no more than journeymen in the trades. And, of course, members of the "liberal" professions, as these have always been understood are also included in the bourgeoisie.

All these higher varieties emerge from the vast family of *chefs d'entreprise,* who constitute the numerical bulk of the class. By *chef d'entreprise*, I mean someone who owns or manages independent means of production and is served by paid labor, who derives his principal means of subsistence from this activity, and who, in particular, claims the profit of the commercial or industrial enterprise. This is a broad family, ranging from the financier, shipper, manufacturer, wholesaler, and merchant down to the lowest categories, the owners of shops and workshops, and independent craftsmen who employ paid help and directly sell the product of their labor to their clientele. Ranking below this level, after several intermediate forms, comes the semiproletarian dependent craftsman employed at home by a commercial capitalist who pays by the piece and provides the raw material. Provisionally, one may situate the frontier of the bourgeoisie between the artisan-merchant and the artisan-worker, the latter living essentially on the sale of his services. Of course, this frontier is permeable, like every frontier in the physical or social world.

The fact that this category of commerce and industry is disparate and troubled by a variety of conflicts is by no means peculiar to it. It is the same everywhere, including even the nobility. In each of the bourgeois categories enumerated above, there are infinitely many degrees and disparate situations. Even the "professionals," apparently the most "bourgeois" of all these groups, can be shown to contain a subgroup of semiproletarians—to be separated out in a subsequent operation.

A *conseiller* in a sovereign court was a world apart from a *huissier* in the Eaux-et-Forêts or a *sergent royal*. So, too, was a wealthy, property-owning *rentier* a world apart from the widow who herself might be a "*rentière*" but reduced to a bare subsistence. The extreme variety of tax roll classifications within a single city or occupational category attests, then as now, to the extent of the social scale. To appreciate its full range, we must remember that the social hierarchy runs from the highest levels in the top categories to the lowest levels in the bottom categories.

No class has ever been homogeneous or all inclusive. In the case of the bourgeoisie, however, it does not follow that the whole of the class born originally from the profit of enterprise did not share certain values vis-à-vis other classes or social groups in Ancien Régime society, which would endure in western and central Europe until some time between 1789 and the middle of the nineteenth century, depending on the place.

The international project proposed here for the eighteenth century and the first half of the nineteenth century should include, at a minimum, the following goals:

· to count and classify by occupation.

· to establish a hierarchy within each occupational category.

· to compare occupations and establish a hierarchy among them, or to group hierarchically in some fashion other than by occupation some or all of the categories considered to be "bourgeois" (and rapidly outlined above), the collection of which is of course subject to revision according to each country's social structure.

Preferably, this work should be undertaken in a limited geographical setting—a city or sections of a large city. Of course, broader studies of occupational or nonoccupational categories (such as military society or the society of notables) may in some cases be extended to the nation as a whole.

By virtue of its structure and the nature of its sources (autonomous or serving as a control), this study of social composition should provide at least sample data for another study having to do with social psychology: a kind of "group biography" that would pay attention (in addition to other matters equally worthy of consideration) to the geographic and social milieu of origin, to relationships, to the environment in which people live, to material and cultural activities, and to symptoms of ideological choices. This additional study can also be carried out in either a narrow or a broad geographical setting, depending on the milieu under study and the nature and location of the sources.

Is there any need to add that such research in social composition and social biography can in no way be construed as replacing the information to be gleaned from personal memoirs, journals, and correspondence or, alternatively, from traditional or innovative studies of genealogy, indi-

vidual and group biography, and "dynasties"? Research of this kind has
already been able to put together a collection of individual cases in such
a way as to yield preliminary conclusions about groups. Our task is not
situated above other kinds of work but, rather, alongside and around
them. It should help to situate this other work in a certain milieu; and it
should provide other approaches with massive documentation.

The present report is devoted to the preliminary problem of sources,
to the ways and means of investigating social composition.

The primary objectives of the statistical history of bourgeois groups are
categories and hierarchies. There is much information to be gleaned
already from major printed collections, chiefly English and Prussian,
concerning that portion of the nineteenth century which falls within the
purview of our investigation. English census data, compiled every decade since 1801, can be used to study the distribution of the population by
occupation, in some instances (1851, for example) with an extraordinary
wealth of detail. Basic information about the pyramid of fortunes can be
found in the *Returns Rendered to Parliament* and, from 1855 on, in the
Report of the Inland Revenue Commissioners. On the Prussian side, one can
find in the compilations of the *Gewerbestatistik*, including the *Tabellen* of
1849, the number of master craftsmen, journeymen, and apprentices in
various trades, as well as the number of factory workers and mills.

But these diverse collections, far superior to any available for France,
concern only the first half of the nineteenth century or, in some cases,
the latter part of that period, and even that time frame is treated in
very unequal fashion. Despite the wealth of data, the figures are rather
superficial and schematic. By their very nature, they neglect problems
essential for the history of the bourgeoisie, most notably the problem of
personalities, of the very important group of notables. A far richer and
more concrete source of information on this subject would appear to
exist in archival sources.

If we concentrate our attention on the major French documentary
collections likely to have their equivalent in other western and central
European archives, we may divide the existing sources, which are in any
case woefully incomplete, into three groups:

· electoral sources, which contain that incomparable catalogue of
  notables, the lists of *censitaires* (that is, of those wealthy enough
  to pay the tax known as the *cens*, which qualified them to vote).

· fiscal sources, namely, direct tax rolls complemented both by the
  archives of the registry and disputed claims office and by information to be gleaned from notarial documents, with which it is

possible to arrive at a complete occupational classification of the bourgeoisie in a limited geographical area, such as a city. The same sources also make it possible to sketch a portrait of the various groups within a given occupation or of the hierarchy of wealth in a particular city.

· demographic sources, which provide more ample documentation of the occupational distribution of the population than the two previous categories. Other important information can be gleaned from military census registers, namely, the occupations of conscripts and their parents. A completely different type of source, which for the time being must be regarded as supplementary, consists of private business files or official files, which can sometimes provide a particularly rich portrait of a profession or of society itself.

[*In the next section of this article—omitted here—Labrousse offers a lengthy exploration of the French sources to be exploited in this research program.*]

All three types of document collections—electoral, fiscal, and demographic—are found in many countries. Lists of the most highly taxed individuals were drawn up for the whole of the Grand Empire. The system of notables, of property qualifications for voting, was familiar throughout western and central Europe, to speak only of the vast area that concerns us here. A professional electorate existed everywhere, as did consular tribunals and institutions. Everywhere there were direct tax rolls, offices to adjudicate disputed tax claims, a registry, a census, and military recruitment. What is more, we still have very incomplete knowledge of the resources available to us, despite what has been done thus far in regard to eighteenth-century manuscript collections. New categories of documents will emerge within existing major collections or perhaps even from new collections. In the absence of classifications and catalogues, moreover, we have no idea of the extent of existing archives scattered among many repositories. Perhaps the destruction of documents in other countries was even more extensive than it was in France, or perhaps the treasures to be found elsewhere are far greater.

The important thing is to find out what the situation is. Looking ahead to an international study of the bourgeoisie, what we need now is a "preliminary" inventory, a first general overview to tell us what the major collections are, especially in local, municipal, and provincial archives, which are by far the richest sources of documents in this domain. Looked at in isolation, local "collections" may not amount to much— a record of vital statistics, perhaps, or a tax roll. But combined with other, similar sources, they can make an important contribution to the subject.

The next order of business is to classify and inventory what we have. The resulting inventories should be published and made available to all the major archives and universities. In that way, they can serve not only as a guide but also as a goad to further research.

Everyone knows full well that nothing really useful or far-reaching can be done until such tools and aids are in place. Is this a dream for another time? No one expects to get everything we need at once, but we do need some things right now. First, steps must be taken to conserve existing documents. Strict instructions must be issued that none of these records be destroyed on any pretext; much of this material is stored in disorganized fashion in local repositories, and records still in the possession of the bureaucracies that produced them originally are often in great danger. Second, a preliminary survey of the major collections is an immediate imperative. Third, we need a few inventories of the most important collections, which would set an example for other inventories and begin to establish a basis for international comparisons.

A proposal to this effect will be presented to the [International Congress of Historical Sciences meeting at Rome in 1955].

Perhaps more should be done: an International Study Commission, similar to the Commission Internationale d'Histoire des Mouvements Sociaux that was established in Paris in 1950, could be created. I hope that we would be unanimous in wanting this commission to be as broadly international as possible, in order to open up the investigation to the largest possible number of European countries.

It would also be useful for reasons of principle as well as opportunity to expand the object of the study still further. Boundaries should not deter us unduly. The bourgeoisie shares common boundaries with both the nobility and the proletariat. A single document will often prove useful for research into all orders or all classes. Can we study the *censitaire* list of 1790, the universal suffrage list, the tax roll, or the census but refuse to look beyond the boundaries of the bourgeoisie? Can we close our eyes to the riches available? Can we study a class without also studying its relative numbers or its exchanges with its neighbors? As we produce works for the purpose of raising social history to the quantitative plane on which economic history is already firmly established, can we refuse to take the measure of the major contenders?

The study should not be expanded without limit. Limited to a relatively narrow geographical setting—the city is often mentioned—it will remain practicable and gain a useful amplitude.

We therefore call for the creation of an international commission for the history of social structures, which will keep us in contact with one another, facilitate and monitor the implementation of our decisions, and administer the investigation of the major problems discussed above in the best interests of the research. This project clearly belongs in the domain of collective research, which can be conducted only by teams working together.

It would be a good thing if our Congress resulted in the creation of one such team, charged with developing the preliminary instruments needed for collaborative international research of this kind.

TRANSLATED BY ARTHUR GOLDHAMMER

PIERRE VILAR

History After Marx

(1969)

A few years younger than Fernand Braudel, Pierre Vilar (b. 1906) is not the best known of the great French historians of the postwar period. At any rate, this is the case in France itself (where Vilar was very late to succeed Ernest Labrousse at the Sorbonne in 1965) and in the English-speaking world. In the Spanish-speaking countries of Europe and Latin America, however, his reputation is immense (indeed, much of his work was first published in Spanish). One reason for this is that Vilar is above all the author of a single great three-volume work, La Catalogne dans l'Espagne moderne: Recherches sur les fondements économiques des structures nationales *(1962). A geographer by training but soon influenced by Simiand, Labrousse and Febvre (as a young man he published in the early* Annales*), this economic historian discovered the importance of nationalism as a political reality during the Spanish Civil War (1936–1939) and as a historical reality during the course of his work on Catalan identity. He also discovered Marx and can be considered one of the few true Marxists among French historians. He is a Marxist in the sense that, following Joseph Schumpeter, he sees Marx as the man who described "how economic theory can be converted into historical analysis and how historical exposition can be converted into rational history." His outspoken taste for theory, his commitment to a "total" history, and his high view of the historian's "craft" led him to engage in celebrated polemics with Raymond Aron, Louis Althusser, and Michel Foucault (see* Une Histoire en construction: Approche marxiste et problématiques conjoncturelles *[Paris: Gallimard/Seuil, 1982], from which this text is excerpted). Through his teaching at the Ecole des Hautes Etudes and later at the Sorbonne, this atypical historian actually exerted considerable, if not always highly visible, influence; someday it will have to be measured. Written in January*

Pierre Vilar, "L'Histoire après Marx," in *Une Histoire en construction: Approche marxiste et problématiques conjoncturelles* (Paris: Gallimard/Seuil, 1982), pp. 376–81.

1967 and published in 1969 at the height of the structuralist tide, the following text reaffirms the author's strong convictions and commitments.

Over the past thirty or forty years, history has indeed established itself as a science in Marx's sense. That sense is what needs to be explained first, and the way to do that is to go back to the point at which Marx first accorded primacy to the *economic*. If Marx, a young philosopher passionately interested in social and political issues, transformed himself into an economist after 1840, it was because he saw political economy as *the first human domain that scientific reasoning had been able to penetrate.*

Once one recognizes that the apparently free exercise of individual human will *has an objective aggregate effect* (a price, say, or a wage or an interest rate), then one can attempt to *model* that effect in terms of concepts, hypotheses, and theories which can and should be first *derived from and then verified by statistical observation.* Economics, which today is equipped with a considerable array of mathematical and statistical instruments, can thus explain, predict, intervene, and plan. Just because it has not yet mastered all of reality does not mean that one ought to place stylistics above it in the hierarchy of science.

Marx's genius, however, was to have seen beyond the limits of the economic model, which he was able to specify in advance. He recognized that if the objectification of the subjective can exist in the economic sphere, there is no reason why human interests of other kinds, from the most sordid to the most noble, should not also lead, through combination and conflict, to an objectification in the facts that constitute the rationality and necessity of history. Thus, the entire realm of the human, in space and in time, can be brought within the compass of scientific analysis.

In particular, if the abstract models of economics appear to be disturbed by "exogenous" factors, there is no reason to do as "pure" economists do when they hasten to dismiss those factors as "contingent" or "historical." The exogenous can have its own internal necessity in the context of a more complicated model. Moreover, the economic "laws" discovered by the classical economists are not universal in space or time, because they apply only within a specific technological, institutional, and psychological framework that, while stable enough perhaps to define a "structure," is *by no means eternal.* Hence, there is a science of the *historical*, which is in fact the science of these structures, including their emergence, transformation, and disappearance.

To be sure, the historical is so complex that no mathematics has yet been conceived to capture it. Economics has the advantage of stating nearly all its results in quantitative form, and this happens less often (though more often than many people believe) in other areas open to historical research.

It is nevertheless possible, even without calculation, to have rational arguments, *schemas* if not models. This, according to Joseph Schumpeter, was precisely what Marx discovered: "Marx was the first top-flight economist to recognize and teach in systematic fashion how economic theory can be converted into historical analysis, and how historical exposition can be converted into rational history." This judgment carries particular weight, since Schumpeter was a man with a considerable gift for abstraction and one of the great historians of economic theory.

Other economists subsequently recognized the possibility of (and need for) "causal analysis" and the inadequacy of any theory of growth that fails to take the *historical factor* into account. More than many historians are willing to admit, therefore, their discipline has been called upon by others to penetrate, in *scientific* fashion, the secrets of the multifarious, ever-changing human condition.

At this point, someone may object that many professional historians remain skeptical of the word "science," and even of the word "theory," when applied to their everyday task. In "academic, western" historiography, attacks on "theory" are always welcome, whereas in "Marxist, eastern" historiography, salutes to theory are often followed by insipid, old-fashioned narrative accounts. Yet did not Marcel Mauss once say that a history becomes sociology to the extent that it is intelligent, and did not Lenin say that a stupid Marxist would always be less of a Marxist than an intelligent bourgeois? Of course, the reasons for the uneven development of historical science are much broader than this. But among the things that slow progress everywhere are superficial ideas and the entrenched habits that ensure the success of those historians who limit their efforts to amassing "petty true facts," while handling dense historical materials is by no means an easy profession.

In France, at least, the battle seems won, however. Lucien Febvre, who was suspicious of theory but who, like Marx, loved to exercise his brilliant mind in criticism and polemic, dared to hold out to the young historians of my generation if not the immediate hope of a science of history based on models at least the continuous application of intelligence to a history centered on *problems*. In so doing, he was neither allying himself with Marx nor invoking him as a reference, but he was lifting many of the taboos against theory in history. To proclaim the historian's right to a "working hypothesis" was to authorize him to think within a *theoretical* framework. It was, in any case, to grant history a penetrable rationality.

Last but not least, it was also to embrace a fundamental aspect of Marx's outlook: the refusal to accept any firm division or "watertight" separation among the various sectors of history. Analysis of course remains an essential part of any investigation, and the historical profession cannot do without specialization. But economics alone can never fully account for all economic phenomena, nor political theory for all political phenomena, nor the theory of the spiritual for all spiritual phenomena. In each concrete instance, the *problem* lies in the *interaction* of all of these.

Thus, the Marxist notion of "totality," unknown to positivist history, has been resurrected in notions such as Henri Berr's idea of "synthesis." To gauge the influence of this idea, one has only to compare today's collections of works on general history with those of fifty years ago. While the old periodizations remain standard, none of the recent works fail to precede their narratives with descriptions of the economy's deep structures and major conjunctures. None skimps on space for discussion of the social mechanisms affecting law, daily life, and psychological attitudes. None fails to examine societies in their aesthetic and spiritual climates or to relate shades of ideology to the way of life of different social groups. Economies, societies, civilizations: the Marxist hierarchy seems to have become the most natural thing in the world. Nowadays, the publisher of Jacques Bainville and Pierre Gaxotte commissions works by Pierre Goubert and Eric Hobsbawm. For a while, as a consequence of the reaction against the *événementiel* [excessive concentration on events], political and military matters were sacrificed (as they never were by Marx!). Recently, however, a "politicology" and a "polemology" have developed to cap off historical totality's arsenal.

We still need to make sure that static description does not overwhelm narrative, that a concern with structures does not do away with a concern with structural changes. In Marx, history has a motor and a meaning. Can the same be said of our historians?

"Evolutionism" is currently out of favor. It has been portrayed as a nineteenth-century mental form, which would place Darwin and Marx at a considerable distance from today's scholars. Some historians worry that these condemnations of "historicism," said to be "naive," may be a mere cover for condemnations of the introduction of *historical time* into science. Evolutionism, the triumph of the nineteenth century, is far from having been transcended and remains to be exploited—even in the exact sciences and obviously in the human sciences. Not to do so would be to turn one's back not only on the tasks that Marx set us but also on the goal that Lucien Febvre and Henri Berr set as history's ultimate objective, namely, *the evolution of humanity* (as certain well-known titles will attest).

In this respect, there is no reason why we cannot remain faithful to them, no reason why we cannot base our hope for an "anthropology" of the future not on the least historical of human facts (for there are no "ahistorical" facts) but, rather, on *historical* analysis of the *technical, economic*, and *social* stages that brought man to where he is today—the threshold, but only the threshold, of a *scientific era.*

That brings us to another point of contact between Marx's thought and our most secure discoveries, the idea of the *technological factor* as the motor of history. In this regard, there are certain misconceptions that need to be dispelled. When Marx spoke of the "economic" factor as determining the course of history "in the last analysis" and of the technological factor as determining the economy in the last analysis, he was merely taking note of the fact that man's essential originality lies in his capacity to control nature. This does not mean that technology and the economy are the only "interesting" subjects; it means that they alone cause human groups to take *decisive* and *irreversible* steps. If technology leads to rapid changes in the productivity of labor, the whole organization of the group is called into question. If the organization of the group resists adaptation, technological progress suffers. Technological progress is therefore not a *sufficient condition* for human social development, despite what some impatient economists have argued. It is, however, a *necessary condition*, in the sense that any change not accompanied by a dramatic rise in the productivity of labor is likely to prove fruitless in the medium to long run.

As is well known, the problems of "development" and "underdevelopment" which are of greatest *current* interest have to do with the delicate relationship between technical progress and structural changes of every sort—social, political, psychological, and religious. Historians can draw many useful lessons from current events. Yet history also points up problems that are not identical but, rather, *analogous* to current issues. What makes history sociological is this constant comparison of different ages, which involves the use of theories, conceptualizations, schemes, models, and working hypotheses on the historical as well as on the economic level.

The desired transformation presumably calls for *quantification* and *measurement*. Economists drawn to the study of history have lately proposed either a "totally quantitative" history of goods produced or an analysis of concrete episodes in economic history using abstract models as working hypotheses. While these are interesting technical proposals, they remain incomplete (as even their proponents recognize) because they *isolate* the economic from the historical and thus fail to encompass the *global* phenomenon. Here, theory must precede measurement. Some very instructive exercises in measuring productivity by relating food prices to the purchasing power of wage-earners have led only to the rediscovery of Adam Smith or Marx—and such rediscovery would be far more useful if it were conscious and systematic. Here again, historians have a major role to play, since they, like Marx, never separate the study of texts and theories from that of the objective conditions under which those texts and theories appeared.

For a while, some people thought that "objective, quantitative" history would rise to the unprecedented status of an "experimental theory" under an influence very remote from that of Marx: I am thinking of François Simiand's original idea of "conjunctural history," which had such influence on my generation of historians that it would be unforgivable of me not to mention it here. Simiand's history, however, was systematically antideductive, disdainful of structures, monetarist, and ultimately psychologistic in its conclusions and optimistic in its predictions about the economic cycle—and for all these reasons it seems to me unsuitable as a vehicle for bringing Marx's broad vision back into historical research.

Nevertheless, Simiand did define the notion of objective historical data by laying down rules for the use of quantitative sources, and he did postulate the rationality of history at the statistical level. In so doing, he created the technical and conceptual instruments necessary for studying the relation between economic chance, psychosocial reactions, and events.

Availing himself of this tool, Ernest Labrousse, the most creative of living historians revolutionized the study of the French economy in the eighteenth century by reconstructing its structural dynamics and supplementing price history with income history, thereby revealing class contradictions in the society. The precise dialectic that led to the French Revolution emerged in his work for the first time. He resolved the contradiction between Jules Michelet's thesis ("revolution of poverty") and Jean Jaurès's ("revolution of prosperity") by demonstrating the existence of a relationship between pauperization and enrichment, between the apparent long-term equilibrium and the real severity of recurrent short-term crises.

Admittedly, Labrousse's references to Marx are more implicit than explicit and hedged with reservations. Yet would it have been possible for anyone but a scholar with a profound understanding of Marx's work to have transformed conjunctural analysis into structural dynamics?

Now, it may be that in the 1960s we find ourselves on a plateau similar to that reached in the 1930s, when, no doubt owing to the Depression, economists became obsessed with the notion of "conjuncture." Today, our obsession is rather with "structure," a concept that, in certain respects, seems to have swept away all concerns with the diachronic but has the advantage of offering us certain new instruments to work with, including modern data-processing techniques and subtle formal analyses. Will we be able to match what Ernest Labrousse did when confronted with the work of Simiand, namely, to use the instruments without succumbing to the dogmatism of the doctrine, knowing full well that history is neither all curves nor all cross sections but both at the same time? Until we have mathematized these relationships, can we not discover their principles in the Marxian dialectic—these being simply the principles of rational history?

Rational history already has at its disposal tools that no one could have dreamed of a century ago: an enormous body of macroeconomic statistics and microeconomic models, techniques for social investigation extended through the use of computers and simplified through the use of polling, and "content analyses" that bring the power of statistical methods into the realm of the spiritual itself.

Still, we must be careful not to confuse tools with science. In the days when history meant erudition, such confusion was common. Let us not make the same mistake in an age when history is done with models. Scientific practice is a continuous dialogue between the concrete and the abstract, the real and the rational. Such was Marx's belief, and if historical science has since developed by following the trail he blazed it is quite simply because he was the first to demonstrate the *legitimacy* of doing so. This would be more universally recognized if Marx had acknowledged, and his disciples had demonstrated, the practical implications.

TRANSLATED BY ARTHUR GOLDHAMMER

FERNAND BRAUDEL

The Mediterranean and the Mediterranean World in the Age of Philip II
Preface to the First Edition

1949

Fernand Braudel (1902–1985) is probably the most celebrated French historian of the second half of the twentieth century and certainly the best known outside France. He came to history relatively late, however, his work and career interrupted by World War II. While confined as a prisoner of war in Germany from 1940 to 1945, he wrote, without books or notes, entirely from memory, the book that made his reputation overnight: La Méditerranée et le monde méditerranéen à l'époque de Philippe II (*The Mediterranean and the Mediterranean World in the Age of Philip II*)*, which he defended as a thesis in 1947 and published in 1949. This was an abundant work, the book of a lifetime, and it would undergo several revisions and amplifications. Thirty years later, it was followed by the three volumes of* Civilisation matérielle, économie et capitalisme *(1979), and then by an unfinished, posthumously published three-volume work,* L'Identité de la France *(1986). Braudel's work was thus at once massive and highly concentrated, but it was only one aspect of a life devoted to inspiring and managing the scientific work of others. As Lucien Febvre's successor as both the editor of* Annales *and chairman of the Sixth Section of the Ecole Pratique des Hautes Etudes, Braudel reigned over much of French social science in the 1950s, 1960s, and 1970s. He also headed a powerful international network of collaborating scholars, as J. H. Hexter notes in his article, "Fernand Braudel and the Monde Braudellien . . ." (see pp. 355–366).*

Here, then, are the first and most famous pages of The Mediterranean. *The book deals with the history of a geographic region, a sea,*

From *The Mediterranean and the Mediterranean World in the Age of Philip II*, trans. by Siân Reynolds (New York: Harper and Row, 1972), pp. 17–22. First published as *La Méditerranée et le monde méditerranéen à l'époque de Philippe II* (Paris: Armand Colin, 1949), pp. ix–xv.

*and the countries along its coast, during the second half of the six-
teenth century. Yet the ambition behind it was far more vast. This
experiment in geohistory grew in both time and space. Braudel aimed
at nothing less than a total history of the Mediterranean basin, ranging from its incredibly varied geography to its multiple trade links,
social structures, and patterns of warfare and diplomacy. The author's model for historical study proved enduringly influential, even
though hardly anyone tried to imitate his scope of analysis: the funda-
mentals of topography, climate, and long-term population trends provided the basis for the history of enduring economic and social patterns. Braudel did not ignore political history or even particular
battles, but they definitely came last and were by implication only
explicable in terms of larger, more lasting influences.*

*The book also had another goal, namely, to explore the complexity
of social time in terms of a hierarchy of three time frames: the deep,
almost static, history of the environment, the overlapping cycles of
the economy, and the quick time of events, which for Braudel was of
little concern.*

I have loved the Mediterranean with a passion, no doubt because I
am a northerner like so many others in whose footsteps I have followed. I have joyfully dedicated long years of study to it—much
more than all my youth. In return, I hope that a little of this joy and a
great deal of Mediterranean sunlight will shine from the pages of this
book. Ideally, perhaps one should, like the novelist, have one's subject
under control, never losing it from sight and constantly aware of its
overpowering presence. Fortunately or unfortunately, the historian has
not the novelist's freedom. The reader who approaches this book in the
spirit I would wish will do well to bring with him his own memories,
his own vision of the Mediterranean to add color to the text and to help
me conjure up this vast presence, as I have done my best to do. My feeling
is that the sea itself, the one we see and love, is the greatest document of
its past existence. If I have retained nothing else from the geographers
who taught me at the Sorbonne, I have retained this lesson with an
unwavering conviction that has guided me throughout my project.

It might be thought that the connections between history and geographic space would be better illustrated by a more straightforward example than the Mediterranean, particularly since in the sixteenth century
the sea was such a vast expanse in relation to man. Its character is complex, awkward, and unique. It cannot be contained within our measurements and classifications. No simple biography beginning with date of
birth can be written of this sea; no simple narrative of how things hap-

pened would be appropriate to its history. The Mediterranean is not even a *single* sea, it is a complex of seas; and these seas are broken up by islands, interrupted by peninsulas, ringed by intricate coastlines. Its life is linked to the land, its poetry more than half-rural, its sailors may turn peasant with the seasons; it is the sea of vineyards and olive trees just as much as the sea of the long-oared galleys and the roundships of merchants, and its history can no more be separated from that of the lands surrounding it than the clay can be separated from the hands of the potter who shapes it. *"Lauso la mare e tente'n terro"* ("Praise the sea and stay on land"), says a Provençal proverb.

So it will be no easy task to discover exactly what the historical character of the Mediterranean has been. It will require much patience, many different approaches, and no doubt a few unavoidable errors. Nothing could be clearer than the Mediterranean defined by oceanographer, geologist, or even geographer. Its boundaries have been charted, classified, and labeled. But what of the Mediterranean of the historian? There is no lack of authoritative statements as to what it is not. It is not an autonomous world; nor is it the preserve of any one power. Woe betide the historian who thinks that this preliminary interrogation is unnecessary, that the Mediterranean as an entity needs no definition because it has long been clearly defined, is instantly recognizable and can be described by dividing general history along the lines of its geographical contours. What possible value could these contours have for our studies?

But how could one write any history of the sea, even over a period of only fifty years, if one stopped at one end with the Pillars of Hercules and at the other with the straits at whose entrance ancient Ilium once stood guard? The question of boundaries is the first to be encountered; from it, all others flow. To draw a boundary around anything is to define, analyze, and reconstruct it, in this case to select, indeed adopt, a philosophy of history.

To assist me, I did indeed have at my disposal a prodigious body of articles, papers, books, publications, surveys, some purely historical, others no less interesting, written by specialists in neighboring disciplines— anthropologists, geographers, botanists, geologists, technologists. There is surely no region on this earth as well documented and written about as the Mediterranean and the lands illuminated by its glow. But, dare I say it, at the risk of seeming ungrateful to my predecessors, that this mass of publications buries the researcher, as it were, under a rain of ash. So many of these studies speak a language of the past, outdated in more ways than one. Their concern is not the sea in all its complexity but some minute piece of the mosaic—not the grand movement of Mediterranean life, but the actions of a few princes and rich men, the trivia of the past, bearing little relation to the slow and powerful march of history which is our subject. So many of these works need to be revised, related to the whole, before they can come to life again.

Then, too, no history of the sea can be written without precise knowledge of the vast resources of its archives. Here the task would appear to be beyond the powers of an individual historian. There is not one sixteenth-century Mediterranean state that does not possess its charter room, usually well furnished with those documents that have escaped the fires, sieges, and disasters of every kind known to the Mediterranean world. To prospect and catalog this unsuspected store, these mines of the purest historical gold, would take not one lifetime but at least twenty, or the simultaneous dedication of twenty researchers. Perhaps the day will come when we shall no longer be working on the great sites of history with the methods of small craftsmen. Perhaps on that day it will become possible to write general history from original documents and not from more or less secondary works. Need I confess that I have not been able to examine all the documents available to me in the archives, no matter how hard I tried. This book is the result of a necessarily incomplete study. I know in advance that its conclusions will be examined, discussed, and replaced by others, and I am glad of it. That is how history progresses and must progress.

Another point is that by its inauspicious chronological position, between the last flames of the Renaissance and Reformation and the harsh, inward-looking age of the seventeenth century, the Mediterranean in the second half of the sixteenth century might well be described, as it was by Lucien Febvre, as a *"faux beau sujet."* Need I point out where its interest lies? It is of no small value to know what became of the Mediterranean at the threshold of modern times, when the world no longer revolved entirely around it, served it, and responded to its rhythms. The rapid decline of the Mediterranean about which people have always talked does not seem at all clear to me; rather, all the evidence seems to point to the contrary. But even leaving this question aside, it is my belief that all the problems posed by the Mediterranean are of exceptional human richness, that they must therefore interest all historians and nonhistorians. I would go so far as to say that they serve to illuminate our own century, that they are not lacking in that "utility" in the strict sense which Nietzsche demanded of all history.

I do not intend to say much about the attraction and the temptations offered by such a subject. I have already mentioned the difficulties, deceptions, and lures it holds in store. I would add just this, that among existing historical works, I found none which could offer general guidance. A historical study centered on a stretch of water has all the charms but undoubtedly all the dangers of a new departure.

Since the scales were so heavily weighted on both sides, was I right in the end to come down on the side of the unknown, to cast prudence aside and decide that the adventure was worthwhile?

My excuse is the story of how this book was written. When I began it in 1923, it was in the classic and certainly more prudent form of a study of Philip II's Mediterranean policy. My teachers of those days strongly approved of it. For them, it fitted into the pattern of that diplomatic history which was indifferent to the discoveries of geography, little concerned (as diplomacy itself so often is) with economic and social problems; slightly disdainful toward the achievements of civilization, religion, and also of literature and the arts, the great witnesses of all worthwhile history; shuttered up in its chosen area, this school regarded it as beneath a historian's dignity to look beyond the diplomatic files, to real life, fertile and promising. An analysis of the policy of the Prudent King entailed above all establishing the respective roles played in the elaboration of that policy by the king and his counselors, through changing circumstances; determining who played major roles and who minor, reconstructing a model of Spanish foreign policy in which the Mediterranean was only one sector and not always the most important.

For in the 1580s the might of Spain turned toward the Atlantic. It was out there, whether conscious or not of the dangers involved, that the empire of Philip II had to concentrate its forces and fight for its threatened existence. A powerful swing of the pendulum carried it toward its transatlantic destiny. When I became interested in this hidden balance of forces, the physics of Spanish policy, preferring research in this direction to labeling the responsibilities of a Philip II or a Don John of Austria, and when I came to think, moreover, that these statesmen were, despite their illusions, more acted upon than actors, I was already beginning to move outside the traditional bounds of diplomatic history; when I began to ask myself finally whether the Mediterranean did not possess, beyond the long-distance and irregular actions of Spain (a rather arid topic apart from the dramatic confrontation at Lepanto), a history and a destiny of its own, a powerful vitality, and whether this vitality did not in fact deserve something better than the role of a picturesque background, I was already succumbing to the temptation of the immense subject that was finally to hold my attention.

How could I fail to see it? How could I move from one set of archives to another in search of some revealing document without having my eyes opened to this rich and active life? Confronted with records of so many basic economic activities, how could I do other than turn toward that economic and social history of a revolutionary kind that a small group of historians was trying to promote in France to the dignity that was no longer denied it in Germany, England, the United States, and indeed in Belgium, our neighbor, or Poland? To attempt to encompass the history of the Mediterranean in its complex totality was to follow their advice, be guided by their experience, go to their aid, and be active in the campaign for a new kind of history, rethought, elaborated in France but worthy of being voiced beyond her frontiers; an imperialist history, yes, if one insists, aware of its own possibilities and of what it had to do, but also desirous, since it had been obliged to break with them, of shattering traditional forms—not always entirely justifiably perhaps, but let that pass. The perfect opportunity was offered me of taking advantage of the very dimensions, demands, difficulties, and pitfalls of the unique historical character I had already chosen, in order to create a history that could be different from the history our masters taught us.

To its author, every work seems revolutionary, the result of a struggle for mastery. If the Mediterranean has done no more than force us out of our old habits, it will already have done us a service.

This book is divided into three parts, each of which is itself an essay in general explanation.

The first part is devoted to a history whose passage is almost imperceptible, that of man in his relationship to the environment, a history in which all change is slow, a history of constant repetition, ever-recurring cycles. I could not neglect this almost timeless history, the story of man's contact with the inanimate, neither could I be satisfied with the traditional geographical introduction to history that often figures to little purpose at the beginning of so many books, with its descriptions of the mineral deposits, types of agriculture, and typical flora, briefly listed and never mentioned again, as if the flowers did not come back every spring, the flocks of sheep migrate every year, or the ships sail on a real sea that changes with the seasons.

On a different level from the first there can be distinguished another history, this time with slow but perceptible rhythms. If the expression had not been diverted from its full meaning, one could call it "social history," the history of groups and groupings. How did these swelling currents affect Mediterranean life in general—this was the question I asked myself in the second part of the book, studying in turn economic systems, states, societies, civilizations, and, finally, in order to convey more clearly my conception of history, attempting to show how all these deep-seated forces were at work in the complex arena of warfare. For war, as we know, is not an arena governed purely by individual responsibilities.

Lastly, the third part gives a hearing to traditional history—history, one might say, on the scale not of man but of individual men, what Paul Lacombe and François Simiand called "*l'histoire événementielle*" that is, the history of events—surface disturbances, crests of foam that the tides of history carry on their strong backs. A history of brief, rapid, nervous fluctuations, by definition ultrasensitive; the least tremor sets all its antennae quivering. But as such, it is the most exciting of all, the richest in human interest, and also the most dangerous. We must learn to distrust this history with its still-burning passions, as it was felt, described, and lived by contemporaries whose lives were as short and as short-sighted as ours. It has the dimensions of their anger, dreams, or illusions. In the sixteenth century, after the true Renaissance, came the Renaissance of the poor, the humble, eager to write, to talk of themselves and of others. This precious mass of paper distorts, filling up the lost hours and assuming a false importance. The historian who takes a seat in Philip II's chair and reads his papers finds himself transported into a strange one-dimensional world, a world of strong passions certainly, blind like any other living world, our own included, and unconscious of the deeper realities of history, of the running waters on which our frail barks are tossed like cockleshells. A dangerous world, but one whose spells and enchantments we shall have exorcised by making sure first to chart those underlying currents, often noiseless, whose direction can only be discerned by watching them over long periods of time. Resounding events are often only momentary outbursts, surface manifestations of these larger movements and explicable only in terms of them.

The final effect then is to dissect history into various planes, or, to put it another way, to divide historical time into geographical time, social time, and individual time. Or, alternatively, to divide man into a multitude of selves. This is perhaps what I shall be least forgiven, even if I say in my defense that traditional divisions also cut across living history which is fundamentally *one*, even if I argue, against Leopold von Ranke or Karl Brandi, that the historical narrative is not a method, or even the objective method par excellence, but quite simply a philosophy of history like any other; even if I say, and demonstrate hereafter, that these levels I have distinguished are only means of exposition, that I have felt it quite in order in the course of the book to move from one level to another. But I do not intend to plead my case further. If I am criticized for the method in which the book has been assembled, I hope the component parts will be found workmanlike by professional standards.

I hope too that I shall not be reproached for my excessive ambitions, for my desire and need to see on a grand scale. It will perhaps prove that history can do more than study walled gardens. If it were otherwise, it would surely be failing in one of its most immediate tasks, which must be to relate to the painful problems of our times and to maintain contact with the youthful but imperialistic human sciences. Can there be any study of humanity, in 1946, without historians who are ambitious, conscious of their duties and of their immense powers? "It is the fear of great history which has killed great history," wrote Edmond Faral, in 1942. May it live again!

TRANSLATED BY SIÂN REYNOLDS

The Annales and Postwar Programs for Systematic Research

The prewar Annales *(1929–1939) sought to promote collaborative research and reflection on various historical topics. An article in the form of a questionnaire, or* enquête, *served as an invitation to collaboration. At Marc Bloch's initiative, various themes in agrarian history or the definition of types of nobility thus appeared as* enquêtes *in the journal. When this format was revived in the 1950s, its focus was sharpened and there was an array of new resources to draw upon. The* Annales *were now supported by a research institution, the Centre de Recherches Historiques of the Ecole Pratique des Hautes Etudes (Sixth Section). Research was also organized, not only at the Ecole but in the Centre National de Recherche Scientifique and the universities. New technologies were available to research teams. This was the golden age of collaborative research, of programmatic, disciplined historical labor, which enjoyed a substantial budget, a considerable and replenishable workforce of students and technical assistants, and often the intellectual authority of leading names in the field. The systematic exploitation of serial data and other quantitative sources, soon enhanced by the use of computers, proved remarkably effective in a variety of areas, as we shall see. The* enquête *was a way of defining new subjects and trying out working hypotheses.*

The very different research programs outlined in the three excerpts that follow give some idea of the range of inquiries suggested in the pages of the postwar Annales. *Roland Barthes, soon to be an internationally renowned cultural critic, demonstrates the early influence of semiotics (the analysis of cultural objects as systems of signs) and structuralism in his tantalizing piece on the psychosocial meaning of food. François Billacois lays out a program for systematic research into crime and criminality, a topic that would attract many historians' attention in the 1970s. Jacques Le Goff shows that medieval spiritual trends could be subjected to systematic analysis by linking the placement of mendicant orders to the growth of towns. Although collaborative research was carried out in organized seminars and re-*

search teams on many of these suggested topics, most research was still carried out by individuals working more or less on their own.

———

ROLAND BARTHES

For a Psychosociology of the Contemporary Diet

1961

Americans consume nearly twice as much sugar as the French—a statistic important to both economics and politics.[1] But is that the end of the story? Not at all: one has only to move from consideration of sugar as a commodity—abstract, quantified—to sugar as a concrete element of diet, something "eaten" rather than "consumed," to get an idea of the magnitude of the phenomenon (which has probably never been explored). Americans must of course do something with all that extra sugar. Anyone who has spent any time in the United States knows that sugar is ubiquitous in American cooking. It permeates not only foods ordinarily made with sugar in France (such as pastries) but also a proliferation of new varieties (frostings, jellies, syrups), and is even used in dishes not usually sweetened in France (such as meats, fish, vegetables, salads, and condiments). Economists are not the only people interested in this: psychosociologists, for example, have argued that there is a consistent relation between sugar consumption and standard of living. (Is that relation really consistent today? If so, why?[2]) And also historians, who might well not deem it unworthy of them to investigate how sugar established itself in American culture (perhaps through the "salt/sugar dichotomy" in the diet of Dutch and German emigrants).

Sugar, moreover, is not just a food, even in an extended sense. It is, if you will, an "attitude." It is associated with customs and "protocols" that transcend the alimentary realm. Using sweet condiments and drinking Coca-Cola with dinner are dietary facts, to be sure; but going to "dairy bars," which instead of alcoholic beverages serve various sweet drinks, is not just a way of consuming sugar but a way of life, a mode of relaxation,

Roland Barthes, "Pour une psycho-sociologie de l'alimentation contemporaine," *Annales ESC* 16 (1961), pp. 977–86.

travel, and leisure which surely tells us a great deal about Americans. Who would say that wine in France is simply wine? Ubiquitous substances such as sugar and wine are institutions. And these institutions inevitably give rise to certain images, dreams, taboos, tastes, choices, and values. How many songs about wine are there in France? In America there was once a hit tune called "Sugar Time." Sugar is a time, a social category.[3]

I chose the case of sugar in the United States because French readers are apt to overlook what is all too familiar in their own diet. We do not see what we eat, or, worse still, we see nothing significant in it. Eating, we tend to say (especially if we are academics), is at best a pastime and for many a culpable predilection.[4] Perhaps this is why most work on the psychosociology of the French diet has approached the subject only indirectly, in the course of dealing with more substantial matters such as lifestyle, household budgets, or advertising. Recently, however, sociologists, contemporary historians (for we are concerned only with today's diet), and economists have begun to acknowledge the subject as a legitimate area of inquiry.

Paul Henri Chombart de Lauwe, for example, has studied the behavior of French working-class families in regard to food. He was able to highlight certain areas of frustration and to outline some of the themes that govern the transformation of needs into values and necessities into alibis.[5] In her book on Le Mode de vie des familles bourgeoises, de 1873 à 1953, Marguerite Perrot minimizes the role of economics in the transformation of the bourgeois diet over the past hundred years and emphasizes instead the role of taste, or ultimately ideas, especially dietetic ideas.[6] Finally, the development of advertising has given economists a much clearer sense of the ideal nature of consumer goods. It is by now a commonplace that the product purchased by the consumer (as a subjective experience) is by no means the actual product. The two are separated by the production of innumerable false perceptions and values. Consumers remain loyal to certain brands and justify their loyalty on "natural" grounds, thus providing a market for a range of products that in many cases exhibit no intrinsic differences, not even under laboratory analysis: this is true, for example, of various kinds of oils.[7]

Of course, these distortions and reconstructions involve not just anomic individual prejudices but elements of a true collective imagination, which together define the outline of a certain mental framework. All of this suggests a need to expand the very notion of what we mean by food. What is food? It is not just a collection of commodities that we can describe in statistical or culinary terms. It is also a system of communication, a body of images, a protocol of customary practices, situations, and behaviors. How can this culinary reality be studied? How can images and signs be brought into the picture? Dietary facts must be sought where they can be found—by direct observation of the economy, cooking techniques, eating habits, and advertising, and by indirect observation of social psychology.[8] The intrinsic meaning of these elements must be analyzed without recourse to any deterministic economic or ideological theory. Here I can do no more than outline the form that such an analysis might take.

When modern man buys or sells or consumes an item of food, he is not dealing with a simple, transitive object. Food epitomizes and communicates a situation. It is a piece of information, an item of meaning. In other words, it is not simply an index of more or less conscious motives but a sign, perhaps a functional unit in a structure of communication. Here, I am not referring solely to food as a form of *display* as used in various rituals of hospitality.[9] Any food can serve as a sign. Whenever a need becomes part of a normative system of production and consumption (in other words, whenever it becomes part of an institution), its function and the sign of that function become inextricably intertwined: this is true of clothing,[10] and it is also true of food. From an (abstract) anthropological point of view, food is *the* primary need, but ever since man ceased to live on wild berries, that need has been highly structured: substances, techniques, and practices form a system of significant differences, a system that makes alimentary communication possible. What proves that such communication exists? Not the more or less alienated awareness of the system's users, but the fact that alimentary facts can easily be shown to form a structure analogous to other systems of communication.[11] Although people may well believe that food possesses the immediate reality of a need or pleasure, it can nevertheless form the basis of a system of communication: food would not be the first object to be experienced as purely functional when it is actually a sign.

If food is a system, what can the elements of that system be? The first step in answering this question for a particular society is to inventory all alimentary facts—products, techniques, and practices. One then applies to those facts what linguists call the "commutation test": simply put, one looks for distinctions that yield differences of meaning. An example may help to clarify what I mean. In France the bread one eats at lunch is not the bread one would serve at a formal dinner party. Similarly, dark bread and light bread can be construed as social signifiers: dark bread, once a sign of poverty, has paradoxically become a sign of refinement. It is reasonable, therefore, to look upon the varieties of bread as signifying elements: that is the case, at least, with these particular varieties, since the same experiment might well show that there are also insignificant differences, differences that are not collective institutions but merely matters of individual taste. Proceeding in this way, one could compile a table of significant differences: these constitute our dietary system. After distinguishing the significant from the insignificant, one constructs a differential system of signifiers—dietary *declensions*, as it were (I trust that the grammatical metaphor will not seem unwarranted).

Now, it is likely that the elements of this system will only rarely coincide with the categories of food normally treated by economists. In France, for example, "bread" is not a significant element; one has to consider the varieties of bread before significant differences appear. In other words, the classes of signifiers are more subtle than the classes in terms of which we describe commerce; more than that, they involve discriminations irrelevant to the process of production: a single product can have more than one meaning. Alimentary significance is established not at the level of food production but at the level of processing and consumption. Natural foods, perhaps, have no intrinsic meaning (other than certain luxury items such as salmon, caviar, and truffles, where price, not preparation, is what matters).

If the elements of our alimentary system are not *products* in the economic sense, what are they? In the absence of any definitive research, one can only speculate. A study that Paul Lazarsfeld did some years ago (limited in scope, to be sure, and therefore cited here only as an example) showed that certain "tastes" varied with income.[12] Low-income people preferred sweet chocolates, smooth fabrics, and strong perfumes, while the relatively well-to-do preferred bitter chocolates, textured fabrics, and light fragrances. Here, the product (chocolate) is the same. The significant difference involves not product categories but flavors—*bitter* versus *sweet*. Hence, flavor is one element of the alimentary system of signifiers. One can envision others, for example, texture or consistency (dry, creamy, watery), whose psychoanalytic implications are abundantly clear. (Indeed, if intellectuals did not disdain the subject of eating, it would be an obvious candidate for Gaston Bachelard's "psychoanalytic poetics.") Claude Lévi-Strauss has shown, moreover, that the category of savoriness can be used to define national oppositions (French/English cuisine, Chinese/French, German, etc.)[13]

One can also imagine broader but more subtle oppositions: in fact, the evidence is so abundant and obvious that one can define what I shall call an "alimentary spirit" (begging the reader's indulgence for using a term with such romantic overtones). By this I mean simply that a set of alimentary traits may exhibit certain consistent (although complex) features which, taken together, delineate a general system of tastes and customs: by combining several significant elements (such as flavor and texture) one obtains interpretable composites (not unlike the suprasegmental prosodic units of language). Here I would suggest two very different examples. The ancient Greeks gathered the notions of succulence, luster, and moistness under the rubric "euphoric," or *ganos*: honey, wine, and grapes were *ganos*.[14] In the Greek alimentary system, this was surely a significant element though not associated with any single product. Or, to take a modern example, it seems that Americans oppose the categories *sweet* (which, as we have seen, includes many different kinds of foods) and *crisp* (anything that crunches, cracks, pops, or sparkles, from potato chips to certain brands of beer). One thing may be crisp simply because it is cold, another because it is astringent, still another because it is brittle (alimentary categories sometimes defy logic). Clearly, such a notion goes beyond the merely physical. In the realm of food, "crisp" denotes an almost magical virtue, a certain power to awaken, an aggressiveness, in contrast to the sticky, tranquilizing nature of sweets.

What is the point of such definitions? It is to construct, semantically rather than empirically, syntactic systems ("menus") and styles ("diets").[15] These can then be compared. The goal is to discover not what *is* but what *signifies*. Why? Because what interests us is human communication, and communication always implies a system of significations, that is, a body of discrete signs separated out from an insignificant mass of interstitial material. Hence, when sociology deals with cultural "objects" such as clothing, food, or (in a more obscure manner) housing, it must structure those objects before investigating what society does with them. For what society does is precisely to structure them for use.

To what do such alimentary significations refer? Not only, as I said earlier, to deliberate *display*[16] but also to a far broader set of themes and situations: one can say, in fact, that what food embodies as its signified is "the world." Nowadays, we can study the themes and situations that food signifies through advertising. To be sure, advertising gives only a projective image of reality. By and large, however, the sociology of mass communications shows that although the mass media are in a technical sense created by specific groups of people, they generally reflect rather than shape the collective psychology. In addition, motivational research is now sufficiently sophisticated that negative responses by the public can be analyzed. (I spoke earlier of the guilt induced by an advertising campaign for sweets based on an idea of indulgence; the advertisement was poorly designed, but the public's response was no less interesting from a psychological standpoint.)

A glance at food advertisements suggests three basic themes. Food can have an essentially commemorative function: it allows individuals to associate themselves with the nation's past (this is particularly common in French advertisements). Kitchen techniques have historical virtue in this regard: they come to us out of the venerable past and are supposed to embody the vast experience of bygone generations, a kind of ancestral wisdom. In French cooking one is never supposed to innovate, unless it be by rediscovering forgotten secrets. This historical theme, so common in advertising, depends on two sets of values. On the one hand, it points toward an aristocratic tradition (dynasties of manufacturers, royal mustards, Napoleon brandy); on the other hand, it stands for the persistence of an ancient rural society in all its variegated splendor (a utopian myth, to be sure).[17] Through food, memories of France's multifarious regions are preserved in the midst of modernity. Whence the paradoxical association of gastronomy with preserves: "cooked" dishes in cans. Of course, the myth of French cuisine that exists abroad (or in the dealings of the French with foreigners) strongly encourages the ascription of such "old-fashioned" values to food. But since the French themselves participate actively in this myth (especially when they travel), it can be said that, in a sense, they experience the continuity of their national past through food. In a thousand ways what they eat gives them roots in their own past and thus allows them to believe in a certain culinary existence of *la France*.[18]

A second group of values has to do with what might be called the anthropological situation of the modern consumer. Motivational research has shown that certain foods are associated with feelings of inferiority and that people are therefore reluctant to eat them. Some foods are "manly," others "effeminate."[19] Indeed, the artwork in many advertisements associates certain foods with images of sublimated sexuality: advertising eroticizes food and thus transforms the culinary consciousness. Food therefore becomes implicated in a pseudo-causal way in a variety of nonalimentary situations.

Finally, a third realm of ideas is associated with a range of ambiguous values, part somatic and part psychological, centered on the concept of *health*. Mythologically speaking, health is simply a mediation between body and spirit, the alibi that food adopts to signify in a material way an immaterial order of realities. In culinary terms, health is interpreted as the body's ability to cope with different social situations. This ability stems from the body but also transcends it. *Energy,* for example, is said to come from sugar, the "strength food," at least in France, which "keeps energy flowing in a steady stream"; from margarine, which "builds solid muscles"; and from coffee, which "dissolves fatigue." Here food is still related to its physiological function: it gives the organism strength, for example. But that strength is immediately sublimated and set in context (more on this in a moment): the energetic man is ready for conquest, the relaxed man is ready to deal with the stress of modern life. The remarkable development of dietetics no doubt has something to do with all this. Indeed, as we saw earlier, one historian has credited dietetics with having shaped consumer spending for the past fifty years. Whence a phenomenon that any psychosociology of eating must tackle head on— "diet-consciousness." In the developed countries, food now comes in for serious attention not only from specialists but from the public at large. That attention, however, is largely shaped by mythology. The rationalization of dietetics is significant, moreover: modern dietetics (in France at any rate) is associated not with asceticism, wisdom, or purity[20] but with *power*. The energy that a conscientious diet is supposed to provide helps the individual adapt to the modern world—so goes the myth. Ultimately, therefore, diet-consciousness reflects an implicit representation of modernity.[21]

Food also signifies situations, hence a way of life. Food does not reflect lifestyle but enacts it. Eating is a much more elaborate form of behavior than its purpose requires. It suggests or signals or takes the place of other forms of behavior, and in this sense it is clearly a sign. What does food signify? Behavior, it is safe to say, of every conceivable kind—business, labor, sport, effort, leisure, celebration. Each of these situations has its alimentary expression. Indeed, one might almost say that food's "polysemy" is characteristic of modernity. In the past, food signified only festive occasions, and in a positive, organized fashion. Today, by contrast, work has its own diet (semiotically speaking). Light, high-energy foods are seen as the essential sign (and not just the accompaniment) of active participation in modern life: the "snack" not only fulfills a new need but gives that need a certain theatrical expression, exhibiting the modernity of those who partake, showing them to be competent managers with power and control over the extremely rapid pace of contemporary life. Snack foods are typically compact, light, and quickly consumed; they have a certain "Napoleonic" quality. On a different plane, one has the "business lunch," a new need on which restaurants have capitalized by developing special luncheon menus. The business lunch is a mythic staging of power in which the conciliatory virtues once associated with the breaking of bread survive in conditions of comfort and quiet suitable for extended discussions. The food served is gastronomically satisfying (if need be in the classic tradition): it is a catalyst whose purpose is to produce the euphoric state most conducive to successful negotiations. Although snacks and business luncheons are similar as working situations, food signals the differences between them in a perfectly legible manner. One can imagine any number of similar cases.

Recently, in France at any rate, the range of culinary associations has expanded dramatically: food is now implicated in an endless variety of social situations. In general, better health and better living have been invoked as reasons for the change. It bears repeating, however, that food is also a signifier of situations: its value is at once nutritive and ceremonial, and, once basic needs are satisfied, as they are in France, the ceremonial value increasingly outweights the nutritive. To put it somewhat differently: *foods in contemporary French society are constantly being turned into situations.*

There is no better illustration of this trend than the mythology around coffee. For centuries coffee was considered a stimulant (Michelet even blamed the Revolution on it). Recently, however, without explicitly denying coffee's stimulative effects, advertisers have tried to associate it, rather paradoxically, with images of rest, repose, and relaxation. Why? Because coffee today is less a substance[22] than a situation. Workers are allowed to take "coffee breaks," during which they revive their energies according to a precise protocol. If this sort of transition from consumption to the circumstances of consumption is typical, there is reason to believe that food will acquire an even greater signifying potential than it already has. It will gain in function what it loses in substance. The signifying function of food will embrace both active situations (the business lunch) and inactive ones (the coffee break). But since work and relaxation are diametrically opposed, the traditional festive function of food may be lost as a result. Society will then organize its system of culinary signification around two pivotal notions—activity (as distinct from work) and leisure (as distinct from celebration). Here, then, is further proof, if proof be needed, of the degree to which food is an organic system, an organic part of a particular type of civilization.

TRANSLATED BY ARTHUR GOLDHAMMER

NOTES

[1] Annual per capita consumption of sugar in the U.S. is 43 kilograms [94 lbs.], compared with 25 kilograms [54.7 lbs.] in France.

[2] See François Charny, *Le Sucre* (Paris: P.U.F., 1950), p. 8.

[3] I will say nothing here about the problem of sugar's "metaphors" and paradoxes—"sweet" rock singers, or young men in black leather jackets drinking sweet milkshakes, for example.

[4] Market research has shown that food advertising based openly on love of eating is apt to fail because it makes readers feel guilty; see Joachim Marcus-Steiff, *Les Études de motivation* (Paris: Hermann, 1961), pp. 44–5.

[5] Paul Henri Chombart de Lauwe, *La Vie quotidienne des familles ouvrières* (Paris: Centre National de Recherche Scientifique, 1956).

[6] Marguerite Perrot, *Le Mode de vie des familles bourgeoises, 1873–1953* (Paris: Armand Colin, 1961), p. 292: "There has been a clear evolution since the end of the nineteenth century in the diet of the bourgeois families studied in this work. It

seems to have been a result of a change not in standard of living but rather of individual taste, influenced by a better understanding of the rules of diet."

[7] Marcus-Steiff, *Les Etudes de motivation*, p. 28.

[8] For recent research methods, see ibid.

[9] Although a great deal is known about this way of using food, this knowledge should be collected and organized. Among the topics to be included: the practice of buying rounds of drinks, holiday meals, degrees and modes of dietary ostentation for different social groups.

[10] Roland Barthes, "Le Bleu est à la mode cette année: note sur la recherche des unités signifiantes dans le vêtement de mode," *Revue française de sociologie* 1 (1960), pp. 147–62.

[11] Here I am using "structure" in the sense that it has in linguistics: "an autonomous entity of internal dependencies," according to Louis Hjelmslev, *Essais linguistiques* (Cophenhagen, 1959), p. 1.

[12] Paul F. Lazarsfeld, "The Psychological Aspect of Market Research," *Harvard Business Review* 13 (1934), pp. 54–71.

[13] Claude Lévi-Strauss, *Anthropologie structurale* (Paris: Plon, 1958), p. 99.

[14] Henri Jeanmaire, *Dionysos* (Paris: Payot, 1951).

[15] Semantically, vegetarianism, in restaurants at any rate, appears to be an attempt to copy meat dishes through various artifices not unlike the use of *simili* (copies) in dress.

[16] Social ostentation is not purely and simply a matter of vanity. Motivational analysis (using indirect questions) shows that there is a concern with appearance even in very subtle reactions, and social censorship is very powerful even in matters of food.

[17] The expression *"cuisine bourgeoise"* originally had the literal meaning of "town cooking" and later acquired the extended meaning of a relatively sophisticated cuisine, but it has lately fallen out of favor, while the "peasant *pot-au-feu*" (stew) is periodically the subject of photographic features in the major women's magazines.

[18] Alimentary exoticism can, of course, be a value, but for the vast majority of Frenchmen it seems limited to coffee (the tropics) and pasta (Italy).

[19] This is a good place to ask what "manly" food is. There is of, course, no inherent psychological quality to distinguish such things. An item of food is virile when for dietetic (hence historical) reasons, women, children, and elderly people do not eat it.

[20] One has only to compare the development of vegetarianism in England and France.

[21] Currently in France there is a battle going on between traditional (gastronomic) and modern (dietetic) values.

[22] The power to awaken, to recharge a person's batteries, seems to have been transferred, in France at any rate, to sugar.

FRANÇOIS BILLACOIS

For a Survey of Criminality in Ancien Régime France

1967

There are now and always will be records lying untouched in the archives. For every document in the Trésor des Chartes and every issue of the *Moniteur* that has received the attention of dozens of scholars, how many bundles of documents, how many registers, how many entire series of records have been totally overlooked? New methods are slowly but surely bringing valuable unexploited documents into general circulation, and in doing so they are changing the face of history: first, fiscal archives; then, over the past few decades, notarial minutes; still more recently, parish registers; and now, judicial archives are gradually giving rise to a *serial* history, a history that is based on massive documentation yet carefully nuanced, one that is qualitative as well as quantitative—a totally human history.[1]

Judicial records constitute one of the richest and, until recently, least exploited documentary series. Among the types of materials included are court decrees, prosecutorial records, hearing transcripts, interrogations of witnesses, and affidavits prepared by the clerks of Ancien Régime courts and preserved by a civilization mired in procedure, attentive to precedent, and apt to spin a whole series of cases out of a single offense.

There are three reasons why these materials have been little exploited until now. First, their very abundance has been a deterrent. Historians working alone have been overwhelmed by the massiveness of the documentation. The records of the Parlement of Paris fill seven kilometers of shelves in the Archives Nationales.[2] There are four hundred bundles of criminal documents from the Parlement of Grenoble (one of the least extensive jurisdictions in France), and these concern some eight thousand cases from the seventeenth and eighteenth centuries. In every departmental archive, Series B is one of the most abundantly stocked, with

François Billacois, "Pour une enquête sur la criminalité dans la France d'Ancien Régime," *Annales* 22 (Mar.–Apr. 1967), pp. 340–49.

judicial records from every level of jurisdiction from the *prévôté, séné-chaussée, bailliage, présidial,* and even *parlement.*

Second, the documentation is not only massive but also dauntingly complex. Even a historian with a firm grasp of Ancien Régime judicial institutions can easily become lost in conflicts over jurisdiction, overlapping customary laws, and transfers of cases from tribunal to tribunal. And then there are the pitfalls of a formalistic style that is at once precise and highly abstract. In short, one is confronted with a maze in which Ariadne's threads take one but a short distance before ending in an impossible tangle. Those inventories which exist are cursory. Some collections are not even classified chronologically. In order to find out whether a particular series is continuous enough to be usefully exploited, one has no choice but to delve into its contents. There are a few irreplaceable aids, such as the *Guide des recherches dans les fonds judiciaires de l'ancien régime,* which not only describes the various collections in the Archives Nationales but also gives a bibliography for each judicial institution, discusses the functioning and evolution of the various tribunals, and suggests types of research appropriate to each set of documents. Other scholarly aids, though, such as the famous and venerable *Tables* of Le Nain are so difficult to use without a patient apprenticeship that they are more in the nature of an additional puzzle than a useful tool opening access to the sources.

Last but not the least among the obstacles we face in dealing with documents from before the second half of the seventeenth century is quite simply the difficulty of reading them. Clerks were slow to adopt italianate script. With cramped hands and worn quills they covered page after page of trial transcripts without breaks for paragraphs or punctuation, following the arguments as best they could with the help of abbreviations, omissions, variant spellings, and syllables tacked onto or lopped off of words without regard to their meaning. The more legible a sentence is, the more likely it was actually written before or after the hearing and simply repeats the usual judicial litany, full of stock flourishes such as *"item"* and *"de ce requis."* By contrast, the closer the document is to the spoken language, to the spontaneous reaction of the accused or the witness, the more palpably authentic the contents, the more apt the writing is to degenerate into impenetrable arabesque.

The Contents of the Criminal Archives

Yet any social history that would be as comprehensive as possible cannot do without this abundant though arduous resource. Here is a brief, somewhat tedious, and by no means exhaustive listing of the contribution that criminal records could make to various branches of history:

Economic History

The crimes of usury and counterfeiting can add to our knowledge of monetary circulation and credit. Thefts, small or large, reveal an economy of substitution without which a portion of the population could not stay alive. The burning of harvests and fraudulent grain shipments are precise symptoms of the agricultural conjuncture.

Demography

Murders of course never account for more than a negligible percentage of all deaths. It would nevertheless be interesting to compare violent deaths (due to murder, brawling, duels, suicides, and so on) with overall mortality and economic indicators in a given geographical region over a given period of time. A study of infanticide would also be instructive: the Parlement of Grenoble heard two cases of this type in the year 1646 alone, both involving the killing of illegitimate children in rural villages.[3] It would also be invaluable to compile a distribution of criminals and victims by age group.

Social Groups

Just as confessors associated certain sins with certain social conditions, judges knew that certain crimes were more likely to occur in different strata of society, in part because of tensions inherent in the relations of production and in part because of social stereotypes attached to each *état*, or social station. Marginals and nomads (itinerant traders, hawkers, vagabonds, beggars, mountebanks) were especially apt to end on the gallows, or at any rate in the dock. There is no more vivid portrait of these "malingering" classes, which were the "dangerous classes" of the Ancien Régime, than that provided by the records of their trials.

The history of domestic servants, another key social group, has yet to be written. Countless larcenies and robberies, as well as murders of masters by servants or of others by servants at the instigation of their masters, could help shed light on the master-servant dialectic, an ambiguous relationship encompassing commitment as well as resentment, complicity as well as hostility, as it was experienced on a daily basis in seventeenth- and eighteenth-century shops, townhouses, and chateaux.[4]

Institutional History

Only statistical analysis of working documents can replace a history that consists of external description of abstract metamorphoses of contentless forms with a real, vital history of legal procedure and institutions. The "slowness of justice" may prove to be something other than a traditional rhetorical complaint of his majesty's subjects if one measures and compares in broad diachronic perspective the duration of cases heard by various courts, the number of cases processed in each session, and the proportion of cases that went to appeal. Other important information to be obtained would include the number and social background of defaulting defendants, the number of criminal appeals, the range of prison terms actually meted out,[5] the ebb and flow of particular types of crime,[6] the use of torture, and the significance of executions in effigy and of public executions.

Religious Life

The royal tribunals had jurisdiction over crimes of blasphemy and sacrilege. Although crimes committed by clerics were judged by the *officialités*, the royal courts dealt with crimes in which ecclesiastics were victims. Clearly, these records can be exploited to study religious feeling, and the reactions of the witnesses are as revealing as the charges themselves. Crimes of religion and common law can also tell us about the Protestant and Jewish communities, and even about groups of deists, atheists, and libertines, as well as about the Catholic majority's attitude toward these groups. Was there, for example, a distinctively Protestant criminality, different from Catholic criminality as to the nature or frequency of the crimes committed? Was the percentage of Protestant defendants in line with the proportion of Protestants in the population? Did it increase in periods of religious conflict (or of social tension and economic difficulty)? Were people of different religions punished equally for the same crime?

Clearly, then, this is a vast area, as vast as the history of material facts and collective representations and sensibilities itself.[7] These are some of the goals to be pursued through serial study of Ancien Régime criminal records. [. . .]

COLLECTIVE INVESTIGATION BEGUN

An investigation has been launched under the auspices of the Sixth Section of the Ecole Pratique des Hautes Etudes in collaboration with a seminar on the history of the penal law. The parameters and sources of the inquiry have been set and a team of researchers is already in place.

Sources

The inquiry will focus on criminal archives from the Paris region (including rural crimes, urban crimes, and crimes associated with the capital): in other words, records of the Châtelet, Parlement, and Bastille.[8] As for the Châtelet, which had initial jurisdiction in the majority of cases, the surviving seventeenth-century records are quite fragmentary. By contrast, its eighteenth-century records are as complete as those of

Parlement, and the loss of certain documents is compensated by the proliferation of written records to which every case gave rise. Two eighteenth-century collections facilitate the approach considerably by including names, ages, occupations, and sentences for important categories of defendants. These are the *Registres de la prévôté d'Ile-de-France* and the *Inventaire alphabétique du grand criminel du Parlement de Paris.*[9]

The Method

As each investigator examines trial depositions related to his own work, he will also prepare a file card containing all the information that might be useful for a history of criminality, along with other items and references that could be needed for more specialized studies. At the conclusion of this project these criminal records should be available in a form suitable for treatment using modern data-processing methods. Our initial goal is more modest, namely, to reduce the sources to a standard form (a sample is appended to the end of this article). To begin with, we are also making only periodic samples of the records (one year in every ten). Starting with the year 1785, we plan to work backward in time, beginning with the most complete and legible records as well as the ones least alien to our habitual ways of thinking, so as to perfect our method before tackling more difficult cases.

The Team

It is currently small, which justifies the modesty of our initial goals. Students will probably soon be added. We are confident, moreover, that the utility of such a study for all areas of the history of the final years of the Ancien Régime will bring additional collaborators for shorter or longer periods of time, people who will be led to our work by their own problems and who will leave us with those problems partly solved and with our joint program that much further advanced—for a collective labor is an ethical test.

TRANSLATED BY ARTHUR GOLDHAMMER

CRIMINAL CASE STANDARD FORM

I. The Trial
  A. Judgment
    1. Date
    2. Reference
  B. Procedural file
    1. Date
    2. Reference
  C. Other documents (if any)
  D. Initial judgment or appeal of judgment of _____
II. The Offense
  A. Nature
  B. Date
  C. Place
III. The Accused
  A. Social characteristics
    1. Last name, first name, alias
    2. Sex
    3. Age
    4. Rank or occupation
    5. Place of birth
    6. Place of residence
    7. Religion
    8. Signature
    9. Miscellaneous
  B. Absent, present in court, in custody, or deceased?
  C. Has he been involved in other cases?
  D. Were there accomplices?
IV. The Victim
  A. Social characteristics
    1. Last name, first name, alias
    2. Sex
    3. Age
    4. Rank or occupation
    5. Place of birth
    6. Place of residence
    7. Religion
    8. Signature
    9. Miscellaneous
  B. Relation to the accused (if any: kin, employment, neighbor, creditor/debtor)
V. Succinct analysis of the case with mention of accomplices, if any (optional)
VI. Decision of the Court

NOTES

[1] See the excellent analytic piece by Pierre Chaunu, "Une Histoire religieuse sérielle: À propos du diocèse de La Rochelle (1648–1724) et sur quelques exemples normands," *Revue d'histoire moderne et contemporaine* 12 (1965), pp. 5–86.

[2] This bit of information is taken from Charles Braibant's introduction to the *Guide de recherches dans les fonds judiciaires de l'Ancien Régime* (Paris: Direction des Archives de France, 1958).

[3] Archives départementales de l'Isère, B 2118.

[4] An anonymous review of E. Thomas's *Les Pétroleuses* in the *Times Literary Supplement* (Jan. 14, 1965), pp. 17–19, entitled "Women in Arms," points out that in revolutionary times servants are always found on both sides. In 1871, for example, the chambermaid of the lady of the house sided with the Versailles government (just as Mirabeau's chambermaid would later be an anti-Dreyfusard), whereas the governess often sided, at least in her heart, with the Commune, along with female industrial workers and shopgirls. But what about 1789, or 1798, or the riots and uprisings of the eighteenth century? Were valets foot soldiers on the side of the established order, or did they lead the "populace" in pillaging wealthy residences?

[5] Statistical methods are essential here, because the law, barring a few exceptions, did not fix prison terms, which were left to the judge's discretion.

[6] In the early seventeenth century L'Estoile in his *Journal* makes frequent mention of death sentences for sorcery, bestiality, and sodomy. In the eighteenth century, these offenses, while still illegal, no longer ended up in Parlement, much less on the scaffold. When and how did the transition take place?

[7] Court trials are an excellent touchstone for understanding religious beliefs and notions. Henri Hours has described a riot that occurred when a group of women rose up to ward off a hailstorm they expected to strike their village owing to a threat of excommunication. Trials also tell us about such collective notions as crime itself, which in the eighteenth century still encompassed such diverse offenses as "domestic theft," "blows and excesses," blasphemy, and murder.

[8] The archives of the Bastille are preserved in the Bibliothèque de l'Arsenal. Many of these documents (along with documents of other provenance scattered through archives across Europe) have been published by François Ravaisson, *Archives de la Bastille* (Paris, 1866–1884), 16 vols.

[9] Archives Nationales, Y 18 792-18 795 and Inventaire 450.

JACQUES LE GOFF

The Mendicant Orders in Urban France

1968

The Centre de Recherches Historiques of the Sixth Section of the Ecole Pratique des Hautes Etudes has begun an *enquête* in the historical cultural anthropology of France. It began with nineteenth-century military archives, and its purpose is to trace as far as possible into the past the various features whose interaction formed France's historical personality. (Eventually the investigation may be broken down into smaller geographical and/or chronological units: it may, for example, turn out to be useful to study southern France separately from northern France. The traits in question are to be grounded in, and explained in terms of, something other than the superficial effects of political forces and conjunctures.) There are, however, certain obvious difficulties in delving, as we propose to do here, into the depths of the past.

For the Middle Ages, nothing like the documentation available for more recent periods is to be found. In particular, it is well known that there are few sources that lend themselves to statistical treatment. For the time being, at least, there are no methods or research programs designed to develop substitutes for the kinds of documentation needed for quantitative research and thus for achieving something more than an impressionistic understanding of history's underlying realities. In view of these shortcomings, we have designed a more modest approach to the anthropological foundations of medieval France.

DEFINITION OF THE INVESTIGATION

We are interested in the urban phenomenon. Although we are well aware that the civilization of medieval France was primarily rural, we felt that a historical study of urbanization could yield useful information about one aspect of France's deep historical development. Although there are excellent works on specific aspects of the subject as well as some very good overviews, there is no systematic quantitative study.

Jacques Le Goff, "Apostolat mendiant et fait urbain dans la France médiévale: L'Implantation des ordres mendiants," *Annales* 23 (Mar.–Apr. 1968), pp. 335–45.

What approach should one take toward urban France in the Middle Ages? Although archaeological methods are important, their usefulness is limited. Urban excavations can yield invaluable, indispensable information, but these findings must be supplemented by other approaches. Furthermore, for obvious practical reasons, it is impossible to excavate every site known to have been developed in the Middle Ages.

A demographic approach might at first sight seem a safer bet. But this, too, runs up against major difficulties and objections:

1. How should one choose the urban areas in which to conduct demographic studies for the medieval period?

2. Where is the necessary documentation to be found? There are, of course, virtually no quantitative demographic sources prior to the fourteenth century, and even for later periods interpretation of the documentation is a delicate matter.

3. Although population is one criterion of "urbanness," there is no hard and fast rule for defining a "city." Some large villages were more populous than small cities.

4. It is hard enough for geographers and statisticians to agree today on what defines a city, and to expect to define any firm criterion for medieval cities therefore seems unrealistic and ultimately unscientific.

Legal criteria are no more suitable than population criteria, moreover, since we cannot say what, if any, institutions were purely urban or identify any particular institution common to all medieval cities. We will, however, use legal criteria in the course of our study, even if we cannot use them to define our subject.

We have therefore chosen to focus not on quantitative factors such as population or external qualitative factors such as legal institutions but, rather, on internal qualitative factors. We propose to study an aspect of the urban phenomenon capable of shedding light on the specific functions that define "urbanness" in sociological terms, namely, the localization of the mendicant orders, which we believe is a phenomenon that can tell us a great deal about urban France in the Middle Ages.

Our investigation is therefore based on the following two working hypotheses, the first of which is the more necessary if not the more important:

1. The urban map of medieval France coincides with the map of mendicant convents. In other words, (a) there are no mendicant convents outside urban areas, and (b) there are no urban centers without a mendicant convent.

It is important to note that we are well aware that these two propositions may turn out to be less than one hundred percent correct. It will suffice if there are few exceptions (mendicant convents outside urban centers or, more likely, urban centers without mendicant convents), and if most of the exceptions can be explained by external factors.[1] Of course, in order to avoid the danger of tautology (if one defines any development in which there is a mendicant convent as a city, then one will have assumed what one wants to demonstrate), we will analyze places with convents but unlikely to be cities as well as places without convents that we suspect might be cities (for example, episcopal sees without a mendicant convent).

> 2. There is a connection between the demographic and social structure of urban centers and the location of mendicant convents in those centers. More precisely, mendicant convents were situated in or close to cities so as to be able to reach new social groups, composed mainly of recent immigrants from the countryside. In order to reach these groups, the Church was obliged to develop a new type of preaching, and mendicant convents were established in or on the fringes of urban centers, often in the *faubourgs*.

This second hypothesis is independent of and complementary to the first, and less important for our purposes. There were no doubt many exceptions. Later we will discuss various reasons for diversity, but the special case of university towns should be mentioned at once: the "Latin quarter" was always a favorite location of mendicant convents. It would be interesting to study the various centripetal and centrifugal forces at work in these cities.

RESEARCH PROGRAM

I. Geographical and chronological setting
   A. Geographical setting: the borders of present-day France.
   Ultimately we are interested in historical structures in the territory that constitutes present-day France. Bear in mind, however, that the convents and towns studied were not all in France at the time.
      One advantage of this geographical framework is that it allows us to make direct use of the present organization of the French archives. As a starting point for our work, we can also draw on the extensive and solid information contained in Richard W. Emery's study, *The Friars in Medieval France*.[2]
   B. Chronological framework: ca. 1200–1550
   This was the period chosen by Emery. The *terminus ante quem*, which corresponds to the foundation and establishment of the

Mendicant Orders, is indisputable.[3] Emery justifies the date 1550 by the argument that it falls between a half century during which the Mendicant Orders were in decline and a period of renaissance (p. xvii). As the investigation proceeds, the *terminus post quem* may be called into question. It may turn out, for example, that 1525 is a better choice, for particular reasons (the foundation of the Capuchins) as well as general ones.

II. Data collection

We need to develop a data form for recording all the information needed for in-depth study of each individual case (location, date of foundation, archival and bibliographic sources), including:

A. All mendicant convents in medieval France

B. All places in which one or more mendicant convents were located

According to Emery's catalogue, there were 882 convents and 536 locations. According to our hypothesis, those 536 locations (a number that may eventually be corrected as the investigation proceeds) constitute urban France in the medieval period. At the present time, December 1967, information has been collected from Emery and other research concerning these 882 convents and 536 locations.

III. Maps

We need to prepare:

A. Maps of France indicating the locations of all mendicant convents (maximum: eleven in Paris), with notations indicating those locations with one or more convents.

B. Maps of all places in which mendicant convents were located, indicating as far as possible the layout of the place and the location of the convent.

IV. The Conjuncture

We need to ascertain and map all relevant changes in convent emplacement (creation of new convents, disappearance of old ones, and changes of location within a given town):

A. At the national level:

Emery has identified four key periods: 1200–1275, 1275–1350, 1350–1450, and 1450–1550. This periodization needs to be examined closely, and we need to develop a fuller chronology, particularly for the thirteenth century, which saw the largest number of foundations (Emery's figures for the four periods indicated are 423, 215, 110, and 134 respectively). Preliminary maps have already been drawn up for each decade (1200–1210, 1210–1220, and so on).

B. At the local level:

Was there a conjuncture during which convents moved locally (generally moving inside city walls or closer to the center of town)? If so, was this related to a more general conjuncture (shrinking of cities due to fourteenth-century economic and demographic crises or disasters, such as plague and violence)? Or were such moves due mainly to fortuitous circumstances, such as a change in the mendicants' relation to urban society (as, for example, with the Dominican convent at Cahors)?

Already at this stage we encounter problems of interpretation.

Problems

I. Establishing data

A. Archival documents

Archives of the convents and mendicant orders: specific gaps (no direct wealth or property).

Documents suitable for revealing the relation of the mendicant convents to the urban environment: documents relating to conflicts of jurisdiction, wills.

B. Convents

Possible errors in Emery's list: forgotten convents (absence of Corsica, for example), fictitious convents.

[...]

C. Dates

What is the date of a mendicant convent's foundation: for example, for a convent of Preachers, is it the date when a site was identified (suggested by a monk or nun, an ecclesiastic or lay person, sometimes with solicitation of an endowment), or when an exploratory mission was sent, or a decision was made (*receptio* or *promotio loci*, theoretically requiring a decision of the chapter general), or the date of the actual foundation *(tenere fratres, erigere altare)*, itself evolving over several phases (see Celestin Douais, *Acta capitulorum provincialium O.F.P. 1re province de Provence*)?[4]

We must also be attentive to possible errors in Emery's dates and give more precise dates wherever possible.

D. The population of the convents

Can we determine at least the approximate number of friars living in a convent? Is there a conjunctural pattern to these numbers? Is the number related to the "urbanness" of the location (the size of the city or the regional, national, or international role it might play)?[5] Here again, convents in academic towns are a special case (for example, the Dominicans' Saint-Jacques convent in Paris was overcrowded and therefore repeatedly obliged to call upon the order for material assistance).

E. Maps

Are there any usable "old" maps?

Are there any modern catalogues of convent maps or historical maps of cities?

What factors bearing on the relation between the mendicant orders and urbanization should be included on the maps or in legends?

1. For national maps: political boundaries (which ones?), ecclesiastical boundaries (dioceses), relief, roads, maps of other contemporary orders.

2. For local maps: jurisdictional boundaries, churches, other convents, centers of political power and economic activity.

II. Definition and delimitation of the scope of the inquiry

What is a mendicant order? Are all the orders considered to be mendicant good indicators of urbanization?

A. Are the Preachers the only order that really fits the fundamental hypothesis?

B. For the other mendicant orders, were there other factors that determined their location and diminished the importance of their relation to urbanization?

1. The hermitic tendency (among the Minorites, Augustines, and Sachets, for example)?

2. A marked regional character (such as the location of the Sachets in Provence)?

3. Particular aims, such as founding hospitals and, above all, redeeming captives. Can the Mercedarians and Trinitarians be regarded as mendicant orders, and, if so, were they related in any direct sense to urbanization?

C. What list of mendicant orders should be adopted?

1. Emery's list: Augustines, Carmelites, Dominicans, Croisiers (*Ordo Sanctae Crucis*), Franciscans, Mercedarian Minimes, Friars of Pica (?) (*Ordo Beatae Mariae Matris Christi*), Sachets (*Ordo Penitentiae Jesu Christi*), Servites, Trinitarians, Guillelmites?

2. What were the small mendicant orders abolished by the Second Council of Lyon (1274)?

3. How interesting are these orders for our purposes? An important special case is that of the Sachets, for whom we have found 111 convents founded between 1248 and 1274, 51 of them in (present-day) France, including, in addition to the dense Provençal kernel, the majority of "large" cities.

D. Should we look at convents of female mendicants (the sisters were cloistered)?

III. Problems of localization and its sociological interpretation
  A. The role of local factors:
    1. Attitude of the secular clergy: in particular, the attitude of bishops (and chapters) and conflicts around parochial rights.
    2. Attitude of the regular clergy previously settled in the town or its surroundings: relations between Benedictines and Mendicants in the urban setting.
    3. Attitude of the lay authority or authorities.
    4. Donations: social geography of donations and protections. Was there a particular connection between the urban bourgeoisie and the mendicant orders?
    5. Did the presence of heretics affect the location of mendicant convents to the point of obscuring the relation of the mendicants to urbanization? Or was urbanization more important than the antiheretical motive? Or perhaps urbanization was related to both heresy and mendicant location.
    6. What role did contingent local factors play in (a) the establishment and (b) the location of mendicant convents? Did such factors hasten, delay, or prevent the establishment of convents? Did they play an important role in the relegation of mendicant convents to the fringes of the city?
    7. To explain the frequent choice to locate convents initially in suburbs, should we ascribe greater importance to the mendicants' own sense of the areas in which their apostolic labors were most urgently needed or to material or contingent factors such as donations, the location of the property of the social groups most likely to give, and the availability of land and/or housing at reasonable prices? Can mendicancy be related to a sociotopographic evolution of urban development: division of communal lands, settlement of artisans in the suburbs, policies of the authorities (religious communities, lay and ecclesiastical lords, bourgeois patriciate) in regard to land and buildings?
  B. Topographic policy of the orders
    1. Was there competition between orders and therefore between convents of different mendicant orders in the same town or region? Or was there some agreement about dividing the territory? What motivated arbitration in this area, particularly papal arbitration, and what was its influence?
    2. Was the number of mendicant convents in a city proportional

to the size of the city? Was it directly proportional, or did competition between orders play a role?

C. Diversity of urban phenomena with respect to location of mendicant convents

    1. Do contemporary documents, and particularly documents dealing with mendicant convents, allow us to establish a typology and hierarchy of urban developments (definitions of such words as *civitates, villae, loca, loci,* etc.).

    2. In view of a study of the urban factor in the historical cultural anthropology of France, can study of the location of mendicant convents help us to define types of urbanization and, in particular, to distinguish between dynamic types (northern France?) and traditional types (southern France?)? Were the different types of urbanization related to functional economic differences (predominance of artisanal production, role of the rural market, size of surrounding trading region, etc.)?[6]

D. The hinterland

    1. Did all the mendicant orders extend their activities into rural areas? Case of the Dominican *praedicationes* and *termini.*

    2. Did the mendicant hinterland correspond to the urban hinterland: in other words, were alms collection and preaching aimed at the same populations that already gravitated toward the urban center in which the convent was located?

    3. The definition of these rural zones of influence sometimes led to conflicts, and these conflicts often left traces in the archives. Is there hope of finding enough documentation of this sort to establish a map of urban zones of influence in medieval France?

E. Mendicant orders and urban culture

Did the urban location of the mendicant orders have an influence on the type of piety and spirituality they proposed? Were the city's social stratification, problems, and spirit reflected in mendicant practices? What was the cultural role of the mendicant convents (with their libraries, schools, sermons, manuals of hagiography and devotion, art, ceremonies and liturgy)? What did they contribute to urban culture generally, as well as to such particular aspects of urban culture as local patriotism?

CONCLUSION: GENERAL AND COMPARATIVE PROSPECTS

Assuming that this investigation succeeds in demonstrating a close relationship between the mendicant phenomenon and urbanization in medieval France, does it follow that the same is true across Europe? Did such a connection exist throughout medieval Christendom? Can one map urban Christendom by mapping mendicant convents? Do other civilizations and other religions exhibit comparable organic links between an ecclesiastico-religious phenomenon and urbanization?

We are aware that in order to bring out the distinctive features of the mendicant phenomenon and its relation to urbanization, we must also study and map the monastic world as it existed prior to and contemporaneous with the mendicant world. It is simplistic and misleading to suggest that the mendicant orders relegated the Benedictines and other monks and canons to the shadows.

TRANSLATED BY ARTHUR GOLDHAMMER

NOTES

[1] For example, around 1300, in the Dominican province of Provence, the combined influence of powerful laymen (the King of Majorca, the King of Sicily/Count of Provence, and various nobles) and of the papacy led to the foundation of Dominican convents in places whose urban character is doubtful (Collioure, 1290; Puigcerda, 1291) or unlikely (Saint-Maximin, 1295; Genolhac, 1300; Buis-les-Baronnies, 1294–1310). See Bernard Gui, *De fundatione et prioribus conventuum provinciarum Tolosanae et Provinciae O.P.*, ed. P. A. Amargier (Rome, 1961), pp. 271–74, 275–77, 278–79, 282–83.

[2] Richard W. Emery, *The Friars in Medieval France: A Catalogue of French Mendicant Convents, 1200–1550* (New York: Columbia University Press, 1962).

[3] One should not, however, neglect an earlier religious movement associated with urban growth: the canonial movement of the eleventh and twelfth centuries, to which Canon J. Chatillon and Dom J. Becquet have drawn our attention. Referring to the period 1050–1150, Becquet speaks of "quantities of small collegiate churches founded in symbiosis with a pre-urban nucleus."

[4] Celestin Douais, *Acta capitulorum provincialium O.F.P. 1ʳᵉ province de Provence, Provence Romaine, Provence d'Espagne* (Toulouse, 1894), pp. xliv–l.

[5] Note that the Dominicans (and other orders that adopted their constitution) required a minimum of twelve friars to form a convent.

[6] See Georges Duby, "Recherches récentes sur la vie rurale en Provence au XIVᵉ siècle," *Provence historique* (1965), pp. 97–111.

Braudel's Emphasis on the Long Term

FERNAND BRAUDEL

History and the Social Sciences: The *Longue Durée*

1958

This is probably one of the most influential texts in postwar French historiography; it certainly did a great deal to establish the identity of that historiography in other countries. In this manifesto, Braudel systematically organized the themes of La Méditerranée *(a work perhaps more celebrated than read) and underplays the complexity of social time, instead emphasizing the primacy of the* longue durée *in the analysis of social phenomena. When reading this text, it is important to remember that Braudel had recently become the chairman of the Sixth Section of the Ecole Pratique des Hautes Etudes, at the time the most powerful center of social science research and teaching in France. His responsibility was, in fact, to formulate and implement a scientific policy, a program, as will be seen, that frames the thinking of this contribution. At a time when French social science was growing increasingly restive under history's domination (a restiveness that would soon express itself in the structuralist offensive), and when it seemed that interdisciplinarity might be in jeopardy, Braudel, with great lucidity and singular modesty, proposed assigning history ("perhaps the least formalized of the sciences of man") the role of serving as a common ground—even as he recognized the value of the* longue durée *in providing "one possibility of achieving a*

Fernand Braudel, "Histoire et sciences sociales: La longue durée," *Annales ESC* 13 (1958), pp. 725–53. Also published in Fernand Braudel, *On History*, trans. Sarah Matthews (Chicago: University of Chicago Press, 1980).

common language for the purpose of comparing results in the social sciences."

There is a general crisis in the human sciences: they are all overwhelmed by their own progress, if only because of the accumulation of new knowledge and the need to work together in a way that is yet to be properly organized. Directly or indirectly, willingly or unwillingly, none of them can remain unaffected by the progress of the more active among them. But they remain in the grip of an insidious and retrograde humanism no longer capable of providing them with a valid framework for their studies. With varying degrees of clear-sightedness, all the sciences are preoccupied with their own position in the whole monstrous agglomeration of past and present researches, researches whose necessary convergence can now clearly be seen.

Will the human sciences solve these difficulties by an extra effort at definition or by an increase in ill temper? They certainly seem to think so, for (at the risk of going over some very well trodden ground and of raising a few red herrings), today they are engaged more busily than ever in defining their aims, their methods, and their superiorities. You can see them vying with each other, skirmishing along the frontiers separating them, or not separating them, or barely separating them from their neighbors. For each of them, in fact, persists in a dream of staying in, or returning to, its home. A few isolated scholars have managed to bring things together: Claude Lévi-Strauss[1] has pushed "structural" anthropology toward the procedures of linguistics, the horizons of "unconscious" history, and the youthful imperialism of "qualitative" mathematics. He leans toward a science that would unite, under the title of "communications science," anthropology, political economy, linguistics . . . But is there in fact anyone who is prepared to cross the frontiers like this, and to realign things in this way? Given half a chance, geography would even like to split off from history!

Yet we must not be unfair. These squabbles and denials have a certain significance. The wish to affirm one's own existence in the face of others is necessarily the basis for new knowledge: to deny someone is already to know him. Moreover, without explicitly wishing it, the social sciences force themselves on each other, each trying to capture society as a whole, in its "totality." Each science encroaches on its neighbors, all the while believing it is staying in its own domain. Economics finds sociology closing in on it, history—perhaps the least structured of all the human sciences—is open to all the lessons learned by its many neighbors, and is then at pains to reflect them back again. So, despite all the reluctance, opposition, and blissful ignorance, the beginnings of a "common market" are being sketched out. This would be well worth a trial during the coming years, even if each science might later be better off readopting, for a while, some more strictly personal approach.

But the crucial thing now is to get together in the first place. In the United States, this coming together has taken the form of collective research on the cultures of different areas of the modern world, "area studies" being, above all, the study by a team of social scientists of those political Leviathans of our time: China, India, Russia, Latin America, the United States. Understanding them is a question of life and death! But at the same time as sharing techniques and knowledge, it is essential that each of the participants should not remain buried in his private research, as deaf and blind as before to what the others are saying, writing, or thinking! Equally, it is essential that this gathering of the social sciences should make no omissions, that they should all be there, that the older ones should not be neglected in favor of the younger ones which seem to promise so much, even if they do not always deliver it. For instance, the position allotted to geography in these American exercises is almost nil, and that allowed to history extremely meager. Not to mention the sort of history it is!

The other social sciences are fairly ill informed as to the crisis that our discipline has gone through in the past twenty or thirty years, and they tend to misunderstand not only the work of historians but also that aspect of social reality for which history has always been a faithful servant, if not always a good salesman—social time, the multifarious, contradictory times of the life of men, which not only make up the past, but also the social life of the present. Yet history, or rather the dialectic of duration as it arises in the exercise of our profession, from our repeated observations, is important in the coming debate among all the human sciences. For nothing is more important, nothing comes closer to the crux of social reality, than this living, intimate, infinitely repeated opposition between the instant of time and that time which flows only slowly. Whether it is a question of the past or of the present, a clear awareness of this plurality of social time is indispensable to the communal methodology of the human sciences.

So I propose to deal at length with history, and with time in history. Less for the sake of present readers of this journal, who are already specialists in our field, than for that of those who work in the neighboring human sciences: economists, ethnographers, ethnologists (or anthropologists), sociologists, psychologists, linguists, demographers, geographers, even social mathematicians or statisticians—all neighbors of ours whose experiments and whose researches we have been following for these many years because it seemed to us (and seems so still) that we would thus see history itself in a new light. And perhaps we in our turn have something to offer them. From the recent experiments and efforts of history, an increasingly clear idea has emerged—whether consciously or not, whether accepted or not—of the multiplicity of time, and of the exceptional value of the long time span. It is this last idea that, even more than history itself—history of a hundred aspects—should engage the attention and interest of our neighbors, the social sciences.

HISTORY AND TIME SPANS

All historical work is concerned with breaking down time past, choosing among its chronological realities, according to more or less conscious preferences and exclusions. Traditional history, with its concern for the short time span, for the individual and the event, has long accustomed us to the headlong, dramatic, breathless rush of its narrative.

The new economic and social history puts cyclical movement in the forefront of its research and is committed to that time span: it has been captivated by the mirage and the reality of the cyclical rise and fall of prices. So today, side by side with traditional narrative history, there is an account of conjunctures which lays open large sections of the past, ten, twenty, fifty years at a stretch ready for examination.

Far beyond this second account, we find a history capable of traversing even greater distances, a history to be measured in centuries this time: the history of the long, even of the very long time span, of the *longue durée*. This is a phrase which I have become accustomed to for good or ill, in order to distinguish the opposite of what François Simiand, not long after Paul Lacombe, christened "*l'histoire événementielle*," the history of events. The phrases matter little; what matters is the fact that our discussion will move between these two poles of time, the instant and the *longue durée*.

Not that these words are absolutely reliable. Take the word "event": for myself I would limit it, and imprison it within the short time span— an event is explosive, a "*nouvelle sonnante*" ("a matter of moment") as they said in the sixteenth century. Its delusive smoke fills the minds of its contemporaries, but it does not last, and its flame can scarcely ever be discerned.

Doubtless, philosophers would tell us that to treat the word thus is to empty it of a great part of its meaning. An event can, if necessary, take on a whole range of meanings and associations. It can occasionally bear witness to very profound movements, and by making play, factitiously or not, with those "causes" and "effects" so dear to the hearts of the historians of yore, it can appropriate a time far greater than its own time span. Infinitely extensible, it becomes wedded, either freely or not, to a whole chain of events, of underlying realities which are then, it seems, impossible to separate. It was by adding things together like this that Benedetto Croce could claim that within any event all history, all of man is embodied, to be rediscovered at will. Though this, of course, is on condition of adding to that fragment whatever it did not at first sight appear to contain, which in turn entails knowing what is appropriate— or not appropriate—to add. It is the clever and perilous process that some of Jean-Paul Sartre's recent thinking seems to propose.[2]

So, to put things more clearly, let us say that instead of a history of events, we would speak of a short time span, proportionate to individuals, to daily life, to our illusions, to our hasty awareness—above all, the time of the chronicle and the journalist. Now, it is worth noting that side by side with great and, so to speak, historic events, the chronicle or the daily paper offers us all the mediocre accidents of ordinary life—a fire, a railway crash, the price of wheat, a crime, a theatrical production, a flood. It is clear, then, that there is a short time span which plays a part in all forms of life, economic, social, literary, institutional, religious, even geographical (a gust of wind, a storm), just as much as political.

At first sight, the past seems to consist in just this mass of diverse facts, some of which catch the eye, and some of which are dim and repeat themselves indefinitely. The very facts, in other words, that go to make up the daily booty of microsociology or of sociometry (there is microhistory too). But this mass does not make up all of reality, all the depth of history on which scientific thought is free to work. Social science has almost what amounts to a horror of the event. And not without some justification, for the short time span is the most capricious and the most delusive of all.

Thus, there is among some of us, as historians, a lively distrust of traditional history, the history of events—a label that tends to become confused, rather inexactly, with political history. Political history is not necessarily bound to events, nor is it forced to be. Yet except for the factitious panoramas almost without substance in time which break up its narrative,[3] except for the overviews inserted for the sake of variety, on the whole the history of the past hundred years, almost always political history centered on the drama of "great events," has worked on and in the short time span. Perhaps that was the price that had to be paid for the progress made during this same period in the scientific mastery of particular tools and rigorous methods. The momentous discovery of the document led historians to believe that documentary authenticity was the repository of the whole truth. "All we need to do," Louis Halphen wrote only yesterday,[4] "is allow ourselves to be borne along by the documents, one after another, just as they offer themselves to us, in order to see the chain of facts and events reconstitute themselves almost automatically before our eyes." Toward the end of the nineteenth century, this ideal of history "in the raw" led to a new style of chronicle, which in its desire for exactitude followed the history of events step by step as it emerged from ambassadorial letters or parliamentary debates. The historians of the eighteenth and early nineteenth centuries had been attentive to the perspectives of the *longue durée* in a way in which, afterward, only a few great spirits—Jules Michelet, Leopold von Ranke, Jacob Burckhardt, Numa Denis Fustel de Coulanges—were able to recapture. If one accepts that this going beyond the short span has been the most precious, because the most rare, of historiographical achievements during the past hundred years, then one understands the preeminent role of the history of institutions, of religions, of civilizations, and (thanks to archeology with its need for vast chronological expanses) the groundbreaking role of the studies devoted to classical antiquities. It was only yesterday that they proved the saviors of our profession.

The recent break with the traditional forms of nineteenth-century history has not meant a complete break with the short time span. It has worked, as we know, in favor of economic and social history, and against the interests of political history. This has entailed upheavals and an undeniable renewal, and also, inevitably, changes in method, the shifting of centers of interest with the advent of a quantitative history that has certainly not exhausted all it has to offer.

Above all, there has been an alteration in traditional historical time. A day, a year once seemed useful gauges. Time, after all, was made up of an accumulation of days. But a price curve, a demographic progression, the movement of wages, the variations in interest rates, the study (as yet more dreamed-of than achieved) of productivity, a rigorous analysis of money supply all demand much wider terms of reference.

A new kind of historical narrative has appeared, that of the conjuncture, of the cycle, and even of the "intercycle," covering a decade, a quarter of a century, and, at the outside, the half century of Kondratiev's classic cycle. For instance, if we disregard any brief and superficial fluctuations, prices in Europe went up between 1791 and 1817, and went down between 1817 and 1852. This unhurried double movement of increase and decrease represents an entire intercycle measured by the time of Europe, and more or less by that of the whole world. Of course these chronological periods have no absolute value. François Perroux[5] would offer us other, perhaps more valid, dividing lines, measured with other barometers, those of economic growth, income, or the gross national product. But what do all these current debates matter! What is quite clear is that the historian can make use of a new notion of time, a time raised to the level of explication, and that history can attempt to explain itself by dividing itself at new points of reference in response to these curves and to the very way they breathe.

Thus, Ernest Labrousse and his students, after their manifesto at the last Rome Historical Congress (1955), set up a vast inquiry into social history in quantitative terms. I do not think I am misrepresenting their intention when I say that this inquiry must necessarily lead to the determination of social conjunctures (and even of structures) that may not share the same rate of progress, fast or slow, as the economic conjuncture. Besides, these two distinguished gentlemen—the economic conjuncture and the social conjuncture—must not make us lose sight of other actors, though their progress will be difficult if not impossible to track, for lack of a precise way of measuring it. Science, technology, political institutions, conceptual changes, civilizations (to fall back on that useful word) all have their own rhythms of life and growth, and the new history of conjunctures will be complete only when it has made up a whole orchestra of them all.

In all logic, this orchestration of conjunctures, by transcending itself, should have led us straight to the *longue durée*. But for a thousand reasons, this transcendence has not been the rule, and a return to the short term is being accomplished even now before our very eyes. Perhaps this is because it seems more necessary (or more urgent) to knit together "cyclical" history and short-term traditional history than to go forward, toward the unknown. In military terms, it has been a question of consolidating newly secured positions. Labrousse's first great book, published in 1933, was thus a study of the general movement of prices in France during the eighteenth century,[6] a movement lasting a good hundred years. In 1943, in the most important work of history to have appeared in France in twenty-five years, this very same Ernest Labrousse succumbed to this need to return to a less cumbersome measure of time when he pinpointed the depression of 1774 to 1791 as being one of the most compelling sources, one of the prime launching pads, of the French Revolution. He was still employing a demi-intercycle, a large measure. In his address to the International Congress in Paris in 1948, *Comment naissent les révolutions?*, he attempted this time to link a new-style pathetic fallacy (short-term economic) to a very old-style pathetic fallacy (political, the "revolutionary days"). And behold us back up to our ears in the short time span. Of course, this is a perfectly fair and justifiable procedure, but how very revealing! The historian is naturally only too willing to act as theatrical producer. How could he be expected to renounce the drama of the short time span, and all the best tricks of a very old trade?

Over and above cycles and intercycles, there is what the economists without always having studied it call the "secular tendency." But so far only a few economists have proved interested in it, and their deliberations on structural crises, based only on the recent past, as far back as 1929, or

1870 at the very most,[7] not having had to withstand the test of historical verification, are more in the nature of sketches and hypotheses. They offer nonetheless a useful introduction to the history of the *longue durée*. They provide a first key.

The second and far more useful key consists in the word "structure." For good or ill, this word dominates the problems of the *longue durée*. By "structure," observers of social questions mean an organization, a coherent and fairly fixed series of relationships between realities and social masses. For us historians, a structure is of course a construct, an architecture, but over and above that it is a reality that time uses and abuses over long periods. Some structures, because of their long life, become stable elements for an infinite number of generations: they get in the way of history, hinder its flow, and in hindering it shape it. Others wear themselves out more quickly. But all of them provide both support and hindrance. As hindrances they stand as limits ("envelopes," in the mathematical sense) beyond which man and his experiences cannot go. Just think of the difficulties of breaking out of certain geographical frameworks, certain biological realities, certain limits of productivity, even particular spiritual constraints: mental frameworks too can form prisons of the *longue durée*.

The example that comes most readily to mind is once again that of the geographical constraint. For centuries, man has been a prisoner of climate, of vegetation, of the animal population, of a particular agriculture, of a whole slowly established balance from which he cannot escape without the risk of everything's being upset. Look at the position held by the movement of flocks in the lives of mountain people, the permanence of certain sectors of maritime life, rooted in the favorable conditions wrought by particular coastal configurations, look at the way the sites of cities endure, the persistence of routes and trade, and all the amazing fixity of the geographical setting of civilizations.

There is the same element of permanence or survival in the vast domain of cultural affairs. Ernst Robert Curtius's magnificent book,[8] which has at long last appeared in a French translation, is a study of a cultural system that prolonged the Latin civilization of the Byzantine Empire, even while it distorted it through selections and omissions. This civilization was itself weighed down by its own ponderous inheritance. Right up to the thirteenth and fourteenth centuries, right up to the birth of national literatures, the civilization of the intellectual elite fed on the same subjects, the same comparisons, the same commonplaces and catchwords. Pursuing an analogous line of thought, Lucien Febvre's study *Rabelais et le problème de l'incroyance au XVIe siècle*,[9] is an attempt to specify the mental tools available to French thought at the time of Rabelais. Febvre was concerned to define the whole body of concepts which regulated the arts of living, thinking, and believing well before Rabelais and long after him, and which profoundly limited the intellectual endeavors of the freest spirits from the very outset. Alphonse Dupront's subject too appears as one of the freshest lines of research within the French school of history.[10] In it, the idea of the crusade is examined in the West after the fourteenth century, that is, well after the age of the "true" crusade, in the continuity of an attitude endlessly repeated over the *longue durée,* which cut across the most diverse societies, worlds, and psyches, and touched the men of the nineteenth century with one last ray. In another, related field, Pierre Francastel's book *Peinture et société*[11] demonstrates the permanence of "geometric" pictorial space from the beginnings of the Florentine Renaissance until cubism and the emergence of intellectual painting at the beginning of our own century. In the history of science, too, all the many model universes are just as many incomplete explanations, but they also regularly last for centuries. They are cast aside only when they have served their turn over a long period. The Aristotelian concept of the universe persisted unchallenged, or virtually unchallenged, right up to the time of Galileo, Descartes, and Newton; then it disappeared before the advent of a geometrized universe, which in turn collapsed, though much later, in the face of the Einsteinian revolution.[12]

In a seeming paradox, the main problem lies in discerning the *longue durée* in the sphere in which historical research has just achieved its most notable successes—that is, the economic sphere. All the cycles and intercycles and structural crises tend to mask the regularities, the permanence of particular systems that some have gone so far as to call civilizations[13]—that is to say, all the old habits of thinking and acting, the set patterns that do not break down easily and, however illogical, are a long time dying.

But let us base our argument on an example, and one that can be swiftly analyzed. Close at hand, within the European sphere, there is an economic system which can be set down in a few lines: it preserved its position pretty well intact from the fourteenth to the eighteenth century or, to be quite sure of our ground, until about 1750. For whole centuries, economic activity was dependent on demographically fragile populations, as was demonstrated by the great decline in population from 1350 to 1450, and of course from 1630 to 1730.[14] For whole centuries, all movement was dominated by the primacy of water and ships, any inland location being an obstacle and a source of inferiority. The great European points of growth, except for a few exceptions that go only to prove the rule (such as the fairs in Champagne, which were already on the decline at the beginning of the period, and the Leipzig fairs in the eighteenth century), were situated along the coastal fringes. As for other characteristics of this system, one might cite the primacy of merchants; the prominent role of precious metals, gold, silver, even copper, whose endless vicissitudes would only be damped down, if then, by the decisive development of credit at the end of the sixteenth century; the repeated sharp difficulties caused by seasonal agricultural crises; let us say the fragility of the very basis of economic life; and, finally, the at first sight utterly disproportionate role accorded to one or two external trade routes: the trade with the Levant from the twelfth to the sixteenth century and the colonial trade in the eighteenth century.

These are what I would define, or rather suggest, in my turn following many others, as being the major characteristics of mercantile capitalism in Western Europe, a stage that lasted over the *longue durée*. Despite all the obvious changes that run through them, these four or five centuries of economic life had a certain coherence, right up to the upheavals of the eighteenth century and the Industrial Revolution from which we have yet to emerge. These shared characteristics persisted despite the fact that all around them, amid other continuities, a thousand reversals and ruptures totally altered the face of the world.

Among the different kinds of historical time, the *longue durée* often seems a troublesome character, full of complications, and all too frequently lacking in any sort of organization. To give it a place in the heart of our profession would entail more than a routine expansion of our studies and our curiosities. Nor would it be a question of making a simple choice in its favor. For the historian, accepting the *longue durée* entails a readiness to change his style, his attitudes, a whole reversal in his thinking, a whole new way of conceiving of social affairs. It means becoming used to a slower tempo, which sometimes almost borders on the motionless. At that stage, though not at any other—this is a point to which I will return—it is proper to free oneself from the demanding time scheme of history, to get out of it and return later with a fresh view, burdened with other anxieties and other questions. In any case, it is in relation to these expanses of slow-moving history that the whole of history is to be rethought, as if on the basis of an infrastructure. All the stages, all the thousands of stages, all the thousand explosions of historical time can be understood on the basis of these depths, this semistillness. Everything gravitates around it.

I make no claim to have defined the historian's profession in the preceding lines—merely one conception of that profession. After the storms we have been through during recent years, happy not to say naif the man who could believe that we have hit upon true principles, clear limits, the Right School. In fact, all the social sciences find their tasks shifting all the time, both because of their own developments and because of the active development of them all as a body. History is no exception. There is no rest in view, the time for disciples has not yet come. It is a long way from Charles-Victor Langlois and Charles Seignobos to Marc Bloch. But since Marc Bloch, the wheel has not stopped turning. For me, history is the total of all possible histories—an assemblage of professions and points of view, from yesterday, today, and tomorrow.

The only error, in my view, would be to choose one of these histories to the exclusion of all others. That was, and always will be, the cardinal error of historicizing. It will not be easy, we know, to convince all historians of the truth of this. Still less, to convince all the social sciences, with their burning desire to get us back to history as we used to know it yesterday. It will take us a good deal of time and trouble to accommodate all these changes and innovations beneath the old heading of history. And yet a new historical "science" has been born, and goes on questioning and transforming itself. It revealed itself as early as 1900, with the *Revue de synthèse historique*, and with *Annales,* which started to come out in 1929. The historian felt the desire to concentrate his attention on *all* the human sciences. It is this which has given our profession its strange frontiers, and its strange preoccupations. So it must not be imagined that the same barriers and differences exist between the historian and the social scientist as existed yesterday. All the human sciences, history included, are affected by one another. They speak the same language, or could if they wanted to.

Whether you take 1558 or this year of grace 1958, the problem for anyone tackling the world scene is to define a hierarchy of forces, of currents, of particular movements, and then tackle them as an entire constellation. At each moment of this research, one has to distinguish between long-lasting movements and short bursts, the latter detected from the moment they originate, the former over the course of a distant time. The world of 1558, which appeared so gloomy in France, was not born at the beginning of that charmless year. The same with our own troubled year of 1958. Each "current event" brings together movements of different origins, of a different rhythm—today's time dates from yesterday, the day before yesterday, and all former times.

THE QUARREL WITH THE SHORT TIME SPAN

These truths are of course banal. Nonetheless, the social sciences seem little tempted by such remembrance of things past. Not that one can draw up any firm accusation against them and declare them to be consistently guilty of not accepting history or duration as dimensions necessary to their studies. The "diachronic" examination that reintroduces history is never absent from their theoretical deliberations.

Despite this sort of distant acknowledgment, though, it must be admitted that the social sciences, by taste, by deep-seated instinct, perhaps by training, have a constant tendency to evade historical explanation. They evade it in two almost contradictory ways: by concentrating overmuch on the "current event" in social studies, thanks to a brand of empirical sociology that, disdainful of all history, confines itself to the facts of the short term and investigations into "real life"; by transcending time altogether and conjuring up a mathematical formulation of more or less timeless structures under the name of "communications science." This last and newest way is clearly the only one that can be of any substantial interest to us. But there are enough devotees of the current event to justify examining both aspects of the question.

We have already stated our mistrust of a history occupied solely with events. To be fair, though, if there is a sin in being overconcerned with events, then history, though the most obvious culprit, is not the only guilty one. All the social sciences have shared in this error. Economists, demographers, geographers are all balanced (and badly balanced) between the demands of yesterday and of today. In order to be right they would need to maintain a constant balance—easy enough, and indeed obligatory, for the demographer, and almost a matter of course for geographers (particularly ours, reared in the Vidalian school)—but rare for economists, held fast to the most short lived of current events, hardly looking back beyond 1945 or forecasting further in advance than a few months, or at most a few years. I would maintain that all economic thinking is trapped by these temporal restrictions. It is up to historians, so economists say, to go back further than 1945, in search of old economies. Economists thus voluntarily rob themselves of a marvelous field of observation, although without denying its value. They have fallen into the habit of putting themselves at the disposal of current events and of governments.

The position of ethnographers and ethnologists is neither so clear nor so alarming. Some of them have taken great pains to underline the impossibility (but intellectuals are always fascinated by the impossible) and the uselessness of applying history within their profession. Such an authoritarian denial of history would hardly have served Bronislaw Malinowski and his disciples. Indeed, how could anthropology possibly not have an interest in history? History and anthropology both spring from the same impulse, as Claude Lévi-Strauss[15] delights in saying. There is no society, however primitive, that does not bear the "scars of events," nor any society in which history has sunk completely without trace. This is something there is no need to complain about or to insist on further.

On the other hand, where sociology is concerned, our quarrel along the frontiers of the short term must necessarily be a rather bitter one. Sociological investigations into the contemporary scene seem to run in a thousand different directions, from sociology to psychology to economics, and to proliferate among us as they do abroad. They are, in their own way, a bet on the irreplaceable value of the present moment, with its "volcanic" heat, its abundant wealth. What good would be served by turning back toward historical time: impoverished, simplified, devastated by silence, reconstructed—above all, let us say it again, *reconstructed*. Is it really as dead, as reconstructed, as they would have us believe, though? Doubtless, a historian can only too easily isolate the crucial factor from some past age. To put it in Henri Pirenne's words, he can distinguish without difficulty the "important events," which means "those which bore consequences." An obvious and dangerous oversimplification. But what would the explorer of the present-day not give to have this perspective (or this sort of ability to go forward in time), making it possible to unmask and simplify our present life, in all its confusion—hardly comprehensible now because so overburdened with trivial acts and portents? Lévi-Strauss claims that one hour's talk with a contemporary of Plato's would tell him more than all our classical treatises on the coherence or incoherence of ancient Greek civilization.[16] I quite agree. But this is because for years he has heard a hundred Greek voices rescued from silence. The historian has prepared his way. One hour in modern Greece would tell him nothing, or hardly anything, about contemporary Greek coherence or incoherence.

Even more to the point, the researcher occupied with the present can make out the "fine" lines of a structure only by himself engaging in *reconstruction*, putting forward theories and explanations, not getting embroiled in reality as it appears, but truncating it, transcending it. Such maneuvers allow him to get away from the given situation, the better to control it, but they are all acts of reconstruction. I would seriously question whether sociological photography of the present time is any more "true" than the historical portrayal of the past, more particularly the more it tries to get any further away from the *reconstructed*.

Philippe Ariès has emphasized the importance of the unfamiliar, of surprise in historical explanation:[17] you are in the sixteenth century, and you stumble upon some peculiarity, something that seems peculiar to you as a man of the twentieth century. Why this difference? This is the question that one then has to set about answering. But I would claim that such surprise, such unfamiliarity, such distancing—these great highways to knowledge—are no less necessary to an understanding of all that surrounds us and that we are so close to that we cannot see clearly. Live in London for a year and you will not know much about England. But by contrast, in light of what has surprised you, you will suddenly have come to understand some of the most deep-seated and characteristic aspects of France, things you did not know before because you knew them too well. With regard to the present, the past too is a way of distancing yourself.

In this way, historians and social scientists could go on forever batting the ball back and forth between dead documents and all-too-living evidence, the distant past and the too-close present. But I do not believe that this is a crucial problem. Past and present illuminate each other reciprocally; and in exclusively observing the narrow confines of the present, the attention will irresistibly be drawn toward whatever moves quickly, burns with a true or a false flame, or has just changed, or makes a noise, or is easy to see. There is a whole web of events, as wearisome as any in the historical sciences, which lies in wait for the observer in a hurry, the ethnographer dwelling for three months with some Polynesian tribe, the industrial sociologist delivering all the clichés of his latest investigation, or who truly believes that he can thoroughly pin down some social mechanism with cunningly phrased questionnaires and combinations of punched cards. Social questions are more cunning game than that.

In fact, what possible interest can we take, we the human sciences, in the movements of a young girl between her home in the sixteenth arrondissement, her music teacher, and the Ecole des Sciences–Po, discussed in a sound and wide-ranging study of the Paris area?[18] They make up a fine-looking map—but if she had studied agronomy or gone in for water-skiing, the whole pattern of her triangular journeys would have been altered. It is nice to see on a map the distribution of all domiciles belonging to employees in a large concern—but if I do not have an earlier map, if the lapse of time between the two maps is not sufficient to allow the tracing of a genuine movement, then precisely where is the problem without which any inquiry is simply a waste of effort? Any interest in inquiries for inquiry's sake is limited to the collection of data at best. Yet even then these data will not all be ipso facto useful for future work. We must beware of art for art's sake.

In the same way I would question whether any study of a town, no matter which, could be the object of a sociological inquiry in the way that Auxerre[19] was, or Vienne in the Dauphiné,[20] without being set in its historical context. Any town, as an extended social entity with all its crises, dislocations, breakdowns, and necessary calculations, must be seen in relation to the whole complex of districts surrounding it, as well as in relation to those archipelagos of neighboring towns which Richard Häpke, the historian, was one of the first to discuss. Similarly, it must also be considered in relation to the movement, more or less distant in time, sometimes extremely distant, that directs this whole complex. It cannot be of no interest; rather, it must surely be crucial to note down particular urban/rural exchanges, particular industrial or mercantile competition, to know whether you are dealing with a movement in the full flush of its youth or at the end of its run, with the beginnings of a resurgence or a monotonous repetition.

One last remark: Lucien Febvre, during the last ten years of his life, is said to have repeated: "History, science of the past, science of the present." Is not history, the dialectic of time spans, in its own way an explanation of society in all its reality, and thus of contemporary society? And here its role would be to caution us against the event: Do not think only of the short time span, do not believe that only the actors which make the most noise are the most authentic—there are other, quieter ones too. As if anybody did not know that already!

COMMUNICATION AND SOCIAL MATHEMATICS

Perhaps we were wrong to linger on the tempestuous borders of the short time span. In actual fact, that debate proceeds without any great interest, certainly without any useful revelations. The crucial debate is elsewhere, among our neighbors who are being carried away by the newest experiment in the social sciences, under the double heading of "communications" and mathematics.

But this will be no easy brief to argue. I mean it will be by no means easy to prove that there is no sort of social study that can avoid historical time, when here is one that ostensibly at least, has its being entirely outside it.

In any case, the reader who wishes to follow our argument (either to agree or to dissociate himself from our point of view) would do well to weigh for himself, one after another, the terms of a vocabulary which, though certainly not entirely new, have been taken up afresh and rejuvenated for the purposes of these new debates. There is nothing more to be said here, obviously, about events, or the *longue durée*. Nor a great deal about *structures,* though the word—and the thing—is by no means entirely free from uncertainty and debate.[21] Nor would there be any point in dwelling on the words "synchronous" and "diachronous": they are self-defining, though their function in the actual study of social questions might be less easy to make out than it appears. In fact, as far as the language of history is concerned (insofar as I conceive it) there can be no question of perfect synchrony: a sudden halt, in which all time spans would be suspended, is almost an absurdity in itself, or, and this comes to the same thing, is highly factitious. In the same way, a descent following the onward stream of time is conceivable only in terms of a multiplicity of descents, following the innumerable different rivers of time.

These brief summaries and warnings must suffice for now. But one must be more explicit when dealing with *unconscious history*, *models*, and *social mathematics*. Besides, these commentaries will, I hope, without too much delay, link together what is problematic in all the social sciences.

Unconscious history, is, of course, the history of the unconscious elements in social development. "Men make their own history, but they do not know that they are making it." [22] Marx's formula pinpoints the problem but does not explain it. In fact, it is the same old problem of short time span, of "microtime," of the event, that we find ourselves confronted with under a new name. Men have always had the impression, in living out their time, of being able to grasp its passage from day to day—but is this clear, conscious history delusory, as many historians have agreed? Yesterday, linguistics believed that it could derive everything from words. History was under the illusion that it could derive everything from events. More than one of our contemporaries would be happy to believe that everything is the result of the agreements at Yalta or Potsdam, the incidents at Dien Bien Phu or Sakhiet-Sidi-Youssef, or again from that other event, important in a different way it is true, the launching of the Sputniks. Unconscious history proceeds beyond the reach of these illuminations and their brief flashes. One has, then, to concede that there does exist, at some distance, a social unconscious; and concede, too, that this unconscious might well be thought more rich, scientifically speaking, than the glittering surface to which our eyes are accustomed. More rich scientifically, meaning simpler, easier to exploit—not easier to discover. But the step from bright surface to murky depths—from noise to silence—is difficult and dangerous. Equally, let it be said that "unconscious" history, belonging half to the time of conjunctures and wholly to structural time, is clearly visible more frequently than one would willingly admit. Each one of us can sense, over and above his own life, a mass history, though it is true he is more conscious of its power and impetus than of its laws or direction; and this consciousness is not only of recent date (like the concerns of economic history), although today it may be increasingly sharp. The revolution, for it is an intellectual revolution, consisted in confronting this half darkness head on, and giving it a greater and greater place next to, and even to the detriment of, a history purely of events.

History is not alone in this prospecting (quite the reverse, all it has done has been to follow others into the area, and to adapt the perspectives of the new social sciences for its own use), and new instruments of knowledge and research have had to be created: hence *models,* some more or less perfected, some still rather rough and ready. Models are only hypotheses, systems of explanations tied solidly together in the form of an equation, or a function: this equals that or determines the other. Such and such a reality never appears without that one, and constant and close links are revealed between the one and the other. The carefully constructed model will thus allow us to inquire, throughout time and space, into other social environments similar to the observed social environment on the basis of which it was originally constructed. That is its constant value.

These systems of explanation vary infinitely according to the temperament, calculations, and aims of those using them: simple or complex, qualitative or quantitative, static or dynamic, mechanical or statistical. I am indebted to Lévi-Strauss for this last distinction. A mechanical model would be of the same dimensions as directly observed reality, a reality of limited dimensions, of interest only to very small groups of people (this is how ethnologists proceed when dealing with primitive societies). When dealing with large societies, where great numbers come in, the calculation of the average becomes necessary: this leads to the construction of statistical models. But what do these sometimes debatable distinctions really matter!

In my opinion, before establishing a common program for the social sciences, the crucial thing is to define the function and limits of models, the scope of which some undertakings seem to be in danger of enlarging inordinately. Whence the need to confront models, too, with the notion of the time span—for the meaning and the value of their explanations depend fairly heavily, it seems to me, on their implied duration.

To be more clear, let us select our examples from among historical models,[23] by which I mean those constructed by historians. They are fairly rough and ready as models go, not often driven to the rigor of an authentic scientific law, and never worried about coming out with some revolutionary mathematical language—but models nonetheless, in their own way.

Above we have discussed mercantile capitalism between the fourteenth and the eighteenth centuries—one model that, among others, can be drawn from Marx's work. It can be applied in full only to one particular family of societies at one particular given time, even if it leaves the door open to every extrapolation.

There is already a difference between this and the model that I sketched out in an earlier book,[24] of the cycle of economic development in Italian cities between the sixteenth and eighteenth centuries. These cities became in turn mercantile, "industrial," and finally specialists in banking, this last development being the slowest to grow and the slowest to die away. Though in fact less all-embracing than the structure of mercantile capitalism, this sketch would be much the more easily extended in time and space. It records a phenomenon (some would say, a dynamic structure, but all structures in history have at least an elementary dynamism) capable of recurring under a number of common circumstances. Perhaps the same could be said of the model sketched out by Frank Spooner and myself,[25] which dealt with the history of precious metals before, during, and after the sixteenth century: gold, silver, copper—and credit, that agile substitute for metal—all play their part too. The "strategy" of one weighs on the "strategy" of another. It would not be particularly difficult to remove this model from the special and particularly turbulent world of the sixteenth century, which happened to be the one we selected for our observations. Have not economists dealing with the particular case of underdeveloped countries attempted to verify the old quantitative theory of money, which was, after all, a model too in its own fashion?[26]

But the time spans possible to all these models are brief compared with those of the model conceived by the young American social historian Sigmund Diamond.[27] Diamond was struck by the double language of the dominant class of great American financier contemporaries of Pierpont Morgan, consisting of a language internal to their class, and an external language. This last, to tell the truth, was a brand of special pleading with public opinion to whom the success of the financier is presented as the typical triumph of the *self-made man,* the condition necessary for the nation's prosperity. Struck by this double language, Diamond saw in it the customary reaction of any dominant class that feels its prestige waning and its privileges threatened. In order to camouflage itself, it is necessary for it to confuse its own fate with that of the City or the Nation, its own private interests with the public interest. Sigmund Diamond would willingly explain the evolution of the idea of dynasty or of empire, the English dynasty or the Roman empire, in the same way. The model thus conceived clearly has the run of the centuries. It presupposes certain conditions, but these are conditions with which history is abundantly supplied: it follows that it is valid for a much longer time span than either of the preceding models, but at the same time it puts into question much more precise and exact aspects of reality.

At the limit, as the mathematicians would say, this kind of model is kin to the favorite, almost timeless models of sociological mathematicians. Almost timeless, in actual fact, traveling the dark, untended byways of the extreme *longue durée.*

The preceding explanations must of necessity provide only an inadequate introduction to the science and theory of models. Also, historians are far from standing in the forefront. Their models are hardly more than bundles of explanations. Our colleagues are more ambitious and advanced in research, attempting to establish links between the theories and languages of information or communications theory or of qualitative mathematics. Their merit—and it is a great one—is in absorbing the subtle language of mathematics into their domain, though this runs the risk, should our attention flag even slightly, of its escaping from our control and running off, Heaven only knows where! Information and communications theory, qualitative mathematics, all come together under the already substantial patronage of social mathematics. And we must try, as far as we are able, to light our lantern by their flame too.

Social mathematics[28] is made up of at least three languages, and there is still scope for them to mingle and develop more. Mathematicians have not yet come to the end of their inventiveness. Besides, there is not *one* mathematics, *the* mathematics (or, if there is, it is only as an assertion, not a fact): "one should not say algebra, geometry, but an algebra, a geometry" (Th. Guilbaud)—which does not make our problems, or theirs, any easier. Three languages, then: that of necessary facts (a given fact, and its consequence), which is the domain of traditional mathematics; the language of contingent facts, dating from Blaise Pascal, which is the domain of the calculation of probabilities; and, finally, the language of conditioned facts, neither determined nor contingent but behaving under certain constraints, tied to the rules of a game, to the "strategic" axis in the games of John von Neumann and Morgenstern,[29] those triumphant games which have gone on developing on the basis of their inventors' first bold principles. Game theory, with its use of wholes, of groups, and of the calculation of probabilities, opens the way to "qualitative" mathematics, and from that moment the move from observation to mathematical formulation does not have to be made along the painful path of measurements and long statistical calculations. One can pass directly from an observation of social reality to a mathematical formulation, to the calculating machine, so to speak.

Of course, the machine's diet has to be prepared in advance, since there are only certain kinds of food that it can cope with. Besides, the science of information has evolved as a function of true machines and their rules of functioning, in order to promote *communication* in the most material sense of the word. The author of this article is by no means a specialist in these complex fields. The research toward creating a translating machine, which I followed from afar but nonetheless followed, has left me and many others deep in thought. All the same, two facts remain: first, such machines, such mathematical possibilities, do exist; and second, society must prepare itself for social mathematics, which is no longer our old accustomed mathematics of price curves and the graphs of birthrates.

Now, while the workings of the new mathematics may often elude us, the preparation of social reality for its use, fitting it out and trimming it appropriately, is a task we can well cope with. The preliminary treatment has up till now been almost always exactly the same: choose some unified limited object of observation, such as a "primitive" tribe or a demographic "isolate," in which almost everything can be seen and touched directly, then establish all possible relationships, all possible games among the elements thus distinguished. Such relationships, rigorously worked out, provide the very equations from which mathematics will be able to draw all possible conclusions and projections in order to come up with a *model* that sums them all up or, rather, takes them all into account.

Obviously a million openings for research exist in these areas. But one example is worth any amount of prolonged explanation. We have Claude Lévi-Strauss as an excellent guide, let us follow him. He can introduce us to one area of these researches, call it that of a science of "communications." [30]

"In any society," writes Lévi-Strauss, "communication operates on at least three levels: communication of women, communication of goods and services, communication of messages." [31] Let us agree that these are, at their different levels, different *languages*, but languages nonetheless. If that is so, are we not entitled to treat them as languages, or even as *language*, and to associate them, whether directly or indirectly, to the sensational progress made by linguistics, and even more by phonemics, which "will certainly play the same renovating role with respect to the social sciences that nuclear physics, for example, has played for the physical sciences"? [32] That is saying a lot, but sometimes one has to say a lot. Just as history is caught in the trap of events, linguistics, caught in the trap of words (the relation between word and object, the historical evolution of words), was set free by the phonemic revolution. It became aware, beneath the word, of the unit of sound which is the phoneme, at that point paying no attention to its sense, but carefully noting its placing, the sounds accompanying it, the grouping of these sounds, the infraphonemic structures, and the whole underlying *unconscious* reality of language. On the basis of the few dozen phonemes that occur in every language in the world, the new mathematical calculations set to work and, in so doing, set linguistics, or at least one aspect of linguistics, free from the realm of social studies to scale the "heights of the physical sciences."

To extend the meaning of language to elementary structures of kinship, myths, ceremonial, economic exchanges is to attempt that difficult but worthwhile route to the summit. Lévi-Strauss showed this sort of courage initially when dealing with matrimonial exchanges—that first language, so essential to all human communication that there is no society, whether primitive or not, in which incest, marriage within the nuclear family, is not forbidden. Thus, a language. And beneath this language he sought the one basic element that would, so to speak, correspond to the phoneme. That element, that "atom" of kinship, was put forward by our guide in its most simple format in his thesis of 1949:[33] the man, his wife, their child, and the child's maternal uncle. On the basis of this quadrangular element and of all known systems of marriage within these primitive worlds—and they are many—the mathematicians were enabled to work out all possible combinations and solutions. With the help of the mathematician André Weill, Lévi-Strauss was able to translate the observations of the anthropologist into mathematical terms. The resulting model should provide proof of the validity and stability of the system, and point out the solutions it implies.

The procedure of this research is clear: to get past superficial observation in order to reach the zone of unconscious or barely conscious elements, and then to reduce that reality to tiny elements, minute identical sections, whose relations can be precisely analyzed. It is at this "microsociological [of a certain kind, I would add] stage that one might hope to discover the most general structural laws, just as the linguist discovers his at the infraphonemic level or the physicist at the inframolecular or atomic level."[34] This is, of course, an activity that can be pursued in a good many other directions. Thus, what could be more instructive than to see Lévi-Strauss coming to grips, this time, with myths, and in a lighthearted way with cooking. Myths he reduced to a series of individual cells, or "mythemes"; the language of cookbooks he reduced (none too seriously) to "gustemes." Each time, he has sought the deepest, least conscious layers. I am not concerned, while I speak, with the phonemes in my speech; nor, unless very exceptionally, when I am at the table, do I concern myself with "gustemes," if gustemes in fact exist. Yet, each time, the subtle and precise interplay of relationships is there, keeping me company. As far as these simple, mysterious relationships go, will the final act of sociological research be to grasp them where they lie beneath all languages, in order to translate them into one Morse code that is the universal language of mathematics? That is the prime ambition of the new social mathematics. But that, if I may say so, is another story.

But let us get back to the question of time spans. I have said that models are of varying duration: they are valid for as long as the reality with which they are dealing. To the social observer, that length of time is fundamental, for even more significant than the deep-rooted structures of life are their points of rupture, their swift or slow deterioration under the effect of contradictory pressures.

I have sometimes compared models to ships. What interests me, once the boat is built, is to put it in the water to see if it will float, and then to make it ascend and descend the waters of time, at my will. The significant moment is when it can keep afloat no longer, and sinks. Thus, the explanation that Frank Spooner and I proposed for the interplay of precious metals seems to me to have little validity before the fifteenth century. Earlier than that, the competition between metals was of a violence quite unparalleled in previous observations. It was up to us, then, to find out why. Just as, going downstream this time, we had to find out why the navigation of our overly simple craft became first difficult and then impossible in the eighteenth century, with the unprecedented growth of credit. It seems to me that research is a question of endlessly proceeding from the social reality to the model, and then back again, and so on, in a series of readjustments and patiently renewed trips. In this way the model, in turn, is an attempt at an explanation of the structure, and an instrument of control and comparison, able to verify the solidity and the very life of a given structure. If I were to construct a model on the basis of the present, I would immediately relocate it in its context in reality, and then take it back in time, as far back as its origins, if possible. After which, I would project its probable life, right up to the next break, in accordance with the corresponding movement of other social realities—unless I should decide to use it as an element of comparison and take it off through time and space, in search of other aspects of reality on which it might shed new light.

Would I be wrong to believe that the models put forward by qualitative mathematics, at least insofar as they have been shown to us up till now,[35] would lend themselves ill to such excursions, above all because they are committed to traveling along only one of time's many possible highways, that of the extreme *longue durée*, sheltered from all accidents, crises, and sudden breaks? I will refer, once again, to Claude Lévi-Strauss, because his experiments in this field seem to me the most well thought out, the clearest, and the most securely rooted in the social experience that any such undertaking should be based on and return to. Let us note that each time he is concerned with questioning a phenomenon that develops only very slowly, almost timelessly. All kinship systems persist because there is no human life possible beyond a certain ratio of consanguinity, so that, for a small group of people to survive, it must open onto the outside world: the prohibition of incest is a reality of the *longue durée*. Myths too, developing slowly, correspond to structures of an extremely long duration. Without even bothering to pick out the oldest, one could collect together all the versions of the Oedipus story, so that, classified according to their different variations, they might throw light on the underlying impulse that shapes them all. But let us suppose for a moment that our colleague was interested not in myths but in, say, the images projected by and succeeding interpretations of "Machiavellianism," and that he was seeking the basic elements in this fairly straightforward and very widespread doctrine, which came into being in the middle of the sixteenth century. Everywhere here he would find rifts and reversals, even in the very structure of Machiavellianism, for it is not a system that has the theatrical, sempiternal solidity of myth. It is sensitive to any action and reaction, to all the various inclemencies of history. In a word, it does not have its being solely within the calm, monotonous highways of the *longue durée*. Thus, the process recommended by Lévi-Strauss in the search for mathematizable structures is valid not only on the level of microsociology but also in confronting the infinitely small and the extreme *longue durée*.

Does this mean that this revolutionary qualitative mathematics is condemned to follow only the paths of the extreme *longue durée*? In which case, after a hard struggle, all we find ourselves with are truths built rather too much on the dimensions of eternal man. Elementary truths, aphorisms amounting to no more than mere common sense, are what the disappointed might be inclined to say—to which would come the reply, fundamental truths, able to cast new light on the very bases of all social life. But that is not the whole question.

I do not in fact believe that these experiments—or analogous experiments—cannot be conducted outside the scope of the very *longue durée*. The stuff of qualitative social mathematics is not figures but links, relationships, which must be fairly rigorously defined before they can be rendered into a mathematical symbol, on the basis of which one can study all the mathematical possibilities of these symbols, without having to trouble oneself any more about the social reality they represent. Thus, the entire value of the conclusions is dependent upon the value of the initial observation, and on the selection of essential elements within the observed reality and the determination of their relationships. One can thus see why social mathematics has a preference for what Lévi-Strauss calls mechanical models, that is to say, models based on fairly narrow groups in which each individual can, so to speak, be directly observed, and in which a highly homogeneous social organization enables a secure definition of human relationships, in a simple and concrete way, and with few variations.

So-called statistical models, on the other hand, deal with large and complex societies, in which observation can be carried out only according to averages, or, in other words, according to traditional mathematics. But once the averages have been arrived at, should the observer be able to establish, on the scale of groups rather than of individuals, those basic relationships we have been discussing, which are necessary to the formulation of qualitative mathematics, then there would be nothing to stop him from making use of them again. So far as I know, there have not been any attempts made along these lines. These are early days for such experiments, though. For the moment, whether one is dealing with psychology, economics, or anthropology, all the experiments have been carried out in the way I discussed when speaking of Lévi-Strauss. But qualitative social mathematics will not have proved itself until it has confronted a modern society with involved problems and different rates of development. I would wager that this venture will tempt one of our sociologist-mathematicians; I would wager equally that it will prompt a necessary revision of the methods according to which the new mathematics has operated so far, penned up in what I would call, in this instance, the excessive *longue durée*. It must rediscover the diversity of life—the movement, the different time spans, the rifts and variations.

TIME FOR THE HISTORIAN, TIME FOR THE SOCIOLOGIST

And here I am, after an incursion into the timeless realms of social mathematics, back at the question of time and time spans. Incorrigible historian that I am, I stand amazed yet again that sociologists have managed to avoid it. But the thing is that their time is not ours: it is a great deal less imperious and less concrete and is never central to their problems and their thoughts.

In truth, the historian can never get away from the question of time in history: time sticks to his thinking like soil to a gardener's spade. He may well dream of getting away from it, of course. Spurred on by the anguish of 1940, Gaston Roupnel[36] wrote words on this subject that will make any true historian suffer. Similar is the classic remark made by Paul Lacombe who was also a historian of the grand school: "Time is nothing in itself, objectively, it is only an idea we have."[37] But do these remarks really provide a way out? I myself, during a rather gloomy captivity, struggled a good deal to get away from a chronicle of those difficult years (1940–45). Rejecting events and the time in which events take place was a way of placing oneself to one side, sheltered, so as to get some sort of perspective, to be able to evaluate them better, and not wholly to believe in them. To go from the short time span, to one less short, and then to the long view (which, if it exists, must surely be the wise man's time span); and having got there, to think about everything afresh and to reconstruct everything around one: a historian could hardly not be tempted by such a prospect.

But these successive flights cannot put the historian definitively beyond the bounds of the world's time, beyond historical time, so imperious because it is irreversible, and because it flows at the very rhythm of the earth's rotation. In fact, these different time spans we can discern are all interdependent: it is not so much time that is the creation of our own minds, as the way in which we break it up. These fragments are reunited at the end of all our labors. The *longue durée*, the conjuncture, the event all fit into each other neatly and without difficulty, for they are all measured on the same scale. Equally, to be able to achieve an imaginative understanding of one of these time spans is to be able to understand them all. The philosopher, taken up with the subjective aspect of things, interior to any notion of time, never senses this weight of historical time, of a concrete, universal time, such as the time of conjuncture that Ernest Labrousse[38] depicts at the beginning of his book like a traveler who is constantly the same and who travels the world imposing the same set of values, no matter the country in which he has disembarked, nor what the social order with which it is invested.

For the historian everything begins and ends with time, a mathematical, godlike time, a notion easily mocked, time external to men, "exogenous," as economists would say, pushing men, forcing them, and painting their own individual times the same color: it is, indeed, the imperious time of the world.

Sociologists, of course, will not entertain this oversimplified notion. They are much closer to the *dialectique de la durée* as put forward by Gaston Bachelard.[39] Social time is but one dimension of the social reality under consideration. It is within this reality just as it is within a given individual, one sign of particularity among others. The sociologist is in no way hampered by this accommodating sort of time, which can be cut, frozen, set in motion entirely at will. Historical time, I must repeat, lends itself less easily to the supple double action of synchrony and diachrony: it cannot envisage life as a mechanism that can be stopped at leisure in order to reveal a frozen image.

This is a more profound rift than is at first apparent: sociologists' time cannot be ours. The fundamental structure of our profession revolts against it. Our time, like economists' time, is one of measure. When a sociologist tells us that a structure breaks down only in order to build itself up afresh, we are happy to accept an explanation that historical observation would confirm anyway. But we would wish to know the precise time span of these movements, whether positive or negative, situated along the usual axis. An economic cycle, the ebb and flow of material life, can be measured. A structural social crisis should be equally possible to locate in time, and through it. We should be able to place it exactly, both in itself and even more in relation to the movement of associated structures. What is profoundly interesting to the historian is the way these movements cross one another, and how they interact, and how they break up: all things that can be recorded only in relation to the uniform time of historians, which can stand as a general measure of all these phenomena, and not in relation to the multiform time of social reality, which can stand only as the individual measure of each of these phenomena separately.

Rightly or wrongly, the historian cannot but formulate such opposed ideas, even when entering into the welcoming, almost brotherly realm of Georges Gurvitch's sociology. Did not a philosopher define him recently as the one "who is driving sociology back into the arms of history"?[40] But even with him, the historian can recognize neither his time spans nor his temporalities. The great social edifice (should one say "model"?) erected by Georges Gurvitch is organized according to five basic architectural aspects:[41] the deeper levels, the level of sociability, the level of social groups, the level of global societies, and the level of time. This final bit of scaffolding, temporalities, the newest and the most recently built, is as if superimposed on the whole.

Gurvitch's temporalities are various. He distinguishes a whole series of them: the time of the *longue durée* and slow motion, time the deceiver and time the surpriser, time with an irregular beat, cyclic time running in place, time running slow, time alternating between running slow and fast, time running fast, explosive time.[42] How could a historian believe in all this? Given such a range of colors, he could never reconstitute a single, white light—and that is something he cannot do without. The historian quickly becomes aware, too, that this chameleonlike time barely adds any extra touch, any spot of color to the categories that had been established earlier. In the city that our friend has built, time, the last to arrive, cohabits quite naturally with all the other categories. It fits itself to the dimensions of their homes and their demands, according to the "levels," sociabilities, groups, and global societies. It is a different way of rewriting the same equations without actually changing them. Each social reality secretes its own peculiar time, or time scale, like common snails. But what do we historians get out of all this? The vast edifice of this ideal city remains static. History is nowhere to be seen. The world's time, historical time is there, but imprisoned, like Aeolus in his goat's skin. It is not history that sociologists, fundamentally and quite unconsciously, bear a grudge against, but historical time—which is a reality that retains its violence no matter how one tries to bring it to order and to break it down. It is a constraint from which the historian is never free, while sociologists, on the other hand, almost always seem to manage to avoid it, by concentrating either on the instant, which is always present as if suspended somewhere above time, or else on repeated phenomena that do not belong to any age. So they escape the two contradictory movements of the mind, confining them within either the narrowest limits of the event or the most extended *longue durée*. Is such an evasion justifiable? That is the crux of the debate between historians and sociologists, and even between historians of differing persuasions.

I do not know whether this rather excessively cut and dried article, relying overmuch, as historians have a tendency to do, on the use of examples, will meet with the agreement of sociologists and of our other neighbors. I rather doubt it. Anyway, it is never a good thing, when writing a conclusion, simply to repeat some insistently recurrent leitmotif. Should history by its very nature be called upon to pay special attention to the span of time and to *all* the movements of which it may be made up, the *longue durée* appears to us, within this array, as the most useful line to take toward a way of observing and thinking common to all the social sciences. Is it too much to ask our neighbors that, at some stage in their reasoning, they might locate their findings and their research along this axis?

For historians, not all of whom would share my views, it would be a case of reversing engines. Their preference goes instinctively toward the short term. It is an attitude aided and abetted by the sacrosanct university courses. Jean-Paul Sartre, in recent articles, strengthens their point of view when he protests against that which is both oversimplified and too ponderous in Marxism in the name of the biographical, of the teeming reality of events.[43] You have not said everything when you have "situated" Flaubert as bourgeois, or Tintoretto as petty bourgeois. I entirely agree. But in every case a study of the concrete situation—whether Flaubert, Valéry, or the foreign policies of the Gironde—ends up by bringing Sartre back to its deep-seated structural context. His research moves from the surface to the depths, and so links up with my own preoccupations. It would link up even better if the hourglass could be turned over both ways—from event to structure, and then from structure and model back to the event.

Marxism is peopled with models. Sartre would rebel against the rigidity, the schematic nature, the insufficiency of the model, in the name of the particular and the individual. I would rebel with him (with certain slight differences in emphasis) not against the model, though, but against the use that has been made of it, the use it has been felt proper to make. Marx's genius, the secret of his long sway, lies in the fact that he was the first to construct true social models, on the basis of a historical *longue durée*. These models have been frozen in all their simplicity by being given the status of laws, of a preordained and automatic explanation, valid in all places and to any society; whereas if they were put back within the ever-changing stream of time, they would constantly reappear, but with changes of emphasis, sometimes overshadowed, sometimes thrown into relief by the presence of other structures that themselves would be susceptible to definition by other rules and thus by other models. In this way, the creative potential of the most powerful social analysis of the last century has been stymied. It cannot regain its youth and vigor except in the *longue durée*. Should I add that contemporary Marxism appears to me to be the very image of the danger lying in wait for any social science wholly taken up with the model in its pure state, with models for models' sake?

What I would like to emphasize in conclusion is that the *longue durée* is but one possibility of a common language arising from a confrontation among the social sciences. There are others. I have indicated, adequately, the experiments being made by the new social mathematics. The new mathematics draws me, but the old mathematics, whose triumph is obvious in economics—perhaps the most advanced of the human sciences— does not deserve to be dismissed with a cynical aside. Huge calculations await us in this classic field, but there are squads of calculators and of calculating machines ready too, being rendered daily yet more perfect. I am a great believer in the usefulness of long sequences of statistics, and in the necessity of taking calculations and research further and further back in time. The whole of the eighteenth century in Europe is riddled with our workings, but they crop up even in the seventeenth, and even more in the sixteenth century. Statistics going back an unbelievably long way reveal the depths of the Chinese past to us through their universal language.[44] No doubt, statistics simplify the better to come to grips with their subject. But all science is a movement from the complex to the simple.

And yet, let us not forget one last language, one last family of models, in fact: the necessary reduction of any social reality to the place in which it occurs. Let us call it either "geography" or "ecology," without dwelling too long on these differences in terminology. Geography too often conceives of itself as a world on its own, and that is a pity. It has need of a Vidal de la Blache who would consider not time and place this time, but place and social reality. If that happened, geographical research would put the problems of all the human sciences first on its agenda. For sociologists, not that they would always admit it to themselves, the word "ecology" is a way of not saying "geography," and by the same token of dodging all the problems posed by place and revealed by place to careful observation. Spatial models are the charts upon which social reality is projected, and through which it may become at least partially clear; they are truly models for all the different movements of time (and especially for the *longue durée*), and for all the categories of social life. Amazingly, though, social science chooses to ignore them. I have often thought that one of the French superiorities in the social sciences was precisely that school of geography founded by Vidal de la Blache, the betrayal of whose thought and teachings is an inconsolable loss. All the social sciences must make room "for an increasingly geographical conception of mankind."[45] This is what Vidal de la Blache was asking for as early as 1903.

On the practical level—for this article does have a practical aim—I would hope that the social sciences, at least provisionally, would suspend their constant border disputes over what is or is not a social science, what is or is not a structure . . . Rather, let them try to trace across our research those lines which, if they exist, would serve to orient some kind of collective research, and make possible the first stages of some sort of coming together. I would personally call such lines mathematization, a concentration on place, the *longue durée* . . . But I would be very interested to know what other specialists would suggest. For it goes without saying that this article has not been placed under the rubric *Débats et combats* by pure chance.[46] It claims to pose, but not to resolve, the obvious problems to which, unhappily, each one of us, when he ventures outside his own specialty, finds himself exposed. These pages are a call to discussion.

TRANSLATED BY SARAH MATTHEWS

NOTES

[1] Claude Lévi-Strauss, *Structural Anthropology,* trans. Claire Jacobson and Brooke Grundfest Schoepf (London: Allen Lane, Penguin, 1968), vol. 1, p. 300 and passim.

[2] Jean-Paul Sartre, "Questions de méthode," *Les Temps modernes* 139, 140 (1957).

[3] "Europe in 1500," "The World in 1880," "Germany on the Eve of the Reformation," and so on.

[4] Louis Halphen, *Introduction à l'histoire* (Paris: P.U.F., 1946), p. 50.

[5] See his *Théorie générale du progrès économique*, Cahiers de l'I.S.E.A., 1957.

[6] *Esquisse du mouvement des prix et des revenus en France au XVIIIᵉ siècle*, 2 vols. (Paris: Dalloz, 1933).

[7] Considered in René Clémens, *Prolégomènes d'une théorie de la structure économique* (Paris: Domat-Montchrestien, 1952); see also Johann Akerman, "Cycle et structure," *Revue économique* 1 (1952).

[8] Ernst Robert Curtius, *Europäische Literatur und lateinisches Mittelalter* (Berne, 1948).

[9] *Rabelais et le problème de l'incroyance au XVIᵉ siècle* (Paris: Albin Michel, 1943; 3d ed., 1969).

[10] Alphonse Dupront, "Le Mythe de croisade: Essai de sociologie religieuse," thesis, Sorbonne.

[11] Pierre Francastel, *Peinture et société: Naissance et destruction d'un espace plastique, de la Renaissance au cubisme* (Lyon: Audin, 1951).

[12] Other arguments: I would like to suggest those forceful articles in which all of them advance a similar thesis, such as Otto Brunner's (*Historische Zeitschrift*, 177. 3) on the social history of Europe; Rudolph Bultmann's (ibid., 176. 1), on humanism; Georges Lefebvre's (*Annales historiques de la Révolution française*, 114 [1949]) and F. Hartung's (*Historische Zeitschrift*, 180. 1), on enlightened despotism.

[13] René Courtin, *La Civilisation économique du Brésil* (Paris: Librairie de Médicis, 1941).

[14] As far as France is concerned; in Spain, the demographic decline was visible from the end of the sixteenth century.

[15] Lévi-Strauss, *Structural Anthropology*, p. 23.

[16] "Diogène couché," *Les Temps modernes* 195, p. 17.

[17] *Les Temps de l'histoire* (Paris: Plon, 1954), especially p. 298 et seq.

[18] P. Chombart de Lauwe, *Paris et l'agglomération parisienne* (Paris: P.U.F., 1952), 1:106.

[19] Suzanne Frère and Charles Bettelheim, *Une Ville française moyenne: Auxerre en 1950,* Cahiers des Sciences Politiques, no. 17 (Paris: Armand Colin, 1951).

[20] Pierre Clément and Nelly Xydias, *Vienne sur-le-Rhône: sociologie d'une cité française,* Cahiers des Sciences Politiques, no. 71 (Paris: Armand Colin, 1955).

[21] See the Colloquium on Structures, Sixth Section of the Ecole Pratique des Hautes Etudes, typed summary, 1958.

[22] Quoted by Lévi-Strauss, *Structural Anthropology*, vol. 1, p. 23.

[23] It would be tempting to make room here for the "models" created by economists, which have, in fact, been a source of inspiration to us.

[24] *The Mediterranean and the Mediterranean World in the Age of Philip II*, trans. Siân Reynolds, 2 vols. (New York: Harper and Row, 1972–74).

[25] Fernand Braudel and Frank Spooner, *Les Métaux monétaires et l'économie au XVIᵉ siècle, Rapports au Congrès international de Rome* 4 (1955), pp. 233–64.

[26] Alexandre Chabert, *Structure économique et théorie monétaire*, Publications du Centre d'Etudes Economiques (Paris: Armand Colin, 1956).

[27] Sigmund Diamond, *The Reputation of the American Businessman* (Cambridge, Mass., 1955).

[28] See, in particular, Claude Lévi-Strauss, *Bulletin international des sciences sociales,* UNESCO 6. 4, excerpted at pp. 191–194 and in general the whole of this very interesting issue, entitled *Les Mathématiques et les sciences sociales.*

[29] *The Theory of Games and Economic Behavior* (Princeton, 1944). See also the brilliant summary by Jean Fourastié, *Critique* 51 (Oct. 1951).

[30] All the following quotations are drawn from his most recent work, *Structural Anthropology.*

[31] Ibid., vol. 1, p. 296.

[32] Ibid., vol. 1, p. 33.

[33] Claude Lévi-Strauss, *Les Structures élémentaires de la parenté* (Paris: P.U.F., 1949). See *Structural Anthropology,* vol. 1, pp. 36–51.

[34] Lévi-Strauss, *Structural Anthropology,* vol. 1, p. 35.

[35] I am careful to say qualitative mathematics, according to games strategy. As far as classic models and those used by economists are concerned, a different sort of discussion would be called for.

[36] Gaston Roupnel, *Histoire et destin* (Paris: Bernard Grasset, 1943), p. 169 and passim.

[37] *Revue de Synthèse historique* (1900), p. 32.

[38] Ernest Labrousse, *La Crise économique française à la veille de la Révolution française* (Paris: P.U.F., 1944), introduction.

[39] *Dialectique de la durée*, (2d ed., Paris: P.U.F., 1950).

[40] Gilles Granger, *Evénement et structure dans les sciences de l'homme,* Cahiers de l'Institut de Science Economique Appliquée, Series M., no. 1, pp. 41–42.

[41] See my doubtless too polemical article "Georges Gurvitch et la discontinuité du social," *Annales ESC* 3 (1953), pp. 347–61.

[42] Cf. Georges Gurvitch, *Déterminismes sociaux et liberté humaine* (Paris: P.U.F., 1955), pp. 38–40 and passim.

[43] Ibid. See also Jean-Paul Sartre, "Fragment d'un livre à paraître sur le Tintoret," *Les Temps Modernes* (Nov. 1957).

[44] Otto Berkelbach, Van der Sprenkel, "Population Statistics of Ming China," BSOAS, 1953; Marianne Rieger, "Zur Finanz- und Agrargeschichte der Ming Dynastie, 1368–1643," *Sinica* (1932).

[45] P. Vidal de la Blache, *Revue des synthèse historique* (1903), p. 239.

[46] A well-known rubric of *Annales ESC*.

Orders or Classes: Debate Between Mousnier and Labrousse

MOUSNIER, SOBOUL, LABROUSSE

Description and Measurement in Social History: A Discussion

1965

The debate of the late 1950s and 1960s between Ernest Labrousse and Roland Mousnier has come with the passage of time to seem at once topical and outdated. It remains topical in the sense that it deals with a problem that all professional social historians encounter, and one around which debate still rages (see "The City and the Trades," by Simona Cerutti, p. 588), the question of the social taxonomies that enable us to make sense of past societies. Yet it seems outdated because of the ideological antagonism that underlies the discussion at every point. Both powerful Sorbonne professors, Labrousse and Mousnier occupied opposite extremes of the ideological spectrum. Labrousse, the veritable founder of French social history in its original form, was a man of the left, more a disciple of Jaurès than of Marx. Along with his many students he instigated numerous research projects that generally relied on the classical categories of sociographic analysis: occupation, source and amount of income, types of wealth. His opponent, Roland Mousnier (1905–1993), was more interested in the early modern period, the sixteenth and seventeenth centuries. A man

---

Discussion between Mousnier, Soboul, and Labrousse in *L'Histoire sociale: Sources et méthodes,* Proceedings of the Colloque de l'ENS de Saint-Cloud, 1965 (Paris: P.U.F., 1967), pp. 26–30.

of the right, he believed that the societies of the past could be understood only in terms of their own criteria, which for him meant membership in an "order" or estate and social prestige. "Orders or classes?" In this simplistic, highly ideological form, there was apparently no resolution to the disagreement, for reasons that were not purely scientific. No one today would follow either of the two protagonists, but the questions that Mousnier raised would probably be welcomed with a more open mind today than they were thirty years ago.

The occasion for this vigorous debate was a 1965 colloquium on "Social History: Sources and Methods," which served both to sum up recent work and to set a course for future research. Mousnier responded to the interventions of Labrousse and Albert Soboul.

Mousnier: Labrousse, a moment ago you alluded to the need for national as well as international colloquia and for us to discuss issues among ourselves. After listening to this first paper and hearing Soboul and studying the program of this colloquium, I have a confession to make: right now, here in Saint-Cloud, a few miles from Paris, I feel as though I were in a foreign country. Not that I disagree with what our friend Soboul said and in large part with what you said. In many respects, as Soboul pointed out, there is already general agreement. And to begin with, there is agreement on a point that no longer even needs to be mentioned, that we must always have a working hypothesis. Following Lucien Febvre, you drew a contrast between the traditional historian and the modern historian. But that contrast is illusory: there is no such thing as a traditional historian or a modern historian. Take Fustel de Coulanges, whose name you mentioned, and who could be considered the very type of the traditional historian. Fustel told us repeatedly that all his research was undertaken in order to answer specific questions, questions that were research hypotheses. It is impossible to do research without asking questions and making hypotheses. Let's just say that in every period there are real historians who ask questions, who formulate the best possible research hypotheses, and who achieve certain results, and there are historians who are simply curious, who are in fact just ragpickers filling their baskets, to borrow an image that Claude Bernard took from François Magendie. But such historians exist in 1965 just as they did in the past, and they will exist in 1985 and in 2075 if there still are historians then. The contrast is between two human types, not between two periods.

As for quantitative methods, we are in agreement, entirely in agreement. We must count. We must measure. Statistics are indispensable. We cannot do without them, and we cannot do genuine social history or anything truly scientific unless we adopt statistical methods, unless we measure and count. I am in full agreement with what you said.

So, why is it, after listening to Soboul and Labrousse, who reminded us of forebears whom we all venerate and from whom we draw daily inspiration, that I felt I was living in an intellectual world that was, well, let me say "different from yours" if the word "foreign" seems too strong? The plain fact is that I saw nothing in what you said that I would call social history.

You spoke of historians who do not believe in the existence of classes in society prior to the nineteenth century. I do not know if such historians exist. But I believe that while we do indeed find societies prior to the nineteenth century in which there were no classes, we also find that classes did exist in many societies. Yet we come now to the crucial problem, the most difficult problem, one that is never confronted head on, and one with which we cannot grapple adequately if we approach it tangentially—namely, the problem of social structures and social groups. Yes, we must count, but we must first know what it is that we are going to count. We agree, don't we? And what strikes me in Soboul's and Labrousse's papers, and so far as I can tell in the program for the sessions of the next few days, is that there is never any specific discussion of social groups and social structures. As Labrousse said, the problem that should be raised first when one begins to study any society is never mentioned: namely, the society must first be considered as a whole. When you said that measurement must come before monographs, you may have misspoken, for one can perfectly well consider a society as a whole and yet not begin with measurement, for measurement is a very difficult thing. Inevitably we come back to the same problem: What are we going to count, what are we going to measure? One must first establish what the society's organizational principle is and what, in view of that principle, the fundamental groups in the social stratification are.

Let me offer a brief example in order to make my meaning clear. I take it from an introduction I wrote for an edition of two *cahiers* of the nobility from 1649 and 1651.[1] Above all, I sought to distinguish clearly between three types of society that are often confused by students of sixteenth-, seventeenth-, and eighteenth-century France. Some historians speak of class struggles in those centuries. I do not berate them—I did the same thing myself in my thesis, twenty years ago, with certain nuances. At that time, I was working solely with the concept of class, which is insufficient.

Some historians say "this society is a caste society." And one does find aspects of caste as well. But if one takes a closer look, it becomes clear that there is a third type of society, a society of orders. I do not claim that these are the only three types of society that exist. There are many others.

But for sixteenth-, seventeenth-, and eighteenth-century France, these are the relevant types, because these are the types at issue among historians. Each type gives rise to a different social stratification, different forms of social mobility, different social groups, and a completely different kind of life. Now, in studying any type of society, the first thing to do, it seems to me, is to determine what type one is dealing with, and this can be done only by a descriptive method—because different types of society and organizational principles will lead to different social structures, groups, and relations among groups. Only after this determination of type has been made can one usefully begin to count. That is why I am disappointed not to find this problem directly addressed in the program of this colloquium (perhaps it will come up in the next two days of discussion). How many types of society are presently known? And, given the social structures that almost invariably result from each type, how can we apply statistical methods to their study? What you have told us is very interesting and very useful. At times, for example, you say that what you are really after is an economic scale, an economic stratification. You are looking for tax records, notarial records, estimates of wealth, and so on. Well and good: an economic stratification is one kind of stratification, but it is not necessarily the social stratification of the society you are studying. The social stratification may be quite different. It may be based on appreciations of rank and honor or status. A status ranking is another form of stratification, but it, too, may well fail by itself to yield the full social stratification unless it is combined with something else. There are also many factors that can be grouped under the heading of *power*—all the means by which one individual can influence the will of other individuals. There, too, you can establish a quantitative social stratification with as many numbers and measurements and samples as you like. This will yield a third type of social stratification, which once again may not be *the* social stratification. My point is that we need a far more thorough study of the concepts involved than we have had in what we have heard so far or than is promised in the program we have before us.

SOBOUL: Perhaps I summarized my thoughts a bit too quickly. I believe that it is necessary to have a hypothesis, a central working model to be subjected to theoretical and empirical criticism. Surely it is possible to come to agreement on this point. One also needs a set of clearly elaborated basic concepts. The crux of the issue, then, is the set of criteria involved in defining the concept of class.

Insofar as early modern society (of the sixteenth, seventeenth, and eighteenth centuries) is concerned, I am inclined to believe that it is both a society of orders and a society of classes. By the end of the Ancien Régime, the juridical structure of orders (clergy, nobility, third estate) scarcely concealed the class structure (aristocracy, bourgeoisie, and so on). The order is the juridical form, the appearance; class is the social reality. For example, the aristocracy, with its privileges as well as its economic underpinnings—landed property, feudal rights. Of course, it is necessary, in dealing with any society as complex as that of the Ancien Régime, to have recourse to more than one set of criteria. But one can be taken in by the juridical structure of orders, which is merely a mask for the social reality of classes.

MOUSNIER: In studying any society, it is obvious that we must find out what we are dealing with and what kinds of relations may exist among orders and classes. At the end of the Ancien Régime, as you are quite correct to point out, the juridical structure by orders was a mask. On that point we are in total agreement. But this was not the case earlier, and you must not avert your eyes from the reality: the classification by juridical orders, the legal classification, was not the whole classification by orders. Societies of orders frequently have part of their organization inscribed in law, but only part. The rest is the result of a social phenomenon, namely, the behavior of individuals toward one another. And that can never be inscribed in law. Yet in such behavior you have something that expresses the relations of a society of orders and not a society of classes.

SOBOUL: May I ask you a simple question? Do you believe that the aristocracy existed as a class in the eighteenth century?

MOUSNIER: As a class, not at all.

SOBOUL: That is precisely the problem.

LABROUSSE: May I say a word here, Mousnier? You have raised fundamental issues, and I shall confine my answer to fundamental matters as well. Let me say at once that in some respects I agree with you. As you well know, in a work I published a long time ago I contrasted the society of orders with the society of classes. Today, I would no longer express myself in the same terms. Let us distinguish between a state of orders and a state of classes. Let us distinguish between a society of orders and a society of classes. But let us also distinguish between state and society, despite the relations between the two. The Revolution was not a transition from a society of orders to a society of classes, as I once wrote, but from a state of orders to a state of classes. That is what the French Revolution was.

But it is the eighteenth century that I have in mind, for reasons having to do with both sources and method. We start where the data are abundant and "work backward" from the better-known to the lesser-known. The project currently under way focuses primarily on the eighteenth century but goes all the way back to the final years of the previous century. And what do we see when we look at the eighteenth century? A society of orders and a society of classes juxtaposed, in coexistence. I do not believe, moreover, that this state of affairs is peculiar to the eighteenth century alone. Every society must be studied with research methods appropriate to it. Our enumeration of classes is therefore valid for the eighteenth century, in coexistence with our enumeration of orders. I now move from the defensive to the offensive and ask you to what extent a society of orders exemplifies the criteria and characteristics of a society of classes. Of course it has its own specific characteristics, on that we agree. But it also seems to me beyond doubt that it has criteria and characteristics in common with the other classification, the other type of society.

MOUSNIER: But since men are men, you will always find that different societies have certain common features—it's a virtual certainty.

LABROUSSE: No, the classification by orders is a juridical classification.

MOUSNIER: No! Not at all! In the sixteenth and seventeenth centuries the classification by orders was a social reality, part of which was reflected in law. From 1750 on, in my view, France was no longer a society of orders; it was already a society of classes. And as you rightly said a moment ago, the Revolution blew off the legal masks, the juridical structures, but the Revolution was already accomplished before the social revolution, the deed was already done. I think we agree on that. A part of the system of orders of the old French society was embodied in legal texts, but only a part. You want to see the society of orders as nothing but a legal construct, a juridical mask, but it was nothing of the kind: it was a matter of social behavior on the part of groups and individuals, and such behavior comes under the head of the social, does it not?

LABROUSSE: I think it should be possible to build bridges between the various parts of the eighteenth century and even between the seventeenth and eighteenth centuries. Between two forms of society, slow mutation is the rule. If I spoke earlier of the juridical character of the society of orders, it was because that juridical character does not appear in the society of classes, and the two types of society can be contrasted on these grounds. There is, of course, a whole range of behavior and social priorities that works in favor of notables of the orders. Don't you think, though, that if we look at the essential aspects of the problem, there isn't a similar behavior that develops in the nineteenth century and, as you point out, in the second half of the eighteenth century, in favor of the notables of the society of classes? This social esteem or social consideration you mention attaches to any form of social superiority, to all notables, whether of orders or classes. The fundamental difference between them is, of course, that in the society of orders notability is classified, hierarchical, and "legalized." There are other differences as well. But we agree that social esteem or consideration is a factor in both types of society. It has an influence in both cases.

MOUSNIER: It has an influence in both cases, but not at all according to the same principles.

TRANSLATED BY ARTHUR GOLDHAMMER

NOTE

[1] R. Mousnier, J.-P. Labatut, and Y. Durand, *Problèmes de stratification sociale: Deux cahiers de la noblesse pour les états généraux de 1649–1651* (Paris: P.U.F., 1965). An excerpt of this book appears as the next piece in this volume, pp. 154–158.

Problems of Social Stratification

1965

Roland Mousnier was not satisfied with polemic. His goal was to work toward a descriptive sociology based on a functional typology, invoking Weber against Marx, a typology fairly rigid in principle but made more supple in practice by a clear interest in "intermediate types." When Mousnier dropped his polemical stance, his historian's predilection for complex cases was quick to emerge. This text was written as a preface to one of the first publications of the Mousnier "school," and it can be read as that school's "manifesto."

Whereas the society of castes and the society of orders consist of closed, officially hierarchized social groups, the society of classes is in principle an open society in which individuals are free and enjoy equal rights. The law recognizes only individuals, not groups. Classes have only a de facto, not a de jure, existence. A social class is not represented by any legally constituted council or governed by any official regulation; there are no legal sanctions for violations of tacitly accepted behavioral norms. The concept of social class is based on the purely factual observation that a certain number of people behave and react in similar ways and share certain fundamental ideas, coupled in some cases with a consciousness of this similarity and of virtually identical basic interests. In theory, social mobility attains its maximum. Individuals climb the social ladder as they acquire wealth and turn it into capital. The only social heredity that subsists is that of property. Virtually the only official social group is the "nuclear family," consisting of father, mother, and children. In theory there is no endogamy, but in practice endogamy is often nothing more than the expression of a concern to match or balance wealth or capital.

R. Mousnier, J.-P. Labatut, and Y. Durand, *Problèmes de stratification sociale: Deux cahiers de la noblesse pour les états généraux de 1649–1651* (Paris: P.U.F., 1965), pp. 20–24.

Of course, the heritability of property in fact gives, from the start, a tremendous advantage to the son of the bourgeois capitalist in matters of education, social contacts, and capital formation. Lineages survive and defend themselves, moreover, more effectively than the theory predicts. In addition, social mobility is often limited by the fact that in order to rise in the hierarchy and be accepted in a higher stratum, an individual must not only accumulate wealth but also acquire a style of life. Further-more, despite theoretical social equality, the European bourgeois enjoys certain legal privileges, because in European class society the law often bans trade unions and workers' guilds, prohibits strikes, bestows certain legal advantages on employers in labor conflicts, and subjects workers to special surveillance.

In taking note of such correctives, however, we move from consider-ation of pure types to intermediate types. In England, for example, be-tween the sixteenth and twentieth centuries we find a group of "gentle-men," a group that apparently enjoyed a peak of ascendancy in the nineteenth century and reflects the slow transition from a society of or-ders and estates to a society of classes. "Gentility" was never a legal condi-tion or estate in England, although in the Middle Ages the word "gentle" was applied to those entitled to bear arms. Since the sixteenth century, however, "gentlemen" have had no legal or political status, no special rights enforceable by the courts, and no special titles or functions. One is or is not a "gentleman" solely in virtue of a consensus, a tacit judgment based on the joint appreciation of those belonging to the "gentlemen" group. That group includes the nobility, the gentry, and members of the bourgeoisie—landowners, professional men, and select representatives of the world of affairs. Yet "gentlemen" and "ladies" constitute a true social group. The essential criteria of membership include education, manners, bearing, appearance, a gentlemanly countenance, cultivation, lifestyle, and abstention from manual labor of any kind. Birth, family background, wealth, and the means to live as a "gentleman" are also important. The symbol of membership is the right to avenge an insult through dueling: a gentleman crosses swords only with his peers.

Conversely, we find social groups whose existence demonstrates the passage from a society of classes to a nascent but not yet legally recog-nized society of orders. In the United States in the twentieth century, the number of self-employed businessmen has experienced a sharp decline. The likelihood of achieving economic independence has evaporated. American society is moving from atomic capitalism to molecular capital-ism. Capital is increasingly subject to the power and policies of major capitalists, on the one hand, and organized labor, on the other. Mean-while, the "new middle class," consisting mainly of lesser professionals and salaried white-collar employees, a group destined always to remain in the middle of the capitalist hierarchy, is growing. Within this group a new preoccupation with social status has emerged, and with it a growing importance attached to all marks and symbols of social rank, to everything that places members of the group above workers and confers on them a special dignity: proper manners, correct pronunciation, formal education, old school ties. Society is closing: "estates" are in the process of formation.[1]

Max Weber noted some time ago that rapid changes in technology and economic position favored the creation of classes and, conversely, that long periods of economic stability and, a fortiori, of economic recession encouraged the emergence of orders. When a certain type of social stratification remains basically unchanged in a given region over a period of centuries, it may happen that in certain places at certain times new forms of stratification will appear which are reminiscent of other social types—forms of classes in the midst of a dominant society of orders or forms of orders in the midst of a dominant society of classes.

For example, when in 1933 W. Lloyd Warner and Paul S. Lunt studied Newburyport, Massachusetts, they found, in this city of relatively small industry and reduced economic activity with a population of families that could in some cases trace their ancestry back to the seventeenth century, a social stratification reminiscent of a society of orders, even though the dominant society in the United States was, of course, a society of classes. The upper crust in Newburyport consisted of old families or lineages that could trace their ancestry back without interruption to if not the seventeenth then at least the eighteenth century. These families regarded themselves as forming a group and stood aloof from all other groups. Among themselves the members of this upper crust called each other "cousin" even if there was no actual kinship: "She is my cousin. Well, not really, but my father and mother grew up with her." These lineages behaved as if they formed a single kinship group. The "upper crust" was endogamous. Family ties linked nearly all its members, who often compared genealogies. Disputes erupted if a new family claimed ties to the upper crust. Such "uppitiness" was bitterly denounced. First-cousin marriages were frequent. Z said: "My children are descended from the first of the T's in sixteen different ways, nine on their mother's side and seven on mine." Many women remained spinsters rather than marry outside the group.

The upper crust of Newburyport had its own special froms of behavior, manners, and lifestyle. Family meals were veritable rituals, and there were rituals covering many other aspects of life, including the storage of toys. Objects inherited from ancestors had ritual and symbolic value, which linked the members of the household to one another and the living to the dead. The family home became a sort of ancestral temple, a symbol of the lineage. Money played a secondary role. Some relatively poor families belonged to the upper crust: "You don't have to have a lot of money. What counts is how you use it."

The members of the city's other social strata were fully aware of the existence of this upper crust and its peculiar characteristics. When asked why "the richest man in town" was not included, people responded that "he and his family don't behave properly," "they don't do what they ought to do," meaning not that their morals were questionable but that their lifestyle was not that of the upper crust. With time, obviously, the wealth that made such a style possible should have been enough to gain acceptance, but the important point is that wealth alone was not enough for social recognition; the proper lifestyle was also necessary, and for a period of at least two generations.

Newburyport society even generated its own myths to explain and justify the social order. The upper crust, people believed, were the descendants of sea captains who had settled in this port city. The middle class were the descendants of first, second, and third mates; the lower classes were the offspring of ordinary sailors. Thus, Newburyport fulfilled the conditions defining a society of orders.[2]

Conversely, in certain economic conjunctures it is possible for classes to emerge within a society of orders. In Segovia, in Castille, in the first third of the sixteenth century merchants may have become the leading social group through their activity as capitalist entrepreneurs, that is, as a class. Jean-Paul Le Flem, who is now doing research on the economic life and social structure of Segovia in the sixteenth and seventeenth centuries, will no doubt enlighten us on this point. Indeed, it may even be possible in certain economic conjunctures for classes to emerge in a society of castes. In *Caste, Class, and Occupation*, G.-S. Ghurye explains that in southern India in 1670 castes of artisans challenged the social supremacy of the Brahmins. If this is true, these artisans could not have been acting in the name of religious purity. Their struggle must have been motivated, in a more or less confused way, by a sense of the superiority of productive labor over religious activity. If so, it might be interesting to relate their movement to the development of commerce between India and Europe and within India itself, as well as to the rise of capitalist activities drawing on the fruits of their labor. It would require solving an important problem in order to do so.[3]

TRANSLATED BY ARTHUR GOLDHAMMER

NOTES

[1] T. H. Marshall, *Class, Citizenship, and Social Development* (Garden City: Doubleday, 1964).

[2] W. Lloyd Warner and Paul S. Lunt, *The Social Life of a Modern Community:*

Yankee City (1941), pp. 82–84, 99–110. Lloyd Warner published five volumes of research on Yankee City between 1945 and 1959. His methods and results drew numerous criticisms, most recently from Stephen Thernstrom, *Poverty and Progress: Social Mobility in a Nineteenth-Century City* (Cambridge, Mass.: Harvard University Press, 1964). However, two key facts remain intact: the existence of classes based on prestige in the 1930s and the existence of the "upper crust."

[3] G.-S. Ghurye, *Caste, Class, and Occupation* (Bombay: University Department of Sociology, 1961), ch. 1, p. 6. Roland Mousnier, *Les XVIᵉ et XVIIᵉ siècles: La grande mutation intellectuelle de l'humanité, l'advenement de la science moderne, et l'expansion de l'Europe*, Histoire générale des civilisation, vol. 4 (4th ed., Paris: P.U.F., 1965), pp. 541–61.

Classes or Elites: Debate Between Soboul and Furet–Richet

The debate about social categories involved much more than academic nitpicking. A social interpretation of the passage from the Ancien Régime to the new "bourgeois" society was essential to Marxism and to Marxist historians' identification of a political and historical trajectory leading from the Jacobins of the French Revolution to Marx, then Lenin, and Marxism-Leninism in the present. The connection between 1789 and 1917 was for them of the highest importance. In the mid-1960s, the debate about this social and political interpretation took a new and more bitter turn with the controversy provoked by the publication of François Furet (b. 1927) and Denis Richet's (1927–1989) two-volume history The French Revolution *(1965–1966). Both had been members of the Communist Party themselves until 1956. They now contested the Jacobin-Marxist "orthodoxy" about the "bourgeois revolution," arguing that the bourgeoisie and the nobility were united by many common interests into a more general elite, and that the Marxist categories of class and class conflict could not explain the dynamics of the French Revolution.*

In the article excerpted here, Richet further developed their position on the elite and its conflicts with a "despotic" monarchy. In response, Albert Soboul (1915–1982) defended the "classical" interpretation. A student of Georges Lefebvre, Soboul heatedly rejected the view that the urban lower class and rural peasant movements had only fortuitously or accidentally conjoined with the bourgeois or middle-class revolution. The Furet-Richet line of argument eventually expanded and coalesced with similar currents from the Anglophone world to form a new school of "revisionist" historiography on the French Revolution in the 1970s and 1980s. By the 1980s, it had largely displaced the Marxist school as the reigning "orthodoxy." In the meantime, though, the debate ceased being exclusively Franco-French; it became international and, in particular, Anglo-American.

DENIS RICHET

The Ideological Origins of the French Revolution

1969

Assuming that there is a necessary relation between "infrastructure" and "superstructure," why should one expect a priori that the ideological elaboration will reveal traces of a major conflict of interest between nobility and bourgeoisie? Of course, we all know that there were *some* conflicts, magnified by various offenses to pride. We also know that there were other, just as important and no less durable conflicts, such as that between Court and provincial nobles for access to high military rank. The problem, in my view, lies elsewhere. Did Enlightenment society possess *shared* representations in which the urbanized nobility played no less important a role than the upper spheres of the third estate? In the realm of literary, artistic, and musical taste, Alphonse Dupront has shown that there were such common models and that the aristocracy played a key role in elaborating them.[1] Was it otherwise when it came to the idea that this society forged of itself? To answer this question, one must look beyond accidents of biography (after all, Mirabeau and Condorcet were no less noble than Montesquieu) and search the whole corpus of texts for the obsessive presence of a fundamental division between noble and bourgeois ideology.

In the absence of any quantitative study,[2] and without claiming to be familiar with so much as one percent of the literary production of the time, one can examine the greatest works. At the heart of the "philosophical" debates that followed the publication of Montesquieu's *De l'Esprit des lois*, at the center of the polemics triggered by the convocation of the Estates General, we find not the concept of nobility but the notion of *privilege*. The word takes on a particular resonance: it refers only secondarily to the rights and duties peculiar to each *corps* of Ancien Régime

Denis Richet, "Autour des origines idéologiques lointaines de la Révolution française: Elites et despotisme," *Annales ESC* 24 (Jan.–Feb. 1969), pp. 11–14, 20, 22–23, reprinted in *De la Réforme à la Révolution: Études sur la France moderne* (Paris: Aubier, 1991), pp. 389–416.

society, and despite appearances it does not coincide with the question of fiscal exemptions (which the nobility of course relinquished before the Estates General met).[3] Nor, of course, did it cover all the advantages that a twentieth-century democrat would find worthy of reproach in the elites. Privilege was that which confined the elite within the narrow boundaries of noble birth. In attacking privilege, neither the Physiocrats nor Condorcet nor the Patriots of 1789 condemned nobility. All—except Sieyès—recognized its preeminence and distinguished, with Roederer, between the "legal prerogative of the nobility," which they rejected, and the "advantages afforded it by public opinion," which they considered natural and just.[4] Indeed, in "Qu'est-ce que le tiers-état?," Sieyès himself gave a remarkably succinct explanation of why the nobility had been a pioneer in the fight for liberty: "I am by no means surprised," he wrote, "that the first two orders provided the first champions of justice and humanity. Talent stems from the exclusive use of intelligence and long habit. The members of the order of the Third Estate should, for a thousand reasons, excel in its use. But the light of public morality *must first appear among the men best placed to grasp the great social relations* and among whom the basic thrust is less commonly thwarted: for there are forms of knowledge that owe as much to the soul as to the spirit."[5] This passage offers a marvelous explanation of the continuous movement that I have been attempting to describe. What the philosophes and Patriots wanted was an open elite accepting the preeminence of the nobility but integrating property, wealth, and talent, an elite that had been in gestation since the sixteenth century. As Pierre Louis de Lacretelle wrote in 1789, "Today landowners and rentiers, noble or not, have an equal interest in public prosperity."[6]

At no time did consciousness of the fundamental barrier between the elite and the lower classes disappear from the consciousness of these innovators. The word "equality" was either rejected or more commonly understood as the opposite of privilege, that is, in the sense of equality among property owners. D'Holbach, who is sometimes portrayed as a democrat, carefully distinguished between the propertied and the "imbecile populace who, devoid of enlightenment and common sense, may at any moment become the instrument and accomplice of troublesome demagogues bent on disrupting society. We must never raise our voices against this inequality, which was always necessary."[7] Condorcet gave a clearer statement of what "equality" meant to the men of the Enlightenment: "The right of equality is not hindered if only the propertied enjoy the *droit de cité,* because they alone are the possessors of land, because their consent alone bestows the right to inhabit it. But it is hindered if the *droit de cité* is shared unequally among the various classes of the propertied, because such a distinction does not grow out of the nature of things."[8] Three centuries in the making, this image of *la notabilité* would flourish in 1791, triumph still more explicitly in the constitution of Year III, and ultimately dominate the early decades of the nineteenth century.

This expansion of the elite was opposed, however, by part of the nobility: therein lay the drama of the moment. "Aristocrats" expressed their historic refusal by stubbornly insisting on the vote by orders, and later through emigration and counterrevolution.[9] That refusal may account in part for the Revolution's veering out of control, which I have described elsewhere.[10] The contrast between this attitude and that of the English nobility inspired Tocqueville[11] and Balzac[12] to write some well-known pages. Nowadays, though, no one agrees with Tocqueville that the *franc-fief* was a decisive obstacle to the osmosis of the elites, or with Balzac that the French aristocracy was swept away in torment because it "clung fatally to symbols." Do the reasons for this historic refusal lie in the existence of an impoverished and overabundant rural nobility, which found itself humiliated first in the army of the Ancien Régime and later in emigration?[13] Or in the resistance of recently ennobled *parlementaires* all the more firmly attached to their privileges? Keep in mind as well the court nobility, which, under the system of pensions, lived off the Ancien Régime. In any case, this division of the elites over the question of privilege would weigh heavily on the fate of the *censitaire* monarchies of the nineteenth century.

We do not find a similar division in the way in which the elites conceived of their relations with the government. It was at this level that the veritable revolution took place, and, despite the model magnificently set forth by Marx in his preface to *A Contribution to the Critique of Political Economy*, it took place before the development of new "productive forces." In order to understand this, we must once again work backward in time and follow various theoretical challenges to the regime emanating from the nobility of both sword and robe as well as the upper strata of nonnoble society. [. . .]

The elites, though divided over the issue of privilege, were profoundly united around one fundamental demand: liberty. This was not, as is often said, an unnatural alliance, an accidental and deceptive cartel, but the fruit of a shared hope and a unified will. All the philosophes were perfectly well aware that the opposition of the Parlements to Louis XV reflected not only sincere desires but also petty interests, but that did not stop them. D'Holbach, who detested all the privileged *corps* and saw in them the vestige of a barbarous past, nevertheless believed that in the absence of any other representation they ought to form "the always necessary rampart between supreme Authority and the liberty of subjects."[14] Mably, though he disapproved of Montesquieu's praise for *corps intermédiaires*, believed that the Parlements could play a useful role and predicted that some day they would call for a convocation of the Estates General.[15] [. . .]

Must we therefore give up the concept of bourgeois revolution? On this point I want to be absolutely clear. In the broadest economic terms, a slow but revolutionary mutation occurred between the sixteenth and the nineteenth centuries, nothing less than the advent of capitalism, which is one of the major phenomena of modern times. This development of many centuries can, if one wishes, be baptized a "bourgeois revolution," the decisive phase of which was located in the second half of the nineteenth century. But I do not believe that the French Revolution of 1789 can be encompassed within the Marxian theory of revolution, one of the weakest and least coherent aspects of Marx's gigantic work.[16] There are two reasons for my belief. First, there was no development of the productive forces prior to the end of the eighteenth century sufficient to bring about a violent substitution of new "relations of production" for old ones. Second, and more important, the Revolution of 1789 was the result of two shifts in elite consciousness that had been a long time in the making. First, the elites became aware of their autonomy with respect to the political order, and second, they became aware of their need to control the government. This was a shared consciousness, in which the nobility played the role of an initiator and educator but which grew to embrace nonnobles of wealth, property, and talent. It was the Revolution of the Enlightenment.

TRANSLATED BY ARTHUR GOLDHAMMER

NOTES

[1] Alphonse Dupront, *Art, littérature et société au XVIIIe siècle* (Paris: C.D.U., 1963–1965).

[2] See François Furet, *Livre et société dans la France du XVIIIe siècle* (Paris: Mouton, 1966).

[3] Egret, *La Pré-révolution française* (Paris: P.U.F., 1962).

[4] Ibid.

[5] Emphasis added.

[6] Cited by Egret, *La Pré-révolution française*.

[7] D'Holbach, *Politique naturelle, ou discours sur les vrais principes du gouvernement* (1773).

[8] Condorcet, *Idées sur le despotisme* (1789).

[9] Jacques Godechot, *La Contre-Révolution* (Paris: P.U.F. 1961).

[10] François Furet and Denis Richet, *La Révolution française* (Paris: Hachette, 1966).

[11] Alexis de Tocqueville, *L'Ancien Régime et la Révolution* (Paris: Gallimard, 1953), vol. 2, n. 150.

[12] Honoré de Balzac, *La Duchesse de Langeais.*

[13] Godechot, *La Contre-Révolution*; Emile-G. Léonard, *L'Armée et ses problèmes au XVIIIᵉ siècle* (Paris: Plon, 1958).

[14] D'Holbach, *Politique naturelle.*

[15] Mably, *Les Droits et devoirs du citoyen* (1789; written 1758–59).

[16] See the perceptive analyses in Kostas Papaioannou, "Classe et luttes de classes," *Contrat social,* vol. 5, nos. 2 and 3 (1961), and B. Wolf, *Le Marxisme, une doctrine politique centenaire* (Paris: Fayard, 1967).

ALBERT SOBOUL

Classical Revolutionary Historiography and Revisionist Endeavors

1974

At the moment when Elizabeth Eisenstein's article was reviving the discussion among American historians of the bourgeois nature of the French Revolution, in France itself in 1965 a revisionist undertaking on a completely different scale was begun and has since been stubbornly pursued.[1] Here the historical context is no longer that of the Cold War, but it would not be possible to abstract this endeavor from the social conditions and political struggles of the France of 1965. The goal is still the same: while denying the reality of classes, find an alternative explanation for the revolutionary upsurge. Thus, we have this effort to modernize and reassert the value of the liberal theme of the duality of the French Revolution, but without the rationality and necessity that characterized the analysis of a Adolph Thiers or a François Guizot. What is proposed is an aristocratic and bourgeois revolution of the Enlightenment, followed, with no necessary connection, by a popular revolution, violent and reactionary. Thus, a reformist way and a revolutionary way would confront each other.

This interpretation was first expressed in the work of Edgar Faure, *Turgot's Disgrace (May 12, 1776)*, published in 1961. But could the liberal reform then undertaken succeed with the persistence of the feudal structures and aristocratic privilege that this minister, however enlightened, never intended to touch? ... In a similar vein is the work *The French Revolution* by François Furet and Denis Richet. Of the various themes developed and tirelessly taken up again, two are worth retaining—that of the "revolution of elites," and that of the "skid" of the revolutionary movement, both implying the contingent nature of the Revolution. "Was the

From "Classical Revolutionary Historiography and Revisionist Endeavors," in Soboul, *Understanding the French Revolution*, trans. April Ane Knutsen (New York: International Publishers, 1988), pp. 255–73. "Historiographie classifique et tentatives revisionnistes" first appeared in *La Pensée* 177 (Sept.–Oct. 1974), and was reprinted in Soboul, *Comprendre la révolution* (Paris: Maspero, 1982).

Revolution inevitable?" No, without a doubt, for our authors: "All still depends on the ability of the King of France to arbitrate and reform."

"Revolution of elites": revolution of the Enlightenment, revolution of 1789. All during the eighteenth century, a community of ideas and states, a common society life doubtless brought together the aristocratic and bourgeois elites still characterized by an equal aspiration to political freedom, as well as an equal revulsion to the popular masses and democracy. The revolution was made in these enlightened minds before being transposed into law and order. The men of '89 had been won over to the spirit of reform, generally widespread, whether it was that of aristocratic liberalism or that of bourgeois thought. There would thus have been "a tactical convergence against absolutism," a provisional alliance of the diverse leading social forces of the pre-Revolutionary period. Thus, 1789 would have been the outcome of this awakening of consciousness of the elites, a revolution of the Enlightenment, and ideology would constitute the driving element of history. "The 1789 Revolution resulted from a double awakening of consciousness of the elites effected through a long progression. Consciousness of their autonomy, first, in relation to the political order, of their necessary control, then of power. Unanimous consciousness where the nobility played the role of initiator and educator, but that broadened out to include wealth, property and talent. That was the Revolution of the Enlightenment."

We cannot but underscore the simplifying nature of these views. First of all, did the Enlightenment really have a unifying function? It does not seem so, if we follow the ambiguous "fortune" of such and such a philosopher. Louis Althusser has stressed in his *Montesquieu* (1959) "the paradox of posterity" for this theoretician of the aristocratic reaction, claimed not only by the Constituents of 1789, but even by Marat and Saint-Just.[2] As for Rousseau, who as we know so nourished Jacobinism, he was also one of the doctrinal sources of the counterrevolution. The pragmatism of the Enlightenment—it is deformed as it is refracted into the various social milieus following diverse ends.

As for the elites, Richet concedes that, despite their common will, they were divided on the problem of privilege—that's putting it mildly. In fact, there was no unified French elite. Jean Meyer, the most recent historian of the nobility strongly affirms: "The French nobility neither knew how nor wanted to integrate the intelligentsia and the new social forces. . . . The State did not know how to conduct a policy acceptable to the most dynamic elements of the bourgeoisies."[3] There is the heart of the problem. The revolution of the Enlightenment, that is, the reform, stumbled against privilege. Neither the nobility nor the monarchy could accept, without repudiating themselves, the suppression of privilege; on the other hand, the bourgeois elites could not accept its preservation. An internal necessity impelled the confrontation of the two categories. As for the "ability of the King of France to arbitrate and reform," an in-depth analysis, not of the government of Louis XVI but of the monarchial State at the end of the Ancien Régime, would show that it could in fact only swing "to one side." Well before the Revolution, the monarchy had proved that it was the State of the aristocracy, a position that the speech and Declaration of Louis XVI on June 23, 1789, was to illustrate again.

"Skid of the Revolution": this theory is even more dangerous than that of the so-called revolution of elites. Our authors in fact distinguish three revolutions in 1789: that of the Constituent Assembly which bears the mark of the "triumphant" eighteenth century as the *cahiers de doléances* allow us to define it; that of the Parisians who "did not rise to safeguard the National Assembly and its conquests; that was only an objective consequence of their desire to save themselves"; finally that of the peasants who "knocked loudly at the door of the bourgeois Revolution reluctant to open up to them."

Certainly, we no longer conceive of the French Revolution as that of the third estate, unrolling without contradiction its majestic course, as it is represented to a certain extent by Jean Jaurès in his *Socialist History*. Georges Lefebvre has shown the existence of an autonomous and specific peasant current within the revolution of the third estate; his disciples, of a popular urban current, called *sans-culotte*, also autonomous and specific. The general course of the bourgeois revolution cannot, however, be altered. Would there not be, therefore, any organic link between these various currents?

Our authors are astonished by the alliance between this opulent bourgeoisie of the eighteenth century and the people of the cities and countryside. They judge it "unexpected," for lack of having given sufficient attention to the structures of the society of the Ancien Régime characterized by privilege and remnants of feudalism. It is in view of this meeting—contingent, in their eyes—between the bourgeoisie and the popular urban and rural masses that the root of their hypothesis lies, that of the "three revolutions of 1789," a notion indispensable to the following hypothesis, without a doubt the most astonishing and the most dangerous, that of the "skid" of the revolution from 1792 to 9 Thermidor (July 27, 1794: the fall of Robespierre).

The reformist revolution of 1789, defined by the program of its enlightened leaders and by a compromise *from above*, having thus failed through the inability "of the monarchy to arbitrate and to reform," was definitively turned from its initial course in 1792 by popular intervention. A "skid" implies that this intervention was neither indispensable to the success of the bourgeois revolution nor fundamentally motivated by it. Just as the meeting of the three revolutions of 1789 had been purely fortuitous, so the revolution of 1792–1794 would be merely contingent, an accident. "Let us dare to say it: as a consequence of such accidents, didn't the liberal revolution born of the eighteenth century, and that the French bourgeoisie would effect decades later, fail for the time being?" Our authors don't ask themselves if it is not precisely in this period, which they call "a skid," that the bourgeoisie was able to exterminate all the forms of counterrevolution and thus render possible, in the long run, the liberal system that prevailed definitively after 1794. Nor do they ask about the profound causes of the intervention of the popular masses; for them, it depended only on the myth of the aristocratic plot. As for the war, it would be due in the last analysis to the "passionate expansionism of France." Thus, everything is reduced to mental determinations. There is no question of daily bread, the essential motivation of the popular masses from 1789 to 1795. "The Revolution was led by the war and the pressure of the Parisian crowd off the great path traced by the intelligence and wealth of the eighteenth century." The popular masses would be moved only by myths and fantasies; the war would be only an accident.

Thus, these authors reintroduced the chance and the irrational into history, which is, however, a thinkable and thus rational subject. The theory of the "skid," by making the revolution a contingent phenomenon ("the limited and contingent events of 1789–1793," writes Richet elsewhere, without fear of ridicule[4]), without internal historical necessity, breaks with the line of classical revolutionary historiography, from Barnave to Thiers and Tocqueville, from Jaurès to Lefebvre.

Antoine Barnave, in his *Introduction to the French Revolution* (1792), had already indicated with prophetic lucidity the rooting of the Revolution in the deep structures of the French society of the Ancien Régime.[5] In the Restoration period, this historian of the liberal school in turn insisted on the internal logic of the revolutionary movement from 1789 to November 1799—François Guizot, certainly, but also Adolphe Thiers and Auguste Mignet, each publishing a *History of the French Revolution* in 1823 and 1824. This was a "fatalist" school, to use Chateaubriand's expression, in the sense that they saw in the Revolution the logical development of given cause and in the Terror an evil necessary to the salvation of the nation. The idea of necessity presides over their work, giving them methodological unity and clarity. "The interior resistance," according to Mignet, "led to the sovereignty of the multitude, and the aggression from outside led to military domination." And again: "Three years of the dictatorship of the Committee of public safety, if they were lost for liberty, they were not lost for the Revolution." We see the same point of view in the work of Thiers, and the same idea of a "fatal force" that stimulated the course of the Revolution and surmounted all obstacles until the goal was reached. This is a concept of a global and necessary revolution, although historical necessity does not exclude free will, for man retains full responsibility for his acts. Certainly, we must here acknowledge the role of circumstances: it was a question of justifying the hopes and assuring the positions of the liberal party against the ultrareaction. These historians had not, however, subordinated historical truth to their political position. They had determined one of the constants of classical revolutionary historiography.

Tocqueville, in turn, with his customary perception, had indicated the necessity of the Revolution. "The Revolution was least of all," he writes in *The Ancien Régime and the Revolution* (1856), "a fortuitous event. It is true that it took the world by surprise, and yet it was only the complement of a much longer work, the sudden and violent termination of an undertaking on which ten generations of men had worked."[6] Jaurès and his introduction to *Socialist History* must be read again. Lefebvre must be read again. . . .

But let us conclude. There were not three revolutions in 1789, but a single one, bourgeois and liberal, with popular support, particularly among the peasants. There was not a skid of the Revolution in 1792 but a will of the revolutionary bourgeoisie to maintain the cohesion of the third estate through an alliance with the popular masses, without whose support the gains of 1789 would have been forever compromised. Year II was not a "time of distress," but a moment of radicalization necessary to assure victory over the counterrevolution and the coalition, and thus the salvation of the bourgeois revolution.

We cannot leave the current state of historiography of the French Revolution and the critics of the classical social interpretation without some reflections on methodology.

The history of the Revolution, like any historical subject, is structured and thus thinkable, scientifically knowable, like any other reality. The goal of the historian is to achieve if not certitudes at least probabilities or networks of probabilities—or even better, as Georges Lefebvre said, tendential laws. Tocqueville wrote in *The Ancien Régime and the Revolution*: "It is not by chance that aristocracies were born and maintained; like all the rest, they are subject to fixed laws, and it is perhaps not impossible to discover them." Abandoning this constant line of our classical historiography, departing from this requirement of rationality, reintroducing into history the contingent and the irrational seems not to constitute progress in the profession of historian but, indeed, retreat and almost a surrender.

In his concern for rationality, the historian must ceaselessly go from scholarly research to critical reflection. He advances between two pitfalls: on the one hand, an all-purpose schematization that impoverishes and dessicates the rich historical subject, on the other, a cursory empiricism that, in the name of the complexity of the real, considers and treats only one particular case. As for the French Revolution, if the historian intends to understand and arrive at some explanation of causes and effects, it is essential to have recourse to some theory connecting ideas to the needs and pressures of society.

This explains the necessity of definitions and the requirement of conceptualization; let us think about the discussions concerning the word "bourgeoisie." History can progress only if it is supported by basic concepts, clearly elaborated. Rejecting this necessity has the effect of challenging history and particularly social history as an explicative discipline. Again it's a matter of reaching an understanding on necessary concepts and their definitions; modifiable, certainly, and always perfectible. Theory ceaselessly solicits every reflection of the historian, and it is through the expedient of conceptualization and theorization that he can hope to draw the anatomy and physiology of societies and revolutions.

We are a long way from accepting the criticism of the classical social interpretation of the French Revolution. The historians who reject this interpretation are no longer capable of a global vision of the revolutionary phenomenon nor of giving it a total explanation. The polemic basically turns on the nature and role of the aristocracy and the bourgeoisie, and on the nature and role of the urban masses. The peasantry is not brought into play, yet it accounts for at least twenty-two million souls out of a total of twenty-eight million in the whole country. Scholarly research since J. Loutchisky and Georges Lefebvre, and critical reflection have stressed the importance of the agrarian question and affirmed that it occupies an "axial position" in the French Revolution. This fundamental problem is perfectly concealed by revisionist criticism.

We are forced to state that there is no longer any total history of the Revolution; there are only partial histories that carve out particular areas and thus break the links that unite them to other aspects of this living and rich subject that is history. It is certainly not a question of saying everything about everything but, rather, of emphasizing how the particular depends on the whole (and reciprocally). Far be it from us to deny the necessity of partial histories; they can also give us the historic specificity of their object of study, but on the condition that they are joined in a necessary manner to the heart of the historic totality. Too often, however, we see these partial histories confining themselves to their limited object, and no longer emerging with anything but remarks for internal use; they have therefore missed their goal of true historical reflection. How can historians write about the nobility in the society of the Ancien Régime without at the same time posing the peasant question in all its breadth? Every particular problem must be thought about historically; it cannot be detached from its historic context in order to abstract from it certain ideal aspects for stranger and stranger extraneous ends. The practice of partial history, without a global vision, contains the germ of true adulteration; in the end it is destined to sterile abstraction. The revisionist designs on the classical social interpretation of the French Revolution seem indeed to have arrived at that point. What scientific global interpretation have Alfred Cobban and his emulators offered as a substitute? Obeying fads, transitory by definition, criticizing without constructing, denying all rationality in the historical movement, they have made only a partial history, purely circumstantial, old before its time and already outdated.

"In order to discover the historical life," writes Jules Michelet, "it would be necessary to patiently follow it in all its paths, all its forms, all its elements. But it would also be necessary, with a still greater passion, to remake, reestablish the play of all that, the reciprocal action of these various forces in a powerful movement that would become life itself."

TRANSLATED BY APRIL ANE KNUTSEN

NOTES

[1] Elizabeth L. Eisenstein, " 'Who Intervened in 1788?' A Commentary on *The Coming of the French Revolution*," *American Historical Review* 71 (Oct. 1956).

[2] Louis Althusser, *Montesquieu: La politique et l'histoire* (Paris, 1959).

[3] Jean Meyer, *Nobles et pouvoirs dans l'Europe d'Ancien Régime* (Paris, 1973), p. 253.

[4] Denis Richet, *La France moderne: L'esprit des institutions* (Paris, 1973), p. 7. "Everything happens as if the events, limited and contingent, of 1789–1793 had imposed a decisive break between a before and after." For the idea of revolution, this author tends to substitute in a significant manner that of transition. See Denis Richet, "Autours des origines idéologiques lointaines de la Révolution française," *Annales ESC* (1967): "In the broadest economic terms, a slow but revolutionary mutation occurred between the sixteenth and the nineteenth centuries, nothing less than the advent of capitalism, which is one of the major phenomena of modern times. This development of many centuries can, if one wishes, be baptized as 'bourgeois revolution,' the decisive phase of which was located in the second half of the nineteenth century." (p. 22).

[5] *Introduction à la Révolution française*, pt. 1, ch. 3. Written in 1792, this work was published in 1843 in the first volume of the *Oeuvres* of Barnave, edited by Bérenger de la Drôme. Jaurès places great emphasis on this work in his *Histoire socialiste*, vol. 1, p. 98.

[6] *L'Ancien Régime et la Révolution* (Paris, 1952), introduction by Georges Lefebvre. Tocqueville adds: "If it had not taken place, the old social edifice would have nonetheless fallen everywhere, sooner here, later there—only it would have continued to fall bit by bit instead of all at once. The Revolution achieved suddenly, by a convulsive and painful effort, without transition, without precaution, without regard, what would have been achieved slowly by itself, in the long run. That was its work" (p. 96).

Remarkable Outsiders

ALPHONSE DUPRONT

Pilgrimage and Sacred Places

1985

The name Alphonse Dupront is certainly not one of the best known either in France or abroad. Dupront (1905–1990) belonged to the second generation of Annales *historians, the generation of Braudel and Vilar. He had a brilliant academic career at the Sorbonne and the Ecole des Hautes Etudes, yet his considerable influence has remained discrete. One reason for this is that much of his work is scattered in many articles, which only decades later were beginning to be anthologized, while his magnum opus,* Le Mythe de croisade, *will finally be published posthumously in 1996, forty years after he first defended it as a thesis. Another reason is the complexity of his thought, which is sinuous, full of nuances, and often formulated in a complex style.*

Today, however, we are increasingly aware of the importance of Dupront's thought and teaching. Many whose names are more famous than his readily acknowledge how much they owe him: from Mona Ozouf to François Furet, from Daniel Roche to Jean-Louis Flandrin and Dominique Julia, all attest to the existence of a brilliant and powerful intellectual "network." Dupront's primary interest was the anthropology of western Christianity in three main areas: crusades, pilgrimages, and images of sanctity, which he approached using a variety of methods, ranging from historical semantics to local surveys, from content analysis to Jungian psychoanalysis. The following excerpt, from the conclusion to an essay on "pilgrimage society," illustrates Dupront's manner well.

Alphonse Dupront, "Pèlerinages et lieux sacrés," in *Du Sacré: Croisades et pèlerinages, images et langages* (Paris: Gallimard, 1987), pp. 406–12.

In analyzing the act of pilgrimage we have thus far confused, or at any rate not yet differentiated, the individual and the collective. In pilgrim society, the act of pilgrimage is essentially collective, so the problem does not really exist. Pilgrimage is in fact a mass social phenomenon, with "mass" understood in an organic rather than a quantitative sense. Even the pilgrim who wishes to be alone is nevertheless part of a powerful collective flow that has chosen its "sacred place"—a flow that, in its crude vitality, is an irrational force of panic. In other words, a human group driven by an irresistible impulse that becomes all the more intense as it gathers strength of numbers. The group is carried along by a transcendent force that seeks its own sacralization. As the group expands in space and time, it constitutes an extraordinary if ephemeral society.

Extraordinary in several senses. To begin with, it is a society that, in its spatial quest, becomes itinerant in search of a land of transfiguration rather than nostalgic for a physical "elsewhere." Unlike the compartmentalized, hierarchical society from which it stems, moreover, pilgrimage society is a society in which differences and groups are confounded: distinctions of age, sex, and rank disappear, and even clergy and laity are joined in a panic-stricken communion of fervor, hope, light, and joy. Yahweh told his people, "Thou shalt rejoice before the Lord thy God, thou, and thy son, and thy daughter, and thy manservant, and thy maidservant, and the Levite that is within thy gates, and the stranger, and the fatherless, and the widow, that are in the midst of thee, in the place which the Lord thy God shall choose to cause His name to dwell there" (Deuteronomy 16:11). Finally, the act of pilgrimage is experienced as a quest marked by anguish, by a demand for or lack of the absolute in both physical plenitude (health of body and soul) and spiritual awakening or accomplishment, these being strengths or nourishments not afforded by the society that the pilgrim temporarily, but only temporarily, abandons.

Pilgrimage society is indeed a society of the ephemeral. It lasts only as long as it takes to complete the pilgrimage. The ordeals of space and manifold rituals are too harsh, and the discovery of the "other" within and of the sacred presence are too spiritually transmuting, not to be an instant of the eternal. The intensity of the pilgrim experience is generally inversely proportional to its duration: it comes in lightning flashes, which leave their mark. The memory of the ephemeral experience is all the more vivid as a result: all who were joined in ephemeral unity bear the stamp, by which they recognize one another. After their return, that memory subsists and is nostalgically cherished through the tedium of everyday life. In societies where soteriological tensions ran deep, where certain great pilgrimages were highly valued and intensively practiced, that memory became a source of social consecration. The community looked forward to the pilgrims' return as a common grace. When returning pilgrims marched on foot, people residing along the route lined up to celebrate those who came home on bare feet from the precincts of the extraordinary. After the hubbub of homecoming died down, a dignity remained, a name: *hadji* for the pilgrim from Mecca, *mecchedi* for the pilgrim from the great Iranian temple at Meched, *roumieu* for the pilgrim from Rome, *jacquaire* for the pilgrim from Compostella. Each of these various appellations connotes collective gratitude to those who have set out on the great sacred adventure. The reverential title that such experience awarded made the pilgrim the living embodiment of a memory as well as the repository of grace bestowed upon the entire community to which he returned.

Pilgrim society was also festive. When the gods of ancient Egypt left to visit neighboring gods, an entire pilgrim community jostled for places at the sacred drama that was about to unfold. Herodotus reports, not without a certain malice, that wine flowed abundantly on such occasions. The pilgrimages to Jerusalem prescribed in Exodus and Deuteronomy coincided with Passover, Tish b'Av, and Succoth, Jewish festivals marking the annual cycle of the harvest. The Hindu pilgrimage was a huge gathering with some of the tumultuous aspects of a fair. In Western Christendom, it is astonishing to discover the persistent and almost orchestrated zeal with which many bishops in the late seventeenth and throughout the eighteenth century attempted to prohibit pilgrimages to sites in their dioceses, many of which had drawn large numbers of visitors. The reason repeatedly given for such actions was that "abuses" were too often committed at such places. What this chaste and obscure word concealed, what modern bishops ever-more ethically exigent and intent on purging the sacred of all contamination by the profane denounced, were the temptations and excesses of the night, temptations and excesses only too likely to mar pilgrimages that lasted, like the present-day Spanish *romerias*, for two days, with pilgrims spending the night either within the sanctuary or in the surrounding countryside. It was the Counterreformation lashing out at the centuries-old complexity of pilgrim society, whose roots stretched all the way back to the agricultural monastic culture of the early Middle Ages.

In those remote centuries, pilgrimages brought impressive numbers of people together. In fact, they expressed three kinds of practices at once, together defining an "extraordinary" expanse of time: a sacred rite, a festival in the most physical sense (that is, a popular celebration) and a fair. This combination of features was an ancient tradition, an intrinsic part of the act of pilgrimage over the *longue durée,* and it persists or at any rate is attested even today, if only in the imbalance that has slowly disrupted the organic harmony of the triad. Take, for example, the fair of Saint Ursus at Aosta, soon to be a thousand years old, which takes up the entire first week of February. It is closely associated with the saint's pilgrimage, Ursus being the patron of the collegiate church of Aosta and protector of the Val d'Aosta. The ancient fair of Saint-Michel d'Ousse-Suzan in the Gascon Landes perpetuates a cult of the archangel at an isolated sacred site in the middle of a forest, consisting of a chapel and three fountains of diverse healing virtues. Or in Auvergne, outside the walls of Besse-en-Chandesse, the fair of Saint Matthew, which takes place on the very same day when, in a climate of generalized sacrality and exuberant secular celebration, the Black Virgin of Vassivière comes down with the flocks from her high temple at Sancy to spend the winter in the small town's collegiate church. From these examples the complexity of the pilgrimage phenomenon should be obvious. For those who participated, it was an avid, insistent search for total festive celebration. The fundamental impulse driving pilgrim society was a festive drive to celebrate. The festive abounded in grace: in the underlying hope for a better state whether of body or soul, in the awesome discovery of the sacred, in the replenishment of vital forces this made possible, in the revelation of something "hidden" in oneself, and in the recognition of a supernatural presence somehow made palpable and, thus, yielding something like physical certainty of an "other world," hence of latent immortality.

Yet this religious reading, in the usual and linear sense of the term, obviously does not cover the whole phenomenon. Beyond the more or less personal experience of an enlightened devotion, the mass of pilgrims—and this is a constant psychological feature of popular religion—had a hard time distinguishing between the sacred and the profane and even habitually confounded the two. The more liberated in the profane sense, the more charged with sacredness they became. In contrast to the pilgrim's ordinary experience, of a time overburdened with work and woe, here was an opportunity for truly extraordinary experience, an opportunity to live virtually all together in a time that was nothing less than solemn. Such a day was truly festive because all needs could be satisfied at once, the characteristic of the festival being precisely that of being different from all other days. So in Western Europe in times past, when the liturgical calendar still enjoyed some priority over the civil calendar, the day of pilgrimage was a joyful day on which no one was required to work. Thus, the tripartite combination of pilgrimage, profane festival, and fair—elements among which pilgrim society in the West gradually, over a period of centuries, established an equilibrium—clearly tells us a great deal about the existential need for acts of pilgrimage. With moving simplicity the pilgrimage supplied all wants: its rituals took care of that holy experience of the hereafter which the pilgrims came looking for in the first place, and it left its mark on subsequent daily life; repressed or disruptive instincts could be unleashed in a vital debauch that might reach the point of physical exhaustion or intoxication yet be concluded in a single day, like a saturnalia or festival of fools; and meanwhile, life's material needs could be attended to in the exalting, dangerously euphoric climate of the fair, in what was at once an expression of unchained power and a crushing proof of weakness. Thus, in a single time and place the pilgrim, who in everyday life was compartmentalized, "trichotomized," and forced inward, found the freedom to explore his unity and discover within himself powers of "otherness." This type of pattern, obviously, was much less apparent in the major pilgrimages, which in the West at least were strictly regimented by the ecclesiastical authorities, yet the "merchants of the temple," a necessity of pilgrimage, were always present, numerous if not invariably prosperous, and in the undifferentiated society of pilgrim fervor many customary taboos were of course weakened. In any case, it is characteristic of a society panic-striken, which a mass society in movement invariably is to some degree, to strive, in an effort of self-transcendence that may reach the point of self-annihilation, to experience all things at once, in an existential plenitude. Pilgrimage society was, as I have said, ephemeral, but it was also a successful quest for fulfillment in joy, which left its mark in the depths of every pilgrim's being.

If pilgrim society was unified in its undifferentiated mass, what organic reality did it possess? Our classifications quickly reveal themselves to be treacherous, for it was not specifically ecclesiastical, nor was it secular. It is enough to observe its life. It could subject itself to the orders, guidance, and practices of a church or inscribe itself within an ecclesial institution as a form of religious existence. Yet across many different cultures and religions, it clearly maintained its independence of such institutions, which it could do without. The forces, irrational and terrifying, that drove the pilgrim could only be disciplined, eroded, weakened, or rationalized by institutions that in themselves were routine, organically established, confident of their supernatural investiture, and in control of the liturgy. In Western Christendom, the liturgical calendar regulated and controlled the pilgrim drive but with revealing compensations. Discreet but incontrovertible evidence for this can be seen in the quantitatively obvious fact that, in the old Christian regions of the West, the oldest pilgrimages, those reputed by oral tradition to be "immemorial," were those that occurred on the day after the major religious feast days, when pilgrims from a parish or city and often from the surrounding countryside would gather at some open-air sanctuary. The Monday after

Easter or Pentecost (and, in some cases, another day or two as well, as in the *grand' Pâque* of the Morvan) was an occasion, with the solemn intensity of the holy day now subsided, for a sort of explosion to take place in the fields in a climate of free communion with nature. The community, in some cases still adhering to the discipline of ritual, could frolic in search of the cosmic while perpetuating, if only subconsciously, age-old traditions, some of which antedated Christianity itself. The holiness of the cosmos, which the church liturgy translated into symbolic terms and internalized, was made tangible as well by pilgrimage rituals that were centered either on relics preserved inside churches or on holy fountains at some distance away. When it came to choosing between relics, churchly, institutional objects, and fountains, natural holy places at which healing waters sprang from the earth, the verdict was clear: most pilgrims preferred the fountain.

While institutions may have regulated or more often inspired pilgrimages, all signs are that they were not in control of pilgrimage society. They often pretended to ignore what they could not control, namely, the essence of the pilgrim's needs. The Church channeled the pilgrim's yearning, but that yearning was not an intrinsic, organic part of the Church, even if the Church knew itself to be a pilgrim to the end of its earthly existence. The need of the masses had a different source, however. Witness the sheer number of pilgrimage cults that grew out of spontaneous popular demand, which was responsible for the canonizations that created cults around saintly remains in both the Christian West and the Muslim world. Or the striking fact that in modern times, right up to the present, both "inventions" and apparitions of the Virgin out of which cults arose have been the privilege of humble people, of simple folk living in natural surroundings and, increasingly often, adolescents and even children. Such involuntary appropriation tells us where the need burns hidden. In Europe today, moreover, there are pilgrimage sites not recognized by the Church, some of which have been drawing crowds of the faithful for years. The legends that generally arise to "naturalize" the shock of an apparition or discovery, legends that are usually polished up by the clergy, nevertheless bear the vigorous imprint of the collective popular imagination, which will accept no substitutes when it comes to the particular grace bestowed or message delivered.

In the West, therefore, there is a clear difference between the Church and pilgrimage society, a difference that tells us a great deal about the authentic nature of the latter. The Church is, of course, an institution with a stable order, a mastery of time, and a more or less ethically oriented soteriology, whereas pilgrimage society is driven by a sacral need that seeks satisfaction and possession, even a moment of pure white heat generated by the kind of violence that bestows consecration. In pilgrimage society, the social group attempts, alone if need be, to achieve what it calls its salvation—that is, it attempts to test its strength so as to achieve, with sacred help, omnipotence. In the terms of anthropological phenomenology, the essence of a pilgrimage society is its dynamic power. The product of a complex collective drive, of the irresistible appeal of an "elsewhere" and an anxious quest for the "other," such a society is a manifestation and therefore a source of collective energy. The group gathers strength until a cure is achieved in one or another of its members—until, above all, the ephemeral pilgrimage attests to what lurks in the depths of the social body from which the group has momentarily detached itself, a drive for biological fulfillment in bodily unison and cosmic communion with the whole created world, a deliverance enabling man to see through to the other side of things and of himself. What churches and institutions temporalize on the scale of eternity and yet dissolve in the routine of works and days, pilgrimage society experiences in an instant of eternity. It is neither ecclesiastical nor secular but organically sacral.

TRANSLATED BY ARTHUR GOLDHAMMER

PIERRE CHAUNU

Long-Term Factors in Seventeenth-Century Society and Civilization: Demographics

1975

Pierre Chaunu (b. 1923) is probably the most prolific of contemporary French historians, the author of hundreds of articles and more than fifty books. An indefatigable worker and prodigious writer as well as the leader of numerous groups, he has tried his hand at every genre from the economic and social history of Europe and the Americas, where he followed in the footsteps of his one true teacher, Fernand Braudel, with his thesis (Séville et l'Atlantique, 1504–1650, published in twelve volumes between 1956 and 1960), to religious history and the history of mentalités *(Le Temps des réformes, [1975]; La Mort à Paris, [1977]) as well as demographic history, not to mention his tireless activity as a militant on the religious, moral, and political fronts.*

Surely, no one has read all of Chaunu. Yet anyone who has read him will recognize the hallmarks of his style: lyrical flights, scientific enthusiasms, vast empirical knowledge coupled with sometimes peremptory and often repetitive generalizations, a liking for large-scale models, adventurous comparisons, and what he calls "global assessment," not always encumbered with subtlety. Chaunu exemplifies practically every tendency in French historiography, but he does so in his own inimitable and probably unrepeatable way. His work and his style refuse to be ignored: the impetuous author, a ubiquitous presence on the French academic scene, would in any case not allow them to be. Some find him irritating, but it is hard not to acknowledge his energy and generosity and just as hard to remain indifferent to the

Pierre Chaunu, "Les Eléments de longue durée dans la société et la civilisation du XVIIe siècle: La démographie" in *Histoire quantitative, histoire sérielle*, Cahier des Annales (Paris: Armand Colin, 1978), pp. 87–92.

work. Here is a sample of the Chaunu style. It is an essay on the Western demographic model, which has played an important role in the author's populationist activism over the past twenty years.

Things took a different direction after J. Hajnal's article and the change in outlook of the Cambridge group.[1] The essence of the matter escaped our notice because on this point the standard but now-outdated demographic theory of the mid-twentieth century was basically identical with this supposedly old-fashioned view, despite the artificial contrast that was set up between the two. And that essence was, of course, a very distinctive marital structure.

The universal model of pubescent marriage at a definite time and place was now challenged by a new structure.[2] Late marriage became the keystone, or more precisely the *sign* of a new system of civilization. By now, Hajnal's case is well accepted, and there is no need to dwell on its details. In several recent works, I have simply tried to systematize, formalize, and explore in depth a theory for which the English demographic historian deserves full credit.

At the very heart of the history of Western Christendom, the demographic system of the seventeenth century, which is identical with the system of previous and subsequent centuries, is a product of culture, not nature: as Lévi-Strauss observes, nature *was* culture in human society well before the Neolithic period. No other system controlled sexual drives more completely or as successfully. A whole array of institutional controls had been long in the making: we glimpse an early transitional state in England, thanks to documents stemming from the poll tax of 1377, a gift of England's ancient tax system, and elsewhere—for example, on the periphery of Europe, in Castilian parish registers as early as the second half of the sixteenth century. As a consequence of this system, anywhere from 30 to, ultimately, 50 percent of women of procreative age were held in reserve, on the sidelines as it were. Various factors contributed to this result. First, females tended to marry later, as much as ten to twelve years after the onset of puberty. Demographers speak of an "adolescent sterility" affecting girls between fourteen or fifteen and seventeen or eighteen years of age, a period during which the fertility rate is relatively low compared with the period from ages 18 to 25 when fertility is maximum. In fact, average female fertility reaches a peak between ages 18 and 20–21, after which it decreases very slowly from 21 to 30, then more rapidly from 30 to 37–38, dropping sharply at 40 and tending toward zero just before menopause, which generally occurs between 48 and 50, perhaps slightly earlier under the harsh conditions of traditional peasant society. Delayed marriage must be understood in relation to another factor, sexual continence, which was observed by 80–90 percent of the unmarried female population. Extramarital sexual relations were infrequent enough to have little social impact. The work of our English and American colleagues, conveniently summarized in a recent article by Edward Shorter, shows that there was probably more variety in this respect than the relative homogeneity of the seventeenth-century French case would suggest.[3] I hasten to add that the variations stem from two sets of factors. One set, of relatively minor importance, can be gathered under the head of "archaic behaviors," in which dominant males exerted sexual pressure on the females of the dominated classes. The second, apparently more important set of factors has to do with a variant form of marriage observed in certain northern regions (several English counties, nearly all of Wales, as well as various places in Friesland and Baltic Germany). In these areas, marriages took place in two stages. In the first stage, called "engagement," the young couple was permitted to have sexual relations in the home of either set of parents; only when the young woman became pregnant did things progress to the second stage of marriage proper, which called for setting up an independent household. This was a less dramatic, possibly more gradual, and certainly archaic conception of constituting a household. If the word "engagement" is substituted for "marriage," these special cases can be fitted into the general model without too much difficulty. Sexual continence and chastity outside not just marriage but also engagement as well were the norm in these regions as elsewhere.

Spinsterhood was a second factor. This eminently aristocratic and, later, urban phenomenon was still relatively rare in the seventeenth century, but it spread—at first fairly slowly in the eighteenth century and then more rapidly in the nineteenth. Though not very common among the lower or peasant classes (on the order of 5–7 percent), spinsterhood was proportionately, and paradoxically, more widespread in seventeenth-century rural France than in the British India of the late nineteenth and early twentieth centuries, as reported in the first reliable censuses (that is, after 1871).

A third factor was the failure of widows to remarry immediately after the husband's death. The time elapsed between death and remarriage was typically short when the widow was either young and unencumbered by children or close to (or past) menopause; but it was quite long (on average, three years minimum) if the widow was between twenty-seven and forty years of age.

Together, these three factors sidelined up to 50 percent of the potentially fertile women of Western Latin Christendom in the seventeenth century.

However, delayed marriage, a reaction to massive socialization in sexual asceticism, was only one element of a more complex structure, a veritable system of civilization that endured for at least five hundred years.

The origin of that system of civilization can be dated with precision: it gradually established itself in the period between 1100 and 1350. (In 1377, England with its poll tax and average female age at marriage of 20.5–21, was already in flagrant transition and closer to the France of Louis XIV than to the India of Mrs. Gandhi. It encompassed England in the narrow sense, the Netherlands, France, the Lotharingian corridor, a narrow strip of western Germany, the western Alpine regions, the Po Valley, Tuscany, and perhaps a bit of northern Catalonia. Roughly 1–1.5 million square kilometers of densely packed territory, in which for the first time in the history of the world people lived in a territory stripped of 80 percent of its natural vegetation, at densities of 35–40 inhabitants per square kilometer, even as high as 60–80 per square kilometer in places like Picardy (studied by Robert Fossier), Flanders, and the central Po Valley. Never had people lived so close together: in a world of steeples, towns were so close that if a person climbed a church belltower in one, he could see seven or eight others on the horizon. Before long, as bells took over and their language was fixed, it was possible for news to travel at the speed of sound through the damp air of the north, where bells have a prettier, clearer, louder, more musical sound than in the south. Delayed marriage was just one aspect—the most visible if not necessarily the most important—of a whole structure. It coincided with a first step toward the dismantling of lineage structures. Even if, as Peter Laslett has shown, the nuclear family is older and more widespread than is often said, it is nevertheless the case that a system in which lineages and nuclei, stem families and nuclear families, coexisted was replaced by one in which nuclear families increasingly predominated.[4] Following Laslett and his students, I have tried to investigate the extent and significance of this transformation.[5]

The decline of the lineage was a necessary condition for other structures to progress, namely, the circle of communal sociability, that of the modern state. Furthermore, as I have shown, the decline of the lineage coupled with a lengthening of the interval between generations was a necessary condition for increased investment in education.[6] Delayed marriage, which depended on broad inculcation of ascetic attitudes toward sexuality, had an influence on the religious climate of the Reformation and Counterreformation.[7] In short, between the twelfth and fourteenth centuries, a new system of civilization slowly emerged in response to the challenges of a fully populated world. This system was not a consequence of mechanical population processes, although such processes were surely the force driving the transformation. Small farms were a consequence of the reclamation of marginal land. Population growth and overcrowding imposed the small farm model, which became the material basis of the nuclear family (which was not only an emotional unit but also, as Gouesse[8] and Laslett[9] have shown, an economic unit). In some ways, delayed marriage was a consequence of overpopulation. In a society in which households coincided with economic units, a place had to be freed up by death before a new household could be founded. Contradicting long-held views, Gouesse found a positive correlation between death and marriage (except in unusual crisis periods, such as in 1693 or 1709).[10] Applications for marriage dispensations reveal a link between deaths of near kin and requests to marry. "My mother has died," one petitioner wrote to the bishop of Coutances by way of his parish priest, "and there is no one to prepare my soup." Marriage dispensations reveal the psychoeconomic mechanisms underlying delayed marriage in an overpopulated world.

It would be a mistake, however, to end the analysis here. I had occasion to show that the response to the challenge took a specific form, which Western Christendom elaborated by drawing upon the values of an earlier system of civilization.[11]

The demographic system that developed in the heart of old Latin Christendom after the fourteenth centry was too rigorous, too deeply rooted, and too logical to have receded before the warning shot of the great plagues. We know that over a long period, from 1300 to 1740, the population of France oscillated between a ceiling of twenty million and a floor of nine million (it was 17 million in 1300, fell to 9 million in 1420, and rose to 19–20 million in 1650 and again in 1700). Most of the time it was closer to the ceiling than to the floor, as Emmanuel Le Roy Ladurie has recently reminded us. This observation holds true for the whole of Latin Christendom. With sufficient distance, one can see that the demographic system that established itself around 1300 tended to attenuate fluctuations. Even the great oscillation of the fourteenth and fifteenth centuries pales into insignificance in comparison with the population fluctuations observed in the Mediterranean basin in late antiquity or in China or among Amerindian peoples.

After five centuries of remaining close to its ceiling, however, the population of Europe began to grow once again, owing to improvements in the quality of life. Between 1750 and 1800 or 1850, population levels began to rise all across the continent, breaking through the old ceiling and helping to bring about the conditions for a major technological mutation, which ultimately destroyed the all too well known Malthusian system of checks and balances.

What we see is nothing less than the emergence of a unique new system, the groundwork for which was laid in the laboratory of Western

Latin Christendom at the peak and tail end of a great semimillennial wave of (re)population. The change began between the seventh and fourteenth centuries, especially in the period spanning 1100 and 1350. Between 1500 and 1700 it was gradually extended to the periphery of Europe (the revolution of delayed marriage came to Spain and eastern Germany, for example, two centuries late). A semimillennial wave runs from 1300 to 1800 or 1850 in the center, from 1500 to 1900 on the periphery. Through a series of relatively minor transformations, it gave rise to the demographic system of industrial Europe, which from 1880 on began to influence other cultures and civilizations not directly descended from western Latin Christianity.

We can now study the demographic reality of the seventeenth century with the aid of a surprising number of excellent monographs (based on peasant genealogies), together with studies based on urban and tax data.[12] When we do so, it becomes clear that there is nothing distinctive about the seventeenth century that is not also true of European demographics over a much longer period, including several centuries before the seventeenth and at least a century after: delayed marriage, attenuated sensitivity to a roughly thirty-year fluctuation, seasonal patterns of birth, marriage and death, ecological, meteorological, and cultural compromises, extraordinary control of the sexual drive, and a marked tendency for the population to remain stable or decline slightly over time. All these features are characteristic not only of the seventeenth century but of the longer period as well.

Virtually none of these characteristics can be ascribed to anything peculiar to the seventeenth century—a few minor features at most. Old cultural features were fading; seasonal sexual abstinences were on the way out. Sexual asceticism increasingly affected the whole society, not just certain age groups. Of course, we know little about abstinence during Lent and Advent. People did not marry during these two seasons of the year, during which sexual relations had traditionally been if not forbidden at least strongly discouraged. Thus, everything depended on the delay of marriage and the control of sexual drives outside marriage. Conjugal behavior remained beyond control. This dichotomy would facilitate the introduction of Malthusian practices. Contraception through withdrawal was promoted in the eighteenth and nineteenth centuries. Toward the end of the seventeenth century, attempts to reintroduce seasonal abstinences (during May) appear to have failed, although we know little about them. In short, a long period of postpubescent abstinence became the chief means of controlling birth for much of the population.

A second key feature of the system was the effectiveness of controls on extramarital sexual activity. Maximum effectiveness appears to have been achieved in France at the end of the seventeenth century and, to a lesser extent, in England. This was the height of a period of reform. Forms of sexual subordination still viable in the sixteenth century (see Gilles de Gouberville's *Journal*) were on the wane. Controls began to break down in the second half of the eighteenth and early nineteenth century, however, leading to a sharp rise in illegitimacy, as Shorter has pointed out. Note, moreover, that in areas of France where asceticism of an Augustinian stripe was practiced, the extreme culpabilization of even legitimate sexual relations probably encouraged the practice of coitus interruptus as early as the late seventeenth or early eighteenth century. The same phenomenon is found in England, but without the same effects, in well-to-do milieus between 1670 and 1730.

A third feature has to do with the overall importance of factors tending to slow population growth. The periphery of Europe, setting aside an area of traditionally dense population including eastern Germany, Russia, and to a lesser extent Poland but including northern Italy and Spain, experienced its last major population downturn. The decline in the population of the empire between 1620 and 1650 was as deep and as rapid as that of France between 1320 and 1420. In France, negative populations swings of up to two million were not unknown, as the number of deaths exceeded the number of births.

Two factors contributed to this. First, the peripheral population reached and even passed its fourteenth-century ceiling. Second were the negative effects of the first phase of building bellicose nation-states with powerful fiscal systems and bureaucratic administrations. According to my calculations, the state doubled what it took from each inhabitant of France between 1620 and 1650.[13] From the time that the fiscal system was introduced in France, the level of taxation changed sharply only twice, in the fourteenth century under Louis XI and in the seventeenth century under Richelieu and Mazarin. Apart from those two periods, the inflation-corrected curves of per capita taxation are virtually horizontal. The germ-carrying armies of the early seventeenth century were eminently lethal, as Le Roy Ladurie has shown.[14] I fully subscribe to his analysis. The generally flat population curves for the seventeenth century (with their modest recurrences of periods of excess deaths), as well as the declining life expectancy in England, were perhaps the price to be paid for the abrupt intensification of international communication and the sharp increase in state exactions benefiting the upper echelons of the technostructure.

The years 1693 and 1709 witnessed the last of what scholars generally refer to as the economic or economic-demographic crises of the Ancien Régime: a lethal drop in production with no possibility of compensation over a vast period, positively correlated with prices and mortality and negatively correlated with conceptions and marriages. Crises of this type were by then exceptional and archaic. They were the result of negative climatic anomalies at the end of the century and of clashes between young Moloch states, before warfare was tempered and before enlightened, life-saving bureaucracies began to achieve positive results in the eighteenth century. In the face of all the challenges, the system allowed for an infinite number of combinations, which, in the context of what I call "molecules" of demographic behavior, range from a net coefficient of reproduction of 0.7 to a coefficient determined by the highest possible indices of impediments to growth: late marriage, lengthy lapses of time before remarriage, and a tendency toward spinsterhood. Broadly speaking, the second half of the seventeenth century combined a slightly archaic rise in mortality with maximum inhibition of births through marital practices. There was, in other words, a massive recourse to "ascetic Malthusianism" coupled with a much lesser degree of "hedonistic Malthusianism."

TRANSLATED BY ARTHUR GOLDHAMMER

NOTES

[1] J. Hajnal, "European Marriage Patterns in Perspective," in D. V. Glass and D. E. C. Eversley, *Population in History* (London, 1965), pp. 101–43.

[2] Pierre Chaunu, *La Civilisation de l'Europe des lumières* and especially *L'Histoire, science sociale*, pt. 3: *L'Homme* and *De l'Histoire à la prospective* (Paris: Robert Laffont, 1975), p. 148.

[3] Edward Shorter, "Female Emancipation, Birth Control, and Fertility in European History," *American Historical Review* 78.3 (June 1973), pp. 606–40.

[4] See the important collection of papers edited by Peter Laslett, *Household and Family in Past Time* (Cambridge, Eng.: Cambridge University Press, 1972).

[5] P. Chaunu, *Histoire, science sociale.*

[6] P. Chaunu, *Civilisation de l'Europe des lumières.*

[7] P. Chaunu, *Le Temps des réformes: L'éclatement* (Paris: Fayard, 1975).

[8] J.-M. Gouesse, thesis in progress under my direction on the formation of the couple in the West.

[9] Peter Laslett, *The World We Have Lost.*

[10] J-M. Gouesse, op. cit.

[11] Chaunu, *Histoire, science sociale* and *Le Temps des réformes.*

[12] Jacques Dupâquier, *La Population rurale du Bassin parisien, à l'époque de Louis XIV* (Paris, 1979).

[13] P. Chaunu, *Histoire économique et sociale de la France,* vol. 1 (Paris: P.U.F., 1977).

[14] Emmanuel Le Roy Ladurie, *Leçon inaugurale au Collège de France,* Nov. 30, 1973.

PART II

The Structuralist Moment (Mid-1960s to Mid-1970s)

The Major Positions

CLAUDE LÉVI-STRAUSS

Scientific Criteria in the Social and Human Disciplines

1964

If any one individual can be credited with founding the movement known as "structuralism," it is the anthropologist Claude Lévi-Strauss (b. 1908). Elaborated in his pathbreaking work Structures élémentaires de la parenté *(*The Elementary Structures of Kinship*), his structuralist anthropology rested on field research among Indian tribes of Brazil, but his models of analysis derived from European and especially eastern European studies of linguistics, particularly the phonology of Roman Jakobson. Lévi-Strauss aimed to uncover the unconscious, collective rules of social behavior, especially the rules governing kinship relations. He would later apply his approach to myths (*Mythologiques*, 4 vols., 1966–1973). He believed that these relations could be mapped on a rigorously formalized grid, just as languages could be precisely compared in terms of their grammar and syntax. He spent the years during World War II in the United States, and eventually held the chair of social anthropology at the Collège de France. In this excerpt, Lévi-Strauss explains his idea of the relationship between the natural sciences and the human or social sciences. In his view, ethnography is much more scientific than history because it is able to develop stable and rigorous models like those of the exact sciences. In other words, he worked from a hard or pure model of science, one that might be qualified as "scientistic." Lévi-Strauss's structuralist emphasis on formal models soon influenced almost every field of scholarship, from the social sciences to history and even literature.*

Claude Lévi-Strauss, "Critères scientifiques dans les disciplines sociales et humaines," *Revue internationale des sciences sociales* 16 (1964), pp. 579–97.

The author of this article has devoted his entire life to the practice of the social and human sciences. Yet he feels no embarrassment in acknowledging that it is impossible to pretend that any real parity exists between those disciplines and the exact and natural sciences; that the latter are sciences while the former are not; and that if the same term is nevertheless applied to both, it is by virtue of a semantic fiction and a philosophical hope still in want of confirmation.

Let us begin, then, by trying to give a precise definition of the difference in principle involved in the use of the word "science" in the two cases. No one doubts that the exact and natural sciences are indeed sciences, yet not everything done in their name is of equal quality: there are great scientists and there are mediocre ones. Still, the common connotations of all the activities that take place under the cover of the exact and natural sciences are beyond doubt. To borrow the language of logicians, one might say that in the case of the exact and natural sciences the definition "in extension" coincides with the definition "in comprehension": the characteristics in virtue of which a science deserves that name also apply, broadly speaking, to the various concrete activities whose inventory corresponds empirically to the domain of the exact and natural sciences.

If we now turn our attention to the social and human sciences, however, we find that the definitions *in extension* and *in comprehension* no longer coincide. The term "science" is merely a fictive designation applied to a range of unrelated activities, only a small number of which can claim to be scientific in character (assuming that one is willing to define the notion of science in a similar way). In fact, many specialists in the fields of research arbitrarily classified as social and human sciences would be the first to repudiate any claim that their work is scientific, at least in the sense and spirit in which their colleagues in the exact and natural sciences use the term. Various dubious distinctions, such as Pascal's between the *esprit de finesse* and the *esprit de géométrie,* have long been used to argue this case. [. . .]

One thing is absolutely clear: Among the social and human sciences, only linguistics can be placed on a footing of equality with the exact and natural sciences. There are three reasons for this: it possesses a universal object, namely, articulated language, which is found in all human groups; its method is homogeneous, that is, it remains the same no matter what language it is applied to, modern or archaic, "primitive" or civilized; and that method is based on certain fundamental principles accepted as valid by all specialists (despite differences over secondary issues).

No other social or human science fully satisfies these conditions. Take the three disciplines whose ability to discovery necessary relations among phenomena puts them closest to linguistics: the object of economic science is not universal but narrowly circumscribed to a small portion of human development; demography's method is not homogeneous, apart from the special case of large numbers; and ethnologists are a long way from achieving the kind of unanimity as to principles now taken for granted in linguistics.

In my view, therefore, only linguistics is directly suitable to the kind of investigation that UNESCO is proposing. One might add certain "advanced" areas of research in fields usually classified as belonging to the social and human sciences, using methods that are obviously derived from the method of linguistics.

What about the rest? The most reasonable method, I think, would be to conduct a preliminary survey of specialists in all disciplines, putting this basic question: Do you or do you not believe that all or some of the results obtained in your discipline meet the same standards of validity as those applied in the exact and natural sciences? If so, please enumerate those results.

Presumably one would obtain a list of questions and problems alleged to exhibit a certain "measure of comparability" relative to some general understanding of scientific method. The items on this list would be quite disparate, however, and I suspect that there would be two observations that one would want to make about them.

First, the points of contact between the social and human sciences, on the one hand, and the exact and natural sciences, on the other, would not always occur in the disciplines that one might expect. In some cases, the most "literary" of the human sciences would turn out to be the most advanced. For example, some very traditional branches of the classical humanities such as rhetoric, poetics, and stylistics are already able to use mechanical and statistical models to treat certain problems with methods derived from algebra. Through the use of electronic calculators, stylistics and textual criticism are on the way to achieving the status of exact sciences. In the pursuit of scientific rigor, many "outsiders" have already established their claims, and it would be quite wrong to believe that the so-called social sciences start out with an advantage over certain of the sciences simply called "human."

The study of these apparent anomalies would be extremely instructive. It will be found, in fact, that the disciplines coming closest to a scientific ideal are those most successful in limiting themselves to the consideration of a readily isolable object with well-defined outlines, one whose various states, as revealed by observation, can be analyzed in terms of a relatively small number of variables. In the sciences of man, the number of variables is probably always greater than is generally the case in the physical sciences. Hence, the comparison should be carried out at a level where the gap is not so apparent, for example, between the physical sciences in which the number of variables is greatest and the human sciences in which the number of variables is smallest. The fact that the former are obliged to work with small-scale models (as in aerodynamics, where models are used in wind tunnels) may shed light on the need to use models in the human sciences, as well as yield a fuller appreciation of the fertility of so-called structuralist methods. Such methods have the effect of systematically reducing the number of variables by treating the object under analysis as a closed system and by dealing at any one time only with variables of a given type (possibly repeating the analysis at several different levels).

Second, the diversity of the list of scientific results may come as a surprise. It will also be far too long, for those asked to respond to the survey have every reason to be indulgent. I except those specialists who may decline to participate on the grounds that their research partakes more of art than of science or that it reflects a type of science fundamentally different from that embodied in the exact and natural sciences. [. . .]

TRANSLATED BY ARTHUR GOLDHAMMER

LOUIS ALTHUSSER

Reply to John Lewis

1972

Louis Althusser (1918–1990) is considered to have been one of the founding fathers, along with Claude Lévi-Strauss, of the structuralist movement in France. After spending World War II in a German prison camp, Althusser became professor of philosophy at the Ecole Normale Supérieure in Paris and a prominent member of the French communist party. Althusser proposed a structuralist reading of Marx that he himself characterized as "antihumanist." For Althusser, history—above all, the history of class struggle—was a process without a subject and the product of interacting structural relations. On the basis of this interpretation, he also proposed looking at Marxism as a purely scientific instrument, on the grounds that it had allegedly achieved an "epistemological break" separating it from ideology. This scientism also made Althusserism consonant with the structuralist agenda. In his For Marx *(1965) and* Reading Capital *(1965), Althusser reinterpreted the writings of Marx to emphasize their scientific and structuralist claims. In fact, his views generated controversy within Marxist circles all over the world and helped to shape the intellectual interests of the generation of '68. These positions are summarized in the following reply, first published in 1972, to the English Marxist critic John Lewis. Althusser argues that the chief motors of history are broad structures and processes (such as class struggle), not individual actions. His insistence on analyzing society as a structured system of social relations, rather than as an aggregate of individuals, further aligned him with the general structuralist impulse in intellectual life.*

I

I want to thank *Marxism Today* for having published John Lewis's article about the books I have written on Marxist philosophy: *For Marx* and

From Louis Althusser, *Essays on Ideology* (London: Verso, 1984), pp. 76–86. First published in *Marxism Today* 16 (Oct.–Nov. 1972), pp. 310–18, 343–49.

Reading Capital, which appeared in France in 1965. He took care to treat me in a special way, in the way a medical specialist treats a patient. The whole family, as it were, together with his silent colleagues, stood motionless at the bedside, while Dr. John Lewis leaned over to examine "the Althusser case."[1] A long wait. Then he made his diagnosis: the patient is suffering from an attack of severe "dogmatism"—a "mediae-val" variety. The prognosis is grave: The patient cannot last long.

It is an honor for this attention to be paid to me, but it is also an opportunity for me to clear up certain matters, twelve years after the event. My first article, reprinted in *For Marx,* which was concerned with the question of the "young Marx," actually appeared in 1960, and I am writing in 1972.

A good deal of water has flowed under the bridge of history since 1960. The Workers' Movement has lived through many important events: the heroic and victorious resistance of the struggle, whether it is helped or hindered by them. It is here that petty-bourgeois *liberty* meets *necessity.*

John Lewis now, in 1972, takes up the old arguments in his turn, in the theoretical journal of the British communist party. He can, if I may say so, rest assured: he is not "crying in the wilderness!" He is not the only person to take up this theme. He is in the company of many commu-nists—everyone knows that. But why should it be that since the 1960s many communists have been resurrecting this worn-out philosophy of petty-bourgeois liberty, while still claiming to be *Marxists?*

We shall see. [. . .]

IV

First, I shall follow the procedure used by John Lewis. I shall compare his "Marxist" Theses with the Theses of Marxist-Leninist philosophy. And everyone will be able to compare and judge for himself.

I will go over the points in John Lewis's order. That way things will be clearer. I am making an enormous concession to him by taking his order, because his order is idealist. But we will do him the favor.

To understand what follows, note that in the case of each Thesis (1, 2, 3) I begin by repeating Lewis's Thesis and then state the Marxist-Lenin-ist Thesis. [. . .]

THESIS NO. 2

John Lewis: "Man makes history by 'transcending' history." Marxism-Leninism: "The class struggle is the motor of history" (Thesis of *The Communist Manifesto,* 1847).

Here things become extremely interesting. Because Marxism-Leninism blows up John Lewis's whole philosophical system. How?

John Lewis said it is man who makes history, to which Marxism-Leninism replied it is *the masses*.

But if we said no more, if we went no further, we would give the impression that Marxism-Leninism gives a *different* reply to the *same* question. That question being: *Who makes history?* This question therefore supposes that history is the result of the action of (what is done by) a *subject* (who)? For John Lewis, the subject is "man." Does Marxism-Leninism propose a *different subject*, the masses?

Yes and no. When we started to sketch out a definition of the masses, when we talked about this idea of the masses, we saw that the whole thing was rather complicated. The masses are actually *several* social classes, social strata and social categories, grouped *together* in a way that is both complex and *changing* (the positions of the different classes and strata, and of the fractions of classes within classes, *change* in the course of the revolutionary process itself). And we are dealing with huge numbers—in France or Britain, for example, with tens of millions of people, in China with hundreds of millions! Let us do no more here than ask the simple question: Can we still talk about a "subject," identifiable by the *unity* of its "personality?" Compared with John Lewis's subject, "man," as simple and neat as you can imagine, the masses, considered as a subject, pose very exacting problems of identity and identification. You cannot hold such a "subject" in your hand, you cannot point to it. A subject is a being about which we can say, "That's it!" How do we do that when the masses are supposed to be the "subject"; how can we say, "That's it?"

It is precisely the Thesis of *The Communist Manifesto*—"the class struggle is the motor of history"—that *displaces the question*, that brings the problem into the open, that shows us how to pose it properly and therefore how to solve it. It is the masses that "make" history, but "it is the class struggle that is the motor of history." To John Lewis's question "how does man make history?" Marxism-Leninism replies by replacing his idealist philosophical categories with categories of a quite different kind.

The question is no longer posed in terms of "man." That much we know. But in the proposition that "the class struggle is the motor of history," the question of "making" history is also eliminated. It is no longer a question of *who* makes history.

Marxism-Leninism tells us something quite different—that it is the *class struggle* (new concept) that is the *motor* (new concept) of history, it is the class struggle that moves history, that advances it—and brings about revolutions. This Thesis is of very great importance, because *it puts the class struggle in the front rank*.

In the preceding Thesis "it is the masses that make history," the accent was put on the exploited classes grouped around the class capable of uniting them, and on their power to carry through a revolutionary transformation of history. It was, therefore, the masses that were put in the front rank.

In the Thesis taken from *The Communist Manifesto*, what is put in the front rank is no longer the exploited classes and so on but the class struggle. This Thesis must be recognized as decisive for Marxism-Leninism. It draws a radical demarcation line between revolutionaries and reformists. Here I have to simplify things very much, but I do not think that I am betraying the essential point.

For *reformists* (even if they call themselves "Marxists") it is not the class struggle that is in the front rank, it is simply the classes. Let us take a simple example, and suppose that we are dealing with just two classes. For reformists these classes exist *before* the class struggle, a bit like two football teams exist, separately, before the match. Each class exists in its own camp, lives according to its particular conditions of existence. One class may be exploiting another, but for reformism that is not the same thing as class struggle. One day, the two classes come up against one another and come into conflict. It is only then that the class struggle begins. They begin a hand-to-hand battle, the battle becomes acute, and finally the exploited class defeats its enemy (that is revolution), or loses (that is counterrevolution). However you turn the thing around, you will always find the same idea here—the classes exist *before* the class struggle, *independently* of the class struggle. The class struggle exists only *afterward*.[2]

Revolutionaries, on the other hand, consider it impossible to separate the classes from class struggle. The class struggle and the existence of classes are one and the same thing. In order for there to be classes in a "society," the society has to be *divided* into classes. This division does not come *later in the story*; rather, it is the exploitation of one class by another—it is therefore the class struggle that constitutes the division into classes. For exploitation is already class struggle. You must therefore begin with the class struggle if you want to understand class division, the existence and nature of classes. *The class struggle must be put in the front rank.*

But that means that our first Thesis (*it is the masses that make history*) must be subordinated to our second Thesis (*the class struggle is the motor of history*). This means that the revolutionary power of the masses comes precisely from the *class struggle*. And *that* means that it is not enough, if you want to understand what is happening in the world, just to look at the exploited classes; you also have to look at the exploiting classes. Better, you have to go beyond the football match idea, the idea of two antagonistic groups of classes, to examine the basis of the existence *not only* of classes but also of the antagonism between classes—that is, the *class strug-gle*. Absolute primacy of the class struggle (Marx, Lenin). Never forget the class struggle (Mao).

But beware of idealism! The class struggle does not go on in the air, or on something like a football field. It is rooted in the mode of produc-tion and exploitation in a given class society. You therefore must consider the *material basis* of the class struggle, that is, the material *existence* of the class struggle. This, in the last instance, is the unity of the relations of production and the productive forces *under* the relations of production of a given mode of production, in a concrete historical social formation. This materiality, in the last instance, is at the same time the "base" (*basis*: Marx) of the class struggle, and its material existence; because exploita-tion takes place in production, and it is exploitation that is at the root of the antagonism between the classes and of the class struggle. It is this profound truth that Marxism-Leninism expresses in the well-known Thesis of class struggle in the infrastructure, in the "economy," in class exploitation—and in the Thesis that *all the forms of the class struggle are rooted in economic class struggle*. It is on this condition that the revolution-ary Thesis of the primacy of the class struggle is a materialist one.

When that is clear, the question of the "subject" of history disappears. History is an immense *natural-human* system in movement, and the mo-tor of history is class struggle. History is a process, and a *process without a subject*.[3] The question about how "*man* makes history" disappears alto-gether. Marxist theory rejects it once and for all; it sends it back to its birthplace—bourgeois ideology.

And with it disappears the "necessity" of the concept of "transcen-dence" and of its subject, man.

That does not mean that Marxism-Leninism *loses sight* for one mo-ment of real men. Quite the contrary! It is precisely in order to *see* them as they are and to free them from class exploitation that Marxism-Lenin-ism brings about this revolution, getting rid of the bourgeois ideology of "man" as the subject of history, *getting rid of the fetishism of "man."*

Some people will be annoyed that I dare to speak about the fetishism of "man." I mean those people who interpret Marx's chapter in *Das Kapital* on "The Fetishism of Commodities" in a particular way, draw-ing two necessarily complementary idealist conclusions—the condem-nation of "reification"[4] and the exaltation of the *person*. (But the pair of notions *person/thing* is at the root of every bourgeois ideology! *Social* relations, however, are not, except for the law and for bourgeois legal ideology, "relations between persons!"). Yet it is the same mechanism of social illusion at work—when you start to think that a social relation is the natural quality, the natural attribute of a *substance* or a *subject*. Value is one example: this social relation "appears" in bourgeois ideology as the natural quality, the natural attribute of the commodity or of money. The class struggle is another example: this social relation "appears" in bourgeois ideology as the natural quality, the natural attribute of "man" (liberty, transcendence). In both cases, the social relation is "conjured away": the commodity or gold have *natural* value; "man" is *by nature* free, *by nature* he makes history.

If John Lewis's "man" disappears, this does not mean that real men disappear. It simply means that, for Marxism-Leninism, they are something quite different from copies (multiplied at will) of the original bourgeois image of "man," a free subject by nature. Have the warnings of Marx been heeded? "My analytical method *does not start from man*, but from the economically given social period" (*Notes on Adolph Wagner's "Textbook"*). "Society *is not composed of individuals*" (*Grundrisse*).

One thing is certain: One cannot *begin* with man, because that would be to begin with a bourgeois idea of "man," and because the idea of *beginning with* man, in other words the idea of an absolute point of departure (= of an "essence") belongs to bourgeois philosophy. This idea of "man" as a starting point, an absolute point of departure, is the basis of all bourgeois ideology; it is the soul of the great Classical Political Economy itself. "Man" is a myth[5] of bourgeois ideology: Marxism-Leninism cannot *start* from "man." It starts "from the economically given social period"; and, at the end of its analysis, when it "arrives," *it may find real men*. These men are thus the *point of arrival* of an analysis that starts from the social relations of the existing mode of production, from class relations, and from the class struggle. These men are quite different men from the "man" of bourgeois ideology.

"Society is not *composed of individuals*," says Marx. He is right: society is not a "combination," an "addition" of individuals. What constitutes society is the system of its social relations in which *its* individuals live, work, and struggle. He is right: society is not made up of individuals in general, in the abstract, just so many copies of "man." Because each society has *its own* individuals, historically and socially determined. The slave individual is not the serf individual nor the proletarian individual, and the same goes for the individual of each corresponding ruling class. In the same way, we must say that even a class is not "composed" of individuals in general: each class has *its own* individuals, fashioned in their individuality by their conditions of life, of work, of exploitation and of struggle—by the relations of the class struggle. In their mass, real men are what class conditions make of them. These conditions do not depend on bourgeois "human nature"—liberty. On the contrary, the liberties of men, including the forms and limits of these liberties, and including their will to struggle, depend on these conditions.

If the question of "man" as "subject of history" disappears, this does not mean that the question of *political action* disappears. Quite the contrary! This political action is actually given its strength by the critique of the bourgeois fetishism of "man": it is forced to follow the conditions of the class struggle. For class struggle is not an individual struggle, but an *organized* mass struggle for the conquest and revolutionary transformation of state power and social relations. Nor does it mean that the question of the revolutionary *party* disappears—because, without it, the conquest of state power by the exploited masses, led by the proletariat, is impossible. But it does mean that the "role of the individual in history," the existence, the nature, the practice and the objectives of the revolutionary party are determined not by the omnipotence of "transcendence," that is, the liberty of "man," but by quite different conditions—by the state of the class struggle, by the state of the labor movement, by the ideology of the labor movement (petty-bourgeois or proletarian), and by its relation to Marxist theory, by its mass line and by its mass work.

Notes

[1] The title of John Lewis's article is "The Althusser Case." Not surprisingly: in his conclusion, John Lewis compares Marxism to . . . medicine.

[2] To clarify this point, this reformist "position" must be related to its bourgeois origins. In his letter to Weydemeyer (March 5, 1852), Marx wrote: "No credit is due to me for discovering the existence of classes in modern society, nor yet the struggle between them. Long before me, bourgeois historians had described the historical development of this struggle of the classes, and bourgeois economists the economic anatomy of the classes." The thesis of the recognition of *the existence of social classes* and of *the resulting class struggle* is not proper to Marxism-Leninism, for it puts the classes in the front rank and the class struggle in the second. *In this form* it is a bourgeois thesis, which reformism naturally feeds on. The Marxist-Leninist Thesis, on the other hand, puts the *class struggle* in the front rank. Philosophically, that means: it affirms the *primacy of contradiction* over the *terms* of the contradiction. The class struggle is not a product of the existence of classes that exist *previous* (in law and in fact) to the struggle: the class struggle is the historical form of the *contradiction* (internal to a mode of production) that *divides* the classes into classes.

[3] I put this idea forward in a study called "Marx and Lenin Before Hegel" (Feb. 1968), published in *Lenin et la philosophie* (Paris: Maspero, 1972).

[4] Transformation into a *thing* (*res*) of everything that is *human,* that is, a *nonthing* (man = nonthing = Person).

[5] The word "man" is not simply a word. Rather, it is the place it occupies and the function it performs in bourgeois ideology and philosophy that gives it its *sense.*

MICHEL FOUCAULT

The Archaeology of Knowledge: Introduction

1969

Philosopher or historian? However one chooses to answer this question, which Foucault himself rejected, his work has stood as a challenge to historians since the 1960s. In many cases, its influence has been the result of misunderstandings or indeed of outright misinterpretations of his project, which was certainly philosophical: "to make philosophical interventions in the field of history." In any case, historians, for better or for worse, plundered his books for a whole range of themes, a vocabulary, a sensibility, and an intellectual style: the problem of social control, the themes of discipline and exclusion, the strategic analysis of power, and the reflections on the history of sexuality thus gave rise to a generation of work, with different accents in different cultural and national contexts (the American Foucault, for example, has little in common with the French Foucault). With consummate, often unnerving skill, the author himself had a hand in perpetuating a considerable degree of uncertainty as to the nature and continuity of a project that underwent several reformulations but can be broadly characterized as a history of the "production of truth," which Foucault regarded as central to Western experience.

Published in 1969, L'Archéologie du savoir (The Archeology of Knowledge), Foucault's (provisional) discourse on method, reflects this perpetuation of ambiguity. At the height of his glory (in France at any rate), the author here systematized the archaeological method that he had developed in several previous books (L'Histoire de la folie, Madness and Civilization, 1961; La Naissance de la clinique, The Birth of the Clinic, 1963; and Les Mots et les choses, The Order of Things, 1966). At the same time, however, he acknowledged the limits of that method and, if Herbert Dreyfus and

---

From *The Archaeology of Knowledge and the Discourse on Language*, trans. A. M. Sheridan Smith (New York: Pantheon, 1972), introduction, pp. 3–17. First published as *L'Archéologie du savoir* (Paris: Gallimard, 1969).

Paul Rabinow are correct, may have recognized a methodological dead-end. This was also the moment when Foucault chose to separate himself somewhat from structuralism, a movement with which his name had rightly or wrongly been closely associated until that time. In particular, he rejects the "hard," scientistic version of structuralism, with which in fact he had very little to do. He also chose to align himself with the historians, or at any rate with history as he liked and wished to see it done. The text that follows is thus a highly personal view of the "situation" of history, or, more precisely, of Annales historiography, in the late 1960s. Note the emphasis on historical method (especially the use of serial data); the somewhat hasty dismissal of the attempt to oppose structure and history as an irrelevant issue; and one of the first challenges to the notion of global history on the grounds that historical inscription and process are essentially discontinuous.

For many years now, historians have preferred to turn their attention to long periods, as if, beneath the shifts and changes of political events, they were trying to reveal the stable, almost indestructible system of checks and balances, the irreversible processes, the constant readjustments, the underlying tendencies that gather force and are then suddenly reversed after centuries of continuity, the movements of accumulation and slow saturation, the great silent, motionless bases that traditional history has covered with a thick layer of events. The tools that enable historians to carry out this work of analysis are partly inherited and partly of their own making: models of economic growth, quantitative analysis of market movements, accounts of demographic expansion and contraction, the study of climate and its long-term changes, the fixing of sociological constants, the description of technological adjustments and of their spread and continuity. These tools have enabled workers in the historical field to distinguish various sedimentary strata; linear successions, which for so long had been the object of research, have given way to discoveries in depth. From the political mobility at the surface down to the slow movements of "material civilization," ever more levels of analysis have been established: each has its own peculiar discontinuities and patterns; and as one descends to the deepest levels, the rhythms become broader. Beneath the rapidly changing history of governments, wars, and famines, there emerge other, apparently unmoving histories: the history of sea routes, the history of corn or of gold-mining, the history of drought and of irrigation, the history of crop rotation, the history of the balance achieved by the human species between hunger and abundance. The old questions of the traditional analysis (What link should be made between disparate events? How can a causal succession be established between them? What continuity or over-all significance do they possess? Is it possible to define a totality, or must one be content with reconstituting connections?) are now being replaced by questions of another type: Which strata should be isolated from others? What types of series should be established? What criteria of periodization should be adopted for each of them? What system of relations (hierarchy, dominance, stratification, univocal determination, circular causality) may be established between them? What series of series may be established? And in what large-scale chronological table may distinct series of events be determined?

At about the same time, in the disciplines that we call the "history of ideas," the "history of science," the "history of philosophy," the "history of thought," and the "history of literature" (we can ignore their specificity for the moment)—in those disciplines which, despite their names, evade very largely the work and methods of the historian—attention has been turned, on the contrary, away from vast unities like "periods" or "centuries" to the phenomena of rupture, of discontinuity. Beneath the great continuities of thought, beneath the solid, homogeneous manifestations of a single mind or of a collective mentality, beneath the stubborn development of a science striving to exist and to reach completion at the very outset, beneath the persistence of a particular genre, form, discipline, or theoretical activity, one is now trying to detect the incidence of interruptions. Interruptions whose status and nature vary considerably. There are the *epistemological acts and thresholds* described by Gaston Bachelard: they suspend the continuous accumulation of knowledge, interrupt its slow development, and force it to enter a new time, cut it off from its empirical origin and its original motivations, cleanse it of its imaginary complicities. They direct historical analysis away from the search for silent beginnings, and the never-ending tracing-back to the original precursors, toward the search for a new type of rationality and its various effects. There are the *displacements* and *transformations* of concepts: the analyses of Georges Canguilhem may serve as models—they show that the history of a concept is not wholly and entirely that of its progressive refinement, its continuously increasing rationality, its abstraction gradient, but that of its various fields of constitution and validity, that of its successive rules of use, that of the many theoretical contexts in which it developed and matured. There is the distinction, which we also owe to Canguilhem, between the *microscopic* and *macroscopic scales* of the history of the sciences, in which events and their consequences are not arranged in the same way: thus a discovery, the development of a method, the achievements and the failures of a particular scientist do not have the same incidence and cannot be described in the same way at both levels; on each of the two levels, a different history is being written.

Recurrent redistributions reveal several pasts, several forms of connection, several hierarchies of importance, several networks of determination, several teleologies, for one and the same science, as its present undergoes change: thus, historical descriptions are necessarily ordered by the present state of knowledge, they increase with every transformation and never cease, in turn, to break with themselves (in the field of mathematics, Michel Serres has provided the theory of this phenomenon). There are the *architectonic unities* of systems of the kind analyzed by Martial Guéroult, which are concerned not with the description of cultural influences, traditions, and continuities but, rather, with internal coherences, axioms, deductive connections, compatibilities. Lastly, the most radical discontinuities are the breaks effected by a work of theoretical transformation "that establishes a science by detaching it from the ideology of its past and by revealing this past as ideological."[1] To this should be added, of course, literary analysis, which now takes as its unity not the spirit or sensibility of a period, nor "groups," "schools," "generations," or "movements," nor even the personality of the author, in the interplay of his life and his "creation," but the particular structure of a given oeuvre, book, or text.

The great problem presented by such historical analyses is not how continuities are established, how a single pattern is formed and preserved, how for so many different, successive minds there is a single horizon, what mode of action and what substructure is implied by the interplay of transmissions, resumptions, disappearances, and repetitions, how the origin may extend its sway well beyond itself to that conclusion which is never given—the problem is no longer one of tradition, of tracing a line, but one of division, of limits; it is no longer one of lasting foundations, but one of transformations that serve as new foundations, the rebuilding of foundations. What one is seeing, then, is the emergence of a whole field of questions, some of which are already familiar, by which this new form of history is trying to develop its own theory: How is one to specify the different concepts that enable us to conceive of discontinuity (threshold, rupture, break, mutation, transformation)? By what criteria is one to isolate the unities with which one is dealing; what is *a* science? What is an oeuvre? What is *a* theory? What is *a* concept? What is *a* text? How is one to diversify the levels at which one may place oneself, each of which possesses its own divisions and form of analysis? What is the legitimate level of formalization? What is that of interpretation? Of structural analysis? Of attributions of causality?

In short, the history of thought, of knowledge, of philosophy, of literature seems to be seeking, and discovering, more and more discontinuities, whereas history itself appears to be abandoning the irruption of events in favor of stable structures.

But we must not be taken in by this apparent interchange. Despite appearances, we must not imagine that certain of the historical disciplines have moved from the continuous to the discontinuous, while others have moved from the tangled mass of discontinuities to the great, uninterrupted unities; we must not imagine that in the analysis of politics, institutions, or economics we have become more and more sensitive to overall determinations, while in the analysis of ideas and of knowledge we are paying more and more attention to the play of difference; we must not imagine that these two great forms of description have crossed without recognizing one another.

In fact, the same problems are being posed in either case, but they have provoked opposite effects on the surface. These problems may be summed up in a word: the questioning of the *document*. Of course, it is obvious enough that ever since a discipline such as history has existed, documents have been used, questioned, and have given rise to questions; scholars have asked not only what these documents meant but also whether they were telling the truth, and by what right they could claim to be doing so, whether they were sincere or deliberately misleading, well informed or ignorant, authentic or tampered with. But each of these questions, and all this critical concern, pointed to one and the same end: the reconstitution, on the basis of what the documents say, and sometimes merely hint at, of the past from which they emanate, which has now disappeared far behind them. The document was always treated as the language of a voice since reduced to silence, its fragile but possibly decipherable trace. Now, through a mutation that is not of very recent origin, but which has still not come to an end, history has altered its position in relation to the document: it has taken as its primary task not the interpretation of the document, nor the attempt to decide whether it is telling the truth or what is its expressive value, but to work on it from within and to develop it: history now organizes the document, divides it up, distributes it, orders it, arranges it in levels, establishes series, distinguishes between what is relevant and what is not, discovers elements, defines unities, describes relations. For history, then, the document is no longer an inert material through which it tries to reconstitute what men have done or said, the events of which only the trace remains; history is now trying to define within the documentary material itself unities, totalities, series, relations. History must be detached from the image that satisfied it for so long, and through which it found its anthropological justification—that of an age-old collective consciousness that made use of material documents to refresh its memory. History is the work expended on material documentation (books, texts, accounts, registers, acts, buildings, institutions, laws, techniques, objects, customs, and so on) that exists, in every time and place, in every society, either in a spontaneous or in a consciously organized form. The document is not the fortunate tool of a history that is primarily and fundamentally *memory*; history is one way in which a society recognizes and develops a mass of documentation with which it is inextricably linked.

To be brief, then, let us say that history, in its traditional form, undertook to "memorize" the *monuments* of the past, to transform them into *documents*, and to lend speech to those traces which, in themselves, are often not verbal, or which say in silence something other than what they actually say. In our time, history is that which transforms *documents* into *monuments*. In that area where, in the past, history deciphered the traces left by men, it now deploys a mass of elements that have to be grouped, made relevant, placed in relation to one another to form totalities. There was a time when archaeology, as a discipline devoted to silent monuments, inert traces, objects without context, and things left by the past, aspired to the condition of history, and attained meaning only through the restitution of a historical discourse. It might be said, to play on words a little, that, in our time, history aspires to the condition of archaeology, to the intrinsic description of the monument.

This has several consequences. First of all, there is the surface effect already mentioned: the proliferation of discontinuities in the history of ideas, and the emergence of long periods in history proper. In fact, in its traditional form, history proper was concerned with defining relations (of simple causality, of circular determination, of antagonism, of expression) between facts or dated events: the series being known, it was simply a question of defining the position of each element in relation to the other elements in the series. The problem now is to constitute series—to define the elements proper to each series, to fix its boundaries, to reveal its own specific type of relations, to formulate its laws, and, beyond this, to describe the relations between different series, thus constituting series of series, or "tables": hence the ever-increasing number of strata, and the need to distinguish them, the specificity of their time and chronologies; hence the need to distinguish not only important events (with a long chain of consequences) and less important ones, but types of events at quite different levels (some very brief, others of average duration, like the development of a particular technique, or a scarcity of money, and others of a long-term nature, like a demographic equilibrium or the gradual adjustment of an economy to climatic change); hence the possibility of revealing series with widely spaced intervals formed by rare or repetitive events. The appearance of long periods in the history of today is not a return to the philosophers of history, to the great ages of the world, or to the periodization dictated by the rise and fall of civilizations; it is the effect of the methodologically concerted development of series. In the history of ideas, of thought, and of the sciences, the same mutation has brought about the opposite effect; it has broken up the long series formed by the progress of consciousness, or the teleology of reason, or the evolution of human thought; it has questioned the themes of convergence and culmination; it has doubted the possibility of creating totalities. It has led to the individualization of different series, which are juxtaposed with one another, follow one another, overlap and intersect, without one being able to reduce them to a linear schema. Thus, in place of the continuous chronology of reason, which was invariably traced back to some inaccessible origin, there have appeared scales that are sometimes very brief, distinct from one another, irreducible to a single law, scales that bear a type of history peculiar to each one, and which cannot be reduced to the general model of a consciousness that acquires, progresses, and remembers.

Second consequence: The notion of discontinuity assumes a major role in the historical disciplines. For history in its classical form, the discontinuous was both the given and the unthinkable; the raw material of history, which presented itself in the form of dispersed events—decisions, accidents, initiatives, discoveries—the material that, through analysis, had to be rearranged, reduced, effaced in order to reveal the continuity of events. Discontinuity was the stigma of the temporal dislocation that it was the historian's task to remove from history. It has now become one of the basic elements of historical analysis. Its role is threefold. First, it constitutes a deliberate operation on the part of the historian (and not a quality of the material with which he has to deal)—for he must, at least as a systematic hypothesis, distinguish the possible levels of analysis, the methods proper to each, and the periodization that best suits them. Second, it is the result of his description (and not something that must be eliminated by means of his analysis)—for he is trying to discover the limits of a process, the point of inflection of a curve, the inversion of a regulatory movement, the boundaries of an oscillation, the threshold of a function, the instant at which a circular causality breaks down. Third, it is the concept that the historian's work never ceases to specify (instead of neglecting it as a uniform, indifferent blank between two positive figures); it assumes a specific form and function, according to the field and the level to which it is assigned. One does not speak of the same discontinuity when describing an epistemological threshold, the point of reflection in a population curve, or the replacement of one technique by another. The notion of discontinuity is a paradoxical one, because it is both an instrument and an object of research; because it divides up the field of which it is the effect; because it enables the historian to individualize different domains but can be established only by comparing those domains; and because, in the final analysis, perhaps, it is not simply a concept present in the discourse of the historian but, rather, something that the historian secretly supposes to be present. On what basis, in fact, could he speak without this discontinuity that offers him history—and his own history—as an object? One of the most essential features of the new history is probably this displacement of the discontinuous: its transference from the obstacle to the work itself; its integration into the discourse of the historian, where it no longer plays the role of an external condition that must be reduced, but that of a working concept; and therefore the inversion of signs by which it is no longer the negative of the historical reading (its underside, its failure, the limit of its power) but, instead, the positive element that determines its object and validates its analysis.

Third consequence: The theme and the possibility of a *total history* begin to disappear, and we see the emergence of something very different which might be called a *general history*. The project of a total history is one that seeks to reconstitute the overall form of a civilization, the principle—material or spiritual—of a society, the significance common to all the phenomena of a period, the law that accounts for their cohesion—what is called metaphorically the "face" of a period. Such a project is linked to two or three hypotheses. It is supposed that between all the events of a well-defined spatiotemporal area, between all the phenomena of which traces have been found, it must be possible to establish a system of homogeneous relations—a network of causality that makes it possible to derive each of them, relations of analogy that show how they symbolize one another, or how they all express one and the same central core. It is also supposed that one and the same form of historicity operates upon economic structures, social institutions and customs, the inertia of mental attitudes, technological practice, political behavior, and subjects them all to the same type of transformation. Lastly, it is supposed that history itself may be articulated into great units—stages or phases—that contain within themselves their own principle of cohesion. These are the postulates that are challenged by the new history when it speaks of series, divisions, limits, differences of level, shifts, chronological specificities, particular forms of rehandling, possible types of relation. This is not because it is trying to obtain a plurality of histories juxtaposed and independent of one another—that of the economy beside that of institutions, and beside these two those of science, religion, or literature. Nor is it because it is merely trying to discover between these different histories coincidences of dates, or analogies of form and meaning. The problem that now presents itself—and defines the task of a general history—is to determine what form of relation may be legitimately described between these different series; what vertical system they are capable of forming; what interplay of correlation and dominance exists between them; what may be the effect of shifts, different temporalities, and various rehan-

dlings; in what distinct totalities certain elements may figure simultaneously; in short, not only what series, but also what "series of series"—or,
in other words, what "tables" it is possible to draw up. A total description
draws all phenomena around a single center—a principle, a meaning, a
spirit, a worldview, an overall shape; a general history, on the contrary,
would deploy the space of a dispersion.

Fourth and last consequence: The new history is confronted by a
number of methodological problems, several of which, no doubt, existed
long before the emergence of the new history, but which, taken together,
characterize it. These include: the building-up of coherent and homogeneous corpora of documents (open or closed, exhausted or inexhaustible
corpora), the establishment of a principle of choice (according to whether
one wishes to treat the documentation exhaustively or to adopt a sampling method as in statistics, or to try to determine in advance which are
the most representative elements); the definition of the level of analysis
and of the relevant elements (in the material studied, one may extract
numerical indications; references—explicit or not—to events, institutions, practices; the words used, with their grammatical rules and the
semantic fields that they indicate, or again the formal structure of the
propositions and the types of connection that unite them); the specifica-
tion of a method of analysis (the quantitative treatment of data, the
breaking-down of the material according to a number of assignable features whose correlations are then studied, interpretive decipherment,
analysis of frequency and distribution); the delimitation of groups and
subgroups that articulate the material (regions, periods, unitary processes); the determination of relations that make it possible to characterize a group (these may be numerical or logical relations; functional,
causal, or analogical relations; or it may be the relation of the "signifier"
to the "signified.")

All these problems are now part of the methodological field of history.
This field deserves attention, and for two reasons. First, because one can
see to what extent it has freed itself from what constituted, not so long
ago, the philosophy of history, and from the questions that it posed (on
the rationality or teleology of historical development, on the relativity of
historical knowledge, and on the possibility of discovering or constituting a meaning in the inertia of the past and in the unfinished totality of
the present). Second, because at certain points it intersects problems that
are met with in other fields—in linguistics, ethnology, economics, literary analysis, and mythology, for example. These problems may, if one
so wishes, be labeled "structuralism," but only under certain conditions:
they do not, of themselves, cover the entire methodological field of history, they occupy only one part of that field—a part that varies in importance with the area and level of analysis; apart from a number of rela-

tively limited cases, they have not been imported from linguistics or ethnology (as is often the case today); but they originated in the field of history itself—more particularly, in that of economic history and as a result of the questions posed by that discipline. Lastly, in no way do they authorize us to speak of a "structuralism of history," or at least of an attempt to overcome a "conflict" or "opposition" between structure and historical development: it is a long time now since historians uncovered, described, and analyzed structures, without ever having occasion to wonder whether they were not allowing the living, fragile, pulsating "history" to slip through their fingers. The structure/development opposition is relevant neither to the definition of the historical field, nor, in all probability, to the definition of a structural method.

This epistemological mutation of history is not yet complete. But it is not of recent origin either, since its first phase can no doubt be traced back to Marx. But it took a long time to have much effect. Even now—and this is especially true in the case of the history of thought—it has been neither registered nor reflected upon, while other, more recent transformations—those of linguistics, for example—have been. It is as if it was particularly difficult, in the history in which men retrace their own ideas and their own knowledge, to formulate a general theory of discontinuity, of series, of limits, unities, specific orders, and differentiated autonomies and dependences. As if, in that field where we had become used to seeking origins, to pushing back further and further the line of antecedents, to reconstituting traditions, to following evolutive curves, to projecting teleologies, and to having constant recourse to metaphors of life, we felt a particular repugnance to conceiving of difference, to describing separations and dispersions, to dissociating the reassuring form of the identical. Or, to be more precise, it is as if we found it difficult to construct a theory, to draw general conclusions, and even to derive all the possible implications of these concepts of thresholds, mutations, independent systems, and limited series—in the way in which they had been used in fact by historians. As if we were afraid to conceive of the *Other* in the time of our own thought.

There is a reason for this. If the history of thought could remain the locus of uninterrupted continuities, if it could endlessly forge connections that no analysis could undo without abstraction, if it could weave, around everything that men say and do, obscure syntheses that anticipate for him, prepare him, and lead him endlessly toward his future, it would provide a privileged shelter for the sovereignty of consciousness. Continuous history is the indispensable correlative of the founding function of the subject—the guarantee that everything which has eluded him may be restored to him; the certainty that time will disperse nothing without restoring it in a reconstituted unity; the promise that one day the subject—in the form of historical consciousness—will once again be able to appropriate, to bring back under his sway, all those things kept at a distance by difference, and find in them what might be called his "abode." Making historical analysis the discourse of the continuous and making human consciousness the original subject of all historical development and all action are the two sides of the same system of thought. In this system, time is conceived in terms of totalization and revolutions are never more than moments of consciousness.

In various forms, this theme has played a constant role since the nineteenth century: to preserve, against all decenterings, the sovereignty of the subject, and the twin figures of anthropology and humanism. Against the decentering operated by Marx—by the historical analysis of the relations of production, economic determinations, and the class struggle—it gave place, toward the end of the nineteenth century, to the search for a total history, in which all the differences of a society might be reduced to a single form, to the organization of a worldview, to the establishment of a system of values, to a coherent type of civilization. To the decentering operated by the Nietzschean genealogy, it opposed the search for an original foundation that would make rationality the telos of mankind, and link the whole history of thought to the preservation of this rationality, to the maintenance of this teleology, and to the ever-necessary return to this foundation. Lastly, more recently, when the researches of psychoanalysis, linguistics, and ethnology have decentered the subject in relation to the laws of his desire, the forms of his language, the rules of his action, or the games of his mythical or fabulous discourse, when it became clear that man himself, questioned as to what he was, could not account for his sexuality and his unconscious, the systematic forms of his language, or the regularities of his fictions, the theme of a continuity of history has been reactivated once again; a history that would be not division but development; not an interplay of relations but an internal dynamic; not a system but the hard work of freedom; not form but the unceasing effort of a consciousness turned upon itself, trying to grasp itself in its deepest conditions—a history that would be both an act of long, uninterrupted patience and the vivacity of a movement, which, in the end, breaks all bounds. If one is to assert this theme—which, to the "immobility" of structures, to their "closed" system, to their necessary "synchrony," opposes the living openness of history—one must obviously deny in the historical analyses themselves the use of discontinuity, the definition of levels and limits, the description of specific series, the uncovering of the whole interplay of differences. One is led, therefore, to anthropologize Marx, to make of him a historian of totalities, and to rediscover in him the message of humanism; one is led therefore to interpret Nietzsche in the terms of transcendental philosophy, and to reduce his genealogy to the level of a search for origins; lastly, one is led to leave to one side, as if it had never arisen, that whole field of methodological problems that the new history is now presenting. For, if it is asserted that the question of discontinuities, systems and transformations, series and thresholds, arises in all the historical disciplines (and in those concerned with ideas or the sciences no less than those concerned with economics and society), how could one oppose with any semblance of legitimacy "development" and "system," movement and circular regulations, or, as it is sometimes put crudely and unthinkingly, "history" and "structure"?

The same conservative function is at work in the theme of cultural totalities (for which Marx has been criticized, then travestied), in the theme of a search for origins (which was opposed to Nietzsche, before an attempt was made to transpose him into it), and in the theme of a living, continuous, open history. The cry goes up that one is murdering history whenever, in a historical analysis—and especially if it is concerned with thought, ideas, or knowledge—one is seen to be using in too obvious a way the categories of discontinuity and difference, the notions of threshold, rupture and transformation, the description of series and limits. One will be denounced for attacking the inalienable rights of history and the very foundations of any possible historicity. But one must not be deceived: what is being bewailed with such vehemence is not the disappearance of history but the eclipse of that form of history that was secretly but entirely related to the synthetic activity of the subject. What is being bewailed is the "development" that was to provide the sovereignty of the consciousness with a safer, less exposed shelter than myths, kinship systems, languages, sexuality, or desire. What is being bewailed is the possibility of reanimating through the project, the work of meaning, or the movement of totalization, the interplay of material determinations, rules of practice, unconscious systems, rigorous but unreflected relations, correlations that elude all lived experience; what is being bewailed is that ideological use of history by which one tries to restore to man everything that has unceasingly eluded him for over a hundred years. All the treasure of bygone days was crammed into the old citadel of this history; it was thought to be secure; it was sacralized; it was made the last resting place of anthropological thought; it was even thought that its most inveterate enemies could be captured and turned into vigilant guardians. But the historians had long ago deserted the old fortress and gone to work elsewhere; it was realized that neither Marx nor Nietzsche were carrying out the guard duties that had been entrusted to them. They could not be depended on to preserve privilege; nor to affirm once and for all—and God knows it is needed in the distress of today—that history, at least, is living and continuous, that it is, for the subject in question, a place of rest, certainty, reconciliation, a place of tranquilized sleep.

At this point there emerges an enterprise of which my earlier books *Madness and Civilization, The Birth of the Clinic*, and *The Order of Things*[2] were a very imperfect sketch—an enterprise by which one tries to measure the mutations that operate in general in the field of history; an enterprise in which the methods, limits, and themes proper to the history of ideas are questioned; an enterprise by which one tries to throw off the last anthropological constraints; an enterprise that wishes, in return, to reveal how these constraints could come about. These tasks were outlined in a rather disordered way, and their general articulation was never clearly defined. It was time that they were given greater coherence—or, at least, that an attempt was made to do so. This book is the result.

In order to avoid misunderstanding, I should like to begin with a few observations.

My aim is not to transfer to the field of history, and more particularly to the history of knowledge, a structuralist method that has proved valuable in other fields of analysis. My aim is to uncover the principles and consequences of an autochthonous transformation that is taking place in the field of historical knowledge. It may well be that this transformation, the problems that it raises, the tools that it uses, the concepts that emerge from it, and the results that it obtains are not entirely foreign to what is called "structural" analysis. But this kind of analysis is not specifically used.

My aim is most decidedly not to use the categories of cultural totalities (whether worldviews, ideal types, the particular spirit of an age) in order to impose on history, despite itself, the forms of structural analysis. The series described, the limits fixed, the comparisons and correlations made are based not on the old philosophies of history but, rather, are intended to question teleologies and totalizations.

Insofar as my aim is to define a method of historical analysis freed from the anthropological theme, it is clear that the theory I am about to outline has a dual relation with the previous studies. It is an attempt to formulate, in general terms (and not without a great deal of rectification and elaboration), the tools that these studies have used or forged for themselves in the course of their work. But, on the other hand, it uses the results already obtained to define a method of analysis purged of all anthropologism. The ground on which it rests is the one that it has itself discovered. The studies of madness and the beginnings of psychology, of illness and the beginnings of a clinical medicine, of the sciences of life, language, and economics were attempts that were carried out, to some extent, in the dark; but they gradually became clear, not only because little by little their method became more precise, but also because they discovered—in this debate on humanism and anthropology—the point of its historical possibility.

In short, this book, like those that preceded it, does not belong—at least not directly, or in the first instance—to the debate on structure (as opposed to genesis, history, development); it belongs to that field in which the questions of the human being, consciousness, origin, and the subject emerge, intersect, mingle, and separate off. But it would probably not be incorrect to say that the problem of structure arose there too.

This work is not an exact description of what can be read in *Madness and Civilization*, *The Birth of the Clinic*, or *The Order of Things*. It is different on a great many points. It also includes a number of corrections and internal criticisms. Generally speaking, *Madness and Civilization* accorded far too great a place, and a very enigmatic one too, to what I called an "experiment," thus showing to what extent one was still close to admitting an anonymous and general subject of history; in *The Birth of the Clinic*, the frequent recourse to structural analysis threatened to bypass the specificity of the problem presented, and the level proper to archaeology; lastly, in *The Order of Things,* the absence of methodological sign-posting may have given the impression that my analyses were being conducted in terms of cultural totality. It is mortifying that I was unable to avoid these dangers: I console myself with the thought that they were intrinsic to the enterprise itself, since, in order to carry out its task, it had first to free itself from these various methods and forms of history; moreover, without the questions that I was asked,[3] without the difficulties that arose, without the objections that were made, I may never have gained so clear a view of the enterprise to which I am now inextricably linked. Hence the cautious, stumbling manner of this text: at every turn, it stands back, measures up what is before it, gropes toward its limits, stumbles against what it does not mean, and digs pits to mark out its own path. At every turn, it denounces any possible confusion. It rejects its identity, without previously stating, "I am neither this nor that." It is not critical, most of the time; it is not a way of saying that everyone else is wrong. It is an attempt to define a particular site by the exteriority of its vicinity; rather than trying to reduce others to silence, by claiming that what they say is worthless, I have tried to define this blank space from which I speak, and which is slowly taking shape in a discourse that I still feel to be so precarious and so unsure.

"Aren't you sure of what you're saying? Are you going to change yet again, shift your position according to the questions that are put to you, and say that the objections are not really directed at the place from which you are speaking? Are you going to declare yet again that you have never been what you have been reproached with being? Are you already preparing the way out that will enable you in your next book to spring up somewhere else and declare as you're now doing: 'No, no, I'm not where you are lying in wait for me, but over here, laughing at you?'"

"What, do you imagine that I would take so much trouble and so much pleasure in writing, do you think that I would keep so persistently to my task, if I were not preparing—with a rather shaky hand—a labyrinth into which I can venture, in which I can move my discourse, opening up underground passages, forcing it to go far from itself, finding overhangs that reduce and deform its itinerary, in which I can lose myself and appear at last to eyes that I will never have to meet again. I am no doubt not the only one who writes in order to have no face. Do not ask who I am and do not ask me to remain the same: leave it to our bureaucrats and our police to see that our papers are in order. At least spare us their morality when we write."

TRANSLATED BY A. M. SHERIDAN SMITH

NOTES

[1] Louis Althusser, *For Marx* (New York: Pantheon, 1969), p. 168.

[2] *Madness and Civilization*, trans. Richard Howard (New York: Vintage, 1965); *The Birth of the Clinic*, trans. A. M. Sheridan Smith (New York: Pantheon, 1973); *The Order of Things*, trans. Alan Sheridan (New York: Pantheon, 1970).

[3] In particular, the first pages of this introduction are based on a reply to questions presented by the Cercle d'épistémologie of the Ecole Normale Supérieure (see *Cahiers pour l'analyse*, no. 9). A sketch of certain developments was also given in reply to readers of the review *Esprit* (April 1968).

FRANÇOIS FURET

French Intellectuals:
From Marxism to Structuralism

1967

The following text is a relatively rare instance of a successful history of the present. The author, François Furet (b. 1927), had just made a name for himself as a historian of the French Revolution. He had been politically committed, in the communist party until 1956, then in the anticolonialist struggle. As a political commentator, he also took part in the adventures of a left-wing intellectual weekly, France-Observateur, *which later became* Le Nouvel Observateur. *From these three types of experience, Furet derived the sensibility that produced the quick, accurate analysis we have here of a moment in French intellectual history in which he was both participant and sharp-eyed observer. By 1967, structuralist methods had already proved influential in a number of fields: linguistics, Lévi-Straussian anthropology, and the history of religion à la Dumézil. However, with Althusser (*Pour Marx, *1965), Foucault (*Les Mots et les choses, *1966), and Lacan (*Ecrits, *1966), structuralism was in the process of turning into a scientific ideology, an ideology that served as cover for a history (real history, that is) whose meaning is no longer so clear and disappoints those who only recently had great expectations from it.*

The "end of ideologies," as diagnosed by Raymond Aron, for instance, in one of his books, refers generally to the developed societies of America and Western Europe. It connects prosperity, economic growth, and social integration, on the one hand, with the

From François Furet, *The Workshop of History*, trans. Jonathan Mandelbaum (Chicago: University of Chicago Press, 1984). This is a revised and expanded version of "The French Left: From Marxism to Structuralism," which appeared in *Survey* 62 (Jan. 1967), pp. 72–83. Also published as "Les Intellectuels français et le structuralisme," in *Preuves* 92 (Feb. 1967), pp. 3–12.

progressive decline of political extremisms, on the other; the car, the refrigerator, and television are said to have killed revolution. This type of analysis has already inspired endless comment on neocapitalism, the Gaullist regime, and the kind of political torpor that has characterized France since the end of the Algerian war, as if one of the functions of Gaullist nationalism were now to counterbalance an objective process of French "Americanization."

But does the end of ideologies mean the end of ideologues? If it is true that present-day France tends in its social depths to be dozing off into a society of abundance and social integration, is the diagnosis also true of the groups and the individuals whose profession is thinking and writing? It may be objected that this question implies a certain modification of our initial proposition, for the relations of intellectuals to ideologies differ in nature from those of the general public; at any rate, they are more complicated (even if they are apparently simple or deliberately simplified). French intellectuals, though, because of the authority they have enjoyed since the Enlightenment, have often been indicative of the problems and choices of society as a whole. There can be no greater historical oversimplification than deifying the intelligentsia's purely protesting role; claiming a long line of great but damned ancestors is a cheap way of entering into an exceptional heritage. But Voltaire was the most acclaimed hero of the eighteenth century, the Revolution put Rousseau in the Pantheon, and Victor Hugo's coffin was followed by an enormous crowd. The intellectual Left has rarely governed the France of its time, but it has supplied its universal values. Neither the Dreyfus affair nor the Popular Front nor the postwar spread of communism is intelligible if the part played by the intellectuals and their ideological elaboration is left out of account.

This is why ideology is far from consisting exclusively of a theory of history, though in the France of yesterday Marxism-Leninism was the most widespread and extreme form it took. Ideology is born of the feeling that a great historical problem can and must be solved by individual commitment—hence the passion inseparable from it, the proselytism, the condemnation of the enemy and even of the indifferent, the identification of personal morality with historical necessity. The class struggle has different aims according to Guizot or Marx. The former hails the triumph of the bourgeoisie, and the second the advent of the proletariat; but both, even if this is denied, as it is by Marx, imply a moral view of politics, distinction between good and evil, and commitment to the side of the good.

Thus, the French Left has no monopoly on ideology; on the contrary, for nearly two hundred years the conflict between Right and Left has been the warp on which ideologies have been woven. The Frenchman of the Right, armed with Maurice Barrès versus Emile Zola, Charles Maurras versus Romain Rolland, and Pierre Drieu La Rochelle versus Louis Aragon, also has his cultural pedigree, whose assumptions and political hypocrisy the Left has frequently denounced. The national masochism of the Pétainist bourgeoisie or, fifteen years later, the nationalist enthusiasm for *l'Algérie française* refers back to the same system of intellectual and moral arguments, only the terms of which vary with the event. Why, then, the privileged position enjoyed today by the ideology of the Left and by the left-wing intellectual? The answer is that the last great battle of right-wing ideology was fought by fascism—and lost. Since the end of the war, ideological elaboration has consequently been a quasi monopoly of the Left.

How the celebrated Hegelian tribunal, which had become the "opium of the intellectuals," was wildly misused by the victorious Left after it had been "proved right" by history was described by Raymond Aron even before the politico-moral tribunal of Stalinism broke down with the death of Stalin. Up to that moment, historical certainty and moral judgment had combined and reinforced each other; now both factors in the apogee of the ideological age were simultaneously punctured by developments in the contemporary world.

Destalinization raised the issue of justice and truth in the communist world; there turned out to be other enemies besides the bourgeoisie, and it came to be seen that the Soviet Union was not always, necessarily, and inherently in the advance guard of human history. This led to a new diaspora of communist and progressive intellectuals; a whole world collapsed, as I well remember, because I was a part of it. Warsaw, Budapest, the Chinese schism have only accentuated the process, providing the last rites for a Marxism-Leninism that had been both incarnate and universal. But during those very years, a new universalist mirage, an ersatz messianism, presented itself to the revolutionary intellectuals, namely, the struggle for independence of the Third World or, in the French context, support for the NLF in the Algerian war. This additional experiment in ideological extremism was the more characteristic of left-wing intellectual circles in that it was experienced in social isolation, disclaimed by the communist party, and not understood by the working class. The Western intellectual looked overseas for his (mythical) tie with the oppressed and the agents of world revolution, in the ranks of an enemy who was assumed by definition to be socialist and internationalist. The Muslim fellah celebrated by Frantz Fanon had become the latest ally of revolutionary defeatism of the Leninist type. The outcome is familiar. The left-wing intellectual had invested his liquid revolutionary capital in religious nationalism; in seeking the bolshevik party of 1917, it found Islam; and, instead of Lenin, it found Hovari Boumediene.

The disconcerting outcome in Algeria and the very victories of the colonial peoples have slowed down left-wing intellectual investment in the Third World, for the difficulties in the way of economic "takeoff" are often too technical in nature to nourish passion, and the love affair between the NLF's French wartime friends and the Algeria of Colonel Boumediene has ended in disappointment. Nevertheless, the economic setbacks that have taken place in most of the recently decolonized countries have in a way restored to honor the idea of a Leninist—or Maoist—dictatorship. For lack of suitable soil for experimentation of this type at home, some Western intellectuals proclaim its necessity in the underdeveloped countries as the only way of demolishing the many obstacles in the path of mobilization of labor and national saving for capital formation. A few years ago it was chiefly the romantic and antibureaucratic character of the Cuban revolution (which contrasted so sharply with socialism of the Soviet type) that roused enthusiasm, but the Chinese model now seems to be restoring priority to economic rationality, and this classic slant may again enable it to be used in defense of totalitarianism. But it is too obviously inapplicable to European conditions, its culture being too "exotic" and its antecedents too well known, and so it is unlikely to rally a great deal of support; and, finally, the hostility of the French communist party deprives it of a great deal of influence.

The irruption into history of the nations of the Third World, instead of promoting a "Chinese" version of Marxism, has in fact contributed to hastening the end of the ideologies in contemporary French culture. Superficially and for a brief moment, it seemed to revive great universal visions of social transformation, but in reality it served to discredit lastingly and in depth the philosophies of history of the nineteenth century. This phenomenon could be crudely summed up by saying that, in the context of French intellectual life—so sensitive to fashion and so prompt to generalize—the prestige of structural ethnology has been partly due to the fact that it offered an "antihistory."

A disappointed intellectual Left, demoralized by history, turned to primitive man, not to decipher mankind's infancy—which would have led back to history—but to find man's "true" situation. The approval of the "savage" by a society that considers itself to be saturated with wealth and "civilization," to use the term already current in Rousseau's time, is not a new phenomenon. But the interesting feature of the present vogue is that the savage has become, for a time, the model for the human sciences. It is probably not by chance, nor is it the mere result of an incidentally only too obvious cultural chauvinism, that structuralism, which has dominated European linguistic research since the first postwar period, was popularized in France not by linguistics but by ethnology. Nor is its success solely attributable to the work of Lévi-Strauss, whose *Structures élémentaires de la parenté* (*The Elementary Structures of Kinship*) dates from 1948—nearly ten years before he achieved notoriety. It took the dislocation of Marxist dogmatism between 1955 and 1960 for ethnology to fulfill a social expectation and meet a historical situation. Decolonization revealed to all the secrets of the ethnologists, those pioneers of anticolonialism: namely, that cultures are multiple, are equally worthy of respect, and manifest themselves in terms of permanence rather than of change. French colonization (which, it must not be forgotten, was often Left in origin) claimed to place them in Western "time," putting them through European stages of progress whether they liked it or not. Now, however, there is perhaps a trace of expiatory masochism in the revaluation of these extra-European worlds.

Furthermore, these exotic and impoverished worlds have the virtue of focusing all the distaste for, and rejection of, the "affluent society": even if they are no longer centers of revolution and are gradually sinking below the survival line, they are at least pure and innocent in the eyes of a Left that is at heart moralistic and more Christian than it thinks. They remain a geographical refuge for the frustration with the historical immobility of a nonrevolutionary West. Provided the flame of revolution keeps smoldering in the Third World (as in South America) or flares up there (as in China), the students of prosperous Europe will someday be able to transmute their despair into hope. Above all, a profound change has taken place in the French intellectual's idea of the world and the part played in it by his country. The transference of his revolutionary hopes to the Soviet Union and then to the Third World was in itself an implicit confession of impotence concerning the possibilities in his own country. Yet it also betrayed the survival of the Jacobin tradition, nostalgia for the France of 1793, a patriotism temporarily frustrated but nevertheless optimistic: France would one day again pick up the torch of revolutionary history. Now, even this dream is fading. Not only has the Soviet flame gone out and the Third World disconcerted or disappointed its friends of the heroic age, but France itself is no longer France. The French intellectual, heir to a prestige less fragile than power and unconsciously used to a universal radiation of his culture, is not yet reduced to the sad state of the Belgian; but he is increasingly aware of being a citizen of a country that, in spite of Gaullist rhetoric, senses it is no longer making human history. Having been expelled from history, the France in which he lives consents the more willingly to expel history. It can look at the world with eyes no longer veiled by its own example and civilizing obsession, with eyes now skeptical about the "lessons" and "meaning" of history. Paul Valéry admirably foresaw this phenomenon after the First World War in his *Regards sur le monde actuel*.

Thus, the recent disappointments of the French intellectuals and the general political situation combine to cast doubt on history—for so long a tyrannical mistress before she became an unfaithful one.

It is without doubt this situation that explains the great impact of the thinking of which Lévi-Strauss is generally regarded as both a model and a representative. It is, however, uncertain—even unlikely—that Lévi-Strauss, who has a passion for accuracy, would accept this vague and general attribution of paternity affixed to him under the label of "structuralism." But, from the point of view of the social character of his audience, that matters little. On the other hand, it is significant that a work as specific and as technical as his should have had so widespread an impact on men of letters, art critics, and philosophers. To enumerate its great themes and aspirations is not to evade the significance of the intellectual movement that reflects the scope of its influence, since that is precisely what has to be understood.

In the first place, however abstract and high-powered it may be, the effect of his work is to revive something like the great Rousseauist paradox that split the eighteenth century. One feels it to be suffused by love of nature, the countryside and flowers, a fondness for "primitive" man that inevitably stimulates nostalgia for a happiness lost by industrial societies. Lévi-Strauss writes of a world in which the eagle, the bear, and meadow sage still exist, but he believes no more than Rousseau, who is one of his favorite authors, in a return to a primitive happiness that has disappeared forever. The heir to Franz Boas and Marcel Mauss knows that there is no such thing as a state of nature but, rather, myriad communities and cultures, each representing a different form of man's confrontation with nature; and he also realizes that there is no objective way of establishing any hierarchy among them. Thus, the industrial society of Europe or America loses the privileged position to which it believes itself entitled in relation to tribes buried in the forests of the Amazon. "A great deal of egocentricity and naiveté is required if one is to believe that the whole of man has taken refuge in a single one of his historical or geographical modes of being, while the truth about man lies in the system of their differences and common properties," he wrote in *La Pensée sauvage* (*The Savage Mind*). Thus, the savage does not provide us with an image of man's childhood, as was believed in the eighteenth and nineteenth centuries in accordance with a naively European model of human history; he does not even provide us with one adequate image among others. As soon as it is granted that he has conceived quite varied societies and uses a logic as profound—or simple—as that of modern science, he no longer exists as a "savage" or as a "primitive." He merely offers us, as the so-called developed societies do, a multiplicity of cultural solutions of the eternal conflict between man and nature.

The role of the ethnologist is thus to classify cultural systems, to undertake for each of them an objective analysis of their systems of symbols and their articulation. The objectives of the psychoanalyst are implicitly transferred from the individual to the collective, from clinical analysis to the "decoding" of a social language such as myth. In his last years, Freud was greatly attracted by the interpretation of ethnological data (which he had not completely mastered). Lévi-Strauss rejects the methodological confusion implied in this illicit ethnology-psychoanalysis relationship; he never extrapolates into his own field the procedures of psychoanalysis. But his ideas about myths extend to the collective sphere the objectives of individual psychoanalytic treatment; they are intended to bring to the surface the subconscious structure of social beliefs, the code that underlies man's thinking and ultimately determines what he does think of himself and of others. On this, Lévi-Strauss agrees with Marx and Freud. Like that of myth, the realm of ideologies is the realm of false consciousness of reality, which must be explained at another level. Unlike Marx, though, he sees no historical remedy for this false consciousness, no reconciliation of man and his true history.

Moreover, structural ethnology at long last promises an advance of the human sciences to a methodology as rigorous as that of the exact sciences, for in one sense the work of ethnological analysis resembles a laboratory experiment. In both cases, the object under observation is treated as a natural object, is laid out in space, is amenable to any amount of experimentation, and there is a great awareness of the distance between the observer and the observed. In another sense, however, the methodological quarrels of the ethnologists threaten the assimilation of ethnology to the exact sciences. Lévi-Strauss is constantly aware both of the kinship and of the gap still to be filled, hence the originality of his work and no doubt also its wide range, which contrasts with the deliberately restricted nature of ethnological description. Working with a few societies into which history has not introduced its chaos and in which reduction to a few variables is relatively easy, he has been able to satisfy his concern for scientific rigor and his obsession with the linguistic "model" in the best possible conditions.

It is true, as he often repeats, that he has never ventured beyond; though, as always happens whenever a book becomes fashionable, imprudent or overzealous disciples tend to extend his method toward building up a general theory of societies. Frivolous or perhaps illusory though this anticipation may be, it underlines the methodological influence of his work. Is not this entomologist of human behavior, capable of the feat of emerging from his own cultural world, the reverse of Sartrian man, on whom engulfment in history and the emergence of a revolutionary practice impose his celebrated commitment? The fact that he belongs to the same generation as Sartre and has lived through practically the same history and is also considered to belong to the Left is thus immaterial; to him, these things belong to the domain of opinion and not to that of science. So in what way does he belong to the Left? The term hardly has meaning to a man who believes that, in their state of babbling infancy, the human sciences to which he has devoted his life and outside which he wishes to say nothing have for the time being nothing serious, still less useful, to offer to the polis and its struggles—except a relapse into ideology. In fact, their chance of one day deserving their name specifically depends on their keeping silent. "One may legitimately ask the exact and natural sciences what they are, but the social and human sciences are not yet in a state to render accounts. If these are required of them, or if on political grounds it is considered clever to pretend to do so, it will not be surprising if all one gets is phony balance sheets" (*Revue internationale des sciences sociales*, 1964).

Is this scruple to be regarded as a real break with history? It would be highly significant for our argument if it were so. But Lévi-Strauss continually denies it and pays explicit tribute to history, allowing it even to "reserve its rights" (*Leçon inaugurale* at the Collège de France, 1960). Until when, though? And what is the history to which he refers? Is it the meaning of history created by Sartre's dialectical reason? Evidently not, for, except at the price of unscrupulous falsification, looking back cannot demonstrate in the present the necessary outcome of the past. To Sartre, a man can always draw logical conclusions; to Lévi-Strauss he can only think that he does so. A stubborn illusion grants the present a rather foolish privilege without seeing that the present itself introduces into successive events a connecting link drawn from its own depths. Thus, the assurance of a retrogressive movement of truth vanishes under the ethnologist's eye, and the philosophy of history becomes a myth, the necessity of which only emphasizes its lack of substance. Lévi-Strauss, criticizing the fabrication of historical meaning by Sartre's dialectical reason, wrote this significant passage on the history of the French Revolution:

> Those described as men of the Left still cling to a period of contemporary history that granted them the privilege of consistency between practical imperatives and patterns of interpretation. Perhaps that golden age of the historical conscience has already passed; and the fact that one can at least imagine the possibility shows that this was merely a fortuitous situation, resembling the chance "focusing" on a heavenly body of an optical instrument with which it happened to be in a state of relative motion. We are still "focused" on the French Revolution; but, if we had lived earlier, we might have been focused on the Fronde. (*The Savage Mind*)

Once this pseudo-science has been exposed, however, the fact remains that societies change and there are histories—if not a single history—that are entitled to their observers. History, like Le Verrier's planet, thus becomes a perpetual "disturbing factor" introducing structural disequilibria. Now, it is impossible to grasp everything at once; synchronism and diachronism cannot be taken in at the same glance. Increasing one's knowledge in one field proportionally diminishes one's chances of acquiring it in another. Thus, structural ethnologists are needed to study order, and historians to study disorder. This division of labor is equal only in appearance, however. The study of structures has a double advantage, chronological and logical: chronological because the description of structures provides it with a starting point, and this gives complete autonomy to the work of the structuralists, while the opposite is not true (the work of the historian is dependent, ornamental, or, at all events, relegated to a distant future); and logical because, contrary to structural analysis, historical analysis pulverizes norms when it deals with events. Moreover, history is very difficult—perhaps impossible—to rationalize.

From this point of view, which is perhaps the most significant for our argument, Marx and Sartre are on the same side of the barricade, that of history, while Lévi-Strauss is on the other, that of structure. Like Hegel and Marx, Sartre still describes an advent, a history of human fulfillment, while Lévi-Strauss reduces multiple man to common mechanisms, dissolves him in a universal determinism, in the last resort displays him like a natural object. His books, written with a rather precious rigor, are a pitiless commentary on man's nothingness, marking a probably fundamental epistemological breach with the "ideological era." This is systematized by Michel Foucault in *Les Mots et les choses* (*The Order of Things*).

I do not wish to lapse into overly facile identifications, unduly confusing books and authors, but from the point of view of this analysis it is permissible to compare the work of Roland Barthes and Foucault with that of Lévi-Strauss, particularly considering the connection that intellectual opinion has spontaneously established among the three. Their fields of work are very different, but the methodological inspiration is the same: it is to try to obtain an ethnological view of contemporary societies and cultures. Foucault, imitating the use of the ethnologist's cultural telescope and reversing it, tries to gain more light from it that way. Lévi-Strauss mingles the Jivaro world with his European outlook, while Foucault sets out to consider European culture from a Jivaro angle in order to conjure away its presence at last and turn it into a scientific object. He tries to describe not individual patterns, which pertain to the study of opinions, but the conceptual structures that in each period make those opinions possible; the present intellectual revolution consists in his view in the breach with historicism and the end of humanist anthropocentrism. This makes Sartre the last "nineteenth-century philosopher"—which cannot be pleasing to him. Foucault's methodological aggressiveness, probably one of the clues to the success of his book, is of interest in that it tries to systematize the general significance of structuralism in present-day European culture; the analysts of man's "dissolution" have succeeded the prophets of his advent.

If what Foucault says is indeed true, and if structuralism confines Marx to a nineteenth century intellectually dominated by history, it is very curious and sociologically extremely interesting that structuralism should have developed in France so systematically and so late and in the same left-wing intellectual circles that (in the broad sense of the term) had been Marxist since the Liberation. This leaves us with the task of trying to describe and understand this paradoxical phenomenon as well as the curious and, I think, specifically French mutual contamination that has taken place between Marxism and structuralism.

At the first level of analysis, it is evident that if Marxism continues to lie at the heart of the French intellectual debate, it is less as a theory than as an ideal, less as an intellectual tool than as a political heritage. Twenty years have now passed since Sartre tried to reconcile the existentialist self with Marxist determinism, that is, his theory of personal liberty with his progressive opinions. It is this that forced him in his last philosophical book to substitute his dialectics of individual liberty for Marxist dialectical materialism while quoting as "self-evident" and approving without the slightest critical analysis the sum total of the propositions put forward in *Das Kapital*, that is to say, the essentials of the Marxist philosophy of history. By this subterfuge, he reconciles his philosophic conscience with his political progressiveness but, at the same time, illustrates the profound duality of his work and the uneven quality of his intellectual rigor. What interests him is the establishment of new existential foundations for human history and the revision of what he considers the mark of "scientism" in Marx. The respectful and distant doffing of his hat to *Das Kapital* does not derive from the same level of analysis; it signifies merely his allegiance to the left-wing intelligentsia, the resistance of yesterday, and the present-day struggles against imperialism. It is the historical symbol of an age that is the ideological age. Sartre speaks and will always speak as an elder brother to all those who lived profoundly through the times of fascism and communism. The genius of this professional philosopher resides, paradoxically perhaps, in the secret of his sensibility and art rather than in the clarity of his thought. In vain, he refuses to be what he has become, for he is caught up in the pitiless history of literature. He has turned into a patriarchal figure, a revered elder aging in glory, a Nobel Prize winner in spite of himself, but a Nobel Prize winner all the same. That is the last trick played on him by "words."

It is true that Lévi-Strauss has also emphasized his debt to Marxism, but his debt is of a different kind. Having deliberately abstained from postwar political struggles, shut in his academic ivory tower, he has felt no need to state his position in relation to communism or anticommunism; the few interviews that—obviously without pleasure—he has given the press betray more than prudence: a professional desire to keep his distance from his own cultural world and the chaotic history that introduces its disorders into it. Nevertheless, he can perhaps be considered more faithful than Sartre to Marx's philosophic premises and materialist determinism. He has inherited from Marx the scientific ambition of interpreting in intelligible terms the ideas that men form about the natural and social worlds by another system underlying them; he accepts the idea of a homogeneous society in which the determining factors will, in the last resort, be the relations between man and nature. Yet he transforms it profoundly by drawing up a veritable theory of superstructures. One of the plainest symptoms of the end of the ideological age among French intellectuals is, incidentally, this passion for the study of superstructures, as if they desire to track down, unveil, and understand the intellectual products of men and groups from their most hidden motivations. This is also the weakest point in Marx's analysis. To Lévi-Strauss, who made himself plain on the subject in *The Savage Mind*, the primacy of infrastructures is like a hand dealt at cards; what societies do with the hand imposed upon them depends on man's cultural inventiveness. However, this inventiveness does not suggest an unlimited number of variables. On the contrary, it is governed by structures and logical systems whose appearance and mutations, far from being necessary and inevitable as so many stages in an identical human evolution, depend on a calculation of probabilities; this accounts for the concomitant multiplicity of societies and cultures.

Admittedly, from other passages in his books, less materialist and less Marxist interpretations can be drawn, for one can never be sure whether the logical structure brought to light by the analysis is the same nature as the material produced by it or whether it informs reality. In fact, the problem of whether it is materialist or Kantian (a Kantianism without transcendental subject, Paul Ricoeur has said) is of little interest to Lévi-Strauss, who seems to accept both hypotheses; that is to say, he takes little interest in his philosophical relations with Marxism.

Moreover, he has always refused all extrapolation of his analytic procedures to mythologies, beliefs, or "historical" societies; he did so explicitly in reply to Edmund Leach, the British anthropologist, who suggested a Lévi-Straussian "decoding" of the book of Genesis—and the contrast between the theoretical ambition implicit in his ideas and the narrowness of their field of application rouses the mistrust of many of his colleagues in the English-speaking world, who remain attached to the empirical accumulation of facts. In France, however, it is this ambition or, rather, its special contribution to South American ethnology that has roused the enthusiasm of intellectuals and led rapidly to discussions at the most general level—existentialism, Marxism, and structuralism. The left-wing periodicals bear witness to this: the ethnologist has been consecrated a philosopher rather in spite of himself. Perhaps this should be regarded, as do certain English-speaking anthropologists, as a special feature of the French national tradition. But in this instance the fascination exercised by Lévi-Strauss over many Marxist or formerly Marxist intellectuals seems to me to have a more specific explanation. It is born neither of fraternity of political opinion (for Lévi-Strauss is the opposite of a "committed" man) nor of philosophical kinship (which is highly problematic, if it exists at all, and is in any case a matter of indifference to Lévi-Strauss) but from an inverse relationship in which nostalgia for Marx has been able to insert itself. Stated simply, the structural description of man as object has, in every respect, taken the place of the historical advent of the man-god.

There is yet another and still more surprising aspect of the relationship between the Marxists and the structuralists. It is significant that a whole trend of communist thought implicitly relies on structuralism, not to break with Marxism but to renovate it. That is the meaning of the work of Louis Althusser and his friends, who are trying to restore the theoretical value of the work of Marx and Lenin by rigorous analysis of their operative concepts in order to free it of the banally humanist ideology with which Roger Garaudy diluted it. Instead of being concerned, like Sartre, with reconciling an epistemology with progressive ideas, they aim to marry structuralist method and Marxist theory. From this there emerges a Marxism purged of its Hegelian paternity and of all contamination by bourgeois humanism and differing from Marx's ideas about his own doctrine, since the latter is redefined by the bringing to light of its fundamental conceptual structures. It is on this condition alone, in Althusser's view, that Marxism can again become what it really is (which was masked by the huge amount of social and historical sedimentation that has taken place): that is to say, *the* theory, *the* science par excellence, as opposed to the ideologies. This explains the curious path taken by Althusser: trying as he is to "deideologize" Marxism, he nevertheless uses it both as an object of study and as his sole point of scientific reference. Structural analysis, an attempt to extend the methods of natural science to the "human sciences," is thus subtly diverted in the direction of Marxist dogmatism, which is assumed as a self-evident premise—for the Marxist model is assimilated from the outset to the scientific model. Hence the epistemological contradiction and political ambiguity of the works of Althusser and his friends, which are devoted to restoring life to Marx by rigorous analysis but are blocked by bigoted adherence to a conceptual apparatus that, brilliant though it may have been, dates from another age and another world.

Perhaps on another plane this ambiguity is significant of the development of some communist intellectuals who have remained in the party since the destalinization crisis, and of younger ones who have since joined it in a climate that has become much more tolerant and much more critical than that of the 1950s. Althusser simultaneously offers structuralism and Marxism, critical study and doctrinaire intransigence, loyalty to the French communist party and reservations about it. There are many reasons to suppose that a sociological study of his present audience would disclose these factors, which are so characteristic of the present and recent past of communist intellectuals. No matter that they are contradictory; it is precisely because they are contradictory that a structuralist interpretation of Marx is able to offer them a temporary home. Intellectual and sociological contradictions mutually explain and reinforce each other; the structuralist "deideologizing" of Marxism undoubtedly offers a way of living through the end of the ideologies inside the communist world.

If this analysis is as a whole correct, if there is indeed a link between a general phenomenon like the end of ideologies and the attractiveness of structuralism in the special environment of the French intellectuals, it will strike one as surprising that the disintegration of ideological certainties and of the "meaning" of history has not led to a return to favor of empirical research and the gathering of factual information in the manner of the English-speaking world. Not that such research and the accumulation of factual information is not growing in France; on the contrary, there as elsewhere sociological surveys, public opinion polls, and large-scale investigations of archives are multiplying. However, everything is more than ever subordinated, even more than it was yesterday, to the search for a general theory. Everything is happening as if the crisis of Marxism had cleared the way for a methodology of another kind but at the same level, heir to the same ambition for total, systematic understanding. What for lack of a better term is called the Parisian "passion" for structuralism—that is, its social success and its timing— would thus be explained by its deep relationship, both contradictory and homogeneous, to Marxism. The natural sciences model has displaced the history model, man as object has taken the place of man as subject, structure has taken the place of determinist ambition and derives from the same desire to decipher what underlies the apparent or merely conscious meaning of human behavior.

It is probable that the end of the ideological age among the French intellectuals embraces two distinct phenomena differing in nature. Destalinization, the Sino-Soviet schism, the crisis of the Third World—and French and European prosperity—have punctured the progressivism of the 1950s that was so characteristic of the ideological age. Hence, there was a receptiveness of intellectual opinion, a kind of expectation—rather as, a century ago, the inglorious failure of the romantics of 1848 preceded and facilitated the formation of the realist and positivist generation. But it helped this generation to emerge, it did not create it: this intellectual change does not itself call for sociological explanation. At the present time, the political disappointments suffered by progressivism have profoundly weakened the influence of Marxism among the left-wing intellectuals, but it is Lévi-Strauss and not Raymond Aron who reigns in the void thus created. What prevails is not a liberal and empirical criticism of Marxism but, rather, a hyperintellectual and systematic way of thinking that aims at a general theory of man. Not only have Marxists or former Marxists been able to invest their past in this without repudiating it; they have also rediscovered in it their ambition for a comprehensive science of man and their old all-embracing dream, "deideologized" and freed from the naivetés of commitment and of the meaning of history. To that extent perhaps the case of the French intellectuals deserves to become a classic; the end of the ideological age has found its doctrinaires.

TRANSLATED BY JONATHAN MANDELBAUM

The Historians Respond

ANDRÉ BURGUIÈRE

History and Structure

1971

André Burguière, at the time secrétaire de rédaction *of the* Annales, *began his introduction to a special issue of the journal devoted to "History and Structure" by parodying Jean Giraudoux: "The war between history and structuralism will not take place." It was a reassuring diagnosis, perhaps because it came late, in 1971. It was in the mid-1960s that the structuralist movement posed its most aggressive challenge to the historical point of view. By the early 1970s, there were already signs that the challenge was on the wane. Historians chose that moment to take back the initiative. In the case of the* Annales, *they did so, once again, by occupying the terrain of social science to point out the deep similarities that existed, in their view, between the project initiated by Marc Bloch and Lucien Febvre forty years earlier and the recent claims of social scientists anxious to declare their independence from history. Indeed, the historians went so far as to proclaim "rights of paternity to the structural approach." This intellectually as well as strategically important special issue of the journal was devoted to rediscovering this alleged common heritage, as well as to a purely empirical definition of a program of interdisciplinary comparison.*

The war between history and structuralism will not take place. In this special issue of the *Annales*, we have no intention of reviving a rhetorical duel that was fashionable for a time but later forgotten.[1] We prefer to profit from this period of relative calm. While theoret-

---

André Burguière, "Histoire et structure," *Annales ESC* 3–4 (1971).

ical debate temporarily lies fallow, research can once again raise its voice. The time has come for a preliminary assessment of structuralism's influence on historical research.

The confrontation that some wished to arrange between history and the latest human sciences transformed a genuine problem into a false debate. While historians saw no need for a dramatic choice between diachrony and synchrony, they felt directly concerned by methodological realignments going on all around them. At this level, structuralism never constituted a school: it merely reflected the convergence of various lines of research, some already well established (in comparative mythology and general linguistics, for example), others more recent (such as structural anthropology and semiology), temporarily brought together by similar methodological requirements.

If the rejection of history seemed to crystallize this diverse movement and afford it a certain cohesiveness, it was because these disciplines needed first of all to break the historicist mold in which they were all originally cast—by "historicism" I mean a constant tendency to shift the analysis from study of the phenomenon to study of its origin (genetic explanation), as well as a tendency for various approaches to toss the ball back and forth among themselves through endless recourse to dialectical reasoning (explanation in terms of external causes).

Yet a return to history is already beginning. Ethnologists are increasingly interested in restoring to so-called primitive societies the historical dimension that is compressed in myths and institutions; epistemology, as Michel Foucault has pointed out in *L'Archéologie du savoir* (*The Archaeology of Knowledge*), nowadays attaches great significance to points of rupture and transition—accidents of a sort—that emerge from the complexity of the history of science; while history has more than ever shown itself to be attentive to movements over the *longue durée*, to that which changes slowly. By contrast, what remains of the structuralist *aggiornamento*, its irreversible contribution, is its refusal to treat social reality as a mere aggregate of elementary units (facts, events, symbols, ideas)—to isolate phenomena and begin with details that are supposed either to speak for the whole or allow one to move from the particular to the general yields nothing of significance.

Discipline after discipline hit upon the idea that, in the human sciences, messages are never discrete. Observable phenomena and sources are not willed phenomena but emergent fragments of an underlying system. In comparative mythology, for example, Georges Dumézil, a structuralist *avant la lettre*, found that it made no sense to focus exclusively on how myths derived from one another. In the corpus of Indo-European mythology the identification of symbolic representations of certain social functions (such as the warrior function) had given rise to a diffusionist hypothesis, which, since it involved a homogeneous ethno-cultural entity, found ready acceptance while providing no explanation for the presence or persistence of the symbolic representations in question. By contrast, the fact that the warrior function in Indo-European myths always appeared in conjunction with (or implicitly referred to) the religious and agricultural functions revealed the durable importance of a cultural model based on a tripartite organization of society. The persistence of this model should be seen not as an ideological consequence floating on the surface of history but as the projection of a system of thought essential to the functioning of Indo-european societies.

If structural analysis consists in uncovering permanent features, in revealing, in the words of Jean Piaget, "a system of transformations governed by certain systematic laws,"[2] then historians must recognize that they have long been familiar with the approach, even at the risk of seeming to be asserting yet again certain rights of priority. For them, structure was at first a deliberately vague methodological notion, useful for understanding imperceptible changes and for bringing into history phenomena that had seemed to stand outside of time. This early structuralism overlaps with the history of the *Annales*. I would be reluctant even to mention it, for by now it has become the common property and tool of all historians, if some structuralists, and not the least of them, in their criticisms of historians had not repeatedly neglected the *Annalistes'* contribution. For instance, Louis Althusser wrote that "Hegel merely reconceptualized, in terms of his own theoretical problematic, the number-one problem of historical practice, the problem that Voltaire evoked when he distinguished, for example, the century of Louis XV from that of Louis XIV. This is still the major problem of modern historiography."[3] If by this Althusser means periodization as a means of classification, it has and will continue to have in history the same heuristic value that the classification of species has in the natural sciences. However, if he means a sort of dissection of historical reality in all its "thickness" into a mere sequence of isolated scenes, each of which, with its complex architecture of social ills, commercial exchanges, wars, and works of art, is then to be symbolized by a king or pope, what historian nowadays would accept this as a description of his practice?

And what historian would resign himself to the division of labor proposed some time ago by Claude Lévi-Strauss, when he stated that history organizes its data "in relation to conscious expressions, ethnology in relation to unconscious expressions, of social life."[4] All that history has incorporated over the past half century, from geographical history to the history of *mentalités*, from the quantitative history of prices, demographic data, food consumption, and climate to the history of social relations and institutions, it has done by crossing the boundary between conscious and unconscious data. When it returns to the most conscious of all forms of expression, to works of literature and art, it still must look beyond the work's stated meaning and base its analysis on the organization of the unconscious, or at any rate of the implicit, which Lucien Febvre dubbed *l'outillage mental*. It sometimes seems as if history's mission were to serve as a scapegoat for the human sciences. Its place? "That which belongs by right to irreducible contingency."[5] Its object? "The power and inanity of the event."[6] It was good for all the indigestible refuse of social reality, for all that could not be reduced or formalized, as if it must forever remain the empire of the accidental.

What history are these critics talking about? The history that grows with the passage of time? The history that historians write or some metaphysical dimension of the human condition whereby man exercises his freedom and creates his meaning in the element of time? The ambiguities of the vocabulary, it must be granted, are perpetuated by historians themselves, as if they hoped thereby to preserve the ambivalence of their knowledge. In this respect, the debate with structuralism and with structural anthropology in particular deserves credit for forcing history to choose between the science and the ideology of change. By claiming to be concerned with societies without history, ethnology challenged the beliefs of historians for whom a society becomes intelligible only as it fulfills its destiny over time. But "historyless" is hardly an accurate description of societies that are neither static nor without memory. Today, of course, ethnologists, especially Africanists, are casting a critical eye on ahistorical conceptions of primitive society. Every society bears the burden of history, and the histories of some of the societies studied by ethnologists have been very eventful indeed, full of migrations, wars, economic transformations, and social tensions. Only our inability (or reluctance) to discover their histories forces us to adopt an ethnocentric point of view, from which some societies seem static and determined never to change the way they function, to reproduce themselves endlessly.

These histories remain undiscoverable not because they have sunk into oblivion (the impressive wealth of myths and oral literature is proof that it has not) but because history's conceptual framework has not been able to accommodate them. What is at issue here is the whole system of chronological divisions that our educational system from elementary school to the university religiously perpetuates and thereby invests with an almost transcendental value. How are exotic societies to be fitted into the ubiquitous scheme of four major historical epochs that have become a fundamental fixture of our intellectual development—Antiquity, Middle Ages, Ancien Régime, modern times? (Indeed, the last great division is marked by the French Revolution, which is scarcely relevant outside

France.) How is their history to be squared with those constant pressures of reality that are the cause of evolution and revolution—productive techniques, social groups, nations, institutions, beliefs, and so on?

Beyond this inadequate system of references, what is called into question is the historian's claim to define every society by comparing its level and pace of development with those of Europe. This claim, inspired by generosity as much as by dogmatism, grew out of the ideology of progress with which historical science was closely associated in its early days. As various studies in historical lexicology have shown, the eighteenth century hesitated between a fixed and a dynamic conception of history, between history as portrait and history as narrative reconstruction of a sequence of events. Evolutionism, in which historical science ultimately found its roots, was a militant philosophy that expected history to furnish experimental proof of progress. It was also quite simply a response to new economic conditions. Extending theory beyond all reasonable limits, it projected the values of industrial Europe, its cult of change and innovation, onto other epochs and civilizations. It transformed the growth process that propelled Europe into a phase of high-temperature development, the age of accumulation that made Europe distinct, into the unique time of history. As if Europe, while equipping itself with the means to achieve objective knowledge of the past (through erudition, critical scrutiny of the sources, and other requirements of historical method), sought above all to justify its destiny after the fact.

Can a particular experience, an accidental or at least recent acceleration of change through industrial revolution, be turned into the universal standard against which all history is measured? Indeed, such a conception of history, a veritable Procrustean bed into which a wide variety of civilizations have been forced, provides too many justifications and too few explanations. It is being challenged today by students of other cultures as well as those of our own historical bailiwick.

If, in this effort to achieve a new outlook, historians can claim certain rights of paternity to the structural approach, much of the credit must go to Marxism. Although Marxism may nowadays appear to be the most fully developed of various unilinear theories of history, it taught historians to define a society or period in terms not of a series of events but of an operational system, namely, the mode of production. It undertook to decipher in a systematic way the results of a historical method that was content simply to verify the authenticity of its sources, and in so doing discovered behind what societies admitted about themselves (the language of the superstructure, that is) their unavowed logic.

Marxism's legacy was therefore perfectly ambiguous. Every tendency in historical science today has been influenced by Marxism even when there is no explicit reference to it. Yet, thus far, no important historical work has been totally Marxist in inspiration. Although Lévi-Strauss acknowledges a direct relation between the Marxist method and the structuralist approach,[7] some Marxist historians charge that structuralism underestimates the strivings toward human liberation that emerge in the course of social development, strivings that they accuse structuralists of diluting in a dispiriting tincture of historical pluralism.[8]

In fact, in affirming the need for historical pluralism in anthropology, Lévi-Strauss was responding to the same need that impelled French historians of the 1930s to emphasize the importance of various kinds of cycles. The static history of "cold" or traditional societies is not necessarily immutable or repetitive, he argued, but their "line of development means nothing to us" because it falls outside our frame of reference.[9] It is something different from cumulative history, the history of technological progress, industrial production, and also (provided one is clear about the defining indices) intellectual progress.

In Europe's eventful past, historians have recently identified intervals of equilibrium during which change has been more or less minimal over a relatively lengthy period. The great cycle of European agrarian history that runs from the thirteenth to the eighteenth century is one of these. By the middle of the eighteenth century, some regions had just returned to the levels of population density and economic output they had achieved on the eve of the Great Plague, yet despite this broad equilibrium they experienced all the contradictions and tensions of a "hot" history: social tensions whose peaks coincided with demographic "troughs," and poor harvests together with an absolute decrease in food consumption (marked by the virtual disappearance of meat from the average market basket) in the sixteenth and seventeenth centuries. At the same time, however, cities were growing and commercial capitalism was grafting early forms of accumulation onto a basically growthless agrarian society.

Cyclic theories also had the merit of making crises a part of the system's logic. For a long time, historians viewed the periodic catastrophes that afflicted Ancien Régime society, with their cortege of rebellion and epidemic, as nothing more than accidental disturbances of a backward economy, due in part to civil unrest, in part perhaps to the birth pangs of a new social order. But then Ernest Labrousse revealed the socioeconomic implications of subsistence crises, Jean Meuvret and Pierre Goubert showed how they served to regulate the Ancien Régime's demographic system, and Emmanuel Le Roy Ladurie demonstrated their close association with climatic cycles, that other implacable reality of agricultural societies bereft of technological progress, so that we now recognize cyclical crises as one of the linchpins of Ancien Régime society.

The disparity that exists within any given period between repetitive change, regression, and progress leads to the identification of several distinct rhythms within historical time, indeed to a contrast that, since

Fernand Braudel's celebrated article, is often invoked between the *longue durée* and the *temps court* (short time span).[10] It also obliges the historian to look upon historical development as a matter not of necessity but of intersecting probabilities. In rural Languedoc, for example, impoverished by debt and fragmentation of the land and condemned to economic stagnation by saturation of the cultivable territory, Le Roy Ladurie has found signs of cultural growth (literacy, availability of reading matter) as early as the sixteenth century, a development with important consequences for ensuing religious conflicts. Lévi-Strauss's image of a dice game nicely captures the discontinuity of progress: "What can be won on one throw can always be lost on the next, and it is only occasionally that history is cumulative, that the winnings add up to make a jackpot."[11]

As a result, historians, once again following in the wake of economists, formulated the concept of a model, which can be used to analyze and interrelate these various temporalities. Models come in many varieties. Homogeneous models are used to study the possibility and pace of economic growth. Simulated models are used to test the rationality and efficiency of certain historical choices in the spirit of the alternative hypotheses studied by so-called new economic historians in the United States. And complex models combine quantitative data with behavioral symptoms, as historical demographers have done in studying the austere seventeenth century.

Models, which increase the likelihood of success in comparative history, can also be coupled with the structural approach that ethnographers now use to study myth and ritual. Rather than compare civilizations or forms of development point by point, fixing on the most prominent features, one tries to measure similarity statistically by looking at sets of features susceptible of creating comparable historical conditions.

In a first phase, exemplified by the work of Fernand Braudel, historians used the concept of structure to study the *longue durée*, to identify "an almost immobile history, a history of slow changes and transformations often involving crushing setbacks and endlessly repeated cycles."[12] At this level, history uses mainly quantitative data, which naturally call for structural analysis. Formalization, for which the notions of cycle and model are useful, is for this purpose not merely a possible style but a necessary step for making sense of complex, apparently incoherent phenomena.

By contrast, the data with which the studies in this volume of the journal concern themselves are positively bursting with meaning. Written texts, symbolic language—different registers of what can be called "cultural history" defined by a common intention, namely, to signify. The historian's problem in this area is that his reflection does not enable him to give meaning to what seemed incomprehensible but only to replace one meaning with another. His research thus moves along a razor's edge, between the deceptive clarity of classical historical analysis in which everything seemed already to have its explanation and the arbitrariness of a method that requires everything to be called into question.

Yet it may well be in the realm of cultural history, where anachronism is only too apt to rear its head, that the structural approach can be most effective. The mind is always tempted to abolish the distance that separates it from those who bear witness to the past by adapting their discourse to its own system of reasoning. If the studies presented here draw their inspiration largely from methods developed recently in linguistics, ethnology, and comparative mythology, it is first of all in order to restore the historical dimension to cultural forms, that is, to take note of the distance that separates those forms from our own intellectual universe.

The organization of this issue follows the paradoxical progression of structural analysis from the manifest sense to the latent sense. *Myths* and *Institutions,* whose significance is often condensed in enigmatic symbols, lend themselves readily to analytic decoding. *Texts and Images* and *Other Logics* are areas in which our rationality all too easily projects itself, and these therefore put up greater resistance to a similar reduction. That is why most of these studies argue for an open structuralism. The materials with which historians work are too impure for ordinary structural analysis, but that impurity is also what makes those materials so rich. "It is as if wherever structure grew impoverished, praxis yielded its utmost," in Luc de Heusch's admirable formulation, "as if a first degree of articulation of culture with nature gave way to a second." [13]

To place oneself in a historical perspective it is not enough to pay attention to a certain erosion of mental habits or systems of organization. After a crisis or confrontation of some kind, time will in some cases completely engulf the structure that one wants to observe. For the historian, there is a real danger in sticking with dead forms (at the level of vocabulary, for example) out of a prejudice in favor of continuity while neglecting the forces that are in the process of transforming a society.

A little structuralism takes us away from history; a great deal of structuralism brings us back. The following survey will have served its purpose if it succeeds in demonstrating both the value and the modesty of structuralism's contribution to history. In the end, what the historian asks of structuralist methods is not a pretext to flee the sound and fury or to exorcise the instability of historical reality but a tool to observe how transformations work while remaining as close as possible to his task— the analysis of change.

TRANSLATED BY ARTHUR GOLDHAMMER

Notes

[1] On this aspect of the problem, see François Furet, "Les Intellectuels français et le structuralisme," *Preuves* 2 (Feb. 1967). Excerpted here as "French Intellectuals From Marxism to Structuralism," pp. 217–230.

[2] Jean Piaget, *Le Structuralisme* (Paris: P.U.F., 1968).

[3] Louis Althusser, *L'Objet du "Capital"* (Paris: Petite Bibliothèque Maspero, 1968), p. 116.

[4] Claude Lévi-Strauss, *Anthropologie structurale* (Paris: Plon, 1958), p. 25.

[5] Claude Lévi-Strauss, *Du Miel aux cendres* (Paris: Plon, 1966), p. 408.

[6] Ibid.

[7] Claude Lévi-Strauss, *Tristes tropiques* (Paris: Plon, 1955), p. 49.

[8] See especially Maxime Rodinson, "Ethnologie et relativisme," *La Nouvelle critique* (Nov. 1955).

[9] Claude Lévi-Strauss, *Race et histoire* (Paris: Gonthier, 1961), p. 42.

[10] Fernand Braudel, "La Longue durée," *Annales ESC* 13 (1958).

[11] Lévi-Strauss, *Race et histoire*, p. 39.

[12] Fernand Braudel, *La Méditerranée et le monde méditerranéen à l'époque de Philippe II* (Paris: Armand Colin, 1966), 2nd ed. preface.

[13] Luc de Heusch, *Pourquoi l'épouser? et autres essais* (Paris: Gallimard, 1971), p. 136.

New Interdisciplinary Alliances

———

JACQUES LE GOFF

Mentalities: A History of Ambiguities

1974

Jacques Le Goff was not the first historian to tackle the difficult task of defining the notion of mentality. *Robert Mandrou and Georges Duby, not to mention Lucien Febvre, were among those who had also tried. However, Le Goff's effort came under rather special circumstances: his article was published in the multivolume manifesto* Faire de l'histoire *(1974), which he coedited with Pierre Nora. The aim was to acquaint a broad public with the breadth and diversity of the "historian's territory," as well as to reestablish a sort of community of reflection and collaboration between history and the social sciences, a community that had been seriously shaken by the structuralist movement. This situation accounts perhaps for the call for interdisciplinary collaboration, which added still more uncertainty to the definition of an already "ambiguous" notion. To be sure, the theme of mentalities was a familiar part of the* Annales *tradition. Yet in the intellectual climate of the early 1970s, to point this out was something of a gesture of goodwill toward anthropology in particular, as it had become a "discipline of reference" for French historians. Indeed, it was about to take its place, after geography and economics, as their preferred partner. The revival of the history of* mentalities, *a genre that had for the most part lain fallow after World War II,*

From Jacques Le Goff and Pierre Nora, eds., *Constructing the Past: Essays in Historical Methodology* (New York: Cambridge University Press, 1984), pp. 167–68. First published as "Les Mentalités: Une histoire ambiguë," in Jacques Le Goff and Pierre Nora, eds., *Faire de l'histoire*, vol. 3 (Paris: Gallimard, 1974), pp. 77–79.

would take place under the aegis of what people were just beginning to call historical anthropology. As a leading practitioner of the art, Le Goff in this article offered an overview of the situation as it existed at the time. Notwithstanding the author's intention, however, the text can also be read as an attempt to secure new alliances and propose new strategies.

For the historian today, the term "mentality" is still a novelty and already devalued by excessive use. There is much talk of the history of mentalities, but convincing examples of such history are rare. It represents a new area of research, a trail to be blazed, and yet, at the same time, doubts are raised as to its scientific, conceptual, and epistemological validity. Fashion has seized upon it, and yet it seems already to have gone out of fashion. Should we revive or bury the history of mentalities?

The primary attraction of the history of mentalities lies in its vagueness: it can be used to refer to the leftovers, the indefinable residue of historical analysis.

After 1095, something stirs in Western Christendom, and individuals and masses alike throw themselves into the great adventure of the crusades. In attempting to analyze this momentous period, we may refer to demographic growth and nascent overpopulation, the commercial ambitions of Italian city-states, the papacy's desire to reunite a fragmented Christendom by taking on the infidel. But none of these factors is sufficient to explain everything, or indeed, perhaps, to explain what is most important. For this, we need to understand the pull of Jerusalem, the earthly equivalent of the Celestial City, and its central position within a certain collective imagery. What are the crusades without a certain religious mentality?

What is feudalism? A set of institutions, a mode of production, a social system, a particular type of military organization? Georges Duby maintains that we must go further, "extend economic history into the history of mentalities," and analyze "the feudal concept of service." Feudalism must be seen as a "medieval mentality."

The period since the sixteenth century has seen the birth of a new kind of society in the West—capitalist society. Is it the result of a new mode of production, of an economy based on money, a construction of the bourgeoisie? It is all those things, but it is also the product of new attitudes toward work and money, of a mentality that, since Max Weber, has become associated with the Protestant ethic.

The notion of "mentality," then, refers to a kind of historical beyond. Its function, as a concept, is to satisfy the historian's desire to "go further," and it leads to a point of contact with the other human sciences.

Attempting to define the "religious mentality" of the Middle Ages, Marc Bloch sees within it "a whole series of beliefs and practices ... some of them passed down from age-old forms of thaumaturgy, others of relatively recent origin, produced within a civilization still endowed with a great myth-making capacity." In this respect, the historian of mentalities will tend to move toward the ethnologist: both seek to discover the stablest, most immobile level of a society's existence. As Ernest Labrousse put it, "the social changes more slowly than the economic, and the mental more slowly than the social." Keith Thomas, in his work on the religious mentality of the Middle Ages and Renaissance, explicitly employs ethnological methods, principally inspired by Edward Evans-Pritchard. Through the study of ritual and ceremony, the ethnologist tries to reconstruct beliefs and value systems. Medieval historians like Percy Ernst Schramm, Ernst Kantorowicz, and Bernard Guinée, following the lead of Marc Bloch, have enriched the political history of the Middle Ages with their description of a political mentality, a mystical conception of monarchy, based on analysis of coronations, miraculous healings, the insignia of authority and the receptions accorded to kings by towns. Formerly, the hagiographer was interested in the saint, but interest now focuses on saintliness—its basis in the mind of the believer, the psychology of credulity, the mentality of the ancient hagiographer. The anthropology of religion has radically altered the perspective of religious history.

The historian of mentalities must also assimilate some of the techniques of the sociologist, for the object of both is by definition collective. The mentality of any one historical individual, however important, is precisely what that individual shares with other men of his time. Take the example of Charles V of France: he is unanimously praised by historians for his thrift, his administrative ability, his statesmanship. He is the wise king, the reader of Aristotle who rebuilds the kingdom's finances, keeps strict accounts, and wages on the English a war of attrition which does not stretch the public purse. Now, in 1380, on his deathbed, Charles V abolishes the hearth tax—and historians have busily sought to explain this unexpected gesture either as some obscure political strategy or as the aberration of a man no longer in control of his faculties. But why not adopt an explanation consistent with fourteenth-century attitudes: the king who is afraid of death and does not wish to face the Last Judgment burdened with the hatred of his subjects? The king who, in his dying moments, allows his mentality to outweigh his political judgment, the commonly shared beliefs of his time to override his personal political ideology?

There are particularly close links between the historian of mentalities and the social psychologist. For both, the notions of behavior and attitude are crucial. What is more, the increasing tendency of social psychologists like Clyde Kluckhohn to emphasize the role of cultural control in biological behavior represents a bridge between social psychology and ethnology, and therefore a link with history as well. The reciprocal attraction between social psychology and the history of mentalities is particularly clear in two areas: the study of crime, marginality, and deviance in the past, and the parallel growth of the contemporary opinion poll and of historical analysis of electoral behavior.

Here, historical psychology has a great opportunity to develop links with another central area of contemporary historiography: quantitative history. The history of mentalities, whose object would appear to be characterized by nuance and constant flux, can in fact, if it is prepared to accept certain modifications, use the quantitative methods developed by social psychology. As Abraham A. Moles has indicated, the attitude-scales method takes as its starting point "a mass of fact, opinions and verbal statements, initially totally incoherent," but in the end produces a "scale of measurement" commensurate with the facts being treated; this in turn allows the facts in question to be defined. Thus, the ambiguous term "mentality" may perhaps be defined satisfactorily, in a manner reminiscent of Alfred Binet's famous phrase, "Intelligence is what is measured by my test."

Similarly, the link with ethnology will allow the history of mentalities to draw on structuralist methods, one of the great tools of modern human sciences. Is not mentality itself a structure?

Over and above the links with some human sciences which the history of mentalities opens up, though, one of its main attractions is the new perspectives it offers to historians who have become too dependent on economic and social history and, above all, on vulgar Marxism.

Certainly, economic and social history, Marxist in inspiration or not, has established a solid basis for historical explanation by wresting historiography from the dei ex machina of providence and great men, and their positivist equivalents, chance and events. But for all this, the aims of history as defined by Jules Michelet in his 1869 preface have not been achieved: "History . . . still appeared to me to be weak in two respects: neither sufficiently material . . . nor sufficiently spiritual, speaking of laws and political acts but not of ideas and manners." Within Marxism itself, historians who emphasized modes of production and the class struggle as historical mechanisms failed to develop a convincing analysis of the relationship between infrastructure and superstructure. The economic mirror they held up to society revealed only a pale reflection of abstract theories: there were no faces, no living people. Man does not live by bread alone, but in this history there was no bread at all, just skeletons automatically repeating the same danse macabre. These fleshless mechanisms needed a new dimension, and that new dimension was provided by mentalities.

The history of mentalities, then, represents a link with other disciplines within the human sciences, and the emergence of an area that traditional historiography refused to consider. Yet it is also a meeting point for opposing forces that are being brought into contact by the dynamics of contemporary historical research: the individual and the collective, the long-term and the everyday, the unconscious and the intentional, the structural and the conjunctural, the marginal and the general.

The history of mentalities operates at the level of the everyday automatisms of behavior. Its object is that which escapes historical individuals because it reveals the impersonal content of their thought—that which is common to Caesar and his most junior legionary, Saint Louis and the peasant on his lands, Christopher Columbus and any one of his sailors. The history of mentalities is to the history of ideas as the history of material culture is to economic history. People of the fourteenth century see the plague as a divine punishment, and that reaction is the fruit of the assumptions present in the teachings of Christian thinkers from Saint Augustine to Thomas Aquinas; it is a reflection of the equation, disease = sin, developed by the clerics of the Early Middle Ages, but it retains only the rough form of the idea and pays no heed to logical articulations and rational subtleties. In the same way, everyday utensils and the clothing of the poor are derived from prestigious models created by superficial developments in the economy, fashion, and taste. It is at this level that we may grasp the style of a period—deep in its everyday behavior. When Johan Huizinga calls John of Salisbury a "pregothic mind," thus seeing him as a precursor of subsequent historical developments, his expression evokes the notion of mentality: the historical figure becomes the collective expression of a period, as when Lucien Febvre, rejecting the anachronisms of the historians of ideas, situated Rabelais in the concrete historicity that is the object of the historian of mentalities.

What men say, whatever the tone in which they say it—conviction, emotion, bombast—is more often than not simply an assemblage of readymade ideas, commonplaces, and intellectual bric-a-brac, the remnants of cultures and mentalities belonging to different times and different places. This determines the methods that the historian of mentalities must use. Two stages may be noted: first, the identification of different strata and fragments of what, following André Varagnac's term "archaeocivilization," we may call "archaeopsychology"; and second, since these remnants are nevertheless ordered according to certain criteria of mental, if not logical, coherence, the historian must determine these psychic systems of organization, comparable to the principles of *bricolage intellectuel* which Lévi-Strauss sees as the distinguishing feature of primitive thought.

TRANSLATED BY ARTHUR GOLDHAMMER

JEAN-PIERRE VERNANT

Myth and Thought Among the Greeks: Introduction

1965

Born in 1914, Jean-Pierre Vernant has had an unusual career. Trained as a philosopher, he came to historical anthropology by way of social psychology, a discipline that enjoyed a moment in the sun in France but has since been somewhat neglected. A disciple of Louis Gernet, a Hellenist and student of Emile Durkheim, and above all of Ignace Meyerson, the tireless promoter of historical psychology, Vernant has devoted many works to the world of the Greeks: Mythe et pensée chez les Grecs *(1965)* [Myth and Thought Among the Greeks], Les Ruses de l'intelligence: La métis des Grecs [Cunning Intelligence in Greek Culture and Society] *(with Marcel Detienne, 1974),* L'Individu, la mort, l'amour *(1989). He was also the driving force behind a brilliant research team, including such eminent scholars as Pierre Vidal-Naquet, Marcel Detienne, Nicole Loraux, and François Hartog. In focusing on ancient Greece, these investigators were trespassing on territory already claimed by classical studies, philosophy, and ancient literature and history. The approach Vernant describes in the following text, which his work illustrates, is quite different (which is why it has often been greeted with dismay by classicists). He set out to construct a historical anthropology of the ancient world with which it would be possible to understand the "Greek miracle" in terms of mutations in mental categories and systems of thought, or, more generally, representations (and the reader will note that Vernant is not loathe to use the word* mentality*). He aims to see mental structures and psychological functions in the particular contexts that gave them meaning. Instead of judging myth in the light of reason, he seeks to understand it as a coherent, rigorous, logical, and distinctive mode of knowledge. This approach, as well as*

From *Mythe et pensée chez les Grecs* (Paris: Maspero, 1965). This translation appeared as the introduction to *Myth and Thought Among the Greeks* (London: Routledge and Kegan Paul, 1983), pp. ix–xv.

the object of his studies, explains why Vernant, long known only to specialists, did not emerge as a leading figure until relatively late in his career—in the structuralist years (when the affinity of his work with that of Lévi-Strauss became apparent), and even more in the 1970s, when it was seen as offering a remarkable illustration of the fruitfulness of the dialogue between history and anthropology.

For ten years, we have attempted to apply to the field of Greek studies the methods in historical psychology that Ignace Meyerson has initiated in France.[1] The subject matter for our investigation is material that has been worked on by specialists—scholars of both Greek and ancient history. However, we shall be considering it from a different point of view. Our material includes religion (with its myths, rituals, and illustrated representations), philosophy, science, art, social institutions, and technical or economic data. But whatever we are dealing with, we shall consider it as having been created by the human mind, as the expression of organized mental activity. By studying these phenomena, we shall seek to understand the individual, in ancient Greece, a being inseparable from the social and cultural environment of which he is at once the creator and the product.

The task is difficult because it is necessarily indirect in character, and it runs the risk of being unfavorably received. In dealing with the evidence, the texts, the archaeological data, the realities that we too must use, the specialists are all faced with particular problems for which they must use special techniques. In most cases, the study of the individual and his psychological functions appears to them to be foreign to their own particular fields. The psychologists and sociologists, on the other hand, are too involved in the contemporary world to be interested in a study of classical antiquity, and so they abandon this to what they take to be the somewhat outdated curiosity of the humanists.

Yet, if there is a history of the inner being, to complement the history of civilizations, we must again adopt the shibboleth first advanced a few years ago by Zevedei Barbu in his *Problems of Historical Psychology: Back to the Greeks.*[2] If we approach the matter from the point of view of historical psychology, there seem to us to be several reasons why a return to the Greeks is unavoidable. The first is of a practical nature: documentation of life in ancient Greece is more extensive, more varied, and has been more thoroughly researched than the evidence for any other civilization. There is at our disposal a large number of substantial and detailed original works relating to the social and political history, the religion, art, and thought of ancient Greece. To this practical advantage can be added more fundamental reasons: the writings that have come to us from ancient Greek civilization embody ideas sufficiently different from those expressed in the framework of our own intellectual universe to make us feel not only a historical distance but also an awareness of a fundamental change in man. At the same time, these ideas are not as alien to us as are some others. They have come down to us through an uninterrupted process of transmission. They live on in cultural traditions to which we constantly refer. The Greeks are sufficiently distant for us to be able to study them as an external subject, quite separate from ourselves, to which the psychological categories of today cannot be applied with any precision. Yet they are sufficiently close for us to be able to communicate with them without too much difficulty. We can understand the language used in their writings, and reach beyond the literary and other documents to their mental processes, their patterns of thought and feeling, their system of relations between will and action—in sum, to the structure of the Greek mind.

There is one final reason why the historian of the inner being should turn to classical antiquity. Within the span of a few centuries, Greece underwent decisive changes both in its social and its mental life. The city was born, and, with it, law. Among the first philosophers there was the emergence of rational thought and the progressive organization of knowledge into a body of clearly differentiated disciplines—ontology, mathematics, logic, natural sciences, medicine, ethics, and politics. New forms of art were created, and different modes of expression were invented in response to the need to validate hitherto-unknown aspects of human experience: these were lyric poetry and tragedy in literature, and in the plastic arts, sculpture and painting, seen as having an imitative function.

These innovations in so many different fields indicate a change in mentality so marked that it has been seen as the birth of "Western man," a true flowering of mind and spirit in every sense of the term. These transformations relate not only to progress made in intellectual matters or the techniques of reasoning. From the *homo religiosus* of the archaic cultures to this political, reasoning individual (referred to in Aristotle's definitions, for example), the transformations affect the entire framework of thought and the whole gamut of psychological functions: the modes of symbolic expression, and the manipulation of signs, ideas of time and space, causality, memory, imagination, the organization of action, will, and personality—all these categories of the mind undergo a fundamental change in terms both of their internal structure and their interrelationships.

Two themes in particular have fascinated Greek scholars during the last fifty years: these are the progression from mythical to rational thought and the gradual development of the idea of the individual.

These two questions have not been accorded an equal amount of space. The first is the subject of a general study, whereas in dealing with the second we have concentrated on one particular aspect. We feel, however, that in order to avoid misunderstandings we should attempt to explain our position with regard to each of these two problems. The title of the last study in this book is "From Myth to Reason." However, by this we do not claim to be considering mythical thought in general, any more than we admit to the existence of rational thought in an immutable form. On the contrary, in our closing remarks, we emphasize that the Greeks did not invent reason as such but, rather, a type of rationality dependent on a historical context and different from that of today. Similarly, we believe that in what is known as mythical thought there are diverse forms, multiple levels and different modes of organization, and types of logic.

Where Greece is concerned, intellectual evolution appears to have followed two main lines of development between the time of Hesiod and that of Aristotle. First, a clear distinction was made between the world of nature, the human world, and the world of supernatural powers. Distinctions between these tend to become blurred or intermingled by the mythical imagination, which sometimes confuses the different areas, sometimes operates by slipping over from one plane to another, and sometimes establishes a network of systematic correspondences among all these aspects of reality. On the other hand, "rational" thought tends to ignore the ambivalent or extreme notions that play so important a part in myth. Rational thought avoids the use of associations by means of contrast, and does not couple and unite opposites or proceed by overturning a succession of theories. On the principle of noncontradiction and unanimity, it condemns all modes of reasoning that proceed from an ambiguous or equivocal basis.

Stated this generally, our conclusions are of a provisional nature, aimed above all at outlining a pattern of inquiry. They make use of more restricted and more precise studies focusing upon a particular myth recounted by a particular author, or upon a particular body of myth having variants in different Greek traditions. The only way to trace the transformations in the mental processes, techniques, and logical procedure is to undertake concrete studies to determine just how the vocabulary, syntax, modes of composition, and the choice and organization of themes evolved from Hesiod and Pherecydes through to the Presocratic philosophers. Thus, the last study in this book should be read with reference to the first. We have carried the structural analysis of a particular myth, Hesiod's myth of the races, as far as we can, in order to describe a manner of thought which is anything but incoherent, but whose movement, rigor, and logic have their own particular character; the structure of the myth depends, both for its overall plan and for the details in its various parts, upon the balance and the tension between the poles of ideas. Within the context of the myth, these ideas express the polarity of the divine powers that are at the same time set in opposition and associated. Thus, in Hesiod's work we find a "model" of thought which is in many respects close to the one that, as expressed in the couple of Hestia and Hermes, seems to us to dominate the earliest Greek religious experience of space and movement.

It may seem surprising that we have not given a larger place in this collection of studies to the analysis of the individual. This is indeed the one area where Greek scholars have been led by the very nature of their investigations to touch on psychological problems. The transformations in the individual from Homer to the classical period seem quite startling, for Homeric man had no real unity and no psychological depth but, instead, was subject to sudden impulses and inspirations that were thought to be of a divine origin. The Homeric individual was, in a sense, alienated both from himself and from his action. Then, however, man began to discover the inner being; the body was seen as something distinct, psychological impulses were treated as a whole, and the individual emerged (or at least certain values linked with the individual as such). The sense of responsibility developed; the agent was seen as more answerable for his own actions. All these developments in the individual have been the subject of specialists' inquiries and of discussions that have a direct bearing upon historical psychology.

We have not sought to make an overall assessment of these studies partly, but not solely, because one psychologist has already attempted to do this. Barbu has studied what he terms the "emergence of personality in the Greek world"[3] from a point of view similar to our own. While we fully accept many of his analyses and would advise the reader to consult them, we are inclined to express reservations of two kinds with regard to his conclusions. First, it seems to us that the author rather forces the issue in the picture that he paints of the development of the individual. Because he has not taken account of all the different kinds of evidence, and particularly because he has not studied them closely enough, he sometimes imposes upon them too modern an interpretation and projects onto the Greek personality certain features that, in our opinion, did not emerge until a later period. Second, although his study is undertaken from a historical point of view, it is not entirely free from normative preoccupations. Barbu's view is that the Greeks discovered the *true* individual. By basing their inner being upon a balance maintained between two opposed psychic processes—on the one hand, of "individuation" which integrates the internal forces of the individual around a single center, and on the other, one of "rationalization," which integrates indi-

viduals into a higher form of order (be it social, cosmic, or religious)—
they constructed a perfect form or model for the individual. Quite apart
from specific objections we have to points of psychology in this, we do
find that the work of certain Greek scholars has a tendency to underesti-
mate not only the complexity of a psychological category such as the
individual, with all its many dimensions, but also its historical relativism.
They consider the individual as a category whose development is now
complete, which can be defined in simple and general terms, and so they
sometimes tend to pursue their inquiries as though the question were
one of finding out whether or not the Greeks were aware of the individual or at what moment they discovered it. For the historical psychologist,
the problem should not be posed in these terms. There is not, and there
cannot be, a perfect model of the individual, abstracted from the course
of the history of mankind with all its vicissitudes and all its variations
and transformations according to place and time.

The purpose of the inquiry, then, is not to establish whether the individual personality existed in ancient Greece but, rather, to seek to discover what the ancient Greek personality was and how its various characteristics differed from personality as we know it today. Which of its
aspects become defined, in greater or lesser detail, at particular moments,
and what form do they take? Which aspects remain ignored? Which
features of identity already find expression in particular types of works,
institutions, and human activities, and to what degree? Along what lines
and in what directions did the Greeks develop the concept of personality? What groping or abortive attempts were made to grasp it? What
blind alleys were followed? And, finally, how far is personality organized? What is its core? What are its most characteristic features?

An inquiry of this kind presupposes that a scholar should first have
isolated from the body of evidence offered by Greek civilization those
facts which are especially relevant to one or another aspect of personality.
The scholar should also have been able to define the types of works and
activities through which the ancient Greeks explored the inner being
just as, through science and technology, they explored the physical
world. The inquiry therefore has to cover an extremely vast and varied
field, including linguistic facts and the development of vocabulary (especially psychological vocabulary); social history, particularly the history
of law, but also the history of family life and of political institutions;
large chapters of the history of thought, those, for instance, which pertain
to the concepts of the soul, of the body, and of individuality; the history
of moral ideas—for instance, shame, guilt, responsibility, and merit; the
history of art, and in particular the problems arising from the emergence
of new literary genres such as lyric poetry, tragedy, biography, autobiography, and the novel (insofar as these last three terms are appropriate

with reference to the Greek world); the history of painting and of sculpture, with the development of portraiture; and, finally, the history of religion.

Since it would not be possible to encompass all these problems within a short study, we have decided to limit ourselves to the evidence provided by religion. Furthermore, we shall consider only the religion of the classical period, and shall not concern ourselves with any innovations introduced in the Hellenistic period. The limitations thus imposed from the start upon our inquiry are bound to make it all the more demanding. Since it is confined to religion, we have had to draw careful distinctions within this domain. We have had to consider, in each instance, the effect any particular aspect has had on the history of personality and how far religious beliefs and practices, through their psychological implications, affect the inner state and contribute toward developing identity. As will be seen, our conclusions are in general negative, and we have been led to emphasize especially the differences and the distance that, in terms of religious life, separate the fifth-century Greek from the believer of today. [. . .]

NOTES

[1] Ignace Meyerson, *Les Fonctions psychologiques et les oeuvres* (Paris, 1948).

[2] Zevedei Barbu, *Problems of Historical Psychology* (London, 1960).

[3] Ibid., ch. 4, pp. 69–144.

[4] Cf. Meyerson, ch. 3, "L'histoire des fonctions," especially the pages devoted to the history of personality, pp. 151–85.

JACQUES LE GOFF AND PIERRE VIDAL-NAQUET

Lévi-Strauss in Broceliande: A Brief Analysis of a Courtly Romance

1979

The historical anthropology that came into being (as both a project and a rallying cry) in the 1970s soon extended its reach over a large territory, from the analysis of myth to the uses of the body, from kinship systems to attitudes toward death, from religious experience to the political imagination. It never established a unified approach. Its practitioners borrowed whatever existing models and theories seemed most useful (and the same thing happened outside of France as well). A few important figures did, however, play a fundamental role, among them Claude Lévi-Strauss, Georges Dumézil, and Jean-Pierre Vernant.

The text that follows is a good (and early—a first version appeared in 1974) example of deliberate mingling of history with anthropology, as its title suggests. Not only does it invoke the name of a great anthropologist, but it also proposes using structural analysis to study an episode in Chrétien de Troyes's romance, Yvain ou le Chevalier au lion *(late twelfth century). There are also references to Georges Dumézil, Tzvetan Todorov, and others. Equally significant is the fact that the piece is the product of a seminar that brought together two well-known historians, the medievalist Jacques Le Goff, and the historian of ancient Greece, Pierre Vidal-Naquet. As a result, the authors were able to add a crucial comparative dimension to their analysis, as well as to suggest a novel way of looking at the* longue durée.

From Jacques Le Goff, *The Medieval Imagination,* trans. Arthur Goldhammer (Chicago: University of Chicago Press, 1988), pp. 107–31. First published, in abbreviated form, in *Critique* 325 (1974), pp. 543–71; the complete version (translated here) first appeared in *Claude Lévi-Strauss* (Paris: Gallimard, 1979), pp. 265–319.

The episode that we have chosen for comment[1] is taken from Chrétien de Troyes's *Yvain ou le Chevalier au lion,* written some time around 1180.[2] Yvain, a knight in King Arthur's court, following a series of adventures about which we shall have more to say in a moment, obtains the permission of his wife Laudine to leave her for a year "in order to accompany the king and go to tournaments" (lines 2561–62). Should he remain away for more than the allotted time by so much as a single day, he will forfeit his wife's love. Inevitably—for this is a fantastic tale, in which conditions are set only to be transgressed[3]—Yvain allows the deadline to pass. A damsel from his wife's household, riding a symbolic black palfrey, comes to tell him that all is lost, and that he must never attempt to see his wife again. Yvain, losing his wits at this news, flees the court and heads for the forest.

A word needs to be said about the setting of the action. Like other of Chrétien's works (most notably *Perceval* and *Erec et Enide*) and many other courtly romances, the story unfolds in two series of episodes of radically different, even opposite, meaning (or *sen,* as one would have said in twelfth-century French).[4] The narrative opens with the story of a failure, a bungled "adventure." Calogrenant, another knight in Arthur's court and a cousin of Yvain, is unable to defeat Esclados le Roux, the guardian of a magic fountain in the heart of Broceliande. Yvain follows the same route and succeeds everywhere where Calogrenant has failed. Not only does he defeat and slay the lord of the fountain but he also marries the man's widow and, like the king of Nemi studied by Frazer, replaces him on the throne. Yvain's feats are what might be called gratuitous adventures, exploits for exploits' sake, in which the magical interventions of Lunette, maid to the lady of the fountain, were of crucial assistance.

> 2166　*Mes or est mes sire Yvain sire,*
> *Et li morz est toz obliez*
> *Cil qui l'ocist est mariez;*
> *Sa fame a, et ensanble gisent. . . .*

Now Sir Yvain is lord and the dead man is completely forgotten. His murderer has married and taken his wife, and now they sleep together.

The poet, who is not an adventurous knight but most probably a clergyman, does not disguise his feelings about the matter. Indeed, subsequent to Yvain's madness, the episode that chiefly interests us here, the knight ceases to make conquests for himself and works only on behalf of others, as a defender of widows and orphans. Having legitimated his lordship, he regains his wife's love.

The episode that is most important for our purposes occupies lines 2783–883:

> Yvain was beside himself. Everything he heard upset him, and everything he saw tormented him. He wished he were far away in a land so wild that no one would know where to look for him, and that neither man nor woman would know more of him than if he were at the bottom of an abyss. His trouble mounted. He hated nothing so much as himself, and he knew not where to seek consolation. He saw that he was responsible for his own disgrace, that he had ruined himself. Rather than fail to take vengeance against himself for the theft of his happiness, he preferred to lose his mind. He parted without a word, so afraid was he of raving in the presence of the barons. The latter paid no heed. They allowed him to wander off on his own. Their words and their concerns, they believed, would be of little interest to him.
>
> Soon he was far from their tents. Madness took hold of his mind. He flayed himself and shredded his garments and fled across fields and furrows. His worried companions looked for him everywhere, among the tents, in the hedges, and through the orchards, but they did not find him.
>
> Yvain ran like a madman until near a park he encountered a boy with a bow and very broad and sharp barbed arrows. He had just enough sense to take them away from the youth. He lost all memory of what he had done until then. He lay in wait in the woods, slew whatever animals happened by, and ate their meat raw.
>
> He wandered among the hedgerows like a frenzied man of the wild until he came to a small, low house. There lived a hermit who was out grubbing for roots. When the hermit saw the naked figure of a man, he realized that the fellow had lost his wits and ran into his house to hide. But out of charity the good man placed some bread and water out through the window.
>
> The madman drew near and, his appetite whetted, took the bread and ate. Never had he tasted such bad-tasting stale bread. The flour from which it was made had cost no more than five sous per measure, for it contained barley with the straw mixed in and was more bitter than yeast and mildewed and dry as bark. But hunger tormented him, and the bread seemed good, for hunger is sauce for any dish well prepared and well preserved. He ate all the bread and drank the cold water from the pot.
>
> When he was finished he fled into the woods in search of stags and does. And the good man under his roof, when he saw him run away, prayed to God to protect him but never to allow him to stray again into that part of the woods. But nothing could prevent the lunatic, witless though he was, from returning to a place where someone had done him a good turn.

Thereafter, as long as his madness lasted, not a day went by when he did not bring some wild beast back to the hermit's hut. He spent his time hunting, and the good man spent his skinning and cooking the game, and every day there was bread and water in the window for the wild man. He had to eat venison without salt or pepper and drink cold water from the fountain. And the good man took it upon himself to sell the skins and buy oat or barley bread of which the other man ate his fill. This continued until one day when a lady and two damsels from her household found the madman sleeping in the forest.

The lady and one of the damsels then healed Yvain's madness with a magic ointment that the lady had previously obtained from the fairy Morgue (Morgan).

We shall have much more to say about Yvain's reintegration into the human world, for a lot more was involved than the damsel with the magic ointment. The "wild man theme" was a common topos of medieval Latin literature. The prototype can be found in a well-known episode of the *Vita Merlini* (1148–1149) by Geoffroy of Monmouth, a text that draws heavily upon ancient Celtic tradition.[5] Responsible for a battle in which two of his brothers die, Merlin takes to the woods (*fit silvester homo,* line 80), where he leads a miserable life but acquires prophetic powers. The theme occurs frequently in courtly romance,[6] and brilliant use was made of it by Ariosto in *Orlando furioso* (which is why Frappier would call the episode in question "Yvain furioso").[7] Our goal, however, is to comment on the text in detail, avoiding facile "psychological" explanations in which Chrétien appears to have been almost a psychiatrist: "All the details, all the precise little indications, suggest that, in describing his character's madness, Chrétien did not allow himself to diverge very far from certain observed facts."[8] That Chrétien transformed courtly romance into a kind of psychologization of mythology is not without importance, to be sure, but the significance of this particular episode lies elsewhere; no matter how fine an observer he was, Chrétien undoubtedly met very few madmen in the forest of Broceliande. Yvain was not just any madman, moreover: he was neither the mad Heracles of Euripides nor the mad Orestes of Racine; nor was he a client of Charcot's.[9]

It is useful to reread this episode with an eye to what structural analysis can reveal.[10] Yvain first abandons his companions, the "barons," who stand for all society and mankind. He crosses cultivated fields and is soon beyond the limits of the region in which the knights of King Arthur's court search for him (among tents, orchards, and hedgerows). His madness is situated in the forest,[11] a more complex place than it first appears. In the medieval West, the forest was the equivalent of what the desert was in the East: a refuge, a hunting ground, a place of adventure, impenetrable to those who lived in cities and villages or worked in fields.[12] In England or at any rate in "Britain," it was even more—a place where in a sense the hierarchy of feudal society broke down. Offenses committed in the forest did not fall under the jurisdiction of the regular courts. The laws of the forest issued "not from the common law of the kingdom but from the will of the prince, so that it was said that what was done according to those laws was just not in an absolute sense but according to the law of the forest."[13] Henry II, king of England and Anjou, in 1184 prohibited "bows, arrows, or dogs in his Forests to anyone without surety."[14] The forest was royal property not only because of the resources it supplied but perhaps even more because it was a "desert." Here Yvain ceases to be a knight and becomes a hunter-predator:

2826   *Les bestes par le bois agueite*
        Si les ocit; et se manjue
        La venison trestote crue.

In the woods he lay in wait for beasts and killed them, and he ate the venison raw.

He strips his body of its clothing and his mind of its memory. He is naked and without memory. Yet between the world of men and that of wild beasts, Chrétien has provided a rather curious mediation—a "park," that is, an enclosed area for grazing,[15] a place for raising livestock (and thus different from both the world of agriculture and that of gathering). There he finds a "boy," that is, a servant, a person who stands at the bottom of the social scale.[16] No sooner does the lad appear than he is robbed of his bow and arrows:

2818   *Un arc*
        Et cinq saietes barbelées
        Qui molt erent tranchanz et lées.

A bow and five barbed arrows, broad and sharp.

Now, bow and arrow are the weapons of a hunter, not of a knight in battle or tournament. To digress for a moment, there was a time long before the twelfth century when a contrast was drawn between the fully equipped warrior and the isolated, even savage archer, namely, in archaic and classical Greece. In Euripides' *Heracles*, the king of Argos contrasts the archer of the title to a valiant hoplite and finds him wanting: "a nullity of a man who fought with apparent bravery in his contests with animals but was incapable of any other prowess. He never held a shield on his left arm or confronted a lance. Carrying a bow, the most cowardly of weapons, he was always ready to flee. For a warrior, the test of courage is not firing arrows but standing at his post and watching, without averting his eyes, as a whole field of raised lances runs toward him, always steadfast in his rank." [17] From the time of Homer until the end of the fifth century, the bow was the weapon of bastards, traitors (such as Teucros and Pandaros in the *Iliad*), and foreigners (such as the Scythians in Athens)—in a word, of subwarriors (in the sense in which one speaks of "subproletarians"). Yet it was also the weapon of the super-warriors, in particular of Heracles, whom only a tragedian influenced by the sophists could have portrayed as a second-class fighter. For it was Heracles who passed on to Philoctetes, the lonely hero, the weapon that would decide the fate of Troy, and it was Ulysses who, wielding his bow at Ithaca, affirmed his sovereignty.

The distinction between the "heavy" and the "light" warrior, between the solitary, wily hunter and the soldier who fights as part of a unit, predates archaic Greece. To confine our attention to Indo-European sources, Georges Dumézil has found it in an Indian epic, the *Mahabharata*, certain elements of which date from Vedic times. Here, however, the bow is the sign not of the isolated hunter but of the armed combatant: "As a warrior, Arjuna was different from Bhima"—they are two of the five brothers who are heroes of the Indian epic. "He fights not naked but clad in breastplate and mail and armed, indeed 'superarmed': he wields a huge bow.... He is not like Bhima a solitary warrior, an advance guard." [18] In other words, the bow is a sign whose value is determined solely by its *position* in a system, obviously a fact that calls for comment in any Lévi-Straussian analysis of the work.

Let us return, however, to the twelfth-century works with which we are primarily concerned. In Béroul's *Roman de Tristan,* [19] roughly contemporary with Chrétien's *Yvain*, the hero, about to plunge into the forest with Isolde, obtains a bow from a forest warden along with "two feathered, barbed arrows" (lines 1283–84), which he uses to hunt game to keep himself and his companion alive. Later in the Morois forest episode, he fabricates a new "bow" (or, more precisely, an infallible trap for wild animals):

1752   *Trova Tristan l'arc Qui ne faut*
          En tel manière el bois le fist
          Riens ne trove qu'il n'oceïst.

Tristan made the Unerring Bow of wood in such a way that there was nothing that it failed to kill.

In line 1338 of Béroul's poem, the "laburnum" bow is also the emblematic arm of Tristan's prince and Isolde's husband, King Mark— emblematic because, unlike Tristan, Mark does not make use of his bow,[20] any more than Charlemagne does of the emblematic bow he gives to Roland as a sign of his mission in the *Chanson de Roland* (lines 767ff.). Thus, the bow can be a royal symbol (as for Ulysses) or it can be the emblem of a solitary hunter. In the Middle Ages, it was predominantly the latter. If further proof is needed, it can be found in the late thirteenth-century anthology of *Merlin's Prophecies*,[21] in which two knights, Galeholt the Brown and Hector the Brown,[22] land on a desert island teeming with wild animals and in a sense reinvent civilization at its most primitive level. Their first act is to make a bow.[23] Thus, the bow is an ambiguous symbol, capable of signifying either a lapse from civilization or a revival of civilization. What is more, the "unerring bow" made famous by Béroul's poem[24] was also the name applied to the weapon used by the traitor Eadric to assassinate Edmund II (The Ironside), king of Wessex, according to the Anglo-Norman historian Geffrei Gaimar's *Estoire des Engleis*.[25] A weapon like Tristan's, though a legitimate arm when used against wild animals in the Morois forest or against the criminal lords at King Mark's court who drove the hero into exile, became illegitimate in knightly combat.

The text cited above is not isolated. It is easy to cite similar examples in chronicles, *chansons de geste*, and church documents. For example, the Latin chronicle of the murder (on March 2, 1127) of Charles the Good, count of Flanders, written by the notary Galbert of Bruges tells us about the knife-wielding Benkin *in sagittando sagax et velox*.[26] Many other documents portray archers among brigands and other "wild men" living on the fringes of society and engaged in inferior forms of military activity.[27] As for *chansons de geste*, consider Bertrand of Bar's *Girard de Vienne*, whose hero shouts: "A hundred curses among which archers are first. They are cowards, they dare not draw near." For the knight, to be an archer is to become a "shepherd boy."[28] In 1139, the Second Lateran Council anathematized in its twenty-ninth canon "the murderous art, hated by God, of crossbowmen and archers. We forbid the use of this art against Christians and Catholics."[29] This text is particularly interesting in that it was not the product of knights and their entourage: the ninth canon of the same council prohibited tournaments, but in a rather different tone. Courtly romance encoded this prohibition by likening the archer to a wild animal or even a centaur, the sign of Sagittarius. In the *Roman de Troie*, for example, Benedict of Sainte-Maure describes one of Priam's allies as an infamous criminal yet an infallible archer: "Whatever he aims at he strikes at once. His body, his arms, his head were like ours, but he was not at all handsome. He never wore cloth, for he was as hairy as a beast. . . . He carried a bow that was made not of laburnum but of boiled leather joined together by a strange technique."[30]

Thus far, we have concentrated primarily on French and Anglo-Norman sources. In other words, we have been looking at a sector in which chivalric norms and values, ways of life and forms of thought predominated. But just as what was true of Greece was not true of India, what was true of France and England was not true of Wales, where the bow was a noble weapon. Now, it so happens that we possess a Welsh version of Yvain's adventures, similar in some ways to Chrétien's version but different in others. It is highly unlikely that the two versions are directly related.[31] Yet the Welsh version is far from being utterly alien to the civilization of French chivalry; a book has even been written on the influence of chivalric culture on Welsh tales.[32] Nevertheless, the Welsh resisted the French denigration of the bow as a weapon of war. The episode that corresponds to Yvain's madness does not involve the theft of a bow and its use against wild animals. In the fortress where, in the French version, first Calogrenant and later Yvain encounter a vavasor, or minor noble, and a girl familiar with the weapons used by knights, the Welsh storyteller has his heroes meet two youths practicing archery with ivory bows.[33] Similarly, in the *Gest of Asdiwal* the concrete details of the myth change in a manner reflecting the local ecology and customs but without altering the myth's structure.[34]

But let us get back to our archer, a naked savage and eater of raw meat.[35] No sooner is his metamorphosis complete than his reintegration into society begins. Yvain "finds" a man who is living at a primitive level of civilized technology: he has a "house" and engages in a rudimentary form of agriculture. A conquest of the wild by civilization is clearly implied. The man "grubs for roots," in other words, he gathers food from land that had been cleared by burning. He also purchases bread. The hermit thus belongs to an intermediate status between the constituted orders of society and the chaos of barbarism. He recoils and hides from Yvain, whose naked body marks him as a savage.[36] He barricades himself inside his hut. At this point, the hermit and the knight-cum-savage enter into a form of commerce motivated, according to the Christian interpretation, by the hermit's charity. The hermit offers the madman bread and cooked venison, at the bottom of the scale in terms of food preparation. Yvain has never tasted bread so bad or stale, eating it dry rather than in a kind of porridge, the basic dietary staple of the Middle Ages. Water is served in a pitcher, but it is very cold spring water, that is, "natural" water. The venison is cooked but served without salt or pepper. Thus, the poet implicitly or explicitly points out a series of absences—of porridge, wine, salt and spices, and table manners. Yvain eats alone, in a sense clandestinely. In exchange, the savage brings the hermit stags, does, and other wild beasts. This commerce even gives rise to a surplus, which allows this de facto society to enter into trade with others. The hermit skins the animals, sells their hides, and with the profits buys unleavened barley and rye bread to satisfy Yvain's needs. The arrangement between the two men is one of silent barter, with contact between them reduced to a bare minimum: the mad knight hurls his prey in front of the hermit's door, and the hermit sets bread, water, and cooked meat in the hut's narrow window. Communication between the world of the hunt and the world of agriculture, the raw and the cooked, thus takes place at the lowest possible level.

The opposition is apparent at two levels: between Yvain and the hermit, who represents an enclave of "culture" in the midst of "nature," and between Yvain and the environment in which he moved prior to entering the forest. Yvain has chosen nature in the wild, that is, the forest and what it has to offer. Nudity replaces clothing; raw foods replace prepared and especially cooked foods. Impulsive behavior and repetitive actions supplant memory. Yvain has abandoned culture. He has fled organized society with its economic system encompassing plowed fields and orchards surrounded by hedgerows. He has abandoned tents, houses, and military camps for open-air campsites. And he has given up agriculture in favor of hunting with bow and arrow.

Yvain and the hermit are guests of the forest. Both lead solitary and frugal lives. But the hermit leaves the forest occasionally to sell hides and buy bread in transactions with "civilized" men. Although the hut in which he lives is rudimentary, it is nevertheless a product of human construction. He wears clothing and is shocked by Yvain's nakedness. And he barters hides for bread. He lives by basic dietary rules. Although we are not told how he cooks the venison that Yvain supplies, there is little doubt that the meat is roasted. In Béroul's *Tristan* the lovers, with help from Gouvernal the squire, live on venison roasted directly over the fire without milk or salt.[37] Thus, we see here what Lévi-Strauss has called the "culinary triangle," with roast meat in the mediating role, though boiled meat is present only metaphorically.[38] In other words, the meeting between Yvain and the hermit is possible because the former stands at the upper limit of "nature" (whose lower levels comprise the forest flora and fauna), while the latter stands at the lower limit of "culture" (the upper levels of which are represented by the court and its knights, whose superiority is called into question, as we shall see).

In making provisional use of the concepts of "nature" and "culture" here, we do not mean to suggest that they were clearly and consciously distinguished in Chrétien's mind.[39] The oppositions we have identified are all based on a further opposition, between the dominant world of humans and the dominated world of animals (dominated by hunting as well as domestication). The "wild" is not what is beyond the reach of man but, rather, what is on the fringes of human activity. The forest (*silva*) is wild (*silvatica*) not only because it is the place where one hunts for animals but also because it is the haunt of charcoal burners and swineherds.[40] Between the asymmetric extremes of savagery and culture the mad and savage hunter is an ambiguous mediator, as is the hermit, but in a different way.

Twelfth-century thinkers reflected a good deal on the concept of nature, largely stripping it of its sacred qualities. Figurative art accomplished much the same thing, as with the sculpture of Eve in the flesh at Autun.[41] The concepts wildness, matter, and nature, though they had many points in common, were not identical.[42] When Chrétien played on the opposition between *Nature* and *Norreture* (which the Greeks called *paideia*), he did not mean to oppose culture to wildness, for there were good "natures" (like Yvain's) as well as bad.[43] Nature is not the same as animality. In courtly literature, moreover, the juxtaposition of madman or savage (they were not always the same) with hermit was commonplace, one couple among others deserving systematic study: the knight and the shepherdess, the knight and the female savage,[44] the lady and the leper (an instance of which can be found in Béroul). The list could be extended. Courtly romance contains numerous examples. In Béroul, for instance, the lovers' sojourn in the forest of Morois (after they have been driven mad by a potion) is framed by two dialogues with the hermit Ogrin, the very person who facilitates Isolde's return to the court of King Mark. In Chrétien de Troyes's *Conte du graal,* Perceval "has lost his memory so completely that it no longer reminds him of God."[45] Not until he meets in the forest a hermit who turns out to be his uncle does his adventure begin to take on a meaning.[46]

A romance written after Chrétien's time, *Li Estoire del chevalier au cisne,*[47] describes a man who is much more fully a savage than Yvain, for he exhibits all the traits of the savage of folklore: he is as hairy as an animal, he meets a hermit with certain Christian characteristics, and he attains the summit of knightly glory. In *Valentine and Orson*, a romance that enjoyed immense popularity in the late Middle Ages and beyond,[48] we find a variant of the theme in which Orson, the reeducated savage, himself becomes a hermit.[49] Again it would be worthwhile to study systematically the savage-civilizer couple (in which the civilizer himself lives a half-savage life), in this case a noteworthy variation on the theme of Yvain and the hermit.[50]

In the thirteenth-century allegorical romance *Quête du graal,*[51] certain of the characters are in essence enlightened interpreters of God. As Tzvetan Todorov has observed, the "possessors of meaning are a distinct group among the characters.[52] They are 'wise men,' hermits, abbots, and recluses. Just as the knights could not know, these men could not act. None of them takes part in any episode except those involving interpretation. The two functions (action and interpretation) are strictly divided between the two classes of characters." Twelfth-century romances were "symbolic" in the sense that their authors discussed the hidden significance (*sen*) of their poems. By "symbol" we mean here simply "the attribution by any literary means of an intellectual value to a physical reality (object, place, gesture, and so on) that does not attach to that reality in normal language and usage."[53] In this sense, the encounter between the savage and the hermit is indeed "symbolic," but it does not exhaust the *sen* of the romance or even of an episode whose significance extends far beyond. The admirable ambiguity of the text is perhaps that this encounter is pure action, that the exchange is at no time cast in dialogue form.

It is not easy to define precisely what the notion of "wild man" involves and how the mad knight relates to that notion. Societies in fact define their relations to alien beings by way of their representations of wild men; indeed, historical societies were not interested in the wild man as such. In both written documents and images, and even with respect to institutions, the whole interest is in the relations between the wild man and his "cultivated" brother. Every culture has its own way or ways of classifying aliens, whether by viewing them as radically different, interchangeable, or in terms of a series of intermediaries. From Enkidu, the wild brother of Gilgamesh, the Mesopotamian king of Uruk, to Tarzan and the Yeti, to say nothing of Polyphemus the Cyclops and Caliban, literature has defined man in relation to the gods, the animals, and other men. Depending on the period and person, this definition has been either exclusive or inclusive.[54] Societies also define their relation to the proximate and remote environment and explicate the concept of seasonal time through the wild man theme.[55]

The same theme might also be worth studying in folklore. Its significance is ambiguous, for the wild man is classified in thematic indices both as a "supernatural helper" (in which case he is generally destined to rejoin society) and as a dangerous adversary, perhaps an ogre, of which Homer's Polyphemus is one example among others.[56]

There were moments in Western history when things were relatively simple. The men who interpreted the age of discovery classified the "new men" in one of two fundamental ways, either as domesticable animals or as wild animals.[57] The former were to be converted to Christianity and put to work, the latter to be exterminated. Such is the conclusion that emerges from a reading of travel literature, although it should be noted that Montaigne in the *Essays* and Shakespeare in *The Tempest* gave a critical reading whose ambiguity must be respected—and saluted: Caliban is neither a mere animal nor a simple colonial rebel.[58]

The Middle Ages, in their way, are far more complex. Medieval classifications were more commonly series than discrete entities. (The tympanums of Vézelay and Autun, for example, portray monsters as capable of understanding the divine Word.) Yet even near neighbors could be cast as devils—women, shepherds, Jews, foreigners.[59] Medieval forests were populated not only by hermits but also by demons. Wild men in the forests could therefore appear as innocents of the golden age, as in the *Estoire del chevalier au cisne*, which portrays men who

329 *Rachinetes manjuent et feuilles de pumier*
Ne savent que vins est ne nus autres daintiés.

Eat tiny roots and leaves of apple trees; they know nothing of wine or any other sophisticated refreshment.

But they could also appear as minions of Satan.

We do not intend to explore systematically this vast domain but, rather, are simply making a modest attempt to understand, with the aid of structural analysis, the text with which we began, by restoring the context from which we extracted it,[60] and, further, to show how this kind of analysis, which originated in the study of "cold" societies, can be incorporated into historical research as such.[61]

The story of Calogrenant at the beginning of Chrétien's romance is something like a dress rehearsal (albeit ending in failure) for the first part of Yvain's adventures, which culminates in his marriage to Laudine. Wherever his predecessor went Yvain too will go, but he will succeed where Calogrenant failed. The world into which Calogrenant ventures "alone like a peasant, seeking adventure ... armed with all armors as every knight should be" (lines 174–77) is, in a spatial sense, oddly laid out and curiously populated. As in any chivalric romance the setting is the forest, Broceliande, portrayed as the wilderness par excellence.[62] It is an abstract forest, not a tree of which is described.

177 *Et tornai mon chemin à destre*
Parmi une forest espesse
Molt i ot voie felenesse
De ronces et d'espinnes plainne.

Mounted on my charger I followed my path through a thick forest, along trails thick with thorns and brambles.

The knight takes his bearings and chooses the right-hand path, the "good" direction.[63] Yvain's adventure would take him down the same path but with a redundancy heavily stressed by the poet:

762   *Erra, chascun jor, tant*
        Par montaignes et par valées,
        Et par forez longues et lées
        Par leus estranges et salvages
        Et passa mainz félons passages
        Et maint péril et maint destroit
        Tant qu'il vint au santier estroit
        Plain de ronces et d'oscurtez.

He wandered every day through mountains and valleys and through forests long and broad, through strange and wild places and through many a difficult passage, and braved many perils and straits, until he came to a narrow path, dark and full of brambles.

The *félons passages*, the characteristic treachery of the forest, thus give way to an incipient order symbolized by the path. By way of the forest the knight gains access to another very different kind of place, having nothing to do with either the culture symbolized by court and fields or savage nature. It is a kind of moor (line 188), an "otherworld" of sorts, in which the hero encounters at a castle gate a vavasor who holds a goshawk in his hand, indicating that he is a hunter, but a cultivated one.

In courtly romance, the vavasor is the traditional host, and it is in the role of hosts that he and his daughter, "a beautiful and gentle virgin" (line 225) greet the knights-errant whom they welcome into their fortress. Hosts and not guides: the vavasor confirms that the route taken was the right one (lines 204–205) but gives no indication as to how to proceed. Here the thread of the plot is interrupted. The signs of otherworldliness are discreet but incontrovertible. Although this is a warrior's castle, no object is made of iron. Everything is copper, a metal of superior value:

213   *Il n'i avoit ne fer ne fust*
        Ne rien qui de cuivre ne fust.

There was nothing of iron, nothing that was not made of copper.[64]

And there is also an orchard (or, more precisely, a walled garden or meadow), an unambiguous sign for anyone familiar with the symbolism of "Breton" romance:

237   *El plus bel praelet del monde.*
        Clos de bas mur à la reonde.

The most beautiful meadow in the world, enclosed by a low wall.

An "enclosed place, separate from the rest of the world, in which all connections with normal social life and its concomitant responsibilities are broken"[65]; the otherworldly quality of the place is also signified by sexual temptation: the hero is attracted by the presence of the young maiden and does not wish to leave (lines 241–43).

The return to the forest leads the knight[66] to a place that is the antithesis of the one he has just left. In the midst of the forest, "in a clearing," he comes upon "terrifying wild bulls" that "were fighting among themselves and making so much noise, with such pride and ferocity" (lines 277–81) that the narrator backs off.[67] These bulls have a master, a "peasant who looks like a Moor,"[68] a giant and an authentic wild man in the sense that he is not just a man who has returned to the wild but one whose features and body and clothing are all borrowed from the animal world: "His head was larger than that of a horse or any other animal, and he had bushy hair, a broad, hairless forehead more than two hands wide, large, soft ears like those of an elephant, enormous brows, a flat face, owlish eyes, a cat's nose, a cleft mouth like a wolf's, sharp, reddish teeth like a boar's, a black beard, a curly mustache; his chin touched his chest, and his backbone was long, humpbacked, and twisted. He leaned on a club and was clad in a strange outfit that was made not of linen or wool but of two pieces of cowhide attached to his neck" (lines 293–311).[69] Unlike the vavasor, who is only a host, this savage "peasant," this "anti-knight," is a guide,[70] of the sort known to specialists in medieval folktales as a "helper," in this case a human (as opposed to a supernatural) helper. He is called upon to identify himself and explain how he is able to control beasts that *appear* to be totally wild: "By Saint Peter of Rome, they know nothing of man. I do not believe that it is possible in plain or hedgerow to keep a wild animal unless it is tied up or penned in" (lines 333–38). Whereupon he demonstrates his mastery and explains himself in such a way that his humanity is evident: "And he told me that he was a man" (line 328). "I am the sire of my beasts" (line 334). Indeed, he is a lord who can not only question the knight as an equal but also guide him on the road to discovery, showing him the way to the magic fountain that guards the castle whose lady is Laudine. He gives a meaning to the forest:

375   *Ci près troveras or en droit*
         Un santier qui là te manra
         Tote la droite voie va,
         Se bien viax tex pas anploier
         Que tost porroies desvoier:
         Il i a d'autres voies mout.

Nearby you will find on the right a path that will take you there. Follow the right hand if you wish to avoid going astray. There are many other ways.

This guardian is therefore an ambiguous figure. He possesses most of the features typical of the medieval wild man as we know him from art and literature,[71] but certain details seem out of place: his technical (rather than magical) mastery over the wild animals and the fact that his animals, while ferocious, belong to a species domesticated by man.[72] The wild man is not merely a guest of the forest but its master. The knight is searching for an "adventure or marvel" (line 366), but the peasant "knows nothing about adventure" (line 368). He does know something about a marvel, however, namely, a magical country, which brings us to a new theme in *Yvain*.

This new thematic space encompasses all three spaces already traversed—culture, nature, and the otherworld of hospitality and femininity—but at a higher level, thanks to magic. At its center is a fortress adjacent to a town and surrounded by cultivated fields whose defense in case of enemy attack poses a number of problems.[73] The food eaten here is, of course, cooked, and Yvain can eat roast capon and good wine served on a white tablecloth. This feudal domain, graced by the same institutions as King Arthur's court (a seneschal, numerous knights, and so on), is guarded by a magic fountain adjacent to a chapel. The fountain is a most artful work, described by the savage as made of iron but actually of gold (lines 386 and 420) with stairs of emeralds and rubies. The water in it is cold yet boiling, and when poured it creates a terrifying tempest.

Yet access to this courtly society is via a supernatural wilderness. The peasant tells Calogrenant: "You will see this fountain, which is boiling yet colder than marble. The most beautiful tree ever shaped by Nature covers it with its shadow" (lines 380–83).[74] When combat begins between Esclados la Roux, the defender of the fountain, and Yvain, Chrétien resorts to animal imagery that he never uses in clashes between two knights of equal rank. Esclados attacks Yvain "as if he were hunting a rutting stag" (line 814), and Yvain is compared to a gyrfalcon stalking cranes (line 882).

Finally, once Yvain has killed the knight, this world is predominantly female, and Laudine's beauty, like that of the tree beside the fountain, is supernatural: "Yes, I swear that Nature could not dispense such beauty, it was beyond all measure. Perhaps Nature had nothing to do with it! How could that be? Where did such great beauty come from? God created it with his own hands for Nature to ponder. No matter how much time it took to counterfeit such a work, it would never succeed. Even God, were he to apply himself to the task, could never with all his efforts produce its like" (lines 1494–1510). Here, sexual temptation, previously encountered at the vavasor's, is so present that Yvain, after being threatened with death and saved by the ring given him by Lunette, marries Esclados's widow and becomes master of the castle.

Thus, this is a world with three aspects: savagery, culture, and courtliness. But from another point of view it is also a divided world, as Chrétien continually emphasizes. The approaches to the fountain are, successively and alternatively, paradisal and infernal. The marvelous singing of the birds gives way to the terrifying tempest. Yvain himself describes the ambiguity of the situation:

> 1457
> *Ce qu'Amors vialt doi je amer*
> *Et doit me elle ami clamer?*
> *Oïl, voir, par ce que je l'aim*
> *Et je m'anemie la claim*
> *Qu'ele me het, si n'a pas tort*
> *Que ce qu'ele amoit li ai mort*
> *Donques sui ge ses anemis?*
> *Nel sui, certes, mes ses amis.*[75]

She, whom Cupid wants me to love, must she call me friend? Yes, surely, because I love her. And I call her my enemy, because she hates me, and with good reason, because I killed the man she loved. Am I therefore her enemy? Surely not, because I love her.

What takes place inside the fortress can be classed under the head of courtly spirit, refined love, and culpable ruse. Lunette brings Yvain and Laudine together through a series of lies. The feminine world is itself divided, for servant and mistress in a sense share roles.

Yvain's madness marks the severance of the hero's ties with both Arthur's court and the world just described. The bulk of the text (from line 2884 to the end, line 6808) is taken up with describing the stages of Yvain's return: cured of his madness, he regains the love of his wife and legitimate possession of his estate. In order to make sense of the previous interpretation, we must examine the stages of this return. The madness episode is indeed of crucial importance. Previously, the savage world is represented by the forest, the scene of adventure and initiatory exploits. But madness turns Yvain himself into a savage and simultaneously makes the status of the forest seem more complex. In terms of structural analysis, there is no forest as such. Even within the context of a single work, the forest exists only in relation to that which is not forest. Oppositions come into play even within what appeared to be simple.[76]

When Yvain, healed by the magic ointment given him by the Lady of Noroison, reawakens—

> 3029
> *Si se vest*
> *Et regarde par la forest*
> *S'il verroit nul home venir.*

He dressed and looked into the forest to see if anyone was coming.

—the forest effectively becomes populated. The very presence of the lady is a sign that a castle is nearby, "so near that it was no more than a half league away, just a short walk, according to the measurement of leagues in that country, two of whose leagues equal one of ours, and four, two" (lines 2953–57). It is as though the spaces that are so carefully distinguished in the first part of the text have ceased to be separate. The forest, the moor with its orchard, the court, and the magic fountain are no longer isolated from one another. Laudine's estate has been integrated into Arthur's court,[77] and the characters go from one space to the other without the aid of mysterious guides and without submitting to rites of passage. To be sure, the forest still exists, and a maiden comes close to losing herself in it:

> 4842
> *Si pooit estre an grant esmai*
> *Pucele au bois, et sanz conduit*
> *Pas mal tans, et par noire nuit,*
> *Si noire qu'ele ne veoit*
> *Le cheval sor qu'ele seoit.*

With great emotion the damsel took to the woods without a guide, in bad weather and in the dark of night, so dark that she could not see the horse on which she was sitting.

But the maiden, who calls upon God and her friends "to rescue her from this bad pass and guide her toward some inhabited place" (lines 4851–52) is in fact guided by Yvain, who uses exclusively human means (one of his helpers is Lunette, who makes no use of magic), and it is on "flat and level terrain" (line 5031) that she ultimately encounters the knight who will rescue her.

The forest is no more than an element—a humanized element[78]—of the landscape, but the savage wilderness still exists, and Yvain's sojourn in it is not without consequences. After his recovery, he enters the service of the lady of Noroison and does battle against the knights who have pillaged Count Allier. Chrétien compares him to a falcon hunting ducks and to a "lion tormented and pursued by hunger loosed among the deer" (lines 3191 and 3199–3200). This is the last animal metaphor used in connection with Yvain.[79] The metaphorical lion is made flesh. Yvain, again traveling through the forest, sees locked in struggle two creatures of the wild, a lion and a serpent, the latter in fact almost a dragon, for it breathes fire (line 3347).[80] The lion is about to succumb. If Yvain saves it, he risks death himself. Yet Yvain does not hesitate for a moment between the "venomous and criminal" animal (line 3351) whose vices are well known to readers of Genesis[81] and the noble beast depicted in the *Roman de Renart* as the king of the wild, "the frank and gentle beast" (line 3371). As it happens, however, the lion loses the tip of his tail—a rather obvious symbol of castration or at least domestication—to the knight's sword. The grateful lion renders a vassal's homage to Yvain and subsequently becomes his companion and even his pet (line 3435). Yvain is henceforth the "knight with lion."[82] The lion took part in his battles, at least in those in which the rules of chivalry, which prescribe combat between equals, are not respected.[83] The striking fact, not yet taken seriously by any commentator, is that the relations that are established between Yvain and the lion from the outset reproduced the relations established between the hermit and Yvain during his madness. But in this case it is obviously Yvain who plays the human role.[84] The lion *hunts* on behalf of Yvain. He detects the scent of a kid within a *bowshot* (line 3439), a word that calls to mind the bow of Yvain the hunter—but now it is Yvain who slits the animal's hide, roasts it on a spit (roasting is explicitly mentioned in lines 3457–60), and shares the meat with the animal (who receives the surplus). The absence of "table manners" and, in this case, of bread (there being no commerce involved, in contrast to the situation with the hermit) is emphasized, but it is of course Yvain and not the lion who complains about the savage nature of the repast: "This meal gave him little pleasure, for he had no bread or wine or salt or tablecloth or knife or other utensil" (lines 3462–64).

In fact, Yvain's encounter with the lion and the elimination of the serpent remove the ambiguities associated with the savage world in the first part of the romance. From this point on, Yvain will confront only wild creatures about which there is no ambivalence.[85]

He first saves a damsel threatened with being delivered into prostitution by a "giant criminal" (line 3850) named Harpin of the Mountain, who possesses certain characteristic traits of the savage.[86] He is armed not with a sword but with a pike (lines 4086–98), he has a hairy chest (line 4217), and he is covered with a bearskin (line 4191). He is compared to a bull (line 4222) and goes down "like a felled oak" (line 4238), but this time the connotation is entirely diabolical. The battle with the Maufé (the Evil One) takes place not in the forest but in the plain under the sign of God, Christ, the Virgin, and the angels (line 4106).[87] Yvain has heard mass (line 4025), which is mentioned for the first time.

In the chateau de Pême-Aventure (the Worst Adventure), which in some respects resembles the residence of the hospitable vavasor,[88] Yvain comes upon a group of captive girls forced to work with silk. Here Yvain, accompanied by his lion, does battle not with a metaphorical devil but "with two sons of the devil, and this is no fable, for they were born of a woman and of one Netun" (lines 5265–67).[89] The fight with these "hideous and black" creatures (line 5506) is a struggle against diabolical savagery.[90] Yvain the victor will finally be able to return to the castle by the fountain. His fight with his peer Gawain so that he may return home is clearly a knightly combat in which there is neither victor nor vanquished. Nor is any low trick used in securing his return to the good graces of Laudine, which is negotiated, without the aid of magic, by Lunette. Laudine agrees to help the knight with the lion to return to his lady, unaware that he and Yvain are one and the same. There is no deception involved, only a play on the hero's two identities.

The lion, which is inseparable from Yvain as he makes his return to humanity, and which is gladly welcomed by Laudine, is simply merged with Yvain when his itinerary is complete and disappears from the story.

Let us, then, review the characters that populate the wild in Chrétien's tale.[91] At the two extremes are the lion and the serpent, and in between is a whole range of other figures. The helpful hermit may be paired with the giant ogre Harpin of the Mountain and the two sons of diabolical Netun.[92] A central figure, monstrous but human, is the "peasant who looks like a Moor," about whom Yvain asks "how nature could have done such foolish work, so ugly and common" (line 798); this is the savage in the strict sense. Yvain himself traverses all the degrees of the scale, confronting his enemies and helped by his helpers. At a critical moment in his adventure, he himself becomes a savage, thus assimilating that aspect of the wild needed by the perfect knight.

Certain of the codes that underlie Chrétien's tale have emerged in the course of the analysis. But we owe it to readers of *Yvain* to sketch out more fully than we have done thus far the relations between the tale and the society from which it issued and to which it returned. To be sure, we have already had occasion to make extensive reference to twelfth-century society. Such references were an expository convenience, permitting us to shorten the argument and to verify certain points. But narrative elements such as the bow, the hermit, the savage, the lion, the serpent, God, and the Devil could have been decoded without reference to the outside world. Yet that world did exist, and in the final analysis it is what interests historians.[93]

The question is made more complex by the fact that an image of the world of chivalry is available in two very different sorts of twelfth-century literary works—different in terms of both the audience addressed and the underlying ideology. The *chanson de geste* appeared somewhat earlier than the courtly romance,[94] but in the twelfth century the two genres were mutual influences and rivals.[95] For the positivist historians of the last century (who have more than one imitator today), it was essential to choose between the two. Thus, Léon Gautier, in his celebrated work on chivalry, stated authoritatively that "the romances of the Round Table, which to biased or hasty judges seem so profoundly chivalric, actually number among the works that hastened the end of chivalry."[96] Having made this judgment, he can then tranquilly and with admirable knowledge of the texts trace the life of the knight from birth to death using evidence drawn almost exclusively from *chansons de geste* without once asking himself whether those sources were indeed written for the purpose of providing positivist historians with data and footnotes. Historians nowadays are less confident; we know that we are mortal, and that our errors will be as transparent to our successors as those of our predecessors are to us. At least we have learned that fiction, like myth, and indeed like society, cannot be treated as though it were a thing.

"The relation of the myth to the idea is definite, but it is not one of *representation*. It is dialectical in nature, and the institutions described in myths may be the inverse of the real institutions. Indeed, that may always be the case when the myth seeks to express a negative truth. . . . Mythological speculations seek in the final analysis not to portray reality but to justify its rather rough construction, since extreme positions are *imagined* only in order to show that they are *untenable*."[97] What is true of myth is even more true of the literary work, whose complex texture must be respected. We must not seek to decompose literature into primary components to which the narrator adds an ideological dimension and a set of personal choices.[98] There is, admittedly, a kind of literature that is nothing but a degraded form of myth, as Lévi-Strauss has said of the serialized novel. To be sure, some courtly romances resemble the serialized novel[99]; but, taking a broader view, the whole genre attests to a comprehensive ideological project. That project, which has been described in great detail by Erich Köhler,[100] concerned what Marc Bloch has called the "second age of feudalism," in which the nobility transformed itself from a de facto into a de jure class. Threatened by the rise of royal authority and by urban development, the new class aimed to restore an order that was subject to continual challenge. Romances were written as works intended to be read; as such, they deliberately excluded the mixed public that listened to the *chansons de geste*. Only the two major orders, knights and clergy, were consumers of courtly romance,[101] as was stated in these well-known verses by the author of the *Roman de Thèbes*[102]:

> *Or s'en tesent de cest mestier,*   13
> *Se ne sont clerc ou chevalier*
> *Car aussi pueent escouter*
> *Comme li asnes al harper*
> *Ne parlerai de peletiers*
> *Ne de vilains, ne de berchiers.*

Nothing will be said here about those whose trade is not that of cleric or knight, for if asses can listen to the harp, so can they. I shall not speak of furriers or peasants or shepherds.

Clergy and knights were not on the same plane, however. The ideal of adventure was held out to the knight, not to the cleric. To be sure, this was a complex ideal, ambiguous by nature and subject to a variety of internal tensions: Think of Chrétien's critique of *Tristan* in *Cligès*.[103] Köhler, however, has summed up its intentions quite well: "Adventure was a way of overcoming the contradiction that had come to exist between the ideal life and the real life. Romance idealized adventure and thus conferred upon it a moral value. Adventure was dissociated from its concrete origins and situated in the center of an imaginary feudal world in which a community of interests among the various strata of the nobility, already a thing of the past, still seemed possible to achieve."[104] Courtly love, a "precious and holy thing" (*Yvain,* line 6044), was at once the point of departure and the point of return for an adventure that left the feudal court for the wild only to prepare the way for a triumphant return. In the meantime, the hero secured his salvation in accordance with the wishes of the clergy, saving himself by saving others. At the center of Chrétien's romance the hermit preserves Yvain's humanity and the lady of Noroison begins his return to chivalry. However, medieval ideology reduced all the diversity of society to just three functions (enumerated most recently by Georges Dumézil, after so many others). Besides the clergy, who prayed, and the knights, who fought, there were those who worked. This third function is represented in the romance by the peasant: his humanity is acknowledged, but his hideous appearance marks him as a member of his class.

To further our knowledge of an imaginary world, recognized as imaginary by courtly writers themselves,[105] we must proceed by investigating what Freud called "displacements" and "condensations," as well as by examining the extensions and inversions introduced by the poets. Consider, for example, the problem of initiation. As has been known for some time, dubbing, the ceremony by which young men were inducted into knighthood, was an initiatory rite comparable to similar rituals found in many societies.[106] It is clear, moreover, that courtly romances can readily be interpreted as revealing an initiatory pattern, with a departure followed by a return.[107] Yet it is striking that the dubbing rite experienced by so many aspiring knights on the battlefield or on the night of Pentecost plays but a limited role in Chrétien's romances, among others.[108] It is not mentioned in *Yvain*, and although it is present in *Perceval* and *Cligès* it is in no sense a turning point of the story. The knights who head into the "forest of adventure" are already dubbed. The theme of childhood, so important in the *chansons de geste*, is of relatively minor interest in courtly romance. Compared with "real" initiation, therefore, the initiation described in the romances is disproportionately extended in time and space.

In an important article, Georges Duby has suggested another comparison.[109] Duby calls attention to the existence of a special class in twelfth-century aristocratic society—the youths (*juvenes*). Duby writes: "A 'youth' was in fact a grown man, an adult. He was admitted to a group of warriors, given arms, and dubbed; in other words, he became a knight. . . . Youth can therefore be defined as that part of life comprised between dubbing and fatherhood,"[110] which could be a very long time indeed. Youths were footloose, vagabond, and violent. They were the "leading element in feudal aggressiveness."[111] And their long, adventurous quest—"a long sojourn shames a young man"—had a purpose: to find a rich mate. "The intention of marrying seems to have governed all of a young man's actions, impelling him to cut a brilliant figure in combat and to show his prowess in athletic matches."[112] Marriage was made more difficult by the proscriptions of the Church, which often made it impossible to find a bride close to home. Duby himself has noted the inescapable parallel between this situation and that described in courtly literature: "The presence of such a group at the heart of aristocratic society fostered certain attitudes, certain collective images, certain myths, of which one finds both reflections and models in literary works written in the twelfth century for the aristocracy and in the exemplary figures that those works proposed, which encouraged, perpetuated, and stylized spontaneous emotional and intellectual reactions."[113] Indeed, Yvain, husband of the wealthy widow Laudine of Landuc, accords rather well with the model proposed by Duby.

Let us take a closer look, however. Note first that in *Yvain* as well as *Erec et Enide* marriage takes place not *after* but *before* the great adventure that demonstrates the hero's mettle. Among the reasons for youthful restlessness suggested by Duby are certain inevitable conflicts—between father and son and especially between younger brother and older brother (and heir). Many "youths" were younger sons who became knights-errant because of their position in the family. Yet such conflicts are apparently absent in Chrétien's romances.[114] What is more, it is as if *all the poet's heroes* were only sons: this is true of Yvain, Cligès, Lancelot, Perceval, and Erec.[115] Brothers and sisters belong to the *previous generation*. Yvain and Calogrenant are first cousins. Erec, Enide, and Perceval discover uncles and aunts in the course of their adventures. Cligès becomes the rival of his paternal uncle for possession of Fenice, daughter of the emperor of Germany.[116] The adventures of the youths are collective, moreover: the chroniclers portray bands of *juvenes* furnishing the "best contingents for all remote expeditions."[117] Yet adventure in courtly as opposed to epic literature is always individual.[118] Thus, it would appear that the courtly writers refracted the social facts in such a way that their interpretation often amounts to an inversion of reality. The mechanisms employed to accomplish this deserve further study—shift from the present to the past, from the plural to the singular, from the masculine to the feminine.

Yet much of the real economic and social evolution of the twelfth century is present in *Yvain,* but at an unconscious level: the transformation of the rural landscape and of seigneurial and clerical revenues, and the changes in peasant life that resulted from vast efforts to clear the land begun in the tenth century and apparently culminating in the twelfth.[119]

Shortly before *Yvain* was written the Norman poet Wace in the *Roman de Rou* described the magic fountain of Broceliande, which plays so central a part in Chrétien's story, as a thing of the distant past: [120]

6386
Mais jo ne sai par quel raison
Là sueut l'en les fées véeir
Se li Breton nos dïent veir
E altres merveilles plusors
Aires i selt aveir d'ostors
E de grans cers mult grant plenté
Mais vilain ont tot désesrté
Là alai jo merveilles querre
Vi la forest e vi la terre
Merveilles quis, mais nes trovai
Fol m'en revinc, fol i alai,
Fol i alai, fol m'en revinc
Folie quis, pour fol me tinc.

I do not know, however, why people were in the habit of seeing fairies there. If the Bretons tell of these and other marvels, there were buzzards and lots of huge stags, but the peasants soon left. I went in search of marvels and saw forest and earth but of marvels found none. Mad I came back and mad I went, mad I went and mad I came back. What I was asking was mad, and I consider myself mad.

Obviously we cannot prove that Chrétien read this text, which so eloquently bears witness to the disenchantment of the forest as it was cut down to make way for new fields. Instead, we shall turn to *Yvain* itself, for the text of the romance provides us with our best argument.

In interpreting *Yvain,* we have stressed the importance of the hero's three encounters in the forest[121]: with the savage who gives him directions, with the hermit who saves him and restores his humanity, and with the lion that he tames. Now, the meeting with the peasant takes place on cleared land (lines 277, 708, 793) as does the meeting with the lion (line 3344); the hermit is grubbing for roots on cleared land (line 2833).[122] Finally, the encounter with Harpin of the Mountain takes place after the

poet has described him "galloping through the woods" (line 4096)—
"before the gate," to be sure," but "in the middle of a *plain*" (line 4096),
where the word "plain" was commonly used at the time to refer to recently cleared land. The only encounter that does not take place on
cleared land is that with the sons of diabolical Netun, but this is not
situated in any concrete location.[123] Turning now from the savage world
to the magical world, we find, as J. Györy has observed, that one consequence of the use of the fountain is the destruction of the estate's trees
despite their admirable, almost paradisal qualities: "But if I could, sir
vassal, I would shift to you the suffering caused me by the obvious injury
of which proof surrounds me, in my wood that has been cut down" (lines
497–501). The theme disappears, however, after the Calogrenant story.
The magical world—and perhaps the interests of the lords, not all of
whom benefited from the clearing of land—is here in contradiction with
the savage world.

The peasant and the lion were both encountered in clearings, then,
but only the hermit is actively clearing land and modifying space. The
three characters are therefore both similar and different.[124] The active
role ascribed to the hermit is not particularly surprising, since it corresponded to reality: hermits played a far greater role than the monks of
the great abbeys in the major episodes of land-clearing.[125] Admittedly,
peasants played no less important a role, but the ideology of the clergy
was opposed to acknowledging this fact, deplored by Wace, in the marvelous world into which Chrétien introduces us.[126]

Yvain's itinerary, as we have reconstructed it with the aid of structural
analysis, intersects with and sheds light on several historical schemata.
The key space, the clearing, corresponds to a very important economic
phenomenon of the twelfth century, the clearing of land. Yvain's adventure follows in the footsteps of the groups of "youths" identified by
Georges Duby, whose contradictory relations with the rest of society
have been analyzed by Erich Köhler. Finally, the Christian atmosphere
of the time is present in the very texture of the analysis, in the implicit
judgment on chivalric behavior, and, more specifically, at critical transitional stages in Yvain's trajectory: a chapel watches over the stairs, the
pine, and the magic fountain where everything begins; a hermit preserves Yvain's humanity; and Yvain's rehabilitation is accomplished
through a confrontation with the world of the devil. In order to return
to the world of culture, Yvain himself must first be Christianized, and
even the forest is marked by Christian signs.

We hope that the reader will forgive us for ending our analysis here.
In order to carry it further, we would have to move to another plane,
one explored by Chrétien himself in *Perceval*.[127]

TRANSLATED BY ARTHUR GOLDHAMMER

NOTES

[1] The title of this essay is obviously inspired by Edmund Leach's well-known paper "Lévi-Strauss in the Garden of Eden: An Examination of Some Recent Developments in the Analysis of Myth," *Transactions of the New York Academy of Science* 2(23) 1967. We wish to thank Claude Gaignebet, a true savage, and the very civilized Paule Le Rider for the valuable information they provided.

[2] For this date and general information about the sources and composition of the romance, see J. Frappier, *Etude sur "Yvain ou le Chevalier au lion" de Chrétien de Troyes* (Paris, 1969), which contains a nearly complete bibliography. We use and cite from, with minor correction, the modern French adaptation by André Mary (Paris, 1944). [The English translations here are from the French cited in the original text.—Trans.] Not until it was too late to make use of it did we learn of the translation by C. Buridant and J. Trotin (Paris, 1972). The numbering of the verses is that of the "edition" (based on Guiot de Provins's copy) of Mario Roques, *Les Romans de Chrétien de Troyes*, vol. 4: *Le Chevalier au lion* (Paris, 1967). The best edition is still that of W. Foerster, 2d ed. (Halle, 1891); cf. P. Jonin, *Prolégomènes à une édition d'Yvain* (Aix-Gap, 1958).

[3] See C. Brémond, *Logique du récit* (Paris, 1973), which builds on the work of Vladimir Propp.

[4] This was noticed by R. Bezzola, *Le Sens de l'aventure et de l'amour (Chrétien de Troyes)*, 2d ed. (Paris, 1968), pp. 81–134. See also W. S. Woods, "The Plot Structure in Four Romances of Chretien de Troyes," in *Studies in Philology* (1953), pp. 1–15; J. C. Payen, *Le Motif du repentir dans la littérature française médiévale* (Geneva, 1968), p. 385; and W. Brand, *Chrétien de Troyes* (Munich, 1972), pp. 72–73, which clearly summarizes the different views concerning the two parts of *Yvain*. Comparative structural analysis of Chrétien's five romances can be found in the fundamental work of Eric Köhler, *Ideal und Wirklichkeit in der Höfischen Epik* (Tübingen, 1956), pp. 257–264 (a second edition with an important appendix was published in 1970).

[5] Published in English translation by J. J. Parry in the *University of Illinois Studies in Language and Literature,* vol. 10, no. 3 (Urbana, 1925). For a recent comment on Merlin's madness see D. Laurent, "La gwerz de Skolan et la légende de Merlin," in *Ethnologie française* 1 (1971): 19–54. On Merlin as a man of the woods and on a similar figure in Scottish mythology who was taken up by Christianity in the legend of Saint Kentigern see M. L. D. Ward, "Lailoken or Merlin Sylvester," in *Romania* (1893), pp. 504–526.

[6] See the examples collected in the excellent work of R. Bernheimer, *Wild Men in the Middle Ages: A Study in Art, Sentiment, and Demonology*, 2d ed. (New York, 1970), pp. 12–17. As Bernheimer rightly notes, "to the Middle Ages wildness and insanity were almost interchangeable terms" (p. 12). Merlin is of course mentioned numerous times in this work.

[7] Frappier, *Etude*, p. 19.

[8] Ibid., p. 178. The psychologization of the episode dates as far back as the Middle Ages. The German poet Hartmann von Aue in his *Iwein* gives a sort of interpretation of Chrétien's romance that frequently emphasizes its structural aspects. Nevertheless, he insists that courtly love, or "'Minne," is so powerful that a member of the weaker sex can reduce a valiant warrior to madness. See J. Fourquet, *Hartmann d'Aue: Erec-Iwein* (Paris, 1944), and for a comparison of the two poems and a commentary on Hartmann's work, see H. Sacker, "An Interpretation of Hartmann's Iwein," in *Germanic Review* (1961), pp. 5–26, and M. Huby, *L'Adaptation des romans courtois en Allemagne aux XIIᵉ et XIIIᵉ siècles* (Paris, 1968), especially pp. 369–370. We are indebted to Raymond Perrenec for several useful comments on Hartmann's poem.

[9] J.-C. Payen, *Le Motif du repentir*, goes so far as to compare Yvain's remorse with "that . . . of Cain hiding in a grave to escape from his bad conscience."

[10] Few structural analyses of medieval literature have been attempted in France. See, however, F. Barteau, *Les Romans de Tristan et Iseut* (Paris, 1972). A recent bibliography and a brief general introduction may be found in P. Zumthor, *Essai de poétique médiévale* (Paris, 1972), pp. 352–359.

[11] Hartmann von Aue underscores the opposition between cultivated fields and wild forest by systematically rhyming *gevilde* (cultivated rural lands) with *wilde* (the wilderness), as in lines 3237–3238 in the Benecke, Lachmann, and Wolff edition: "Thus he crossed the fields (*über gevilde*) and headed for the wild (*nach der Wilde*)" The German poet is also playing on the relation between *Wilde* and *Wald* (forest).

[12] See Jacques Le Goff, *La Civilisation de l'Occident médiéval* (Paris, 1964), pp. 169–171.

[13] Charles Petit-Dutaillis, *La Monarchie féodale*, 2d ed. (Paris, 1971), pp. 140–142, citing *De necessariis observantiis scaccarii dialogus*, ed. A. Hughes, C. G. Crump, and C. Johnson (Oxford, 1902), p. 105. Compare H. A. Cronne, "The Royal Forest in the Reign of Henri I," in *Essays in Honor of J. E. Todd* (London, 1949), pp. 1–23.

[14] Petit-Dutaillis, *La Monarchie féodale*.

[15] This park remains rather mysterious. In the Welsh version of Yvain's adventures the park is the place where the mad knight meets the lady who will save him. It thus becomes a kind of seigneurial "paradise."

[16] It is tempting to speculate that this episodic lad has a female counterpart in the person of the "Wild Damsel" (line 1624), who warns Laudine of the impending arrival of King Arthur and his court in her mysterious domain in the heart of Broceliande, which will establish contact between the City and the Forest.

[17] *Heracles*, lines 157–164. On these questions see Pierre Vidal-Naquet, "Le Philoctète de Sophocle et l'Éphébie," *Annales ESC* (1971), pp. 623–638, reprinted in Jean-Pierre Vernant and Pierre Vidal-Naquet, *Mythe et tragédie en Grèce ancienne* (Paris, 1972), pp. 167–184, especially pp. 170–172.

[18] Georges Dumézil, *Mythe et épopée* (Paris, 1968), vol. 1, p. 64.

[19] Béroul, *Le Roman de Tristan*, ed. E. Muret and L. M. Defourques (Paris, 1972); translated into modern French by D. Grojnowski (Lausanne, 1971).

[20] This point bears emphasis because certain modern and widely known versions of *Tristan* (such as those of Joseph Bédier and René Louis) portray King Mark threatening Tristan with an arrow in the famous scene of the observed rendez-vous. But nothing like this can be found in the versions of Béroul or Eilhart of Obert or Gottfried of Strasburg. The scene is also absent from what has survived of Thomas's version. See J. Bédier, *Le Tristan de Thomas* (Paris, 1902), pp. 198–203, an instructive text for anyone interested in knowing how a medieval romance is reconstituted or fabricated.

[21] *Merlin's Prophecies*, ed. L. A. Paton (New York, 1926).

[22] The names suggest bears.

[23] *Merlin's Prophecies*, pp. 424–425.

[24] An erotic song by Jean Bretel d'Arras (G. Raynaud, ed., *Bibliothèque de l'Ecole des chartes* 41 (1880): 203–202) has as its refrain "Je sui li ars qui ne faut" (I am the unerring bow). On the theme and image of the unerring bow, see M. D. Legge, "The Unerring Bow," *Medium Aevum* (1956): 79–83.

[25] Geffrei Gaimer, *Estoire des Engleis*, ed. A. Bell (Oxford, 1960), line 4392.

[26] Galbert of Bruges, *Histoire du meurtre de Charles le Bon, comte de Flandre*, ed. Henri Pirenne (Paris, 1891), p. 59; see also pp. 121–122.

[27] See Georges Duby, *Le Dimanche de Bouvines* (Paris, 1973), pp. 103ff.

[28] Bertrand of Bar, *Girard de Vienne*, ed. P. Tarbé (Paris, 1850), p. 7.

[29] R. Foreville, *Latran I, II, III et Latran IV* (Paris, 1965), p. 89.

[30] Benedict of Sainte-Maure, *Le Roman de Troie*, ed. L. Constans (Paris, 1905), vol. 2, lines 12354–12374, pp. 231–232. See also A. M. Crosby, *The Portrait in Twelfth-Century French Literature* (Geneva, 1965), pp. 21–22 and 87.

[31] R. L. Thomson, ed., *Owein or Chwedgl Iarlles y Ffynnawn* (Dublin, 1968). Very likely the two versions shared a common source. The works of Frappier, *Etude*, pp. 65–69, and A. C. Brown, "Iwain, A Study in the Origins of Arthurian Romance," in *Studies and Notes in Philology and Literature* (Cambridge: Harvard University Press, 1903), pp. 1–147, may also be consulted, though both works suffer from nationalist and pro- or anti-Celtic prejudice.

[32] Morgan Watkin, *La Civilisation française dans les Mabinogion* (Paris, 1963). Jean Marx, not one to minimize the importance of Celtic sources, also recognizes "the influences of Franco-Norman romances and mores" on the Welsh *Owein*. See his *Nouvelles Recherches sur la littérature arthurienne* (Paris, 1969), p. 27, note 5. Neither of these authors has considered the role of the bow in *Yvain* or *Owein*, however.

[33] Cf. Thomson, *Owein or Chwedgl Iarlles y Ffynnawn*, pp. xxx–xxxi. These are sumptuous bows, strung with the muscles of stags and equipped with whalebone handles.

[34] Claude Lévi-Strauss, *Annuaire de l'Ecole pratique des Hautes Etudes*, Sections des sciences religieuses (1958–1959), pp. 3–43; reprinted in *Anthropologie structurale II* (Paris, 1973), pp. 175–233.

[35] The nature/culture, savage/courtly dialectic was a feature of the period's mental and literary schemata. In a text roughly contemporary with *Yvain*, an *exemplum* taken from the Cistercian Geoffroy of Auxerre's commentary on Revelation, we find a process of acculturation of a savage woman that is more or less the exact opposite of the process of deculturation that Yvain undergoes. Yvain first abandons the company of the civilized, then sheds his clothing, then changes his diet. In Geoffroy's text a young man returning from a swim in the ocean brings with him a Melusina, to whom he gives clothing, food, and drink in the company of his relatives and friends: *"Suo nihilominus opertam pallio duxit domum et congruis fecit a matre sua vestibus operiri. . . . Fuit autem cum eis manducans et bibens, et in cunctis pene tam sociabiliter agens, ac si venisset inter convicaneos, inter cognatos et notos"* (see F. Gastaldelli, ed., *Super Apocalipsim* [Rome, 1970], p. 184). Compare G. Lobrichon, "Encore Mélusine: un texte de Geoffroy d'Auxerre," *Bulletin de la société de mythologie française* 83 (1971): 178–180.

[36] This nudity is mentioned five times, in lines 2834, 2888, 2908, 3016, and 3024. See M. Stauffer, *Der Wald: Zur Darstellung und Deutung der Natur im Mittelalter* (Zurich, 1958), p. 79.

[37] Béroul, *Le Roman de Tristan*, lines 1285–1296.

[38] Claude Lévi-Strauss, "Le triangle culinaire," *L'Arc* 26 (1966): 19–29.

[39] That it is important not to reify these concepts is a point made by Serge Moscovici, *La Société contre nature* (Paris, 1972), as well as by Claude Lévi-Strauss, *Structures élémentaires de la parenté*, 2d ed. (Paris–The Hague, 1967), p. xvii.

[39] That it is important not to reify these concepts is a point made by Serge Moscovici, *La Société contre nature* (Paris, 1972), as well as by Claude Lévi-Strauss, *Structures élémentaires de la parenté*, 2d ed. (Paris—The Hague, 1967), p. xvii.

[40] On the relation between *silva* and *silvaticus* (or *Wald* and *Wild* in German), see W. von Wartburg, *Französiches Etymologistes Wörterbuch* 11 (Basel, 1964), pp. 616–621, and especially J. Trier, *Venus, Etymologien und das Futterlauf*, in *Münsterische Forschungen 15* (Cologne, 1963), pp. 48–51.

[41] See M. D. Chenu, "La nature et l'homme: La Renaissance du XIIe siècle," in *La Théologie au XIIe siècle* (Paris, 1957), pp. 19–51.

[42] The semantic commonality is among the most disturbing. *Silva* meant both forest and matter (from the Greek *hyle*), and medieval thought played on this fact. J. Györy has attempted to use this as the basis for an interpretation of Chrétien's romance in "Le cosmos, un songe," in *Annales Universitatis Budapestinensis, Sectio philologica* (1963), pp. 87–110.

[43] See P. Gallais, *Perceval et l'initiation* (Paris, 1972), especially pp. 28–29 and 40–43, whose conclusions need to be verified by close examination of the text.

[44] See M. Zink, *La Pastourelle: Poésie et folklore du Moyen Age* (Paris-Montreal, 1972), especially pp. 100–101, whose conclusions are similar to ours in a number of respects.

[45] Chretién de Troyes, *Perceval le Gallois ou le Conte du Graal*, translated by L. Foulet (Paris, 1972), p. 147.

[46] This episode is commented on several times in Gallais, *Perceval et l'initiation* (see the index under *ermite*).

[47] See J. B. Williamson, "Elyas as a Wild Man in Li Estoire del Chevalier au Cisne," *Essays in Honor of L. F. Solano* (Chapel Hill, N.C.: University of North Carolina Press, 1970), pp. 193–202.

[48] See A. Dickson, *Valentine and Orson: A Study in Late Medieval Romance* (New York, 1929).

[49] Ibid., p. 326; Bernheimer, *Wild Men*, p. 18.

[50] Think of the centaurs of antiquity and their role as educators. Bernheimer's *Wild Men* is an initial attempt to pursue this theme, which bears further investigation.

[51] *Quête du Graal*, edited by A. Pauphilet (Paris, 1923), translated by A. Béguin as *Quest for the Grail* (Paris, 1965).

[52] Tzvetan Todorov, "La Quête du récit," in *Critique* (1969), pp. 195–214 (the passage cited here is on p. 197). There is in thirteenth-century literature an allegorical reading of an episode involving Yvain: Huon de Méry, *Le Tornoiemenz Antecrit*, ed. G. Wimmer (Marburg, 1888). On the transition from symbolism to allegory, see for example H. R. Jauss, "La transformation de la forme allégorique entre 1180 et 1240: d'Alain de Lille à Guillaume de Lorris," in A. Fourrier, ed., *L'Humanisme médiéval dans les littératures romanes du XIIe au XIVe siècle* (Paris, 1964), pp. 107–144.

[53] P. Haidu, *Lion-Queue-Coupée: L'Ecart symbolique chez Chrétien de Troyes* (Geneva, 1972); see especially the classic pages of M. D. Chenu, "La mentalité symbolique," in *La Théologie au XIIe siècle*, pp. 159–190.

[54] Overviews for a single era are relatively rare. On the Middle Ages, see Bernheimer, *Wild Men*, whose interests are extremely broad. Also worth consulting is L. L. Möller, "Die Wilden Leute des Mittelalter," the catalogue compiled for an exposition at the Museum für Kunst und Gewerbe of Hamburg (1963); W. Mulertt, "Der Wilde Mann in Frankreich," *Zeitschrift für französische Sprach und Literatur* (1932), pp. 69–88; O. Schultz-Gora, "Der Wilde Mann in der provenzalischen Literatur," in *Zeitschrift für Romanische Philologie* 44 (1924): 129–137.

[55] In Europe, for example, there was both a wild man of the winter, naked, hairy, wielding a club, and often likened to a bear, and a wild man of the spring, or "May man," girt with a symbolic belt of leaves. Concerning the rites associated with the capture of the wild man, that is, the subsumption of the forces that he represents, see A. Van Gennep, *Manuel de Folklore français*, vol. 3 (Paris, 1947), pp. 922–925, and vol. 4 (Paris, 1949), pp. 1488–1502.

[56] See A. Aarne and S. Thompson, *The Types of the Folktale*, 2d ed. (Helsinki, 1964), FFC 184, T. 502, pp. 169–170, and, for France, P. Delarue and M. L. Ténèze, *Le Conte populaire français*, vol. 2 (Paris, 1964), countertype 502, "l'homme sauvage," pp. 221–227. On the wild man as a motif in folktales, see S. Thompson, *Motif-Index of Folk Literature*, vol. 6 (index) (Copenhagen, 1958), under the head "Wild Animal," especially III, F. 567.

[57] Not everyone made such interpretations, but this was the majority attitude.

[58] See the fine study of R. Marienstras, "La littérature élisabéthaine des voyages et *La Tempête* de Shakespeare," in Société des Anglicistes de l'enseignement supérieur, *Actes du Congrès de Nice* (1971), pp. 21–49. For a colonial interpretation of *The Tempest*, see R. Fernandez Retamar, *Caliban cannibale*, translated by J. F. Bonaldi (Paris, 1973), pp. 16–63.

[59] Bernheimer's *Wild Men* lacks a chapter on the wild man and the devil.

[60] We are not, of course, proposing a comprehensive interpretation of *Yvain* but merely attempting to bring out one level of meaning.

[61] See the special May–August 1971 issue of *Annales ESC*, devoted to "History and Structure."

[62] On the forest as the natural setting of knightly adventure, see Stauffer, *Der Wald*, especially pp. 14–115 (on Broceliande, cf. pp. 45–53). "Were the handsomest forms of prowess those of the city or those of the forest?" seems to have been a standard question in the Middle Ages, the answer to which was obviously that "the prowess of the city is worthless." See C. V. Langlois, *La Vie en France au Moyen Age*, vol. 3 (Paris, 1927), pp. 239–240.

[63] Haidu, *Lion-Queue-Coupée*, emphasizes the symbolic value of this "Christian moral topos" (p. 37). See also the lucid comments of Eric Auerbach, *Mimesis*, trans. W. Trask (Princeton, 1953).

[64] These lines are omitted from the Mary translation.

[65] Haidu, *Lion*, p. 38, which draws upon a chapter in the celebrated work of E. R. Curtius, *European Literature and the Latin Middle Ages*, trans. W. Trask (Princeton, 1953).

[66] In speaking of the knight or the hero we are referring to both Calogrenant and Yvain.

[67] The translation is based on the text as established, we think in convincing fashion, by F. Bar, "Sur un passage de Chrétien de Troyes (*Yvain*, v. 276–285)," *Mélanges I. Siciliano* (Florence, 1966), pp. 47–50. In any case, it has been known since Foerster's edition that line 278 of the Guiot manuscript (*tors salvages, ors et lieparz*) should not be read as "wild bulls, *bears and leopards*," for the latter animals are never mentioned again. The word *orz*, plural of *ord* (frightful, terrifying) was originally misread as *ors* (bear), and this mistake led to others. Buridant and Trotin, *Yvain*'s most recent translators, were also persuaded by this emendation (see p. ix of their version).

[68] Hartmann borrows this comparison: "*Er was einem Möre gelich*" (line 427), but in striking detail, which underscores the kinship between the mad Yvain and the wild man, he also applies it to the "mad noble" (*der edele Töre*, line 3347). The master of the bulls, though not "mad" in the psychological sense, is described in line 440 as a "*walttör*," a "madman of the woods."

[69] Many of these features were a topos of medieval romance, and some can be traced back to late Latin literature. See Crosby, *The Portrait*, index under "giant herdsman."

[70] Despite what is said by Gallais, *Perceval*, pp. 132–139, the "hideous damsel" of the *Grail* (lines 587–612, Lecoy edition, pp. 109–111 of the Foulet translation) does indeed offer Perceval a salutary warning, which is later completed and corrected by the hermit. Her portrait parallels that of the "peasant."

[71] See especially Bernheimer, *Wild Men*, pp. 1–48. Note, however, that sexual aggressiveness is missing. On the other hand, the character's declaration that he is human is part of the medieval topos of the wild man. Among the many comparisons that one might make, one seems inevitable because it is with another herdsman who is also a helper of the hero: see *Aucassin et Nicolette*, Dufournet edition, chap. 24, pp. 15–16.

[72] The corresponding figure in the Welsh tale reigns over true wild animals: serpents and mountain lions. As is common in Celtic tales, fantastic features are accentuated. The herdsman has only one foot and one eye, for example. See Loth, p. 9. In Hartmann there are no mountain lions, bears, serpents but there are bison and wild oxen, in other words, wild counterparts of the bull.

[73] Cultivated lands are mentioned in lines 1619, 1808, 2086, and 2472.

[74] The tree is a pine, and apart from the great oak mentioned in line 3012, near which Yvain regains his mental health, it is the only tree in the forest that is described. Because the pine is an evergreen, there is something magical about it (lines 384–385).

[75] Such passages (and there are many others) provide some justification for Huon de Méry's allegorical interpretation, according to which Heaven precedes Hell on the approach to the fountain, as well as for A. Adler's modern interpretation, "Sovereignty in Chrétien's *Yvain*," in *Publications of the Modern Language Association of America* (1947), pp. 281–307, which attempts to identify instances of the philosophical concept of *coincidentia oppositorum* throughout the romance.

[76] On this subject see the pertinent remarks of Tzvetan Todorov, *Introduction à la littérature fantastique* (Paris, 1970), pp. 21–24, criticizing Northrop Frye, *The Anatomy of Criticism* (Princeton, 1957).

[77] As noted by E. Köhler, "Le rôle de la coutume dans les romans de Chrétien de Troyes," in *Romania* (1960), pp. 386–397: "The misuse of the fountain is stopped by incorporating it into Arthur's kingdom" (p. 312). Of course this incorporation is not actually effected until the end of the romance.

[78] This change of sign is characteristic of initiation rituals and of the stories told in connection with or in place of such rituals. The initiatory wilderness is brought into the world of culture. See on this matter the enlightening remarks of A. Margarido, "Proposiçòes teoricas para a leitura de textos iniciáticos," *Correio do Povo* (Porto Alegre), 21 August 1971.

[79] Except that when he nearly goes mad again, he is compared to a "frenzied boar" (line 3518).

[80] Chrétien's German "translator" actually makes the serpent a dragon. On the significance of dragons in medieval art and literature, see Jacques Le Goff, "Culture ecclésiastique et culture folklorique au Moyen Age: Saint Marcel de Paris et le dragon," in *Mélanges C. Barbagallo* (Bari, 1970), pp. 53–90, which contains a lengthy bibliography; reprinted in *Pour un autre Moyen Age* (Paris: Gallimard, 1978), pp. 236–279; English translation, pp. 159–188.

[81] The comparison between the soul's concupiscent parts and the serpent was a twelfth-century topos. Yet a positive image of the serpent persists in medieval symbolism: even that creature was ambiguous. See Le Goff, "Culture ecclésiastique et culture folklorique."

[82] On the symbolism of the lion and its origins in the legend of Saint Jerome and the story of Androcles, see J. Frappier, *Etude sur Yvain*, pp. 108–111, and Haidu, pp. 71–73. We do not believe, however, that Yvain's lion is a symbol of Christ, although the lion commonly figured as such in medieval symbolism. In the *Queste del Saint Graal*, ed. A. Pauphilet, pp. 94–98 and 101–104, Perceval repeats Yvain's adventure with the lion and the serpent and then, in a dream, sees two ladies, one riding a serpent, which is identified with the synagogue, the other riding a lion, which is identified with Christ. The two systems of images were thus combined.

[83] This has been analyzed by G. Sansone, "Il sodalizio del leone e di Ivano," in *Mélanges I. Siciliano* (Florence, 1966), pp. 1053–1063. Concerning the eastern and monastic background of this friendship, see G. Penco, "L'amicizia con gli animali," in *Vita monastica* 17 (1963): 3–10, and M. J. Falsett, *Irische Heilige und Tiere im mittelalterlichen lateinischen Legenden* (Diss. Bonn, 1960).

[84] This was noted by Brand, p. 78.

[85] Here we omit the detail of the narrative, which is quite complex: in particular, Yvain intervenes in a quarrel between two heiresses. We are emphasizing only what is pertinent to the main line of our analysis and certainly one of the main lines of the story, namely, Yvain's relations with the wild.

[86] The giant intends to turn the girl over to *garçons* (servants of the lowest sort) for their pleasure (lines 3866, 4110, and 4114). On the erotic connotations of the savage, see Bernheimer, *Wild Men*, pp. 121–175.

[87] On possible meanings of the word *plain*, see p. xx below.

[88] The parallel is carried to great lengths in the Welsh *Owein* (cf. Thomson, pp. xx and lii–liv). Both castles are inhabited by twenty-four maidens. In Chrétien's version both Pême-Aventure and the vavasor's castle have orchards (lines 5345, 5355). In both the heroes eat sumptuous meals. Sexual temptation is also present, but rejected. Yvain, faithful to Laudine, refuses to marry the girl he delivers, though she, too, is "beautiful and gentle" (line 5369). One point of difference is that there is no wife in the vavasor's castle, but there is one at Pême-Aventure.

[89] Netun is derived by phonetic evolution from the latin name of the god Neptunus.

[90] Netun's son wields a sort of club "covered with metal and brass wire." Concerning this "horned club," normally proscribed in knightly combat, see F. Lyons, "Le bâton des champions dans *Yvain*," in *Romania* (1970), pp. 97–101.

[91] Here we are referring to characters that live *in* the wild, not to those who are merely passing through, such as the lady of Noroison whose magic ointment cures Yvain.

[92] In Delarue and Ténèze's brief analysis of the "Conte de l'homme sauvage," the polarity between savage helper and savage enemy is clearly noted. In this story a child delivers a captive savage. Threatened with death and banished to the wild, the child encounters giants against whom the savage helps to protect him. The story ends with the child's return and the reintegration of the savage into society. It is clear, however, that this final sequence is redundant with respect to what goes before.

[93] Obviously it would be possible to give a general anthropological reading of the text based on the theory of rites of passage and initiatory schemes, but such a reading is not within our area of expertise and in any case beyond the scope of this essay.

[94] For a comprehensive and up-to-date introduction to the subject, see P. Le Gentil, *La Littérature française du Moyen Age*, 4th ed. (Paris, 1972), pp. 24–29.

[95] The controversial issues are well stated in the anthology entitled *Chanson de geste und Höfischer Roman* (Heidelberg, 1963) (*Studia Romanica* 4), especially in the contributions of E. Köhler, "Quelques observations d'ordre historico-sociologique sur les rapports entre la chanson de geste et le roman courtois," pp. 21–30, and H. R. Jauss, "Chanson de geste et roman courtois au XIIᵉ siècle (Analyse comparative du *Fierabras* et du *Bel Inconnu*)." See also·R. Marichal, "Naissance du roman," in *Entretiens sur la renaissance du XIIᵉ siècle*, ed. M. de Gandillac and E. Jeauneau (Paris and The Hague, 1968), pp. 449–482; J. Le Goff, "Naissance du roman historique au XIIᵉ siècle," in *Nouvelle Revue française* 238 (1972): 163–173.

[96] Léon Gautier, *La Chevalerie*, new edition (Paris, undated), p. 90.

[97] Lévi-Strauss, *La Geste d'Asdiwal*, pp. 30–31.

[98] "Explain structurally what can be explained structurally, which is never everything. As for the rest, try insofar as possible to grasp a determinism of another kind, which must be gleaned from statistics and sociology and which has to do with individual history, the society, and the environment." Claude Lévi-Strauss, *L'homme nu* (Paris, 1971), p. 560.

[99] Claude Lévi-Strauss, *L'Origine des manières de table* (Paris, 1968), pp. 105–106.

[100] Especially in his magisterial work, *Ideal und Wirklichkeit in der Höfischen Epik*.

[101]Ibid., pp. 37–65.

[102]*Roman de Thèbes*, ed. G. Raynaud de Lage (Paris, 1966).

[103]Chrétien de Troyes, *Cligès*, ed. A. Micha (Paris, 1970), lines 3105–3124.

[104]Erich Köhler, "Quelques observations," p. 27.

[105]See Jauss, "Chanson de geste et roman courtois," pp. 65–70.

[106]The comparison was first made, as far as we know, by J. Lafitau, *Moeurs des sauvages amériquains comparées aux moeurs des premiers temps* (Paris, 1724), vol. 1, pp. 201–256, and vol. 2, pp. 1–70, 283–288.

[107]The point can be made without relying on the rather dubious comparisons with oriental material suggested by P. Gallais in *Perceval et l'initiation*.

[108]On dubbing see Marc Bloch, *La Société féodale*, vol. 2 (Paris, 1940), pp. 46–53, and J. Flori, "Sémantique et société médiévale: Le verbe *adouber* et son évolution au XIIᵉ siècle," *Annales ESC* (1976), pp. 915–940.

[109]"Au XIIᵉ siècle: les 'jeunes' dans la société aristocratique," *Annales ESC* (1964), pp. 835–896, reprinted in *Hommes et structures du Moyen Age* (Paris, 1973), pp. 213–226; references here are to the paper in the *Annales*. See also E. Köhler, "Sens et fonctions du terme 'jeunesse' dans la poésie des troubadours," in *Mélanges René Crozet* (Poitiers, 1966), pp. 569ff.

[110]Duby, "Au XIIᵉ siècle," pp. 835–836.

[111]Ibid., p. 839.

[112]Ibid., p. 843. On the complexity of courtly attitudes toward marriage, see E. Köhler, "Les troubadours et la jalousie," in *Mélanges Jean Frappier* (Geneva, 1970), pp. 543–559.

[113]Duby, "Au XIIᵉ siècle," p. 844.

[114]Gawain has a brother, but he plays the role of antihero in the story of the Grail.

[115]We make these brief remarks in the hope that someone will undertake a systematic study of kindship structures in courtly romance.

[116]Duby, "Au XIIᵉ siècle," p. 839.

[117]On this subject see the illuminating remarks of J. Frappier, *Chrétien de Troyes: L'homme et l'oeuvre* (Paris, 1957), p. 15.

[118]There is a conflict over an inheritance in *Yvain*, but it is between sisters, both daughters of the Seigneur de la Noire Espine (lines 4699ff.). Yvain restores the rights of the dispossessed younger sister.

[119]We are here borrowing and to some extent elaborating upon a suggestion made by J. Györy in his previously cited article, pp. 107–108. On the matter of land-clearing itself, see Georges Duby, *L'Économie rurale et la vie des campagnes dans l'Occident médiéval* (Paris, 1962), pp. 142–169 and, more briefly, *Guerriers et paysans* (Paris, 1973), pp. 225–236. Duby places the "moment of maximum intensity of the phenomenon" between 1075 and 1180 (*Guerriers et paysans*, p. 228). The latter date is roughly when *Yvain* was written.

[120]Wace, *Le Roman de Rou*, ed. A. J. Holden (Paris, 1971), lines 6372ff. The text has often been cited and commented on, notably by Frappier, *Etude sur Yvain*, pp. 85–86, and Stauffer, p. 46.

[121]Note that our reading is based on the hero's encounters with three characters of the male sex (including the lion). Another reading, which would stress encounters with female characters, is surely possible.

[122]This detail is found only in Chrétien's version. Whatever relations there may be between the Welsh tale and the French romance, the text of *Owin*, in which the hermit does not appear, places the savage in a clearing but situates the fight between the lion and the serpent on a low hill. See Loth, pp. 9 and 38. Harmann von Aue's interpretation is again interesting: Calogrenant comes to a vast clearing (*geriute*)

whose paradoxical character is underscored by the absence of any humans (*âne die liute*, lines 401–402). The savage herdsman is in a field (*gevilde*, line 981). The hermit is not grubbing for roots but is standing on newly cleared land (*niuweriute*, line 3285). The encounter with the lion and the serpent takes place in a clearing (*bloeze*), to which the hero comes after "crossing a huge pile of felled trees," (lines 3836–3838). The trees do not appear to have been felled by the man but by natural and magical means, as after the storm unleashed by Yvain.

[123]The word *essart* (clearing) occurs again in line 4788 when the elder daughter of the Seigneur de la Noire Espine announces that she will not share with her sister "either castle or city or clearing or wood or plain or any other thing."

[124]Adler, p. 295, notes the parallel between the hermit and the savage guardian: "The Gestalt of the Hermit assumes the feature of a spiritualized replica of the Herdsman."

[125]Duby, *L'Économie rurale*, pp. 146–47.

[126]The argument could be pursued further by comparing *Yvain* with tales and myths in which land-clearing plays an essential role, such as the story of Melusina. See J. Le Goff, "Mélusine maternelle et défricheuse," *Annales ESC* (1971), pp. 587–622, and E. Le Roy Ladurie, *Le Territoire de l'historien* (Paris, 1973), pp. 281–300. In the authentic peasant folklore of Kabylie, the land clearer, the one who "clears away brush to create a garden or orchard," is none other than Sultan Haroun al-Rashid, "here promoted to almost supernatural rank," according to Camille Lacoste-Dujardin, *Le Conte kabyle* (Paris, 1970), p. 130.

[127]See P. Le Rider's remarkable *Le Chevalier dans le conte du Graal de Chrétien de Troyes* (Paris: S.E.D.E.S., 1978).

ROGER CHARTIER

Intellectual History or Sociocultural History? The French Trajectories

1982

In the late 1970s and early 1980s, historians began to cast a critical eye on the work that had gone before. This criticism took two forms. The first, a relatively new genre, was historiographical critique, focused in particular on specific aspects of French, and especially Annales, *history. The second involved critical thinking about the conceptual tools that historians used implicitly or explicitly. The following text is a good example of both of these concerns. Roger Chartier (b. 1945) wrote it originally for an American audience, with the purpose of explaining certain unusual features of French historiography by setting them in context. He did this by situating historical work in contemporary French history, and by comparing French historical work with other attempts to answer a similar set of questions. The exercise was salutary: at a time when the history of* mentalités *was belatedly becoming emblematic of French historiography, especially in the United States, Chartier subjected it to rigorous and closely argued analysis.*

As of the 1960s, the notion of *mentalité* became essential to French historiography in characterizing a history that proffers as its object neither the ideas nor the socioeconomic foundations of societies. More practiced than theorized about, this history of mentalities "à la française" is informed by several conceptions more or less shared by its users.[1] First, the definition of the word as suggested by Jacques Le Goff: "the mentality of any one historical individual, however important, is precisely what that individual shares with other men of his time." Or: "the level of the history of mentalities is that of daily life and

From "Intellectual History or Sociocultural History? The French Trajectories," trans. Jane P. Kaplan, in Dominick LaCapra and Steven L. Kaplan, eds., *Intellectual History: Reappraisals and New Perspectives* (Ithaca, N.Y.: Cornell University Press, 1982), pp. 13–46.

habits; it is what escapes the individual subjects of history because it reveals the impersonal content of their thoughts." Thus, there is constituted as a fundamental historical object the very opposite of the object of classical intellectual history: to the idea, the conscious construction of an individualized mind, is opposed, term for term, the always-collective mentality that regulates, without their knowing it, the representations and judgments of social subjects. The relationship between consciousness and thought is therefore posed in a new way, close to the formulation of sociologists in the Durkheimian tradition, placing the accent on the schemas or the contents of thought which, even if they are expressed in the style of the individual, are, in fact, the "unthought" and internalized conditionings that cause a group or a society to share, without the need to make them explicit, a system of representations and a system of values.

Another common point is a very broad conception of the field covered by the notion of *mentalité*, which includes, as Robert Mandrou writes, "what is conceived and felt, the field of intelligence and of emotion." Starting from that shared concept, attention is directed toward psychological categories at least as much as and probably more than toward intellectual categories: hence a supplementary distinction between a history of mentalities identified with historical psychology and intellectual history in its traditional definition. The identification with psychology is very evident in Febvre, who was an attentive reader of Charles Blondel (*Introduction à la psychologie historique*, 1929) and of Henri Wallon (*Principes de psychologie appliquée*, 1930)[2] and in his successors (Mandrou, for example, whose book *Introduction à la France moderne*, published in 1961, was subtitled *Essai de psychologie historique*). This identification is also at the very core of the work of Ignace Meyerson, whose importance has been paramount for the transformation of Greek studies.[3] Well beyond the project of reconstituting the sentiments and sensibilities belonging to the people of a certain time period (which is essentially Febvre's project), Meyerson's enterprise concerns the essential psychological categories—those at work in the construction of time and space, in the production of the imaginary, in the collective perception of human activities—which he places at the center of observation and captures in their precise historical specificity. For example, the notion of person as it is treated by Jean-Pierre Vernant, following Meyerson: "there is not, there cannot be, a perfect model of the individual, abstracted from the course of the history of mankind with all its vicissitudes and all its variations and transformations according to place and time. The purpose of the inquiry, then, is not to establish whether the individual personality existed in ancient Greece but, rather, to seek to discover what the ancient Greek personality was and how its various characteristics differed from personality as we know it today."[4] Starting from a similar intellectual position, Alphonse Dupront proposed to constitute the history of collective psychology as a specific discipline in the field of the human sciences, and to do this by giving it maximal extension since it included "the history of values, mentalities, forms, symbols, and myths."[5] In fact, under the guise of a definition of collective psychology, he suggested a total reformulation of the history of ideas. One of the major objects of the history of collective psychology is constituted by the idea-forces and the concepts that make up what Dupront calls the *mental collectif* of the people of an epoch. Grasped through the circulation of the words that designate them, located in their social roots, considered as much in terms of their affective or emotional charge as of their intellectual content, ideas become, like myths or complexes of values, one of these "collective forces by which men live their time" and thus one of the components of the "collective psyche" of a civilization. Therein one can see something like the fulfillment of the *Annales* tradition, both in the fundamentally psychological characterization of the collective mentality and in the redefinition of what the history of ideas must be, reinserted into an inquiry into the whole of the *mental collectif*.

It is clear, moreover, that the history of mentalities (considered as a part of sociocultural history), having as its object the collective, the automatic, the repetitive, can and must employ quantitative methods: "The history of collective psychology needs series that are, if not exhaustive, at least as broad as possible."[6] We see, then, what this approach owes to the history of economies and societies which, spurred on first by the great crisis of the 1930s, then by the post–World War II crisis, became the "heavy" sector (by number of collective investigations and the striking successes of some of them) of historical research in France. When, in the 1960s, cultural history emerged as the most popular and the most innovative domain in history, it did so by taking up and then transposing the problematics and the methodologies that assured the success of socioeconomic history. The project is simple, as stated a posteriori by Pierre Chaunu:

> The problem consists of attaining the third level [the level of the affective and mental] with the help of the techniques of regressive statistics, that is, with the help of the mathematical analysis of the series and of the double interrogation of the document, first of all in itself, then in relation to its position in the midst of the homogeneous series in which the fundamental information is integrated. It amounts to as complete an adaptation as possible of the methods that were perfected first by historians of the economy, then by social historians.[7]

This preeminence accorded to the series, and therefore to the collection and to the treatment of homogeneous, repeated, and comparable givens, has several implications. The most important is the central position bestowed upon the massive documentary collections, widely representative socially and allowing the categorization of multiple data over the long run. This orientation leads to the rereading and the exploitation of sources classically used in social history (for example, the notarial archives). It also results in the invention of new sources that permit the reconstitution of ways of thinking or feeling. Beyond the methodological similarity, Chaunu's "serial history of the third level" shares a double problematic with the history of economies and societies. The first is that of duration: How to articulate together and reconcile the mentalities of the long run, which tend to be more or less immobile, with the brusque changes and transfers of belief and sensibility of the short run? This issue (posed, for example, about the dechristianization of France) prefigures the central question of Braudel's *La Méditerranée*: How to conceptualize the formation of hierarchies, the articulation and imbrication of different durations (short time, *conjoncture*, long run) of historical phenomena?[8]

The second problematic inheritance, a bequest of cultural history, is found in the manner of conceiving the relationship between social groups and cultural levels. In fidelity to the work of Ernest Labrousse and the French "school" of social history, the categorizations elaborated in order to classify facts of *mentalité* are always those resulting from a social analysis that places levels of fortune in a hierarchy, distinguishes types of revenues, and classifies professions. It is then, on the basis of this social and professional grid, that the reconstitution of different systems of thought and of cultural behavior can take place. There results a necessary commensurability between the intellectual or cultural divisions on the one hand and the social boundaries on the other, whether it be the frontier that separates the little people from the notables or the dominated from the dominating, or the gradations that mark a social ladder. This almost tyrannical preeminence of the social dimension, which initially defines cultural cleavages that subsequently have only to be characterized, is the clearest trace of the dependence of cultural on social history which marks postwar French historiography. (We can note, moreover, that this dependence does not exist in the work of Febvre or Bloch, both of whom were more sensitive either to categories shared by all the people of a time period, or to differential usages of available intellectual equipment.)

It is upon these methodological bases, affirmed or unconscious, that the history of mentalities has developed in French historiography during the past fifteen years. Indeed, it has responded much more tellingly than intellectual history to French historians' new levels of awareness. Of these, the most significant is the recognition of a new equilibrium be-

tween history and the social sciences. Contested in its intellectual and
institutional primacy, French history reacted by annexing the terrains
and the modes of questioning of neighboring disciplines (anthropology,
sociology) that challenged its domination. Attention was thereby displaced toward new objects or objectives (collective thoughts and gestures
vis-à-vis life and death, beliefs and rituals, educative models, and so on),
which until then had belonged to ethnological investigation, and toward
new questions, largely foreign to social history, which were principally
concerned with ranking the constitutive groups of a society. Second,
there was the recognition that social differentiations cannot be conceptualized solely in terms of fortune or dignity, but are either produced or
mediated by cultural differences. The unequal division of cultural com-
petencies (for example, reading and writing), cultural goods (for example, books), and cultural practices (attitudes toward life or death) becomes the central object or objective of multiple inquiries conducted
according to quantitative procedures and aiming to provide another sort
of content for social hierarchies, without placing these hierarchies in
question. Finally, there was the realization that, for taking on these new
domains, classical methodologies did not suffice: consequently, as we
have seen, historians have recourse to serial analysis where testamentary
formulas, iconographic motifs, and the printed word replaced the price
of wheat, and we witness the flowering of work on historical language
or languages, from the description of semantic fields to the analysis of
"énoncés."[9] Therefore, because it transposed the approaches and the
problems that belonged to socio-economic history as part of a far-reaching transformation of the historical problematic, the history of mentalities (as part of sociocultural history) was able to occupy the front of the
intellectual stage and seem (as Dupront implicitly suggested) to reformulate—and thereby disqualify—the old way of doing the history of ideas.

But such a reformulation was also undertaken within the field of
intellectual history, and resulted in positions completely contradictory to
those of historians of mentalities. The major work here—which was,
incidentally, well received by the *Annales*—is Lucien Goldmann's.[10] At
the outset, a similar distance from the traditional modalities, biographical and positivistic, of the history of ideas seems to mark Goldmann's
project. As with Febvre, and as in the history of mentalities, the question
was first and foremost one of investigating the articulation between
thoughts and the social worlds. The concept of "vision of the world,"
borrowed from Georg Lukács, is the instrument that makes such an
approach possible. Defined as "the ensemble of aspirations, sentiments,
and ideas that unite the members of a given group (most often of a social
class) and oppose them to other groups,"[11] it makes possible a threefold
operation: to assign a defined social significance and a defined social

position to literary and philosophical texts, to understand the kinships between works of opposing forms and natures, and to discriminate within an individual work the "essential" texts (Goldmann's adjective), constituted as a coherent whole, to which each individual work must be related. For Goldmann the concept of world vision has simultaneously the functions of Febvre's mental equipment and the "habitus" of Erwin Panofsky (and Pierre Bourdieu). The *Dieu caché* gave an application, debatable but exemplary, of these propositions, construing Pascal's *Penseés* and nine of Racine's tragedies, from *Andromaque* to *Athalie*, as the corpus expressing most coherently "a tragic vision of the world," identified with Jansenism, and connecting this collective conscience to a particular group, that of the officials of the robe dispossessed of their political power, and hence of their social leverage, as a consequence of the construction of the absolutist state.

Whatever may be the historical validity of such an analysis, it brought out one crucial idea that is the complete opposite of one of the postulates of the history of mentalities: it is the "great" writers and philosophers who depict with the greatest coherence, throughout their essential works, the conscience of the social group of which they are members; it is they who attain "the maximum possible consciousness of the social group they represent." Hence the primacy accorded to the major texts (defined in a new way, by their relationship to a vision of the world), and hence its corollary: suspicion, if not outright refusal, of quantitative approaches in the field of cultural history. Well before the present-day mistrust of such approaches, nourished by an anthropological conception of culture, Goldmann's kind of intellectual history first alerted us to the illusions of quantification. "A sociological history of literature owes it to itself to privilege the study of the great texts," wrote Jean Ehrard.[12] That meant, on the one hand, that it is in the singularity of these texts that shared ideas are to be found most clearly and completely, and, on the other hand, that the counting of words, titles, and collective representations is literally "insignificant," that is, incapable of reconstituting the complex, conflicting, and contradictory significance of collective thought. This sort of numerical collection of the superficial, the banal, and the routine is not representative, and the collective conscience of the group (which is collective "unconsciousness" for the greatest number) can be read only in the imaginative or conceptual work of the few authors who carry it to its highest degree of coherence and transparency.

The debate joined here touches upon the very definition of intellectual history, thus upon the constitution of its proper object or objective. In 1961, Dupront pleaded against the history of ideas as follows: "The history of ideas, as ever amorphous and capable of absorbing, a bit like a thirsty sponge, everything that traditional history cared so little about treating, leans too far toward pure intellectuality, the abstract life of the idea, often isolated beyond proportion from the social milieux where it takes root and which give varying expression to it. . . . What is as important as the idea and maybe even more important is the embodiment of the idea, its significance, the use one makes of it." [13] From this attitude emerges the call for a social history of ideas, taking as its object the implantation and circulation of ideas. In a text published ten years later, Franco Venturi challenges the pertinence of such a project which, for him, misses the essential point: "The risk of the social history of the Enlightenment, as we see it practiced today, especially in France, is that of studying ideas when they have already become mental structures without ever grasping the creative and dynamic moment of their birth, and of examining the whole geological structure of the past without investigating the soil itself from which fruits and plants grow." [14] Ideas against mental structures: the opposition clearly shows the location of the divergences and the rejection of the supposed reductionism of the social (therefore quantitative) history of intellectual production. Moreover, this reductionism has two faces. The first is sociological, viewing the significance of ideas in terms of their foundation, whether it be indicated by the position of the individuals or the milieus that produce them, or by the social field of the reception of ideas. [15] It should be noted that this criticism, directed against the undertakings of cultural sociology, does not impugn Goldmann's perspective but, in reality, is situated in his own tradition. Without conflating the two questions, the notion of the world vision enables one to relate the significance of an ideological system, described in its own terms, to the sociopolitical conditions that cause a well-defined group or class, in a given historical moment, more or less to share, consciously or unconsciously, this ideological system. We are here far from the summary characterizations that sacrifice the ideological to the social, for example, by viewing the Enlightenment as simply bourgeois on the pretext that the philosophes and their readers were for the most part bourgeois themselves. Confronted with the ideas, or better, with the concepts utilized by the people of a specific time in a specific sense, the historian of ideas then has as his task "to abandon the search for a determination in favor of the search for a function," a function that can make sense only if one takes into account the entire ideological system of the epoch in question. [16]

Criticism addressed to the social history of ideas has recently aimed at another target and denounced another form of reductionism. Under attack is no longer the reduction of an idea or an ideology to its conditions of production or reception, but the assimilation of thought contents to cultural objects through a process of reification. "Serial history of the third level" carries such a reduction in its enterprise, since its quantifying vocation supposes either that the analyzed cultural and intellectual facts are from the outset coherent universes of objects (for example, books whose subjects can be treated statistically or pictures whose themes can be inventoried), or that collective thoughts, captured in their most repetitive and least personal expression, can be "objectified," that is to say, reduced to a limited number of formulas that need only to be studied in terms of their differential frequency in the diverse groups of a population. The sociological temptation here consists then of considering the words, the ideas, the thoughts, the representations as simple objects to be counted in order to bring out their unequal distribution. This is tantamount to ejecting the subject (individual or collective) from the analysis and denying any importance to the personal or social relationships that social agents entertain with cultural objects or thought contents. A study that focuses exclusively on distribution perforce fails to take into account the fact that any use or appropriation of a product or an idea is an intellectual "work": "with respect to the quantitative history of ideas only an awareness of the historical and social variability of the figure of the reader can truly establish the bases of a history of ideas that is also qualitatively different." [17] As Carlo Ginzburg has shown, what readers make of their readings in an intellectual sense is a decisive question that cannot be answered either by thematic analyses of printed production, or by analysis of the social diffusion of different categories of works. Indeed, the ways in which an individual or a group appropriates an intellectual theme or a cultural form are more important than the statistical distribution of that theme or form. [18]

Sure of their quantitative methodology, united in a definition of the history of mentalities less blurred than has been supposed, French historians have long remained deaf to these sharp challenges. Implicitly their representation of the field of intellectual history reduced these criticisms to so many rearguard battles in the name of a worn-out tradition. They envisioned the absorption of the history of ideas into a broader categorization that could be baptized sociocultural history or history of mentalities or history of collective psychology or social history of ideas. We can see today that according to this way of thinking, nothing had changed since the 1930s in the domain of intellectual history. The French historians have been guilty twice over of neglect or misunderstanding. First of all they paid no attention to the models that the epistemologies of Gaston Bachelard, Alexandre Koyré, and Georges Canguilhem offered for any undertaking in intellectual history. It is symptomatic to encounter in the *Annales* only a single review devoted to Bachelard (two pages by Lucien Febvre in 1939 on the *Psychanalyse du feu*) and none on the works of Canguilhem or Koyré (the only article published by Koyré in the *Annales* did not appear until 1960). This extraordinary blindness is laden with consequences. It deprived French historians of a whole world of concepts that might have put them on guard against the overly rough certainties drawn from statistical inquiry. These concepts might have permitted them to substitute for a nonarticulated description of the cultural products or thought contents of an epoch (such as quantitative research presents) a comprehension of the relations that exist, at a given moment, among the different intellectual fields. This approach would have made it possible to think in terms inaccessible to quantitative inquiry. First, one could examine the bonds of reciprocal dependence that unite the representations of the world, the technologies, and the state of development of different branches of knowledge. Then, by using an insightful idea such as the notion of epistemological obstacle (which brings out in another way what is the sharpest idea in mental equipment), one could explore the articulation among common representations (the accumulated fund of sensations, images, theories) and the progress of knowledge designated as scientific.[19] Had they listened to the epistemologists, the French historians might also have learned a different way to pose the problem on which all history of mentalities stumbles, that of the reasons for and modalities of the passage from one system to another. There, too, the quantitative lenses through which one perceives major changes are radically unable to pick up the deep processes of transformation, which can be understood only by examining together the dependence and autonomy of the different fields of knowledge, as Koyré has done. The passage from one system of representations to another can, from this perspective, be understood at the same time as a drastic break (in branches of knowledge but also in the very structures of thought) and as an itinerary composed of hesitations, of steps backward, of roadblocks.[20]

In addition to their failure to appreciate epistemology, which has deprived them of the intellectual instruments capable of articulating what the social history of ideas allowed them only to observe, historians have been guilty of another: the failure to consider the new manner of conceptualizing the relations between works (in the broadest sense) and society, proposed by historians of literature and ideas. The familiar historical problematic was modified by this manner of conceptualizing in two senses: first, by suggesting a nonquantitative conception of representativeness and, second, by dislocating the ideological systems of the society whose conflicts they were supposed to reflect or continue or translate. This dislocation does not mean affirming the absolute independence of the ideological systems vis-à-vis the social domain but, rather, posing this relationship in terms of structural homologies or global connections. Today, historians of mentalities are rediscovering the validity of this line of inquiry, heretofore neglected. Having renounced the project of a total history, they now pose the problem in terms of articulations between intellectual choices and social position on the scale of well-defined segments of society or even on the scale of the individual.[21] It is on this reduced scale, and probably only on this scale, that we can understand, without deterministic reduction, the relationships between systems of beliefs, of values and representations on one side, and social affiliations on another. Techniques of analysis fashioned for a history of ideas from above, at the summit, are thus transposed to another terrain, in order to grasp how an "ordinary" man appropriates for himself and in his own way (which risks deforming or mutilating) the ideas or beliefs of his time. Far from being drained, intellectual history (understood as the analysis of "work" done on specific ideological material) then annexes the terrain of popular thought that seemed to be the domain par excellence of quantitative history. The relationship between the history of mentalities and the history of ideas must thus be conceptualized in an infinitely more complex way than that characteristic of the French historians of the 1960s. [. . .]

TRANSLATED BY JANE P. KAPLAN

NOTES

[1] See Georges Duby, "L'Histoire des mentalités," in Charles Samaran, ed., *L'Histoire et ses méthodes* (Paris, 1961), pp. 937–66; Robert Mandrou, "L'Histoire des mentalités," in *Encyclopedia universalis* (1968), vol. 8, pp. 426–38; Georges Duby, "Histoire sociale et histoire des mentalités—le Moyen Âge: Entretien avec Georges Duby" (1970), in *Aujourd'hui l'histoire: enquête de la nouvelle critique* (Paris, 1974), pp. 201–17; Jacques Le Goff, "Les Mentalités: une histoire ambiguë," in Jacques Le Goff and Pierre Nora, eds., *Faire de l'histoire*, 3 vols. (Paris, 1974), vol. 3, pp. 76–94 [the piece is excerpted here as "'Mentalities': A History of Ambiguities," pp. 241–246]; Philippe Ariès, "L'Histoire des mentalités," in Jacques Le Goff et al., *La Nouvelle histoire* (Paris, 1978), pp. 408–23; Roger Chartier, "Outillage mental," in *La Nouvelle histoire,* pp. 448–52.

[2] See the following three articles: "Méthodes et solutions pratiques: Henri Wallon et la psychologie appliqué," *Annales d'histoire économique et sociale* (1931); "Une Vue d'ensemble: histoire et psychologie," in *Encyclopédie française* (1938); and "Comment reconstituer la vie affective d'autrefois? La Sensibilité et l'histoire," *Annales d'histoire économique et sociale* (1941), reprinted in *Combats pour l'histoire* (Paris, 1956), pp. 201–38.

[3] Ignace Meyerson, *Les Fonctions psychologiques et les oeuvres* (Paris, 1948).

[4] Jean-Pierre Vernant, *Mythe et pensée chez les Grecs: Études de la psychologie historique* (Paris, 1967), pp. 13–14. [The work is excerpted here as *Myth and Thought Among the Greeks*: Introduction pp. 247–253].

[5] Alphonse Dupront, "Problèmes et méthodes d'une histoire de la psychologie collective," *Annales ESC* 16 (1961), pp. 3–11.

[6] Ibid., p. 8.

[7] Pierre Chaunu, "Un Nouveau champ pour l'histoire sérielle: Le quantitatif au troisième niveau," in *Mélanges en l'honneur de Fernand Braudel,* 2 vols. (Toulouse, 1973), vol. 2, pp. 105–25.

[8] Fernand Braudel, *La Méditerranée et le monde méditerranéen à l'époque de Philippe II*, 2. vols. (2d. ed., Paris, 1966), vol. 1, pp. 16–17 [the work is excerpted here as *The Mediterranean and the Mediterranean World in the Age of Philip II*, pp. 82–88]; "Histoire et sciences sociales: la longue durée" (1959), in *Ecrits sur l'histoire* (Paris, 1969), pp. 41–83 [the work is excerpted here as "History and the Social Sciences: The Longue Durée, pp. 115–145].

[9] Compare Régine Robin, *Histoire et linguistique* (Paris, 1973).

[10] Lucien Goldmann, *Le Dieu caché: Étude sur la vision tragique dans les* Pensées *de Pascal et dans le théâtre de Racine* (Paris, 1955), and Robert Mandrou, "Tragique au XVIIe siècle: A propos de travaux récents," *Annales ESC* 12 (1957), pp. 305–13.

[11] Goldmann, *Le Dieu caché*, p. 26.

[12] Jean Ehrard, "Histoire des idées et histoire littéraire," p. 79.

[13] Dupront, "Problèmes et méthodes d'une histoire de la psychologie collective."

[14] Franco Venturi, *Utopia e riforma nell'Illuminismo* (Turin, 1970), p. 24.

[15] Jean Ehrard, "Histoire des idées et histoire sociale en France XVIIIe siècle: Réflexions de méthode," in *Niveaux de culture et groupes sociaux,* Actes du colloque réuni du 7 au 9 mai 1966 à l'Ecole Normale Supérieure (Paris, 1967), pp. 171–78.

[16] Ibid., p. 175, and the comments of Jacques Proust, pp. 181–83.

[17] Carlo Ginzburg, *Il Formaggio et i vermi: Il cosmo di un mugnaio del' 1500* (Turin, 1976), pp. xxi–xxii.

[18] Pierre Bourdieu, *La Distinction: Critique sociale du jugement* (Paris, 1979), pp. 70–87.

[19] Gaston Bachelard, *La Formation de l'esprit scientifique: Contribution à une psychanalyse de la connaissance objective* (Paris, 1939).

[20] Alexandre Koyré, *From the Closed World to the Infinite Universe* (Baltimore, 1957).

[21] For example, see Ginzburg, *Il Formaggio et i vermi*, concerning the cosmology of a miller; see also the essays of Natalie Z. Davis, which, on the basis of several case studies, pose the problem of the connections between religious choice and social rank, in *Society and Culture in Early Modern France* (Stanford, Calif., 1975).

Radical Doubts About Historical Method

PAUL VEYNE

Writing History: Essay on Epistemology

1971

When it appeared in 1971, Paul Veyne's book Comment on écrit *l'histoire (*Writing History*) was received as an iconoclastic pamphlet. Born in 1930, the author was not yet well known outside his specialty, the history of ancient Rome, and this was his first book. In it, he mounted an impetuous, energetic, argumentative case against the scientific credo of the day's historians. Bear the date in mind: the target of Veyne's attack was not only history's pretension to produce scientific knowledge but also the whole climate of scientism that the structuralist movement had been fostering for a decade. Fortified by wide reading, Veyne poured withering scorn on a whole list of reigning scientific beliefs: No, he argued, history is not a science, it does not explain, it is at best a literary genre capable of constructing coherent, convincing plots. Two years before Hayden White's* Metahistory: The Historical Imagination in Nineteenth-Century Europe *(1973), Veyne, working from very different premises, developed a skeptical view, an ultracritical epistemology that ultimately placed history, and indeed the social sciences generally, somewhere between subjectivity, rhetoric, and the gratuitous pleasure of scholarship.*

It was a time of prescriptive epistemology, and on the whole the book was not well received. To declare oneself "an obsolete empiricist" at a time when structuralism was still burning bright and "the-

---

From *Writing History: Essay on Epistemology,* trans. Mina Moore-Rinvolucri (Middletown, Conn.: Wesleyan University Press, 1984); first published as *Comment on écrit l'histoire* (Paris: Seuil, 1971).

ory" was everywhere staking its claims was taken as a provocation. Furthermore, Veyne's intellectual references were alien to idiosyncratic French taste: he cited German historicists, Max Weber, and British and American positivists. Raymond Aron, who had met with similar incomprehension thirty years earlier, was one of the few who hailed the originality of Veyne's book ("Comment l'historien écrit l'épistémologie," Annales ESC 26 [1971]), a work that admittedly staked out its position largely within Aron's own intellectual camp. As a result, many issues that have returned to the limelight in recent French debate thanks to the work of Paul Ricoeur and Jean-Claude Passeron went unnoticed at the time.

History "in Depth"

Every historical account is a plot out of which it would be artificial to cut discrete causes, and this account is directly causal, comprehensible; only the comprehension it gets is more or less deep. "To look for the causes" is to relate the fact in a more penetrating way, to bring to light the noneventworthy aspects, to pass from the comic strip to the psychological novel.[1] It is pointless to oppose a narrative history to another that aspires to be explanatory; to explain more is to narrate better, and in any case one cannot relate without explaining—the "causes" of a fact, in the Aristotelian sense, the agent, the matter, the form, and the end are, in truth, the *aspects* of that fact. It is toward this deepening of the account, this making explicit data, aims, and means of action, that today's historiography is often oriented; it ends in analyses (in the sense in which one speaks of the analytical novel)—which, though not accounts in the usual sense of the word, are nonetheless plots, for they include interaction, chance, and goals. It is usual to call this kind of analysis, in a metaphor coming from the theory of economic cycles, the study of the different temporal rhythms: in the foreground, the policy of Philip II day by day; as background, the Mediterranean data, which hardly change. The poles of the action thus serve to construct a temporal scenography in depth, and it is understandable that a baroque artist like Fernand Braudel enjoyed this. In the same way, the history of science will be that of the relations between the biography of a scientist, the techniques of his time, and the categories and problems limiting his field of vision at that time.[2]

What justifies the metaphor of the multiple temporal rhythms is the unequal resistance to the change in the different poles of action. At every period, unconscious diagrams, topoi that are in the air of the time, impose themselves on a scientist or an artist, *geprägte Formen* that classical philology studied in the time of its greatness:[3] those "readymade forms" that impose themselves with surprising strength on the imagination of artists and that are the matter of the work of art. For example, Heinrich Wölfflin discloses, beyond the quite varied personalities of the artists of the sixteenth century, the passage from a classical structure to a baroque structure and the "open form." For all is not possible at every moment of history; an artist expresses himself through the visual possibilities of his time, which are a kind of grammar of artistic communication, and that grammar has its own history, its slow rhythm, which determines the nature of styles and the manner of the artists.[4]

But since a historical explanation does not descend by parachute from the sky, it remains to be concretely explained how the "readymade forms" could almost imperatively impose themselves on an artist, for the artist does not "submit" to "influences"; the work of art is a doing, which uses sources and "influences" as material causes, in the same way that the sculptor uses marble as the material cause of his statue. So we shall have to study the education of painters in the sixteenth century, the atmosphere of the studios, the demands of the public that made it more or less difficult for an artist to break with the fashionable style, the authority of recent works as opposed to the works of the previous generation. The influence of visual grammar, of the "pedestal" supporting figuration in the sixteenth century, which Wölfflin analyzes so brilliantly, passes through the psychosocial mediations that are taken up by historical study and of which the art historian cannot be ignorant.

But if there is mediation and interaction, other mediations will function in the opposite sense and will explain that the baroque structure of figurative space and the open form may have appeared, lasted a long time, and disappeared; if readymade forms are a material cause of the work, the work is the material cause of those forms. The grammar of forms, in slowly passing time, would be a realized abstraction, if it existed otherwise than through and among the artists who make it last, by continuous creation, in swiftly passing time or among those who revolutionize it. At most, one can say that these two poles of artistic activity evolve at different speeds, that forms die less quickly than artists, and that we have more difficulty in being conscious of the existence of that grammar of forms than of the personality of the artists.

The plurality of historical times is a manner of speaking which means two things—that the innovators who upset the data of their period are fewer than the imitators, and that the historian must react against a laziness urging him to be satisfied with what the documents say in black and white or with the facts as conceived by the most eventworthy history.

Every fact is both causing and caused; the material conditions are what men make of them, and men are what the conditions make of them. Thus, since Leopold von Ranke's *Wallenstein*, we see in biography the account of the interactions of a man and his time; interaction is today called "dialectic," which means that the individual whose life is being written about will be considered as the son of his century (how could he not be?), but that he also acts on his century (for one does not act in a void) and that, in order to do so, he takes into account the data of his century, for one does not act without a material cause. [. . .]

How History Is a Work of Art

Can it be that historical synthesis is no more than positivism? It is indeed so, and the most famous books contain no more. It is easily forgotten what an extremely small place general ideas occupy in history books; to what are they reduced in Marc Bloch's *La Société féodale* (*Feudal Society*). To the idea that ground was the only source of wealth and to a few pages that illustrate more than analyze the need of every man to find a protector and the weakness of the central power. In any case, there was undoubtedly nothing more to be said. The beauty of *Feudal Society* comes from what it reveals—a society with its human types, its habits, and its constraints, in its most irreducible and most everyday originality at the same time. The naturalness of this picture, obscured by no abstraction (few books are less abstract), is what deludes us: as Bloch makes everything understandable, it seems to us that he explains more powerfully than the others. This naturalness is also that of Ronald Syme's *Roman Revolution* or of the Hellenistic-Roman civilization shown by Louis Robert, in whom the contemporaries of Cicero, Augustus, or Hadrian are seen with as much realism as a traveler sees a neighboring people that he has come to know well; the characters are in vain in period costumes, their clothes are not more crumpled and dirtied by everyday life. The past then becomes neither more nor less mysterious than the moment we are living.

The interest of a history book is not in the theories, the ideas, and the conceptions of history, packed up to be handed to philosophers; it is, rather, in what makes the literary value of that book. For history is an art, like engraving or photography. To affirm that it is not science but that it is an art (a minor art) is not to sacrifice to an annoying commonplace or to clear the ground: it would be, if it were affirmed that history, whatever one does, will be a work of art in spite of efforts it makes to be objective, the art being an ornament or incompressible margin. The truth is a little different: history is a work of art *by* its efforts toward objectivity in the same way that an excellent drawing by one who draws historical buildings, who shows the document and does not make it banal, is a work of art to some degree and supposes some talent on the part of its author. History is not one of those arts of knowledge in which, to quote Etienne Gilson, it is enough to have understood the method to be able to apply it; it is an art of production in which it is not enough to know the methods—talent is also needed.

History is a work of art because, while being objective, it has no method and is not scientific. Similarly, if one tries to specify where the value of a history book lies, one will find oneself using words that would be applied to a work of art. Since history does not exist, there are only "histories of . . ." and histories of which the eventlike atom is the plot. The value of a history book will depend first of all on the cutting out of that plot, the unity of action it requires, the boldness with which this unity has been extricated from more traditional cutouts—in short, on its originality. Since history is not a scientific explanation, but understanding of the concrete, and since the concrete is one and without depth, a comprehensible plot will be a coherent plot, without the solution of continuity or the deus ex machina.

Since the concrete is a development and concepts are always too fixed, the notions and categories of the historian must try to equalize the development by their flexibility. Since development is always original, you will have to be rich in ideas in order to perceive all its originality and know how to multiply the questions. Since the field of the eventworthy is surrounded by a zone of shadow which we cannot yet conceive, much subtlety will be needed to explain this noneventworthy area and to see what is taken for granted. Finally, history, like the theater and the novel, shows men in action and requires some psychological sense to make them alive; for mysterious reasons, there is a connection between the knowledge of the human heart and literary beauty. Originality, cohesion, flexibility, richness, subtlety, and psychology are the qualities necessary to say with objectivity "what really happened," to use Ranke's words.

Starting from this, one can amuse oneself by designating the worst history book known—I propose Oswald Spengler's—and the best—*Feudal Society,* for example. The work of Bloch does not mark a final point in knowledge, or progress in the method, for that progress no more exists than does that point. Its merit lies in the qualities enumerated above—that is, in its Attic qualities, which a reader seeking in history something other than it can give, would pass by without even seeing them, and which, while conferring its objectivity and its naturalness on the work and by being a quality of the historian, are fully revealed only in a literary analysis. [. . .]

THE CONFUSION OF ESSENCES

There is more. The contemplation of a historic landscape is like that of a terrestrial landscape: not only are the forms of relief like the statement of a problem, but they further seem to suggest solutions or indicate where a future science lies. For, after all, apples might not fall to the ground,[5] and men might not obey some of the solutions. Authority, religion, economics, art have a hidden logic; they are so many regional essences.[6] Their relief is not the result of chance; their slopes are not oriented haphazardly; there is some rugged exigency in them. The most astonishing characteristic of this scenery is its hugeness; everything in it turns to the institution, to differentiation, or to diffusion, everything in it develops and grows complicated: empires, religions, systems of relationships, economics, or intellectual adventures. History has a curious tendency to raise giant structures, to make human works almost as complicated as those of nature.

The result is that, even if one writes from beginning to end the history of a human work, one has not yet the feeling of having really explained it: the historian spends his time turning around essences that have their secret praxeology, without ever knowing the last word of what he is speaking about. He has to admit, on the one hand, that there is not much in common between an ancient "state" and the modern state; that when he speaks of the Greek religion and of the Christian religion, he is misusing a homonym. On the other hand, though, he does not cease to feel that there is an essence of public authority or of religion behind their historical variations. No one knows what those essences are; yet to want to write history while pretending to be ignorant of what is known immediately by any traveler who, disembarking on an unknown island, recognizes that the mysterious gestures made by the natives are a religious ceremony, is to reduce history to chaos. So, from Plato to Edmund Husserl, history, like all experience, has not ceased to pose the problem of the essence; our vision of experience is a vision of essences that, although confused, alone give a meaning to the scene.

In brief, we never, in history, succeed (and what historian has not known the exasperation of that powerlessness?) in finding what Ludwig Wittgenstein calls the hard of the soft, to seize which is the condition and the beginning of all science; everywhere, on the contrary, experience is at hand. Doubly so. First, causality is not constant (a cause does not always produce its effect; moreover, they are not always the same causes—for example, economic causes—which are the most efficacious). Second, we do not succeed in passing from the quality to the essence. We can recognize that a certain conduct may be termed "religious," but we cannot say what religion is; this inability is translated in particular by the existence of confused frontier zones—for example, between the religious and the political, where one is reduced to platitudes ("Marxism is a millenarist religion") that one cannot resign oneself to formulate, but that one also cannot ignore, for they contain, somewhere, a bit of truth. However, that bit slips through the fingers in quarrels about words, as soon as one tries to determine it. This jumble, these contradictions, this confusion induce us to state, beyond experience, the order of the formal, of the scientific; for science is born of contradiction and of the confusion of phenomena, much more than it is inferred from their resemblances. Thus, there is repeated unceasingly the old conflict between Aristotelian experience and Platonic formalism; all science is more or less Platonic.

The historian keeps to experience, so he must constantly resist the temptation to settle its confusions, at least expense, by going in for reductionism. Yet it would be simple to explain everything by bringing everything back to something else, the wars of religion will come back to political passions. Those passions will not be related to a sickness of the body social, as such, which the individual feels within himself and which, through anguish or shame, prevent him from sleeping, even if he does not suffer from them in his private life; they will be reduced to the sphere of his personal interest, and that interest itself will be of the economic order. That is a materialist reductionism, but there are others that will be idealist and are worth nothing more. Thus, politics will be reduced to religion; instead of considering that the Roman emperor or the king of France was surrounded by a charismatic aura (the cult of the imperial, the annointing and coronation, the curing of scrofula) because he was the sovereign, because the love of the people for the sovereign is a feeling expressed in all times, and because all authority appears more than human, it will be thought that the monarchic cult was the "basis" of royal power. Similarly, economics will be reduced to psychology: if primitive peoples exchange goods, it will be in virtue of a psychology of the countergift and of a seeking for prestige. Everything will be brought back to something more banal than itself. If emperors were accustomed to leave behind monuments of their reign—triumphal arches or Trajan's column—it will not be out of a desire to leave a trace of their reign in the open and to proclaim their glory, even if no one listens; it will be for "imperial propaganda."

We may consider that, today, the personal education of a historian, the acquisition of that clinical experience of which we were speaking before, is largely spent in getting rid of those reductions that are in the air and in rediscovering the originality of different essences. To reach a contradictory and deceptive conclusion: Each essence is explained only by itself—religion by the religious sentiment, and monuments by the desire to leave monuments. The human soul is formless; it does not have a hierarchical structure that would allow the bringing-back of these diverse sentiments to one more profound sentiment, class interest, or innermost religion. And yet, although one sees no foundation for them, those sentiments persist no less fiercely; they coexist, independent, arbitrary, and irreducible as old nations. The surprising contrast between their absence of principles and their tenacity can be explained only by some hidden reason and reference to a future science.

IT HAS LITTLE TO EXPECT FROM SCIENCE

Yet what will be the effect of that future science on the historian's profession? It will be weak, because, as we are not unaware, there are no laws *of* history. The result is that the historian will have "to know everything," like the ideal orator or like the detective and the criminal, but will be able to be content, like them, to know as an amateur. The detective and the criminal must have information on everything, for they cannot foresee to what lengths the execution or the reconstitution of a criminal plot may take them; but if that plot can work up scientific knowledge, at least there is no science of the plot itself, whose unfolding has no laws. How far away it already seems, the epoch, only a half century old, when François Simiand advised that in history one should seek generalities and regularities, in order to draw from them an inductive science of wars and revolutions—when it was hoped to succeed one day in explaining the growth and evolution of a given society.

Not only is no event enfiladed by a law, but even laws that interfere with the course of an event will never explain more than a small part of it. Talcott Parsons spoke truly, more than he perhaps thought, when he wrote that history is "an empirical, synthetic science which needs to mobilize all the theoretical knowledge necessary to explain the historical processes."[7] To put it more precisely, "the knowledge that is necessary"—laws in detail—in the measure that they complete the understanding of the plot and are inserted in sublunary causality. Spinoza's dream of a complete determination of history is only a dream: science will never be able to explain the novel of humanity, taking it in whole chapters or only in paragraphs. All it can do is to explain a few isolated words of it, always the same ones, which you come across on many a page of text, and its explanations are sometimes instructive for the understanding, sometimes only idle commentaries.

The reason for this separation between history and science is that history has as a principle that all that has been is worthy of it; it has not the right to choose, to limit itself to what is susceptible of scientific explanation. The result is that, in comparison with history, science is very poor, and repeats itself terribly. Whatever economy or whatever society you describe, the general theory of the state as a crossroads and of the economy as the market equilibrium will be true; for the equations of Léon Walras to become an event, the earth would have to become an Eden in which goods would no longer be scarce, or a demi-Eden where they would all be substitutable for each other. What would be the use of a future mathematics of political authority to a historian of the Roman Empire? Not to explain that the emperor was obeyed for exactly the same reasons that every government is obeyed: that theory would, rather, do him a negative service—it would help him not to give way to reductionism and to false theories, not to speak too much of charisma. It would, in short, render him the services of a culture. Let us conclude, with Ludwig von Mises, that "when history brings into play certain scientific knowledge, the historian has only to acquire an average degree of knowledge (a moderate degree of knowledge) of the science in question, a degree that will not exceed what is normally possessed by every cultured person."[8]

So much the more because science may be so abstract that one has no real idea of what to do with it. The theory of games of strategy is presently as magnificent as it is useless, like the calculation of probabilities in Blaise Pascal's time; and the whole problem is to succeed in applying it to something. You have only to see the precautions of writers who are tempted to use it, their way of touching it gingerly.[9] It is so easy, indeed, to get burned by it. Here is the famous "prisoners' dilemma": two suspects know that if they both keep quiet, they will get off with a light punishment, but that if one of them confesses, he will be released, whereas his comrade will receive a severe sentence because he was not the first to confess.[10] There is enough there to excite anyone who has the slightest sociological imagination. That is, therefore, why social life is sustained by a dialectal of "all" and "each";[11] all want the government to work, but no one wants to pay taxes if he is not sure that the others will pay too. That is why authority, order, is needed; that is the explanation of the solidarity, of the prudence of *homo historicus*; that is the definitive refutation of anarchism—and that is why revolutions do not happen. Better still, from that insoluble dilemma will be deduced the necessity for a formal rule: "Do what you have to do, come what may," and you will have created the Kantian ethic. It is too beautiful, there is too much of it, it is nothing more than an allegory; the slightest monographic study in which the dilemma would have testable effects would suit us much better. Alas! Man is so wavering and diverse a being that the human sciences cannot be other than very abstract, for they have to go very far before finding an invariant. [. . .]

TRANSLATED BY MINA MOORE-RINVOLUCRI

NOTES

[1] History is narration; it is not determination nor is it explanation; the opposition of "facts" and "causes" (Taine, Langlois, and Seignobos) is an illusion rising from a misunderstanding of historical nominalism. That history is not determination goes without saying (when one thinks it has been proved that "Napoleon could not" take a certain decision, it would remain true that, during the night before the decision, the emperor might have had a fit of mysticism or one of apoplexy). There is, on the other hand, a widespread idea that a historiographer worthy of the name and truly scientific must pass from "narrative" to "explanatory" history. For example, in Josef Gredt's textbook of Aristotelian-Thomist philosophy, we read that history is not truly a science in the sense that its object is a mass of factual data that it does not deduce, but that it does become scientific in a certain way by connecting those facts with their causes. But how would it not connect them with their causes, since every account immediately has a meaning, since it is impossible to gather a fact without bringing its causal roots with it, and since, conversely, to find a new cause of "a" fact is to disengage, in the form of a consequence, a new aspect of "the" fact in question?

To find economic causes of the French Revolution is to shed light on the economic aspects of that revolution. The illusion comes from believing that the Revolution is "a" fact other than nominally; that it is not *a* fact means it is not a *fact*, since "being and one are convertible"—it is a nominal aggregate. Certainly, when one writes "What are the causes of the Revolution?" and when one is hypnotized by this statement, one has the impression that the fact is there and that it remains to find its causes; thus one imagines that history becomes explanatory and that it is not directly comprehensible. The illusion disappears as soon as the word "Revolution" is replaced by what it covers: an aggregate of little facts. As R. Aron writes (more or less) in his *Dimensions de la conscience historique*, "the" causes taken together do not entail "the" Revolution as their resultant; there are only *detailed* causes that each explain one of the numberless *detailed* facts grouped together under the name "Revolution." Similarly, when Max Weber related puritanism to the beginnings of capitalism, he did not claim to discover the several causes or the one cause of "the" capitalism; he simply brought to light one aspect of capitalism that was misunderstood before his time and whose cause he simultaneously indicated: a religious attitude. This aspect is not a perspective on the geometrical figure that capitalism might be, for that geometrical figure does not exist; the aspect in question is only a new historical fact that will quite naturally integrate with the aggregate we call capitalism. In other words, under the same name of capitalism we shall continue to designate an event that in reality is no longer quite the same, because its composition has been enriched.

We shall see, in chapter X, that the progress of history is not to pass from narration to explanation (every narration is explanatory), but to push narration further into the non-eventworthy.

[2] G. Granger, "L'histoire comme analyse des oeuvres et comme analyse des situations," in *Médiations*, I (1961), pp. 127–143, which states: "Every human work is something more than the product of its conditioning, but, on the other hand, that something in no way obliges us to hypostatize the frameworks of consciousness to subordinate to them all apprehension of reality."

[3] The classical example is the formal analysis of St. Paul's speech before Areopagus by E. Norden, *Agnostos Theos, Untersuchungen zur Fromengeschichte religiöser Rede* (1923; repr. 1956).

[4] H. Wölfflin, *Principes fondamentaux de l'histoire de l'art: Le problème de l'évolution du style dans l'art moderne*, Fr. trans. (Plon, 1952), pp. 262 f., 274 f. The work of A. Warburg, with his study of the *Pathosformeln*, gives a fairly similar meaning.

[5] The story of Newton's apple is authentic: A. Koyré, *Études newtoniennes* (Gallimard, 1968), p. 48, n. 35.

[6] Compare the pluralist materialism of J. Freund, *Essence du politique* (Sirey, 1965). Of course, we do not give the words "regional essence" the very precise meaning they have in Husserl.

[7] Parsons, *The Social System*, p. 555.

[8] *Epistemological Problems of Economics*, p. 100. Let us stress the great interest of this book for the epistemology of history and of sociology; we deplore not having been able to get *Theory and History*, by the same author (Yale University Press, 1957), which is out of print. The clarity of mind regarding the epistemology of history, shown by the authors whose education is primarily scientific (either physics, like Popper, or economics, like Mises or Hayek), is a lesson to be meditated on.

[9] For instance, G. Granger, *Essai d'une philosophie du style* (A. Colin, 1968), p. 210. Another example: in *Théorie économique et analyse opérationnelle*, p. 395, W. J. Baumol declares that the "game of the two prisoners" reveals the fundamental reason for the prolongation of state control in the most democratic society; on that he refers to his book *Welfare Economics and the Theory of the State* (Longmans, 1952). When we have read the latter book, we note that there is not the slightest reference to the theory of games, but the reader will find many situations described there to which he might be tempted to apply that theory, as the author himself was surely tempted to do when writing his book.

[10] R. D. Luce and H. Raiffa, *Games and Decisions*, p. 94; W. J. Baumol, *Théorie économique* . . . , p. 396; W. Edwards, "Behavioral Decision Theory," in W. Edwards and A. Tversky, eds., *Decision Making* (Penguin, 1967), p. 88. The *Times Literary Supplement* has announced the publication of a book by A. Rapoport and A. Chammath, *Prisoner's Dilemma* (Ann Arbor: University of Michigan Press, 1970).

[11] Sartre, *Critique de la raison dialectique*, pp. 306–377.

MICHEL DE CERTEAU

A Transitional Epistemology: Paul Veyne

1972

The essay that follows was one of the most interesting reactions to the preceding excerpt, Paul Veyne's 1971 Comment on écrit l'histoire (Writing History). It was interesting because it did not try to defend the scientific ideology so prevalent at the time but, instead, responded to Veyne's criticisms by proposing an epistemology of history not as a genre but as a set of procedures, of ways of doing things. It was significant, too, because Certeau also published, at around the same time, an important critical reflection on the practice of the discipline entitled "Faire de l'histoire" (1970). Some of the themes of that essay are adumbrated here.

In a review of Paul Veyne's recent book, Raymond Aron was quite correct when he saw the David of Aix doing battle against "the sectarian squabbles and fashions of Paris."[1] [. . .] Since the capital is "structuralist," Veyne is antistructuralist. Since Paris is doing quantitative history, and since formal analysis is thriving there, he is against those things. Yet his is a guerrilla war. His "epistemology" does not march in serried ranks of propositions. He pursues his adversaries on their own terrain, taking to the bush when necessary. At times, he seems out for a lark and nothing more. Nevertheless, another author falls to his sallies on every page. In the blink of an eye, the victim finds himself "rectified," hit with unerring accuracy just where he is weakest. Veyne's footnotes are filled with the names of scholars cut down in their glory and laid to rest. He is a keen and avid marauder.

His erudition is as tireless as his zeal for demystification. As a scourge of orthodoxies, he is unbeatable. His text sparkles with references and citations. He juggles bibliographies. He has read everything, or nearly so, and conceals none of it. His book-learning is dazzling. He has explored every kind of scientific literature with an alert eye. He cites the

Michel de Certeau, "Une Epistémologie de transition: Paul Veyne," *Annales ESC* 27 (1972).

telling page. He zeroes in on the avowal hidden away in the details of an analysis. He extracts the relevant theory from a mass of irrelevancies and detects the sentence with which an author gives himself away. He also knows how to engrave the crystal of his transparent style with the silhouette of a thought, revealing its strengths and weaknesses.

Yet his very versatility arouses suspicion. As he roams his textual battlefield, his various positions begin to overlap as reading is heaped upon reading. Where exactly does he stand? He seems never to be *anywhere*. His mobility leaves him in no place at all. It hides the place from which the author speaks and from which what he says derives its authority. He never reveals the line of his discourse, which is ultimately a *literary* line. The brilliant game in which he brings together so many different authors unfolds on the endless, flat surface of the text in which he reduces, transforms, and organizes the "pretexts" that all his readings constitute for him. Looked at in this way, his variegated oeuvre can be linked to a typical form of academic literature. It is a form of the rhetoric of erudition.

Its purpose and interest, however, lie in the claim that historiography can only be a rhetoric of curiosity. This book is therefore defined by the connection and tension that exist between a rhetoric of erudition and a rhetoric of pleasure. [. . .] For Veyne, historiography is defined as an intelligible object by the rules of a literary genre and as a referent by the pleasure of the investigator. In short, it is the text of a desire.

That is what is new about the book. However, before attempting to gauge its importance, we must dwell for a moment on the book's structure, which is pieced together from the debris of an epistemology that I am tempted to describe as a sort of practical joke or bluff. Fortunately, there is reason to believe that the author shares this view.

The first criterion is external. Can a book really be about history if the great works of French historiography have been winnowed out? There is no analysis of the methods or practices of Fernand Braudel, Ernest Labrousse, Emmanuel Le Roy Ladurie, Jean Meuvret, Jean-Pierre Vernant, or Pierre Vilar, to mention only the names that first come to mind. Many other authors are barely touched on. Is this exclusion meant perhaps as an attack on historiographical orthodoxies? How can that be, when René Baehrel, Philippe Ariès, and others are scarcely treated any better? What is the author talking about, then, if he considers the leading historians of the day unworthy of his attention? If he fails to articulate an epistemology based on an examination of their actual techniques and procedures? And if, out of excessive wariness of institutional "traps," he refuses to situate himself in relation to institutions of learning (universities and historical institutes) to which he himself belongs, and which constitute the platform from which he speaks? In view of all this, it should come as no surprise that nothing is left of history but a literature that discusses the things of the past. Of the logic invested in the organizations and operations that produce historiography, nothing is left. [. . .]

As for the facts with which Veyne, as historian, declares himself to be "content," they are merely the product of the empiricism on which the author prides himself when he identifies himself on the first page of his book as "an obsolete empiricist." As such, he defines, within the borders of the real, a boundary between the known and the unknown: knowledge, he alleges, stems from particular realities. Thus for Veyne, "history" can be "a narrative of *true* events": "As long as one recounts things that are *true*, [history] is satisfied." It relates them in a form "that is *natural* to them." From what well is this "truth" drawn? The "fact" is the result of some procedure of analytic decomposition. It is a way of laying down or spelling out a signification compatible with some system of interpretation. Yet how could Veyne possibly be suspicious of the ideology that governs his *conception* of "facts" and of "the concrete" when he assigns *ad patres* the task of examining concepts? He grants himself possession of reality and truth from the beginning: "For the historian as for everyone else, what is truly real is individuals," individuality being by definition the real to which history gives access and which allows events to enter into discourse. Still more explicitly, he invokes an "ontology of the individual substance." The rejection of conceptual problems leads him to an ontology. In practical terms, this takes the form of a primacy granted immediately to microunits ("facts," "events," "individuals," and so on) over macrounits ("society," "mentality," "period," and so forth), whereas fundamentally both derive to the same degree from a conceptual decomposition.

Veyne's whole epistemology seems to be organized around a series of dichotomies: concrete/abstract, contingent/necessary, phenomenon/essence. These cleavages all recapitulate in one form or another the split between the *experiential* and the *formal*, or between *fact* and *law*. Presumably, history takes the side of "experience" and "facts" for the simple reason that these are the things of which it speaks. In this literary realm, words allegedly give us things. Language ostensibly yields an adequate (in some respects) picture of its referent. It supposedly captures the articulations of reality and can therefore tame it, becoming a transparent window onto "true" facts (or at any rate a series of windows yielding fragmentary views thereof).

It is hardly surprising that Veyne continually dismisses present-day historiographical issues as the subjects of "old debates." [2] Ultimately, his philosophy of language takes us back to good old Aristotle. Does not Veyne argue that, when it comes to knowledge, "the answer was set forth in the *Posterior Analytics* and has not changed essentially since"?[3] In fact, that famous and often-commented text enables us to measure what has "changed since," namely, the relation of language to its referent. For Aristotle, knowledge derives from precisely that which has become unthinkable for us, the possibility of a language associated with an "intuition" which "apprehends principles" and, hence, "is the principle of knowledge," thus positing an original coincidence of knowledge and truth. In today postulating an epistemological situation of this type, Veyne dismisses what is characteristic not only of the construction of scientific language but also of the scientific analysis of language. Indeed, for reasons that do not have to do with personal ideological choices but, rather, with the general conditions of discursive practice, the hypothesis of a language of *presence* has become nostalgic.

HISTORICAL DISCOURSE

In addition, Veyne declares that history is "nominalist." Insolent reader that I am, I shall allow myself to choose among the author's successive positions: this declaration of nominalism coincides most fully, I think, with his intention. I shall therefore omit any discussion of the disputes connected with the old-fashioned epistemology of subject-object relations. At the very least, these deserve acknowledgment for having provided the author with the jewel case in which he displays the wonders "invented" by his indefatigable curiosity: innumerable astute remarks about a wide range of historical issues and authors, and countless observations owing to an acute sensitivity to people and things. There is something of Montaigne in Veyne. That is his attractive side, unlike his epistemology, which is too distant from the procedures of historiography and the analysis of language to be convincing. What is a theory, if not the articulation of a practice? And what is an epistemology, if not a discourse that elucidates that relationship? However, that is not where Veyne's interests lie.

Indeed, his tastes and curiosities have taken him well beyond a conceptual apparatus borrowed from American and German followers of late-nineteenth-century German historical criticism. Some singularly new and important questions have emerged from Veyne's experience as a historian. These questions can be grouped around two themes: first, historiography is a *discourse,* a "literary genre" organized in the form of a "plot" consisting of a series of "episodes," and second, historiographical practice grows out of a *desire* for knowledge, a "curiosity" on the part of the historian. "To sum up," Veyne writes, "history is an intellectual activity that uses time-honored literary forms to satisfy simple needs of curiosity."

If we read Veyne with these themes in mind, rather than as the scholastic continuator of "old debates" about whether historical knowledge is objective or subjective, the significance of his book becomes clear. Paradoxically, his thoughts on the subject echo, in their own distinctive way, the work of Roland Barthes and Michel Foucault on history as discourse as well as Foucault's current work on history as a form of textual organization articulated around a "will to know," a desire for knowledge.[4] Yet Veyne rejects (or at any rate neglects) the theoretical and methodological sophistication that this work offers in order to speak in his own way about "literary genre" and "curiosity."

As to genre, he considers historiography to be a "narrative" and a "staging." He emphasizes the "literary nature" of the "plot." For him, moreover, "explanation" is a matter of the order of exposition: "What is called explanation is scarcely more than the way in which the narrative is organized into a comprehensible plot." Furthermore, "the progress of the plot" from "episode to episode" (each of which figures in the narrative as a "cause") is governed by certain rules. In short, we are dealing with "time-honored literary forms" whose structure can therefore be isolated.

This way of looking at things is a form of discursive analysis, carried on perhaps with sly discretion, perhaps with aristocratic disdain for technical jargon, or perhaps in blissful ignorance of what is going on in Paris (but how can one suspect such a thing of a reader like Veyne?). It opens the door to semiotics. It allows us to consider the way in which the discourse in question is governed by rhetorical rules and serves as a playground for a code of verisimilitude, the use made of techniques such as what A. J. Greimas calls "expansion" and "condensation" to slow or hasten referential time, and so on.[5]

Veyne does not discuss any of these things. He would rather explore byways. He defends his views with a critique of concepts (such as "causes," "main lines of development," "period frameworks," and the like) and with an apologia on behalf of historical "detail" and "facts." He threads a narrow course between two reefs, as if he felt himself to be in possession of new questions but without the means to treat them on their own terms. He therefore contents himself with turning old positions into metaphors, which become parables about (as well as camouflage for) his subject, which is the discourse or "literary genre" of history. He makes a baroque object out of an epistemology that is in fact already alien to him.

This internal tension is indicative of a transitional moment. It is the sign by which a transitional epistemology can be recognized. Its *mezza voce* accompaniment takes the form of a series of allusions to the "woes" of the historian (the negative aspect of his pleasure). Its quintessential defining characteristic is the resurgence of different ways of interrogating historical interrogations of the problematics with which historians must deal. Because Veyne is too lucid to forget his interrogations when facing the *discourses* of economics and sociology, he is forced to circle the walls of Jericho.

The problem that he opens up is fundamental. It has to do with the fact that epistemology, which once hinged on the relation of subject to object and to reality, now centers on language. More than any other discipline, history has been affected by this change, for in the nineteenth century it to a large extent took up philosophy's cudgels and claimed to give access to the real through the mediation of "historical facts." This accessibility of the real by way of transparent historical discourse (however fragmentary or distorting it may have been) became inconceivable once the technical apparatus of history began to *forge* its own formal postulates and objects for the purpose of *producing* interpretive "works"; once historical work became a *series of transformations* by which texts or "pretexts" (documents) were turned into other texts (the historical operation); once discourse itself became definable in terms of characteristic *rules*; and once adequacy to a referent (the real) became in history, as in the "realist" novel, a mere "reality effect," that is, a mode of enunciation peculiar to a literary genre. A transition took place from a situation in which a historical reality (history, or *Geschichte*) was "received" in a text to one in which a textual reality (historiography, or *Historie*) is "produced" by an operation whose rules are fixed in advance.

At the risk of falling victim to "fashion" and "sectarianism," I must say that, in Barthes, Foucault, Greimas, Julia Kristeva, and Tzvetan Todorov, I think Veyne has the "Open Sesame" to "concepts" tailor-made to answer his questions. And if those concepts are too Parisian, he can find similar riches in the gardens of Aix tended by Gilles Granger, Jean Molino, and Georges Mounin.

THE HISTORIAN'S DESIRE

Veyne is even more original when he turns away from orthodoxies and formalisms to express his desire as a historian, his curiosities and pleasures. It is nothing less than a revolution to propose pleasure as the standard and rule of historical work, which over the years has been governed by various ideas of the historian: first as a person with a political "mission" or office, later as someone with a "vocation" to uncover the social "truth," and finally as a research worker applying to the technocratic law laid down by the institutions of knowledge. With this suggestion, Veyne has stood the "discipline" on its head.

In rejecting the "laws" that would justify history's claim to be a science, Veyne's first target, I think, is the traditional asceticism (or should

I say Jansenism?) of academic teaching. In piercing the walls of the academic cloister, he is aiming not so much at an epistemology as at the ethical outlook which that epistemology surreptitiously justifies. He shifts the focus from law to pleasure. By substituting "plot" for "cause," "details" for "structures," "items" (Veyne's word for sidetracks to the main theme) for categories and sequential periodizations, and "experience" for "formalism," he gives himself room to get back to the *subject* of history.

Clearly, this "return of the repressed" flies in the face of a whole historical epistemology. Here, to be sure, evocation and practice outweigh theory. The "liberation" of the subject, for example, can be seen in Veyne's rejection of macrounits (*mentalité,* century, economic structure, and the like) in favor of microunits (events, facts, and so on), although both pose the same kinds of problems at the level on which he chooses to treat them. Yet, by pulverizing "history" into a cloud of facts and details, hence subjective decisions, he indirectly evokes the historian as subject. Although this pulverization is still described in traditional epistemological terms, it is the metaphor that Veyne uses to bring the maker of historical texts back into the analysis. He thus focuses attention on the place of the locutory *I* in the production of historical narrative.

Recent historical work shows that the resurrection of the narrative *I* in historical discourse has begun. Growing (but still secondary) importance has been attached to the history of the historian as subject: frequently, prefaces are used to relate the history of the object under study and to indicate the place of the writer in that history.[6] This trend is but a sign, limited by the norms of thesis-writing. Ultimately, however, the pressure to which Veyne bears witness is aimed at breaking what Barthes rightly analyzes as a "censorship of enunciation" through an "overwhelming discursive emphasis on what is stated, and even (in the case of the historian) on the referent: no one is there to assume responsibility for the statement."[7]

Looked at in this way, the "objectivity" of historical discourse can be seen as a "deficiency of signs of the stating agency." It is the product of what one might call "the referential illusion" ("since here the historian pretends to allow the referent to speak for itself").[8] Veyne is thus changing a narrative structure when he shakes the columns of an "objective" methodology to make room for the stating agency. Marked by its heterogeneous conceptualization, his investigation is concerned with "enunciation," that is, with what semioticians since C. S. Peirce have been accustomed to analyze as the subject's capacity to assume responsibility for its statements. Various contemporary researchers have followed this path. Starting with signifying systems, they orient themselves toward signifying practices in the hope of relating problematics of "communication" (characteristic of the first view) to those of "production." More precisely, they consider the relations that exist between the subject of what is stated with the stating subject.[9]

Veyne's contribution takes us even further. It is meant to place the historian's pleasure at center stage. Once again, his aphorisms and ideological decrees are subject to the laws of a complex ballistics. The issue of subjectivity, for example, comes up at once: "All historiography is subjective," Veyne writes. However, against the background of the work as a whole, I cannot read these characteristically peremptory statements as depositing reality in the account of the *knowing* subject. All of Veyne's Aristotelian and Germano-American panoply is not enough to persuade me on this point. What his work signals, I think, is the subversion of a problematic of knowledge by a problematic of desire and its relation to the text; it is the substitution of a science of the subject for a science of man qua object.

"There is no science of man, because the man of science does not exist; only its subject does."[10] Lacan has proposed a theory of this reversal, the sentiment of which is already apparent here. Indeed, when Veyne talks about "curiosity" without invoking a Freudian vocabulary, he states the "question of the subject" more accurately than do some who use the vocabulary of psychoanalysis to exhume a timeless, silent positivity which they may call "the unconscious" while treating it as an *object* of knowledge. Veyne is at once more modest and more honest. Yet his allusion to "curiosity" is not enough to show how historiography shapes the text of the desire that arises out of an ambivalent relation to the "other," reiterated in the figure of the "past" or the "foreigner." It is even less justifiable to assume that singular facts reveal this desire better than general categories do, or that desire is identifiable with the individual, who represents it in the manner of an enticement.

Despite the connection afforded by the problems he raises, Veyne stands aloof from analytical treatments of those same questions largely because he speaks as an historian. He comes from somewhere: history. He describes how the central problematics have shifted within a field that all too often is ignored by others—semioticians and psychoanalysts—who have elucidated those problematics for themselves in other areas. His text recounts changes occurring on his terrain as they appear in the vocabulary of the milieu. Thus, he is describing the shredding of an epistemology with the tattered threads it has left behind.

In placing his own thinking, along with history in general, under the sign of nominalism, Veyne is again using a metaphor, but a very precise one. It points toward the end of a body of thought organized in relation to real "objects" and toward the need to analyze historiography as a discourse articulated on other discourses within the system of language. One whole school of historiography took for its slogan, "I, the past, now speak." Veyne has reoriented historiography toward the transformations of textual organizations in which what is speaking is the desire to know.

In the end, however, important questions remain unanswered. What connection will develop between this treatment of *discourse* and the *practices* determined by the technical institutions of a discipline? And how will an epistemology so defined modify historiographical procedures and styles, that is, historiographical production itself?

TRANSLATED BY ARTHUR GOLDHAMMER

NOTES

[1] Raymond Aron, "Comment l'historien écrit l'épistémologie," *Annales ESC* 26 (1971), p. 1320.

[2] In his article "Contestation de la sociologie," *Diogène* no. 75 (1971), he says that the problems of the theory of knowledge are matters for "old debates" already discussed by Leibniz, Saint Thomas Aquinas, and Aristotle.

[3] Ibid., p. 5.

[4] Roland Barthes, "Le Discours de l'histoire," *Social Science Information* 6.4 (1967), pp. 67–75, and "L'Effet de réel," *Communications* no. 11 (1968), pp. 84–90; Michel Foucault, *Les Mots et les choses* [The Order of Things] (Paris: Gallimard, 1966), ch. 7–10, and *L'Archéologie du savoir* [Archaeology of Knowledge] (Paris: Gallimard, 1969). See also A. J. Greimas, *Du Sens: Essais sémiotiques* (Paris: Seuil, 1970), pp. 103–16, and Julia Kristeva, *Sémiotiké: Recherches pour une sémanalyse* (Paris: Seuil, 1969), esp. pp. 208–45. Veyne himself invokes Saussure and perhaps Foucault when he rejects "deceptive continuities [and] misleading genealogies."

[5] The narrative moves quickly over times in which "nothing happens" and slows to relate "feverish periods."

[6] See, for example, Emmanuel Le Roy Ladurie's preface to his *Paysans de Languedoc* (Paris: SEVPEN, 1966), and especially the preface and introduction to Pierre Vilar's *La Catalogne dans l'Espagne moderne* (Paris: SEVPEN, 1962), pp. 11–165, in which the author discusses the evolution of his methods and his experience of contemporary Spain in relation to four centuries of Spanish history.

[7] Barthes, "Le Discours de l'histoire," p. 71.

[8] Ibid., p. 69.

[9] See the special issue of *Langages* no. 17, edited by Tzvetan Todorov (March 1970), "L'Enonciation," and the previously cited work of Julia Kristeva, or "Sémanalyse et production de sens," in A. J. Greimas, ed., *Essais de sémiotique poétique* (Paris: Larousse, 1972), pp. 207–34.

[10] Jacques Lacan, *Ecrits* (1966), p. 859. This statement is one of the central propositions of the important Lacanian text, "La Science et la vérité," pp. 855–77.

PART III

The Territory of the Historian (1970s–mid-1980s)

New Objects and New Methods

JACQUES LE GOFF AND PIERRE NORA

Constructing the Past

1974

Published in 1974, the three volumes of Faire de l'histoire *(Constructing the Past) marked an important moment in French histori-cal scholarship. The innovation was not fundamentally scientific in nature: the structure of the work, with sections on "new problems," "new approaches," and "new objects," was mainly rhetorical, and the pieces selected offered an eclectic sample of the historical work of the moment, particularly of the kind of work being published in the* Annales. *What was new was the enterprise itself, in three respects. First of all, it was a publishing venture aimed at a broad audience, beyond professional circles. It is of some interest in this connection that the work had two editors: Jacques Le Goff, a noted medievalist but also one of the editors of the* Annales *and, at the time, chairman of the Ecole des Hautes Etudes en Sciences Sociales, and Pierre Nora, a "historian of the present" but perhaps best known as Gallimard's history and social science editor. Second, the book was an affirmation of a new group of historians with both intellectual and social affini-ties, a group that was almost exclusively French and even Parisian, centered (though not exclusively) on the* Annales, *the Ecole des Hautes Etudes, and the Collège de France, two elite research institu-tions, rather than the university. Most of the members of this group belonged to the post-Braudel generation: besides the two editors, it*

Jacques Le Goff and Pierre Nora, eds., *Faire de l'histoire* (Paris: Gallimard, 1974), 3 vols, table of contents and preface. Many of the contributors are included in this volume.

included Pierre Chaunu, Georges Duby, François Furet, Emmanuel Le Roy Ladurie, and Pierre Vidal-Naquet, to name a few. There were also a few illustrious elders (Alphonse Dupront, André Leroi-Gourhan, and Pierre Vilar), some relatively unknown younger historians, and a few brilliant outsiders (Michel de Certeau, Michel Serres, and Jean Starobinski). Many of the members of this group would participate together in future projects. Finally, the table of contents confirms the profoundly empirical character of the project. This was no theoretical manifesto but, rather, a statement and illustration of historiography's revitalized and broadened outlook: the political even made a discreet reappearance. The book demonstrated the variety of current work in history and the fruitfulness of collaboration with other social sciences. It was thus a manifesto without a doctrine, and some, though not all, of what it proposed was new at the time (and has therefore aged since). The work's success both in France and abroad was a testament to the confidence of historians in the resources of their discipline as well as to the interest of a new and wider audience for what can conveniently be called "the new history."

Table of Contents

Preface

The title of this work is borrowed from Michel de Certeau.[1] This title will at once allow the reader to gather what this work is not about. It is not a panoramic view of contemporary historical practice. To begin with, our ambition is not to offer a comprehensive view of the field of history or of what historians are producing. The domain of history today is unlimited, and it is expanding into new areas while leaving others exhausted or untouched. We are concerned here only with advances already made by various historians, only some of whom actually contribute to this volume. Our text, moreover, is not an outside look at what is being produced in history but, rather, a contribution to historical reflection and research.

Though shaped by many hands, this book is intended to illustrate and promote a new type of history. It is not the history of any research team or school. While readers may find traces of the so-called *Annales* school in the essays of many of the authors as well as in the spirit of the work as a whole, this is because the new history owes so much to Marc Bloch, Lucien Febvre, Fernand Braudel, and others who have carried on their innovative work. Yet there is no orthodoxy here, not even of the most open-ended sort.

In a work that seeks to defy limits and overcome prejudices, it may seem surprising that all the authors are French (or nearly so). Although the leading role that French historians have played in the renovation of history partly justifies this decision, it would be paradoxical if a work intended to move beyond the Eurocentrism that was all too prevalent in the old history were to fall into the trap of nationalism. We wanted, however, to maintain a certain consistency. Although the historians represented here reflect various outlooks and belong to different generations, they reflect similar training, concerns, and aims.

In a collection that proclaims the current fragmentation of history and accepts the coexistence of different but equally valid types of historical research, we did not seek to justify this disparateness by juxtaposing samples of the various kinds of history in question. Instead, we have tried to show how the different avenues of historical research relate to one another. Profound changes are occurring in the basic scientific disciplines today, and fundamental intellectual techniques are undergoing a thorough overhaul. What is alive in linguistics and mathematics today is what is called "modern." The epithet does not lend itself to history, where it has traditionally designated a period rather than a type, so we have instead coined the phrase "new history." That is what we wish to present here.

In our view, the novelty of the new history lies in three areas: *new problems* have called history itself into question; *new approaches* have modified, enriched, and revolutionized traditional areas of history; and *new objects* have appeared in history's "epistemological field."

History has been forced to redefine itself first of all because historians have become aware of the relativism of their science. It is no longer the absolute that it was for the historians of the past, whether providentialist or positivist, but the product of a situation, a history. The singular nature of a science that has only one term for both its object and itself, that oscillates between history as lived and history as constructed, between the endured and the fabricated, forces historians who have become aware of this unique relationship to question yet again the epistemological underpinnings of their discipline.

History has also come under attack from the social sciences, such as demography and economics, in which quantification reigns supreme. It has become, for those disciplines, an experimental laboratory for testing hypotheses, and it has been obliged to abandon impressionism in favor of statistical rigor and forced to reconstruct itself using countable, quantifiable data. What historians must do, however, is not sever their ties to a humanism that has been based, since the Middle Ages if not since Greek antiquity, on the qualitative, but rather evaluate the risks and benefits of erecting measurability as a supreme standard, a standard that may entail as much impoverishment and mutilation as it brings consolidation and enrichment.

The new history, which rejects more firmly than ever the philosophy of history and does not recognize itself in Vico or Hegel or Croce, much less Toynbee, has nevertheless shed the illusions of positivism. Moving beyond the critique, altogether convincing, of historical "facts" and "events," it has begun to exhibit a conceptualizing tendency that raises the danger of hitching history to something other than itself, whether it be Marxist eschatology, Weberian abstraction, or structuralist atemporality.

This brings us to the major challenge to which the new history must respond, that of the other human sciences. The domain that it once occupied alone, that of explaining societies over time, has been invaded by other sciences whose boundaries are ill defined and which threaten to engulf or dissolve it. Ethnology is the most enticing of these disciplines; rejecting the primacy of the written and the tyranny of the event, it is drawing history toward the slow, almost static realm of the Braudelian *longue durée*. It is reinforcing history's tendency to dig down to the level of the quotidian, the ordinary, the "little people."

The most secure systems of historical explanation have been called into question by this expansion of the field. The most global and coherent of synthetic historical views (in both senses of the word "synthetic"), Marxism, has come under attack from the new human sciences. Social history has extended its influence into the history of social representations, ideas, and mentalities. There it has discovered a complex world of interactions and delays that rules out any simplistic use of the notions of infrastructure and superstructure.

Last but not least, the most serious challenge to traditional history is perhaps that raised by the new conception of contemporary history, which is still trying to define itself in terms of such notions as "immediate history" or "history of the present," refusing to reduce the present to an inchoate past and thus challenging the well-established definition of history as the science of the past.

Along with these major controversies, the new history is also being made by deepening and adding to certain traditional areas of history without challenging their basic assumptions. What is involved, in most cases, is a tendency for fragmentary histories to come together as totalities. Modern archaeology has turned archaeological excavation into a way of deciphering the meaning of systems of objects. Economic history has focused in on notions such as "crisis" and "conjuncture," which help to reveal how economic systems operate. Going beyond serial economic history, other investigators have combined economic with political, psychological, and cultural data in order to study whole systems. Similarly, demographic history has added complexity to its models by bringing in information about mentalities and cultural systems. Religious history, literary history, the history of science, political history, and the history of art are also moving toward total history by focusing on such globalizing concepts as the sacred, texts, codes, power, and monuments.

Finally, history has made itself new by incorporating new objects that previously lay beyond its reach and outside its territory. History's voracious appetite of late would have made it easy for us to multiply examples, but we have limited ourselves, not without regret, to a significant sample of typical new objects. Some of those selected may seem paradoxical choices: climate, the body, myths, and festivals, for instance, may appear atemporal rather than historical, while mentalities and youth might seem fairly static. The unconscious of psychoanalysis, language as studied by modern linguistics, cinematographic images, public opinion polls—all these things are connected with new human sciences; yet history has, in a sense, confiscated them. Still other objects were once considered too unimportant for historians to notice: cooking, for instance, which attests to the growing importance of two new realms of history, the history of material civilization and that of techniques. Finally, one of our new objects is not new in itself but only by virtue of a "scandalous" change in the way recent historians have chosen to view it—the book, considered as a product not of elites but for the masses, a special case of the quantitative revolution in history.

One might conclude from this preface that the new history has fallen victim to the invasive and destructive aggression of the other human sciences. Do historians still have a territory of their own? Does history deceive us because it incorporates by definition the realm of human experimentation, which is time? Beyond the diversity of coexisting histories, is there *a* history? Does History (with a capital *H*) exist?

History, as this work should make clear, has recently undergone an unprecedented expansion, yet it almost always emerges intact from the confrontation with its sister sciences owing to the soundness of its tried and true methods, its chronological moorings, and its reality. If danger threatens, it lies rather in the risk that history might lose itself in its all too successful adventures. There is reason to wonder whether, after a period of openness whose triumphs we wish to celebrate here, the time has not come for a period of discreet reflection and redefinition. Progress in science is as much the product of rupture as of extension, if not more. History may be awaiting its Saussure.

The new history, as should be apparent to readers of this book, is in any case characterized by its awareness of being determined by the conditions of its production. Hence, there are reasons for the growing interest of history in itself, in the increasing space and emphasis being devoted to the history of history. History is a product, but it also asks about its producer, the historian. The modern historian—a pioneer, an adventurer, and a conqueror—is also ill at ease. Though increasingly specialized, historians have yet to develop techniques sophisticated enough to protect themselves from amateurs and vulgarizers, or to share in the prestige that the late twentieth century affords to its scientific heroes, those who split atoms and work with magical formulas and win Nobel Prizes. They can no longer be Jules Michelet, that giant with feet of clay, a model discouraging both for what is great in him and for what is vile. They cannot be Albert Einsteins. The historian (as Marc Bloch said) is a craftsman, at once too much of an artist and not enough.

However, the most important item on today's agenda is not to dream of yesterday's prestige or tomorrow's. It is to learn how to do the kind of history needed now. A science of the mastery of the past and the consciousness of time, history must still define itself as a science of change, of transformation. Hence, this work is intended to be something more than a summary or diagnosis of history's place at the present time. We hope that it will show where history is and ought to be headed. Its ambition is not just to show how history is done but to illuminate what is left to do.

TRANSLATED BY ARTHUR GOLDHAMMER

NOTE

[1] Michel de Certeau, "Faire de l'histoire," *Recherches de science religieuse* 58 (1970), pp. 481–520.

The Triumph of
Quantitative Approaches

EMMANUEL LE ROY LADURIE

The Historian and the Computer

1973

History did not wait until the 1960s and 1970s to make use of statistics and quantitative measures. Research in price history was already under way early in the century. In France, the work of the sociologist, economist, and historian François Simiand and of his most immediate disciple, Ernest Labrousse, not only established quantitative history but made it a model of the scientific approach to the past. In the late 1960s, however, it became possible to move from the artisanal stage (data maintained by hand on slips of paper and perhaps tabulated mechanically) to more elaborate processing by means of computers. Emmanuel Le Roy Ladurie (b. 1929), who published his first great book, Les Paysans du Languedoc *(The Peasants of Languedoc), in 1966, and who was then director of the Centre de Recherches Historiques of the Ecole des Hautes Etudes as well as coeditor of* Annales, *was one of the first to assess the new possibilities, which he did with a neophyte's enthusiasm that now seems part of a distant past (Who would dare to affirm today, as he did in 1968, that "historians will either be programmers or they will no longer exist"?). Bear in mind that, however extreme these ringing declarations may seem, they did lead to a number of successful studies in economic, social, and cultural history—among them, Christiane Klapisch-Zuber and Daniel Herlihy's study of the Florentine* Catasto, *Le Roy Ladurie's*

From *The Territory of the Historian,* trans. T. B. and Siân Reynolds (Chicago: University of Chicago Press, 1979), pp. 3–5. First published in *Le Territoire de l'historien* (Paris: Gallimard, 1973).

*work with collaborators on nineteenth-century military archives, and
François Furet and Jacques Ozouf's work on French literacy in the
sixteenth to the nineteenth centuries.*

Once upon a time, not so very long ago, a specialist in German history decided to use a computer to analyze *the social composition of the entourage of Wilhelm II.* So he compiled biographies of all the individuals at the kaiser's court, encoded their particulars, with details of their family ancestries and birthplaces, then took a deep breath and fed all his material, duly transferred to punched cards, into a computer. The machine's verdict was categorical: Wilhelm's entourage was composed essentially of ... *aristocrats born east of the Elbe.* The computer had told him what everyone knew in the first place.

This anecdote illustrates an obvious point: in history as in everything else, what matters is not so much the machine as the question one asks it. A computer is only interesting in that it allows one to tackle problems that are new and original in their subject matter, method, and, above all, their scope.

This said, many promising research possibilities are of course opened up to those historians who have access to computer science. One that immediately springs to mind is the analysis of those vast deposits of documents, containing vital data, but whose sheer bulk has until now daunted all researchers.

One such is the 1427 *Catasto* (land register) of Florence: it has been waiting five hundred years for historians to take any notice of the prodigious wealth of demographic data contained in its bulging registers. For in these documents, the Florentine inspectors of the fifteenth century had listed in detail information about the family circumstances of fifty thousand households.

Two medievalists, David Herlihy and Christiane Klapisch-Zuber, have now taken the opportunity offered by modern techniques for analyzing the contents of these ancient files. Thanks to these historians, the university computer at Madison, Wisconsin, will shortly have made a mere mouthful of the *Catasto.* For the first time, massive records of a medieval population in the century following the Black Death will be fully revealed. What is more, a machine-readable tape, easily stored and reproduced, and containing all the information collected, will make available for further research, calculations, and correlations data previously buried in the massive and unreadable Florentine documents, which by good fortune survived the flooding of the Arno.

Not only has it a voracious appetite for data, but the historical computer can also accommodate any number of approaches or ideologies.

One of the earliest "machine history" studies, which appeared some time ago in the review *Annales,* was the work of a Soviet historian seeking to establish the degree to which the Russian peasants were exploited by wealthy landowners in the past: this was pure Marx or Lenin, but tailored to the computer age. In a somewhat different perspective, the new generation of radical historians like Kenneth Lockridge in the United States, who are engaged in reinterpreting the American Revolution, putting greater emphasis on its revolutionary or even Castroist content, are using the most sophisticated technology in their work. With the aid of computers that can digest the hundreds of thousands of figures contained in the tax records of the thirteen colonies, they are seeking to show that the upheavals of the War of Independence had their origins in a situation of social crisis as the small farmers, victims of the depression and impoverished by the division of their land, directed their concentrated resentment against their British masters.

In Europe, particularly in England and above all in France, where quantitative history has made so much headway in the last thirty years, the computer is gradually becoming central to one of the most promising disciplines of the new school—historical demography. The most difficult and above all exhausting task in this area always used to be the laborious reconstitution of families who were alive in, say, the seventeenth and eighteenth centuries.

Researchers who embarked upon this task were until now obliged to index by card all the records for any village they were studying: the marriages, baptisms, and burials entered in the registers kept up over a period of two hundred years by successive parish priests. These tens of thousands of entries then had to be reclassified on files for each family, so that for every couple the births, marriages, and deaths of parents or children were recorded. This labor of classification was both Herculean and depressing: it could last months or more, without the slightest glimmer of an intellectual discovery on the horizon. Only afterward, when all the families had been reconstituted, did it become possible to make any meaningful calculations of fertility, family size, mortality, and so on. A number of researchers in Cambridge and Paris are now working out programs so that the computer can take care of this thankless preliminary phase, from the initial data collection to the reconstitution and statistical analysis of the family files. The historian will then have virtually nothing to do but apply thought—which should, after all, be his or her proper task.

To take another kind of research, a team of historians from the Ecole des Hautes Etudes recently completed a study of Parisian rents from the fifteenth to the seventeenth century. Here again, the computer was the key to success. The basic data on these rents had been lying unread in notarial files or in hospital and convent accounts. Thanks to this study, which was considerably accelerated by the use of computers, the data could at last be extracted from these dusty ledgers and some of the basic questions that preoccupy quantitative historians could be asked of them, for instance: When did the real economic renaissance occur in Paris? Is it true that the city experienced a "sixteenth-century boom," a "seventeenth-century crisis," or a depression at the end of the Middle Ages? The computer made it possible for these problems to be tackled with a far greater margin of safety than the traditional procedures of reckoning permitted. And, indeed, within a fairly short time the team had obtained not merely a single graph of average Parisian rents, but over a hundred graphs, providing corroboration for each other and casting light on all kinds of aspects of the question; charting rent movements according to occupation of tenant, district, type of housing or landlord, and so on.

Computer-based history does not merely lead to a single, well-defined category of research. It can also bring about the institution of a new kind of archive. Once information has been placed on computer cards or tape and used by one trailblazing historian, it can be stored for the purposes of future researchers seeking to make previously unattempted comparisons. An "archive bank" of this kind already exists in the Interuniversity Consortium for Social Sciences at the University of Michigan, Ann Arbor: the consortium at present holds census returns and American election records since the beginning of the nineteenth century. A new kind of archivist is to be found there too—a sort of historical technologist very different from the traditional scholarly graduate of the Ecole des Chartes.

I need hardly add that, here as elsewhere, there is an "American challenge." For twenty or thirty years, the French school of history has been living—rather well—on the heritage of the founding fathers, Lucien Febvre and Marc Bloch. And, in the field of social, economic, and quantitative history at least, this school has come to be regarded as a trendsetter and an avant-garde for historians of other countries. The technological revolution we are now experiencing bids fair to change all that.

TRANSLATED BY T. B. AND SIÂN REYNOLDS

FRANÇOIS FURET

Quantitative History

1971

This article first appeared in Annales *in 1971 and was reprinted three years later in the collective work* Faire de l'histoire *(Constructing the Past). The precise chronology is important, because it sets the proper context for Furet's critical reflections, which coincided with the beginnings of the great wave of quantitative history. Trained by Ernest Labrousse among others, Furet was himself a practitioner of quantitative history as well as a student of the French Revolution: he did work in economic history (with Jean Bouvier and Marcel Gillet), in social history (with Adeline Daumard), and in cultural history (as a participant in the important study of* Livre et société dans la France du XVIIIe siècle, 1965 and 1970), before joining with Jacques Ozouf to do extensive research on the rise of "written culture" in France between the sixteenth and nineteenth centuries (*Lire et Ecrire, 1977 [*Reading and Writing*]).*

His thoughts on the epistemological implications and other consequences of large-scale quantification are therefore those of a practitioner. The position staked out here is notable for its radicalism (quantitative history was supposed to usher in the age of "problem-oriented history" advocated by the founders of the Annales*) as well as for its caution (statistics were not the only way of doing history). The piece is remarkable for its call to arms against "intellectual indolence," a call less heeded, perhaps, than it deserved.*

Quantitative history is fashionable just now both in Europe and in the United States. Since the 1930s, historical research has been making rapidly increasing use of quantitative sources and of calculation and quantification procedures. But, like all fashionable

From *The Workshop of History,* trans. Jonathan Mandelbaum (Chicago: University of Chicago Press, 1984), pp. 40–53. The article first appeared as "L'Histoire quantitative et a construction du fait historique," *Annales ESC* 26 (1971), pp. 63–75, which was reprinted as "Le Quantitative en histoire," in Jacques Le Goff and Pierre Nora, eds., *Faire de l'histoire,* vol. 1: *Nouveaux problèmes* (Paris: Gallimard, 1974), pp. 42–61.

phrases, "quantitative history" has come to be used so sweepingly that it covers almost everything, from critical use of the simple enumerations of seventeenth-century political arithmeticians to systematic application of mathematical models in the reconstruction of the past. Sometimes quantitative history refers to a type of source, sometimes to a type of procedure; always, in some way or other, explicit or not, to a type of conceptualization of the past. It seems to me that if one goes from the general to the particular and tries to pinpoint the specific nature of historical knowledge in relation to the other social sciences, one can distinguish three groups of problems relating to quantitative history.

1.   The first group concerns the methods of treating the data: problems having to do with the formation of different families of data, the geographical unity of each family, and its internal subdivisions; with correlations between different series; with the values, in relation to the data, of different models of statistical analysis; with the interpretation of statistical relationships; and so on.

These problems belong to the *technology* of research in the social sciences. It is true, they may also include questions of methodology, not only because no technique is "neutral" but because, more specifically, all statistical procedures are bound to raise the problem of whether, and to what extent, historical or sociological knowledge is compatible with, or can be dealt with exhaustively by, mathematical conceptualization of a probabilistic kind. But neither the technical nor the theoretical debate is specific to history: both arise in connection with all the social sciences. In this respect, quantitative history is no different from, for example, what is now called "empirical sociology," which in this context is simply contemporary quantitative history.

2.   Quantitative history also refers, at least in France, to the aims and researches of certain economic historians, who attempt to turn history into a kind of retrospective econometrics, or, in other words, on the basis of modern national accounting, to fill in all the columns of an imaginary input-output table for past centuries. The champions of this econometric history advocate total and systematic quantification, in their view indispensable both for the elimination of arbitrariness in selecting data and for the use of mathematical models in their processing. This processing is based on the concept of general equilibrium as imported into economic history from political economy.

According to this argument, genuine quantitative history would be the result of a twofold reduction of history: first, at least provisionally, the reduction of its field to economics; and, second, the reduction of its descriptive and interpretive system to the one worked out by the most rigorously constituted of the social sciences today, political economy. The same analysis could be applied to demography and demographic history: here again, a conceptually constituted science indicates the data and supplies the methods for a particular historical discipline, the latter thus becoming a sort of by-product of the other discipline, whose questions and concepts it merely transposes into the past.

Of course, there have to be data for the past just as for the present; or at least it has to be possible to work them out with a sufficient degree of accuracy or to reconstruct or extrapolate them. This necessity sets the first limit to the complete quantification of historical data. Complete quantification, even if possible at all before the nineteenth century, could not go back beyond the introduction of the statistical or protostatistical recording of data, which coincides with the centralization of the great European monarchies. However, history did not begin with William Petty or Sébastien Vauban.

Moreover, there is no reason why the historian should agree, even provisionally, to have his field of research reduced to economics or demography. There are two alternatives. Either history is only the study of a previously determined, limited sector of the past, into which mathematical models established by certain social sciences are imported in political economy, which seems to me the only one of the social sciences with such models at its disposal. History then becomes nothing more than an additional field of data. Or—the second alternative—one takes history in the widest sense, that is, as a discipline not strictly reducible to a set of concepts and with countless different levels of analysis, and then addresses oneself to describing these levels and establishing simple statistical connections between them on the basis of hypotheses that, whether original or borrowed, depend on the intuition of the researcher.

3.   This is why, even if one qualifies history as "quantitative," one cannot escape what is the specific object of historical research—the study of time, of the diachronic dimension of phenomena. But, looked at from this point of view, quantitative history's most general and elementary object is to form historical fact into temporal series of homogeneous and comparable units, so that their evolution can be measured in terms of fixed intervals, usually years. This fundamental and logical operation constitutes what Pierre Chaunu has called "serial history," a necessary though not sufficient condition of strictly quantitative history as defined above. For serial history offers the conclusive advantage, from the scientific point of view, of substituting for the elusive "event" of positivist history the regular repetition of data selected or constructed by reason of their comparability. It does not, however, claim to give an exhaustive account of the whole body of evidence nor to be a comprehensive system of interpretation nor to be a mathematical formulation. On the contrary,

the division of historical reality into series leaves the historian confronted with his material broken down into different levels and subsystems, among which he is at liberty to suggest internal relationships if he chooses.

Defined in this way, quantitative and serial history emerge as at once connected with and distinct from each other. Yet they share an elementary basis in that both substitute the series for the event, both make a construction from historical data in terms of probabilistic analysis. To the classic question *What is a historical fact?* they both give a new answer that transforms the historian's raw material—time. It is about this internal transformation that I should like to put forward a few ideas.

To avoid any misunderstanding, let me say at once that this essay does not set out to prescribe quantitative history as the only kind permissible. During the last ten or twenty years, serial history has turned out to be one of the most fertile approaches in the advancement of historical knowledge. It also has the immense advantage of introducing into the ancient discipline of history a rigor and efficiency superior to those of qualitative methodology. But it is nevertheless true that there are important sectors of historical reality that it is by nature unable to treat or even to approach, either for circumstantial reasons such as irremediable lack of data or for fundamental reasons such as the irreducibly qualitative nature of the phenomenon concerned. This explains why, for example, historians of antiquity, who work with data very discontinuous in time, or specialists in intellectual biography, concentrating particularly on what is unique and incomparable in creativeness, are usually less attracted by serial history than, say, historians of the agrarian structures of modern Europe.

From this point of view, another, and perhaps more basic, problem should be raised. Serial history undoubtedly provides accurate methods for measuring change, but to what extent does it enable the historian to interpret change? By definition, data series are composed of identically constructed units, in order to make comparisons possible. The long-term variation of these units in time, when it takes the form of cycles, brings us back to what one could call change within stability and thus to an analysis in terms of equilibria. But sometimes the temporal variation of one or more series takes the shape of an open-ended growth trend, that is, a cumulative process. If one breaks down this trend into relatively small units (annual or ten-year periods, for example), it becomes harder to define the threshold beyond which the time structure and the rates of change are transformed. This raises tremendous problems of dating and periodization. Moreover, the decisive historical change cannot be inserted into any series endogenous to a given system; instead, it must be the product either of an innovation unrecorded in any previous quantification or of an exogenous factor that upsets the centuries-old equilibrium of the system. These methodological problems lie at the heart of the present debate over the question of industrial takeoff. In other words, if it is true that no methodology is innocent, then serial history, by concentrating on the long term and on the equilibrium of systems, seems to me to put a premium on conservation. It is a good antidote to the identification of history with change—a nineteenth-century inheritance—and thus a crucial phase in the development of history as a discipline. Nevertheless, the premises and limits of serial history must also be realized.

But the fact that serial history has limits—a subject that might be discussed on another occasion—does not excuse intellectual indolence or uncritical observance of tradition. If a number of historians today are breaking away from narrative in order to concentrate on problems, this is largely due to changes in the pieces of the puzzle used by historians to reconstruct the picture of the past. Because of serial history, they are now confronted with a new panorama of data and a new awareness of the premises of their profession. It is likely that we have not yet exhausted the possibilities offered by quantitative methods.

The Historian and His Sources

Quantitative history presupposes the existence and elaboration of long series of homogeneous and comparable data, and the first problem that presents itself in new terms is that of sources. In general, European archives were formed and classified in the nineteenth century, in accordance with procedures and criteria reflecting the ideological and methodological preoccupations of the period. This meant that national values predominated and that priority was given to politico-administrative sources. It also meant that documents were preserved and classified in accordance with the special and limited purpose of a particular inquiry: archives were built up to witness to events rather than to time. They were constituted and criticized in themselves and not as factors in a series; the point of reference was external. What was in question was the historical "fact" of the positivists, the naive mind's illusory sheet anchor in what is supposed to be real, as distinct from mere testimony—a particular, discontinuous, elusive sequence within either an indefinite flux or a chronology preestablished in terms of centuries, reigns, and ministers. In short, archives are the memoirs of nations, just as the letters a person keeps show what an individual has chosen to remember.

However, the data of quantitative history refer not to some external, vaguely outlined "fact" but to internal criteria of consistency. A fact is no longer an event selected because it marks a high spot in a history whose meaning has been predetermined but, rather, a phenomenon chosen and sometimes constructed by reason of the recurrence that makes it comparable with others in terms of some unit of time. The whole conception of history based on archives is radically transformed at the very time when its technical possibilities are multiplied by the electronic processing of information. This simultaneous and interconnected revolution in methodology and technique enables us to think in terms of a new kind of archive preserved on perforated tapes. Such archives would not only be built up according to a deliberately planned system; their criteria would also be quite different from those of the nineteenth century. Documents and data exist no longer for themselves but in relation to the series that in each case precedes or follows: it is their comparative value that becomes objective, rather than their relation to some elusive "real" substance. Thus, incidentally, the old problem of the *critique* of historical documents moves on to different ground. "External" criticism is based no longer on credibility as derived from contemporaneous texts of another kind but, instead, on consistency with a text of the same kind occurring elsewhere in the temporal series. "Internal" criticism is simplified inasmuch as many of the necessary cleaning-up operations can be entrusted to the memory of the computer.

Consistency is introduced at the outset, when the data are first sorted out, by a minimal formalization of each document that makes it possible to retrieve, over a long period and for each unit of time, the same data in the same logical order. From this point of view, the historian's use of computers is not only an enormous practical advance in the time it saves (especially when the sorting is done verbally by tape-recording, as in the Couturier method); it is also a very useful theoretical discipline, in that the formalization of a documentary series that is to be programmed forces the historian from the very beginning to abandon epistemological naiveté, to construct the actual object of his research, to scrutinize his hypotheses, and to make the transition from implicit to explicit. The second critical process, this time an internal one, consists in testing the consistency of the data themselves in relation to those which come before and after—in other words, in eliminating errors. It thus emerges as a sort of consequence of the first process and can in fact be done largely by automation through programmed methods of verification.

Naturally enough, serial history in its manual form began by using those historical series that were easiest to handle, that is, economic, fiscal, and demographic documentation. The revolution introduced by the computer into the collection and processing of data has steadily multiplied the extent to which such numerical series can be explored. The technique can now be applied to any kind of historical data reducible to a language that can be programmed—not only tax rolls and market price lists but also series of relatively homogeneous literary collections, such as medieval chartularies or the *cahiers* of the Estates General of monarchical France.

Thus emerges the first task of serial history, the imperative of its development: the constitution of its subject matter. Classical historiography was constructed from archives worked on and processed according to the critical rules bequeathed to us by the Benedictines of the age of Enlightenment and the German historians of the nineteenth century. The serial history of today has to reconstruct its archives in terms of the dual methodological and technical revolution that has transformed the rules and procedures of history.

This being so, the question arises of the problematic nature of history's subject matter, the hazards of its survival, its partial destruction and sometimes total disappearance. I am not sure this question distinguishes history as much as is sometimes alleged from the other human sciences whose objects are more specifically defined. The characteristic feature of history is the extraordinary and almost unlimited elasticity of its sources. As the researcher's curiosity roves further and further, huge dormant areas of documentation are revealed. What nineteenth-century historian bothered with the parish registers that have now become, especially in England and France, one of the surest sources of our knowledge of pre-industrial society?

Moreover, if the researcher invests them with a new significance, sources already exploited once can be used again for other purposes. Descriptions of price movements can lead to sociological or political analyses; Georges d'Avenel is followed by Ernest Labrousse. Demographic series studied from the point of view of, for example, the use of contraception by married couples can also throw light on problems of mental attitude or religious practice. Signatures to legal documents can give statistics about the spread of literacy. Biographies systematically grouped in terms of common criteria, on the basis of a given working hypothesis, can build up documentary series imparting an entirely new life to one of the oldest kinds of historical narrative.

Hitherto, history has been almost exclusively based on the written traces of men's existence. No doubt, live interrogation, which provides empirical sociology with so much of its data, will always be beyond the reach of the historian except for the period in which he lives. Yet how much unwritten evidence there is still to be cataloged and systematically described! The physical conditions of rural life, the divisions of the land, iconography sacred and profane, the layout of early towns, what the houses were like inside—one could go on forever listing the elements of civilization that, once cataloged and classified in detail, would make it possible to establish new chronological series and put at the historian's disposal the new subject matter that the conceptual enlargement of history demands. For it is not the sources that determine the approach but the approach that determines the sources.

Of course, this type of argument must not be pressed too far. To the documentary demands of certain contemporary social sciences, history can answer only with irreparable gaps. It is difficult to see what substitutions or extrapolations could ever fill in the columns of an input-output table of the French economy in the time of Henry IV, not to mention periods even more distant. All this means, though, is that, conceptually, history is not reducible to political economy. The problem of sources, for the historian, lies not so much in absolute lacunae as in series that are incomplete, and this not only because of the difficulties of interpolation and extrapolation but also because of the chronological illusions they may lead to.

Take the classic example of popular revolts in France at the beginning of the seventeenth century. Because of the great abundance of administrative documents relating to the subject at that time, this period has become the best-known chronological sector in the history of peasant risings between the end of the Middle Ages and the French Revolution. The hazards of survival have even seen to it that a large part of these archives, the Fonds Séguier, ended up in Leningrad, enabling Soviet historians to advance a Marxist interpretation of France's Ancien Régime. The subsequent controversy has enhanced the interest of the documents still further. But another problem arises before that of interpretation, and this concerns the presupposition common to both interpretations here: that is, that there really was, during the period when the absolutist state was coming into being and there was probably a rapid increase in taxation, a special chronological concentration of that classic phenomenon in French history, the jacquerie. The existence of such a concentration could be definitely established only by the study of a long homogeneous series and comparison between this section of it and those before and after. But for several reasons such a series cannot be constructed. In the first place, there is no unique and homogeneous source for such revolts over a long period. Moreover, there is every reason to believe that the survival of such a collection as the Fonds Séguier in St. Petersburg, a collection especially rich in this respect but limited to the papers of one family and thus subject to the hazards and possible distortions of individuals' careers, falsifies our chronological perception of the subject. In any case, a jacquerie is a story without direct sources, a rising of illiterates. We can glimpse it today through the medium of administrative or legal archives, but by this very fact, as Charles Tilly has remarked, every revolt that escapes repression escapes history. The relative richness of our sources during a given period may be a sign of changes that are institutional (reinforcement of the apparatus of repression) or purely individual (special vigilance on the part of a particular official), rather than of any unusual frequency in the phenomenon itself. The difference between the number of peasant risings under Henry II and under Louis XIII may reflect first and foremost the progress of monarchic centralization.

Therefore, in handling serial sources the historian is forced to think carefully about the influence that the way they were constituted may have on their quantitative application. I think we may distinguish between such sources as follows, in order of increasing complexity in their conversion into series:

1. Structurally numerical sources, grouped together as such and used by the historian to answer questions directly connected with their original field of investigation; for example, French parish registers for the demographic historian, prefectoral inquiries into industrial or agricultural statistics in the nineteenth century for the economic historian, the data on American presidential elections for the specialist in sociopolitical history. These sources sometimes need standardizing (as when there is a variation in local units or a modification of the classifying criterion); also, when there are gaps in the documentary sequence, one may have to extrapolate certain elements. But in such cases both operations are carried out with the minimum of uncertainty.

2. Sources that are structurally numerical but used by the historian substitutively, to find the answers to questions completely outside their original field of investigation; for example, the analysis of sexual behavior on the basis of parish registers, the study of economic growth through price series, the socioprofessional evolution of a population through a series relating to taxes. Here the historian encounters a double difficulty. He has to define his questions all the more meticulously because the documentary material was not assembled with them in mind, and the question is constantly before him of the relevance of such material to such questions. He usually has to reorganize the material completely in order to make it usable and in so doing makes it more arbitrary and this more open to objection.

3. Sources that are not structurally numerical but that the historian wants to use quantitatively, by a process involving two substitutions. In such cases, he has to find in his sources a univocal significance in relation to the question he is asking. He also has to be able to reorganize them in series, that is, in comparable chronological units, and this demands an

even more complex process of standardization than in the preceding paragraph. Data of this third type, which become more and more frequent the further one goes back into the past, can be subdivided into two classes: first, nonnumerical sources that are nevertheless serial and thus easily quantifiable, such as modern European marriage contracts drawn up by notaries, which, according to the historian's choice, can give evidence about endogamy, social mobility, income, literacy, and so on; and second, the sources that are strictly qualitative, and therefore not serial, or at least particularly difficult to standardize and arrange in series, such as the administrative and legal series referred to above or iconographic survivals of forgotten faiths.

Whichever kind of source he is dealing with, the historian of today has to rid himself of any methodological naiveté and devote a good deal of thought to the way in which his knowledge is to be established. The computer gives him the leisure to do so by freeing him from what used to take up most of his time—the recording and card-indexing of data— but at the same time it demands from him rigorous preliminary work on the organization of series and their meaning in relation to the inquiry. Like all the social sciences, but perhaps with a slight time lag, history is passing from the implicit to the explicit. The encoding of data presupposes their definition; their definition implies a certain number of choices and hypotheses, made all the more consciously because they have to conform to the logic of a program. Thus, the mask finally falls away from that historical objectivity that was supposed to lie concealed in the facts and to reveal itself at the same time as them. Henceforth, the historian is bound to be aware that he has constructed his own "facts" and that the objectivity of his research resides in the use of correct methods for elaborating and processing them and in their relevance to his hypotheses.

So serial history is not only, or even primarily, a transformation of the raw material of history; it is a revolution in the historiographical consciousness.

THE HISTORIAN AND HIS "FACTS"

The historian, working systematically on chronological series of homogeneous data, is really transforming the specific object of his knowledge—time or, rather, his conception and representation of it.

1. The so-called *histoire événementielle* is not to be defined by the preponderance it gives to political facts. Nor is it made up of a mere narrative of certain selected "events" along the time axis. First and foremost, it is based on the idea that these events are unique and cannot be

set out statistically, and that the unique is the material par excellence of history. That is why this kind of history paradoxically deals at one and the same time in the short term and in a finalistic ideology. Since the event, a sudden irruption of the unique and the new into the concatenation of time, cannot be compared to any antecedent, the only way of integrating it into history is to give it a teleological meaning. And as history, especially since the nineteenth century, has developed primarily as a mode of interiorizing and conceptualizing the sense of progress, the "event" usually marks some stage in the advent of a political or philosophical ideal—republic, liberty, democracy, reason, and so forth. The historian's ideological consciousness can assume very subtle forms. It may group knowledge relating to a certain period around unifying schemas not directly linked to political options or values; for example, the spirit of an age, its weltanschauung. Basically, though, the same compensating mechanism is at work: in order to be intelligible, the event needs a general history apart from itself and independently determined. Hence, the classic conception of historical time as a series of discontinuities described in the mode of continuity—that is, as narrative.

Serial history, on the other hand, describes continuities in the mode of discontinuity: it is a problem-oriented history instead of a narrative one. Because it has to distinguish between the levels of historical reality, it breaks down all previous conceptions of general history, calling in question the old postulate that all the elements of a society follow a homogeneous and identical evolution. The analysis of series has meaning only if it is done on a long-term basis, so as to show short or periodic variations within trends. The series reveals a time that is no longer the mysterious occasional spurt of the event but an evolutionary rhythm that is measurable, comparable, and doubly differential in that it can be examined within one series or as between two or more.

A wedge has thus been driven into the old carefully enclosed empire of classical historiography, and this by means of two distinct but connected operations. First, by the analytical breakdown of reality into different levels of description, serial history has opened history in general to concepts and methods imported from the more specifically constituted social sciences, such as political economy. This opening has probably been the operative factor in the recent historical revival. Second, by quantitatively analyzing the different evolutionary rhythms of the different levels of reality, it has at last turned into a scientifically measurable object the dimension of human activity that is history's raison d'être—time.

2.   Now that the historian's hypothesis has shifted from the level of the philosophy of history to that of a series of data both particular and

homogeneous, it usually reaps the advantage of becoming explicit and formulable; but, at the same time, historical reality is broken down into fragments so distinct that history's classic claim to give a universal view of things is endangered. Must the claim be abandoned?

I would say it may probably be kept as a goal on the horizon but that, if history wants to go forward, it should abandon this ambition as a point of departure. Otherwise, it might fall once more into the teleological illusion described above. Present-day historiography can progress only insofar as it delimits its object, defines its hypotheses, and constitutes and describes its sources as carefully as possible. This does not mean it has to restrict itself to microscopic analysis of one chronological series. It can group several series together and put forward an interpretation of a system or subsystem. But today, a comprehensive analysis of the "system of systems" is probably beyond its power.

We may take as examples demographic and economic history, the most advanced sectors now in France and probably elsewhere. It so happens that for the past twenty years or so the period that in France is called "modern"—that is, the period between the end of the Middle Ages and 1789—has been the subject of the largest number of studies in serial history, both demographic and economic. So it is the one we are least ignorant about from this point of view. French historiography, starting out from reconstructed commodity price series, has compared these with the evolution in the number of people as shown in demographic series. Thus, there has gradually been built up the concept of an "economic Ancien Régime," based on the preponderance of a cereal production exposed to the vagaries of meteorology and on the periodic purging of the system by recurrent crises. These crises are indicated by sudden steep rises in price curves and the collapse of those indicating size of population.

But the price series, the meanings of which can be quite varied and ambiguous, have been supplemented by more specific indications concerning volume of production and by the use of series relating to the evolution of supply and demand, itself a factor in the evolution of prices. On the subject of production, though the tithe records concern the same percentage of the harvest every year and so tell us nothing absolute, they are valuable because of their relative comparability. For production, we also have the protostatistical sources brought together by the administration of the Ancien Régime and possibly reorganized on a national scale. On the subject of demand, in addition to general demographic records, we can also turn to the reconstruction of the great masses of liquid money—the treasuries of communes and seigneuries, tithes, rents, profits, wages.

The combination of many demographic and economic series has recently enabled Emmanuel Le Roy Ladurie to make a wider analysis of the old agrarian economy. His book gives a sampling of data covering the whole of the Languedoc, a long-term chronology (from the fifteenth to the eighteenth century), and a rich and varied quantitative documentation. Thanks to the cadastral surveys, the latter makes possible a study of rural property owning. The fifteenth to the eighteenth centuries tell the story of a very long agrarian cycle characterized at the same time by a general equilibrium and by a series of states of disequilibrium. The general equilibrium roughly corresponds to the Malthusian model—the model that Malthus discovered and made immortal at the very moment it ceased to be true, at the time of England's takeoff. The economy of early rural Languedoc was dominated in the long term by the relation between agricultural production and the number of men. Society's inability to raise agrarian productivity and the absence of an unlimited reserve of cultivable land, together with the famous "monetary famine" beloved of the price historians, presented structural obstacles to decisive growth. Though the monetary explanation loses its central role, it is integrated into an interpretation both more complex and more unified.

The structure of the old economy acted in the long term as an internal regulator. Nevertheless, within the system, the different variables— number of men, evolution of property, distribution of income from rents, fluctuations in productivity and prices, and so on—make it possible to distinguish separate periods in accordance with the position each variable occupies in relation to the whole, in terms of the annual rhythms and cycles of each particular curve. The complete structure thus chronologically comprises several types of combinations of series, that is, several different situations. And, in fact, it is through the careful examination of these successive situations, and the features they have in common or in which they differ, that the structure itself emerges. This, incidentally, may shed some light on the dispute over synchronic and diachronic, which often divides anthropologists and historians, and which at present is at the heart of the evolution of the social sciences. The short- or medium-term periodic movement that constitutes an "event" on the economic plane does not necessarily clash with the theory of general equilibrium; on the contrary, an empirical description of such movements may make it possible to define the theoretical conditions of the equilibrium, whose elasticity indicates the limits within which it operates.

3.   The Languedoc example quoted above is a special case in that the correlation there between the different demographic and economic series is made within a comparatively homogeneous region and a limited

sphere of human activity (agrarian economy). The sectional application of serial history to different areas usually leads to the analysis of regional or national disequilibria. And general, or would-be general, serial history, even when restricted to a limited geographical area, tends to lead to the analysis of temporal disequilibria between the different evolutionary rhythms of each level of human activity.

The first point is now well known, thanks to the increasing number of studies on regional economic history. The specialist is used to the idea of there being measurable differences between different countries and between areas influenced in different degrees by the same situation or reacting in different ways to similar situations occurring at different times. There are countless examples, some of which raise problems that have become classic in European history. Such, for instance, are the recently revived question of the comparative growth of France and England in the eighteenth century; the antithesis between the rise of agriculture in Catalonia in the eighteenth century and its decline in Castile, which has been shown by Pierre Vilar; and the contrast in seventeenth-century France between the Beauvaisis revealed by Pierre Goubert, poor and seriously stricken by the middle of the century by economic and demographic recession, and the Provence described by René Baehrel, comparatively fortunate, or at least not affected by the downturn of expansion until much later. More generally, the date of this reversal, this plunge into the "tragedy" of the seventeenth century, varies considerably according to region and to the nature of the local economy. It becomes increasingly unlikely that there was only one economic *conjuncture* for both urban and rural economies.

Thus, serial history opens out at once into the analysis of situations either differential or simply separated from one another in time (in other words, into what might be called the "geography" of serial history's chronology) and into the study of structural differences that may be indicated by chronological discrepancies. Cycles occurring at different times in the same or different regions, but fundamentally comparable internally, exhibit only geographical variations of the same theme. Contradictory developments, on the other hand, whether within the same geographical area (for example, between town and country) or between two different areas, may present the historian with differences in economic structure.

But history cannot be reduced just to the description and interpretation of economic activity. If it has a specific character distinguishing it from the other social sciences, this consists precisely in having no specific character and in claiming the right to explore time in all its dimensions. It is easy to see why economics has been the primary sphere of quantitative history—because of the necessarily measurable character of its indicators; by the preciseness of the concepts it makes available; and by its theoretical approach in terms of growth, the favorite image for historical change in Western thought today. But man is not merely an economic agent. The contemporary world offers too many examples of cultural resistance to the general adoption of growth on the Western model for the historian not to mistrust the Manchester-school approach to progress (or its Marxist inversion). He is bound to want to analyze the societies of the past in terms of politics and ideology as well as economics.

Even so, he does not and cannot revert to the old teleological history of progress, which extrapolates into cultural life the rhythms of economic development, whether this is supposed to occur by a kind of peaceful, natural adaptation or through the necessary medium of revolution. These ideological postulates of another age are useless now; it is not by clinging to them that the historian can preserve the universality of history. The only way to do so is by setting out to list and describe by the methods of serial history the other levels of human activity besides the objective processes of economics; by starting from the hypothesis that chronological rhythms, and the researcher's attitude to time, may vary according to the different levels of reality or to the particular part of the system being analyzed.

On the practical plane, almost everything still remains to be done. The historian must look for the possible indicators, quantifiable or not, of what may be called a "politico-ideological" society; he must establish its documentation and what constitutes representativity and comparability from one period to another. For all this, there are sources as abundant and series as homogeneous as in the field of economics or demography: they exist for popular literacy, the sociology of education and religious sentiment, the absorption of ideas by elites, the manifest or latent contents of political ideologies, and so on. On the theoretical plane, the main task, of course, is to build up gradually the components of a comprehensive history but first and above all to analyze the different rhythms of development at various levels of a historical complex. This is the only way to achieve two of the priorities of historiography today. These are:

I.   To revise the traditional general periodizations, which are mainly an ideological inheritance from the nineteenth century and which presuppose precisely what is still to be demonstrated, that is, the roughly concomitant development of the most diverse components of a historical complex within a given period. Instead of beginning from a set of periodizations, it is probably more useful to start by examining the components concerned. It is probable, for example, that while the concept of the Renaissance is relevant to many of the indicators of cultural history, it is devoid of meaning in relation to the data for agricultural productivity.

2.   Then to define, within a complex of data of different kinds, which levels are developing rapidly or changing decisively and which in the medium or long term are in a state of inertia. It is not clear, for example, that the dynamism of French history from, say, the great expansion of the eleventh and twelfth centuries is economic in character; it may be that education, culture (in the broad sense), and the state (the latter through the various public offices) played a more fundamental role here than the increase in the national product. Perhaps I shall be allowed to conclude on this bold hypothesis if I add that it will remain unverifiable until general history has sat at the feet of serial history.

TRANSLATED BY JONATHAN MANDELBAUM

America Discovers the *Annales*

Braudel's La Mediterranée *(The Mediterranean and the Mediterranean World in the Age of Philip II) rapidly gained an international reputation, even before it was translated, and it was widely viewed as the flagship for a new armada of French historical scholarship. As the following review by Bernard Bailyn demonstrates, however, the reception in the United States was not always enthusiastic; the sheer massiveness and ambition of the work seemed to trouble many American scholars. (Bailyn, who wrote this review as a young historian, went on to a brilliant career as a specialist in the ideological origins of the American Revolution.)*

J. H. Hexter's consideration of Braudel and the Braudelian world echoes some of Bailyn's criticisms of Braudel's approach as an "exhausting treadmill." By 1972, Hexter, an American specialist in English history, could only grant that La Mediterranée *had achieved indisputable classic status; why devote a long article to it otherwise? Hexter's article is notable not only for analyzing Braudel's work in the increasingly influential institutional context of the* Annales *and the Ecole des Hautes Etudes but also for its rollicking sense of humor; the grandeur of French historical aims and accomplishments calls forth a kind of Rabelaisian satire, especially of French quantitative methods. Yet beneath the humor is a serious examination of the new historical approaches being advocated in France.*

Braudel and the Annales *also had fervent admirers in the United States. In 1977, the Fernand Braudel Center was inaugurated at the State University of New York, Binghamton. The center published the journal* Review, *which claimed to be directly inspired by Braudel's work and by the approaches advocated in the* Annales. *The focus on the* Annales, *by then international in its influence on historical scholarship, is evident in the editorial by Immanuel Wallerstein. (How often is a journal started to comment and extend upon the work of another journal?!)*

BERNARD BAILYN

Braudel's Geohistory—A Reconsideration

1951

S ince its publication in 1949 Fernand Braudel's *La Méditerranée et le monde méditerranéen à l'époque de Philippe II* has been received as a major addition to the literature of early modern history. In France, the excitement over this eleven-hundred-page work has centered on what would appear to be its revolutionary innovations in historical method. Lucien Febvre, for example, in an article in the *Revue historique*, after describing the book as more than a "perfect work of an historian with a profound grasp of his métier" and even more than a "professional masterpiece," declared that the book introduces a revolution in the mode of conceiving history. "It marks," said Febvre, "the dawn of a new time, of that I am certain." His article concluded with this charge to youth: "Read, reread, and meditate on this excellent book.... Make it your companion. What you will learn of things, new to you, about the world of the sixteenth century is incalculable. But what you will learn simply about man, about his history and about history itself, its true nature, its methods and its purposes—you cannot imagine in advance." Braudel himself devoted an article in the *Revue économique* to elaborating the method used in his book and presented it to economic historians for their consideration.

Braudel's book is an attempt to set the story of Philip II's reign in what the author hoped was a description of the total "world" to which those events were relevant. It was not simply Spain or the empire that he sought to examine but rather "the history of *the Mediterranean* in its complex mass" (p. xi, emphasis added). And the scope of his study was expanded not only spatially but also structurally, for politics was only one expression of the life of this "world." Philip's actions were to be seen in relation to the other less obvious but perhaps ultimately more efficacious elements at work in the Mediterranean world of the sixteenth

From *Journal of Economic History* 11 (1951), pp. 277–82.

century. The book is built on the architecture suggested by the classification of these elements.

The first aspect of this "world" is geographic: "man in his relations with the environment that surrounds him" (p. xiii). Here, the significant movement is almost imperceptible and is complicated by the ceaselessly revolving inner cycles of seasons and years. Its "time" is that of geography (p. xiv). The second aspect is that usually dealt with by social and economic historians: the histories "of the groups, of the structures, of the collective destinies, in a word, of the group movements" (*des movements d'ensemble*; p. 308). Here, the motion is "slowly rhythmed" (*lentement-rythmée*), and the time may be called "social." In practice, this is a 409-page essay on the social and economic history of the area mainly during the sixteenth century. The third element is that usually dealt with by the traditional historians: the "short, quick, nervous oscillations" of men of action. It is thus only in the last section of the book (354 pages) that the events of Philip's reign are recounted.

This organizational scheme and the theory of three separate movements in history constitute Braudel's methodological innovation. It is by means of this formulation that he sought "to grasp the history of the Mediterranean in its complex mass."

But this schematization proves to have been an exhausting treadmill. For all his diligence, the author has not advanced toward his goal. To the extent that the divisions between the sections are effective, a comprehension of the organic totality of Mediterranean life is blocked. There are fine pages that illuminate their subject; but they do so, not because of these lines of demarcation so carefully laid out, but in spite of them. The parts of his "world" are all there, but they lie inert, unrelated, discrete.

If, for example, one is to set political events in a meaningful relationship with the other aspects of society, a satisfactory explanation of the Turkish successes in the East must include a discussion of geography, social structure, and economics. But the actual events of the Turkish problem are discussed in routine fashion in several parts of section three, particularly on pages 791ff. No reference at all is given in this passage to the treatment of geography and climate in part one or to the problems of space, transport, and economics in section two. Is there no demonstrable relationship between the general situation of the Ottoman Empire (pp. 509–16) and the Turkish impact on Balkan society (pp. 571–76), on the one hand, and the political developments of "the last six years of the Turkish supremacy, 1559–1565" (pp. 791–856), on the other? Or, again, can one interested in explaining the totality of the Mediterranean world be content to discuss the coastal areas and their inhabitants on pages 105ff., the transportation and supply of food on pages 447ff., the forms of war on pages 661ff., and then recount separately, and with no reference to these deeper dimensions, the transportation of troops and sea warfare in concrete situations on pages 798ff.?

Yet, there are passages in the book where the reader is led toward an understanding of the dynamic unity of at least a portion of the Mediterranean world. Such a discussion, original and illuminating, is that of the effect on economic life in the sixteenth century of the geography of the Mediterranean lands (pp. 324ff.). For an evaluation of Braudel's method, the significance of this section is that the divisional scheme of the book is temporarily laid aside. Economic development, according to the outline, belongs properly where it is, in section two, but the quality of the passage is a result of the author's bringing to bear on it considerations that belong in section one—geography and space. And there are repeated references in the pages on this subject to the "short, quick, nervous oscillations" of the world of men and events that one might have expected only in section three.

The author was aware that his scheme was to some extent arbitrary and protested in the preface that it was "only a means of exposition," and that he "was not blocking the pathways that led from one to another" (p. xiv). Yet if the separations of his material along the lines of his outline are of any use at all, it must be that they separate things that are most valuably discussed apart from one another. The fact is that Braudel reached closest to his goal of an integrated study of a "world" only when he neglected the means he had chosen to lead to this end.

The root of the difficulty is that Braudel has mistaken a poetic response to the past for an historical problem. To him, the area of the Mediterranean is charged with drama and slicked with affection. The first words in the book are, "I have passionately loved the Mediterranean." There is, of course, nothing wrong with an historian's being emotionally involved with his subject; but the formulation of a valid problem is as much the necessary ingredient for superior work in history as the sympathetic identification of scholar and subject. Such problems must first of all be concerned with movements through time in the affairs of men living in organized groups. How did it come about, the historian properly asks, that the Roman Empire ceased to be, that the Republican Party lost the last election, that the people of Europe became embroiled in religious wars in the sixteenth century? Or, perhaps, what was the process by which the structure of feudal society developed or decayed?

A comparison with Marc Bloch's *La Société féodale* is unavoidable, and it is interesting to note Braudel's statement in his preface that, though he came in contact with Bloch only just before the war, "no detail of his rich thought has remained unknown to me" (p. xv). But *La Société féodale* is organized around the clear historical problems that follow from the question: What was the nature of feudal society? Bloch's introduction, entitled "General Orientation of the Inquiry," cleared the ground by defining his subject and limiting it in time and place. The similarity in titles between the first sections of Bloch's and Braudel's works, respectively "Le Milieu" and "La Part du Milieu," is not carried over into the subject matter. Where Braudel wrote a 304-page essay on topography, routes, deserts, climate, seasons, and cities, Bloch started with a two-chapter summary of the invasions of the ninth and tenth centuries, events which Braudel's scheme would have relegated to an isolated third level. The third chapter, which lays the foundation for all that follows, is Bloch's discussion of the origins of certain regional differences in social structure and other less tangible results of the invasions. Within these twenty-eight pages, all three of Braudel's "times" are woven into a pattern of significant statements about the milieu of early feudalism. The parts of this chapter would never have been brought together by Braudel's scheme. They would have served to illuminate not feudalism but an idea about history.

The problem of the nature of feudal society meant to Bloch duration in time, a beginning, growth, and change. Feudalism for this historian was not something hard and permanent but the condition of European society at a particular period in its past. Feudalism of the tenth century was different from feudalism of the thirteenth century: relationships change and words lose their meanings. Frederick M. Powicke wrote of Bloch and his famous book, "He loves to trace the changes in the meanings of words, to show how each meaning connotes a particular phase of society, and to explain how the relationship or the institution which a term describes outgrew its usefulness or altered its characteristics."

Bloch's problem was not to present the whole of the medieval world but, rather, to make this portion of the past intelligible by organizing the sources around the questions the contemporary mind asks of any society. It was to satisfy this desire for intelligibility that Bloch drew on his knowledge of geography, economics, sociology, literature, as well as the "short, quick, nervous oscillations" of men in action.

There was no central problem Braudel wished to examine. He hoped to describe something he called "the Mediterranean world" in a certain period, though, significantly, he nowhere defined this term carefully. A proper formulation would have started with a broad and important movement in the affairs of men living in this time and area, and on the hooks of this movement elements from every aspect and level of this "world" would have been drawn together to form a satisfactory and hence complex and subtle answer. Sources will yield historical answers only to historical questions, and Braudel started by wanting to know not the wherefores of a movement or condition in the Mediterranean world but rather *everything* about it. It is scarcely surprising that he spent over twenty years on the book. The wonder of it is that, having approached the subject thus, he could ever have been content to call a halt to his research. Unlike the historian who wants to satisfy himself about how such and such came about or functioned, Braudel never reached a point where further research merely buttressed his conclusions. Indeed, there are no conclusions to such a book, and the last eleven pages of text (1089–1100), which are entitled "Conclusion" testify only to Braudel's love for the Mediterranean and his fascination with problems of why civilizations decay and with historical method. This small section includes references to Ernest Labrousse, Robert Montagne, Carlo Levi, Paul Vidal de la Blache, Jules Sion, Roger Dion, Earl J. Hamilton, François Simiand, Georges Gurvitch, and Lucien Febvre—but not a mention of Philip II.

What is painfully lacking in this huge, rambling book is the integration of its parts that could result from the posing of proper historical questions. In place of this, one finds an attempt to tell all, to investigate every cranny of the Mediterranean periphery, and to call in the witness of the allied social sciences. Confronted with the task of expressing in historical terms his desire to embrace the Mediterranean world of the sixteenth century, Braudel could overcome the naturally resulting incoherence only by classifying, separating, compartmentalizing.

Braudel's difficulties are worth discussing at length not only because his book has been uncritically heralded but also because these problems will become increasingly puzzling as our knowledge of the workings of society grows. Satisfactory discussions of large historical movements can never again be simple. As sociologists lay bare the mazed complex of society, the historian fulfills his obligation by rephrasing his own questions to take account of these new findings. And surely the most elementary teaching of the sociologists about social change is that no important element moves in isolation. Consequently, the one thing that assuredly can never be understood about a "world" by laying it out in three slices is its movement, which is to say, its life.

Febvre's passionate encomium of *La Méditerranée* is in itself significant. It reflects the deep need modern historians have for a subtler historiography. Faced with an avalanche of specialized monographs as well as the historical studies of the social scientists, they feel more keenly perhaps than did Henri Berr the need for new principles of *synthèse*. What these new formulations will be one cannot anticipate, for historical questions change as present situations alter both the historian's focus and the criteria of explanation. But if it is to fulfill its function of making man's past intelligible, history must remain the empirical study of the process of human affairs. Students of sixteenth-century history will find in Braudel's book not a revolution in historical method but rather a summary in three parts of a large body of knowledge.

J. H. HEXTER

Fernand Braudel and the *Monde Braudellien . . .*

1972

In 1949 a *thèse* in fulfillment of the requirement for the degree of *Docteur ès Lettres* at the Sorbonne was published in Paris. It was 1,175 pages long.[1] It had no illustrations, maps, or graphs. Its author was a French scholar then forty-seven years old. His name was Fernand Braudel. The title of the *thèse* was *La Méditerranée et le monde méditerranéen à l'époque de Philippe II*. Seventeen years later, in 1966, a revised and corrected edition of *La Méditerranée* in two volumes appeared, replete with tables, maps, graphs, and handsome illustrations, its length 1,218 pages.[2] Now, an English translation of the first volume of the revised edition of *La Méditerranée* has been published.

The preface to the second edition begins as follows:

> It was with much hesitation that I undertook a new edition of *The Mediterranean*. Some of my friends advised me to change nothing, not a word, not a comma, arguing that a work that had become a classic should not be altered. But how could I decently listen to them? With the increase in knowledge and the advances made in our neighbouring disciplines, the social sciences, history books age more quickly now than in the past. A moment passes, and their vocabulary has become dated, the new ground they broke is familiar territory, and the explanations they offered are challenged.

And so we have a historical problem, one of those problems with which, according to Professor Braudel, historical investigation should start: What made *La Méditerranée* a classic in 1949? What makes its second edition a classic in 1972? For it stretches credulity to the breaking point to believe that an English commercial publishing house would undertake the translation and issue of a twelve-hundred-page history book, unless it were a classic.

In terms of the view of history set forth in *La Méditerranée* and propagated by Braudel ever since, however, the historical problem we have just raised is a *question mal posée*. Or better, perhaps, a question raised

From "Fernand Braudel and the *Monde Braudellien* . . . ," *Journal of Modern History* 44 (1972), pp. 480–539.

out of order, too soon. It is a question that has to do with a mere event, and in Braudel's tiered or three-layered image of the past and of the way historians should deal with it, what has to do with events, the *événemen-tielle,* is the least important layer, and the one to be dealt with last. The study of events gains whatever value it has (not very considerable in Braudel's view) only insofar as it rests on the two more substantial layers that underlie it. The base layer is what Braudel calls *structures.* In the case in point, the *structures* are the *mentalités,* sets of mind, points of view, paradigms embedded in institutions, durable organisms, that give French historical scholarship its particular posture and quality. Of its quality, we may think it is the best and must think it is the most ecumenical in the world today. Of its posture, we must say that it has been more successful than historical scholarship in any other nation in assuming a position that brings it into favorable and fruitful relations with the social sciences. In France, those relations enrich the study of history and continuously confront the social sciences not only with the existence of History as a discipline but with its importance both intellectual and institutional for them. No need to point the contrast between France and the United States in this respect. Here the social scientists have been able to turn their backs upon History, and without vigorous challenge have tended to define their central problems in ways that spare them from thinking about history at all.[3] Of this, nothing is more symptomatic than a phenomenon that Braudel himself observed. After the Second World War programs of "area studies" began to proliferate in American universities. An "area" is a large territorial and population group marked by major significant interrelations of some of its parts—shared economic level, political tradition, language, historical experience, religious outlook, social institutions, and so on. The purpose of area studies is to investigate such regions—Latin America, the Middle East, black Africa—in the round, "globally," bringing to bear on each the joint expertise of specialized social scientists. What Braudel noticed was that initially in the United States such clusters of area studies experts often did not include a historian. In France, such an institutional expression of an ahistorical view of the proper study of man would not have passed, as it did in the United States, without serious challenge. It would have had to deal with and confront two powerful institutions. One is a journal, *Annales: Economies, Sociétés, Civilisations.* Its chief directors were successively two historians, Lucien Febvre and Fernand Braudel. The other is the now-famous Sixth Section, the sixth section or division of the Ecole Pratique des Hautes Etudes: Sciences Economiques et Sociales. Its presidents, unthinkably from an American perspective, have been successively two historians, Lucien Febvre and Fernand Braudel. Any inquiry into the structural relation of history to the social sciences in France must start with the *Annales* and the Sixth Section.

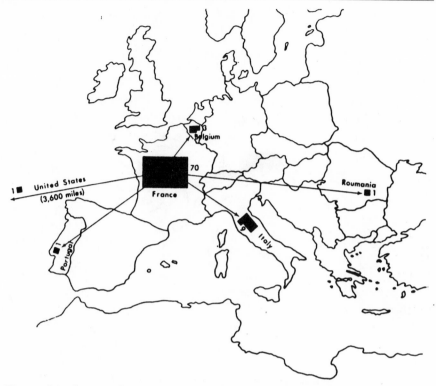

Fig. 1   Distribution of contributors to *Eventails de l'histoire vivante: Hommage à Lucien Febvre*.

Braudel did more than nurture the institutions that he succeeded to. He spread their influence beyond the bounds of France. Of this, the qualitative evidence is abundant: the international fame of the *Annales* and of the Sixth Section, the hospitality that both extend to foreign scholars, the former in its pages, the latter in its seminars. Consider the issue of the American journal *Daedalus*, published last year, devoted to "Historical Studies Today." Articles by eleven contributors. Three from members of one American department of history, the one most closely associated with the Sixth Section.[4] One by a Cambridge University historian who has researches in progress at the Centre de Recherches Historiques.[5] Three from *directeurs d'études* of the Sixth Section itself.[6]

From an adventitious source, there is yet more impressive evidence of the internationalization of the *Annales* structure. In 1953, two volumes were published, *Eventails de l'histoire vivante: Hommage à Lucien Febvre*, with eighty-five contributors, one of them Fernand Braudel, who, one imagines, had a larger hand in the project than his introductory essay indicates. Figure 1 shows how those contributors were distributed geographically. One contributor, if indeed one, behind a curtain effectively iron in the last days of Stalin.[7] One from the United States, none

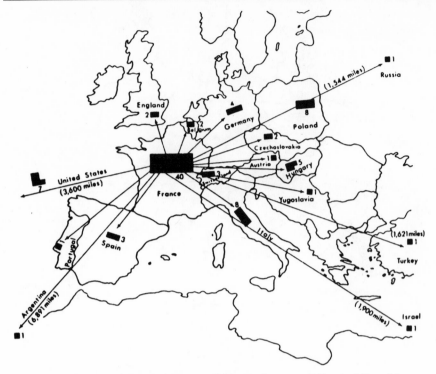

Fig. 2   Distribution of contributors to *Mélanges en honneur de Fernand Braudel.*

from Germany, a cluster from bordering neighbors; from France, 80 percent.

This year, a two-volume *Mélanges en honneur de Fernand Braudel* is to be published, ninety-three announced contributors. Figure 2 shows how they are distributed geographically. From France, 43 percent; none, oddly, from Brazil, where Braudel taught for two years; none, even more oddly, from the North African shore of the Mediterranean which he loved so well, not even from Algeria where he taught more than a decade. But 57 percent, fifty-three scholars from sixteen other lands, with large clusters from Hungary, Poland, and the United States. It is hard to look at the two maps without getting the eerie feeling that with a solid base in France and with Fernand Braudel in command, the *Annalistes* are on a march that, by friendly persuasion, is about to conquer the historical world.

Why, an American tends to ask: Why France? Why not the United States, with its enormous resources, with the traditional collective outlook on history of its professional historians far less rigidly confined to national boundaries than any other equivalent group? Among certain American historians in the United States in the 1930s and 1940s, there prevailed a view similar in many respects to that of the *Annalistes.* And there were historians with the qualities of Febvre and Braudel. There was at least one such in my generation—Oscar Handlin of Harvard University. A historian of the broadest learning, deeply and early concerned to draw on the achievements of the social sciences. A historian who need not and would not shrink from a comparison of his scholarly work with that of Braudel. A historian, moreover, with an extraordinary command of languages and early linked by personal ties with historians of what may be called the Historical "international set." A historian, finally, with enormous energy and high administrative skills, an imperial vision, and not devoid of a proper ambition. Why, we may well ask, does Braudel serenely preside over a great school of historians, firmly based in Paris but spread throughout the world, while Handlin attends meetings of the American Historical Association to deliver public threnodies on the decay of History as a humane science and a profession in the United States?

In one of the most engaging chapters of *The Prince,* Machiavelli ponders the role of *Necessità* and *Fortuna* in human affairs. *Fortuna* is a bitch goddess who is likely to capitulate to an ardent assault. But not always. For *necessità*, the solid order of things may not be favorable. It was favorable in France for the *Annalistes*, for Febvre and Braudel; there circumstances came to the aid of the vigorous. Consider by contrast what was lacking in the United States. First, no tradition of historical journals that reflected the historical outlook of their editor, a tradition already created in France before 1900 by Henri Berr's *Revue de synthèse.* Indeed, for a long while there was no great editorial tradition at all in the United States, no truly outstanding editor of a historical journal since Franklin Jameson. In America, too, a parochial conception of science, which only slowly opened up to the social sciences, and did not open up to History at all. This became a matter of consequence with the establishment of the National Science Foundation. Up to the present, History receives no direct support from the NSF.[8] Up to 1966 there was no federal support at all for historical research. Only recently has the National Endowment for the Humanities been sufficiently funded to render more than nominal assistance to History. A historical project or two rode into NSF support on the coattails, so to speak, of sociology, but only because a sociologist applied for the assistance. Again a different situation from that in France, where exclusion of History (or even literature) from the *sciences humaines* was structurally improbable. Finally, the polycentrism of higher learning in America. In France, who doubts where the center is? Paris. But in the United States—New York? Cambridge? Chicago? The Bay Area? But what about Ann Arbor, Madison, New Haven? Here again, the heart of the matter was to concentrate in a capital of learning a critical mass of historians with a shared point of view or set of paradigms. The *Programme d'enseignement* of the Sixth Section for 1972–73 offers forty-nine research seminars in History, all inclined in the *Annaliste* direction. Where in the United States would one find an advanced History faculty of such dimension, not to speak of such shared inclination? Indeed, where in the United States would one find a university ready to concern itself with the care and feeding of such a gaggle of advanced historical scholars? To achieve in the United States what Febvre and Braudel achieved in France was beyond the capacities of Handlin, beyond the capacity of any historian in the United States. It would, I believe, have been beyond the capacities of Febvre and Braudel. All the *structures* of the scholarly and educational enterprise that favored the *Annales* school in France were lacking in the United States. No bold historians seized *Fortuna* here, because there was no *Fortuna* to seize.

Braudel is candid and specific about his disaffection to history that concerns itself with people as persons. Such persons are *individus*; they belong to the ephemeral realm of the *événementielle*; and they have little impact on history in the *longue durée* or even in the *moyenne durée*. The *longue durée*, however, he populates with nonpeople persons—geographical entities, features of the terrain. Thus, in the Mediterranean peninsulas "are key actors ... have played leading roles.... They are almost persons ... who may or may not be conscious of themselves."[9] Towns are vested with intentions—Constantinople, for example, with "the determination to impose settlement, organization and planning" on the Ottomans. It "triumphed over and betrayed" them, luring them into the wrong wars with the wrong goals.[10]

The protagonist of this somewhat peculiarly cast historical drama, of course, is the Mediterranean itself, or rather herself. She has designs or purposes of her own, which she sometimes succeeds in fulfilling. She "contributed ... to preventing the unity of Europe, which she attracted toward her shores and then divided to her own advantage."[11] And in the sixteenth century through Genoa she "long allocated the world's wealth."[12]

Times, too, get personalized. "The sixteenth century had neither the courage nor the strength" to eradicate the ancient evils of the great cities, and "modern times suddenly projected the territorial state to the center of the stage."[13]

One geographical phenomenon, the big city, is subjected to a veritable trial, with Braudel serving as historical *juge d'instruction*. First the evils for which big cities were responsible in the sixteenth century are laid out. They were "parasites"; they "gave virtually nothing" and consumed a great deal. Then, on the other hand, "one cannot launch inconsiderately into a prolonged indictment of huge cities.... There are perfectly good reasons for them," and "a plea of not guilty" might be entered "on behalf of these admirable political and intellectual instruments."[14] It is not at all certain that our historical perceptions are sharpened by the depersonalization of men or by the personification of the features of human geography.

So far, I have criticized defects in details, significant only because their repetition gives them a patterned quality that mirrors certain consistent traits of Braudel as a historian. Two other difficulties of unequal importance are of serious concern. The first, and less important, makes it hard to follow intelligently the large section of *La Méditerranée* devoted to economic activities. Braudel refers to a vast number of weights, of measures of volume, and of moneys, both coined moneys and moneys of account from all over the Mediterranean. For example, a few minutes' search turned up the following names for moneys: ducats, écus d'or, sequins, lire, soldi, zeanars, dobles, soltaninis, livres, sous, écus d'argent, doblones, escudos de oro, reales, aspri, tourrones, escus pistolet, courrones, tallieri, quattrini, bajocci, kronenthäler, marchetti, pesos, reali ad 8, 6, and 4, maravedis, pfennigs, drachmas, reales, déniers, thalers, maidin. Occasionally, either by an explicit statement or by providing means for an inference, Braudel enables the reader to make an equation for two different moneys, for example 375 maravedis equal one ducat. Nowhere in *La Méditerranée,* however, is there a table of coins and moneys of account. Or of weights and measures. And for such helping guides in the morass of moneys, weights, and measures, a reader, at least this reader, feels a pressing need.

The second difficulty is more serious, since it speaks to a nearly blind spot in Braudel's historical vision. Perhaps in self-defense in dealing with *structures,* he attends almost entirely to material structures—peninsulas, islands, mountains, plateaus and plains, seas and oceans, climate and seasons; routes, shipping, and towns. Routines embedded in custom and law receive less attention or none. The Mediterranean world is the world of grain, the olive tree, the vine, and the sheep. As to the shepherds, we hear only of those involved in the migration from high summer pasture to low winter pasture. Of the daily, scarcely changing life and practices of the vineyard, the olive grove, and the wheat field we hear too little. Nor do we learn much about how small communities (guilds, villages, and towns) or large ones (provinces, principalities, city states, realms, or empires) actually ordered their affairs, or of what held them together in durable structures. In the age of Philip II, two great empires, that of the king of Spain and that of the Ottoman sultan, divided and fought over the Mediterranean. Of the bonds that held each of those unwieldy conglomerates together, more or less, we catch only fleeting glimpses. Of the religious structures, Christianity and Islam, that at once held each together and divided it,[15] we see nothing from the inside. They are recurrent names, but what gave them life—their interlaced institutions, practices, and beliefs—is nowhere to be found.

So *La Méditerranée* has flaws, is in some ways a flawed book. But here we need to pause. To judge a great work such as *La Méditerranée* by its flaws is like judging an economy during a boom solely on the record of concurrent proceedings in bankruptcy. There is much more to the book than casual mistakes or even than systematic ones. Indeed, all the remarks so far under the heading of *Evénement* might rightly be condemned as myopic. They are certainly the work of a historian more exclusively admiring than he need be or should be of tightly built historical works, works that in all their lineaments, articulation, and composition bear the marks of fine, delicate, and patient craftsmanship. His first instinct, and not a very ingratiating one, is to pry away at the places in a historical work that show haste or careless handiwork. It is the wrong instinct for approaching *La Méditerranée*, for to such an approach that book is bound to be vulnerable; indeed, its vulnerability to the above criticism is, I think, an inevitable concomitant of the two qualities in continuous tension with each other that make it indeed a classic.

The first of these great qualities is Braudel's vast appetite for extending the boundaries of his undertaking, the perimeter of his vision. We become aware of it when we ask what the book is about. The Mediterranean in the age of Philip II—that is, a bounded body of water between A.D. 1556 and 1598? Of course not. As to time, King Philip II begins being king in 1556 and stops in 1598—two events; but the Mediterranean, a structure of geohistory, does not begin and end like that; it goes back to man's settlement on its shores, and to the ways of life that such settlement mandated. And it goes forward to today, when some of those ways of life still survive. Other ways of Mediterranean life, born long before Philip, continue long after he was laid to rest. Philip was not the master of structural time, the *longue durée*; the creations of that time were silent constraints on all he did. Nor does the time of *moyenne durée*, of *conjoncture*, accommodate itself to the ephemeral span of his reign. The discernible rhythms of economies, societies, and civilizations lie to both sides of him, before he began, after he ended—the whole sixteenth century at least. But not the sixteenth century of traditional historians, bewitched by the sign of the double zero. With respect to the cycles of the Mediterranean economy, according to Braudel there are two sixteenth centuries. One ran roughly from about 1450 to about 1550, an economic upswing in the Mediterranean followed by an economic downswing. Then a second sixteenth century, from about 1550 to 1630 or 1650, a revival of the Mediterranean economy and then its final plunge and departure from stage center, thrust out by the Atlantic and the powers of the Atlantic rim of Europe.

And the space of the Mediterranean—is it the blue waters of the inland sea and the men who sailed them or lived on their shores? Of course, but far more than that. *La Méditerranée* starts in the mountains, the Alps, the Pyrenees, the Apennines, the Dinaric Alps, the Caucasus, the mountains of Anatolia and Lebanon, the Atlas, the Spanish Cordilleras, the interior massifs of Sicily, Sardinia, Corsica. Then it moves down from the mountains to the plateaus, to the hills, to the plains, and at last to the sea or the several seas of the Mediterranean basin. But Braudel does not stop there. There is a "Greater Mediterranean" to consider. The desert touches the inland sea, and by caravan routes Braudel takes us through the hot deserts to the Africa of the blacks, whence gold came to the Mediterranean; by caravan again through the cold deserts of Asia to China, whence came silk and fine fabrics and to which the Mediterranean sent gold and silver. By four "isthmuses," combined land and water routes, Braudel stretches the Mediterranean to Russia, Poland, Germany, France; and along those routes he takes us junketing to Moscow, Lublin, Lvov, Nuremburg, Augsburg, Ulm, Lyon, Paris, Rouen. So the terrestrial Mediterranean stretches out. Much more, the watery Mediterranean, through the strait of Gibraltar, first to Bruges, Antwerp, London, Hamburg, Danzig—the route of wool and wheat southward, cloth and alum and oriental goods northward. Then several more great bounds to the islands of the Atlantic, to Mexico and Lima, and at last by the way of Acapulco to Manila and to China. There, by this vast extension of the Mediterranean of the seas westward, we meet ourselves coming east by caravan train across the Mediterranean of the deserts.

Let us not deceive ourselves. No doubt there is a reason or a rationale for some of these flights through time and space, and more or less plausible excuses for others. But we fail fully to understand the historian behind *La Méditerranée* if we pause to quibble over this journey or that one. They may be a piece of Braudel's historical design: they are surely a piece of something more insistent and consistent than any design—his temperament, his feel for history. The countervailing manifestation of that feel is Braudel's inexhaustible delight in piling up concrete detail—detail for detail's sake.

A few examples. The Mediterranean was a sea of small ships: "barques, *saëtes, laudi, luiti,* tartans, frigates, *polaccas.*"[16] Among writers who described caravans there is not only Tavernier, there are also "Gobineau, G. Schweinfurth, René Caillé, Brugnon and Flachat."[17] The transhumance routes that the Mediterranean sheep and their shepherds followed had different names in different places: "*cañadas* in Castile, *camis ramadas* in the Eastern Pyrenees, *drayes* or *drailles* in Languedoc, *carraires* in Provence, *traturi* in Italy, *trazzere* in Sicily, *drumul oilor* in Rumania."[18] The hungry camel driver lives on "famine foods." "The Taureg of the Air use ... the seeds of the *drinn,* the *mrokba,* wild *fonio, cram-cram, tawit,* the rhizomes and young shoots of the *berdi.* Their neighbors the Tibu ... get their bread from the fruit of the *dûm.*"[19] The commerce between Spain and North Africa brought to the African shore "textiles—broadcloths, silks, velours, taffetas, rough village cloths—cochineal, salt, perfumes, gum, coral, saffron, tens of thousands of caps," and brought back "sugar, wax, tallow, cowhides and goat skins, even gold."[20]

What, then, were Braudel's intentions in writing *La Méditerranée?* We look for enlightenment to the prefaces of the two editions—and, having looked, we are perplexed. Not that the prefaces are left without the customary statement of intention. On the contrary. The difficulty is that several intentions are stated, and that they point in divergent directions. The first intention Braudel states is "to discover exactly what the historical character of the Mediterranean has been."[21] A problem, then—the *histoire problème* dear to the heart of Lucien Febvre. But, really? A problem must have manageable bounds—unbelief in the early sixteenth century, for example. But the historical character of a body of water and the surrounding lands that for four millennia have been sites and routes for a half dozen or more civilizations? What *is* the problem? Indeed, the *problem* soon undergoes mitosis and becomes "the *problems* posed by the Mediterranean" which are "of exceptional richness."[22] So, then, which problems? A question put too late, since even before we have time to ask it Braudel turns our attention to "the grand movement of Mediterranean life."[23]

Not really *histoire problème* at all, *La Méditerranée.* Rather, *histoire totale*, history that aspires to embrace the whole of human activity, bringing to bear upon it all the knowledge that the sciences of man can provide—an account of the whole life of the peoples of the Mediterranean in the latter part of the sixteenth century. A task beyond the resources of any historian, even one so magnificently equipped, so learned, and so intelligent as Fernand Braudel. It is indeed a task he commits himself to but abandons quickly enough. Under the heading "Collective Destinies" we find much on certain matters pertaining to "The Economies," on precious metals, moneys and prices, commerce and transport. But on agriculture and industry there are only a few pages. Yet agriculture *was* the life of at least four-fifths of the inhabitants of the Mediterranean world. Still, 255 pages on Mediterranean economies in the second half of the sixteenth century—a generous allotment. On civilizations, only sixty-eight pages; on societies, forty-six. Three durable civilizations in the Mediterranean region—Moslem, Christian, Jewish. But about Islam,

Judaism, and Christianity, only that their followers lived in the Mediterranean in obdurate mutual *refus*. Of what the religions *were*, of their
mentalités, nothing. Of course, to ask this totality of Braudel or anyone is
absurd, it is too much—except that Braudel asked it of himself.

Such is the historiography of *histoire problème*. It is not the historiography of Fernand Braudel or of the *monde braudellien* of the Sixth Section.
That world proceeds under the signs of a deluge of information, of exhaustive documentation, of a torrent of words, of abundance at the risk
of surfeit. Its proudest products are Deyon's Amiens—606 pages, Goubert's Beauvaisis—653 pages, Baehrel's Basse Provence—842 pages,
Gascon's Lyon—999 pages, Le Roy Ladurie's Languedoc—1,035 pages,
and Braudel's Mediterranean—1,218 pages. And why not? History is a
house of many mansions. Its rooms are large, and if we historians are
wise, we will follow the precepts of the *Annalistes* and be ready to add
more rooms as the occasion suggests. If we are even wiser, we will not,
as Braudel sometimes seems to suggest, tear down the rooms we already
have but, rather, preserve them as structures, however ill-furnished. One
never knows when a historian will come along to make something of
them, a Garrett Mattingly, brilliantly to redecorate that stale old attic,
diplomatic history. Indeed, in one of his more expansive moments—he
has many of them—that is Braudel's view, too.

> At the risk of being taxed with an impenitent liberalism, I say ... that in
> order to mount the multiple thresholds of history, all the doors seem to
> me to be good. None of us knows all of them. At first the historian opens
> onto the past the door he is most familiar with. But if he wants to see as
> far as possible, necessarily he will knock on one door, then on another.
> Each time a new vista will open to him, and he is not worthy of the name
> historian if he does not juxtapose some of them: cultural and social vistas,
> cultural and political, social and economic, economic and political.[24]

Histoire problème marches under the standard of elegance; *histoire totale,*
under the standard of abundance; but all history and historians worth
the name march under the standard of curiosity—and excellence. So, a
magnificent entrepreneur of history, a great historian, the author of a
marvellous book, *La Méditerranée et le monde méditerranéen à l'époque de
Philippe II*, let Fernand Braudel have the last word. In a thoughtful
study, he has been seeking to understand and help sociologists understand the relations of history to sociology. He knows, however, that his
effort will be in vain unless sociologists grasp history in a way that very
few of them have. "I would wish that in the years of their apprenticeship
young sociologists would take the time to study even in the most modest
archive the simplest of historical questions; that once at least beyond
sterile manuals they might have contact with a craft that is simple but
one that cannot be understood without practicing it."[25] Amen!

NOTES

[1] These include 1,160 pages of text, bibliography, and indexes; there are fifteen pages of front matter.

[2] An accurate comparison of the length of the two editions is difficult, since the second edition considerably exceeds the first in the number of words per full page of text, but it allows space for maps and graphs lacking in the first edition. Nevertheless, the proportion of approximately four to five between words per page in the first edition and in the second edition far more than offsets the space given to maps and graphs. It indicates that the amount of text in the revised edition may exceed that in the original by 20 percent.

[3] Throughout, I have tried to make the distinction between history as the past and the study of the past, on the one hand, and History as a corporate activity of a group of professionals called "historians," on the other, by using an initial capital in the second case. I am not at all sure that I have succeeded.

[4] *Daedalus* (Winter 1971). Articles by Robert Darnton, Lawrence Stone, and John Talbott of Princeton University.

[5] Ibid. Article by M. I. Finley.

[6] Ibid. Articles by François Furet, Pierre Goubert, Jacques Le Goff.

[7] I am not certain whether Constantin Marinesco lived in Rumania in 1953. His degree was from Paris.

[8] Support is confined to the history of science.

[9] Fernand Braudel, *La Méditerranée et le monde méditerranéen à la époque de Philippe II* (2nd ed., Paris: A. Colin, 1966), 2 vols., p. 48.

[10] Ibid., pp. 171–72.

[11] Ibid., p. 460.

[12] Ibid. "She" really did not, even metaphorically. On the contrary, by working out the means of transfer payments from Spain via Italy to the Netherlands, the Genoese bankers, at the behest of Philip II, drained money out of the Mediterranean to fuel the wars of the Netherlands (ibid., vol. 1, p. 435). Philip allocated the money; the Genoese executed the orders. Braudel's implicit identification of wealth with silver and gold is odd.

[13] Ibid. vol. 1, p. 300.

[14] Ibid., pp. 316–21.

[15] Divided the empire of Philip because of the Reformation; that of the Ottomans because of the tensions between ruling ex-Christian slaves and Moslem subjects.

[16] Braudel, *La Méditerranée*, vol. 1, p. 112.

[17] Ibid., p. 165.

[18] Ibid., p. 86.

[19] Ibid., p. 159.

[20] Ibid., vol. 2, p. 186.

[21] Ibid., p. 13.

[22] Ibid., p. 15.

[23] Ibid., p. 14.

[24] *Annales ESC* 14 (1959), pp. 318–19.

[25] Fernand Braudel, *Traité de sociologie*, vol. 1, p. 97.

IMMANUEL WALLERSTEIN

Annales as Resistance

1978

INTRODUCTORY NOTE

On May 13–15, 1977, the Fernand Braudel Center held its Inaugural Conference on the theme, "The Impact of the Annales *School on the Social Sciences." This special issue is the record, more or less, of that conference. It contains the papers given at that conference, as revised by their authors. In a few cases, the revisions were extensive, and in one case the author scrapped his original "comments" to replace it by a paper inspired by another paper delivered. We have also included part of the discussion following the papers.*

One speaker after another stated that there was no homogeneous Annales *school, or was no longer. Some speakers even vaunted this so-called émiettement. That the* Annales *school is a loose expression covering a variety of interests is borne out by the different ways in which our authors approached the very discussion of the "impact" of the* Annales *school. Many used their discussion of the social history of an intellectual current to suggest substantive ideas of their own, modifications or further development of some theme linked to the* Annales *school. We have left the heterogeneity of approach intact. This issue then becomes itself a source material for further analysis of the topic.*

We devoted the conference and the space in this journal to this topic, not out of a sense of respect nor out of mere intellectual curiosity. Rather, we are convinced that the analysis of our scientific ideologies is an integral part of the analysis of the real world, a belief that itself is part of Annales *ideology. We must constantly hack away at the underbrush if we are to make our path in the forest.*

THE EDITORS

We have assembled here to discuss "the impact of the *Annales* school on the social sciences." We have come together to discover *Annales*, to celebrate *Annales*, to learn from *Annales*. I say "discover *Annales*," knowing full well that the group assembled

From *Review* 3–4 (1978), pp. 5–7.

knows *Annales* well. Indeed, they include those who have created it. But nonetheless I say "discover" and not "rediscover." And I say this in the light of Lucien Febvre's aphorism, "Histoire science du passé, science du présent," which stands in dialectical opposition to Leopold van Ranke's dictum that history is the discovery of "wie es eigentlich gewesen ist." Telling the history of the *Annales* is an act of the present that has its meaning and its justification in the present.

What is the nature of the *longue durée* within which we must interpret *Annales*? For me, it is the existence of a capitalist world economy since at least the long sixteenth century, the conjunctural achievement of definitive (albeit transitory) British hegemony within this structure with the final defeat of France in 1815, and the blossoming of history and the social sciences throughout this nineteenth-century world under the cultural umbrella of that Pax Britannica.

What resulted was a culturally dominant mode of analysis in the social sciences which still prevails today—universalizing, empiricist, sectioning off politics from economics from culture, profoundly ethnocentric, arrogant, and oppressive—Gramsci's hegemonic culture at the world level. Hegemonic cultures breed compliance; they also breed resistance. If we are to discover *Annales*, we must appreciate it as a form of resistance, as one major organized center of resistance.

The first issue of *Annales* in 1929 opened with a statement by Marc Bloch and Lucien Febvre "to our readers," in which they complain of the "evils engendered by a divorce that has become traditional," both the divorce between historians and those who study contemporary economies and societies, and the divorce within history among "cloistered" groups of specialists. "It is," they said, "against these fearful schisms that we intend to stand. Not by means of methodological articles or theoretical disquisitions. But by example and by deed." [1]

When, after the Second World War, *Annales* renewed itself with a new name, Febvre entitled his editorial, "Face au vent." "*Annales* is changing," he said, "because everything around it is changing: men, things; in a word, the world." And if, he continued, they ask me, "Do I, the historian, have the right to continue to write history?" then I shall not hesitate to say yes, "to the extent that History may make it possible, and *only* History may do so, to live in a world of constant instability with reflexes other than those of fear. . . ." [2]

When in 1957 Fernand Braudel took up the cudgels of *Annales*, he reminded us that "neither Marc Bloch nor Lucien Febvre had either the wish or the illusion of creating a school. . . ." Rather, he said, "they searched for all their lives." *Annales* would continue to stand for "history pushed to its outer limits, into the very heart of all the sciences that study man; and up to the contemporary instant, filled with the dangerous flames of the event,"[3] that very event whose episodic quality *Annales* had always warned against.

When in 1969, in the wake of the real events of May 1968, Fernand Braudel passed the journal into new hands, he expressed not only the wish that it would remain "in the forefront of innovation, insofar as it could, and accepting the inevitable risks," but also the hope that "if necessary, tomorrow, [the editors] would not hesitate to make a new *Annales*."[4]

We celebrate *Annales*, however, not because it has innovated, but because it has resisted, and resisted well. It insisted that beneath the episodic event lay the *longue durée*, beneath the political film lay economic and social structures, beyond the urban minority lay the rural majority. And it insisted that there was no such thing as economy or society or civilization—that these words had meaning only in the plural—economies, societies, civilizations. And it has made the world of the social sciences take account of these insistences.

But if we discover that *Annales* was a form of resistance, and we celebrate it for its relative success, what may we learn from it? We learn that resistance has its perils, and that the greatest peril of resistance is success. Within a capitalist world economy, those who resist—politically, economically, culturally—are either crushed or rewarded, rewarded in order to be crushed more subtly. And those who resist oft lend themselves, by their vanity or their fatigue, to the boa constrictor's embrace. Who does not want to come in out of the cold? Who does not want to receive justly deserved honor and recognition? Who does not have the sense that, after a certain point, he has done his share?

The school of the *Annales*—for school there is, despite Bloch, despite Febvre, despite Braudel—is no more guilty of creeping cooptation than other schools of resistance. No more guilty, but no less.

There is only one solution to this deadly call of the sirens. It is renewal in the "dangerous flames" of the present, a renewal that is only possible through History, which alone can make it possible "to live in a world of constant instability with reflexes other than those of fear." Historical social science, which is "the science of the past, the science of the present," is, in Febvre's phrase, a "combat." There is a word central to the tradition of the *Annales,* a word that can define our stance. It is a combat that must be waged with intelligence, by men, using words and ideas but not them alone, to create that which honors man—its object and its subject—and which man is able to create. I end with the call of Lucien Febvre in 1946: "History asking questions of the past, in terms of Humanity's needs today: that yes. There is our doctrine. There is our History."

NOTES

[1] "A nos lecteurs," *Annales d'histoire économique et social* 1 (Jan. 1929), pp. 1, 2.

[2] *Annales ESC* 1.1 (Jan.-Mar. 1946), pp. 2, 6–7.

[3] "Les *Annales* continuent . . ." *Annales ESC* 12.1 (Jan.-Mar. 1957), p. 1.

[4] "Les 'Nouvelles' *Annales,*" *Annales ESC* 24.3 (Jan.-Mar. 1969), p. 1.

The Stages
of Life

—————

PHILIPPE ARIÈS

Centuries of Childhood

1960

*Among the "new historians" who came to prominence in the 1970s,
the presence of Philippe Ariès's name was something of a surprise, for
he came from a different world and belonged to a different generation. Born in 1914, Ariès did not become a professional historian until
the end of his life, when he assumed a position at the Ecole des Hautes
Etudes from 1978 to 1984. Until he was past sixty, he was, as he himself has written, a "Sunday historian." His political background was
also quite alien to the postwar French academic scene: his roots lay
in the traditionalist extreme right-wing movement Action Française.
Hence his early work, from* Traditions sociales dans les pays de
France (1943) *to* L'Histoire des populations françaises et de leurs
attitudes devant la vie depuis le XVIIIᵉ siècle *(1948) remained
largely unknown to academic historians.*

Even his most famous work of 1960, L'Enfant et la vie familiale
sous l'Ancien Régime (Centuries of Childhood: A Social History
of Family Life), *an excerpt from which follows, was slow to receive
recognition. Perhaps it was Ariès's acceptance of, indeed his pride in,
his marginality that explains the freshness of his way of looking at
history. Ironically enough, it was the protesting students of 1968 who
discovered and called attention to the work of the right-wing historian, whose themes, such as attitudes toward life and death and the*

From *Centuries of Childhood*, trans. Robert Baldich (London: Jonathan Cape,
1962), pp. 54–59. First published as *L'Enfant et la vie familiale sous l'ancien régime*
(Paris: Plon, 1960).

organic forms of social life, gained new currency in the 1960s. His last great book, L'Homme devant la mort *(Hour of Death), published in 1977, received international recognition.*

This analysis has enabled us to pick out certain customs of dress confined to childhood that were generally adopted at the end of the sixteenth century and preserved until the middle of the eighteenth century. These customs distinguishing between children's clothing and adult clothing reveal a new desire to put children on one side, to separate them by a sort of uniform. But what is the origin of this childhood uniform?

The child's robe is simply the long coat of the Middle Ages, of the twelfth and thirteenth centuries, before the revolution which in the case of men banished it in favor of the short coat and visible breeches, the ancestors of our present-day masculine costume. Until the fourteenth century everybody wore the robe or tunic; the men's robe was not the same as the women's—often it was a shorter tunic, or else it opened down the front. On the peasants in the thirteenth-century calendars, it stops at the knee, while on the great and important it reaches to the feet. There was, in fact, a long period during which men wore a long fitted costume, as opposed to the traditional draped costume of the Greeks or Romans: this continued the fashions of the Gallic or Oriental barbarians which had been added to the Roman fashions during the first centuries of our era. It was uniformly adopted in the East as in the West, and it was the origin of the Turkish style of dress as well.

In the fourteenth century, men abandoned the robe for the short coat, which was sometimes even tight-fitting, to the despair of moralists and preachers who denounced the indecency of these fashions, describing them as signs of the immorality of the times. In fact, respectable people went on wearing the robe, whether they were respectable on account of their age (old men are depicted wearing the robe until the beginning of the seventeenth century) or on account of their station in life (magistrates, statesmen, churchmen). Some have never given up wearing the long coat and still wear it today, at least on occasion (barristers, judges, professors, and priests). The priests, incidentally, came very near to abandoning it, for when the short coat had become generally accepted, and when in the seventeenth century the scandal attending its origins had been completely forgotten, the priest's cassock became too closely connected with his ecclesiastical function to be in good taste. A priest would change out of his cassock to go into society, or even to call on his bishop, just as an officer would change out of his uniform to appear at court.[1]

Children too kept the long coat, at least children of good family. A miniature in the fifteenth-century *Miracles de Notre-Dame* shows a family gathered around the mother's bed; the father is wearing a short coat, doublet, and breeches, but the three children are dressed in long robes.[2] In the same series, the child feeding the infant Jesus has a robe split down the side.

However, in Italy most of the children painted by the artists of the Quattrocento are wearing the tight-fitting breeches of adults. In France and Germany, it seems that this fashion failed to find favor and that children were kept in the long coat. At the beginning of the sixteenth century, the habit became a general rule: children were always dressed in the robe. German tapestries of the period show four-year-old children wearing the long robe, open in front.[3] Some French engravings by Jean Leclerc on the subject of children's games show the children wearing, over their breeches, the robe buttoned down the front, which became the uniform of their age.[4]

The flat ribbons down the back which likewise distinguished children from adults in the seventeenth century had the same origins as the robe. Cloaks and robes in the sixteenth century often had sleeves that one could slip into or leave empty at will. In Leclerc's picture of children playing at chucks, some of these sleeves can be seen to be fastened only by a few stitches. People of fashion, especially women, liked the effect of these hanging sleeves: they stopped putting their arms into them, with the result that the sleeves became useless ornaments. Like organs that have ceased to function, they wasted away, lost the hollow in which the arm fitted, and, flattened out, looked like two broad ribbons fastened behind the shoulders: the children's ribbons of the seventeenth and eighteenth centuries were all that remained of the false sleeves of the sixteenth century. These atrophied sleeves were also to be found in other clothes of a popular or a ceremonial nature: the peasant cloak that the Ignorantine friars adopted as their religious costume at the beginning of the eighteenth century, the first purely military uniforms such as those of the musketeers, the livery of valets, and finally the page's uniform— the ceremonial uniform of the children and young boys of noble birth who were placed with families for whom they performed certain domestic services. The pages of the age of Louis XIII wore baggy breeches in the sixteenth-century style and false sleeves; this page's uniform tended to become the ceremonial costume that was donned as a token of honor and respect: in an engraving by Lepautre, some boys in an archaic page's uniform are shown serving Mass.[5] But these ceremonial costumes were somewhat rare, whereas the flat ribbon was to be found on the shoulders of all the children, whether boys or girls, in families of quality, whether aristocratic or middle-class.

Thus, in order to distinguish the child who had hitherto dressed just like an adult, features of old-fashioned costumes which the grown-ups had abandoned, sometimes a long time before, were reserved for his sole use. This was the case with the robe or long coat and the false sleeves, also with the bonnet worn by little children still in their swaddling clothes: in the thirteenth century, the bonnet was still the normal masculine head-wear, which the men used to keep their hair in position at work, as can be seen from the calendars of Notre-Dame d'Amiens, and so on.

The first children's costume was the costume that everybody used to wear about a century before, which henceforth they were the only ones to wear. It was obviously out of the question to invent a costume out of nothing for them, yet it was felt necessary to separate them in a visible manner by means of their dress. They were, accordingly, given a costume of which the tradition had been maintained in certain classes but nobody wore anymore. The adoption of a special childhood costume, which became generalized throughout the upper classes as from the end of the sixteenth century, marked a very important date in the formation of the idea of childhood.

We have to remember the importance that dress had in the France of old. It often represented a large capital sum. People spent a great deal on clothes, and when somebody died they went to the trouble of drawing up an inventory of his or her wardrobe, as we would today only when fur coats were involved. Dress was very expensive, and attempts were made by means of sumptuary laws to put a curb on luxury clothes, which ruined some and allowed others to mislead the gullible as to their birth and station in life. Even more than in our present-day society—where it is still true of the women, whose dress is a visible and necessary sign of a couple's prosperity or the importance of their social position—dress pinpointed the place of the wearer in a complex and undisputed hierar-chy: a man wore the costume of his rank, and the etiquette books laid great emphasis on the impropriety of dressing in any other way than that befitting one's age or birth. Every social nuance had its corresponding sign in clothing. At the end of the sixteenth century, custom dictated that childhood, henceforth recognized as a separate entity, should also have its special costume.

We have seen that childhood dress originated in an archaism: the sur-vival of the long coat. This archaizing tendency continued. Toward the end of the eighteenth century, in the time of Louis XVI, little boys were dressed in Louis XIII or Renaissance collars. The children painted by Nicolas Lancret and François Boucher are often dressed after the fashion of the previous century.

But two other tendencies were to influence the development of chil-dren's dress from the seventeenth century on. The first emphasized the effeminate appearance of the little boy. We have seen earlier in this work that the boy "in bib and tucker," before the age of "the robe with a

collar," wore the same robe and skirt as a girl. This effeminization of the
little boy, which became noticeable about the middle of the sixteenth
century, was at first a novelty and barely hinted at. For instance, the
upper part of the boy's costume retained the characteristics of masculine
dress; but soon the little boy was given the lace collar of the little girl,
which was exactly the same as that worn by the ladies. It became impossible to distinguish a little boy from a little girl before the age of four or
five, and this costume became firmly established for something like two
centuries. About 1770, boys stopped wearing the robe with the collar
after four or five, but until they reached that age they were dressed like
little girls, and this would be the case until the end of the nineteenth
century: this effeminate habit would be dropped only after World War
I, and its abandonment can be compared to that of the woman's corset
as symptomatic of the revolution in dress corresponding to the general
change in manners.

It is interesting to note that the attempt to distinguish children was
generally confined to the boys: the little girls were distinguished only by
the false sleeves, abandoned in the eighteenth century, as if childhood
separated girls from adult life less than it did boys. The evidence provided by dress bears out the other indications furnished by the history
of manners: boys were the first specialized children. They began going
to school in large numbers as far back as the late sixteenth century and
the early seventeenth century. The education of girls started in a small
way only in the time of Fénelon and Mme. de Maintenon and developed
slowly and tardily. Without a proper educational system, the girls were
confused with the women at an early age, just as the boys had formerly
been confused with the men, and nobody thought of giving visible form,
by means of dress, to a distinction that was beginning to exist in reality
for the boys but that still remained futile for the girls.

Why, in order to distinguish the boy from the man, was he made
to look like the girl who was not distinguished from the woman? Why
did that costume, so novel and surprising in a society in which people
started adult life at an early age, last almost to the present day, at least
until the beginning of this century, in spite of the changes in manners
and the prolongation of the period of childhood? Here we are touching
on the as yet unexplored subject of a society's consciousness of its behavior in relation to age and sex: so far, only its class consciousness has
been studied.

Another tendency that, like archaizing and effeminizing, probably
originated in the taste for fancy dress led the children of middle-class
families to adopt features of lower-class or working dress. Here, the
child would forestall masculine fashion and wear trousers as early as the
reign of Louis XVI, before the age of the sans-culottes. The costume

worn by the well-dressed child in the period of Louis XVI was at once archaic (the Renaissance collar), lower-class (the trousers), and military (the military jacket and buttons).

In the seventeenth century, there was no distinctive lower-class costume and, a fortiori, no regional costumes. The poor wore the clothes they were given[6] or those they bought from old-clothes dealers. The lower-class costume was a secondhand costume, just as today the lower-class car is a secondhand car. (The comparison between the costume of the past and the car of the present day is not as artificial as it may seem: the car has inherited the social significance that dress used to have.) Thus, the man of the people was dressed like the man of the world a few decades earlier; in the streets of Louis XIII's Paris, he wore the plumed bonnet that had been fashionable in the sixteenth century, while the women wore the hood favored by ladies of the same period. The time lag varied from one region to another, according to the rapidity with which the local gentry followed the prevailing fashions. At the beginning of the eighteenth century, the women of certain regions—along the Rhine, for instance—were still wearing fifteenth-century coifs. In the course of the eighteenth century, this evolution came to a stop, as result of a moral estrangement between the rich and the poor and also a physical separation. Regional dress originated in both a new taste for regionalism (it was the period of the great regional histories of Brittany, Provence, and so on, and also of a revival of interest in the regional languages that had become dialects as the result of the progress of French) and differences in dress due to variations in the time that the fashions of town and court took to reach different parts of the country.

TRANSLATED BY ROBERT BALDICK

NOTES

[1] Mme. de Sévigné, *Lettres*, April 1, 1672.
[2] *Miracles de Notre-Dame*, vol. 1, p. 58.
[3] H. Göbel, *Wandteppiche*, 1923, vol. 1, plate 182.
[4] Jean Leclerc, "Les Trents-six figures contenant tous les jeux," 1587.
[5] Lepautre, engraving, Cabinet des Estampes, Ed. 43 fol., p. 111.
[6] Jan de Bray, 1663, "A Distribution of Clothes," H. Gerson, I, no. 50.

ANDRÉ BURGUIÈRE

Family and Society

1972

As André Burguière points out in the following essay, in the late 1960s the history of the family became one of the major areas of confrontation and collaboration between history and the social sciences. This was the case not only in France but also in England, particularly in the work of Peter Laslett and his Cambridge Group, and soon as well in the United States, Germany, Italy, and elsewhere. In France, however, there was nothing obvious about this development: historically, the family was one of those organic forms of the social favored by conservative and even reactionary thinkers, usually outside the universities. It was also of interest to genealogists, mostly amateurs. Three major factors account for its late emergence as an important object of research. The development of rigorous quantitative methods in historical demography made it possible to exploit extensive but previously neglected documentary sources and to produce reliable data. Second, anthropological work on family systems (particularly that of Lévi-Strauss in Structures élémentaires de la parenté *[*The Elementary Structures of Kinship*]) provided a theoretical and conceptual framework. Finally, some credit must be given to the "atmosphere of the time," in particular the change in French society's perception of itself and attitude toward the past that took place between the mid-1960s and mid-1970s. Signs of this change range from the "rediscovery of the social" in its most communal forms (witness May '68) to the nostalgia for the past in the 1970s. Largely independent of one another at first, these changes converged to thrust the family to the center of historical thinking. In 1972, the* Annales *devoted a large special issue to the subject, an early indication of its importance and a survey of the riches that the theme had to offer.*

André Burguière, "Famille et société," introduction to a special issue of *Annales* 27 (1972), pp. 799–801.

This special issue was not merely inevitable but practically wrote itself. For some years now, work on the family has been flourishing in the four corners of the social sciences. In some disciplines, such as ethnology and sociology, it is already a standard topic. For historians, it is a new problem. It is perhaps the historian's weakness, or vocation, not to be able to gauge the importance of a social institution until cracks begin to appear in it, until it enters into crisis. Is historical knowledge, like the owl of Minerva, condemned to fly only at night?

Rather than ask what the sudden interest in the problems of the family portends for present-day society, we should ask why historians remained uninterested for so long. Historical science crystallized around the notions of state and nation. Part of the explanation for this is simply practical: the sources on which historians work are more numerous and more accessible in public archives than in private collections. History redefined itself as a research enterprise when the first public archives were instituted, and those archives shaped history's content.

An obvious ideological preference also drove history toward the state. In contrast to the natural sciences, which seek to isolate the simple elements of complex experience, history was built on the romantic idea that man fulfills his destiny collectively: in order to work in the field of history, the historian must shed all that is merely individual in his thinking. This romanticism had its uses, moreover—the elaboration of a national history justified the rise of nationalities and nationalisms. The value ascribed to political history (conceived as a history of the state) justified the reinforcement of the state.

In this context, the family was not only neglected but rejected as superfluous matter, refractory to change and to history. Scholars drew on it only for anecdotal, biographical information, but never for generalizable explanations. Genealogists and biographers kept the family confined in a minor historical genre, nearly always of reactionary inspiration. Ethnology and sociology rehabilitated it as an object of research but without challenging the logic of the traditional division of labor. Families provided a useful framework of analysis and served as a factor of explanation, but only in societies said to be "without history" (or without a state).

Hence, it is tempting to see this refusal to treat the family as a legitimate subject of historical discourse as more than a mere rejection. Historical science is the daughter of the bourgeois nineteenth century. I would venture to guess that history aimed to be the history of states and nations not out of indifference to the role of the family but, on the contrary, out of an excess of deference, for it was afraid to subject to critical analysis something so intimately intertwined with bourgeois values and the functioning of bourgeois society.

The utopian aspect of past historical work should not be underestimated: history's goal was to reconstruct the past in the light of an imagined future so as to be able to draw a straight line of progress leading from one to the other. From Thomas More to Tommaso Campanella, from Charles Fourier to Etienne Cabet, utopian writers exalted the state and suppressed the family. The reinforcement of the family during the bourgeois period, not only as the matrix of a new morality and sensibility but also as the guardian of property and agent of capitalist accumulation, by no means led to a withering away of the state. Yet if the recent application of historical methods to the problems of the family has any value, it lies in having demonstrated that the concurrent institutions of family and state were constantly at odds as societies evolved: the moment the state grew weak and lost the power to intervene and protect, the family expanded its prerogatives, asserted its authority over the individual, and transformed itself into a fortress. Whenever the state gained strength, the family receded, loosened the emotional bonds it imposed on individual members, and allowed them to integrate more fully into the larger society. The rise of the family that Georges Duby described in the case of the seigneurial class in the Mâconnais around the year 1000 coincided with a period of political uncertainty and vacuum as the feudal regime was being established. And the rise of the family that Emmanuel Le Roy Ladurie found among fifteenth-century peasants in the Languedoc coincided with the breakdown of feudal power.

Return of the repressed? The family is once again forcing its way into history, in large part thanks to sociology, anthropology, and psychoanalysis, which historians have at last begun to take seriously. Hence, in this special issue it was only natural for us to pay attention, unabashedly, to what was going on in related disciplines. For the most part, however, we have been guided by the progress of historical research itself. It is now almost twenty years since Ernest Labrousse urged historians to undertake a systematic exploration of notarial archives for a vast study of the bourgeoisie. A reconstruction of the family through marriage contracts, estate inventories, and so on seemed, at that time, the best way to arrive at a genuine social history. This kind of approach to the family, which sees it as the repository of patrimonial property and economic power, has played such an important part in recent historical work that it seemed unnecessary to dwell on it further in this issue.

Instead, we have chosen to devote a great deal of space to historical demography. Using methods developed by Louis Henry, it has become possible to analyze family realities in ways that historians have only begun to exploit. Although Henry's methods were originally developed to investigate changes in fertility, they have yielded such valuable results that one sometimes has the illusion of looking at the very tissue of society cell by cell through a kind of historical microscope.

We shall therefore be testing accepted theories of family structure (such as typologies based on family size and degrees of kinship represented within the family group, the relation between family size and systems of authority, and so on). We shall also be looking at behavior and the moral norms that govern it. It makes sense to look at the history of the family on three levels: biological (using demographic data to study the conjugal family in the strict sense); social (family structures determine the elementary forms of social organization); and emotional. This ambitious program is a product of the recent expansion of historical demography, and it is our hope that this issue will serve to bring it to the attention of researchers in other areas of the social sciences.

TRANSLATED BY ARTHUR GOLDHAMMER

MICHEL VOVELLE

Death and the West

1983

*Collective attitudes toward life and death were a favorite subject of
historical research in the 1960s and 1970s, and not only in France.
Philippe Ariès was a pioneer in this area. In the next generation, he
was followed by, among others, Jacques Gélis and Mireille Laget
(on birth), Jean-Louis Flandrin (on love), and André Burguière (on
marriage). Michel Vovelle (b. 1933) was one of the first and most
prolific of the historians of death. In a book that immediately became
a* classic, Piété baroque et déchristianisation en Provence au
XVIIIᵉ siècle *(1971), he attempted a social history of behavior based
on the detailed examination of some two thousand wills. Yet his ambitions went even farther—nothing less than a history of the social
forms of death in the West since the Middle Ages, based on a very
wide spectrum of sources from cemeteries to sermons, from figurative
representations to clothing and even comic strips. If one compares the
resulting work to the book that Philippe Ariès published on the same
subject in 1977, the similarities are apparent but so are the differences: in particular, Vovelle, a disciple of Labrousse, is intensely interested in the social characterizations of collective behaviors.*

HOW THE IMAGE OF DEATH CHANGES

Death is not a constant but changes over time. It would be artificial to
think of this change as somehow reflecting a regular rise and fall of
human fear, as if fear could be measured and graphed as a sine wave
without a beginning or an end. The social history of death is a composite
of relatively slow changes, which often leave traces in memory, image,
and gesture.

The evolution of death also reflects successive changes in ideology:
the Middle Ages to the early eighteenth century saw the Christianization

Michel Vovelle, *La Mort et l'occident, de 1300 à nos jours* (Paris: Gallimard, 1983),
pp. 23–26.

of death (involving both conquest and compromise), and this was followed, from the second half of the eighteenth century to the present, by a series of desacralizations. The resulting void was filled by new ideological constructions based on philosophy, science, and even nationalism. Meanwhile, unsanctioned mystics arose to feed or feed off of the irrationalism of elites as well as masses, whose anxieties were unassuaged.

These were long-term changes, each, apparently, with its own rhythm and its own dynamic. Is this picture correct? In any case, my intention in giving this rapid summary is not to add anything new to the theories previously examined but, rather, to formulate a fundamental question. This has to do with the hierarchy of reciprocal actions, or causes and effects, in what Louis Althusser calls the "skein of time."

I am well aware of the limits of demographic explanation and have little faith in the idea that the collective imagination takes off on adventures of its own. Forgive me for resorting to technical jargon, which I hope I am not misusing: in my opinion, one must search elsewhere for the "overdetermining totality" that governs changes in collective representations. Still, I hope that no one will catch me in any flagrant display of "vulgar Marxism," which brings smiles to the lips of the best and the brightest on both sides of the Atlantic.

My view is quite simple—namely, that the image of death at any particular point in time nicely fits the definition that Marx gave of the mode of production as the "general illumination or special ether that determines the specific weight of all the forms of existence associated with it." The formula is deliberately vague, the opposite, in any case, of a mechanically reductive explanation. Still, in my opinion, the history of death quite aptly illustrates both the complexity and richness of Marx's assertion. To be concrete, consider the example of "baroque" death as reflected in early seventeenth-century imagery: to reduce the baroque era's bombastic inflation of death to a mere reflection of the demographic difficulties of the day is to give an impoverished interpretation of the facts. The seventeenth century's tragic outlook was more than a matter of plagues and the Thirty Years War: it was the "pathetic" mentality of a time of tension and conflict. The invasion of mysticism and its poor cousin, piety; the accentuation of eternal torment and the Last Things; the eradication of the popular religion of death, which was relegated to the status of superstition and suppressed along with witchcraft; and, conversely, the organization of the ceremonial surrounding the death of great personages and the influence of that model on the not so great; the unprecedented use of the hereafter as a bulwark of order and social hierarchy, with emphasis on the abyss between the chosen and the damned, while at the same time Catholics, at least, left the door open to a possible future redemption through a strengthening of the belief in

Purgatory—all of these things are interrelated, and together they give us an indirect but very profound image of the social climate of a time and, more generally, of the worldview of a society of which the baroque image of death was one expression, just as absolutism was its political translation.

And why can't we say the same thing about "bourgeois death" in the nineteenth century? We can look at this new system after it has been established or, better yet, while it was still taking shape between 1770 and 1820. Or again, we can consider what became of it in a period of profound crisis, the twilight of bourgeois values, ending in 1914, when Thomas Mann's hero Hans Castorp fled the enchantment of the "magic mountain" for the death that awaited him at the front.

Death is thus the reflection of a society, but surely it is an ambiguous reflection. The image of the hereafter as a Machiavellian invention of the powerful intended to frighten the humble into docile obedience, an image first crafted by the libertines and later polished by the Enlightenment, is so inaccurate that today one can only regard it as a caricature. Some fashioned counterimages that seized upon death as a means of symbolically overturning the power hierarchy, as in the medieval danse macabre. Others camouflaged their thoughts of violent subversion of the established order as dreams of the millennium and the end of time. Nevertheless, death is not revolutionary: in Rabelais's time, popular culture waged a rearguard action through laughter and derision in the face of death, while the French Revolution affirmed a new ethic through the sublimation of heroism as a victory over death.

In taking a social approach to the changing image of death, I do not seek to discover definitive answers. My ambition is simply to show how one might investigate the ways in which collective representations of death have changed. There are, in my view, long periods of very slow change which can only be dealt with in a *longue durée* perspective, and there are also times when several different behavioral models coexist. In the nineteenth century, the bourgeoisie never made a definitive choice among religious revivalism, scientism, and spiritualism, while rural folk combined now-quaint traditional customs with a vulgarized Christianity. Such cultural stratifications reflected if not tensions within the society then at least crucial social divisions.

This history may have been slow, but it was by no means static: attitudes toward death are an ideal subject for reflection on the applications of "structure" to the history of *mentalités*. Clearly, death is interpreted as part of a larger system or general long-term social project—yet there is nothing rigid or monolithic about such structures. The "symphonic" structure of the Baroque age developed slowly as new elements were added from the late Middle Ages onward, and the process was not without its detours, some of considerable magnitude—the Reformation is a case in point. Then it slowly fell apart over the course of the eighteenth century.

Does the foregoing imply that change is imperceptible? I do not think so: what this history also shows is the importance of leaps of progress brought about by what can be called "crises" in collective sensibility (broadly construed). By this I mean moments of mobility in which many things come together, crystallizing in a challenge to the system: episodes of this type occurred in the late Middle Ages, in the early Baroque period, at the twilight of the Enlightenment, just before the turn of the twentieth century, and perhaps even more recently, somewhere after 1960 or 1965.

Such great upheavals in collective sensibility affect more than just attitudes toward death: attitudes toward the family, life, and conventional values are all interrelated. Some time around 1760, for example, a major change occurred in Western *mentalités,* and all the "indicators" of sensibility reflect this. Crises in sensibility are, of course, social crises, affecting deep social structures. The instability of the waning Middle Ages was a product not just of the Black Plague but of a crisis of chivalrous society generally, of which the outpouring of macabre images was but one extreme manifestation. Similarly, in the late nineteenth century, triumphant bourgeois society was contested by some of its own elites, and one result of this challenge was a surge of interest in morbid subjects; this movement later brought on its own corrective in the form of the contemporary taboo on the subject of death.

Death as a metaphor for the difficulty of life. . . . The investment in death is a product not of increased life expectancies but of greater expectations of happiness, a much more complex, much more significant thing. And surely that is why we are interested today in the history of death. Indeed, this project of discovery (or rediscovery) has a precisely datable history of its own: it began, roughly speaking, fifteen or twenty years ago.

The work of today's historians of death reflects more than just changes in historiographic fashion. Although many were not aware of it at first, they were influenced by a broader social phenomenon, a wholesale rediscovery of death, which deserves to be explored more thoroughly, for it is a significant symptom of our current state of mind.

British and American sociologists, psychologists, and physicians led the way, in small numbers in the 1950s, then in much larger numbers in the 1960s. At the same time, historians, mainly in France—and largely unaware of what was going on elsewhere except for a few pioneering articles by Philippe Ariès—began to look at collective attitudes toward death. Today one can discern certain regional differences in the study of death, with investigators in some parts of the world exploring new avenues while scholars elsewhere lag far behind. In the United States, the study of death was until recently mainly confined to sociologists. In France, it has been dominated by historians and, I would add, philosophers; in Germany the interest was mainly religious. Lately, however, people around the world have become aware of the phenomenon, and the resulting contacts have turned what had been piecemeal research into a general free-for-all.

The recent inflation of thanatological research may be misleading, however. A historian who sets out to write a comprehensive survey of the subject would soon run into difficulty: curiosity about death has been unevenly distributed, and much of the historical work has involved pioneering efforts, with many projects still under way. A bird's-eye view of the subject would reveal a patchwork, and the prospects for successful synthesis might seem bleak. Should the attempt be avoided on that account? I don't think so. Every period asks itself certain questions. Is the recent rediscovery of death a mere detour, as some think, or even a passing fashion? Or might it be, as it has been in the past, an unambiguous expression of a crisis in a liberal democratic society, which has lately been obliged to break the silence it imposed on death at the turn of the century?

In this respect, the detour through history, which until recently has characterized the French approach to the problem, may prove useful. The historian's ambition is not so much to produce a miraculous explanation as to achieve an understanding rooted in the fullness of time. And, in the end, his lack of caution may prove to have been justified: for whatever unspoken personal motives he may have for confronting the problem of death, when he shares his work with others he discovers that they, too, are asking similar questions.

TRANSLATED BY ARTHUR GOLDHAMMER

Social Organization, Social Imagination

GEORGES DUBY

The Three Orders: Feudal Society Imagined

1978

Stretching over more than forty years, the work of the medievalist Georges Duby (b. 1919) has been a dominating force in French historiography. Extremely coherent and centered on a relatively narrow period, from the eleventh to the early thirteenth century, whose crucial importance he has demonstrated, his work embraces all of the major historical subspecialties: social history (in his thesis, La Société au XIe et XIIe siècles dans la région mâconnaise, *1953), economic history (*L'Economie rurale et la vie des campagnes dans l'occident médiéval, *1961 [Rural Economy and Country Life in the Medieval West]* and *Guerriers et Paysans, *1973 [The Early Growth of the European Economy: Warriors and Peasants from the Seventh to the Twelfth Century]), the history of culture and art (*Le Temps des cathédrales: L'art et la société, 980–1420, *1976 [The Age of the Cathedrals: Art and Society, 980–1420]* and *Saint Bernard: L'Art cistercien, *1976), the history of mentalités (*L'An mil, *1967, and* Le Dimanche de Bouvines, *1973) [The Legend of the Bouvines: War, Religion, and Culture in the Middle Ages]), and the history of family structures, kinship relations, and gender (*Le Chevalier, la femme et le prêtre, *1981 [The Knight, the Lady, and the Priest: The Making of Modern Mar-*

From *The Three Orders: Feudal Society Imagined,* trans. Arthur Goldhammer (Chicago: University of Chicago Press, 1980). First published as *Les Trois ordres: Ou, l'imaginaire du féodalisme* (Paris: Gallimard, 1978).

riage in Medieval France], and, with Michelle Perrot as coeditor, L'Histoire des femmes, 1991 [A History of Women in the West]). Duby's abundant output has also helped to win an audience for the "new history" both inside and outside France since the late 1960s.

Les Trois ordres (The Three Orders) is probably not his best known or most widely read work. "A severe book," according to its author, it was a deliberate attempt to explore the area of medieval representations and ideologies. After examining the material and so-cial structures of the early Middle Ages, Duby looks at the persistence, or, rather, the reformulation, of the old tripartite system of social organization whose importance Georges Dumézil had demonstrated in his work on Indo-European culture over a very long time period and across a vast geographical space: according to this scheme, society is divided into three groups, those who make war, those who pray, and those who work. Why was it revived and indeed reorchestrated in the eleventh and twelfth centuries? Why, at that time, did it be-come "good to think with"? What was its purpose? Note that the concept of ideology is explicitly taken from Althusser: it refers to a representation rather than to a reflection of the social organization.

S ome are devoted particularly to the service of God; others to the preservation of the state by arms; still others to the task of feeding and maintaining it by peaceful labors. These are our three orders or Estates General of France, the Clergy, the Nobility, and the Third Estate."

This statement is among those which open the *Traité des ordres et simples dignitez* published in 1610 by the Parisian Charles Loyseau, a work immediately recognized as highly useful and continually reissued throughout the seventeenth century. These words serve to define the social order, that is, the political order, that is, order itself. Here we are confronted with three "estates," three fixed and stable categories, three levels of a hierarchy. It is like a school, that model society where the child learns to remain seated and quiet in orderly rows, to obey, to be classified; it is the class: the older children, those of intermediate age, the youngest; the first, the second, the "third" estate. Or, rather, three "orders"—for that is clearly the word preferred by Loyseau. The mem-bers of the highest order turn their attention heavenward, while those of the two others look to the earth, all being occupied with the task of upholding the state. The intermediate order provides security, the infe-rior feeds the other two. Thus, we have three functions, mutually com-plementing one another. The whole has a triangular solidity, with a base, an apex, and, most important, that ternarity which in some mysterious way bestows a feeling of equilibrium on the construction.

For when Loyseau comes subsequently to talk about the nobility (on page 53 of the 1636 edition), he states clearly that this social body is diverse, with various layers and ranks superimposed on one another. Among the nobility, everything is a matter of rank and precedence, and men will sometimes fight to decide who will be the first to cross a threshold, sit down, or don his hat. Loyseau's concern is thus to introduce some order into this complex situation. He chooses to divide these many gradations into three categories. Why three? No tradition, custom, or authority dictates a tripartite division in this instance. "Because," says Loyseau, "the most perfect division is that into three species." "The most perfect"—that is what is in question—perfection itself. What matters is to seek, in the disorderly jumble of the sublunary world, the proper bases for a harmonious and reasonable construction which would appear to reflect the intentions of the Creator.

Indeed, if the monarchy of the Ancien Régime thought of itself as established on a threefold foundation of Estates General or orders, this was because the fitting of social relations into ternary structures made it possible to integrate these into global structures, which extended over the entire visible and invisible universe. Loyseau makes this point in a long preliminary discussion. This prologue should not be read as a bravura exercise. It is essential; it justifies the whole argument.

"There must be order in all things, because it is seemly that it should be so, and so that these things may be given direction." So that each "thing" may be assigned its proper rank and so that all may be governed. Consider, for example, the hierarchy of created beings, with its three levels. At the lowest level are the inanimate objects: these are obviously classified according to their degree of perfection. Dominating the rest are the "celestial intelligences," the angels: as we know, these are arranged in an immutable order. Between the two are the animals, made subject to man by God. As for men, the concern of the *Traité,* they live a less stable existence, being free to choose between good and evil; nevertheless, "they cannot subsist without order"; hence, they must be ruled. The key idea is thus one of a necessary "direction," and consequently a necessary submission. Some are made subject to others. The former must obey. Loyseau here makes use of a military analogy; he speaks of the "orders" that proceed from the regiment to the company and thence to the squad, which must be carried out without hesitation or question. Discipline is the source of an army's strength. It is also the source of the strength of the state. The world's solidity depends on it.

Next, it is argued that discipline requires inequality. "We cannot live together with equality of condition, hence some must command and others obey. Those who command comprise several orders, ranks, and degrees." Order comes from above. It is propagated through a hierarchy. The arrangement of the ranks, one above the other, ensures that order will spread throughout the whole. "The sovereign lords have command over all within their State, giving their orders to the great, who pass them on to those of intermediate rank, who pass them on to the small" (we notice that a ternary hierarchy has come into being of its own accord among the agents of sovereign power, under its sole authority), "and the small pass the orders on to the people. And the people, who obey all those mentioned" (on this point, let us be quite precise in marking the real dividing line: between the "smallest" of those who command, and the whole of the people, which must mutely obey; between the officers and the troops; between the state apparatus and its—good or bad—subjects),

> are further divided into several orders and ranks so that each of the latter has its superiors, who answer for the actions of the whole order to the magistrates, who do the same to the sovereign lords. Thus, by means of manifold divisions and subdivisions of this kind, several orders are made into one general order (this is the inflection that leads to the three functions) and several estates into one well-governed State, in which there is a proper harmony and consonance and a correspondence among relationships from the lowest to the highest level; in the end, there is an orderly progress from an innumerable order toward unity.

According to this theory, order is based on the plurality of orders, on a sequence of binary relations, in which some give orders to others, who execute or convey them. This first assertion is coupled with another less evident one: that this sequence tends ineluctably to take on a ternary character, that the three functions, that is, the three "orders," come to superimpose themselves upon the innumerable links in the chain. Why? How? In a way that is, frankly, mysterious, or in any case unexplained. Inexplicable, perhaps? A gap appears at this point in the argument. Despite his concern with proof, Loyseau does not seek to prove that this superimposition is necessary. He merely observes that some are particularly devoted to one duty, others to another, and still others to a third. Trifunctionality is self-evident. It is a part of the order of things.

Nevertheless, Loyseau does feel the need to marshal an additional argument to bolster the assumption on which the whole *Traité* is built. As a conclusion to the prologue, therefore, he adds a Latin text taken from the Decretum of Gratian, "the last canon of the eighty-ninth distinction." He does not suspect—or at least he shows no sign of suspecting—that at the time he is writing this text is more than a thousand years old. It is the preamble to a letter sent by Pope Gregory the Great to the bishops of Chilperic's kingdom in August of 595, urging them to recognize the primacy of the bishop of Arles in questions of ecclesiastical discipline.[1]

> Providence has established various degrees [*gradus*] and distinct orders [*ordines*] so that, if the lesser [*minores*] show deference [*reverentia*] to the

greater [*potiores*], and if the greater bestow love [*dilectio*] on the lesser, then true concord [*concordia*] and conjunction [*contextio*: the word evokes a fabric or weave in a very concrete way] will arise out of diversity. Indeed, the community [*universitas*] could not subsist at all if the total order [*magnus ordo*] of disparity [*differentia*] did not preserve it. That creation cannot be governed in equality is taught us by the example of the heavenly hosts; there are angels and there are archangels, which are clearly not equals, differing from one another in power [*potestas*] and order [*ordo*].

Everything is here. Not, of course, an explanation of trifunctionality, but at least its justification. Because heaven and earth are related by homology, the structures of human society necessarily reflect those of a more perfect society; in an imperfect way, they reproduce the hierarchies, the inequalities, which establish order in the society of angels.

It is quite natural to introduce an essay on the trifunctional model with a citation from the *Traité des ordres*. More surprising in such a context is the following statement: there are only "three courses open to young men, the priest's, the peasant's, and the soldier's. . . . The religious estate, because it incorporates, at a higher and purer level, all the soldier's virtues. . . . Labor on the land, because by placing man in continuous contact with nature and its creator, it inculcates the virtues of endurance, patience, and perseverance and thus naturally fosters the heroism needed on the battlefield." Here we find the three "estates" (the word appears in the quotation), three functions (the same ones we have seen already: to serve God, preserve the state by arms, and extract food from the earth), arranged hierarchically in the same way. There is one additional detail: those to whom Loyseau refers as "some" and "others" are here defined as "men," by which "adult males" is clearly meant; women are not involved in this sort of classification. And there are two differences. Here we find no "orders" but rather "courses," paths, which are chosen, vocations of sorts—although they are clearly stages in an ascent, since the same individual can and should take first the third path, then the second, and finally the first, thus taking up each of the three missions in turn in the course of his life, in order to "raise" himself by degrees from earth to heaven, from "nature" to its "creator." These are thus successive stages of a progress toward perfection or "purification." We have a scale of virtues, in a discourse that is less political than it is moral; what is really being proposed is a kind of ascesis. These three "courses," moreover, are not the only ones. They are merely the good ones. Of the others this Manichaean disquisition says nothing. This is because it condemns them. An entire portion of social life is here cursed, spurned, reduced to nothing. What is being proclaimed is that only the priest, the soldier, and the peasant avoid going astray; only they answer God's call. In this way, a close agreement is established between Loyseau's statement and this much more recent one, which can be found in a work published in Paris in 1951: *Notre beau métier de soldat, suivi d'un essai de portrait moral du chef,* by a M. de Torquat.

A quite similar image of the perfect society is set forth in two statements that echo one another, two Latin sentences that may be translated as follows: (1) "Triple then is the house of God which is thought to be one: on Earth, some pray [*orant*], others fight [*pugnant*], still others work [*laborant*]; which three are joined together and may not be torn asunder; so that on the function [*officium*] of each the works [*opera*] of the others rest, each in turn assisting all." (2) "He showed that, since the beginning, mankind has been divided into three parts, among men of prayer [*oratoribus*], farmers [*agricultoribus*], and men of war [*pugnatoribus*]; he gives clear proof that each is the concern of both the others."

Three functions then, the same three, and similarly conjoined. Yet this time the pronouncement issues from the depths of the ages. Six hundred years before Loyseau, nine hundred and fifty before M. de Torquat, it was put forward in the third decade of the eleventh century by Adalbero, bishop of Laon, and Gerard, bishop of Cambrai.

In juxtaposing these citations, my point is to show that an image of the social order endured in France for a millennium. In erecting their mental image of a society one and triune like the divinity who had created and would ultimately judge it, wherein mutually exchanged services unified the diversity of human actions, the bishops of the year 1000 took for their foundation a triangular figure in no respect different from the one that provided symbolic underpinning for a theoretical justification of the subjection of the regimented populace to the absolute monarchy of Henry IV—a theory that the newly born human sciences wasted no time in challenging. Even today, in certain circles no doubt diminished in importance but not yet extinct, it is to this same triangular image that the yearning for a regenerated humanity clings, the yearning for a humanity that would at last be purged of the twin infections, white and red, that breed in the big city, a humanity that would have rid itself at the same time of both capitalism and the working class. Thirty or forty successive generations have imagined social perfection in the form of trifunctionality. This mental representation has withstood all the pressures of history. It is a structure.

A structure encased within another that is deeper and more ample, which envelops it—namely, that similarly trifunctional system whose place among the modes of thought of the Indo-European peoples has been elucidated by the admirable work of Georges Dumézil. In countless texts patiently collected everywhere from the Indus to Iceland and

Ireland, three functions are found: the first, in the name of heaven to lay down the rules, the law that institutes order; the second, brutally, violently, to enforce obedience; the third, finally, of fecundity, health, plenty, pleasure, to guide the "peaceful labors" discussed by Loyseau to achievement of their ends; between these three functions and this same Loyseau's three "orders," M. de Torquat's three "courses," and the priests, warriors, and peasants of the bishops of Cambrai and Laon, the relationship is clear. So clear that there is no reason to make a point of it, other than to clarify the outlines of the investigation whose results this book will set down.

At the confluence of thought and language, closely associated with the structures of a language (I reiterate: a language—the linguists were the first to notice the functional triangle in written expression, and it must be acknowledged that it is not easy to detect a similar ternarity in symbolic modes of expression not involving words), there exists a form, a manner of thinking, of speaking the world, a certain way of putting man's action on the world—which is indeed what Dumézil has in mind when he speaks of trifunctionality: three constellations of virtues with which gods and heroes are endowed. When a warrior chieftain, sovereign, or mistress has to be celebrated in panegyric rather than ritual, it is natural to reach for this classificatory implement, which is ready at hand. This is often the route by which the trifunctional model is transferred from heaven to earth, from imagination to experience: it is a way of organizing praise bestowed on an individual. Traces of its use in this manner abound in countless biographies, both real and fictitious. In contrast, this model is rarely applied in an explicit way to the body social. The "tripartite ideology" that Dumézil has always described as "an ideal and, at the same time, a means of analyzing, of interpreting the forces which are responsible for the course of the world and human life"[2] is the backbone of a value system; overt use is made of it in myth, epic, and flattery; but ordinarily it remains latent, unformulated; only rarely is it brought into the open in the shape of imperious statements as to the proper ideal of society, order, that is, power. But all the citations above support statements of precisely this kind. In them, trifunctionality is laid out as a framework for an ideal classification of the kinds of men. It serves as a justification of certain normative utterances, certain imperatives—whether calls to action in order to bring about a transformation or restoration of society, or reassuring homilies, justifications. I am thinking of a sort of trifunctionality that serves an ideology, a "polemical discursive formation through which a passion seeks to realize a value by exercising a power over society."[3] Precisely stated, the problem is this: Why, of all the simple, equally instrumental images, was that of the three functions chosen? "The human mind is constantly making choices among its latent riches. Why? How?" The question was raised by Dumézil himself.[4] As a historian, I will broaden it somewhat to include two further questions: Where? And when?

The first of these I shall evade by limiting the scope of the investigation to the region where the various statements cited above were made, namely, France, confining my attention more particularly to northern France, whose political, social, and cultural configuration remained for a long time quite distinct from that of the countries to the south of Poitou, Berry, and Burgundy. Indeed, as a matter of correct method, it seems to me that ideological systems must be studied within a homogeneous cultural and social formation, all the more so if the aim is to date the transformations occurring within such systems. Hence, I shall deliberately remain within the bounds of this area. It may appear tiny. Its peculiar advantages should be noted: it is a province with a particularly abundant literature, and in addition the place where the Frankish monarchy took root. Now, it happens that this form, this manner of classification, of self-classification, whose early history I have chosen to study, is first revealed to us by literature; it is closely associated, moreover, with the concept of sovereignty.

The properly historical problem, that of chronology, remains. Within the region thus circumscribed, I have tried to collect and date all traces of an ideology based on social trifunctionality. Written traces—the only material we have. Which leaves a good deal to be desired. Once we move away from the vicinity of the present, we find that a vast portion of what was written has been lost irremediably: what remains comes virtually exclusively under the head of writing for solemn occasions. Official documents. Never does the historian have anything other than remains to paw over, and such scarce debris as he does have comes virtually without exception from monuments that power has caused to be erected; not only does all life's spontaneity escape him, but also all that is of popular origin; only a few men manage to make themselves heard: those who controlled the apparatus of what Loyseau calls the state. As we are discussing chronology, it should therefore be borne in mind that such few dates as can (sometimes with great difficulty) be established indicate nothing other than the moment of emergence, the point in time at which a certain mental representation gains access to the highest levels of written expression. More than that, those emergences whose traces have fortuitously been preserved are not necessarily the oldest, as it behooves us not to forget. Clearly, the margin of uncertainty is quite large.

At least one fact appears certain, so that I may rely on it from the outset: no text in northern France prior to those containing the statements of Adalbero of Laon and Gerard of Cambrai makes mention of a trifunctional view of society. This is beyond doubt: much care has been devoted to the search, by Georges Dumézil himself, and after him by Jean Batany, Jacques Le Goff, Claude Carozzi, and others. In vain: the rich harvest of writings—theoretical writings—left by the Carolingian renaissance yielded nothing. The two Latin sentences I cited above seem to have burst upon silence. In any case, it is with them that the history of a trifunctional representation of society begins in this tiny part of the world. Yet if the date of the original utterance has been established, the chronology of the reception, acceptance, and diffusion of the model remain to be constructed. All that has been said about trifunctionality in medieval society is imprecise. Consider Marc Bloch, for instance: "a theory at that time very widely current represented the human community as being divided into three orders."[5] "At that time": when? During the "first feudal age," that is, according to the great medievalist, in the centuries prior to the mid-eleventh century? "Very widely current": what is meant by this? Consider Jacques Le Goff, who was the first to formulate the problem in appropriate terms: "around the year 1000, Western literature represented Christian society according to a new model which immediately enjoyed a considerable success."[6] What is meant by "around," "new," "immediately," "considerable"? Are we sure of all this? By carrying the investigation forward into the eleventh and twelfth centuries, pursuing it until the allusions to the three social functions, the three orders, proliferate, until it becomes certain that the "theory" is "quite widespread," that the "model" enjoyed "a considerable success," I would like to dispel the ambiguity as far as possible.

I would particularly like to answer Dumézil's question: Why, how was this choice among latent structures made? For this I think it necessary to be precise about the location of the research. The trifunctional figure, as I have said, is a form. Traces of it may be found in quite a few documents. I am not bent on flushing out every one of them. This book's central character, the trifunctional figure, will concern us only where it functions as a major cog in an ideological system. Which it does in Loyseau's dissertation. Thus, if we are to grasp the why and the how, it will be essential to avoid isolating the formulations of the trifunctional theme from their context—as has nearly always been done. They should rather be left in their proper place within the whole in which they are articulated. What matters is to reconstruct the global character of that whole, to investigate the circumstances surrounding the construction of the ideological system in which trifunctionality is embedded, and to ask what problems and contradictions had to be faced before it could be brought forward, promulgated, flaunted as a banner. For if it is correct to contest the notion that the trifunctional schema was "constructed,"[7] if, as a latent structure, it stands outside history, it is nevertheless beyond doubt that the systems incorporating it as a supporting member belong, for their part, to history. They form and are deformed. By closely observing their genesis and dismemberment we have some chance of finding out why and how the trifunctional schema was chosen at a certain time and place.

Having thus specified the object of the research, we come to another category of problems. The model of three social functions—this postulate, this axiomatic truth, whose existence is never proved, never evoked but in relation to a cosmology, a theology, and certainly a morality, and on which one of those "discursive polemical formations" known as ideologies is founded, thereby providing a power with a simple, ideal, abstract image of the social organization—how is this model connected with the concrete relationships within society? Ideology, we are well aware, is not a reflection of the likelihood of success, the disparity between the imaginary representation and the "realities" of life should not be too great. This being the case, and supposing that the ideological discourse does not go unnoticed, new attitudes may then crystallize, changing the way men look upon the society to which they belong. To observe the system in which the model of the three "orders" is embodied as it comes to light in France, to attempt to follow its course through success and misfortune from 1025 to 1225, is to confront one of the central questions now facing the sciences of man: the question of the relationship between the material and the mental in the evolution of societies.

What is more, to confront that question in circumstances that are not hopelessly unfavorable. True, as has already been mentioned, to take so remote a period for our "terrain" is to condemn ourselves to working with mere shreds of information, and to paying heed only to intellectuals, cut off from the rest of society even more than intellectuals nowadays by the peculiarities of their vocabulary and their mode of thought. But at least the documentary resources are relatively limited. It is not impossible to take them all in with a single glance. More, we are liberated by the fact that our interest is focused on so far distant a past: feudalism's contradictions no longer concern us sufficiently that we are loath to demystify the ideology that did its best to reduce or veil them.

The difficulty lies elsewhere. How are we to compare the imaginary and the concrete? How are we to sever the "objective" study of human behavior from investigation of the symbolic systems that dictated the conduct in question and justified it in men's eyes? [8] Is it within the power of the historian to strip away entirely the ideal garb in which the societies of the past cloaked themselves? Can he see them other than as they dreamed of, as they spoke of, themselves? As medievalists, let us ask ourselves: If to us "feudal society" seems composed of three orders, is it not true that the primary reason for this is that the two sentences cited above still obsess us as they once obsessed our mentors? Are we not ourselves slaves to that ideology I am presumptuous enough to want to demystify? It was in any case a force powerful enough to have led us (I say us because I am one of the guilty) into certain blunders, such as dating knighthood's constitution as an "order" a century and a half too early. If for no other reason than this, for its role in the development of historical research, the trifunctional model deserves to be examined very closely, and held up for comparison with all that we are capable of seeing in the world that gradually adopted it for its own.

The time has now come to examine the words that for the first time in the "sources" stemming from northern France gave clear voice to this model.

TRANSLATED BY ARTHUR GOLDHAMMER

NOTES

[1] *Ep.* 54, *Patrologia latinae*, vol. 77, pp. 785–87.

[2] Georges Dumézil, *Mythe et épopées*, 3 vols. (Paris, 1968–73), vol. 1, p. 15.

[3] G. Baechler, *Qu'est-ce que l'idéologie?* (Paris, 1976).

[4] Georges Dumézil, *Les Dieux souverains des Indo-Européens* (Paris, 1977), p. 210.

[5] Marc Bloch, *La Société féodale* (2nd ed., Paris, 1966), p. 406.

[6] Jacques Le Goff, *La Civilisation de l'occident médiéval* (Paris, 1964), p. 319.

[7] D. Dubuisson, "L'Irlande et la théorie médiévale des trois ordres," *Revue de l'histoire des religions* 190 (1975), p. 61, n. 3, is justified, in correcting me, to assert that the theory of the three orders was not constructed, but merely, as he puts it, "brought up to date."

[8] W. H. Sewell, "Etats, Corps et Ordres: Some Notes on the Social Vocabulary of the French Old Regime," *Sozialgeschichte Heute (Festschrift für Hans Rosenberg zum 70. Geburtstag)* (Göttingen, 1974), pp. 49–68.

MAURICE AGULHON

The Circle in Bourgeois France

1977

*Maurice Agulhon is the author of several very important works deal-
ing for the most part with nineteenth-century social history. Born in
1926, he was, like many other historians of his generation, a disciple
of Labrousse, but he soon moved from the study of social structures
to that of social forms, or distinctive ways of "being together." In his
first book,* Pénitents et francs-maçons dans l'ancienne Provence
*(1968), he used the notion of "sociability" to account for the long-
term persistence of distinctive forms of social aggregation. The same
theme also figures in* La République au village, *1970 (*The Republic in the Village: The People of the Var from the French Revolution to the Second Republic*) and* Le Cercle dans la France
bourgeoise, *from which the following excerpt is taken. With this
flexible and useful notion, Agulhon, a discreet nonconformist, did
much to infuse new energy into a whole area of contemporary French
political history by opening it up to a sociological and anthropological
approach, apparent in all his work, in particular in his important
studies of republican iconography,* Marianne au combat *(1979) and*
Marianne au pouvoir *(1984). This work has allowed for the rethinking of democratic republican culture.*

S ociability or "sociability"? In other words, are we dealing with an
accepted historical category or with the isolated idea of one historian (or of a small group of historians)? The author of these lines
bears his share of responsibility for this small problem. In 1966, I used
the phrase *Southern Sociability* as the title of a book whose subtitle specified its content as follows: *Confraternities and Associations in Eastern Provence in the Eighteenth Century.*[1] In this work, I took the view that the
density and vitality of organized social groups, whether bourgeois or

Maurice Agulhon, *Le Cercle dans la France bourgeoise, 1810–1848: Étude d'une mutation de sociabilité* (Paris: A. Colin, 1977), excerpted from the preface.

popular, secular or religious, could serve as excellent indicators of a population's general aptitude for intense public relations, or sociability. What is more, an acknowledged (or, more precisely, suspected, inferred, or assumed) aptitude for such intensity of social life was supposed to be characteristic of a regional temperament, namely, that of the south of France. Two years later, however, I beat a hasty retreat. When the book came out in a new edition with a Paris publisher, I chose a new title, more representative of its concrete content, *Penitents and Freemasons in Old Provence,* relegating sociability to the subtitle, *An Essay on Southern Sociability.*[2]

Nevertheless, despite this timid backtracking, sociability "took," as one says of a fashion, graft, or sauce. As early as 1967, Emmanuel Le Roy Ladurie welcomed the word without quotation marks into his *Histoire du Languedoc.*[3] Since then, many others have followed his lead, for historical literature is no more exempt than other literatures from the need to innovate, or to appear to be innovating, by changing its vocabulary. Has our thinking on the subject been clarified, however? Ten years later, I am glad to avail myself of this opportunity to assess where things stand.

Sociability, a Historical Category

At first glance, the historians' use of the word "sociability" seems unusual, by which I mean that it appears to be somewhat at odds with the ordinary meaning of the word, to extend beyond the dictionary definitions.[4] Indeed, the dictionaries give two generally accepted definitions. In its first, very general sense, the word refers to an aptitude of the human species for living in society, an aptitude that animal species rarely possess, and then only in a rudimentary, nonevolving fashion (bees, elephants, and so on). Sociability is one of the principal ways in which man differs from beast. The other definition concerns an individual's aptitude for getting on well with others. In this sense, a sociable person is one who is not timid, shy, "antisocial," or misanthropic. Sociability is a character trait, which is currently taken to be a virtue. Clearly, however, the first definition is too broad for historians, the second too narrow. The objects in which history is interested fall somewhere between the two, beyond the individual but short of the species as a whole.

Despite the dictionaries, however, the application of the word *sociabilité* to more or less definite groups of human beings is almost as old as the word itself. Let us look at the matter a little more closely. Nothing is known, apparently, about the use of the word prior to the eighteenth century.[5] It appears in a late-eighteenth-century edition of the *Dictionnaire de l'académie française,* which of course customarily lags well behind usage. According to lexicographers,[6] the first writer to establish sociability as a philosophical category is allegedly the Genevan naturalist and metaphysician Charles Bonnet.[7]

For this Protestant scholar, who sought to reconcile rationalist philosophy with Christian revelation, "man is a sociable being; several of his principal faculties have the State of Society as their direct object." Not only does science prove this (as exemplified by the use of speech as a means of communication), but the teachings of Christ confirm and accentuate it by making love of one's neighbor their primary precept: "Is there a purer, nobler, more active or fruitful Principle of Sociability than this lofty Benevolence, which into the Doctrine of [God's] Emissary brings the little used but eminently expressive name of charity?"

The same semantic connection can also be found somewhat later in a purely rationalist philosophical context. When the historian of law Eugène Lerminier gave a course at the Collège de France in 1832 entitled "On the Influence of Eighteenth-Century Philosophy on the Legislation and Sociability of the Nineteenth-Century,"[8] it is clear that for him sociability was nothing other than civilization, understood in the singular, in the liberal and humanitarian manner, that is, as the reality of man's collective destiny through a policy of progress: our goal, he says, is "to contribute to the work of the progressive sociability of the human race." Later he adds: "Politics raises itself to the level of philosophy. One understands the immense solidarity of modern sociability: it has been made to embrace all the elements and all the nations of humanity. . . . Politics [is] the science and application of the properties of human sociability. . . ."

In both Bonnet's Christian and Lerminier's secularized version, then, sociability is humanity itself, but a humanity whose essential social virtue is to develop itself and fulfill its destiny over time. We are still within the first definition of sociability (that applying to the human species), but note the connection with the idea of progress, which gives the term an interesting left-wing connotation.[9]

In a more intuitive fashion, however, the application of the term to portions of humanity, that is, its extension to collective psychology, had already begun in the seventeenth century. Jean D'Alembert, speaking of the French, characterized them as a "nation whose sociability is its principal characteristic."[10] A half century later, Mme. de Genlis mentioned "the natural temperance of the French, [which] contributes greatly to the sociability that distinguishes them."[11] There is a natural extension from this social psychological sense to the historian's sense of the term; and for a word to be used by Jules Michelet was indeed to be welcomed into history with open arms. I shall cite only two occurrences of the term in Michelet by way of example. One is in the celebrated passage in which the change from the seventeenth to the eighteenth century is symbolized by the substitution of coffee for wine, of the café for the cabaret, and of wit for crudeness: "The vast wave of conversation that gave the age its character, and especially that excessive sociability which so quickly created bonds and brought strangers and passersby together in cafés to gossip. . . ."[12] The other citation relates to the period after Thermidor, which saw an outburst of freedom and joy that found its expression in public dances since there were as yet no new salons or *sociétés*. The success of these dances was astonishing: "Never was the amiable sociability of Paris more apparent."[13]

As an acknowledged feature of collective psychology, sociability is thus a part of human history. In other words, it is appreciated differently in different times and places. In the examples cited, we have instances of both geographic variability (we have the sociability of the French or the Parisians) and chronological variability (the sociability associated with the Enlightenment or with the progress of a more refined civilization or even with democracy). More than one observer has noted that many novel (or allegedly novel) features of today's history largely stem from Michelet. More precisely, today's historians have sought to translate into relatively precise, rational terms what the nineteenth-century's master historian glimpsed in intuitive flashes (*éclairs,* he would have said). It should come as no surprise, then, that historians today are looking in various ways at social psychology, of which sociability is one aspect.[14] However, we must now pause for a closer look at different possible avenues of research, some of which have already been amply explored, while others deserve to be. The geography of temperaments and the history of *mentalités* belong to the first group, while the history of associations (as a possible criterion of sociability) belongs to the second.

SOCIABILITY AND THE HISTORY OF *MENTALITES*

Sociability, Michelet suggested, exists in time. The café is a historical personage, and so is the salon or club. So why can't we say the same thing about the aptitude for creating such institutions or the taste for enjoying them? Yet long after Michelet, the study of this sort of thing remained anecdotal, material fit only for popular histories of everyday life. The nobler genres—academic history and high literary history—had enough to do dealing with religion, politics, economics, and revolutions. Today, though, it is widely felt that *everything* that once was, is worthy of interest, and that it is antiscientific to draw a distinction between noble subjects and supposedly idle diversions. It is also widely believed that everything evolves, even those qualities assumed to be closely related to man's condition and therefore permanent. If family feeling and forms of piety, indeed even love and death, have a history and are a part of History, then why not sociability? If, as I indicated earlier, the word has found easy acceptance in recent historical literature, it is because—and to the extent that—our academic historiography has been staking its claims to everyday life, folklore and festivals, popular culture and rebellion as parts of its territory. For some authors, "sociability" has become a convenient catchall embracing the elementary forms of collective life, which are diverse and ubiquitous. In other words, they have treated it as a new word for denoting old realities—what used to be classified as "everyday life," "civilization," or "manners."

To be fair, though, some scholars have gone further and discovered new things. For example, Yves Castan's innovative study of the "criterion of *honnêteté*" in eighteenth-century Languedoc is admirable for its precision and subtlety. To put a complex case in a pithy way, Castan succeeds because he is able to move from the analysis of objective behavior to that of psychological processes. His book should remain a model. However, to go as deeply into the matter as Castan was able to do, one has to delve into an enormous mass of documents limited to a rather brief time span (in this case less than a century). For the same reason, other scholars, including myself, have had to limit their horizons to a single province or *département*. In the history of *mentalités* and/or of mass social phenomena, chronological comparison is therefore just as desirable as geographical comparison but just as seldom done (or at least seldom done *well*, that is, using comparable data).

If sociability, southern or otherwise, is a part of history, it must evolve. Common sense tells us that it does. Don't our more pessimistic contemporaries moan about the way television has confined people in their homes and killed the good old bistros of the past? If the bistros have declined, though, they must have had their heyday—they must have been born at some point in time and enjoyed a period of youthful vigor as well. The history of sociability is also the history of daily life as it impinges on collective psychology. In other words, the subject's scope and variety are daunting, and there is a danger of amassing countless observations that are doomed to remain unilluminating because they cannot be compared with anything else. It would no doubt be better and more useful to isolate *specific* forms and institutions of sociability for concrete study, even if such a project seems at first sight restrictive and incomplete. The results could well turn out to be less modest than one had feared at the outset. Which brings us, as the reader will have anticipated, to the history of associations, a project that began for me as an empirical test and developed into a carefully thought-out research program.

Sociability and Associations

No one can possibly object to the idea that the vitality of associations is a good indicator of the general sociability of a human collectivity. The greater the number and diversity of interpersonal relations, the greater the variety of groups involved: family, parish, commune, coworkers, and people of similar age constitute a minimal social environment, and these may or may not be supplemented by political parties, athletic clubs, charitable organizations, or what have you. Also, the more active an association is, the more it needs a strong internal organization: a group of young men who play soccer on a vacant lot don't need a team president, treasurer, or secretary, but if they want to join a league and play in a regular stadium with regulation equipment, they may need to transform their informal group into a formal club with an office and a written set of rules. A normal course of evolution, then, will involve the emergence of a *voluntary* association (a party or club, say, in contrast to a family, workshop, or state), at first organized informally (like the young soccer players on their vacant lot) and later *formally* (like the athletic club). If one is willing to admit that sociability defined in this way is an important aspect of the history of civilization in what is commonly called the "modern period" (late eighteenth century to the present), and that the intensity, influence, and character of associative life is feature of culture and social psychology that can be compared from region to region, one may well ask why it has not been studied more.

There are two possible answers, one having to do with our (that is, French) historiography, the other with our sociology. As for historiography, the crucial point has already been made. The study of civilization has suffered from the traditional compartmentalization that has marked our discipline until recently: confraternities are a subject for religious history, parties for political history, learned societies for the "history of ideas," and circles, cafés, and clubs for *la petite histoire,* or anecdotal history. By contrast, today's historiography aspires to total history, which is the only way we can hope to achieve a true history of that important social fact, associational life.

Yet is that the only reason? Perhaps historians needed to pay attention to sociology, and what is more, to a sociology adequate to the purpose.

Classical Sociology and Formalist Sociology

If everything in the past is historical, any method or discipline can become historical if applied to the past. Political history may encompass a historical political science, the history of international relations may include a historical "polemology," the history of material life a historical ethnology, and so on. In our case, of course, we are interested in historical sociology, hence in sociology itself. Now, the French sociologists who trained or, more commonly, inspired and influenced French historians paid little attention to sociability, with the possible exception of Eugène Fournière, a neglected theoretician of reform socialism who, around the turn of the century, described what he regarded as both a necessary and desirable evolution of contemporary society in terms of three developments: toward democracy (in the political sphere), socialism (in the economic sphere), and association, which he also called "sociability" or "sociality" (in what we might call the cultural sphere). Armand Cuvillier barely used the term except in the historical part of his *Manuel de sociologie,* in which he discussed the theories of other scholars with whom he did not agree. At times, it even seems that he looked upon the idea with suspicion, as if tainted by an excess of abstraction. "Sociology," he wrote, "is not primarily, and from an abstract or atemporal point of view, a theory of the relations or forms of sociability. Such a theory belongs more to the realm of philosophical construction than to sociology proper, for there is no sociology without history. Sociology is the science of real, concrete human groups, that is, groups rooted in history."[15]

To be sure, associations were part of this concrete reality, but *association* in the singular was not something that Cuvillier thought it important to study. He did encounter it, however, and recognized its essence—namely, that the creation of associations is a process of social complexification that allows individuals to exist not as members of a single natural group but at the intersection of various social circles, thus allowing them a certain individuality and independence.[16] Elsewhere, moreover, he notes that free associations (in general) are normally counterweights to the state and help to guarantee the freedom of individual citizens.

One can also learn from Georges Gurvitch, who has a more particular claim on the notion of sociability.[17] Admittedly, Gurvitch uses this notion chiefly in a microsociological sense (as pertaining to relations between an individual and others), a sense that corresponds to the second dictionary definition given above (in psychological terms, such as whether a person is or is not timid, and so on), while possible macrosociological applications remain more theoretical. However, we come now to the point on which Gurvitch has something to teach us. Macrosociology, he says, is the study of "global societies" and "particular groups." Now, French sociology, under the combined influence of Karl Marx and Emile Durkheim, has always been mainly interested in classes, while particular groups have been of interest primarily to sociologists in other countries, especially the United States.[18]

Indeed, such terms as "voluntary association" and "formal" (or "informal") organization are far more common in the American sociological literature (as well as the German, apparently, although my knowledge of this is superficial and secondhand) than in the French.[19] Why? Is it because the formalism that Cuvillier deemed overly philosophical provided the Americans and Germans with a more receptive theoretical framework? Or because they lived in countries in which voluntary associations were in fact more prevalent, of longer standing, and apt to attract greater interest than in France? No doubt both answers are correct. The second is empirically accurate, indeed a commonplace.[20] Nevertheless, the first is also important. Basic conceptual distinctions such as that of Ferdinand Tönnies (between *Gemeinschaft* and *Gesellschaft*)[21] or Robert MacIver (between community and association)[22] are particularly useful for directing attention to the study of association, or, if you will, organized sociability. In fact, it was Max Weber[23] who most explicitly defined sociology's task as the study of "all structures commonly called social, that is, everything that falls between organized and recognized authorities such as the state, the village, and the established church, on the one hand, and the natural community and the family, on the other. Essentially, this means the sociology of associations in the broadest sense of the term: from the bowling club to the political party to religious groups, from the artistic circle to the literary sect." "From the bowling club to the political party": what a lovely (dare I say "southern"?) agenda, and what august sponsorship for a research program that no one will henceforth presume to dismiss as idle.

If I am correct in thinking that in Germany, Great Britain, and the United States social theory interacted with the social reality from which sociology drew its topics, similar reasoning may also apply to France: to speak plainly, it may be that the deficiencies of French historical research in this area are also deficiencies of French sociology, and the blame must be shared.[24]

In all areas of sociology, including the sociology of associations, sociologists normally work with two heterogeneous types of data: data from the present (which sociologists themselves collect) and data from the past (for which they depend on the work of historians). The ideal form of collaboration between the two disciplines is a dialectic of reciprocal borrowings. The sociologist provides the historian with sociological ideas that shed light on his research and enable him to provide the sociologist with new material; the sociologist then incorporates that material into his own thinking and provides more refined concepts, and so on. This leads us to a final remark: historians must be cautious in borrowing from sociologists. We borrow the notion of social class, for example, but we would never think of borrowing the occupational classification system used today by the French government's statistical agency, for a study of, say, nineteenth-century society, for which the modern system would be laughably inappropriate.

With respect to the subject that occupies us here, just because we borrow a *general* problematic of sociability, we need not borrow a *current* classification of associations. Indeed, it is fairly common today to define and classify associations in terms of their social function, as if it were self-evident that an association has only one function. In the course of my work, however, I formed the impression, or least the suspicion, that this axiom was false, and that at certain times in France in the eighteenth and nineteenth centuries many associations served several functions at once, hence that it might be useful to consider other types of classification better suited to the period under study—classifications that were, in a word, more "historical," though not for that reason any less sociological.

TRANSLATED BY ARTHUR GOLDHAMMER

NOTES

[1] Maurice Agulhon, *La Sociabilité méridionale: Confrères et associations en Provence orientale dans le deuxième moitié du XVIIIe siècle* (Aix-en-Provence: Pensée Universitaire, 1966).

[2] Maurice Agulhon, *Pénitents et francs-maçons de l'ancienne Provence: Essai sur la sociabilité méridionale* (rev. and expanded ed., Paris: Fayard, 1968).

[3] Emmanuel Le Roy Ladurie, "Difficulté d'être et douceur de vivre," in Philippe Wolff, ed., *Histoire du Languedoc* (Toulouse: Privat, 1967), p. 343.

[4] P. Larousse, *Grand Dictionnaire du XIXe siècle,* 17 vols. (Paris, 1866–76); Adolphe Hatzfeld, Arsene Darmesteter, and Antoine Thomas, *Dictionnaire général de la langue française,* 2 vols. (Paris: Delagrave, 1890–93).

[5] The translation follows the French text. The *Oxford English Dictionary*, however, cites an attestation from 1475 as well as definitions corresponding to the middle range of uses to which the author alludes.—TRANS.

[6] Emile Littré, *Dictionnaire de la langue française,* 4 vols. (Paris: Hachrette, 1863–72); Hatzfeld et al., *Dictionnaire générale.*

[7] Charles Bonnet, *La Palengénésie philosophique ou idées sur l'état passé et sur l'état futur des êtres vivants,* 2 vols. (Geneva, 1770), vol. 2, pp. 341–42.

[8] E. Lerminier, *De l'Influence de la philosophie du XVIIIe siècle sur la législation et la sociabilité du XIXe* (Paris: Prevost–Crotius et Didier, 1833), preface, pp. 14, 19, 27.

[9] From another text of Lerminier's, which I have not been able to locate, Pierre Larousse quoted this passage in his *Dictionnaire*: "The cause of democracy is none other than the cause of sociability itself."

[10] Jean d'Alembert, *Eloges*, preface (cited by Hatzfeld et al., *Dictionnaire général*).

[11] Mme. de Genlis, *Les Mères rivales* (cited by Littré, *Dictionnaire*).

[12] Jules Michelet, *Histoire de France*, XIV, p. 164.

[13] Jules Michelet, Histoire du XIXe siècle, I, p. 130.

[14] For an example of the use of this word by the most philosophical of French historians today, consider this text of Pierre Chaunu's: "The nuclear family offers less protection than the class or lineage. Christendom witnessed an explosion of sociabil-

ity. . . . Sociability is concentrated in the matrimonial nucleus, the atomic couple."
P. Chaunu, "Le Tournant du monde plein," *Revue d'histoire économique et sociale*(1975), p. 16.

[15] The key work is of course that of Philippe Ariès: *Histoire des populations françaises et de leurs attitudes devant la vie, depuis le XVIIIe siècle* (rev. ed., Paris: Seuil, 1971); *L'Enfant et la vie familiale sous l'Ancien Regime* (rev. ed., Paris: Seuil, 1975); and *Essais sur l'histoire de la mort en occident du moyen âge à nous jours* (Paris: Seuil, 1975).

[16] Y. Castan, *Honnêteté et relations sociales en Languedoc au XVIIIe siècle* (Paris: Plon, 1974).

[17] Sociability is just as ambiguous a term in social psychology as in individual psychology.

[18] E. Fournière, *L'Individu, l'association, et l'État* (Paris: Alcan, 1907).

[19] Armand Cuvillier, *Manuel de sociologie* (Paris: P.U.F., 1968).

[20] Ibid., p. 190.

[21] Ibid., p. 347.

[22] Ibid., p. 662.

[23] Georges Gurvitch, *La Vocation actuelle de la sociologie,* 2 vols. (rev. ed., Paris: P.U.F., 1957–1963), and *Traité de sociologie,* 2 vols. (Paris: P.U.F., 1958).

[24] Gurvitch, *Traité de sociologie,* vol. 1, pp. 185ff.

MONA OZOUF

The Festival in the French Revolution

1974

Yet another new object—festivals. Several things combined to make
this a popular theme with historians in the 1970s: the festive sensi-
bility of 1968, the new interest in collective rituals and anthropologi-
cal approaches, and a concern with exploring phenomena of socia-
bility. The festival as celebration, outlet, and revolt: these various
approaches bestowed new importance on a range of phenomena long
regarded as marginal or picturesque.

Mona Ozouf was a pioneer in this avenue of research, and her
1976 book, La Fête révolutionnaire, 1789–1799 *(Festivals and the*
French Revolution*), remains a model unsurpassed to this day. She*
first outlined the book's thesis in an article published in Faire de
l'histoire, *which we excerpt here. Trained as a philosopher before*
becoming a historian and marked by the influence of Alphonse Du-
pront (see pp. 173), she is best known for her work on the French
Revolution. Thus, she brings to the study of festival knowledge not
only of the aspects already mentioned but also of another essential
dimension, that of the political.

No performance today is complete without festival, and every vision of the future includes some kind of celebration. The festival has invaded the vocabulary of the political essay, theater
criticism, and literary commentary. This sometimes reflects a nostalgic
desire to restore the past: the society that speaks of festivals is one in
which rejoicing is a private affair, and the collective memory that folklore is supposed to preserve and celebrate is a false one. The intention
may also be a prophetic one: since May 1968, so often interpreted as an

From "The Festival in the French Revolution," in Jacques Le Goff and Pierre
Nora, eds., *Constructing the Past: Essays in Historical Methodology* (Cambridge, Eng.:
Cambridge University Press, and Paris: Editions de la Maison des Sciences de
L'Homme, 1985), pp. 181–97. First published in *Faire de l'histoire* (Paris: Gallimard,
1974).

act of revenge on the festive poverty of modern society, we have been looking forward to some future festival. We are promised it by political and theological thought alike: the latter is currently engaged in rehabilitating festive gratuity as against the values of patience and tension implicit in the work ethic,[1] while political thought expects the revolution to merge with the eternal present of the festival, and deliver happiness, not at some distant future date, but now.[2]

History was for a long time more concerned with the work and effort of men than with those activities which are variously called "entertainment" or distraction. The festival and feast have now become legitimate objects of historical interest,[3] and this is due to the dual influence of folklore and ethnology. They have taught the historian to look at the ways in which human existence is given a structure by ritualization, even if this is anonymous and lacking in explicit organization and conscious cohesion. Psychoanalysis, at the same time, has taught the historian to attach importance to the apparently meaningless.

The annexation of this new area by historiography is not, however, without its problems. First of all, it is far from certain that the festival itself will accept this annexation without putting up a silent resistance, partly because of the immense problems still involved in cultural history, but also because of the festival's particular relationship with time. The present of the festival opens out onto the past and the future, and thus appears to speak a familiar language to the historian. Every festival involves reminiscence:[4] often an anniversary, it seeks to reenact the past, and it is tempting for the historian to accept its testimony. At the same time, the festival heralds the future, is a kind of approximation of it; it simulates a future that the historian is fortunate enough to be able to compare with what will really happen.

But two dangers may be involved here. The first temptation is to see the repetition that is indeed an element of the festival as a self-conscious repetition, the past that is celebrated being held at arm's length and analyzed. Such scholarly precision is not the festival's concern, and the Freudian analysis of repetition is more pertinent: an irrational attempt to deal with a traumatic event without situating or dating it, without wresting it from the unbearable present and controlling it. Repetition is the ceremonial resort of someone who cannot become the historian of his/her own life, the futile circlings of a mind that is a slave to reality. The repetitive festival, like neurosis, is not so much a pedagogy of time[5] as a strategy of archaism in the face of fear. This attachment to the past is clearly an object of great interest to the historian, but it is clear that the history of the festival will be the history of a phenomenon that is itself blind to history.

The second temptation is the opposite of the first, but no less dangerous: it involves taking at face value the rehearsal of the future which parallels the repetition of the past. First, the beginning that the festival enacts is often an illusory one, a repeated exemplary gesture meant to articulate hope; and, second, rather than enacting an indeterminate future that is open to multiple possibilities and for that very reason a source of fear, the festival is a kind of conjuring trick quite incompatible with notions of prediction and work, enacting in the immediate present a scene of immortality and indestructibility. How, then, can its prophecies be taken as a real anticipation of the future? They belong to the realm of the imagination, and are a projection of desire rather than an anticipation of reality. Here again, the historian is disarmed: we cannot expect the festival to shed light on the future it envisages, since the time it heralds is not historical time.

But is this true of all festivals? Surely, some at least enjoy some connection with history, reflecting the contingent reality of the exceptional circumstances from which they sprang? This is certainly one of the reasons for the attention that has been paid to the festivals of the French Revolution. We can date the first wave of such monographs and general studies very precisely: the period in the Third Republic leading up to the separation of church and state in 1905.[6] Historians at this time take up the theme of the replacement of religious enthusiasm by civic festivals, and do so in terms very similar to those used by the men of the Revolution, and this must be seen as a response to the hidden anxieties caused by the separation of church and state. Today, a second wave of work on the Revolutionary festivals is underway, led by North American historians who are interested in the relationship between politics and propaganda.[7] Three reasons justify continued interest in the subject, in my view. First, the coherent and systematic nature of the Revolutionary festival, which develops over a period of scarcely ten years. Second, the mass of archival material that exists, breaking the silence that usually surrounds festivals and feasts and is part of the timeless dimension of folklore.[8] Third, the Revolutionary festival's place in the history of an extraordinary period: such a rich and complex set of rituals, appearing at a time when another set enters into eclipse, must bear traces of the exceptional circumstances that are both the cause and the object of the festival's celebration.

But the Revolutionary festival must be studied for the right reasons. It is incorrect, for instance, to start from the principle (which has been given new life by the events of 1968) that a relation of similarity or even identity exists between the festival and revolution. It is not sufficient to justify this view by pointing to the obvious need that revolutions have felt for festivals, the urgency with which they have instituted them, or even the well-documented plethora of festivals in revolutionary situations—the extraordinary festive explosion following the October Revolution, for instance. None of this proves that the two are consubstantial. The vision of a festival expanded by revolutionary liberation to encompass the whole of life is based not on observed fact, but on the hope, or illusion, of a nonrepressive society in which the distinction between festival and everyday life ceases to exist.

The historian must also be cautious about the received notion that revolution sharpens and strengthens historical consciousness. The corollary of this view is an expectation that the misoneism which is the mark of the festival in ordinary times—its reluctance to alter its ritual framework—will fall away in revolutionary times. But the time that is celebrated in festivals is one that can be regenerated, and the virtue of revolutionary ferment is that it gives added conviction to this process of renovation. The joy that festivals promote—whether they celebrate the revolutions of the earth or the revolutions of history—is the expression of time's ability to bring forth the new from the death of the old. We should ask ourselves whether this dimension of time made new in which the festival operates—which explains, for instance, the magical qualities of the Festival of the Federation for contemporaries who were present and historians who have written about it [9]—is the same as historical time. Is the revolutionary festival a means of affirming history, or an escape route from it?

NOTES

[1] On this theme, see Harvey Cox, *La Fête des fous*, a theological essay on the notions of festival and fantasy (Paris: Seuil, 1971); and Jürgen Moltmann, *Die ersten Freigelassenen der Schöpfung: Versuche über die Freude an der Freiheit und das Wohlgefallen am Spiel* (Munich: Kaiser Verlag, 1971).

[2] See various works taking as their starting point the lyricism of May 1968: Jean-Marie Domenach, "Idéologie du mouvement," *Esprit* 8–9 (Aug.–Sept. 1968); B. Charbonneau, "L'Emeute et le plan," *La Table ronde* 251–52 (Dec. 1968–Jan. 1969); R. Pascal, "La Fête de mai," *France-Forum* (Oct.–Nov. 1968).

[3] This is shown in a wide range of collective and individual works, too numerous to be listed here. I will mention *Les Fêtes de la renaissance*, ed. and introduction by Jean Jacquot, 2 vols. (Paris: CNRS, 1956, 1960); R. Alewyn and Karl Sälzle, *L'Univers du baroque* (Geneva, 1964); and James E. Oliver, *Seasonal Feasts and Festivals* (London, 1961).

[4] One thinks of the totemic meal, according to Freud a reenactment of the original criminal scene in which the sons devour the father. In this sense, humanity's first festival is already the ramblings of old age. To celebrate is, in fact, always to "chew over," independently of the original meaning that Freud gives the term in this fantasy.

[5] This is Cox's theme in *La Fête des fous*. According to him, the festival is a means of learning about certain temporal dimensions that man habitually fears or misunderstands. He learns to domesticate the past through repetition, and the future by the expression of his hopes. Paradoxically, the break in ordinary time which the festival represents allows him to become attuned to the continuity of time. Cox gives the cu-

rious name "juxtaposition" to this therapeutic aspect of festivals. Yet is our awareness of historical time really increased through the festival? Cox is aware of the difficulty and does not disguise the fact that the festival represents a brief holiday from an everyday reality that is the stuff of history.

[6] Alphonse Aulard's *Le Culte de la raison et de l'Etre suprême* appeared in 1892. Albert Mathiez's *Les Origines des cultes révolutionnaires* in 1904. Tiersot's *Les Fêtes et les chants de la Révolution française* in 1908. A host of local studies belong to the same years.

[7] See, for instance, Stanley J. Idzerda, "Iconoclasm During the French Revolution," *American Historical Review* 60 (Oct. 1954); D. L. Dowd, "Art as National Propaganda in the French Revolution," *Public Opinion Quarterly* (Autumn 1951); Dowd, "Jacobinism and the Fine Arts," *Art Quarterly* 16.3 (1953); Dowd, *Pageant-Master of the Republic: Jacques-Louis David and the French Revolution* (Lincoln, Neb., 1948); J. A. Leith, *The Idea of Art as Propaganda in France, 1750–1790* (Toronto: Toronto University Press, 1965); J. Lindsay, "Art and Revolution," *Art and Artists* (Aug. 1969).

[8] There are immediate sources for analyzing the intentions of the organizers; their justifications are too willingly offered and too self-conscious to be taken at face value. Nevertheless, these sources may be balanced against evidence revealing the diffusion and the reception of their plans, and the degree of resistance they met.

[9] Edgar Quinet felt, perhaps more clearly than anyone else, the astonishing novelty of this festival: "Those who had seen the old France, bristling with obstacles at every step, were astonished to see that all the barriers were down. With old-fashioned naivety, they entered Paris as they would a holy town" (*La Révolution* [Paris, 1865]).

MICHELLE PERROT

Workers on Strike: France, 1871–1890

1984

*Michelle Perrot's intellectual trajectory offers an excellent illustra-
tion of the evolution of historical sensibility from 1950 to 1980. In an
autobiographical essay ("L'air du temps," in Pierre Nora, ed.,* Essais
d'égo-histoire *[Paris, 1987], pp. 241–92), she recalled how as a
young woman she began her career in labor history under Ernest
Labrousse. To study "the working class," as one said at the time, was
not only a scientific choice (to do social history) but also an ideological one, marking a desire "to break with the camp of the exploiters
into which I was born." Her first work, therefore, was a vast project
in quantitative and serial history, a study of strikes between 1871 and
1890. Years later came a major work in historical anthropology,
which still recognizes the need to describe and measure social facts yet
goes on to give central importance to strikes as a social and cultural
experience, a shift attested to by the very title of the work,* Les Ouvriers en grève *(1975). In between, the "scientific" orientation of
her early work may have faded somewhat, but even more important
was a change of sensibility, of which May '68 was the symbol, for the
events of May were in effect a strike in which people ordinarily reduced to silence suddenly felt that they had found their voice. In the
1970s, moreover, Michelle Perrot became one of the leading figures
in French women's history.*

E very thesis and indeed every book takes so long to research and to
write that it develops its own history. This would be of no interest if the author alone were involved, but in spite of the cloistered
nature of academic research, such histories cannot help but assume some
of the coloring of their own time. First of all, no choice can be said to be
completely free or wholly without consequences. In choosing the topic

From *Workers on Strike: France, 1871–1890,* trans. Chris Turner with Erica Carter
and Claire Laudet (Leamington Spa, Eng.: Berg, 1987). First published as *Jeunesse de
la grève: France, 1871–1890* (Paris: Seuil, 1984).

of the present book, I was indeed prey to a twofold obsession, being imbued with that slightly ingenuous seriousness typical of the student generation of the 1950s, an obsession with the working class and with the possibility of writing a "scientific" history. The France in which we had grown up was an old country; indeed, it belonged fundamentally to the nineteenth century, to a past age that was only then finally dying away. There were times when we had a presentiment of the huge economic and social upheavals that were around the corner—growth and underdevelopment, the consumer society and technocracy, the Third World and the "new social strata," the crisis of socialism and of culture— but we did not grasp the full extent of these phenomena. Though we did not realize it at the time, we were on the brink of experiencing a kind of Baroque "Renaissance"; yet our vision of the world remained a soberly classical one.

We had no doubts whatsoever of the existence in our country of a classical capitalism and, under its yoke, of a classical proletariat, which was both exploited and politically aware. That proletariat was our model and our hope, the key to our own destiny and to that of the world. After all, the leading lights of the period—from André Breton to Jean-Paul Sartre and Maurice Merleau-Ponty to Emmanuel Mounier—paid homage to it.

Our purpose, however, was not to identify with the working class. We were not content to adopt the approach put forward by Simone Weil; it was too individualist and ethical for our tastes. As the respectful heirs of humanism, we believed in the power of books and the labor of scholars. Taking the working class as the object of our research seemed to us the best way of becoming part of it; it was our way of "going to the people" and thereby making contact with the present.

There were, however, many risks involved in telling this history. It was a field laden down with romantic tales and full of conflicting passions, and it is one where the temptation to indulge in hagiography, excommunication, or lyricism is still strong today. We rejected the easy formulas of the epic and the false certainties of Zdhanovite schematism. We wanted a warm and open history, one that was both rigorous and all-embracing. We also believed in "Science." Under the influence of a diffuse neopositivism (despite all the sarcasm we heaped upon Charles Seignobos), we dreamed confusedly of a "social physics," of historical laboratories staffed by researchers in white coats, constructing the "facts."

On a quite different level, the work of Ernest Labrousse encouraged us to look at economic series, at statistics and surveys; to work at establishing constants and correlations, all of which seemed capable of rescuing history from its uncertain fate. By that route, we rediscovered the tradition of the French sociologists of the early part of the century, of Emile Durkheim and of François Simiand, Maurice Halbwachs, Marcel Mauss and the Année Sociologique group, which, though curiously forgotten by a sociology tormented by the fiendish complexities of language, found a new lease on life within a history that was anxious to become a sociology of the past.

We were wary of a history that was "literary" or ideological. Every text and every idea aroused our suspicions and had to be carefully sifted. We were haunted by the idea of measurement and by numbers that were pure and solid, whose metallic cutting edge could tear through the soft fabric of a historical discourse, which seemed merely the pleasant reverie of some solitary wanderer.

This was, then, a time when quantitative methods were becoming more and more popular. The various stages in this process are not difficult to trace. Quantitative methods were first finely honed within the field of economics, where the mere amassing of series of isolated facts without their being given some integrated structure was rejected as inadequate. From there, they extended their reach to all aspects of social reality. Only what could be counted seemed to us solid and worthy material: registrations and solicitors' records, tolls and fiscal archives, parish registers and records of wine-growing, lists of notables, copyright records, prison registers and criminal records, voting statistics and figures for religious observance, and so on. The domain of the measurable stretched out as far as the eye could see, and we were discovering the extent to which societies were made up of interlocking patterns of repeated acts. We were in the grip of a statistical madness. We thought in terms of curves and cross-sections, secretly convinced that at the end of our patiently accumulated statistical work, reality would stand before us as imposing as the statue of the Commander in Don Juan.

When, at the beginning of the 1960s, mechanical data-processing—from the most humble and most inconvenient systems of cards and rods to the most complicated of machines—and the computer made their belated entry into historical research, researchers were often already staggering under the weight of their statistics. These new methods provided effective support; and, though sometimes below a certain threshold of complexity they acted as an encumbrance, they also gave a stimulus to further work. The computer brought quantitative perspectives to a fine point, extended and systematized them. It made possible all sorts of operations that could not be performed manually. For some time, a sort of punchcard mania and a computer "philosophy" held sway. However, these are now happily behind us, for, remarkable as this instrument was, it could not replace the outlining of a problematic. Its influence on the method of organization of work, the conduct and even the initial formulation of research, is, however, undeniable, and we are still far from having felt its final effects.

My choice of the strike as a research object is explained by the perspectives, outlined above. It is an object that provides rich and dense material, its roots plunging deep into the life of the working class, it is at the same time eminently quantifiable. It stands at the crossroads of two preoccupations. Before choosing it, however, I meandered for some time around other possible topics. I first considered the possibility of producing a more wide-ranging study, taking in the whole of the late-nineteenth-century working-class universe—structures and movements, conditions and ideologies. I spent quite some time researching into socialism, but before 1893 the various socialist "schools" tempted the working class very little. It was not among Paul Brousse's people, nor Jules Guesde's or Edouard-Marie Vaillant's, nor even Alleman's that I would find them. The working class spilled over on all sides from these categories. Moreover, in the absence of preliminary partial studies, the field was too large. Everything still remained to be done from scratch: figures for wages and employment, demography, levels of skill and class stratification, trades and techniques, language and attitudes to life. On all these points, in spite of the research that has been carried out, much still remains to be done today. Finally, I was wary of a temptation to conflate levels—economy, social structures, attitudes—and equally of the trap of presenting these merely as juxtaposed panels, with their mutual connections likely to disappear into the binding of the book.

Concentrating on the strike seemed a way of avoiding these various pitfalls. The time has now come to list the merits of that decision, which are almost the only absolute certainty I still possess now that my explorations are completed. A strike is an event that speaks and is spoken about. It is a subject that loosens tongues and makes ink flow freely—and not only the ink of the guardians of order, but that of chroniclers and storytellers, of the journalists whom strikes attract out into the working-class areas, along with novelists and artists. Strikes grasp the attention, fuel a climate of disquiet, and demand investigation. They generate an abundance of documentary material. Above all, they break down that dumbness to which the guardians of culture habitually condemn the popular classes—those inhabitants of a "world beneath a world" (the Goncourts) —consigning them, as soon as they disappear from view, to the trivial whisperings of oral tradition or to nocturnal silence. Demands, protests, petitions, graffiti, discussions, harangues, slogans, shouts, cheers, and insults are so many links in a chain of discourse which can give us a great deal of information about the aspirations, desires, and conceptions of the workers. They can tell us about them at the most humble levels. Figures hitherto unknown surface momentarily, taking the stage for an instant, only to be submerged once again seconds after. These are precious, fleeting forms, the skeleton of a movement in which too often we know only the principal actors. Silent sufferings, desires buried beneath the exhausting monotony of everyday life, rise up here and find expression. Full of sound and gestures, a strike is an outpouring of words, a psychodrama in which repressed drives are liberated. It plunges down into the heart of the unknown masses.

Complex in its origins and implications, the strike straddles classifications and defies terminological divisions. In a strike, we find articulated together a variety of "instances" which all too often are merely presented layer by layer, piled one upon the other like a house of cards. The strike forces us to inquire into the connections between them; it compels us to wrestle with the details of multiple correlations and imbrications. As a site of conflict, it multiplies the relations between classes and social groups, which we are accustomed to seeing confined in their own separate compartments. It is not only the worker that it presents to us but the employer class too, the state and public opinion as they appear in the mirror held up to them by the workers. A strike is a dynamic relationship.

Strikes reproduce themselves. They escape from the class of accidental phenomena to acquire the status of "social facts," facts possessed of a constraining power in the Durkheimian sense. By their frequency, they lend themselves to the establishment of series and to analysis along economic lines. Where immediate perception, which is dissociative because it focuses on the exceptional and the sensational, finds only the episodic and discontinuous ("upsurges" and "outbursts" as they are commonly known), Anglo-Saxon and, more recently, French economists are beginning to attempt to discern tendencies and regularities. Identifying the general growth of the strike, its distribution over time—year, month, week—and fluctuations, and locating the relations of these latter with the diverse dimensions of the economic situation offers a means of escape from the apparent incoherence of day-to-day development.

However determined we may be here to flush out the element of chance, we shall, nonetheless, take care to avoid the trap of prejudging or imposing an illusory order on objects and events. We shall be as attentive to troubling discordances as to reassuring concordances, for these discordances are both a source of fresh questions and an invitation to different readings of the strike phenomenon. Indeed, in spite of a certain autonomy of structure, which confers on the strike an existence relatively independent of that of its participants, it should not be seen as an abstraction but as a locus of "human" decision-making which has complex roots, as a process in which external realities are mediated through the consciousness of the actors. In the following, therefore, we shall have to sound out that consciousness by ceaselessly measuring acts against words, seeking to grasp zones of sensibility and indifference, to track down lasting or transient representations, hidden thoughts and even, if possible, what remains unthought. On this difficult path, which research has marked out before us, the guides who will come rushing to our aid will be precious few in number.

Since, however, the strike is a quantifiable phenomenon, there are a large number of points where quantitative methods can gain a purchase—whether direct or indirect—upon it. As the basic unit to be dealt with, each strike (defined according to the unity of the participants, a matter to which I shall return) presents several dimensions: extension (the number of strikers, but also the number of workplaces and *communes* affected), length, and intensity (number of days "lost"), which give a summary measure of its impact in time and (both geographical and social) space.

Conforming to a regular pattern in its fundamental characteristics, every strike behaves as an ensemble constituted by a variable combination of identical elements. These may be listed here. Briefly, they include:

> *Stable components*
> · location, date
> · nature of workers on strike
> · nature of strike
> · types of demand
>
> *Dynamic components*
> · type of outbreak
> · course of the strike: organizations
>   meetings, demonstrations
>   violence
>   negotiations
>   arbitration attempts
>   repression
> · outcome

A questionnaire may therefore be made out for every strike to produce an inventory of these elements. Once these have been counted, they allow us to identify the dominant characteristics and the types of strike within a chosen historical space. Moreover, these elements may serve as a basis for establishing a whole range of correlations (for example, between strikes by women, skilled workers or miners, and so on, and the length and nature of the strike, demands, demonstrations, violence, arbitration, outcome, and so forth). So many types of correlation are possible, that it has in fact only been possible to use the most classical coordinates in this operation (a point that is doubtless open to criticism). Overall, then, the strike lends itself to highly detailed internal investigation.

These possibilities dictate a particular method and demand certain means to carry it out. First of all, they impose a need to accumulate a large quantity of statistical data (in the present study, almost three thousand cases), without which any attempt at establishing correlations would be derisory, since this demands the identification of smaller subsets. We had also to conform to the rule of exhaustivity, not only to establish complete series of strikes but also to enumerate all their aspects. The information had not only to be indicative of the succession of events but to be dense and detailed about their content. For want of homogeneous and complete sources, we had to set up overlapping networks of information, so that material from one source could complement what was provided by another. Fortunately, there was no lack of sources: the novelty of the phenomenon and the interest or fear it aroused provided additional information to supplement the detailed accounts of the administrative services. The combined contributions of the National Archives, the Paris prefecture of police, the *département archives* (sifted through systematically), and the inexhaustible newspaper sources provided extensive documentation, even if it was not always of the type one might have wished for.

All this allowed me to establish a file for each of the strikes identified (2,923 from June 1, 1871, to December 31, 1890) or, at least, a file card containing the largest possible amount of the desired data. The move to processing this data on the computer, which had not originally been intended, was therefore relatively straightforward. Having obtained a grant of ten thousand francs (1965) from the National Center for Scientific Research (CNRS), with the aid of the advice of programmers from SODAM, to whom the work was entrusted, I established a code that was a systematization and transcription of the questionnaire I had gradually worked out by trial and error. It occupied almost all of the eighty columns available on each card. We also had to decide on using a system of multiple punching, which was complicated, and which I was later to regret having chosen, for it made certain correlations impossible. Each strike was therefore transformed into a punched card. This was done in two stages: first, I produced a coded matrix (more than six months' work) and then the punching was done. As will be evident, these were the early days of data-processing; I shall not go any further into this aspect of the procedure, which already has an old-fashioned ring to it. I shall simply, and briefly, indicate in what respects the technique seems to me to have influenced the work itself.

First of all, it considerably reinforced the demand for precise information. Cards containing too many unknown factors jeopardized the whole experiment. The need to reduce the number of such factors, to obtain information that was always complete, made me go back to my sources on many occasions. It also put the emphasis on the structural analysis of the object, since, apart from simply adding up the elements, the tables provided by the computer mapped these diverse constituents against each other. The object was thus subjected to a rigorous internal analysis that augmented its solidity, autonomy, and coherence but at the same time isolated it from its environment—about which, as a result, we have much less precise information. The contrast between this brilliantly illuminated area and the surrounding "darkness" is so great that at first one hardly dares to venture out again into those outer reaches. Contact with the computer (however limited) puts the imprecisions of literary language to the test. But that is perhaps not a bad thing.

Thus, the method adopted, far from overriding my original preoccupations, contributed to reinforcing them. My work was getting further and further away from a history of strikes presented in merely narrative form or as a succession of exemplary monographs; it was tending more and more in the direction of historical sociology, toward a description of strikes as a social phenomenon at a given moment in time.

Now, the reader will doubtless ask why I chose the particular moment that I did. In the first instance, I was dealing with a period that, though located at the heart of a relatively densely populated research terrain, was itself more or less uninhabited—and not by chance. It was an obscure period that had no clear outlines and was seemingly of little interest. Opinion had it that the labor movement was so demoralized after the Commune that it was rendered totally inactive. The scattered nature of the sources—the Office du Travail only began issuing strike statistics in 1890—seemed to confirm this impression. It is curious to note that the great strike waves of 1878–80 and 1888–90 are not mentioned in the classic histories of the workers' movement. In their instinctive attachment to institutional frameworks, they are unable to come to grips with a period in which there was no centralized trade union organization.

I was attracted to the subject by these very reasons. Already certain of not being tied down by other people's interpretations, I was also secure in the knowledge that I was dealing with a brand-new subject about which there was no shortage of historical questions, properly so called. What had become of the labor movement after the Commune? Had it been marked by the experience and, if so, how? How had it greeted the nascent republic? Was the law of 1884 solely a product of Waldeck-Rousseau's benevolence? How was the birth of revolutionary syndicalism, which was soon to step into the breach left by the Commune, to be explained? Quite clearly, something had disappeared here and needed to be rediscovered.

To the attraction of the unknown was added that of origins. To grasp a phenomenon not at source but in its emergence into society has always (and often in a very fallacious manner) fascinated historians! Certainly, strikes were not by this time in their cradle; but the law of 1864, by freeing them from legal fetters, had given them new life. I wanted to know how the workers had used this weapon, how society had reacted and whether, in fact, it had become adapted to strikes. The use of a weapon blunts it and wears it out. Nowadays a strike is a relatively routine occurrence, which only rarely captures our attention. We neglect the sprinkling of little disputes, which are just as revealing as others of life's many trials and tribulations. As a decision made by union leaderships, as part of a broader strategy, strikes have become more a way of applying pressure than a means of expression.

Another factor that attracted me was the very absence of central organizations (the Guesdiste Fédération Nationale of 1886 was of little real significance) and, perhaps, the opportunity this afforded to get at the more obscure factors, at that infrastructure of social movements which most often remains hidden from us. Not that the unorganized have any special claim to creativity. They are no more able than others to escape the conceptions, vocabulary, and stereotypes of their times, by which they, as much as organizations, are surrounded. These latter, however, also secrete a language of their own, which doubtless reveals something of the class they represent, but which can also, on occasion, be an impenetrable mask. This phenomenon of "superimposition" occurs in all organizations. Would one judge the psychology of the faithful on the basis of liturgical texts alone? Studies in the sociology and ethnology of religion have taught us to compare and contrast the text of a commandment or the words of a prayer with the actions and behavior of the majority of believers.

Finally, I must justify my precise choice of dates. The absence of any geographical limitations, which would have been incompatible with the desire to study a social phenomenon in its entirety and to escape the constraints imposed by the historico-geographical monograph, obliged me to set temporal limits upon my work. A twenty-year period gave me a sufficient number of cases; with the means at my disposal I could hardly go beyond that: the weight of documentation available to the historian of the modern period rules out vast canvasses centuries long and pushes us toward the close exploration of precisely defined "moments." The year 1871 offered an acceptable starting point; but 1890 will seem more surprising, in that it corresponds to no great economic or political watershed. But why should we impose a political or economic periodization on a phenomenon that these forces do not necessarily govern? Is not the underlying idea behind such a procedure—the idea that all orders of events bend to the same general pressures—open to question? It seems to me that we must seek breaks that are inherent in the subject itself and have a meaning within its own history before we accord significance to the other phenomena with which it may be connected. May Day 1890, the first attempt at creating a general movement on a national scale, marks a new stage in the history of strikes; it has a very appreciable effect on the graph representing strikes, which suddenly rises to new levels at this point. When the general strike takes on substance for the first time and when, by its very failure, it leads to the formation of a central organization, we are, surely, led on to a new terrain of investigation.

These, then, were the reasons for my choice; they have become more precise and also more nuanced as a result of my research. The somewhat simple object I first perceived in the illusory light of a first encounter—"one knows clearly what one knows crudely" (Gaston Bachelard)—has become more substantial, richer, more complicated. My fine initial certainties have given way to new lines of questioning, prompted both by the ceaselessly reactivated demands of present observation—the strike is once again ablaze on our horizon—and by the resistance of the material. Quantified and enumerated, strikes still lie beyond our reach, just as they elude all the skillful ruses deployed to try to capture them in writing. The strike is a multifaceted object and requires the application of a wide variety of approaches which are beyond the scope of a single individual.

At the same time, however, as the strike was taking on more substance as a research object, my text was becoming heavier. And the reader will doubtless interject here in some surprise: "Why all this defense of numerical methods? You have made too little use of the certainty and conciseness they provide. Your book is very long and, when all is said and done, very 'literary.' " This is true, and I can suggest why it has come about. There is, first, the opacity of things; if words are to penetrate them, they have to strain all their resources. Then there is the inadequacy of a training that has left me unable to take advantage of all that my statistical sources had to offer. And lastly, there is the taste the historian retains for writing, even if she is not—alas—a "writer," but just someone who writes.

All this reflects the uncomfortable situation in which the whole discipline of history finds itself: uncertain and divided, historians are being pulled in different directions by the various languages available to us. Tempted by a variety of methods and plagued by an enormous range of questions, we are engaged in the infernal pursuit of a reality that haunts us and yet escapes our grasp.

Assuredly, ours is a difficult discipline.

TRANSLATED BY CHRIS TURNER WITH ERICA CARTER
AND CLAIRE LAUDET

History Without People

EMMANUEL LE ROY LADURIE

The History of Rain and Fine Weather

1973

Can one write a history without human beings? Aggressive as the question is, it did not seem unreasonable at the height of the structuralist wave, when Emmanuel Le Roy Ladurie (b. 1929), followed his Les Paysans du Languedoc *(1966) with his* Histoire du climat depuis l'an mil *(1967), a determined attempt to treat climate and its measurement as a fit subject for history. In any case, Le Roy Ladurie's close attention to slow and far-reaching environmental changes showed him to be the most faithful of Fernand Braudel's intellectual heirs. At the same time, this "history of rain and fine weather" is an excellent example of the spectacular enlargement of the historian's field of interest. Indeed, one of Le Roy Ladurie's collection of essays is entitled, significantly,* Le Territoire de l'historien *(1973), and the very richness of his oeuvre marks him out as one of the most important historical innovators.*

In recent years, methods in climatic history have undergone some significant and highly interesting developments. Before saying something about them, however, I should like to begin by recalling some of the best known of the various techniques employed in historical writings on climate, as applied to the last thousand years.

1.   Concerning the latter part of this period—the last two centuries—the climate historian's task is, quite simply, to collate, verify, tabu-

---

From *The Territory of the Historian*, trans. Ben and Siân Reynolds (Chicago: University of Chicago Press, 1979). First published in *Le Territoire de l'historien* (Paris: Gallimard, 1973).

late, and publish basic series of meteorological observations. From the eighteenth century and the early years of the nineteenth onward, such records are in fact quite plentiful. As a model, in this respect one may refer to the series of temperature readings for England and Holland for the last three centuries given by Gordon Manley and the Dutch researchers in this field.[1] The advantage of having thermometric series from neighboring regions is that they can be checked for their mutual correlation: consequently, whenever any new records are discovered, they can be tested for correlations and their reliability can be established. Then, once one has an indication of the overall picture, the series enable the historian to detect on a regional, national, or even European scale any intermittent fluctuations of temperature, tending toward warmer or colder weather which may have lasted chronologically a decade, a number of decades, or even a century. And, bearing in mind future research, we should not forget that in addition to such temperature records, there also exist early series of rainfall and barometric pressure records for the nineteenth century, and some even for the eighteenth century. Although often less reliable than the records of temperature, they are nevertheless extremely valuable for defining the weather patterns and atmospheric conditions of the past. Huge numbers of valuable dossiers of this kind still lie buried away, even today, in the archives of observatories, medical and provincial academies, and learned societies.

2.   For periods earlier than the eighteenth century, *dendrochronology* (the study of the growth-rings of trees) produces knowledge of the first importance on the subject of drought in arid or subtropical countries; on rainfall in temperate zones; and on cold conditions in northern lands. In the present article, we shall be concerned principally with the fluctuations of these three phenomena.

3.   *Phenology*, the study of the annual dates of the flowering and fruiting of plants, has so far related exclusively to a series of documents almost unique of its kind: the wine harvest dates (*vendanges*) registered in the archives. From these we may learn whether the March–September period in any given year was, on average, "warm" or "cool." Whenever we have a series of such dates for an area or group of areas, they shed light on the temperature fluctuations from one year to the next, or one decade to the next—though not as yet from one century to the next.[2]

4.   The *"événementiel"* or recorded events method relies on the painstaking accumulation of empirical and qualitative observations of climatic conditions recorded at the time by contemporary witnesses in private correspondence, family diaries, parish registers, and so on. John Titow gave us a model of the method in 1960, in his impressive article

on the climate of England in the fourteenth century (*Economic History Review*), and we also have the 1949 publication by D. J. Schove of a comprehensive study of the climatic fluctuations of sixteenth-century Europe and of the progressive cooling of the winters from 1540–1560 to 1600.[3]

5. The *glaciological* method was recently demonstrated by J. Grove apropos of Norway in the seventeenth and eighteenth centuries (see his article in *Arctic and Alpine Research* [1972]). This method involves a combination of different types of research: analysis of documents (the Chamonix archives, the records of the subglacial farms of Norway, and the Icelandic sagas); investigations calling on *geomorphology* (the study of moraines); *palynology* (the study of marshes and peat bogs situated downstream of glaciers); and *nuclear biology* (the carbon 14 dating of the debris of trees left behind in moraines or found rooted in rocky beds lately uncovered by retreating glaciers). These studies have made it possible to track the secular, sometimes multisecular, ebb and flow of the glaciers; thanks to them we know the movements that have taken place in the ice fields of Europe throughout the whole of the last thousand years. They offer an invaluable, if distorting, guide to weather pattern changes and in particular to changes of temperature.[4]

At this point, however, it seems to me essential to say a few words about the methodology, the fundamental aims even, that are associated with such techniques.

The *aim* of climatic history is not to explain human history, nor to offer simplistic accounts of this or that remarkable episode (for example, the crises of the fourteenth and the seventeenth centuries or the dramatic upturn of the eighteenth), not even when such episodes prompt us, with good reason, to reflect upon the great disasters of history. In the initial stages, its aim is quite different: essentially, it is to produce a clear picture of the changing meteorological patterns of past ages, in the spirit of what Paul Veyne calls "a cosmological history of nature." True, this "chronological cosmology," modestly limited to a study of regional climates, may serve as a discipline for future reference of a quite different and more ambitious project with human history as its object. The "spin-off" of the history of the climate does indeed have a bearing on the chronology of famines and also, perhaps, of epidemics, but these are merely consequences derived from it. However important and even exciting they may be, they remain marginal. The historian of the climate should ignore the tactics of the moment. It seems to me that his strategy should be, first and foremost, to place himself in the front line, shoulder to shoulder in interdisciplinary collaboration with the natural scientists. And if, at the outset, they treat him as an intruder, a deserter from his own discipline with nothing of any value to impart, so much the worse for them. The historian should simply swallow the insult and carry on doing his best to get them to accept the specific contribution that he alone is able to make. Several years ago, Pierre Chaunu said that the first duty of the economic historian was, in all modesty, to supply the professional economist with his basic material. Similarly, the climate historian's first duty is to supply the natural scientists—meteorologists, glaciologists, climatologists, geophysicists, and so on—with archival material. The reasons for such a division of labor are obvious and unsensational: by his training (in paleography, knowledge of Latin, and above all mastery of the "historian's craft") the professional historian alone has the key to certain types of data hidden away centuries ago in bundles of illegible old documents. Meteorologists have long ceased to be Latin scholars, let alone— and who can blame them!—paleographers or "historiometricians."

My second comment concerns the necessarily climatological background to all research conducted along these lines. Unless he is to confine himself to a bare recital of the variations of the climate of the past, the historian of rain and fine weather has a duty to work at his assignment primed with a complete understanding of the basic data relating to movements of air masses and atmospheric circulation. The general theories and syntheses relating to such data are well known and are constantly under review. The latest and most up-to-date account is by H. H. Lamb (in 1970 I published a summary of this major work, but this should not be thought a substitute for consulting the original).[5]

These, then, are the essential presuppositions upon which, for the past fifteen years, my own investigations and those of several other researchers in the field of the recent history of the climate have been based. With these in mind, I shall confine myself to pointing out the most recent developments, some of which are continuing along lines already referred to, while others, on the contrary, are breaking entirely new ground. I shall also, in passing, note some of the most glaring gaps in our knowledge in the hope that one day new laborers in the field will come along and fill them.

TRANSLATED BY BEN AND SIÂN REYNOLDS

NOTES

[1] See Manley and Labrijn.
[2] Angot, 1883. Le Roy Ladurie, 1967 and 1971.
[3] Titow, 1960 and 1970. Schove, 1949.
[4] Le Roy Ladurie, *op. cit.*
[5] Le Roy Ladurie, 1970; and especially H. Lamb, 1966.

Revitalizing Old Forms

—————

PIERRE NORA

The Return of the Event

1974

*Events—a new object? By the early 1970s, this question could surely
be answered in the affirmative. The rejection of* l'histoire événementielle *had been a constant theme of French historiography from
François Simiand (1903) to the* Annales, *most particularly in the
work of Fernand Braudel, who, in* La Méditerranée *and later in his
celebrated article on "La longue durée," (see pp. 115-145) maintained that, seen at the level of events, history was evanescent and
impossible to grasp: events "prick holes in the night without illuminating it." This is even more true if the history in question is contemporary, and its study cannot be conceived in terms of long-range
phenomena. It thus took a certain audacity to herald "the return of
the event." Pierre Nora was surely the man to do it: a specialist in the
history of the present who has taught at the Institut d'Etudes Politiques, he stood on the fringes of the* Annales *network, to which he
nevertheless had ties both personal and professional (he was the editor,
at Gallimard, of an important collection of works in history and social science). He was thus both outsider and insider. In this article,
among those representing the disciplines of contemporary and political history in the collective work* Faire de l'histoire *(1974), the approach to events is of course far from traditional. Events are treated
as symptoms, which give access to the imaginary life of democratic
societies. They are also social constructions, which call into play systems of information, networks of meaning, and particular ways of experiencing time. All these are themes that Nora would revisit and*

———————————————————————————————

Pierre Nora, "Le Retour de l'événement," in Jacques Le Goff and Pierre Nora,
eds., *Faire de l'histoire,* vol. 1: *Nouveaux problèmes* (Paris: Gallimard, 1974), pp. 217–
27.

reformulate, as we shall see, in his later work on history and memory.
It may also be worth mentioning that this essay, an earlier version of
which was published under the title "L'Evénement monstre," was writ-
ten in the aftermath of a major event that, for better or for worse, has
left a deep imprint on contemporary French consciousness: May '68.

Events give a miraculous dimension to democratic society. The very integration of the masses has had the effect of integrating marvels as well. As we know from the popular and working-class literature of the first half of the nineteenth century, the fantastic traditionally took its ingredients from out of this world. Now industrial society itself supplies them. When technology accurately imitates the traditional themes of the fantastic, as in the case of the first American moon landing, the result, to borrow the jargon of economics, is a kind of "hypermultiplier effect."[1] Every aspect of the lunar adventure reflected the contrast between technology and tradition, which the organizers of the interplanetary "show" rightfully exploited. The dreamlike precision of the landing gave proof of inconceivable technological prowess. Viewers could identify with the three carefully selected heroes, their physiques reminiscent of Superman. Shrewd use was made of the futuristic lunar lander, from which men in diving suits emerged onto the television screen, their every gesture giving proof that they had at last been delivered from the earth's gravity. And the immensity of the financial, human, and political investment that made it all possible contrasted starkly with the fragile physical and nervous reflexes of three simple men. In such a moment, imaginations shaped by the fabulous scientific powers of the modern world could also dream humanity's oldest dream. Reality, reportage, and consumption coincided: the lunar landing was the model of the modern event.

The distinctive feature of that event was, of course, that it was telecast live around the world by satellite. The immediacy of television was probably not the sufficient cause of the transformation of the event, but it was surely the necessary cause. Witness the Clay-Frazier heavyweight championship fight, which was an event in countries where it was telecast live but not in France, where only a delayed broadcast was available. Television, by abolishing delay and placing the action before our eyes while its outcome is still uncertain, has at last robbed events of their historical character and projected them into the everyday life of large numbers of people.

Now, moreover, events are transformed into spectacles. Is theatricality an inherent quality of so many of the contemporary events that become objects of public consumption, or is it live broadcasting that bestows an element of theatricality upon them? In any case, events have become more democratic even as they have become more spectacular. Symbolically, contemporary history might well begin with Goethe's remark at Valmy: "And you will be able to say, I was there." The essence of the modern event is that it takes place on an immediately public stage. There is no event without its reporter-spectator or spectator-reporter. The event is seen as it is happening. This "voyeurism" not only distinguishes news from history but already anoints the current event with a certain historical fragrance. One has the impression of participating in a play truer than life itself, a dramatic diversion, a festival that society stages for itself. Everybody attends these events, and yet nobody does—for the "masses" are all of us, even if none of us will admit to belonging. The modern event, the event that needs no historian, is what it is because the masses participate in it emotionally. Indeed, it is the only way in which they can participate in public life. That participation is demanding but alienated, voracious but frustrated, multifarious but remote, impotent yet sovereign, autonomous yet—like that impalpable reality of modern life, public opinion—remote-controlled.

This history still awaits its Clausewitz, who will analyze the strategy of what has become the total event just as war became total war by enlisting the participation of civilians. No place remains "behind the lines" of history, nor is there any single "front." The traditional gap between the masters of information and their subjects, between high culture and popular culture, is vanishing, or, rather, a more stable hierarchy is replacing it inside the world of information itself, in the realm of the media. In a world where no one is completely without knowledge or, for that matter, without power, if only through the ballot box, no one has a permanent monopoly on events. The media force us all to say, "Ask not for whom the bell tolls, it tolls for thee."

When de Gaulle issued his famous call to resistance on June 18, 1940, he issued it for everyone, even if almost no one heard him. When an Olympic skier sets a record on a lonely mountainside, he does it for everyone. When an Israeli tank charges into the desert, it attacks for everyone. Publicity is the iron law of the modern event. Thus, the news is also condemned to be total. So ironclad is this rule that if the news ceases, the ensuing silence itself becomes an event. If the Nigerians restrict access to a Biafra filled with reporters, if Indonesia massacres a million communists while the capitalist world remains indifferent, then the absence of news adds to the tragedy of the event itself. The fact that the Leningrad trials took place at the same time as the Burgos trial and also in closed courtrooms influenced their outcome. If the TV news the day after de Gaulle's death had not begun with the announcement "General de Gaulle died last night," the omission would in itself have constituted the beginning of a political event. The fact that the Chinese did not watch the American lunar landing on TV was an event for the non-Chinese world. The law of the spectacle is the most totalitarian law in the free world.

The news, torn between reality and its spectacular projection, has lost the neutrality it had when it was simply an organ of transmission. Whatever noble distortions it may have introduced, it was by nature only a transmission belt, an inevitable intermediary. The event was emitted, transmitted, and received: narrative carried it from a place in which it was already dead to a place in which its impact was blunted, passing information down a traditional chain from the best to the worst informed. The news referred to real facts that existed outside it, which it signified. However technical a definition one gives, Information (with a capital *I*) always functions in principle to reduce uncertainty. It would remain unintelligible if it did not add to already-organized knowledge, restructuring the preestablished framework into which it is received. Viewed globally, however, the media information system fabricates unintelligibility. It bombards us with interrogative, enucleated knowledge, devoid of meaning, and leaves it to us to provide that meaning, saturating us with evidence that makes no sense. If we didn't instinctively behave like historians, it would ultimately be nothing more than noise hiding its own significance. The featureless uniformity of time in industrial societies creates an anxious craving for ever more events, a need to consume time as we consume objects, to allay our very fear of the event itself. The news machine has its own insatiable appetite, and if need be it provides grist for its own mill every day: the tabloids, for instance, manufacture events that are for the most part stillborn. Daniel Boorstin is therefore wrong to think that there are pseudo-events living as parasites on real events.[2] Artifice (is it really artifice?) is the reality of the system. Say, rather, that once upon a time an event was something extraordinary, whereas today, when nothing is absolute, every event is apt to create its own sensation. There is a Gresham's Law of news: the bad drives out the good. Contemporary history has witnessed the death of the "natural" event, in which, ideally, a true fact could be turned into a piece of information. We have entered the era of inflated events, and one way or another we have no choice but to integrate that inflation into the fabric of our daily lives.

Modernity oozes with events, whereas traditional societies tended to make events scarce. In peasant societies, the only events were those of religious routine, climatic calamity, or demographic disaster—a nonhistory. The authorities and the Church sought to eliminate novelty, to reduce its corrosive power, to swallow it up in ritual. All established societies seek to perpetuate themselves through a system of news whose ultimate purpose is to deny events, for an event is nothing other than a disruption of the equilibrium on which it is based. Events, like truth, are always revolutionary, grains of sand in the machine, accidents that come out of the blue to upset the status quo. There are no happy events—events are always catastrophes. There are two ways of exorcising the new: it can be made to disappear by an information system that dispenses no information, or it can be incorporated into the information system itself. In the East, vast regions of the world live under a regime in which the news never contains anything new. The press prints nothing that is unpredictable, just the internal life of the party, notices of regular anniversaries and commemorations, production reports, news of the West distorted in such a way as to render it pointless, and of course the steady hum of propaganda. No effort is spared to drain the news of anything that might endanger the institution purveying it. In a similar way, medieval hagiographers indicated events in the life of a saint only by the day and the month, omitting the year in order to inscribe the event in an eternity without memory and therefore without temporal efficacy. The second way of getting rid of the new is to make novelty the essence of the narrative message, even to the point of redundancy, with the attendant risk of giving the information system the vocation of destroying itself: this is our way.

This state of perpetual overinformation and chronic underinformation is characteristic of contemporary society. Exhibiting events prevents them from becoming occasions for exhibitionism. The inevitable confusion encourages doubt, anxiety, and social panic. Knowledge is the primary form of power in a democratic information society. The corollary is not always false: whoever holds power is supposed to know. Out of this comes a new dialectic, apt to give rise to events associated with secrecy, law and order, conspiracy, rumor, and gossip. It is both true and false that the more an event is talked about, the less we know about its essence; that the system that promotes the proliferation of events also fabricates illusions (but that is not all that it does); and that so many frank avowals conceal a lie. Think, for example, of the Great Fear that ravaged the French countryside in 1789, or the acute case of spy-itis that afflicted the nation in 1793. Think of the allegations of a conspiracy of Freemasons with the Elders of Zion at the time of the Industrial Revolution, or of Hitler's vituperations against "international Jewry," or of Stalin's against "Trotskyism," or of anti-imperialism in formerly colonial states. All these various outlets and scapegoats have been used by the consummate sorcerers of charismatic power. They became useful tools for dealing with a new historical situation, that of mass participation in public life—that is, with the rise of democracy in Tocqueville's sense. These events reflect, in their brutal, clumsy fashion, both the advent of mass politics and the profound frustration of crowds eager to snatch up a false knowledge to compensate for their lack of power.

To multiply the new, fabricate events, and degrade information are surely ways of defending oneself against them. Yet the ambiguity at the heart of information leads to a paradoxical metamorphosis of the idea of event.

THE PARADOX OF THE EVENT

For the historian of the present, there is even an opportunity in all this: the displacement of the narrative message from reality to the virtual reality of the imagination, of the parasitic spectacle, has the effect of bringing out the nonevent within the event. Or, to put it somewhat differently, the event becomes the neutral, temporal site where it is possible to observe, in isolation, a range of deep-seated social phenomena that would otherwise remain buried in the recesses of the collective mind. The event testifies not so much to what it represents as to what it reveals, not so much to what it is as to what it unleashes. Its meaning is subsumed by its reverberations; it is only an echo, a mirror of society, an empty hole. What would de Gaulle's death have meant if it had come ten years later, when he was a diminished, forgotten old man? However, coming as it did, only a year after he had been driven from office by the voters—long enough for them to feel nothing but guilt and regret for what they had done, and in the early days of a regime that hoped to do no more than duty required in paying respect to the dead and at which its father hurled the supreme insult of changing nothing in the laconic testament he had aimed squarely at the Fourth Republic—his death, made sadder still by the fact that memories of the general had yet to solidify, unintentionally became the greatest performance of an actor perpetually obsessed with his exit. It was a sudden, magical death such as each of us inwardly desires, which in the solemnity of the moment took on a legendary character, as if a still-living saint had been recalled to his Maker. Abroad, it was a death that carried off the last survivor of World War II, the ally of the Soviet Union, the decolonizer, the friend of the Arabs, the symbol of the rebel, the man who had recognized China—in short, something for every one of the world's powers. For the people of France, this death recalled the most ancient and venerable traditions of the monarchy: it was the death of a king. In fact, the double ceremony and the opportune timing refloated the monarchy with capital borrowed from the republican legacy: nostalgia for lost grandeur was combined with a fleeting national reconciliation. In a ruse of history, the Notre Dame ceremony ironically enthroned for a second time the man who found himself in the position of "felling oaks," while the coffin made its way to Colombey escorted by the whole panoply of French nationalism, about which de Gaulle's death providentially said more than his entire life.

In fact, immediacy makes an event both easier and more difficult to decipher: easier because it strikes with one fell swoop, more difficult because it gives you everything all at once. In a more traditional system of information, the content of an event defined the area of its diffusion. Its network of influence was clearly defined by those it touched. Its trace was more linear. If events at one time had not been able to distill their many meanings into one, wouldn't Marx, Tocqueville, Lissagaray, and countless other lesser-known nineteenth-century commentators on the history of the moment have found it more difficult to approach the level of historical analysis in their work? Even lucid contemporaries would have erred more often about the events of the time, as lucid commentators do today. Now, however, the intermediaries are cut out of the loop, a sort of telescoping of event and report takes place, and in the incandescence of multiple meanings we are blinded. An important event such as the assassination of President Kennedy is instantly flashed around the world. Its vocation to eventhood is immediately realized in a universal sense, yet somehow the event proceeds from the depths of the worldwide emotion it arouses back to its source, rather than descending from the circle of initiates down to those who might be affected (and on that journey all sorts of extraneous baggage is introduced). In the intransitive event, without theoretical limits or boundaries, different levels of meaning overlap; exploded constellations intermingle. It is best defined from within: What is this event, and for whom? For if there is no event without critical consciousness, then an event can exist only if it is available to all but not the same for everyone. Limits of meaning, limits of the milieus involved, limits in time: when does an event stop and what does it become? Aftershocks, collective amnesias (like that surrounding France's war in Algeria), and subterranean propagations ultimately define its contours.

A curious reciprocity therefore develops between a type of society and its event-ial (événementielle) existence. On the one hand, to the extent that information networks are social institutions, the succession of events defines a society's surface. For example, Soviet society is exemplified by the information system that produced the Twentieth Congress of the Communist Party; Chinese society by the system that produced the Cultural Revolution; and American society by the system that produced the My Lai affair. Conversely, however, such events bring to the surface a large mass of emotions, habits, routines, and representations inherited from the past. A scene of social projections and latent conflicts, an event is what chance was for Antoine Augustin Cournot—an encounter of several independent series of causes, a rend in the social fabric that the system is designed to weave. The most important events are those which bring up the most ancient legacies. Here, again, the system in the East offers an instructive counterpoint. It is surely of some interest that petty crime and scandal are absent from the news in the socialist bloc. News items of this kind reveal the depths of a society, in a minor key, so to speak. By expurgating them, the socialist information system simultaneously eliminates the uncontrollable, shocking revelations about a society that they contain.

Thus, historians are not interested in events, over whose creation they have no control, but in two systems that come together in the event, a formal system and a system of meaning that they are better equipped than most to understand. For there is nothing arbitrary about the unfolding of an event, however indeterminate it might appear. It is not the occurrence of an event that matters but the prominence, the volume, the pace, the interconnections, the relation to other events, the sequellae, and aftershocks. All these things conform to certain patterns, which establish a certain kinship, a depressing similarity, among apparently unrelated phenomena. Opinion polls, now such a familiar fixture of our world, might usefully be accompanied by comparative analyses of news patterns, media strategies, redundancies, and publicity-induced chain reactions—in short, a formal phenomonology of the event.[3] A brief study was done of the death of Pope John XXIII.[4] Might similar monographs about the deaths of national leaders such as Stalin, Kennedy, Churchill, Adenauer, Togliatti, Nasser, and de Gaulle lead to useful comparisons? What similarities might emerge from comparative study of certain scandals or trials with no apparent connection, such as the Dreyfus Affair and various events associated with the Algerian war? Formal analysis leads naturally to analysis of meaning, if only, as a first step, analysis of the meaning of the formal system's appearance, which is itself an event. What change was implicit in the crucial development of a new idea of the event in the late nineteenth century, at the very moment when scientific history, dominated by victorious positivism, was seizing on the notion of event as something that could be effectively studied only in the past? What correlations might exist between these two contemporary phenomena, the birth of a science interested only in the events of the past and the advent of a distinctive realm of experience sometimes referred to as "contemporary history"?

In the pursuit of meaning, then, the historian of the present uses the same serial methods as the historian of the past, except that his aim is to build up to the meaning of the event rather than reduce it to a series of causal factors. He consciously brings out the presence of the past in the present rather than unconsciously imposing the present on the past. Today we know that the night of August 4, 1789, when the First Estate renounced some of its ancient privileges and rights, was not simply the hysterical masquerade that Raymond Aron saw in the Academic Assemblies of May 1968, which invoked the earlier event. Was that obvious on the morning of August 5, 1789? It was possible to tell only after decrees had been issued and implemented, carrying out the declarations made that night. Conversely, no one would deny that the Academic Assemblies expressed things other than what they explicitly proclaimed. The virtue of an event is that it gathers up scattered meanings. It is up to the historian to separate those meanings, to work from the evidence of the event to the evaluation of a system. If the unique is to become intelligible, there must be a series that what is new somehow brings to light. Even the assertion that "this was the first time that . . ." implicitly assumes the possibility of a second. "Even if one sticks to a cybernetic model of society," Edgar Morin correctly observes, "the information-event is precisely what allows you to understand the nature of the system's structure and function, that is, the 'feedback' process through which the information is integrated (or rejected), as well as the resulting modification either in the system or through the system."[5] Again, the historian of the present has no part in the eruption of the volcano, whereas the historian of the past, availing himself of the passage of time, can artificially turn event-volcanoes into the markers with which he stakes out his terrain. Nevertheless, the historian of the present can regain his sovereignty by studying the volcano as a geologist would: his job is to identify the underlying geological strata; to map the internal explosions and secondary detonations; to locate the basic lines of stress and the mechanisms by which lava, after being expelled, is reabsorbed. A crisis, which is a complex of events, is not fundamentally different in nature from an event, which signals a crisis somewhere in the social system. There is a dialectical relation between the two phenomena, namely, the dialectic of change, with which the historian of the present is just as ill equipped to deal as is the historian of the past.

The future may prove him wrong, making a mockery of his provisional attributions and obliterating the connections he has made, thereby revealing the event as part of a different network altogether. Yet his original arguments would still remain meaningful as part of the event itself. All nineteenth-century histories of the French Revolution proclaimed that the revolutionary event was not yet complete. All the literature on May '68 is inextricably intertwined with its subject, part of a "history of May" that can never be written. Contemporary history, the exploration of the present, is not a matter of applying to the present historical methods tested on the past; it is, rather, the ultimate exorcism of the event, the final consequence of its resolution. Even if contradicted by history, it will, like the event itself, have *taken place.*

The entirety of the present is still groping for ways to understand itself through events in the sense they have lately taken on in industrial society. The problematic of the event, which remains to be elaborated, is intimately related to what is distinctive about "contemporary" history. In so-called consumer society, the way we deal with events is perhaps a way of reducing time itself to an object of consumption and to bestow on it the same kinds of emotions that we associate with consumer goods.[6] If it is true that history begins only when historians draw upon their own time to pose questions to the past that contemporaries could never even have imagined, who at the present moment can say what anxiety lies hidden behind our need for events, what neurosis lies implicit in this tyranny, what major event of our civilization is reflected in the development of the vast system of events that for us constitutes the present?

We cannot master the contemporary event, whose "consequences" we do not know. The positivists unconsciously remarked this development in founding the science of history, and in doing so they declared the present to be fundamentally impotent. Now that history has achieved modernity by erasing events from its consciousness, denying their importance, and dissolving them out of the past, a different kind of event has come to haunt us, bringing with it, perhaps, the possibility of a truly contemporary history.

TRANSLATED BY ARTHUR GOLDHAMMER

NOTES

[1] See the suggestive case studies compiled by researchers at the Centre d'Etudes de Presse in Bordeaux and published by André-Jean Tudesq, ed., *La Presse et l'événement* (Paris: Mouton, 1973).

[2] See *L'Image* (Paris: Julliard, 1963).

[3] See especially Abraham Moles, *Socio-dynamique de la culture* (Paris: Mouton, 1967).

[4] See Jules Gritti, "Un Récit de presse: Les derniers jours d'un 'grand homme,'" *Communications* 8 (1966), and, in general, the other works of this author, especially *L'Evénement, technique d'analyse de l'actualité* (Paris, 1961).

[5] Edgar Morin, "Principes d'une sociologie du présent," in *La Rumeur d'Orléans* (Paris: Seuil, 1969), p. 225.

[6] See especially Jean Baudrillard, *Le Système des objets* (Paris: Gallimard, 1967).

MICHEL DE CERTEAU

History and Mysticism

1973

Michel de Certeau (1925–1986) occupied in every way a special place in contemporary French historiography. A Jesuit, he taught first in Paris at the Institut Catholique and later, in a more temporary capacity, at the University of California at San Diego, ultimately returning to Paris to a chair at the Ecole des Hautes Etudes in the final years of his life. He is scarcely easier to situate within the discipline: a theologian and historian by training, a philosopher and semiologist, and a member of Jacques Lacan's Ecole Freudienne, he was firmly committed to an interdisciplinarity that is more often alluded to than practiced. Because his work is hard to pin down, it was late to win recognition, which did not really come until after '68 and, to an even greater degree, after his death. His work is of major importance; it is also very diverse and difficult to classify. It includes scholarly publications and essays on contemporary politics and Christianity; a sociohistorical analysis of today's cultural practices, Arts de faire, *1980* [The Practice of Everyday Life]; *and reflections on epistemology and historiography that are among the most profound of recent years in* L'Ecriture de l'histoire, *1975* [The Writing of History]. *His intellectual project has a central thread, however: the anthropology of religious belief, with a focus primarily on mystical experience, about which he wrote many articles and several books including his major work,* La Fable mystique *(the first volume of which appeared in 1982;* The Mystic Fable). *Certeau's background may account for this choice. It also explains why it took so long for his complex and difficult thinking to be recognized. Religious history, and especially the history of mysticism, was traditionally an area for specialists only. Certeau deserves credit for revealing its wider significance by joining the resources of historical analysis and the methods of social science to theological erudition. The following text*

Michel de Certeau, "Histoire et mystique," *Revue d'histoire de la spiritualité*, no. 89 (1972), pp. 69–82. Reprinted in *L'Absent de l'histoire* (Tours: Mame, 1973).

is a good example of Certeau's approach in its explicit relation of the construction of an object, mysticism, to an analysis of the historiographic discourse about that object.

The phrase "history of spirituality" characterizes a field of study in terms of a relation between two types of knowledge. Yet a glance at research in that field shows how changeable that relation is. If one assumes, to begin with, that "historical facts" can be called upon to help in the description of "spiritual experience," one is soon forced to admit that whatever analogies may exist between the projects of history and spirituality, there are fundamental differences in their modes of comprehension. Although both seek to organize series of data into a meaningful whole, history uses operations of its own to *create* an *intelligibility* out of material that it isolates and organizes. Spirituality, insofar as it is a form of expression, *recognizes* a way of relating language to what is *impossible to say* and therefore situates itself in that liminal region where "what cannot be spoken of" is also "what cannot not be spoken of."[1] What the historian articulates is the success of an operation defined by rules and models elaborated by a present intellectual discipline. What the spiritual recounts is the failure of that operation, insofar as the Inaccessible is the sine qua non of Christian discourse, and the language of each discipline is organized in a necessary relation with "that power that comes to theologians from the spirit and causes us to cling without words or knowledge to realities that are neither spoken nor known."[2]

This heteronomy cannot be examined exclusively in terms of a comparison between different "objects" of knowledge or different contents. It calls the nature of each approach into question, as well as the implicit subject. The question cannot be addressed without explicit acknowledgment of the position from which one approaches it. To exclude from our scrutiny the specific interrogations to which that scrutiny is a response would be to conceal one of its essential features, leading to unwarranted generalization. I shall therefore analyze some aspects of the relation between history and spirituality in a personal way, shaped by my work and inextricably associated with a position that is solely my own. These observations arise out of work I have done on Jean-Joseph Surin, a seventeenth-century mystic.

A PLACE AND A TRAJECTORY

After various studies of spiritual reform in the early sixteenth century, particularly in Pierre Favre's European microcosm, the work of Jean-

Joseph Surin (1600–1665) was chosen as the subject of a new investigation. The deteriorated condition of the texts, the possible existence of a large number of unpublished documents, the strangeness of the case, and the depth and originality of the doctrine—all these things suggested that this was a body of work worth exhuming. They also offered the hope of entering into the psychological, social, cultural, and intellectual complexity of one man's history, without which there is no possibility of getting at the significance of a "mystical" existence. More fundamentally, they offered a way of explaining precisely how *experience* comes to find embodiment in a *language,* obeying its constraints and yet creating a personal discourse, thus raising the question of the "Other" in a cultural system.

The problem of language was one of the central literary, philosophical, and religious debates of Surin's time. It structured his work as a dialectic between "language" (*langue*: the system that defines the world and fills it with objects) and the "word of God" (*le langage de Dieu*: spiritual experience that "language cannot express" and that "has no name"). For Surin, there is no established language of truth (set alongside everyday language). The word of God is "radically different" from ordinary "language" (a universal a priori given) and can be related to it only through "style," a "manner of speaking." The "wounds" of the spirit gradually stamp language with its status of being dispossessed of its Other without being replaced by something that speaks it directly.

Long days in public and private archives in France and abroad yielded an ample number of unpublished papers and documents. Rescued from the grottoes in which the treasures of the past slumber, these scattered sources could be fitted together like the pieces of a puzzle to reveal the surprising history of a life and a work—a history still riddled with gaps but sufficiently intact that one could at least determine what the nature of the gaps was and where they were located.

The task of reconstituting Surin's work (some of which remains unpublished) brought me into intimate contact with his thinking and took me deep into the maze of the period.[3] This preliminary work entailed various kinds of burrowing and searching that raised new historical and theological questions as preliminary assumptions and beliefs proved inaccurate.

The assumption, implicit in the original project, of proximity between the spirituals of the seventeenth century and ourselves was one that had to be abandoned. Knowing them better revealed them as strangers. In the very realm where some commonality of language, some Christian understanding, had been assumed, they proved unrecognizable. Approaching them revealed how far away they were: this distance took the form of a *difference* not only of ideas and feelings but also of modes of perception, systems of reference, and a form of experience that I could neither deny was "Christian" nor recognize as my own.

Normally, we domesticate the "dear departed" so that they will not seem out of place in our shop windows or our thoughts; we preserve them under glass, isolate them, and deck them out so that they may edify us or serve as examples. All at once, however, these docile figures escaped my clutches. They *became* "savages" to the extent that their lives and works seemed intimately connected with a bygone era. What is more, this mutation of the "object" of my study coincided with a change in the orientation of my research, which gradually *became* "historical." What characterizes a work as "historical," what allows one to say that one is "making history" (we "produce" history as we manufacture automobiles), is not the conscientious application of established rules (although such rigor is necessary). It is, rather, the operation that creates a space of signs proportionate to an absence; that structures the reconnaissance of the past not in the manner of a present possession or yet another science but in the form of *a discourse structured by a missing presence*; that, through its processing of materials presently dispersed in our own time, opens up a place in language and a reference unto death. . . .

THE HISTORICAL DISCOURSE

Historical work, even in its erudite aspects, is thus more than simply finding and collecting objects. Essentially, it involves the correlation of those objects. By multiplying evidence (the role of erudition) and formulating hypotheses and connections (the role of theory), it establishes a system of relations. It thus produces knowledge of a *past,* that is, a *completed unity* (which may be biographical, ideological, economic, or what have you, and is completed, even if it may survive in the form of "vestiges" implicated in other systems).

One consequence of this is that historiography today cannot dispense with references to a "set" of relations, whether a *mentalité,* a period, a milieu, a "figure," or an episteme. Although this operational "model" makes it possible to produce a difference (that is, to make history), it does not yield the reality of the past. It is, rather, an instrument of the present for achieving "distantiation," a procedure for generating a discourse about an absent figure. In other words, historiography inevitably requires a conceptual tool whose uses have been explained by structuralist analysis.[4] It also signifies the absence of what it re-presents.

This connection between "structure" and "absence" is ultimately the central problem of historical discourse. Its locus is a *text.* That operation that gives birth to interpretation culminates in and is judged by the fabrication of a text—a historical article or book.[5] What is a historical text?

A semantic structure whose purpose is to articulate *the other*: a structure associated with the production (or manifestation) of an absence.

Paper has long since lost its power to resurrect the dead, but this open secret is no reason to veer off into subjectivism or relativism. It simply suggests that the relation of the text to the real is necessarily a relation with death. Historiography is a form of writing, not of speech. It assumes a vanished voice.[6] Only after a once-living unity has been decomposed into a thousand fragments—only after its death, in other words—can the scattered traces that attest to what it was be assembled as an object of discourse, a unity whose purpose is to create intelligibility.

Conversely, the elaboration and organization of historical discourse depend on two things: something (the object of study) *once took place* but that something *no longer exists.* The event happened (or no trace of it would remain), but only its disappearance allows the *different* activity of writing about or interpreting it in the present. Both as something real and as something past, the event "gives way" to something else, namely, historiographic discourse, which would not have been possible without it yet which does not flow from the event in the same way as an effect flows from its cause.

History therefore cannot be reduced to its relation with the departed. Although the "events" with which it deals are a necessary condition, the present is even more important. History assumes a *disparity* between itself and what happened, and the construction of that disparity is the condition of someone constituting himself as presently living and thinking existence as a *thinking* presence. My research taught me that by studying Surin, I was distinguishing msyelf from him. Once I chose him as my object of study, I made myself a subject vis-à-vis the space formed by the traces he left behind. I am an other in relation to this stranger; I am life in the presence of death. . . .

MYSTICAL DISCOURSE

In all these respects, my reflection on my historical research did not have the effect of taking me away from the study with which it began, as if in order to begin a "philosophy" of my work I had to quit the work site altogether. In asking myself what I was doing in pursuing a historical investigation, I was, rather, led back to the object of that investigation. Although a lengthy period of scholarly research had taken me away from that object and initiated a second phase of the work, a period of reflecting on the nature of the investigation, this detour led me toward a better understanding of the problems to which seventeenth-century mystical discourse was intended to respond and toward a clearer perception of the questions intrinsic to Surin's own "research."

In the first place, Surin's work forms a corpus: like historiographic discourse but in a different mode, it is a *structure* whose purpose is to represent the *Other*. Surin's text, which can be analyzed using methods similar to those that yielded "models" of the folktale and fantastic narrative,[7] can be viewed as a structured whole designed *to manifest an absent figure* whose presence in the text as such is impossible but necessary. A referent is the sine qua non of such discourse as well as its semantic "product" (what it says, in other words), but not its content. Surin names this referent in his text—God, or Jesus. Yet he also posits that it is "hidden." We thus need to examine the nature of this "mystical discourse," which relates the stated to the unstated, or which perhaps, wavering between the two, simply juxtaposes contradictory propositions.

In other words, is mystical discourse possible? Or are we obliged to concede that Surin was unable to produce such a discourse? If so, then there should be signs of that inability, such as an inconsistent use of opposites or a vague reliance on ineffable "experience," as in the "night in which all cows are black." In that case, the term "experience" would function in the text as a sign connoting the nonexistence of "theological" language.[8]

Admittedly, Surin's language vacillates between saying and not saying. It is riven by a fissure introduced by the "unknown language" that God "himself forms through his Spirit." However, that fissure leads to a reformation of language, organized as a *coincidatio oppositorum,* not to be confused with the "wall" that, according to Nicholas of Cusa, surrounds heaven: "Ultra igitur coincidentiam contradictorium videri poteris et nequaquam citra."[9] Here we are dealing more with a structure of reference than with an enclosure. For Surin, language does not defend meaning but is wounded by it.

In his work, "the ineffable" is more than just an indication and a measure of the relative value and ultimate insignificance of what is stated. It denotes a *relation* between the contrary terms and propositions of language. It is the relation between *gentle* and *violent*, for example, that says something about "God" or love. In a similar fashion, but at the level of literary macro-unities, the fact that prose refers to poetry and poetry to prose, or, in other words, the establishment of a "proportion" between these two different genres, creates *within language* the space of a signified that their difference indicates but does not name.

In other words, the fissure of "the ineffable" itself structures language. It is not a hole in language or a source of leakage. It becomes, rather, something in relation to which language is redefined. This transformation is more visible elsewhere, in Pascal for example, when he shows how the discourse of Epictetus and Montaigne "is interrupted ... to make room for the truth of the Gospel ... which brings opposites into harmony,"[10] or when he sees in that focal point an indefinite tension between opposites of which the broken name of Jesus Christ is the sign. The revolution here is to replace the traditional relation between words (or language) and "things" by relations *internal to language* (that is, by relations between complementary or contrary terms). Then the "thing" is no longer manifested through or in the word but "hidden" (mystical). An absence articulates the antinomies and paradoxes expressive of a mystical reality that is never given, localized, or verbally identifiable with an expression or some propositions.

Discourse is thus restructured in a way determined by the absence of what it nevertheless designates. This "mystical language," which came in for frequent discussion by Surin and his contemporaries, has two fundamental characteristics. First, a certain *spatialization* of language predominates over the relation of *verbum* to *res* (which one might call "vertical"). The relation to the referent is a relation between signifiers, that is, an organization of linguistic space.

Second, mystical language has a *split structure*, in that the only way to establish a "symbolic" expression is to separate two terms that are necessary, but contrary to each other. Contemporaries were especially interested in the smallest unit of language, "the mystical word." It was said that the simplest signifier was in fact a combination of opposites ("furious quietude," to borrow the example given by Diego de Jesus). The mystical word was inevitably two words, already split. This plural inherent in the elementary unit of significance was the mark of a "mystical" meaning too subtle for language to capture in its toils, a meaning that reconstitutes language itself from its "wound," in view of a fundamental disjunction between word and thing. Diego de Jesus referred to this "doctrine," in which "incision and mystical anatomy" were essential, as a "science of circumcision," a "cutting knife."[11] His discourse is organized as the manifestation of a cut.

"The ineffable" is therefore not so much an object of discourse as a marker of the status of language. While it is easy to see parallel changes in the same period, for example in the organization of Baroque art or in theories of language, it is also important to draw out the implications of this "model" for later interrogations of theological discourse, as well as for that discourse which in many respects has taken its place and rediscovered its difficulties, namely, the discourse of history.

The Question of the Other

Once one has shown (in ways of which the foregoing offers only one example) how mystical discourse is organized in terms of a necessary but absent other about which it speaks, there is still more to be said. The texts analyzed cannot be separated from their production. What distinguishes historical research from literary research is precisely a concern with the problem of production. Historical research takes texts (and other kinds of sources) as clues to systems of action. Every product bears the marks of its production. The goal of history is essentially to relate saying to doing.[12]

Historical work is therefore the reverse of the process of literary transmission or proliferating commentary. It "proceeds backward" from the effect to the objective conditions that made its appearance possible. When we receive a work passed down through the centuries and, thus, detached from the initial conditions of its manufacture and introduced into the circuit of activities characteristic of the present (sale, interpretation, conservation, and so on); when we find texts isolated from the sequence of operations to which they belonged, identified by the name "Surin," and made available for consumption and use by religious groups or other carefully "targeted" readers; then, as historians, we must reconstruct the processes of the (religious and social) "economy" of which the work was in part a product and a symptom. In doing so, we work toward our objective, which is to find out both *what no longer exists* and *what once made possible* the traces or products that we can identify today. We can then posit the *other* as the *condition of possibility* of whatever it is we are analyzing.

Seen in this way, our present task as historians is to specify, in combination, the two elements without which we cannot understand a different "economy": a *structure* of action, and a *disparity*, that which distinguishes any particular work within a social system. On the one hand, therefore, we look for what was *common* to a given system of production, while, on the other, we look for what was *distinctive* about a particular piece of writing.

Neither element can be isolated unless we succumb to positivist or edifying mythology. Surin's work cannot "stand" alone, as if the spiritual groups of the seventeenth century or the theological schisms of the time were only "background" or "context." Conversely, the religious *mentalité* of the time and the progressive marginalization of the spirituals cannot be looked upon as the cause or ground of Surin's individual work. Neither element can be posited separately: the two poles of analysis are mutually dependent. They are contained in their (controllable, extensible) relation. They are not stemming from some real located somewhere, and seized by the historian's language. They explain each other in the particular mode of modern historiography and mutually signify an absent reality: the operations of the past, the actions of another era.

It would be easy but tedious to recount the difficulties that caused the study of Surin at times to veer in the direction of global structures, at other times in the direction of his particularity as an individual writer. On the global side, what gradually emerged was the isolation of "mystical discourse" in the seventeenth century and the division of theology into three autonomous sciences; the constitution of spiritual networks "in the Church but almost without needing it,"[13] marginal churches tantamount to miniature, through which globalizing utopian ideas, at once political and mystical, circulated; the new connections between spiritual literature and popular literature that resulted from the "atheism" and politicization of the elite's frame of reference; the proximity of faith and madness when reason married the state; the similarities between diabolical and mystical phenomena in the period 1620–1640; and so on. Similarly, Surin's individuality also posed problems of its own: his madness, of course, as the extreme form of his pushing the boundaries of thought; but also the "individual" unity constituted not so much by any particular "experience" as by the series or sequence of narratives and treatises identified by the same proper name; the distinctiveness of Surin's relation to language and communication; the organization of his discourse in light of what he was seeking to produce; and so on.

Each of these aspects referred back to its complement, however. Surin's awareness of his "madness" or of the "divine wound," for example, led back to the problem of perceptual codes. The sudden appearance of reds on a textual horizon painted in black and white also implied a dictionary of colors. The architectural pulsation that gripped the entire work in the imaginative categories of "the closed" and "the open" referred to a symbolic antinomy of surface and hole in the artistic and scientific language of the time. And so on.

The endless details of the interpretive operation repeatedly raised an issue that also comes up in historical work and the internal dialectic of its object: the relation of continuity (structure) to rupture (event). Here we touch on an essential question, no doubt the central question of Surin's "mysticism," where it comes up in two forms: either in terms of the relation of the divine *universal* to the *particularity* of experience, or in terms of the compatibility between "catholicism" (a universal or human extension) and an always necessary "division" (*coupure*), whether of the "world," the group, or religious tradition itself.

In Surin's doctrine, this tension comes up in the form of the *necessary* connection between the "first step" (division, leap, decision, sudden move) and the "universal and confused notion" (knowledge without cause or understanding). Not that one produces the other, or that there is an obligatory chronological passage from one to the other: the universal of the "notion" *is not possible* without the "first step." That universal constantly refers back to that first step as to a *limit* (a "loss" or death) upon which the *pati divina* falls, or as to a rupture that is never "transcended" because it is repeated in various forms throughout the spiritual journey and thus becomes the driving force that makes each act of spiritual "understanding" the "quasi metaphor" for a new knowledge.[14]

In other words, the sense never appears as a state or an object of knowledge or even a stable, docile relation. It is *given* only in function of an *act*. It is the universal associated with a rupture, never identifiable with one or the other. The truth announced by the movement is the *endless relation of difference and necessity* between the "space" of signification that every rupture opens up and the "loss of place" that is forever renewed through one form or another of the conversion fostered by life in the "region of pure love."

This problematic illuminates our enigmatic relation to the Other in and through history, the nature of Christian mysticism, and the relation of historiography to mysticism: this, at any rate, is the hypothesis that slowly emerged in the course of one historian's journey through the spiritual literature of the seventeenth century.

TRANSLATED BY ARTHUR GOLDHAMMER

NOTES

[1] See Rubina Giorgi, "Le Langage théologique comme différence," *L'Analyse du langage théologique: Le nom de Dieu* (Paris: Aubier, 1969), pp. 75–80.

[2] Pseudo-Dionysus, *Oeuvres complètes*, trans. by M. de Gandillac, p. 67: "On Divine Names," 1.1.

[3] Jean-Joseph Surin, *Guide spirituel* (Paris: Desclée de Brouwer, 1963); *Correspondance* (Paris: Desclée de Brouwer, 1966). Critical editions of the *Catéchisme spirituel*, *La Science expérimentale*, and much of the *Dialogues spirituels* are currently ready for publication.

[4] See Jean Viet, *Les Méthodes structuralistes dans les sciences sociales* (Paris, The Hague: Mouton, 1967), pp. 5–20; and for a more epistemological interpretation, François Wahl, "La Philosophie entre l'avant et l'après du structuralisme," *Qu'est-ce que le structuralisme?* (Paris: Seuil, 1968), pp. 299–442. Note a continuity and a discontinuity: with this contemporary epistemology, the problem posed by German criticism, which exhumed a philosophy of history from every positivist study, is both repeated and reformulated. Indeed, the historian's "ideas," choices, and intuitions can now be analyzed in terms of "strategies" of scientific practice in light of the sociocultural conditions of historical understanding. On the German critique of scientific positivism, see Raymond Aron, *Introduction à la philosophie de l'histoire: Essai sur les limites de l'objectivité historique* (Paris: Vrin, 1938), and *La Philosophie critique de l'histoire* (Paris: Vrin, 1971).

[5] G. R. Elton, *The Practice of History* (New York, 1967), pp. 88–141.

[6] Jacques Derrida distinguishes in his work between voice and writing: the former is characterized by unitary reference to a presence, the latter by a spatial plurality and effacement of its origins. His analyses are useful for clarifying the status of historiography, provided that we do not assume that it is an emergence of the past. See, in particular, *De la Grammatologie* (Paris: Minuit, 1967), pp. 11–142.

[7] See Vladimir J. Propp, *Morphologie du conte* (Paris: Seuil, 1970); Tzvetan Todorov,

Introduction à la littérature fantastique (Paris: Seuil, 1970); Louis Marin, *Sémiotique de la passion* (Paris: Bibliothèque des Sciences Religieuses, 1971); and Erhard Guettgemanns, "Text und Geschichte als Grundkategorien der generativen Poetik," *Linguistica Biblica* 11–12 (Jan. 1972), pp. 2–12.

[8] In which case one would have to follow Ludwig Wittgenstein in using "mystical" to refer to all that lies outside the realm of the sayable: "an ontological catchall." See Jacques Poulain, "Le Mysticisme du *Tractatus Logico-philosophicus* et la situation paradoxale des propositions religieuses," in D. Dubarle et al., *La Recherche en philosophie et en théologie* (Paris: Cerf, 1970), pp. 75–155.

[9] Nicholas of Cusa, *Philosophisch-theologische Schriften* (Vienna, 1964–67), vol. 3, p. 132: "Visio Dei," ch. 9.

[10] Courcelle, ed., *Entretien de M. Pascal et de M. de Sacy* (Paris: Vrin, 1960), pp. 55–61.

[11] Diego de Jesus, *Notes et remarques en trois discours pour donner une plus facile intelligence des phrases mystiques,* in *Les Oeuvres spirituelles du B. Père Jean de la Croix* (Paris: Chevallier, 1652), p. 272 (separate pagination).

[12] This is also a fundamental theological problem, which is all too often obliterated by looking only at constituted discourse. See Michel de Certeau, "L'Articulation du dire et du faire," *Etudes théologiques et religieuses* 45 (1970), pp. 25–44.

[13] Alphonse Dupront, "De l'Eglise aux temps modernes," *Revue d'histoire ecclésiastique* 66 (1971), pp. 440–41.

[14] On the term "quasi metaphor," which W. P. Alston, *Philosophy of Language* (Englewood Cliffs, N.J.: Prentice Hall, 1964), p. 105, proposes as the designation for a type of religious terminology, see also Jean Ladrière, "La Théologie et le langage de l'interprétation," *Revue théologique de Louvain* 1 (1970), pp. 262–64.

Moving Abroad

JOHN V. MURRA AND NATHAN WACHTEL

Anthropological History of
Andean Politics

1986

The historiographic "growth" of the period 1960–1980 stemmed from a proliferation of new research objects and approaches. Less commonly, it also took the form of thought experiments. Although comparative history in France has largely remained in the category of wishful thinking, the most convincing efforts in this direction came in the realm of "area studies," where history and anthropology could fruitfully meet. Two examples are excerpted here.

Social scientists, particularly in France, have been fascinated by South America since the 1930s. There are three reasons for this. First, South America was long untouched by European influence, hence it was a fruitful source of new experience and possibilities of comparison. Second, colonial America was for four centuries a theater and prize of European competition, as if the models and values of old Europe had been put to the test by a different set of historical experiences. Finally, this was new terrain and therefore called for a new approach, calling upon the combined skills of prehistorians, geographers, archaeologists, linguists, anthropologists, and historians.

This was the thrust of the collection of articles that John Murra, an American anthropologist, and Nathan Wachtel, a French historian, prepared for the Annales *in 1978 under the title "Anthropological History of Andean Societies." This was the first in a series of attempts to illustrate the possible heuristic uses of comparative study of unfa-*

From John V. Murra, Nathan Wachtel, and Jacques Revel, eds., *Anthropological History of Andean Politics* (Cambridge, Eng.: Cambridge University Press, and Paris: Editions de la Maison des Sciences de l'Homme, 1986), pp. 1–8.

*miliar worlds. The goal was not to assemble a collection of studies of
different areas (the Andes, the Islamic world, Africa, India) but to
show how a set of analytical categories could be tested against various
historical realities. As the authors state at the outset, "Andean
America is truly a testing ground for human and social disciplines."*

In an environment of violent contrasts, frequently at the very limits
of adaptive possibilities, Andean America is truly a testing ground
for human and social disciplines. The societies developed here, numerous and extremely diverse, lived in isolation from the rest of the
world for thousands of years, achieving most of what they did on their
own. Their history followed an original, pristine course. The culmination of these processes is the emergence of Tawantinsuyu, the Inka state,
one of the larger and more powerful preindustrial polities.

If such independent development were to be appreciated for the rare
opportunity it provides for comparative inquiry, one could expect Andean studies to flourish. This dimension is not yet the dominant one.
Nonetheless, independent of any comparative urge, our understanding
of the Andean world has undergone some major changes during the last
few decades, a progress not only quantitative, through an accumulation
of discoveries, but also qualitative, through changes in the sources used,
our methods, and the very object of our inquiry. How do we explain
this mutation?

For centuries, historians, both from the Andean republics and from
abroad, had centered their fascinated attention on the Inka "empire."
Ever since the sixteenth century, Andean precious metals had fed fantasies of El Dorados; Andean institutions also provided "facts" for the
utopian needs of writers as diverse as the Inca Garcilaso de la Vega and
Marmontel. As recently as 1928, the carefully documented work of Louis
Baudin was entitled *L'Empire socialiste des Inkas*. Although it is no longer
fashionable to use that adjective when discussing the last Andean state,
an ample if discordant bibliography is currently busy documenting "Asiatic," feudal, or slave modes of production in this region. At the third
congress devoted to "Andean man and culture," in 1977, each of the
above characterizations and many another had its articulate partisans.[1]
What hope then for clarifying the puzzle before us?

The newcomer to these debates should note that all of these interpretations, diverse as they may seem, actually draw on the same sources,
few in number and by now treated as classic. We have all been reading
the letters and other eyewitness accounts of the European invasion, plus
the somewhat later "chroniclers." These remain irreplaceable, but one
soon becomes aware of the double filter they project between the Andean

event and us: the first screen was the European observer; the second, his informant, usually a member of the Cusco elite. No doubt, some of these observers, notably Polo de Ondegardo and Cieza de León, tried to get beyond the limitations distorting their queries. Aware of discrepancies among the reports of their informants, they tried to reach those who had been functioning adults before the European invasion. It does not seem too much to claim an ethnological inspiration for their work. Still, the institutions of the Inka state had collapsed with the fall of Cajamarca and the help the Europeans had received from ethnic groups such as the Wanka; whatever information about Tawantinsuyu could still be amassed in the 1540s and 1550s by Pedro Cieza or the lawyer Polo was irremediably fragmentary and much of it unverifiable.

A further consideration: in the history of Andean America, the Inka state is a very recent and brief (no more than a century) experience that was itself the heir to many much earlier political formations. Even the most knowledgeable of the European chroniclers confuse these earlier achievements and attribute to the Cusco armies a civilizing mission. In fact, it had taken centuries, if not millennia, to achieve Andean productivity and managerial capacity. Attempts to reconstruct the Andean experience with the aid of such flimsy data, padded out with exotic theoretical models, seem to us to be destined to frustration.

One should mention here another approach to Andean studies: independent of all of the above, social anthropologists, most of them from the United States but also some others trained under their tutelage, have stressed contemporary monographical research. Asking few questions about the antecedents of present-day Andean populations, they found the *comunidad* a convenient framework for their inquiries. If one ignored even the most recent past, "communities" seemed to be the basic units of the indigenous world.

To treat the community, particularly in its Peruvian context, in that way is a dubious, ahistoric venture; there is no way of projecting seriously from present-day practice to institutions four centuries earlier. Even where these monographs provide interesting information, it is hard to use it to understand the Andean world: there is no way of knowing how these "communities" came to be the heirs of the large polities we know to have been prevalent in the Andes both before and after the Inka. In fact, the communities of today are recent colonial and even republican phenomena. Fortunately, in both Bolivia and Ecuador, ethnic groups are still functioning with their own authorities and federating scores of villages.

Thus, historians as well as social anthropologists have reached their own dead ends. Both have held on to their particular end of a historical continuum: the macrocosm of the Inka state and the microstructure of contemporary comunidades. These two static approaches, bedeviled also by incompatibilities of scale, have remained without an intelligible link between them.

New questions had to be asked both of the traditional sources and of the new ones that were emerging. Sometime around 1960, Andean scholars committed themselves to a more interdisciplinary approach, linking, among other fields, archaeology with historical and ethnographic inquiries.

An example—perhaps an obvious one—of the new approaches: a re-reading of the sixteenth-century dictionaries of the Andean languages. In 1560, Domingo de Santo Tomas had found himself unable to translate adequately the Quechua kin terminology he was compiling for his dictionary. Aware that he was dealing with new ethnocategories, he decided to place the topic in his grammar, since it was plain to him that he was handling more than just an intractable vocabulary. Beginning with such linguistic hints, it has been possible to connect the sixteenth-century kinship terminology with data from the parochial registers of the seventeenth and eighteenth centuries, and eventually with contemporary practice. With such methods, we have begun to formulate a model for the Inka kinship system.

Another dimension of the renewed interest of anthropologists in written sources has been their utilization of colonial administrative archives. Thousands of bundles containing litigation, tax, and census records had been available for four centuries in public and private repositories but had remained unused—perhaps because they did not convey any version of the dynastic oral tradition. When they began to be read, historians and anthropologists could see that the issue in the Andes, as elsewhere, was not so much the availability of sources as the questions asked.

A clear example is the well-known protocols of inspections, the so-called *visitas,* of ethnic groups such as the Lupaqa near Lake Titicaca or the Chupaychu of the Huallaga Valley, both carried out by European officials in the 1560s. The second, undertaken on Phillip II's orders by Iñigo Ortiz de Zúñiga, was republished in 1967 and 1972. It had already been transcribed and printed by Father Domingo Angulo as far back as 1920: one wonders how it escaped the attention of the investigators and why it took forty years to "rediscover" it. These inspections are true field inquiries: in the case of the Chupaychu, we get a thorough door-to-door census of several thousand households. Two detailed questionnaires inquired into overall resources, the kinds of crops cultivated, prestations owed to the Inka as compared to those demanded by the *encomendero,* political organization, matrimonial arrangements, religious beliefs, and so forth. Dozens of witnesses testified, some old enough in 1562 to have known Wayna Qhapaq, who died in 1530. The availability of such sources encouraged the Institute of Andean Research to sponsor in 1963–65 a study of the region covered by the *visita*. Historians looked for further written sources; ethnologists and archaeologists cooperated in locating the abandoned dwelling units of the local lords. The archaeologists could then attempt to excavate the dwellings of these polygynous households. It was also possible to document historical continuities in ethnic organization between 1562 and 1965 in fifteen communities studied by the field-workers.

Obviously, no one would wish to retroject mechanically the present onto the past. The use of multiple tactics, all of them starting from the same series of historical hints, allows us to uncover a truly Andean link between the pre-European past and the desperate present. The tactics outlined above for the Chupaychu cannot reach beyond the local and regional levels: rather, they reveal the extreme diversity of ethnic groups and polities that both preceded the Inka state and endured long after its destruction, in some cases until today. Between the immense "empire" of the travelogues and the artificially shrunken community of today's countryside, we watch the emergence of a whole new set of intermediary structures, both temporal and spatial. The two separate ends of the missing chain can, possibly, now be joined, and with them the links between history and anthropology.

Beyond regional diversity, such a comparison reveals the profound unity of Andean civilization as well as its originality. We are able to identify an extraordinarily enduring model, which explains the Andean organization of space as a function of ecological complementarity among the diverse tiers of this broken environment. The nuclei crowded in the highlands, at altitudes above 3,500 meters, where the land was used by the bulk of the population for camelid herding and the production of tubers, reached for self-sufficiency by dispatching colonies, known as *mitmaq,* to many warmer, peripheral settlements. In this way, the highlanders gained continuous access to the exotic maize, fish, hot peppers, timber, cotton, and coca leaf of the lowlands. Such complementary distribution did not imply control of the intermediate regions, beyond trying to protect the caravan routes against pirates. The pattern that emerges is one that the sixteenth-century Europeans called *salpicado,* a "sprinkled" distribution of dispersed settlements belonging to a single polity. In another metaphor, any one ethnic group's territory formed an "archipelago," grouping "islands" up and down the cordilleras and reaching west to the Pacific and east to the Amazon.

One peculiarly Andean feature is that these complementary outliers were frequently multiethnic: representatives of polities quite distant from each other in the mountains found themselves in close, if tense,

proximity at the periphery. These settlements were five, ten, and sometimes even more days' walk away from their respective power centers.
How the tensions were resolved or how the caravans linking a polity's
outliers were protected is not yet sufficiently understood.

It is nevertheless clear that in such circumstances barter or trade
among the ethnic groups was reduced to a marginal percentage of the
exchange traffic. This is a major difference between the Andes and Mes-
oamerica, where we know that large marketplaces operated on schedule
and that professional merchants, frequently of high status, undertook
not only economic but also political assignments.[2] Since 1972, when the
archipelago model was first outlined at a comparative seminar organized
by Angel Palerm in Mexico, efforts have been made to identify the
model's geographical limits and structural limitations. Archaeologists
have probed for its antecedents and early manifestations. Ethnologists
have discovered its enduring relevance.[3] As a result, it seems that the
model applied most effectively in the Qollasuyu part of the Inka realm.
Polities with a nucleus on the coast or in the tropical highlands of the
northern Inka periphery did not fit the model.

Wherever it did function, the "vertical archipelago" implied a rather
closed economic circuit, linking several tiers through ties of kinship,
ethnic identification, and political subordination. This nesting of *ayllu*,
moieties, and ethnic levels into a single pyramid can still be seen at work
today, albeit in reduced, almost beggared circumstances. When the Inka
state expanded its dominion over hundreds of conquered polities, it attempted to project a familiar model to a vast territory and an unprecedented population. The state set up its own "islands" in the conquered
domain; the local people were expected to work these lands in much the
same spirit as they had harvested the acreage of their own ethnic lord or
local shrine. Again, on the model of these traditional authorities, the
Cusco state was expected to behave with "institutional generosity," so
that this asymmetrical reciprocity would manifest itself at each level of
the pyramid and on every ecological tier.

But the greatly expanded scale of operations, as a result of which the
mitmaq colonies might now find themselves sixty days' walk from their
homelands or assigned to garrison or mining rather than agricultural
duties, argues that the organization of the archipelago had been fundamentally altered. Colonists who were sent far away from their ethnic
homelands could no longer return there easily to exercise residual rights
in farming, marriage choices, or worship. If to this we add the establishment of a completely unprecedented management domain, independent
of local and regional interests, along the Inka highways (administrative
centers, warehouses, military installations), we can assume that the vertical archipelago was undergoing fundamental changes in the decades

immediately before 1532. However, it probably continued at the local, ethnic level, since we find it functioning and affecting the earliest European settlement patterns.

The kingdoms and lesser polities conquered were presumed by their rulers to be incorporated within the "realm of the four parts," Tawantin-suyu: in a way, quadripartition is an elaboration of the underlying dual division found throughout the central and southern Andes. As in many other instances where moieties prevail, we are faced with a system of classification that orders not only society but also space, time, the very universe, through a series of confronted pairs: high and low; male and female; left and right; summer and winter. It is notable that in this part of the world, neither moieties nor their subdivisions have any exogamous functions: preferential marriage is endogamous within the *ayllu* and moiety. Can we then claim that each group affirmed its identity by stressing its opposition to its immediate neighbors at comparable levels?

In fact, the deeper meaning of Andean dualism surfaces in one of its most original traits, the mirror image. The component elements of any of the classificatory categories can undergo endless bisection. Thus, the upper moiety can be divided into a part perceived as the "upper upper," whereas the other becomes the "lower upper." Similarly, the lower half can be partitioned into the "lower and upper halves of the lower" (and so on, indefinitely). Such subdivisions can overlap and cross each other, generating quadripartitions and devising multiple configurations, all of which depend on the observer's stance. Structuralist analyses can in certain cases clarify the internal logic of the permutations, a logic defined by its repetitive and relational character.

One can detect a structural homology in the processes of subdivision of opposed pairs, the nesting arrangement of social groups, and the closed economic circuit within the vertical archipelago. The evidence seems to favor a self-enclosed circuit of production and exchange, which, we think, could not exist in the Andes unless it faced the reflection of a circuit formed by classificatory categories as well as systematic bisection of the ethnic groups. All could be bisected, indefinitely.

We are not dealing with a hypothetical "order of orders" that would provide a definitive key to stratified structures. Most likely we are confronting here a global logic that permeated both experiences and representations simultaneously; these, in turn, were folded back into practice. All of this categorized societies that we cannot parse into the facile traditional categories of economic, social, political, or religious concerns, which are usually summoned from Western norms. The model of the archipelago cannot be reduced to its economic dimension; from its very expansion out of transhumance, it was part of a symbolic network. It presupposes an overall scheme assimilating the allocation of lands and the assertion of kinship ties; attitudes toward work; the distribution of power; agricultural and pastoral rituals; and eventually, relations with the gods.

It is not so much that these elements are linked in terms of some neat parallelism: their homology manifests itself at the level of general principles of organization. They are articulated within a system of relations in which clusters and their subdivisions are defined through mutual opposition, but they are also repeated: they nest, and they correct themselves following a variety of criteria and perspectives (the dominant Aymara, the dominated Uru, and so on). Geographically, these general principles are operative over a vast area; they provide its unity, the one we call Andean civilization.

After the European invasion, the state's institutions crumbled; local polities weakened and were eventually fragmented; the ethnic differences paled, but an overall scheme endured. The indigenous world readjusted under colonial domination. Thus, it is notable that after the European administration ordered massive resettlement into *reducciones,* the inhabitants of the Andes (who had become "Indians") spontaneously organized these strategic villages along dualistic lines. The *ayllu*s continued as their basic component. Many mitmaq of the state abandoned their distant exile to return to their homes; once the authority of the ethnic lords was eroded, local autonomies were strengthened at the moiety and lineage level. Regionally, vertical archipelagoes were consolidated.

The colonial system tried to impose a new logic—that of the marketplace, of a money economy, and of an organization of space based on relations no longer vertical but longitudinal, oriented to a dominant pole: the mines and the city of Potosí. But even Spanish domination could not forgo the partial utilization of certain indigenous institutions such as the *mita*. Although this reuse detaches such institutions from their native context, its continued utilization contributes to the perpetuation of an ancient framework, no matter how distorted. Colonial society was constructed from many more such Andean components than is generally recognized.

This collection is organized along three major axes, which we think are related:

1. Problems of spatial organization and the relations between the ethnic polities and the Inka state.

2. Systems of classification; symbolic representations and practices.

3. The progressive erosion of ethnic groups and the emergence of the "community."

The collection presents contributions of historians, geographers, archaeologists, and ethnologists. It does not pretend to provide an exhaustive balance sheet of Andean studies. We have aimed, rather, to offer a view of the issues under debate and some samples of work in progress that we hope will stimulate further inquiry.

NOTES

[1] The congress met in Lima; its *Proceedings* were edited by Ramiro Matos in 1978. The debate over modes of production can be followed in a collection edited by Waldemar Espinoza, *Los Modos de producción en el imperio de los incas* (Lima, 1978).

[2] For a different analysis of exchange in the Andes, see the paper read by Pedro Carrasco at a comparative seminar held at Stanford University, published in George A. Collier, Renato I. Rosaldo, and John D. Wirth, eds., *The Inca and the Aztec States, 1400–1800: Anthropology and History* (New York: Academic Press, 1982).

[3] See also the symposium organized by Flores Ochoa at Americanist meetings in Paris, published as *Actes, XLIIe Congrès International des Américanistes,* vol. 4 (Paris, 1978).

DENYS LOMBARD

"The Virtues of the Javanese Case"

1990

Another example of the methodical employment of dépaysement
(estrangement, getting away for a clearer view) to rethink our habit-
ual categories is the fruit of many years' labor: Denys Lombard's
Carrefour javanais *(1990, 3 vols., more than 1,000 pages). Lom-*
bard's original model was no doubt Braudel's La Méditerranée: *this*
is the comprehensive history of a complex space over a very longue
durée. *After pinpointing some of the complexities of present-day In-*
donesian society, the author proceeds to a "geological" type of analy-
sis: he identifies what he calls "mental nebulae," or forms of historical
experience similar to superposed strata of the past that still produce
more or less visible surface manifestations.

What is more, Lombard (born 1937) reveals the limits of Western-
ization in this cultural region. The coexistence of several time frames
and several worlds requires novel instruments of analysis to under-
stand what modernity means in a society as intricate and complex
as this.

In our effort to analyze Javanese complexity, we have examined three
successive entities, sociocultural "nebulae" that could, it seemed,
usefully be treated as independent. Although these are of very different ages, it was in some ways arbitrary to treat them separately, since
they have been closely intertwined for more than two centuries. But isn't
it just as arbitrary to distinguish, as we habitually do, antiquity from the
Middle Ages and the Middle Ages from modern times? Our classificatory procedure has at least two benefits: it reveals certain enduring long-
term features without imposing a chronological straitjacket, and it highlights the diverse components of Javanese society today.

It would have been theoretically possible, and perhaps desirable, to
add the outlines of a fourth nebula, the origins of which would have

Denys Lombard, *Le Carrefour javanais: Essai d'histoire globale* (Paris: Editions de
l'École des Hautes études en Sciences Sociales, 1990), pp. 151–57.

remained to be discovered in the remotest epochs of protohistory. Using linguistic data, myths, and above all ethnographic comparisons, one might hope to uncover certain aspects of prestate societies, vestiges of which remain in the exterior isles and even on Java (in the Baduy region, for example); we can only assume that these predated the advent of the concentric kingdoms. In the present work, we have touched on some of these archaic influences in connection with the symbolism of the *maca-pat,* the distribution of basic colors, the calender, and certain residual rituals (the shamanic origins of the shadow theater, the relation between the sacrifice of the water buffalo and the cult of the dead).

Comparison with the easternmost islands, which were less subject to the influence of Asia, is sometimes enlightening. Pushing the comparison with remote Melanesia as far as he could, W. H. Rassers, for example, suggested that the Sumatran *surau* and Javanese *pondok* may simply have been continuations of the old "men's houses" of New Guinea, and that the door pictured on the *kayon,* that essential image of the *wayang kulit,* was in fact that of a house of initiation. Specialists in Indonesia and Asia tend to give priority to the Eurasian side of Indonesia and therefore to neglect its Melanesian side. Since F. A. E. van Wouden, research has largely focused on the middle ground of the Great East. This has given us a better understanding of how the "house societies" that still occupy this area function and organize symbolic space. New data should shed light on the epigraphs of ancient Java and help to clear up some obscure terms. It would be foolish, however, to hope to explain everything with such reductionist comparative methods. In Java as in the rest of Bali, the deepest strata were profoundly affected by the formation of kingdoms, and comparisons with more oriental societies can at best serve to identify and date certain eccentric, isolated entities.

We shall therefore confine our attention to the three nebulae described here, which together cover the last millennium. The reader will have noticed that the three nebulae are not situated on the same plane. Between the first and the second there is essentially no rupture of continuity. In the Westernized cells as in the Asiatic networks, we are dealing with societies open to the winds of the sea and built around a small number of virtually identical port cities. We distinguished one from the other primarily because of the prominence of the colonial presence, or, in other words, the lack of distance, which blinds the observer, whether Western or Indonesian. One can imagine that a time may come when the Western networks will appear as no more than a special case and the European presence as no more than a stage in a longer-term evolution.

Whatever the value of this temporary distinction may be, there is one fact that I believe is essential, namely, that the preliminary signs of modernity appeared not with the arrival of the Portuguese or the Dutch but with the coming of the Muslim merchants and the rise of the first sultanates. Islam, which attaches value to the individual history of Muhammad and proposes, with the concept of *umma,* an ecumenical worldview centered on holy cities, did much to spread the idea of a linear time and a geographic space. We have also seen how the cities fostered a new notion of the "individual" (*diri*) and a more complex notion of *sesama,* which is close to our idea of "the Other." None of this, of course, is meant to diminish the role of those Westerners who later gave currency to their own mental equipment, especially the crucial notion of scientific spirit. Nevertheless, it helps us to understand why Islam today hardly feels shaken by Western modernity and retains a prodigious hold on the minds of its followers.

If we must therefore give up the idea that the West was the only initiator of "modern times," we must also rid ourselves once and for all of the old clichés of oriental despotism and the Asiatic mode of production. The all-but-uninterrupted emergence of Indian island sultanates from Pasai in the thirteenth century to Brunei, which recently regained its independence, as well as Chinese trading centers from Gresik in the fourteenth century to Singapore, suffices to show that the Archipelago was just as familiar as Italy or Flanders with the "model" of the mercantile city open to international trade and relatively liberated from agrarian demands. Several of these cities coined their own currency and established laws governing commercial associations and financial operations.

While the "model" does not seem to have been widespread in other parts of Asia over equally long periods, there is no reason to regard the "Malay sultanate" as an exception or aberration. The study of Chinese and other bureaucracies has led to undue neglect of the role of merchants and of the European trading companies, relegating Asian traders to a secondary role (or a subaltern one, like that of *compradors*). As early as the thirteenth century, we have, in Fuijan, the excellent example of Quanzhou (the Zaitun of Marco Polo and Ibn Battuta), which was home to various foreign communities (Muslim, Hindu, Nestorian), and which fell, for a time at least, under the domination of a great merchant. Numerous other cases could be mentioned in China, Japan (Osaka, Sakai), and India (Calicut, Surat), to say nothing of the caravan cities of Central Asia, where Islam also encouraged the creation of "sultanates."

It is true, however, that not even in the Archipelago were these Asian merchants able to achieve the efficiency and will to power that gave the advantage to their nineteenth-century Western counterparts. The real question here has to do with the relation of trade to politics and, more generally, the place of traders in society. A very interesting case is that of the Javanese Paisir, which, following the rise of Demak, Surabaya, and

Banten, was forced to accept the domination of the interior and to give up its control of trade to agents of Mataram (and later of the VOC). If the authorities in the maritime sultanates were content to collect customs duties and to protect the interests of private merchants, things were very different in the agrarian states, where trade was in the hands of functionaries who could at most accept occasional "gifts" while channeling the bulk of the profits from trade into the public treasury. This coercion by the mercantile state probably accounts as much if not more than the superiority of Western technology for the relative backwardness of the business class.

The continuity of the merchants' historical role nevertheless bears emphasizing. The thread runs unbroken from the great Islamicized network that Ibn Battuta explored in the fourteenth century to the economic successes that one observes today not only in Japan and Korea but in the emirates of the Gulf, in certain sectors of the Indian economy, and even in Southeast Asia, where national bourgeoisies are reinforcing their positions alongside the Chinese of the diaspora. Two characteristic features of these societies are worth recalling. We have already noted them in the case of Java, but they are found throughout maritime Asia: the traditional role of "specialized merchant communities" generally held together by endogamy and distinctive rites, and the ancient affinity between Islam and commerce, one consequence of which is that today's "Islamism" often takes root among modest shopkeepers.

One is immediately struck by the presence on all shores of the Indian Ocean of seemingly closed communities living on trade and moneylending. In Java alone we find, apart from the somewhat mysterious "Khmers" of the epigraphic period, the Khoja Indians, the Armenians, the Hadrami Arabs, and certain especially exclusive Chinese groups such as the Hokchia, originally from Fuqing. Yet the model is also found elsewhere in a variety of forms—for example, the networks of Banyans, Chettiars, Parsees, Gujrati Muslims, Ismailians, and Bohras. Also, bear in mind that Europe, too, had its communities of Syri, Jews, Lombards, and Huguenots long before its bourgeoisies seized control of politics and became "national."

What characterizes all these groups is not the religion they profess, which can be very diverse—the Banyans and Chettiars are Hindus, the Parsees are Mazdeans, the Armenians are Christians, and other groups are Islamic or Jewish—but, rather, the way in which they live, as "minorities" closed off and different from the rest of the society of which they are a part. Always close to the authorities but without direct access to power themselves, these mercantile "castes" enjoy official protection and complicity as long as they are needed. They know full well, however, that sooner or later they will be ransomed or even expelled, and so they insure themselves against such risks by diversifying their business, establishing themselves in numerous locations, and developing what can only be called a "multinational" system *avant la lettre*.

Note, moreover, that Muslim "reformists" have repeatedly had close ties to small entrepreneurs and intermediaries, to the world of the bazaar and the "informal economy." In Java, the Sarekat Islam, the Muhammadiyah, and the Masjumi reflected in turn, at one level or another, the crystallization of consciousness in still-insecure business milieus, which looked to reformed Islam to provide them with a common denominator and a new infusion of energy. Comparisons are possible with reformist movements in Malaysia (the PAS) and the Indian subcontinent (the Jama'at-i-Islami of Maulana Maududi, for example). Despite numerous doctrinal divergences, it is tempting to see all these movements as expressing the reaction of frustrated entrepreneurs and the revival of ancient networks aspiring at last to form full-fledged national bourgeoisies.

By contrast, the third nebula has a very different geographic base—the rice-growing regions of the interior rather than the port cities of the coast. The relative abundance of epigraphic documents made it possible to trace its history much farther back than that of the mercantile networks, which left few significant traces prior to the fifteenth century.

The study of this agrarian society proved to be highly instructive, not so much for what it revealed about the difficult struggle with the forest (for that is a general phenomenon associated with the dawn of any number of civilizations), nor for what it taught us about this society's hierarchical system or conception of royalty (although there is in Javanese nobility no shortage of distinctive features), but because it led us to uncover a unique form of urban concentration, markedly different from what we are used to but unsurprisingly similar to the cities of the Pasisir. To be sure, Europe too was familiar with the notion of an *omphalos,* or umbilicus, and our administrative capitals also function as the concentrated expression of the territory they administer. On the other hand, true "cities" are privileged enclaves in which the atmosphere and spirit are different from elsewhere, as in the celestial Jerusalem that medieval imagery depicted as encircled by walls. Such cities contrast with the flat country that surrounds them, from which they are separated by ramparts and customs barriers; today, suburbs isolate our cities from the countryside just as effectively.

But Mojopahit, along with Surakarta and Yogyakarta, were cosmological and palatial centers that remained in close symbiosis with the surrounding territory from which nothing tangible separated them in either a topographical or conceptual sense. The extraordinary *garebeg* ritual is still there to symbolize, albeit in a somewhat bastardized way, the indissoluble bond between the center and the periphery; and the ubiquity of the *wayang kulit,* which everywhere evokes the same shadows and propagates the same norms, whether at court or in the remotest of villages, attests to this cultural homogeneity. Here, there is no discontinuity between the urban and rural worlds but rather a continuum, which stretches from the palace to the edge of the primal forest, allowing the brilliant light of the center to filter all the way to the edges of the inhabited world.

This "agrarian city" model is not unique to Java. Although it appears not to have existed in Europe, where the castle was not enough to create the city, we find similar phenomena not only in Southeast Asia at Angkor, Pagan, Sukhotai, and Chieng Mai, but also in Ceylon, China, and Japan. Paul Wheatley and others have studied the symbolic aspects of these "hub cities," but much remains to be said about the economic and social structures associated with them. There is also work to be done on comparing the evolution of this model with that of the mercantile city as the two developed in parallel and often in competition with each other.

Whereas, in Java, the two urban types coexisted independently (although some features of the central cities can be found at times in the layout of the ports of the Pasisir), it is fascinating to observe that in the Indochinese peninsula the two mingled and combined. In North Vietnam, the commercial city of Ke-cho attached itself to the administrative city of Thang-long (Hanoi). In Lower Burma, Pegou was also a twin city, and the late-sixteenth-century English traveler Ralph Fitch described the merchant suburb alongside the symbolic city. Finally, in Siam's royal city of Ayuthia one can still see the vestiges of the various quarters in which foreigners settled. A comparative study of different urban plans and their evolution over time would be most valuable.

Let us return one last time to the fundamental conflict that continually pitted the agrarian regions against the mercantile networks. I have no intention of posing as a *dalang* and explaining this permanent struggle in terms of two rival energies. Yet I am inclined to see the antagonism as one of the essential wellsprings of Javanese, and indeed Indonesian, history.

One thing seems certain, though it may pain many of my Javanese friends: the worst blow to the "capitalist" dynamic of the Pasisir was dealt not by the VOC but by Mataram. If the maritime destiny of the Chinese empire had begun to wane by the end of the fifteenth century with the abandonment of the expeditions begun by Zheng He, that of Java was compromised a century later by the decline of Demak and thwarted for a long time to come when Sultan Agung destroyed Surabaya in 1625. The agrarian state's victory over the coast symbolized the route of the free Asian merchants and ultimately ensured Dutch domination over all foreign trade and relations with other countries.

Yet if we are tempted to condemn Mataram for this "historic error," another thought should give us pause. Nothing so vast as today's Indonesia would exist were it not for the federating virtues of that same agrarian state. It is revealing in this respect to compare the fate of the three great concentric kingdoms of Southeast Asia whose moments in the sun we can still observe. Neither the Angkorian nor the Paganian model really succeeded in unifying vast territories, even if one believes that the true heir of Angkor was the Siamese monarchy. By contrast, in the Archipelago, and no doubt because the Javanese monarchy was wise enough to adopt the new Islamic ideology, there exists today a great state that is preparing to play a leading role not only in the near-term evolution of Association of Southeast Asian Nations (ASEAN) but in the future of Asia in general.

The recent history of Indonesia confirms the idea of a gradual diffusion of the Javanese model toward the peripheral islands. We are surely witnessing a rapid modernization of the infrastructure, a considerable rise in agricultural production, and the first signs of an industrial takeoff. Yet numerous problems remain, most of them attributable to the compartmentalization of society, and more precisely to the coexistence of sociocultural nebulae that cannot readily fuse. Despite numerous efforts to create a unique "national" ideology around the key notion of Pancasila, diversities and contradictions remain. Statistically, the economic progress is undeniable, but its positive benefits have thus far been limited to narrow sectors of society, and the multiplicity of private laws (a jungle in which Western minds quickly lose themselves) remains as an undeniable sign of ancient fragmentation.

If we compare Indonesia with other countries of the region that have also undergone intensive modernization, and especially with culturally monolithic Japan, which seems to have fully integrated its "Pasisir," it is clear that Indonesia is suffering from a serious handicap that will take some time yet to overcome. To revert to the geological parable that I have used several times already, the Javanese (and Indonesian) landscape is dotted with many different kinds of rocks, and the ongoing metamorphosis of the state is still a long way from amalgamating them.

There are still other heuristic possibilities in the opposition between the agrarian center and the "Pasisir." In the southern Celebes, for example, the interior kingdoms (Wajo, Soppeng) were unable to resist the domination of the maritime cities (Makassar, Bone). In Sumatra, there is still latent conflict between the Minangkabau high country and the ports of the west (Tiku, Priaman, Padang), and even more between the

Batak high country and the Pasisir of the northeast (Kota Cina and Aru as well as Deli and Medan). The same explanatory scheme might be applicable to other regions of South Asia—Ceylon, obviously, where, like Mataram, the central kingdoms (Anuradhapura, Kandy) resisted the cosmopolitan pull of the coast. Perhaps also Pakistan, where the agrarian society of the Punjab does not always seem compatible with the great port of Karachi.

The "Javanese case" has one last merit: it helps us to free ourselves from the artificial notion of "classicism." Since there was little "metamorphism" here, our orientalists were unable to forge the idea of a "great East Indian civilization." Instead of an imposing edifice whose internal workings we could study piece by piece ("institutions," "thought," "structures"), we were forced to accept the geographical diversity and take change as our starting point. Yet the question that arises is this: Are the civilizations that seem "great" to us today in fact those which, at the dawn of their evolution, had the good fortune to overlap several different worlds and to find themselves, like the Indian Ocean islands, at a crossroads?

TRANSLATED BY ARTHUR GOLDHAMMER

The Risks of Growth

PIERRE NORA

The Library of Histories

1971

This brief text served as the introduction to a new collection, the "Bibliothèque des Histoires," created by the historian Pierre Nora for the publisher Gallimard in 1971. This collection, one of the first of its kind, conveyed to a relatively broad public the work of historians doing what was beginning to be called "the new history": Georges Duby, Emmanuel Le Roy Ladurie, Jacques Le Goff, Maurice Agulhon, François Furet, and Mona Ozouf, among others.

The first sentence of this description, "We are experiencing an explosion of history," caused something of a stir. It was meant not to provoke but to call attention to a phenomenon seen at the time as positive—the proliferation of objects of study and the diversification of approaches which, for practitioners and public alike, seemed to characterize the moment. Yet the doubts soon raised informally and more or less privately about this idea of "explosion" are revealing. Weren't historians renouncing an ambition shared by the founders of the Annales *and Fernand Braudel as well as by the Marxist tradition? Wasn't there a danger that progress of the discipline on many fronts would end up in the abandonment of any unified project or interpretation? Although it was probably not Nora's intention, his phrase stirred a debate that would continue into the 1980s.*

W e are experiencing an explosion of history. New questions, engendered by related disciplines, together with the expansion to the whole world of a historical consciousness that was

---

Pierre Nora, description of the *Bibliothèque des Histoires* series, (Paris: Gallimard, 1971).

for a long time the privilege of Europe, have prodigiously enriched the historical interrogation of the past. History, devoted until recently to the narration of events that struck contemporaries, to the memory of great men, and to the political fates of nations, has changed its methods, its analyses, and its objects.

That is why we have sought to create, alongside the Bibliothèque des Sciences Humaines and in the same spirit, a place for history adequate to its many new dimensions.

The analysis of economies and societies has recently been extended to the study of material cultures, civilizations, and mentalities. Political life has expanded its horizons to include the mechanisms of power. Quantitative methods provide a more secure foundation for the development of demographic, economic, and cultural perspectives. The text is no longer the king of documents: the nonwritten—archaeological remains, images, oral traditions—is expanding history's domain. The whole man—body, diet, languages, representations, technical and mental instruments as they change over time—all these once-neglected subjects have become the bread and butter of historians. Meanwhile, the acceleration of history has encouraged more thorough exploration of the permanent features and inertias of collective history.

This new collection, the latest of Gallimard's Bibliothèques, aims to follow these developments closely. The Bibliothèque des Histoires will welcome classic works as well as pioneering research, monographs as well as synthetic overviews, political as well as social and ideological histories—in short, all that is vital in today's historiography—with no other concern than to reflect today's changing methods and desires.

TRANSLATED BY ARTHUR GOLDHAMMER

FRANÇOIS DOSSE

History in Pieces

1987

Between the "explosion of history" touted by Pierre Nora and the "history in pieces" denounced by a young radical historian, François Dosse, in 1987, there was more than a change in formula. The theme, which had fueled polemics and discussions for some fifteen years, became for Dosse a way to attack the hegemony of the Annales *school, its renunciation of any major intellectual ambition, and its submission to the dictates of fashion and the marketplace. This is not the place to challenge Dosse's assertions or arguments by asking, for example, whether it makes sense to speak as he does of the* Annales *school as a single, coherent collective actor. Nevertheless, other commentators have launched similar attacks in one form or another. Interestingly, Dosse's allegations coincide with those from a very different corner of the ideological spectrum in Hervé Couteau-Bégarie's* Le Phénomène "nouvelle histoire": Stratégie et idéologie des nouveaux historiens *(1983). This paradox, perhaps only superficial, calls for further study. More discreet as well as more ambitious, Georges Duby has hinted at a loss of steam associated with success itself: "Every objective has been conquered, the machine is humming, all sorts of curiosities are popping up here and there." In the 1980s, it became commonplace to diagnose signs of exhaustion in a historiographic movement that was still being heaped with praise only a short while before, and not all the critics were* gauchistes *like Dosse. Fashions might be changing.*

The globalist humanizing perspective was that of the first and second generations, the generation of Marc Bloch and Lucien Febvre, who in 1929 founded the *Annales d'histoire économique et sociale,* as well as that of Fernand Braudel. It was an attempt to create a common market of human sciences, a federation with history at its

---

François Dosse, *L'Histoire en miettes: Des* Annales *à la "nouvelle histoire"* (Paris: La Découverte, 1987), p. 252.

center. These were to be synthesized in a globalizing text out of which would come the *interscience* for which Braudel hoped. The scene changed in the 1960s, however. In order to ward off a new attack from the social sciences, the *Annales* historians gave up all hope of synthesis, laid down their weapons, and began thinking in terms of provisionally redefined disciplines based on a range of historical practices and objects. In this view, man was decentered and history was deconstructed as a series of partial practices with no globalizing ambition. The goal now was to segment society in such a way as to permit the transcription of stable constellations of apparently systematic character. This serialization held out a promise of greater richness if these distinct systems could somehow be related and if, within this mode of being, one could somehow place the forces of nonbeing, internal destructive forces signaling phases of rupture and transition. The deconstruction carried out by this most recent *Annales* generation led to historical writing that was more descriptive than explanatory, more positivist and empirical than scientific. In the new configuration of the social scientific field, the historian gave up the orchestra conductor's baton to become, in Emmanuel Le Roy Ladurie's terms, a miner who went down into the archives in search of material to be studied by the other social sciences—or, in the manner of Michel de Certeau, a prowler lurking on the fringes of society in search of deviance and the repressed. In short, he gave up his august chair to conquer the media.

TRANSLATED BY ARTHUR GOLDHAMMER

JACQUES REVEL

The Paradigms of the *Annales*

1979

One can also attempt to avoid polemic and the fluctuations of fashion and try instead to account for the transformation of historical production, for example by showing, behind the apparent continuity that Annales *insistently proclaimed from the journal's very beginning, a series of revisions, reformulations, and even discontinuities. There is nothing iconoclastic about such an attempt: it comes down simply to recognizing that over the course of more than half a century the context and conditions of the historiographic project have changed profoundly, including, in particular, the relation of history to the social sciences. This, at any rate, was the interpretation proposed by* Jacques Revel (b. 1942), at the time secrétaire de la rédaction *of* Annales, *and published in 1979 on the occasion of the journal's fiftieth anniversary—after Nora's but before Dosse's attack.*

For thirty years beginning around 1930, history became the center-piece of French social science. Indeed, social science was defined no longer by its methods but, rather, by its object—man. French academics took to using the phrase *sciences de l'homme* (or *sciences humaines*) to denote what used to be called "social science," as it still is in other places. The effect of this change in nomenclature was to emphasize "man" as the feature unifying a range of scientific disciplines, all of which were presumed to take man as their object. Implicit in this designation was the possibility of collaborative research. Previously, interdisciplinary exchange had centered on methodology, on shared procedural norms, but now the focus shifted to the sharing of concepts and data. Each discipline was free to define its own methodological rules while borrowing from a shared scientific capital as the needs of the moment required. The general mood was optimistic: the supposed unity of man made it possible to hope that, in the long run at least, a general reconciliation would be achieved. This pattern of thought is implicit in the cele-

Jacques Revel, "Les Paradigmes des *Annales*," *Annales ESC* 34 (1979), pp. 1372–75.

brated concept of *Zusammenhang,* which Lucien Febvre championed and sought to exemplify. He advocated a flexible (some would say spineless) interdisciplinarity of which history, it will come as no surprise, was the principal beneficiary, owing both to its intellectual openness and its institutional dynamism. When it came to experimenting with comparative approaches and imported concepts, history offered the widest range of possibilities; it was also the least cryptic and therefore the most receptive of scientific discourses. In an article written in 1958, at a time when history's prestige and accomplishments might have encouraged boastfulness, Fernand Braudel had the courage to write that "history— perhaps the least structured of all the human sciences—is open to all the lessons learned by its many neighbors, and is then at pains to reflect them back again."

Over the past twenty years, this constellation of knowledge has come undone before our eyes. The field of social scientific research began to fragment, to crumble. Man, the central figure in the previous state of the disciplines, ceased to be the fundamental referent and became instead the transitory, outdated object of a particular configuration of scientific discourse. In this connection, it is significant that among Michel Foucault's obstinately corrosive works, *Les Mots et les choses* occupies an emblematic place: published in 1966, the book is nothing less than an archaeology (that is, a deconstruction) of the human sciences. Having lost the unity inherent in their object, the social sciences were unable to restore the unity once thought to reside in an implausible general method, which, as we were reminded at about the same time, was without an object. The discontinuous thus forced itself upon the attention of social science. It was as if a hypothetical global unity had been replaced by a series of partial, local unities defined by scientific procedures, that is, by a kind of labor. In limited areas, the problem was no longer to reconcile different approaches but to look at the construction of particular objects in order to compare practices and measure differences. True interdisciplinary work may well have begun at this stage. Disciplinary boundaries were questioned not so much in the name of an overall unifying project as of a specific production. It may be that we are witnessing a reorganization of the disciplines in which old institutional boundaries are to be replaced by new fields defined by practice.

Such is the evolution that, over the past ten years has been described as an "explosion of history" or denounced, more harshly, as "history in pieces." Let us for now avoid the polemic. Neither characterization is entirely accurate, for each refers to a different aspect of the same situation: on the one hand, the vitality of a quest that is constantly diversifying its interests and exploring new areas and is open (for better or for worse) to suggestions from all sides, and on the other, the epistemological conditions of that quest—in other words, the "territory of the historian" versus the status of his work. In fact, the relation of one to the other has changed. The question is this: Will the insistence on a more localized practice that will nevertheless subject its scientific procedures to more explicit testing threaten the global outlook that was so essential to the first two generations of the *Annales*?

That question has come up repeatedly over the past few years, often to express anxiety or irritation over the recent direction of historical research, particularly as presented in this journal. It may be that putting the problem in such general terms is not the most useful way of approaching it. It is, however, useful as an opportunity to reflect on the paradigms of the *Annales*.

The call for global or, as it was sometimes called, "total" history (neither term was ever clearly defined) expressed both a rejection and a conviction. The rejection, of course, was directed at unreasonably strict boundaries between and within disciplines—at extreme specialization, in other words. The conviction was that different approaches to the social must be compatible and indeed convergent, and that the integration of the social sciences was possible and therefore necessary. For fifty years, these two orientations distinguished the *Annales,* but they also had certain consequences that it might be worthwhile to point out explicitly.

If historians could not say all there was to say about the past (even though many retained the fond hope of resurrecting the totality of bygone eras), they could nevertheless choose not to rule anything out on principle. They were already in one way or another geographers. Now they became economists, demographers, anthropologists, even linguists and naturalists. They brought new ideas, hypotheses, and comparative perspectives into their research. This inventiveness continued virtually uninterrupted for half a century and opened up new areas of research at an ever-increasing pace. Was this enough, however, to define a "global history"? One has the impression that historians juxtaposed a variety of approaches without ever questioning the overall definition of their project. The major monographs (and in France the monograph, in the form of the *thèse,* remains the dominant historiographic genre) illustrate this ambiguous evolution: ever-lengthier summaries attest to the continual expansion of *questionnaires* and methods, but the investigation itself, the *subject* (as it is still called), generally remains strangely repetitive, as if inert. Of course, allowances must be made for disciplinary constraints, for the concrete conditions under which work that is still usually an individual enterprise is actually done, as well as for academic restrictions and habits. There are also some important recent (and not so recent) books that show how traditional objects can be completely redefined and reconstructed. On the whole, however, the disparity between means and ends remains apparent. The "global history" program appears to have offered a neutral framework within which specialized histories could be piled up without much concern about how they could be fitted together, this being regarded as unproblematic.

Meanwhile, the methodological investment continued to grow, and techniques of analysis and data-processing became increasingly complex, defining new specialties with their own skills and boundaries. An evolution of this kind was no doubt inevitable once historians began to move from the programmatic stage to the stage of implementation. By narrowing the scope of their investigations, sharpening their hypotheses, and developing their methodologies, historians working in certain specialized areas achieved results that were at least verifiable and sometimes cumulative: this was the case in historical demography and in certain areas of economic history. As in any science, though, this progress was possible only at the cost of narrowing focus and limiting ambition. The relation of these specialties to the mother discipline (whose object remains fundamentally undefined) is already problematic. It is hardly surprising that certain offshoots were pruned away or eliminated. One alarming thing about the fragmentation of history is the tendency to turn inward, eventually producing a certain smugness about what has been achieved. But is that all? Surely, the unity of the social sciences no longer seems as obvious as it did twenty years ago. Here again, though, what has apparently been lost in programmatic terms may be in the process of being regained in concrete historical research. In the analysis of social facts, interdisciplinarity is no longer invoked as the universal panacea but is, rather, experimented with locally, in relatively well defined fields in which disciplinary prerogatives are disappearing. Has history "exploded," or is it under construction?

Bear in mind, finally, that global history was initially an interrogation of history itself. Historians abandoned the logic and dynamic of narrative. They dismissed the evolutionary perspectives of teleological interpretation. From then on, the past was no more secure than the present, as historians explored the thickness and complexity of social time. In the global approach suggested by the *Annales,* one resisted the temptation to produce syntheses more seamless or schematic than the data warranted. From the outset, the global outlook acknowledged geographical diversity and uneven development, multiple temporalities and discontinuities—and surely it is no accident that Braudel's *La Méditerranée* remains emblematic of the entire enterprise: the whole conception and structure of the book reflect the ambition to apprehend the social in terms of a system of differences. Here, too, forms and styles of doing history have changed. Yet beyond the apparent multiplicity and diversity of current research, and despite far-reaching changes in the conditions of historical work, the *Annales* continue, perhaps, to stand for a particular way of doing history—a determination not to expunge all disparities and discontinuities but, rather, to treat them as focal points of research, to locate and understand them.

TRANSLATED BY ARTHUR GOLDHAMMER

PART IV
Criticisms and Reformulations

A Critical Turning Point

With these two brief editorials published in Annales *in 1988 and 1989, the editors called on their readers and, more generally, the community of historians to reflect upon the state of the discipline and its procedures. The analysis invoked both a continuity with the* Annales *tradition and a rupture. Continuity: heralding the journal's classic appeal to both "history and the social sciences," these position papers reaffirmed what was distinctive in the French historiographical movement from the beginning. Rupture: the collective authors of the articles acknowledged the transformation of the conditions under which historians worked, the relations between disciplines, and the apparent diminishing returns of certain approaches. Had a time of "uncertainty" arrived, as the first text suggests? In any case, the authors state in no uncertain terms that the scientific landscape is changing rapidly, and that something new will emerge from the process. Not only historians but all other practitioners of the social sciences were urged to take measure of this change. Note the repeated assertion that history somehow fell into a trap created by its own dynamic, that it was too often neglectful of its own procedures, too little inclined to reflect upon itself, if you will, and that it often tended to forget that its constructions were not positive realities but hypotheses that had to be spelled out in detail and then tested. This provisional assessment of the state of the discipline ends with two appeals: a call, first, for collective reflection on this "critical turning point" and, second, for experimentation as an explicit, deliberate form of historical work.*

The second text served as the introduction to a special issue of the Annales, *some of the articles from which are excerpted later in this volume.*

THE EDITORS OF *ANNALES*

History and Social Science: A Critical Turning Point

1988

Over the past sixty years, the project of the *Annales* has been based on an encounter between history and the social sciences. This encounter has taken various forms, not all of them equally successful, yet it has contributed to a profound transformation of the historiographic landscape. When a belief in the convergence of the social sciences was universally shared, and it served to define the goals of practical research, work in relatively circumscribed areas yielded concrete evidence of the fruitfulness of exchange between the disciplines and returned profits to both sides. In a time of intellectual opulence and optimism, the journal stimulated, supported, and accompanied research that, "by example and by deed," attested to the development of new objects, questions, and methods.

Today, we seem to be living in a time of uncertainty. A reorganization of the disciplines is transforming the scientific landscape, raising questions about established priorities and disrupting the traditional channels for the circulation of innovation. The dominant paradigms, which used to be sought in various kinds of Marxism or structuralism or in the confident use of quantification, have lost their organizing capacity at a time when ideologies have fallen into disrepute (reminiscent of the attitudes of those travelers who return disillusioned from yesterday's utopia ready to write their "back from China" exposés). Last but not least, research has progressed in so many different directions that there is no longer any implicit consensus on which to base the unity of the social, identified with the real.

History, much of whose energy derived from its ambition to draw the social sciences together in a kind of federation, has obviously not escaped the general crisis of the social sciences. Paradoxically, its own vitality constitutes a further difficulty. The haphazard proliferation of objects of

---

"Histoire et Sciences Sociales: Un tournant critique," *Annales ESC* 43 (Mar.–Apr. 1988), pp. 291–93.

research has resulted in a canvas that is less and less legible. Attacks, however off the mark, on the "fragmentation of history" have nevertheless been useful in pointing up the inevitable consequences of necessary specialization as well as the eclecticism of a discipline whose production is abundant but anarchic. Because it is impossible to identify, in a shifting intellectual landscape, disciplines with which new alliances might be forged and new paradigms founded, superficial solutions abound. And so we have unsubstantiated attacks on an "*Annales* school" set up just to be knocked down and revivals of old themes (the return of the narrative, of the event, of the political, of biography), as if these alone were enough to restore order to the discipline. The situation is further complicated by history's paradoxical position in French society, the leading practitioners having achieved wide recognition even as recruitment of newcomers to the profession is dwindling.

The time has come to reshuffle the cards. It is not our intention to make a definitive assessment of a situation that is changing before our eyes, much less to issue a sweeping diagnosis of failure. We aim instead to draw on past and present experience in order to gather our bearings and map out avenues for rigorous and innovative new work in a time of uncertainty.

Such a project can only be collective. Faithful to its mission, this journal will welcome it and participate in it. Our pages are open to reflections and debates on the themes we are raising. We plan in 1989 to put together a first set of contributions in the form of a special issue. Such an enterprise makes sense only if it takes account of everyone's experience. We shall be glad to receive, in any form, but before the end of April 1989, your reactions to and reflections on the following two points.

New Methods

We hope to draw attention to two major issues—scaling analyses and writing history. After a long period of exclusive attention to global processes and overarching structures, certain results of microhistory have forced us to engage in a healthy intellectual exercise. In particular, we need to discuss and clarify the relation between the size of the objects we study, the mode of observation, and our problematics. How are observations at different levels, from the individual to the group to society, from the local to the global, to be articulated, and what kinds of generalizations are needed? In another direction, under what conditions can results be coordinated and compared? More fundamentally, how can we move toward comparative history, the need for which has often been proclaimed while the practice remains the exception rather than the rule?

These concerns necessarily lead to questions about history's demonstrative capacities and—the two issues are inextricable—its writing. Proof, to historians, means more than just being properly critical of sources and correct in one's use of analytical techniques. Even more essential, perhaps, is the relation between the nature of one's hypotheses and the evidence adduced to establish them. On this issue, the discipline—whether in its quantitative or more literary guise—has its rhetorical habits and conventions. Are these enough, or are other types of argumentation needed? In either case, how can the uses and effects of these devices be controlled? The forms of historical writing need to be taken seriously. Its traditions are deeply entrenched, yet it is also susceptible in every period to suggestions stemming from other forms, narrative in particular. Over the past half century, the selection of new objects and the primacy of numerical and serial data have profoundly altered historical writing without any serious attention to what was going on or any real effort to gauge the effects of the changes. Here again, things are changing before our eyes: some historians are boldly experimenting with novel solutions. Yet there are constraints on the exercise. How can we make sure that we don't lose sight of the need for logical argument and proof?

New Alliances

There is no need here to dwell once again on the traditional relationships that allowed history to draw inspiration successively or concurrently from geography, sociology, and anthropology. We are looking for new testimony, for new studies from the peripheries. Strangely enough, there are provinces on the fringes of the discipline that history claims for its own, yet it has never really taken the trouble to acquire the means such imperialistic pretensions require: among these are the history of art, the history of science, and the history of remote cultures. Numerous experiments are proceeding, moreover, on various new fronts from cliometrics to literary criticism, from sociolinguistics to political philosophy, and it is still too early to judge how fruitful they may be. How is history to be written in these new territories? How does one practice (or not practice) interdisciplinarity: what kinds of joint interrogations are possible, what are their limits, and what kinds of results have been achieved?

It would not be good for historians, much less French historians, to try to answer these questions alone. If the interdisciplinary project makes sense, it must be based on exchange, and therefore we need evaluations from our partners as well. What use do anthropologists, philosophers, and sociologists make of history today—not just of historical intelligibility but also of historical production? In any case, the *Annales* have never pretended to be alone. Other attempts have been made, particularly abroad, to answer the kinds of questions raised here. We want to hear those answers too, and, overcoming old habits, we shall publish them in the hope that they, too, will contribute to our analyses and proposals.

What we are proposing, then, is neither an assessment nor a soul-searching. We do not believe, as some are only too willing to accept, that history is in crisis. On the contrary, we are convinced that we are taking part in creating a new order. The shape of things to come is still unclear, and it must be clarified if we are to exercise the historian's craft in the future. Our ambition is to understand this critical turn as it is happening.

TRANSLATED BY ARTHUR GOLDHAMMER

Let's Try the Experiment

1989

The legacy of the *Annales* belongs to everyone, and everyone is free to interpret it as he or she pleases, to draw upon it for defining a practice or an intellectual position, or to analyze it in a way that generally reveals more about the evolution of the analyst than of the journal. Is there any reason to suppose, however, that intellectual innovation should be the result of a material inheritance? Innovativeness cannot be passed on; it is a process of constant redefinition within a perpetually changing field of forces. Historical questions are the result of deductions from the practices of the past, of the discipline's present configuration, and of conditions at the time that social knowledge is produced: historians write the most ephemeral of books.

To break down barriers between disciplines ("the walls are so high," Marc Bloch and Lucien Febvre lamented in 1929, "that they often block the view") and to "search, wherever possible and accepting all risks, for the latest innovations," as Fernand Braudel wrote in 1969: the journal has kept faith with both ambitions throughout its existence. In other respects, its project has required continual reformulation. In 1989, the *Annales* is sixty years old. Could there be a better time to undertake such a redefinition and, in so doing, to reject the alternative that some have proposed between petrifaction and dissolution? This issue gathers together a first series of texts—others will follow at regular intervals—stimulated by our 1988 call for papers,[1] and indicates the role we hope to fill: not that of a school (with the attendant risks of becoming a clique or an institution) or a mailing address (however prestigious) but, rather, a site of experimentation.

To carve out a domain within which comparisons of current work can be carried out, to give clear formulation to new questions and methods stemming from many scattered areas of investigation, and to establish new foundations for the historian's craft as well as history's dialogue with the social sciences—these are our ambitions, and whether they are

---

"Tentons l'expérience," *Annales ESC* 44 (Nov.–Dec. 1989), pp. 1317–23.

unbounded or not will depend on their ability to stimulate and attract the interest of other thinkers and researchers. Our first order of business is therefore to lay down the main lines along which it is to be hoped we can all advance together. These will form the basis of our editorial policy. They are intended to encourage collective work.

What is distinctive about history is not fully captured by the chronological definition of the objects it defines for itself, nor by its analytic methods, nor by the nature of its documentation. The historian, it has been said, constructs his problematics at the intersection of a long series of comments on and interrogations of the present, and today he borrows many of his methods from the neighboring sciences of man. Conversely, when an economist follows price changes in the eighteenth century or a philosopher studies the origins of structures of confinement, each seeks in the past a richer lode of experience than the present provides. It is not so much that history brings other disciplines together; rather, its domain, the past, is universal.

Might historians, having taught others to uncover and use historical sources, have nothing left to do but open their territory to an ecumenical practice of the human sciences? The terrain of history might then be abandoned to anthropologists, economists, and sociologists of the past. The danger in this is that if the economist historian, for example, is an economist of the past, then history and economics no longer have much in the way of fundamental truths to learn from each other: the diffusion of innovations assumes potential differences. At a time when some doubt the capacity of the social sciences to elucidate the world, we must argue in a deceptively paradoxical way for an affirmation of disciplinary identities. We shall come back to this point.

In this plural enterprise, the exploration of temporal mechanisms must constitute history's particular contribution. Rejecting the linear time of the chronicles and of positivist history, the *Annales* historians were the first to point out the complexity of social time and to emphasize the *longue durée*. Today, the attention being paid once again to events and the revival of a certain kind of historicism suggest that the initial intuition has all but exhausted its effects. The metaphor of different, superimposed levels of history and the particular concern with phenomena of *longue durée* carried with them a risk of neglecting the processes by which the new arrives. At a time when theories of self-organization are rediscovering that the future is entirely contained in the past yet difficult to predict, historians have remained strangely silent. Rightly so, if one believes that the answers to these questions have thus far been highly rhetorical, but wrongly if one thinks that time is perhaps the only truly specific object of history.

To refuse to see the mechanisms of transformation in the present con-figuration of a system is tantamout to asserting that the causes of change are exogenous. We see a logical difficulty in any historical explanation that would place such a critical variable out of reach, in an external position. In focusing on processes, we assume, by contrast, that human temporalities are multiple, that chronological coincidence is not a suffi-cient basis for true contemporaneity, and that temporal disparities are creative. Innovation is possible because all societies function to some extent outside their formal organization and all economies are only par-tially the conjunctures of their structures. (Or, to put it another way, it is because such categories are rigid that thinking about social change is difficult.) We are thus forced to make the hypothesis that the multiple disparities that exist among forms, structures, and functions are the source of an evolution that is neither allometric nor stationary but, rather, properly historic, that is, irreversible, unpredictable, and deter-minate. And the further hypothesis that every society is constantly in the process of constructing itself, and that the analysis of movement is the only way to avoid not just the insignificance of narratives of events but also the tautology of description within predetermined categories.

In its dominant version social history was initially conceived of as the history of the collective and the numerous. It quickly concerned itself with the measurement of social phenomena in terms of simple (or sim-plified) but massively quantifiable indicators, with establishing tables of distribution and curves of evolution and their description and commen-tary. An enormous mass of material was collected and analyzed. As the research proceeded, however, the accumulation of data took priority over the ambition and sometimes even the desire to interpret. If quanti-tative description was essential, one had to assume that the obtained re-sults corresponded to something real. As a logical consequence of this approach, relatively easily quantified structures obtained priority over relations and certain categories were reified. This journal has long ex-pressed concerns about the direction of price history, for example, and about the way in which the socioprofessional categories of the past used to be analyzed. We might just as easily have questioned the way in which historians, especially in France, have all too often been content to juxta-pose different aspects of historical reality, defining social categories com-patible with the broad outlines laid down by economic history and then pigeonholing cultural facts to fit the socioeconomic structure thus estab-lished. Out of this came a sort of common sociography, whose limits quickly became apparent. For a time, the panacea appeared to lie in the compilation of vast data banks: the greater the volume of data, it was believed, the closer to reality; factorial analysis and other sophisticated statistical techniques were also tried. But all of these ran into the same dilemmas, stemming from a simplistic conception of the historian's relation to sources and archives and leading to reification of analytical structures.

Society is not a thing. Interestingly, researchers in a number of areas are now moving away from the two great models that dominated the social sciences, the functionalist model and the structuralist model, and toward analyses in terms of strategies, which allow memory, learning, uncertainty, and negotiation to be reintroduced into the heart of social interaction. These notions, which are playing a central role in all the social sciences today, are useful conceptual tools. They remind us that social objects are not things endowed with properties but, rather, sets of changing relationships within constantly adapting configurations. Economic exchange in its simplest form presupposes a basic convention or prior arbitrage among alternative conventions. Not all of these conventions belong to the sphere of market equilibrium; some are the products of very different mental representations and social relations and are best understood in a longer time frame that every economic operation reactualizes and, at the same time, undermines. Social identities must be conceptualized as dynamic realities that are constructed and reshaped by social actors as they confront new problems, as formations that can be understood only by examining their development over a sufficiently long period of time. Similarly, the definition of the political is inextricably intertwined with the organization of an unstable field of forces that are subject to constant reinterpretation. The exercise of power is the reward of those who know how to exploit the resources of a situation and take advantage of the ambiguities and tensions of social interaction.

Social relations are part of a dynamic process: they elude analysis if one attempts to freeze them in time in order to examine their makeup. The processes by which social actors constantly redefine the organization of the social in keeping with what they think they are doing (and what they are unaware of doing) are in fact the object of history. It is unacceptable that those processes should be determined a priori. For example, the relation between the behavior of a group, its social composition, and a political consciousness that might seem obviously implicit in that composition need not be presumed in advance. To show how these three terms are related is, in fact, the task of historical explanation. "Economies, Sociétiés, Civilizations": the subtitle of *Annales* should not be taken to imply that total history is somehow an arithmetic sum or even that its various determinants are to be sought in three superimposed levels of social experience. Indeed, the economic is cultural as the social is economic. Every society functions as a generalized system of equivalences among these three categories (whose only value, moreover, lies in how they are used). Analysis of the modalities of these equivalences should be seen as a source for understanding societies and epochs.

History, like other disciplines, does not progress by producing ever-more precise accounts of the processes of the past. Here, the fundamental problem is not lack of information. The purpose of critical evaluation of sources is not to pinpoint reality more accurately (the old "mirror" metaphor is misleading in this respect) but, rather, to appreciate the internal qualities of the documents and refine the questions to be put to them. Explanations must be sought elsewhere. On the one hand, any social process reveals a multitude of existential experiences, individual and irreducible; on the other, history, like all scientific discourse, never just produces commentaries or models of intelligibility. Much of contemporary anthropology hinges on the metaphor of the social as text, and we would do well to take from this understanding the notion of polysemy and the idea that the reader participates actively in the production of meaning. Modeling, moreover, yields the useful idea that a good history book is a substantially coherent system of related explanatory propositions.

Thus, when it comes to inventing new problems, history is not limited to updating old questions, borrowing queries from related disciplines, or crystallizing a social demand. It also creates its own objects. A historical article or book is not a small-scale reproduction of reality but the expression of a structure that dissolves the opacity of reality in accordance with certain initial hypotheses and preordained experimental rules. The objects that history constructs are therefore subject to revision on the basis of different principles of intelligibility or new methods. Yet the propositions that enter into each new construction must not contradict the available data and must be internally consistent.

If the object of history cannot be posited from without and must not be limited by a priori categories, its construction and intelligibility can only be products of research methodologies and experimental procedures. Historical knowledge progresses not by totalization but, to use photographic metaphors, by zooming in and refocusing. A technique that is part of the baggage of every historian, the analysis of temporal series, should make progress in this direction possible. In order to understand the value of a variable quantity at any point in time, one breaks a series down into very-long-run variations, long-run trends, and cyclical fluctuations, and one then looks for specific causalities at each temporal level. In the observation of social processes, a similar approach can be taken by varying the scale of observation in a controlled way. Adjusting the focus in this manner can reveal new patterns, point up the inadequacy or reductiveness of available conceptual categories, and suggest new explanatory principles: at each level of interpretation the texture of reality seems different. Methodologically, this implies the need for particular attention to the role of the observer and his instruments in the elaboration of the analysis. The constricting contrast between micro- and macroanalysis needs to be overcome in order to delve more deeply into the more basic question of how best to adjust questions, methods, and scales of observation to different phenomena. As for explanatory principles, different scales of analysis are of course not opposed but complementary, each scale informing a particular level of explanation (that is why the issue that microhistory raises is not one of representativity, which assumes the homogeneity of explanatory variables, but one of generalization). Historical synthesis thus involves the constitution of new objects, and the change of scale that this implies presupposes changes in the hypotheses that make up the model in question. Furthermore, explanatory principles that are verified at one scale cannot be opposed to those established at some other scale. The exploration of diversity cannot proceed by reducing the number of causal relations or by seeking some hypothetical unique rational principle. Historical models should favor complexification over simplification, enrichment over impoverishment, as the only way of accounting for the complexity of social processes.

The enterprise calls for a redefinition of the means and ends of interdisciplinary study. From the beginning, the *Annales* have advocated interdisciplinarity, claiming for historians the right to shed the constraints of the discipline and take advantage of all the resources of the social and even the life sciences. The history of interdisciplinarity has been a story of intellectual generosity, which is perhaps the best thing the journal has contributed to the historical community. We have no intention of breaking with this tradition, but we hope to clarify what can be expected of it today and how to achieve it.

Interdisciplinarity is a kind of relationship among specialized scientific practices. The nature, function, and effectiveness of interdisciplinary relations at any given time depend both on the internal evolution of the disciplines and on the rapport they establish among themselves. That rapport has changed since the turn of the twentieth century. Emile Durkheim and his disciples had dreamed of a social science unified by a common method shared by many disciplines. In the next generation, Marc Bloch and Lucien Febvre, joined later by Fernand Braudel, emphasized what they felicitously called the "uncloistering" of intellectual work: driven by a healthy appetite for knowledge, they made borrowing, often serendipitous, their rule. Yet the explosion of history, the accelerating occupation of new provinces of historical territory, entailed an unanticipated danger—that of a new compartmentalization not between different social sciences but within the historical discipline itself in the guise of new specializations. A problem once discussed in terms of fragmentation is today being posed in different terms. There is, of course, no longer any paradigm that claims to organize, much less to unify, the social sciences. History has undertaken to redefine its goals and methods, as this special issue attests, but we have the feeling that history is not the only discipline in this situation, even if it is the first to air its questions and uncertainties in public, perhaps because it is the least rigorously codified of the social sciences. In 1989, in any case, no discipline can claim intellectual or institutional hegemony in the social sciences.

The outlook is not necessarily melancholic, particularly since the limiting effects of specialization have perhaps never been as minimal as they are now. A common culture is now widely shared. Actual research, moreover, suggests that investigators are less hindered by established boundaries when it comes to availing themselves of new skills. Nowadays, people are working in relatively narrow areas and trying hard to add complexity and depth to new objects of study. Any method that contributes to that end is welcome, and disciplinary issues are no longer as pressing as in the past.

Positive as these reports from the field may be, there are nevertheless dangers in the new attitude. In the first place, there has been a vast proliferation of isolated, individual experiments, in which each investigator is free to decide in sovereign fashion the rules of his own personal alchemy. The result may be an accumulation of case studies that cannot be reproduced and whose results may not be comparable or synthesizable. The second danger is that this empirical solution to the problems of interdisciplinarity may lend credence to the view that there are no more problems, that each investigator is free to use whatever seems useful, and that, ultimately, this circulation of concepts and methods will suffice to yield convergent results.

We believe, on the contrary, that the time has come to raise the issue of interdisciplinarity once again—not as a general question (for the general question seems to have been resolved) but as a problem of everyday historical practice. We wish to suggest that, rather than conceive of the relation between disciplines in terms of homology or convergence, as many would have us do, it may be useful today to insist on their specificity and indeed irreducibility. The paradox is merely apparent. Every scientific practice constructs reality on the basis of a series of hypotheses open to verification. Because the habits and conceptual instruments of each differ, however, the objects elaborated in this way do not overlap. There are several advantages to this. The comparison of different sets of questions and practices usefully recalls the resolutely experimental character of all social analysis. In addition, innovation, in the intellectual as in other realms, hinges on difference. How are we to escape from the weight of accumulated traditions and established ways of thinking—those *prisons de longue durée*—in order to produce new knowledge? Interdisciplinarity, because it multiplies points of view, allows us to gain a critical distance on each of the modes of representing the real, thus enabling us, perhaps, to avoid becoming the prisoner of any one. It should help us to think differently.

TRANSLATED BY ARTHUR GOLDHAMMER

NOTE

[1] See the preceding excerpt in this volume: "A Critical Turning Point," pp. 480–483.

The Critique of Social History

—————

JACQUES REVEL

"Microanalysis and the Construction of the Social"

1996

It is not accidental that microhistory played a key role in the critical reflections begun by Annales *historians in the 1980s. The term "microhistory" refers to the programmatic pronouncements and even more the practices of a small group of Italian historians who began publishing in the 1970s (the best known of whom are Carlo Ginzburg, Edoardo Grendi, Giovanni Levi, Carlo Poni, and their students). The work of these historians can be distinguished on two fronts: first, they practiced social history in a country where social history was far less dominant than in France; second, as outsiders with respect to the leading French approaches to the subject, they were able to draw on work being done in many other countries, especially England and the United States. Their program (which was in any case quite loosely coordinated: there is more than one concept of microhistory) was not so much a model as a guidepost: some* Annales *historians found it helpful to reflect on the implicit assumptions of their approaches as well as on settled habits and reflexes. Microhistory was thus taken less as an alternative strategy than as an occasion for critical reflection on historical methods. This is the perspective Jacques Revel develops in this essay.*

Jacques Revel, "Micro-analyse et construction du social" in Revel (ed.), *La construction du social* (Paris: Gallimard, 1996).

One of the dominant versions of social history is that which took shape in France around the *Annales* and then spread beyond French borders. Its formulation has changed over the past sixty years, yet it offers certain relatively constant features that can be traced back to the critical program that the Durkheimian sociologist François Simiand proposed to historians a quarter of a century before the *Annales* were born.[1] Simiand reminded historians of the rules of sociological method, which he believed would become the rules governing a unified social science of which the various disciplines would thenceforth exhibit particular modalities. In the future, Simiand argued, historians would have to turn their attention from the unique and accidental (that is, from individuals, events, and singular cases) to that which alone could be the object of true scientific study, namely, the repetitive and its variations, the observable regularities from which laws could be inferred. This initial choice, which the founders of the *Annales* and their successors largely made their own, sheds light on the fundamental characteristics of French-style social history: the emphasis on the study of the largest possible aggregates; the priority granted to measurement in the analysis of social phenomena; the choice of a time frame long enough to make large-scale transformations visible (and, as a corollary, the need to situate analyses within different time frames). Certain consequences of these initial requirements have left a lasting mark on the resulting historical methods. The preference accorded to series and numbers made it necessary to invent suitable sources (or to come up with ad hoc methods for processing traditional sources); it also made it necessary to define simple or simplified indices to abstract a limited number of properties or distinctive features from archival documents, in order to follow their variations over time: prices and incomes were used at first, then measures of wealth and occupational distributions; then later, births, marriages, deaths, signatures, titles of books and editorial genres, pious acts, and so on. Not only did it then become possible to study the evolution of each of these indices over time, but, more important, one could, as Simiand had first done with wages and as Ernest Labrousse did in *L'Esquisse du movement des prix et des revenus en France au XVIIIe siècle* (1933), use the data to construct relatively complex models.

From Simiand and the Durkheimians first Marc Bloch and Lucien Febvre and then, in the following generation, Ernest Labrousse and Fernand Braudel also took a sort of scientific voluntarism: the only objects that one can study scientifically are those constructed according to explicit procedures in light of an initial hypothesis which is then sub-

jected to empirical validation. One has the impression that these elementary rules of method were sometimes neglected later on. Procedures certainly became more complicated, but owing probably to the dynamics of
research itself, their experimental status was often forgotten. Many of
the objects that historians constructed were hypothetical in nature, yet
there was a growing tendency to treat them as if they were real things.
Instances of this can be found quite early in the history of the *Annales*.[2]
Criticisms were sometimes leveled at various procedures in price history,
such as the choice of spatial units of observation and socioprofessional
categories, but these criticisms were not enough to halt the general tendency. Furthermore, these approaches figured in a macrohistorical perspective that was never made explicit or subjected to testing. More precisely, the scale of observation was not treated as an experimental variable, because it was at least tacitly assumed that the social realm was
continuous or homogeneous in such a way that one could without difficulty piece together various results: parish, region, city, and occupation
were thus treated as neutral terms for the collection of data, accepted as
they were given.

   This model of social history entered a period of crisis in the late 1970s
and early 1980s, that is, by a strange irony, just at the moment when it
seemed to be at the height of its triumph, when its results were taken
as authoritative well beyond the boundaries of the profession and the
"territory of the historian" seemed capable of indefinite enlargement.
Clearly, the sense of a crisis was slow to make itself felt, and it is by no
means certain that a majority of historians even today would agree that
we are in the midst of one. Perhaps, then, we should say more modestly
that it was in the early 1980s that criticism of the dominant model, however scattershot, became more insistent. Historians began to reconsider
their practice for reasons of several different kinds. Computers made it
possible to record, store, and process much greater volumes of data than
in the past, yet many historians felt that the questions they were asking
had not kept pace with this technological progress, and that their vast
quantitative projects had begun to come up against the law of diminishing returns. Meanwhile, a growing specialization within the profession
tended to fragment a field of research that had seemed definitively open
and unified. These developments were felt all the more strongly because,
in the meantime, the great paradigms that had unified the disciplines of
the social sciences (or at any rate had given them a common outlook)
came under harsh attack, leading also to doubt about some forms of
interdisciplinary exchange. In the same period, society itself was overcome by doubts in the face of crises it could not understand—or, in many
cases, even describe—and this naturally contributed to the belief that

the hope of achieving a global understanding of the social must at least temporarily be set aside. The foregoing remarks only hint at various aspects of an analysis that remains to be carried out in detail. The developments in question began in different places but converged toward a single end, obviously interacting with one another along the way. Taken together, and no doubt influenced by other factors as well, they helped to undermine the certainties of a macrosocial approach that had previously gone largely unquestioned. The interest in microhistory was a symptom of this crisis of confidence as well as a source of ideas for formulating objections and making them concrete.

· A change in the scale of analysis was an essential element in the definition of microhistory. It is important to understand the significance of this change and the stakes involved. Like anthropologists, historians are in the habit of working on circumscribed units of relatively small scale.[3] It is misleading to refer to these units as "terrains" (although historians have for twenty years been fascinated by ethnology). More prosaically, the monograph, which is the primary vehicle for formulating the results of historical research, is associated with the conditions and rules under which professional work in history is done: the insistence on documentary consistency; the familiarity that is supposed to guarantee mastery of the object of analysis; and a representation of the real that often seems to require that problems be associated with "concrete," tangible, visible units. The monograph is generally defined in terms of practice: it is a text in which one presents data and constructs proofs (and in which one is also well advised to prove oneself). In itself, however, it is assumed to be inert. Hundreds of monographs, all based on the same general set of questions, have laid the foundations of social history. The problem implicit in the proliferation of monographs was not one of the scale of observation but, rather, of the representativity of each sample relative to the whole into which it was supposed to fit as one piece of a puzzle. There were no fundamental doubts about the possibility of relating the results of any particular monograph to a mean or mode or typology or whatever was required.

The microhistorical approach is profoundly different as to purpose and method. It is based on the principle that the choice of a particular scale of observation produces certain effects of understanding useful in conjunction with strategies of understanding. Changing the focal length of a lens not only magnifies (or reduces) the size of the object under observation but also modifies its shape and composition. Or, to use a different metaphor, changing the scale of a map is a matter not simply of depicting a constant reality in a larger or smaller format but of changing the content of the representation (that is, the choice of what is representable). Note, incidentally, that in this sense the "micro" dimension enjoys no particular privilege. It is the principle of variation that is important, not the choice of any particular scale.

Over the past few years, however, the microhistorical view has been particularly successful. The historiographical circumstances briefly summarized above help to explain why. The recourse to microanalysis is to be understood first of all as a move away from the accepted model of social history, which from the beginning has been explicitly or (increasingly) implicitly inscribed in a macro framework. This move made it possible to shed certain old habits and to take a critical look at the instruments and methods of sociohistorical analysis. Furthermore, it has provided a practical historiographical avenue for a new focus on the problem of scale in historical analysis (following the lead of anthropology).[4]

Let us turn now to the effects of understanding associated with (or at any rate expected from) the shift to a microhistorical scale. Take, to begin with, one of the rare programmatic texts that helped define the microhistorical project. In an article published in 1977, Edoardo Grendi observed that because the prevailing model of social history organized data in terms of categories developed to permit maximal aggregation (such as wealth, occupation, and so on), it failed to grasp things associated with social behavior and experience and with the formation of group identities that inhibited the integration of diverse types of data. Grendi contrasted this approach with that of (mostly British and American) work in anthropology, which was notable he argued "not so much for its methodology as for its emphasis on a holistic approach to behavior."[5] This claim may seem overly general, but the characteristic concern of microhistorians is worth noting—namely, a concern to develop a research strategy based not primarily on the measurement of abstract properties but, rather, on integrating and interrelating as many of those properties as possible. Confirmation of this concern came the following year in a rather provocative text by Carlo Ginzburg and Carlo Poni, who proposed using "names"—proper names, that is, the most individual and least repeatable of indicators—as markers for constructing a new type of social history focused on individuals in their relations with other individuals.[6] Here, the individual is not conceptualized as antithetical to the social: the hope was to achieve a new angle of vision by following the thread of a particular destiny—that of a man or group of men—and with it the multiplicity of spaces and times, the complex tangle of relations in which that destiny became involved. Here again, the two authors are preoccupied with "the complexity of social relations as reconstructed by anthropologists working in the field, [which] contrasts with the unilateral character of the archival data with which historians work. . . . Yet if the terrain of research is sufficiently limited, documentary series can be superimposed in time as well as space, making it possible to locate the same individual in a variety of social contexts." Basically, this is the old dream of a total history, but this time reconstructed from the bottom up. For Ginzburg and Poni, this approach should make it possible to "reconstruct lived experience." This formulation is loose and ultimately vague, and one might prefer to describe it as a program for analyzing the conditions of social experience reconstituted in all their complexity.

The key is not to abstract from but initially to enrich reality by including the widest possible range of social experience. This approach is illustrated by Giovanni Levi in his book *L'Eredità immateriale*. His method is intensive: to collect "all the recorded biographical events of all the inhabitants of the village of Santena" over a fifty-year period in the late seventeenth and early eighteenth centuries. The goal is to go beyond obvious general trends to reveal the social strategies developed by various actors (individuals, families, and groups) in light of their respective positions and resources. Of course, "in the long run, all these personal and family strategies seem to run together to produce a relative equilibrium. Yet the participation of each of them in the general history, in the formation and modification of the underlying structures of social reality, cannot be evaluated solely on the basis of tangible results: in the course of the life of each there arise, in a cyclical fashion, problems, doubts, and choices—a politics of everyday life—at the center of which lies a strategic utilization of social rules." Maurizio Gribaudi takes a similar approach to a geographically close but historically and historiographically remote site—the formation of the working class in Turin at the turn of the twentieth century.[7] Where others had insisted essentially on a common set of experiences (urban immigration, work, social struggle, political consciousness, and so on) ostensibly underlying the unity, identity, and consciousness of the working class, Gribaudi sought to trace individual itineraries, which reveal the variety of working-class experience, the many contexts in which it occurs, and the internal and external contradictions that this creates. He reconstructs the geographical and professional moves, the demographic behavior, and the relational strategies that accompany the transition from the rural farm to the urban factory. Like many other historians, Gribaudi began with the idea of a homogeneous, or at least behaviorally homogenizing working-class culture. In the course of his work (and in particular in collecting oral histories of the family background of certain leading figures), he discovered a diversity of ways of becoming a worker and living under working-class conditions:

> The problem was to find out how each family in the sample negotiated the journey and its own social identity; what mechanisms allowed mobil-

ity for some while enforcing stagnation for others; and how individual outlooks and strategies changed, often drastically. In other words, putting the problem from the worker's point of view, this meant investigating the various building blocks out of which workers constructed their diverse experiences and physiognomies, thereby shedding light on the dynamics responsible for pulling things together or tearing them apart.[8]

Clearly, the microhistorical approach set out to enrich social analysis by introducing new, more complex, and more flexible variables. There are, however, limits to such methodological individualism, since we are always trying to discover the rules governing the formation and functioning of a social entity or, rather, a collective experience.

"Classical" social history was mainly conceived as a history of social entities—a community (village, parish, city, district, and so on), an occupational group, an order, a class. One could, of course, discuss the boundaries of these entities and even more their coherence and sociohistorical significance, but their fundamental importance was not open to question.[9] As a result, when one looks through the enormous mass of results accumulated over the past thirty or forty years, one has a certain sense of déjà vu and stagnant categories. From one work to the next, the characters are the same though the casts may vary. Someday someone will have to delve into the reasons, no doubt complicated, for this tendency toward descriptive sociography. It was, in any case, strong enough to impede the influence of a book like E. P. Thompson's *The Making of the English Working Class* (which was published in 1963 but translated into French only in 1988); Thompson, of course, refused to accepted any readymade (or ostensibly well-established) definition of the working class and instead emphasized its "making."[10] After a number of isolated attempts,[11] it was only later that French historians gradually became convinced that an analysis in terms of distributions was no longer possible. There were two main reasons for this, and we would do well to distinguish between them even though they partially overlap. The first has to do with the old problem of the nature of the classificatory criteria on which historical taxonomies are based. The second concerns the recent emphasis on the role of social interaction.

In both cases, the choice of a microhistorical perspective is of crucial importance. With respect to social analytical categories, it is surely at the local level that the disparity between general (or exogenous) and endogenous categories is most pronounced. This problem, though long recognized, has become more acute in recent years, owing to the influence of anthropology, especially American cultural anthropology, which has focused primarily on local analyses. This is not the place to go into detail about the kinds of solutions that have been proposed. The results of this necessary (and not yet complete) change of viewpoint are ambiguous. It has, of course, made it possible to cast a critical eye on categories and decompositions that used to be taken for granted. On the other hand, it tends to encourage cultural relativism, which is one of the tendencies of "Geertzism" (so named after anthropologist Clifford Geertz) in social history.

As for the second direction of research, moving toward a reformulation of sociohistorical analysis in terms of process suggests a way out of this dilemma. The idea is that the historian should not simply borrow the language of the actors he is studying but also use that language to point the way toward broader and deeper inquiry aimed at the construction of multiple, malleable social identities working through a complex network of relationships (of competition, solidarity, alliance, and so on). The complexity of this type of approach makes it necessary to limit the field of observation. Microhistorians are not content, however, to observe this de facto constraint; they transform it into an epistemological principle when they attempt to use individual behaviors to reconstruct the modalities of social aggregation (or disaggregation). Simona Cerutti's recent work on guilds and corporations in seventeenth- and eighteenth-century Turin can serve here as an example.[12] Surely, no historiography is more spontaneously organicist than that of guilds and guild associations: these are obviously functional communities, and they are assumed to have exerted such powerfully integrative effects that they became almost natural constituents of early modern urban society. The boldness of Cerutti's approach is to set these certitudes aside in order to show how professional identities and their institutional expressions are not given in advance but, rather, are elaborated and redefined by dint of constant effort involving individual and familial strategies. Instead of the consensual and, on the whole, stable world of guilds that we see in traditional histories, here everything is conflict, negotiation, and provisional transaction. At the same time, personal and familial strategies are not purely instrumental: they are socialized in the sense that they are inextricably associated with representations of urban relational space, of the resources it offers and the constraints it imposes, for it is these representations that shape the outlooks and choices of the social actors. Cerutti thus denaturalizes (or at any rate "debanalizes") the mechanisms of aggregation and association by emphasizing the relations that make them possible and identifying the mediations between "individual rationality and collective rationality."

The shift in focus that has taken place here is probably more obvious to historians than to anthropologists, because the methodological histories of the two disciplines have not always coincided.[13] In my view, a number of important redefinitions are implicit in the move:

1. A redefinition of the presuppositions of sociohistorical analysis, whose major features I have discussed above. In place of systems of classification based on explicit (general or local) criteria, microanalysis focuses on the behaviors that define and reshape social identities. This does not mean that microhistorians ignore the "objective" properties of the population under study; rather, they treat those properties as differentiating resources whose importance and significance are to be judged in light of the social uses to which they are put.

2. A redefinition of the notion of social strategy. Historians, unlike anthropologists and sociologists, work with the fait accompli, with "what actually happened," which by definition is not repeatable. Rarely do alternatives appear in the sources themselves, especially in view of the uncertainties that the social actors of the past had to contend with. Historians are therefore in the habit of invoking the notion of strategy in an ambiguous sense: often it serves to bolster a general functionalist hypothesis (which normally remains implicit), while sometimes it serves, more prosaically, to characterize the behavior of those individual or collective actors who succeeded (and who are generally those whom we know best). In this respect, the resolutely antifunctionalist attitude of the microhistorians is highly significant. By taking multiple individual destinies into account, they seek to reconstitute a space of possibilities in light of knowledge of the resources available to each individual and group in a given configuration. Giovanni Levi has probably gone farther in this direction than anyone else by reintroducing the notions of failure, uncertainty, and limited rationality into his study of peasant family strategies with respect to the market for land in the seventeenth century.[14]

3. A redefinition of the notion of context. This notion has often been used in a facile and lazy way in the social sciences and, in particular, in history. Rhetorically, the context is often evoked at the beginning of a monograph, where it produces a "reality effect" around the object of research. Argumentatively, the context sums up the general conditions within which a particular reality has its place, and in practice this often means nothing more than a simple juxtaposition of two distinct levels of observation. Interpretively, the notion of context is used, less frequently, as a device for drawing out the general factors with which one can account for particular situations. Much of the historiographical work produced over the past twenty years, including but not limited to work in microhistory, has registered dissatisfaction with these various uses of the notion by attempting to relate text to context in a variety of ways. What is distinctive about the microhistorical approach is the refusal to take any of the uses just mentioned for granted—in other words, a refusal to accept that a unified, homogeneous context exists within which and in relation to which social actors make their choices. This refusal can be understood in two complementary ways:

as a reminder of the multiplicity of the social experiences and representations, in part contradictory and in any case ambiguous, in terms of which human beings construct the world and their actions (this is the main thrust of Levi's critique of Geertz);[15] but also, in analysis, as an invitation to reverse the historian's usual approach, which is to situate and interpret his text in relation to a global context. By contrast, what microhistorians propose is to reconstruct the multiple contexts necessary to identify each and make sense of observed behavior. This of course brings us back to the problem of the scale of observation.

4. A redefinition of the scale of observation. This seems to me the most drastic revision. Instead of a hierarchy of scales of observation, historians instinctively prefer a hierarchy of historical "prizes." To put it facetiously, at the national level one does national history; at the local level one does local history. (One is not necessarily more important than the other, particularly from the standpoint of social history.) At the most basic level, the history of a social entity apparently dissolves into a myriad of minuscule events that are hard to organize in any meaningful way. The traditional conception of the monograph seeks to achieve meaningful organization by providing local verification of general hypotheses and results. The multiple contextualization of the microhistorians is based on very different premises. It is assumed, to begin with, that each historical actor participates to one degree or another in various processes (hence within various contexts) of different dimensions and at different levels from the most local to the most global—thus, there is no discontinuity, much less an opposition, between local history and global history. The experience of an individual, a group, or an area makes it possible to apprehend some particular modulation of global history. It is both particular and unique, because what the microhistorical viewpoint offers is not an attenuated or partial or mutilated version of macrosocial realities but a different version.

TRANSLATED BY ARTHUR GOLDHAMMER

NOTES

[1] François Simiand, "Méthode historique et science sociale," *Revue de Synthèse historique* (1903); on the importance of the Durkheimian influence on the origin of the *Annales*, see Jacques Revel, "Histoire et sciences sociales: Les paradigmes des *Annales*," *Annales ESC* 34 (1979), pp. 1360–76 [the work is excerpted here at pp. 471–477].

[2] See Jean-Yves Grenier and Bernard Lepetit, "L'expérience historique: À Propos de C. E. Labrousse," *Annales ESC* 44 (1989), pp. 1337–60.

[3] It would be interesting to follow the parallel formulation of problems of scale in history and anthropology, noting any time differences between the two: see Christian Bromberger, "Du grand au petit: Variations des échelles et des objets d'analyse dans l'historie récente de l'ethnologie de la France," in I. Chiva and U. Jeggle, eds., *Ethnologies en miroir* (Paris: Editions de la Maison des Sciences de l'Homme 1987), pp. 67–94.

[4] In addition to the general influence of British and American anthropology, micro-historians are indebted to the work of Fredrik Barth, *Scale and Social Organization* (Oslo University of Bergen Press, 1978), and *Process and Form in Social Life* (London, 1980).

[5] Edoardo Grendi, "Micro-analisi e storia sociale," *Quaderni storici* 35 (1977), pp. 506–20; see also Grendi's introduction to the special issue "Famiglia e communità" of *Quaderni storici* 33 (1976), pp. 881–91.

[6] Carlo Ginzburg and Carlo Poni, "Il Nome et il come: Mercato storiografico e scambio disuguale," *Quaderni storici* 40 (1979), pp. 181–90 (partial French translation: "Le Nom et la manière," *Le Débat* 17 [1981], pp. 133–36).

[7] Maurizio Gribaudi, *Itinéraires ouvriers: Espaces et groupes sociaux à Turin au début du XXᵉ siècle* (Paris: EHESS, 1987).

[8] Ibid., p. 25. Once again, the references cited by the author are often to British and American works in anthropology, especially Fredrick Barth and other interactionists.

[9] Recall the debate that Ernest Labrousse initiated in the 1950s in connection with a proposal to undertake a comparative history of the various European bourgeoisies, and the now-outdated debate of the 1960s between Labrousse and Roland Mousnier over "orders versus classes." (Both pieces are excerpted here, pp. 147–153 and pp. 154–158, respectively.)

[10] Note, however, that Thompson's work was conceived within a macrosocial perspective.

[11] Let me mention, for example, Michelle Perrot, *Les Ouvriers en grève* (Paris: Mouton, 1974); Jean-Claude Perrot, *Genèse d'une ville moderne: Caen au XVIIIᵉ siècle* (Paris: Mouton, 1975), 2 vols.; and, from sociology, Luc Boltanski, *Les Cadres* (Paris: Minuit, 1982).

[12] Simona Cerutti, *La Ville et les métiers: Naissance d'un langage corporatif (Turin, 17ᵉ–18ᵉ siècles)* (Paris: Editious de Centre de Recherches Historiques, 1990), pp. 7–23.

[13] Marac Abélès's work on local politics in contemporary France (*Jours tranquilles en 89* [Paris: O. Jacob, 1989]) uses most of the themes and some of the formulas proposed at the same time by microhistorians (with whom Abélès had no contact).

[14] Giovanni Levi, *L'Eredità immateriale: Carriera di un esorcista nel Piemonte del seicento* (Turin, 1985).

[15] Levi, "On Micro-History," p. 202; see also "I Pericoli del Geertzismo," *Quaderni storici* (1985), pp. 269–77.

BERNARD LEPETIT

Quantitative History: Another Approach

1989

Ironically, just when computers became widely available in versions small enough to fit on a desk and with enough power to perform thousands of operations in a flash, quantitative methods in history began to lose favor. The reasons for this were diverse: the results obtained were only weakly cumulative, at times the researcher seemed to gain only minimal returns from his or her massive labors, and, in addition, the epistemological optimism that had for so long justified all this work of accumulating facts now increasingly was bracketed if not put directly into question.

Bernard Lepetit provides some of the reasons for this reversal but also suggests some of the ways in which quantitative methods might be revivified by a more sophisticated understanding both of their limits and their promise. Criticism of interdisciplinarity, in contrast, focused less on particular methods. Here, in fact, the perceived problem was lack of focus: historians might turn in any direction for inspiration, from economic modeling to literary criticism, but did not this very eclecticism endanger the coherence of history as a discipline?

Quantitative history is no longer fashionable.[1] For a generation after World War II, it was one of the dominant forms of historical practice in France, a standard of reference against which other ways of doing history were judged. A graph showing the number of series of economic data from Ancien Régime France published over the past hundred years illustrated this conjuncture quite well.[2] The early record for statistical compilations coincided with the 1929 crash; it was beaten in 1952. Over the next twenty years, the number of statistical series doubled each decade. Meanwhile, historical demography gained the reputation of being in the forefront of research by using sophisticated quantitative techniques to generate new positive knowledge. After

Bernard Lepetit, "L'Histoire quantitative: Deux ou trois choses que je sais d'elle," *Histoire et Mesure* 4 (1989), pp. 191–99.

flourishing in economic and social analysis, quantitative history moved on to conquer cultural history as well: signatures of newlyweds, books in libraries, masses for which provision was made in wills, and household objects were all duly counted up and tabulated.[3]

The methodological principles of quantitative history offered many advantages: working from the facts, developing a critical approach to the sources (in keeping with the historical tradition of skepticism toward documents), producing a numerical representation of man's doings.[4] Quantification, based on techniques borrowed from the exact sciences, plunged *l'histoire événementielle* into disrepute. Modern technology, enhanced by computers, could be wedded to the positivist tradition in history. Responding to perceived epistemological dangers, quantitative historians assumed a more or less direct correspondence between the archives and the real, the sources and the statistical series derived from them, the graphs and their description, thus settling in one stroke the problem of how historical discourse relates to the reality of the past: the former was simply assumed to yield an adequate picture of the latter. The quantitative approach allowed historians to invent new problems and discover new objects.

Today, the trend is in the other direction. There is widespread doubt about the ability of numbers to yield a satisfactory account of the most basic forms of behavior. New questions about the role and impact of events or about how change takes place seem to have diminished interest in, and perhaps even robbed, the meaning of the lengthy series of homogeneous statistics that quantitative history needs to do its work. Areas in which quantification made little headway, such as political history and the history of ideas, are once again active. The rediscovery of genres such as biography from which the quantitative is all but banished has had similar effects: the usefulness of quantitative history is no longer apparent. More fundamentally, practice in the discipline has begun to restructure itself around two opposing principles. History, according to the philosopher Paul Ricoeur, belongs to the class of narrative, notwithstanding protests to the contrary.[5] Certain proponents of microhistory have developed the notion of the "normal exceptional" based on the idea that abnormal situations, which by definition are impossible to organize into series, are more revealing than a thousand documents all cut from the same mold.[6] From this they derive a new approach, which instead of constructing and analyzing statistical indices follows the model of Voltaire's *Zadig* in interpreting clues.[7]

To explain these developments one can suggest several themes, which I shall simply state without attempting to justify them. Some of these are quite sweeping, hence difficult to verify: growing doubts about certain macrohistorical processes and a new emphasis on subjectivity are perhaps the most important of these. Other factors can be classed under the heading of basic sociology of research: more egalitarian conditions in the laboratory and changes in the nature of financing have made it increasingly difficult to employ battalions of low-level researchers assigned to the task of collecting massive amounts of archival data and entering the information into computers. The law of diminishing returns has been felt with particular acuteness in history, since few historians receive any statistical training beyond the most elementary level. In addition, the fragmentation of research specialties makes it difficult to reassemble a picture of the real, which must be decomposed and stratified in order to compile statistical series, thus thwarting the profession's ideal goal of achieving a total history. Finally, historians are as hungry for flesh and blood as the ogre of legend: where in a collection of statistical tables can one find the thickness and density of actual human experience?

In my view, historical research can proceed at the present time in three different ways. To describe them, I shall use agricultural metaphors. The most archaic is modeled on the practice of burning stubble on farmed-out land. Since quantitative history appears to have become unproductive, this low-yield field of research should be abandoned for a time and allowed to lie fallow. I am not in favor of such historiographical "rotation." The second possibility is to clear new land. Quantitative history tried this approach when it moved from the economic and social terrain into the cultural. Some of today's practitioners of the discipline apparently believe in the revivifying powers of the database.[8] To my mind, this is a way of striving to regain the lost paradise of totality while continuing to give priority to sources over methods. The larger the database, some researchers seem to believe, the closer the data will approximate reality. Increasingly massive amounts of formalized data are supposed to provide a neutral framework for different types of historical investigation. To me, this conception seems simplistic, for it assumes once more an immediate relationship between the historian and the document and between the archives and the past. I am only too familiar with databases that have met with the same fate as Borges's perfect one-to-one map, which was abandoned in the desert.[9] The third possibility, of which I approve, is to attempt to improve our techniques for cultivating the terrain.

Because the statistical training most historians receive is rudimentary at best, statistics have been used more often than not for descriptive purposes only. The development, especially in France, of factorial analysis, a sophisticated technique for describing large populations of individuals each characterized by a relatively large number of variables, has reinforced this tendency. Moreover, these techniques seemed to resolve the issue of a priori definition of the categories used in the collection of statistics.[10] Better yet, investigators could easily reify the groups emerging from the analysis on the ground that they were implicit in the data.

Nevertheless, the emphasis on description pointed up the major drawback of quantitative methods—the impossibility of drawing any firm conclusions. As François Furet observed in a 1971 article generally quite approving of quantification, this type of history "yields incontrovertible results and a good description of the localized phenomenon chosen as the object of study. But the interpretation of those results cannot claim the same degree of certainty as the results themselves."[11] In the least successful (and necessarily most numerous?) examples of the genre, the conclusions were little more than literary transcriptions of statistical descriptions, or else the descriptions had little to do with the analyses. Tables and graphs were reduced to mere symbols, to a sort of conventional flourish with little relation to the argument whose function was to attest to the scientific character of the research. Instead of giving priority to relations, the emphasis fell on more easily quantifiable structures, and the reification of categories seemed to be a logical consequence of the approach. If statistical description was indeed in the vanguard of empirical research, one had to assume, in order to make the results persuasive, that they corresponded to something real. Much of the historical analysis of occupational groups can now be read in this way.[12]

Yet quantitative analysis is more than just elementary descriptive statistics.[13] Some of these avoid the sequence described above—compilation of data tables, application to them of statistical techniques, interpretation. Thus, they readily avoid the dilemma I have just described. Consider three simple examples:

1. *The analysis of formal models.* Used first to measure social mobility, formal models are also useful for analyzing processes in such a way as to reveal the complex relations between the fates of individuals within groups and of groups within populations. The transition matrices thus obtained can be interpreted by comparing the actual observed distribution with the theoretical distributions constructed on the basis of simple hypotheses about the transmission of positions (hierarchical, egalitarian, inverse, and so on) and with empirical data characteristic of two successive structures. A probability test can be used to decide whether the discrepancy between the actual distribution and the various theoretical ones is or is not significant. The laws of probability also make it possible to decide whether a given set of variables constitutes a system. In both cases, empirical data patterns are evaluated in relation to predictions derived from theoretical models.

2. *Analysis of variance.* Here the goal is to investigate the influence of a supposedly explanatory factor A with several possible states $(A^1, A^2, \ldots)$ on a variable X whose values have been measured. If, for each modality of A, several observations of X are available, it is possible to use a

so-called null hypothesis (according to which factor A has no significant effect on X, so that the observed differences in X for $A^1, A^2, \ldots,$
are due solely to chance, that is, to other factors not controlled for in
the experiment), to test whether A does in fact influence X. Here, of
course, the goal is no longer to count, but to gauge a relationship with
the help of experimentally manipulable groupings.

3. *Correlation analysis.* Analysis of variance can be used to reveal the influence of a heterogeneous factor on a quantitative variable. When
   that factor is measurable, it is possible to quantify the relation between
   the factor and the variable. The correlation coefficient measures the intensity of the connection, and once again a probabilistic test measures
   the significance.

I hope the reader will excuse the elementary nature of this review. Its
only purpose is to show how the new methods differ from the counting
techniques of "serial" history. What all these statistical tools have in common is that they are designed to pursue previously formulated questions.
For example, did the formation of *départements* in 1789 affect the urban
hierarchy? In the nineteenth century, did the size of cities influence their
rate of growth? In a preindustrial economy, is the rate of urbanization a
function of rural population density and landed wealth? First developed
as decision-making tools in applied research, the new methods make it
possible to test the hypotheses we derive from our questions against empirical data: we find, for example, that the size of cities had no effect on
their growth, that the formation of *départements* had no influence on
the evolution of urban hierarchies, and so on. The interpretive hypothesis is clearly primary; it governs the process of statistical analysis by
which it can be accepted or rejected. There are several advantages to
this procedure.

Some of these are well known, and I shall limit myself to describing
them briefly.

1. Only a misguided, reductive "scientism" would claim that science
   deals only with what is measurable. Better to say, with G. G. Granger,
   that "only the structurable has meaning" and that every effort to
   achieve intelligibility is an exercise in recognizing the forms that structure the apparent disorder of immediate experience.[14] By requiring formalization, quantitative methods force the historian to take a more rigorous approach. Ideally, they require a systematic effort to be explicit
   about one's assumptions, to include all critical variables, and to observe
   the methodological rules that guarantee that the results will have certain desired properties.

2. Historical research can thus claim kinship with any experimental approach based not on accumulating data in order to extract a theory
   but, rather, on developing initial hypotheses and subjecting them to

testing through controlled manipulation of empirical data external to the abstract system the hypotheses define. The fact that hypotheses are essential should serve to remind us that reality never discloses itself of its own accord and that documents alone can never provide conclusive evidence. Historians must do more than define problems; they must construct objects, choose approaches, select and refine indices (the "clue paradigm" also applies to quantitative history), and develop sources appropriate to their questions.

It is often stressed that problem-oriented history is inextricably associated with the construction of historical facts. I would add that along with the construction of facts goes the invention of archives and controlled testing of the data. The effect of this is once again to increase the distance between the historian and the phenomena of the past and the sources in which traces of those phenomena are preserved. In my view, therefore, quantitative history has a substantial contribution to make to current debates about the changing nature of the historical profession. Consider three points:

1. RESEARCH PROGRAMS

Take, for example, the colloquium that the International Commission of Historical Demography at Stuttgart in 1985 devoted to historical testing of Ester Boserup's theses on the effect of demographic pressure on the growth of agricultural production.[15] In retrospect, it was clear that the whole debate was based on a misunderstanding and no dialogue was possible. The problem was a difference of scale. Boserup's theory posited a single causal factor based on very-long-term observation of vast territories (China, sub-Saharan Africa) and was couched in terms of successive stages of development. The historians pointed to the complexity of local or regional situations analyzed over a period of roughly a century, in which the strong cause-and-effect correlation that Boserup found was not apparent. Did the critiques prove that Boserup's hypothesis was false? Not at all. They simply showed that her formulation failed to account for the concrete local situations that the historians chose to study. In these special cases, climatic accidents, renewal of trade, and changes in social relations combined with demographic pressures to yield short-term evolutions different from those predicted by the macro-analytic model.

Demographic pressure, social relations, trade channels: each of these factors in itself constitutes an explanatory hypothesis, and so do their various combinations. Before attempting any quantitative verification or search for pertinent indicators, these factors have to be defined, and to do this one must consider the scope of their applicability, thus revealing the impossibility of effective comparison. Quantification forces investigators to define their research programs as precisely as possible. One has to be clear about how research at different levels fits together, as well as about methods of analysis and scales of observation. One must also break down macro-level hypotheses, which might otherwise become mere matters of opinion, into intermediate propositions that can be subjected to quantitative testing. For example, one can envision a research program to test Max Weber's hypothesis about the relationship between the Protestant ethic and the rise of capitalism. A historical sociological approach might rely on tax documents, parish registers, comparisons of the contents of Protestant and Catholic libraries, and lexical analyses of sermons, day books, and commercial correspondence. In this way, Weber's idea would become intelligible in an entirely new way.[16]

2. HISTORICAL DISCOURSE AS MODEL

Consider a demographic model designed to account for various aspects of French economic growth in the nineteenth century.[17] The choice of a theoretical framework together with a set of historical hypotheses yields a series of equations describing the behavior of thirteen interconnected endogenous variables (production, consumption, and so on), which are explained in terms of a small set of exogenous parameters (climate, technological innovation, and so forth). The empirical data from annual statistical series yield estimates of the various parameters and make it possible to judge the validity of the data and the explanatory power of the historian's hypotheses. Although the method here is more complex than in previous cases, it is compatible with the methodological principle that hypotheses are to be subjected to statistical testing against the empirical data. One can also see just what a model is: a model is, to borrow Fernand Braudel's formulation, a set of "closely coupled explanatory hypotheses and systems taking the form of an equation or function." While not all research in quantitative history explicitly follows this demanding approach, the implicit method is always the same. What is a good history book if not a "closely coupled system of explanation"? The use of an econometric model gives us a better idea of the implications of this basic analogy. The work in question ends with a series of simulations based on a "theoretical copy" of the French economy in the nineteenth century. By changing the value of one or more exogenous variables in a counterfactual way, one exhibits the effects of those variables (assuming that all other relevant factors are equal).

Several of the consequences of any model-building method are particularly apparent, I think, in this explicit use of a "theoretical copy." Such a copy is not a one-to-one representation of "reality." It is a simplified, abstract representation based on functional relations that have been shown to be compatible with the available data and internally consistent. The copy is not a duplicate of reality but, rather, the product of a structure that makes that reality less opaque, a structure consisting of an initial set of hypotheses together with certain rules of logic and mathematics. Such a construct can be revised, therefore, not just at the conclusion of the iterative process by which the macroeconomic model is refined but in response to new interpretive criteria: history, it will come as no surprise, is a product of its times. If we assume that all historical discourse (with or without formal rigor) results in constructions of a similar nature, several consequences follow:

· Like Zeno's arrow, historical analysis never attains its target: the real is beyond our reach.[18]

· No object of historical study is given to us in nature (hence, history is not a mirror of reality). Every object must be constructed, and if that object is not to become the prisoner of a priori categories, it must emerge from the research itself and the principles for interpreting it must be implicit in the method by which it is defined (which raises difficult issues for historical synthesis and general history).

· When expressed in realist terms, the opposition between micro- and macroanalysis is misleading.[19] It is situated not at the level of the real but at the level of representation. Each is a different way of conceptualizing phenomena and making them less opaque. Neither one is more "real" than the other.

3. The Pertinence of the Discourse

If the intelligibility of the past hinges on the projection of some theoretical framework that is always open to revision, it does not follow that one discourse is as good as another, or that Montaigne was right when he said that "there is more to be done in the way of interpreting interpretations than of interpreting things," hence that what historians today ought to be doing is studying an endless sequence of previous historiographical traditions. Experience with quantitative modeling suggests various ways of gauging the pertinence of any particular discourse.[20] Every model is a system, any component of which makes sense only in relation to the set of relations that defines the structure of the system as a whole. There are ways of analyzing macroeconomic models internally, for example, to test their validity. Econometric tests are designed to confirm the consistency of the model. The phenomena themselves figure only in the final stages of the analysis, after the model has been shown to respect certain representational rules. Historical proof cannot be reduced to either a logic of persuasion or a logic of narration. The relevance of any particular model is to be judged in light of the problems it was designed to solve, the methods used to test it, and the results of comparing the model's behavior with the empirical historical data. Each of these could easily be the subject of a lengthy essay. It is already clear, however, that a more flexible use of quantitative tools could help history avoid having to choose between positivism and rhetoric.

TRANSLATED BY ARTHUR GOLDHAMMER

NOTES

[1] This paper was written for a conference on "The *Annales*, Yesterday and Today," organized by the Institute of Universal History of the Academy of Sciences of the USSR, Moscow, Oct. 3–8, 1989.

[2] J.-Y. Grenier, *Séries économiques françaises (XVIIᵉ–XVIIIᵉ siècles)* (Paris: Editions de l'EHESS, 1985); see also the excellent review by G. Béaur in *Annales ESC* 44 (1989), pp. 1127–41.

[3] For example, in early modern history, J. Quéniart, *Culture et société urbaines dans la France de l'Ouest au XVIIIᵉ siècle* (Lille, 1977); Michel Vovelle, *Piété baroque et déchristianisation en Provence au XVIIIᵉ siècle: Les Attitudes devant la mort d'après les clauses des testaments* (Paris: Plon, 1973); Daniel Roche, *Le Peuple de Paris: Essai sur la culture populaire au XVIIIᵉ siècle* (Paris: Aubier, 1981).

[4] François Furet, "L'Histoire quantitative et la construction du fait historique," *Annales ESC* 26 (1971), pp. 63–75; reprinted in *L'Atelier de l'histoire* (Paris: Flammarion, 1982) [The piece is excerpted here as "Quantitative History," pp. 333–348].

[5] Paul Ricoeur, *Temps et récit,* vol. 1 (Paris: Seuil, 1983), and vol. 3 (Paris: Seuil, 1985).

[6] Edoardo Grendi, "Micro-analisi e storia sociale," *Quaderni storici* (1977), pp. 506–20.

[7] Carlo Ginzburg, "Spie-Radici di un paradigma indiziario," in A. Gargani, ed., *Crisi della ragione: Nuovi modelli nel rapporto tra sapere e attività umana* (Turin: Einaudi, 1979); French translation in *Le Débat* 6 (1980), pp. 3–44.

[8] It would be useful to have a detailed study of the assumptions governing the creation of databases. One way of doing this would be to explore the methodological statements usually included with responses to calls for the submission of data. For a methodological survey, see L. Fossier and J.-P. Genet, *Standardisation et échange des banques de données* (Paris: CNRS, 1989).

[9] Jorge Luis Borges, "De la Rigueur de la science," *Histoire de l'infamie, histoire de l'éternité* (Paris: UGE, 1964).

[10] J.-P. Benzecri, *L'Analyse des données* (Paris, 1973).

[11] F. Furet, "L'Histoire quantitative" (see note 4, above).

[12] A. Daumard and François Furet, *Structures et relations sociales à Paris au milieu du XVIIIᵉ siècle* (Paris: A. Colin, 1961); Roland Mousnier, *La Stratification sociale à Paris au XVIIᵉ et au XVIIIᵉ siècle* (Paris: P.U.F., 1976); Jean-Claude Perrot, "Rapports sociaux et villes au XVIIIᵉ siècle," *Annales ESC* 23 (1968), pp. 241–67; M. Gar-

den, "Ouvriers et artisans au XVIIIe siècle: L'Exemple lyonnais et les problèmes de classification," *Revue d'histoire économique et sociale* (1970), pp. 28–54.

[13] I beg the reader's indulgence if I take the following examples from my book *Les Villes dans la France moderne (1740–1840)* (Paris: Albin Michel, 1988). This is of course not the only work of its kind; for an excellent and complementary illustration, see A. Guerreau, "Analyse factorielle et analyses statistiques classiques: le cas des ordres mendiants dans la France médiévale," *Annales ESC* 36 (1981), pp. 869–912. On the statistical techniques used, see, for example, A. Monjallon, *Introduction à la méthode statistique* (Paris, 1963); G. Calot, *Cours de statistique descriptive* (Paris, 1965); F. Viallet, *Statistique et recherche appliquée* (Paris, 1970); Raymond Boudon, *L'Inégalité des chances* (Paris: P.U.F., 1973).

[14] G.-G. Granger, *Pensée formelle et sciences de l'homme* (Paris: P.U.F., 1967), and *Pour la connaissance philosophique* (Paris, 1988).

[15] A. Van Der Woude, "Boserup's Thesis and the Historian," and Ester Boserup, "Agricultural Development and Demographic Growth," in A. Fauve-Chamoux, ed., *Evolution agraire et croissance démographique* (Liège, 1987), pp. 381–89.

[16] P. Benedict, "Weber chez les Huguenots," paper read to a seminar at the Centre de Recherches Historiques, mimeographed. For preliminary applications of these ideas, see "Bibliothèques protestantes et catholiques à Metz au XVIIe siècle," *Annales ESC* 40 (1985), pp. 343–70; "La Population réformée française de 1600 à 1685," *Annales ESC* 42 (1987), 6, pp. 1433–67.

[17] M. Lévy-Leboyer and F. Bourguignon, *L'Economie française au XIXe siècle: Analyse macro-économique* (Paris: Economica, 1985), and the analysis given in A. Strauss, "Econométrie et histoire économique: La France au XIXe siècle," *Annales ESC* 43 (1988), pp. 35–71.

[18] Bernard Lepetit, "Les représentations de la ville: Pour quoi faire?" in F. Walter, ed., *Vivre et imaginer la ville, 18e–19e siècles* (Geneva, 1988), pp. 9–28.

[19] Bernard Lepetit, "La micro-histoire: une vue de l'extérieur," *Problèmes et objets de la recherche en sciences sociales,* Journées d'études de l'EHESS (1987), mimeographed.

[20] This last point is developed in J.-Y. Grenier and Bernard Lepetit, "L'expérience historique: A propos de C.-E. Labrousse," *Annales ESC* 44 (1989), p. 1337–60. The fact that this is a collaborative article indicates that these ideas are not mine alone. I am responsible only for the brief formulation of them given here.

New Protagonists

Faced with the shattering of old paradigms produced by the explosion of historical research into new domains, historians began to look for new sources of theoretical inspiration. Marxism and structuralism faded in significance. Most historians either did not believe in or did not believe themselves able to provide grand histories of broad social and cultural mutations. They might have admired Jürgen Habermas or Michel Foucault, or perhaps Norbert Elias for his global reconstruction of "the civilizing process" based on the development of manners and new sensibilities, but they did not necessarily aim for the same scope of analysis in their own work. Even more significant, perhaps, was what historians looked to these great works to provide: not a general explanatory, interpretive, or epistemological model, as they surely would have done twenty years earlier, but rather lessons of two kinds, one having to do with how history ought to be done, the other with new questions that historians ought to be asking.

The following three examples will help to clarify what took place. Pierre Bourdieu, Jean-Claude Passeron, Paul Ricoeur—all three are authors whose work has been of considerable importance to the critical thinking of a number of French historians in recent years. Two of them are sociologists: they thus represent a discipline with which Annales historians have maintained a long-lasting alliance, which has lately borne new fruit. The third comes from philosophy, which by contrast has been a discipline that historians have long viewed with suspicion and skepticism, but the questions he raises are of interest to historians today and, in some cases, seem central to the future of the discipline.

PIERRE BOURDIEU

In Other Words

1987

The sociologist and ethnologist Pierre Bourdieu (b. 1931) proposed to bridge the growing gap between a functionalist social scientific approach that relied on "objective" measures of social life and research on mentalités *or cultures that focused on "subjective" representations of the social world. In his own work, he emphasized the workings of systems of social and cultural differentiation, as in his best-known work* La Distinction *1979 (*Distinction, *1984). Such systems are not fixed, in his view, but are always being made and remade, and thus the people in them are themselves always acting and being acted upon. Bourdieu's work, which has lately begun to attract an audience in the English-speaking world, has dominated French sociology since the 1970s. It has played, in particular, an essential role in the reformulation of themes and problems associated with the social history of culture.*

Speaking in very general terms, social science, in anthropology as in sociology or in history, oscillates between two apparently incompatible points of view, two apparently irreconcilable perspectives: objectivism and subjectivism, or, if you prefer, physicalism and psychologism (which can take on diverse colorings, phenomenological, semiological, and so on). On the one hand, it can "treat social phenomena as things," in accordance with the old Durkheimian maxim, and thus leave out everything that they owe to the fact that they are objects of cognition—or of miscognition—in social existence. On the other hand, it can reduce the social world to the representations that agents make of it, the task of social science then consisting in producing an "account of the accounts" produced by social subjects.

It is rare that these two positions are expressed and above all realized in scientific practice in such a radical and contrasting way. You know

From *In other Words: Essays Towards a Reflexive Sociology*, trans. Matthew Adamson (London: Polity Press, 1990), pp. 124–128, 129–131.

that Durkheim is doubtless, together with Marx, the person who has expressed the objectivist position most consistently: "We find fruitful the idea that social life must be explained not by the conception of those who participate in it, but by the deep causes which lie outside consciousness." But, as a good Kantian, he was not unaware of the fact that this reality cannot be grasped without bringing logical instruments into operation. That being said, objectivist physicalism is often associatd with the positivist inclination to imagine classifications as "operative" ways of cutting things up or as a mechanical recording of "objective" breaks and discontinuities (for example in distributions). It is doubtless in Schütz and the ethnomethodologists that one could find the purest expressions of the subjectivist vision. Thus Alfred Schütz takes exactly the opposite standpoint to that of Durkheim: "The observational field of the social scientist, social reality, has a specific sense and structure of pertinence for the human beings who live and act and think in it. By a series of commonsense constructions, they have preselected and preinterpreted this world that they apprehend as the reality of their daily life. These are the objects of thought that determine their behaviour by motivating it. The objects of thought constructed by the social scientist so as to grasp this social reality must be based on the objects of thought constructed by the commonsense thinking of people who live their daily lives in their social world. Thus, the constructions of the social sciences are, so to speak, second-degree constructions, that is, constructions of the constructions made by actors on the social stage."[1] The opposition is total. In one case, scientific knowledge can be obtained only by breaking away from the primary representations—called "prenotions" in Durkheim and "ideology" in Marx; this break leads to the positing of unconscious causes. In the other case, scientific knowledge is continuous with commonsense knowledge, because it is only a "construction of constructions."

If I have rather labored this opposition, one of the most unfortunate of those "paired concepts" which, as Richard Bendix and Benett Berger have shown, flourish in the social sciences, this is because the most constant and, in my eyes, most important intention of my work has been to transcend it. At the risk of appearing very obscure, I could sum up in one phrase the whole analysis I am setting out for you today: on the one hand, the objective structures that the sociologist constructs in the objectivist moment, by setting aside the subjective representations of the agents, are the basis of subjective representations, and they constitute the structural constraints that influence interactions; but, on the other hand, these representations also have to be remembered if one wants to account above all for the daily individual and collective struggles that aim at transforming or preserving these structures. This means that the two moments, objectivist and subjectivist, stand in a dialectical relation and that, even if for instance the subjectivist moment, when it is taken separately, seems very close to interactionist or ethnomethodological analyses, it is separated from them by a radical difference: the points of view are apprehended as such and related to the positions in the structure of the corresponding agents.

In order fully to transcend the artificial opposition that tends to be established between structures and representations, one also has to break away from the mode of thought that Ernst Cassirer calls "substantialist," which leads people to recognize no realities except those available to direct intuition in ordinary experience, individuals, and groups. The major contribution of what one has to call the structuralist revolution consisted in applying to the social world a relational way of thinking, which is that of modern physics and mathematics, and which identifies the real not with substances but with relations. The "social reality" that Durkheim talked of is a set of invisible relations, those very same relations that constitute a space of positions exterior to each other and defined by their proximity to, neighborhood with, or distance from each other, and also by their relative position—above or below, or even in between, in the middle. Sociology, in its objectivist moment, is a social topology, an *analysis situs*, as this new branch of mathematics was called at the time of Leibniz, an analysis of relative positions and objective relations between these positions.

This relational way of thinking is the point of departure of the construction presented in *La Distinction*. But it's a fair bet that the space, that is, the relations, will go unnoticed by the reader, despite the use of diagrams (and of correspondence analysis that is a very sophisticated form of factorial analysis): on the one hand, because the substantialist way of thinking is easier, more "natural"; second, because, as often happens, the means one is obliged to employ to construct social space and in order to manifest it risk concealing the results they enable one to obtain. The groups that one has to construct in order to objectify the positions they occupy conceal those positions, and the chapter in *La Distinction* on fractions of the dominant class is read as a description of the different lifestyles of those fractions, instead of being read as an analysis of the way they have to be seen as positions in the space of power positions— what I call the "field of power." (In parenthesis, I would note that changes in vocabulary are, as you can see, both the condition and the result of breaking away from the ordinary representation associated with the idea of *ruling class*.)

One can, at this point of the discussion, compare the social space to a geographical space within which regions are divided up. But this space is constructed in such a way that the agents, groups or institutions that find themselves situated in it have more properties in common the closer they are to each other in this space; and fewer common properties, the further they are away from each other. Spatial distances—on paper—coincide with social distances. The same is not true in real space: it is true that one can observe almost everywhere a tendency toward segregation in space; people close to each other in the social space tend to be close together—by choice or necessity—in the geographical space; however, people who are very distant from each other in the social space can encounter one another, enter into interaction, at least briefly and intermittently, in physical space. The interactions, which are accepted at their face value by people of an empiricist disposition—one can observe them, film them, record them, in short they are tangible—conceal the structures that are realized in them. It's one of those cases in which the visible, that which is immediately given, conceals the invisible which determines it. One thus forgets that the truth of the interaction is never entirely to be found in interaction as it is available to observation. One example will suffice to show the difference between structure and interaction, and, at the same time, between the structuralist vision, which I would defend as a necessary moment of research, and the so-called interactionist vision in all its forms (ethnomethodology in particular). I have in mind what I call "strategies of condescension," by which agents occupying a higher position in one of the hierarchies of objective space symbolically deny the social distance, which does not thereby cease to exist, thus ensuring that they gain the profits of recognition accorded to a purely symbolic negation of distance ("he's unaffected," "he's not standoffish," and so on) which implies the recognition of a distance (the sentences I have quoted always have an implicit rider: "he's unaffected, for a duke," "he's not standoffish, for a university professor," and so forth). In short, one can use the objective distances so as to have the advantages of proximity and the advantages of distance, that is, the distance and the recognition of the distance ensured by the symbolic negation of distance.

How can one thus concretely grasp these objective relations which are irreducible to the interactions in which they are manifested? These objective relations are relations between the positions occupied in the distributions of resources which are or may become active, effective, like the trumps in a game of cards, in competition for the appropriation of the rare goods of which this social universe is the locus. These fundamental social powers are, according to my empirical researches, economic capital, in its different forms, and cultural capital, and also symbolic capital, a form that is assumed by different kinds of capital when they are perceived and recognized as legitimate. Thus agents are distributed in the overall social space, in the first dimension in accordance with the overall volume of the capital that they possess in different kinds and, in the second dimension, in accordance with the structure of their capital, that is, in accordance with the relative weight of the different kinds of capital, economic and cultural, in the total volume of their capital.

The misunderstanding in the reading of the analyses that I set out, especially in *La Distinction*, thus results from the fact that classes on paper risk being apprehended as real groups. This realist reading is objectively encouraged by the fact that the social space is constructed so that agents who occupy similar or close positions are placed in similar conditions and submitted to similar conditionings, and have every chance of having similar dispositions and interests, and thus of producing practices that are themselves similar. The dispositions acquired in the position occupied imply an adjustment to this position, which Erving Goffman called the "sense of one's place." It's this sense of one's place which, in interactions, leads people who are in French called "les gens modestes," that is, "ordinary people," to keep to their "ordinary" place and the others to "keep their distance" or "respect their rank," and "not get familiar." These strategies, it should be noted in passing, may be perfectly unconscious and may take the form of what is called timidity or arrogance. In fact, social distances are written into bodies, or, more exactly, into the relationship to the body, to language and to time (so many structural aspects of practice that are ignored by the subjectivist vision).

But, just as subjectivism inclines people to reduce structures to interactions, objectivism tends to deduce actions and interactions from the structure. So the main error, the theoreticist error that you find in Marx, seems to consist in treating classes on paper as real classes, in concluding from the objective homogeneity of conditions, of conditionings, and thus of dispositions, which all come from the identity of position in the social space, that the people involved exist as a unified group, as a class. The notion of social space allows one to go beyond the alternative of nominalism and realism when it comes to social classes: the political enterprise meant to produce social classes as "corporate bodies," permanent groups, endowed with permanent organs of representation, acronyms, and so on, has all the more chance of succeeding since the agents that it wishes to bring together, unify, and constitute as a group are closer in the social space (and thus belong to the same class on paper). Classes in Marx's sense have to be produced by a political enterprise which has all the more chance of succeeding in that it is sustained by a theory that is well founded in reality, and thus capable of exercising a *theory effect—theorein*, in Greek, means to see—capable, in other words, of imposing a vision of divisions.

With the theory effect, we have left pure physicalism, but without abandoning the experience acquired in the objectivist phrase: groups—social classes, for instance—have to be *made*. They are not given in "social reality." We have to take literally the title of the famous book by E. P. Thompson, *The Making of the English Working Class*:[2] the working class in the form in which it may appear to us today, via the words meant to designate it, "working class," "proletariat," "workers," "workers' movement," and so on, via the organizations that are meant to express it, the acronyms, the offices, secretariats and flags, and so forth, is a well-founded historical artefact (in the sense in which Durkheim said of religion that it is well-founded illusion). But that does not mean that one can construct just anything at all, in any old way, either in theory or in practice.

We have thus moved from social physics to social phenomenology. The "social reality" objectivists talk about is also an object of perception. And social science must take as its object both this reality and the perception of this reality, the perspectives, the points of view that, by virtue of their position in objective social space, agents have on this reality. The spontaneous visions of the social world, the "folk theories" that ethnomethodologists tak about, or what I call "spontaneous sociology," but also scientific theories, and sociology, are all part of social reality, and, like the Marxist theory for instance, can acquire an altogether real constructive power.

The objectivist break with prenotions, ideologies, spontaneous sociology, and "folk theories," is an inevitable and necessary moment of the scientific procedure—you cannot do without it (as do interactionism, ethnomethodology, and all the forms of social psychology that rest content with a phenomenal vision of the social world) without exposing yourself to grave mistakes. But you have to carry out a second and more difficult break away from objectivism, by reintroducing, in a second stage, what had to be excluded in order to construct social reality.

Sociology has to include a sociology of the perception of the social world, that is, a sociology of the construction of the worldviews that themselves contribute to the construction of this world. But, given the fact that we have constructed social space, we know that these points of view, as the word itself suggests, are views taken from a certain point, that is, from a given position within social space. And we know too that there will be different or even antagonistic points of view, since points of view depend on the point from which they are taken, since the vision that every agent has of space depends on his or her position in that space.

By doing this, we repudiate the universal subject, the transcendental ego of phenomenology that the ethnomethodologists take over as their own. No doubt, agents do have an active apprehension of the world. No doubt they do construct their vision of the world. But this construction is carried out under structural constraints. And one may even explain in sociological terms what appears as a universal property of human experience, that is, the fact that the familiar world tends to be "taken for granted," perceived as natural. If the social world tends to be perceived as evident and to be grasped, to use Husserl's terms, with a "doxic modality," this is because the dispositions of agents, their habitus, that is, the mental structures through which they apprehend the social world, are essentially the product of an internalization of the structures of the social world. As perceptual dispositions tend to be adjusted to position, agents, even the most disadvantaged, tend to perceive the world as natural and to find it much more acceptable than one might imagine, especially when one looks at the situation of the dominated through the social eyes of the dominant.

TRANSLATED BY MATTHEW ADAMSON

NOTES

[1] Alfred Schütz, *Collected Papers*, vol. 1: *The Problem of Social Reality* (The Hague, n.d.), p. 59

[2] E. P. Thompson, *The Making of the English Working Class* (London, 1963).

JEAN-CLAUDE PASSERON

Sociological Reasoning

1991

Throughout this volume, we have stressed the role of sociology, and in particular of the Durkheimian tradition, in the practical work and theoretical reflections of twentieth-century French historians. Relations between the two disciplines have not always been easy, however, and troubles have been frequent. Nevertheless, the intellectual agenda of the Annales *historians retains many of the characteristic features of Durkheimian epistemology, especially in the concept of a historical science that aspired to achieve a scientific status comparable to that of the natural sciences. The triumph of quantitative history in the three decades after 1950 only reinforced this particular tendency. In fact, it revealed something deeper, something that has been true of French social science since the late nineteenth century—the predominance of scientistic positivism. To be sure, this was much more sophisticated than earlier versions of positivism, of which French social scientists were critical, but it largely ignored the hermeneutic approaches that were coming to prominence at this time in Germany.*

Against this background the importance of Jean-Claude Passeron's Le Raisonnement sociologique *(1991) stands out. A sociologist, Passeron was a longtime collaborator of Pierre Bourdieu's. The book, which followed a series of important articles that had appeared regularly since the late 1970s, undertook to give a new formulation of the sociological approach to understanding, summed up in the book's subtitle: "The Non-Popperian Space of Natural Reasoning." Following Max Weber, Passeron proposes to rethink the unity of the social sciences and their distinctive form of rationality in terms of the historical character they all share. He seeks to dispel the "nomological illusion" with which the social sciences long justified themselves in their own eyes and to recognize what all share—the characteristic of being descriptive languages of the empirical world, which cannot hope to achieve stability because they are themselves inscribed in and produced by history.*

Jean-Claude Passeron, *Le Raisonnement sociologique* (Paris: Nathan, 1991).

In no sense does this mean that the social sciences must settle for being less than sciences. What they must do, rather, is define their own rules. In a time of intellectual chaos, indeed of a certain episte-mological anarchy, this ambitious and difficult book attempts to re-store order and begin rebuilding. No doubt, this is why it has aroused a discreet but intense debate, particularly among historians, from the moment of its publication.

In order to escape the "experimentalist illusion" that would deprive it of its object, sociological reasoning constantly needs to be "recalled to order," the order of historical contextualization. To see what the experimentalist temptation looks like in its purest form, consider a problem familiar to statisticians, that of correcting for "purely statistical effects." When we do this, we discover the contradiction between the supposed rigor of experimental comparison and comparison in the socio-logical sense.

Sociological reasoning, I have argued, cannot be purely experimental reasoning. Even in its experimental aspects there are limits to the appli-cation of statistics to sociological problems. Take, for example, the "structural effects" that the National Institute for Economic and Elec-toral Statistics, that hotbed of subtle statisticians, is always on the lookout for. A structural effect, of course, is a phantom of the statistical method rather than a true historical find. Statisticians, who are critical of the make-believe inherent in the search for experimental impeccability, are well aware of the dangers[1] and have been so ever since Maurice Halb-wachs first explored François Simiand's paradox: if one is to apply statis-tical methods to distinguish between what is intrinsic to camels and what stems from their environment, one needs a sample that includes camels whose habitat is the North Pole. An argument cannot be made purely experimental unless it can be cast in the form of a proposition in which "all things are equal" other than the variables being subjected to experi-mental scrutiny. Where does this lead? In searching for structural anom-alies, one has to make sure that the relation between variables X and Y does not reflect some unnoticed relation between X and some other vari-able T by testing for the effects of T. In other words, the contingency tables have to be made two-dimensional. If one is skeptical, and the scientific mind must be skeptical, one also has to test for other possible hidden variables: T^1, T^2, T^3, and so on. Social data are, of course, taken from a context in which the number of possible variables is infinite. Unfortunately, the sample quickly becomes unwieldy, and the inves-tigator looking for "structural effects" has to "massage" the data in order to construct those tables *experimentally necessary* for his strategy of "neutralization."

Following the logic of experimental reasoning, the investigator is drawn into a forest of statistics, for it is never possible to "neutralize" all the "parasitic" variables. In order to deal with his sample, moreover, he can no longer give proportional weight to each of the subsamples of which it is composed. He may want to make sure, for instance, that an apparent influence of belonging to the medical profession on behavior does not unwittingly reflect the fact that there are too many doctors from Paris in his national sample. In order to neutralize the relationship between residence in Paris and belonging to the medical profession, he must include proportionally more doctors from Lozère than from Paris in his "corrected" sample. If the proportion of Paris doctors is decreased, he must make a corresponding increase in the proportion of agricultural laborers earning less than the minimum wage within the capital's city limits. I am, of course, caricaturing the kinds of difficulties involved in any attempt to "neutralize structural effects" in order to meet the demands of experimental logic by sacrificing more and more information in the name of the *ceteris paribus* clause. My only purpose is to show how, the more one uses statistical corrections (in either the collection or the processing of data, as in experimental psychology, where no problem arises because one is interested solely in interactions among laboratory variables), the more "massaging" of the data one tries, the more persuasive the argument from the statistical point of view and the more absurd from the standpoint of history and sociology. One loses touch with the way in which the variables are related in social reality. One also loses touch with the set of probabilities that link the values of variables hic et nunc, that is, in a real context in which they act together, *configurationally*. Agricultural laborers are more probable in Lozère than in Paris, hence different: statistical treatment condemns individuals to have nothing sticking to the soles of their shoes other than the variable that defines them in the sample. Everyone knows this, of course, yet we all forget it when we use membership in a socioprofessional group as a variable whose significance we assume to remain invariant in different contexts. In so doing we *naturalize* our variables; they become transhistorical. The tie to history is severed.

When sociological reasoning strays too far in the direction of experimental utopia, the insistence on historical contextualization can be seen as a *recall to order*. The historicity of the object is sociology's *reality principle*. The sociologist remains a sociologist only to the extent that he is pulled back toward historical order. Here I use the phrase "pulled back" in the sense in which one says that the string from which the bob of a pendulum hangs exerts a force that "pulls back" the swinging bob. Sex, age, and social class are not variables in the sense that mass and distance are variables in the law of universal gravitation, or even as mass and time are in the law of falling bodies. In such laws, one can always say what variables and values must be taken into account in order to describe and control the relevant (in the sense of experimentally relevant) context: although Galileo knew nothing of the Newtonian, or eventually the Einsteinian, context of his measurements, the formula that he established, $D = \frac{1}{2}GT^2$ remains in practice universally valid, at least on the scale of variations that it was possible to observe in his day. The theory that emerged from his experimental protocol could be stated in terms of an equation involving all the pertinent variables, with all other variables assigned to a context that could be assumed to remain constant. Later, it became possible to see that Galileo's law was in fact a localized singularity, but only after new measurements were undertaken in response to a more general paradigm that offered a theoretical explanation for the limited scope of the original law: the orders of magnitude that restricted its universality were cast in a new light. In the experimental sciences, in other words, one can speak of "protocols," "variables," and "constant contexts" while limiting oneself to "definite descriptions" and without invoking "proper names."[2] By contrast, the relations among sociological variables, no matter how carefully measured, tested, and repeated, never give rise to *universal* statements or even to *general* extracontextual statements, because there is no way to control the constancy of the context or the collection of data made pertinent by some theory in terms of identifiable variables: the context can be enlarged (at the risk of ending up with a typology), but that is all.

This ambiguity concerning sociology's links to either of the two poles of knowledge, the experimental and the historical, is surely a source of benefits as well as risks. It explains how sociology was able to become at times the theoretical focal point of the social sciences, where all the various parts could be put back together (as was the case when the great sociological systems—Marxist, Durkheimian, Weberian—were created), while at other times—its worst moments—degenerating into little more than a place for facile encounters between vague discourses on history and society and modest, inconsequential empirical findings. History, which like sociology is a discipline of interpretive synthesis, also occupies a somewhat different position at the intersection of several paths. Recent developments have placed it at the center of the social sciences, while its roots as a tool for understanding singular configurations encourage importation rather than exportation of methods. Actually, sociological reasoning, though I call it "sociological" (an adjective that misleadingly suggests a strict disciplinary "nationality"), could also be used to characterize the ambition of both disciplines to produce knowledge about the course of the historical world, thereby protecting history from the tendency to forget the conceptual constructs that enable it to speak and sociology from the tendency to substitute formalist constructs for the empirical world it speaks of.

TRANSLATED BY ARTHUR GOLDHAMMER

NOTES

[1] A. Desrosières, "Un Essai de mise en relation des histoires récentes de la statistique et de la sociologie," *Actes de la journée d'études "Sociologie et statistique,"* pp. 166–68.

[2] In the logical sense of "proper name" (more general than the grammatical sense), in which any statement involving even an indirect indexation of variable with respect to spatiotemporal coordinates brings in a pragmatic "designation," which thus contrasts with a "definite description" in Bertrand Russell's sense. Unlike Russell, who succeeded in eliminating proper names in favor of definite descriptions by means of a purely formal operation (reducing individuals to fixed instances of a variable in propositional logic), most logicians have wished to stick closer to the semantics of natural language and have therefore rejected this "trick." See Gilles Gaston Granger, "A Quoi servent les noms propres?" in *Langages* (Paris: Larousse, 1966), pp. 24–33. Philosophical debate continues, however, over the semiotic status of proper names. See also K. Donnellan, "Reference and Description," *Philosophical Review* 75 (1966) and Saul Kripke, "Naming and Necessity," in Donald Davidson and Gilbert Harman, *Semantics of Natural Languages* (Dordrecht: Reidel, 1972).

PAUL RICOEUR

Time and Narrative

1983

The three volumes of Temps et récit *(1983–85;* Time and Narrative*) mark a moment in contemporary historiographical reflection not only in France but in other countries as well. Paul Ricoeur introduced French historians to themes, references, authors, and ideas that had been largely absent from French debate (as evidenced by the lukewarm reception of Paul Veyne's* Comment on écrit l'histoire *[Writing History] in 1971). Among other things, Ricoeur took note of essential aspects of English-language thinking from the new rhetoric to analytical philosophy, which he expounded, interrogated, commented on, and criticized. A philosopher working in the tradition of Husserl's phenomenology, Ricoeur also stands out for his interest in historians' practices and methods, in how they construct their objects, organize their discourse, and so on. Thus, despite the traditional reluctance of French historians to pay attention to philosophical commentary, Ricoeur's work has been well received and has become a part of the historiographical debate, in marked contrast to an earlier work,* Histoire et récit, *which drew little notice from professional historians when it was published in 1955. True, times had changed: the tranquil scientific certainties of the 1960s and early 1970s had given way to doubts or at any rate to questions. The philosopher had no answers, but he did help in the reformulation of the problems.*

Born in 1913, Ricoeur is the author of many works at the intersection of phenomenology and hermeneutics, fields that define the fundamental context of Temps et récit *(in which historical narrative is just one form of narrative among many). The central thesis of the work is one that calls into question one of the constant ambitions of* Annales *historiography—to eliminate events and narrative from history altogether. Ricoeur, in contrast, treats narrative as the irreducible form of the human experience of time.*

From *Time and Narrative,* trans. Kathleen McLaughlin and David Pellauer (Chicago: University of Chicago Press, 1984), vol. 1, pp. 208–17. First published as *Temps et récit* (Paris: Seuil, 1983).

My thesis is that historical events do not differ radically from the events framed by a plot. The indirect derivation of the structures of history starting from the basic structures of narrative allows us to think that it is possible, through the appropriate procedures of derivation, to extend to the notion of historical event the reformulation of the concepts of singularity, contingency, and absolute deviation imposed by the notion of emplotted event.

I would like to return to Fernand Braudel's work, despite—or even because of—the case made there against the history of events in order to show in what sense the very notion of the history of a long time span derives from the dramatic event in the sense just stated, that is, in the sense of the emplotted event.

I will start from the indisputable achievement of the Braudelian methodology, namely, the idea of the plurality of social times. The "dissecting of history into various planes," to employ the terms of the preface to *The Mediterranean,* remains a major contribution to the theory of narrative time. The method of questioning back must therefore start from here. We must ask ourselves what enables us to make the very distinction between a "history whose passage is imperceptible," a history "of slow but perceptible rhythms," and a history "on the scale ... of individual men," namely, that history of events which the history of the long time span is to dethrone.

It seems to me that the answer is to be sought in the principle of unity which, despite the separation into different spans of time, holds the three parts of Braudel's work together. The reader cannot be content with merely recognizing the right of each of these parts to exist by itself— each part, the preface states, "is itself an essay in general explanation." This is all the more incumbent in that the title of the work, by its twofold reference—on the one hand, to the Mediterranean, on the other, to Philip II—invites its readers to ask themselves in what way the long span of time brings about the transition between structure and event. To understand this mediation performed by the *longue durée* is, in my opinion, to recognize the plotlike character of the whole that is constituted by the three parts of the work.

I would like to base my interpretation not on the declarations concerning method collected in the work *On History*, but on a patient reading of *La Méditerranée et le monde méditerranéen à l'époque de Philippe II.*[1] This reading reveals the important role of the transitional structures that ensure the overall coherence of the work. These structures, in turn, allow us to consider the arrangement of the entire work in terms of its quasi plot.

By "transitional structure," I mean all the procedures of analysis and exposition that result in a work's having to be read both forward and backward. In this regard, I would be prepared to say that if the first part itself retains a historical character despite the predominance of geography, this is by virtue of all the elements that point to the second and third parts and set the stage upon which the characters and drama of the rest of the work will be played out. The second part is devoted to the long time span, properly speaking, and serves to hold the two poles together: the Mediterranean, the referent of the first part, and Philip II, the referent of the third. In this sense, it constitutes both a distinct object and a transitional structure. It is this last function that makes it interdependent with the two parts that frame it.

Let me demonstrate this in some detail.

Consider the first level, whose theme seems to be space rather than time. What is immobile is the Inland Sea. Everything he writes about is already part of a history of the Mediterranean.[2] For example, the first three chapters are devoted to this landlocked sea. They refer to inhabited or uninhabitable spaces, including watery plains. Humans are everywhere present and, with them, a swarm of symptomatic events. The mountains appear as a refuge and a shelter for free people. As for the coastal plains, they are not mentioned without a reference to colonization, to the work of draining them, of improving the soil, the dissemination of populations, displacements of all sorts: migrations, nomadism, invasions.[3] Here, now, are the waters, their coastlines, and their islands; they, too, enter into this geohistory on the scale of human beings and their navigation. The waters are there to be discovered, explored, traveled. Even on this first level, it is not possible to speak of them without mentioning relations of economic and political dominance (Venice, Genoa). The great conflicts between the Spanish and Turkish empires already cast their shadows over the seascape. And with these power struggles, events are already taking shape.[4]

Thus, the second level is not only implied but actually anticipated in the first: geohistory is rapidly transformed into geopolitics. In fact, the first part is essentially concerned with establishing the polarity between the Turkish and Spanish empires.[5] Maritime zones are from the very beginning political zones.[6] Our view may try to concentrate on the silent life of the islands, their slow rhythm of ancient and new, but global history never ceases to come ashore on these islands and to link the peninsulas,[7] so "political supremacy passed from one peninsula to another and along with it supremacy in other fields, economic and cultural." Geography has so little autonomy that the boundaries of the space considered are continually redrawn by history.[8] The Mediterranean is measured by its sphere of influence. The phenomenon of trade is, in the same stroke, already implied. The Mediterranean space must be extended as far as the Sahara and to the European isthmuses. Braudel does not shy from stating right in the middle of his first part: "It is worth repeating that history is not made by geographical features, but by the men who control or discover them." Thus, the final chapter of the first level openly leads from a physical unity to that human unity "with which this book is concerned." Consider human labor ("The different regions of the Mediterranean are connected not by the water, but by the peoples of the sea")—it produces a space-in-motion made of roads, markets, and trade. This is why it is necessary to speak of banks and of industrialism and trading families, and especially of cities, whose appearance changes the face of the land.[9]

The second level is, of course, the one where the historian of the long time span finds himself most at home. Yet the extent to which this level, considered in itself, lacks coherence must be noted. Oscillating between the sphere of structure and the sphere of conjuncture, it places three competing systems of organization on stage: that of economic conjuncture, in overall expansion; that of the political implications of the physical and geographical relations, as observed in the mobile polarity of Spain and Turkey; and that of civilizations. These three systems do not correspond exactly, and this perhaps explains the increasing temptation, from one edition to the next, to give in to the unifying materialism of the economic conjuncture.

Already under the title of "economies"—the first system of organization—relatively disparate problems are considered: the constraints of space and of the number of people with respect to the governing of the empires, the role of the influx of precious metals, monetary phenomena and the evolution of prices, and, finally, trade and transportation. As he is setting up this first system, Braudel raises, with ever-increasing emphasis, the question of the specific level at which the totalizing factor, if there is one, is to be located: "Can the model of the Mediterranean economy be constructed?" Yes, if a content can be given to the notion of a "world-economy," considered as an "internally coherent zone" despite its uncertain and variable limits. But this is a risky endeavor, because of a lack of monetary standards by which to draw up an account of all the exchanges. In addition, a flurry of dated events concerning the four corners of the quadrilateral Genoa-Milan-Venice-Florence, as well as the history of the other marketplaces, confirms the fact that level three continually merges with level two. And the growth of states, joined to that of capitalism, makes the long history of economies repeatedly fall back upon the history of events.[10]

And the second level must also make room for other principles of organization—empires, societies, civilizations. It sometimes seems that empires provide the fabric of history: "The story of the Mediterranean in the sixteenth century is in the first place a story of dramatic political growth, with the leviathans taking their positions," the Ottomans to the east, the Hapsburgs to the west. The characters—Charles V, Suleiman—are accidents, of course, but their empires are not. Without denying individuals and circumstances, attention must instead be directed to the conjuncture persistently favorable to vast empires, with the economic ascendancy of the fifteenth and sixteenth centuries and, more generally, to the factors favorable or unfavorable to the vast political formations which are seen to rise and to begin to decline in the sixteenth century.[11]

Once again, neither economies nor empires occupy the entire stage of the second level. Civilizations are also to be considered: "Of all the complex and contradictory faces of the Mediterranean world, its civilizations are the most perplexing," so fraternal and so exclusive are they, mobile and permanent, ready to spread their influence and determined not to borrow from the outside. Spain has its Baroque. The Counterreformation is its Reformation: "The refusal then was deliberate and categorical." In order to express these "areas of astonishing permanence," Braudel has a magnificent description: "a civilization exists fundamentally in a geographical area which has been structured by men and history. That is why there are cultural frontiers and cultural zones of amazing permanence: all the cross-fertilization in the world will not alter them." Mortal? Of course, civilizations are mortal, but "their foundations remain. They are not indestructible, but they are many times more solid than one might imagine. They have withstood a thousand supposed deaths, their massive bulk unmoved by the monotonous pounding of the centuries." However, yet another factor intervenes. Civilizations are many, and it is out of their points of contact, of friction, and of conflict that once again events are born. Even if the Hispanic world's refusal of any mixing is the cause, "the slow shipwreck of Islam on the Iberian Peninsula" has to be recounted, along with the "drama of Grenada," and even the survivals and infiltrations that allow us to speak of "the aftermath of Grenada," until its destruction.[12]

Everything, then, in the first two parts conspires to crown the edifice with a history of events that puts on stage "politics and people." This third part of the work is by no means a concession to traditional history. In a total history, stable structures and slow evolutions perhaps constitute the essential part, but "they cannot provide the total picture." Why? First, because events provide testimony of the deep-seated, underlying movements of history. As we saw, the first two parts make frequent use of these "ephemera of history," which are at one and the same time symptoms and testimonies. The great historian is not afraid of stating here: "I am by no means the sworn enemy of the event." But there is another reason, namely, that events raise the problem of their coherence at their own level. Braudel himself gives a twofold justification for the inevitable selection that this level of explanation requires. On the one hand, the historian retains only important events, those which have been made important by their consequences. Without naming it, Braudel encounters here the problem of singular causal explanation as it was posed by Max Weber and Raymond Aron, with its logic of retrodiction and its search for "adequation."[13] On the other hand, the historian cannot ignore the judgment made by contemporaries concerning the importance of events, under pain of failing to take into account the way in which people of the past interpreted their history. (Braudel mentions in this regard the turning point that the Saint Bartholomew's Eve massacre represents for the French.) These interpretations, too, are part of the historical object.

I now come to my second thesis, namely, this: It is *together* that the work's three levels constitute a quasi plot, a plot in the broad sense used by Paul Veyne.

It would be a mistake to limit the kinship between this text and the narrative model of emplotment to just the third level. To do so would be to miss the major contribution of this work, which is to open up a new career for the very notion of plot, and, in this, for that of *event*.

Nor am I prepared to look for this new form of plot in the middle level alone, although certain statements by Braudel himself suggest doing this. Does he not speak of the *récitatif de la conjuncture,* the conjuncture narrative? What might serve as a plot in the economic history is its cyclical character and the role that is played by the notion of crisis.[14] The double movement of growth and decline thus represents a complete intercycle, measured by the time of Europe and more or less by that of the entire world. The third, as yet untranslated, volume of *Civilization and Capitalism: 15th–18th Century,* entitled *Le Temps du Monde,* is built entirely upon this vision of the rise and decline of world economies, in accordance with the slow rhythms of conjuncture. The notion of a "trend" tends, then, to take the place of that of a plot.[15]

Nevertheless, I am not inclined to restrict myself to this equation, not only because it does just as much violence to the notion of cycle as to that of plot but also because it does not account for what occurs in the work at these three levels. Economic history lends itself to a plot when an initial term and a final term are chosen, and these are provided by categories other than conjunctural history itself, which, in principle, is endless, unlimited in the strict sense. A plot has to include not only an intelligible order but a magnitude that cannot be too vast, or it will be unable to be embraced by our eye, as Aristotle stresses in the *Poetics* (51a1). What frames the plot of the Mediterranean? We may say without hesitation: the decline of the Mediterranean as a collective hero on the stage of world history. The end of the plot, in this regard, is not the death of Philip II. It is the end of the conflict between the two political leviathans and the shift of history toward the Atlantic and Northern Europe.

All three levels contribute to this overall plot. Whereas a novelist— Tolstoy in *War and Peace*—would have combined all three together in a single narrative, Braudel proceeds analytically, by separating planes, leaving to the interferences that occur between them the task of producing an implicit image of the whole. In this way, a virtual quasi plot is obtained, which itself is split into several subplots, and these, although explicit, remain partial and in this sense abstract.

The work is placed as a whole under the heading of the mimesis of action by the continual reminder that "history is not made by geographical features but by the men who control or discover them." In this respect, the history of conjunctures cannot by itself constitute a plot. Even on the plane of economics, several different economies—or, more precisely, the antagonisms of two economic worlds—have to be placed together. I have already quoted this passage from part one: "Politics merely followed the outline of an underlying reality. These two Mediterraneans, commanded by warring rulers, were physically, economically, and culturally different from each other. Each was a separate historical zone." With one stroke, the fabric of the plot is already suggested: the great opposition between the two Mediterraneans and the decline of their conflict.[16] If this is indeed the history Braudel is narrating, then it is understandable that its second level—which is supposed to be entirely devoted to the long time span—requires beyond its overview of economies the addition of the physics of international relations that alone governs the subplot of the conflict between empires and the fate of this conflict. In its ascending phases, "The story of the Mediterranean in the sixteenth century is in the first place a story of dramatic political growth, with the leviathans taking up their positions." In addition, high stakes are involved: will the Atlantic belong to the Reformation or to the Spanish? When Turks and Spaniards turn their backs on one another at the same time, the narrative voice inquires: In the Mediterranean, earlier than elsewhere, does not the hour toll for the decline of empires? The question is necessary, for, as in drama, reversal brings with it contingency, that is to say, events that could have turned out differently: "The decline of the Mediterranean, some will say—with reason. But it was more than that, for Spain had every opportunity to turn wholeheartedly toward the Atlantic. Why did she choose not to?" In turn, the subplot of the conflict between empires, and the retreat of this conflict from the Mediterranean

area, demands to be linked up with the subplot of the collision of monolithic civilizations. We recall the statement, "Of all the complex and
contradictory faces of the Mediterranean world, its civilizations are the
most perplexing." [17] The reversals of these conflicts have been mentioned
above: the fate of the Moriscos, the fate of the Jews, foreign wars. We
must now speak of the contribution these subplots make to the overall
plot. Referring to the alternation of foreign wars and internal wars as
"plain to see," the dramatist writes: "it offers a new perspective on a
confused period of history, illuminating it in a way which is neither
artificial nor illusory. It is impossible to avoid the conviction that contrasting ideological patterns were first established and then replaced."
Thus, just as Homer picked from the stories of the Trojan War the set
he chose to tell in the *Iliad,* Braudel picks from the great conflict between
civilizations in which the Occident and the Orient alternate the conflict
whose protagonists are Spain and Turkey at the time of Philip II and
whose framework is the decline of the Mediterranean as a historical zone.

Having said this, we must admit that the overall plot that constitutes
the unity of the work remains a virtual plot. Didactic reasons require
that the "three different conceptions of time" remain disconnected, the
aim being "to bring together in all their multiplicity the different measures of time past, to acquaint the reader with their coexistence, their
conflicts and contradictions, and the richness of experience they hold." [18]
However, even if it is virtual, the plot is nonetheless effective. It could
become real only if a total history were possible without doing violence
to any of its parts. [19]

Finally, by his analytical and disjunctive method, Braudel has invented a new type of plot. If it is true that the plot is always to some
extent a synthesis of the heterogeneous, the virtual plot of Braudel's
book teaches us to unite structures, cycles, and events by joining together
heterogeneous temporalities and contradictory chronicles. [20] This virtual
structure permits us nevertheless to judge between two opposite ways of
reading *The Mediterranean.* The first subordinates the history of events
to the history of the long time span and the long time span to geographical time—the main emphasis is then placed on the Mediterranean. But
then geographical time is in danger of losing its historical character. For
the second reading, history remains historical insofar as the first level
itself is qualified as historical by its reference to the second level and, in
turn, the second level derives its historical quality from its capacity to
support the third level. The emphasis is then placed on Philip II. But the
history of events lacks the principles of necessity and of probability that
Aristotle attributed to a well-constructed plot. The plot that includes the

three levels equally authorizes both readings and makes them intersect at the median position of the history of the *longue durée*, which then becomes the unstable point of equilibrium between them.

TRANSLATED BY KATHLEEN MCLAUGHLIN AND DAVID PELLAUER

NOTES

[1] The English translation is of the the second edition of 1966. Fernand Braudel, *The Mediterranean and the Mediterranean World in the Age of Philip II,* trans. Siân Reynolds (New York: Harper and Row, 1972), 2 vols.

[2] Placed under the heading of a certain type of geography that is especially attentive to human destinies, the first-level inquiry is "the attempt to convey a particular kind of history" (Braudel, *The Mediterranean,* p. 23). A "history in slow motion from which permanent values can be detected" (ibid.), which therefore makes use of geography as one of its media. In this respect it is striking that the author waits until past page 200 before making any reflections on the "physical unity" of the Mediterranean. We may readily admit that the "Mediterranean itself is not responsible for the sky that looks down on it" (ibid., p. 232), but the physical unity that is in question here is, above all, the permanence of certain constraints—the hostile sea, the harsh winters, the burning sun—and all that contributes to the identity of the Mediterranean people, as they make up for all that is lacking, and adjust their wars, their treaties, and their conspiracies to the rhythm of the seasons, under the sign of the eternal trinity: wheat, olive tree, and vine—"in other words an identical agrarian civilization, identical ways of dominating the environment" (ibid., p. 236).

[3] "Man has been the laborer of this long history" (ibid., p. 64). "Spain sent all her sons down to this southern region opening to the sea" (ibid., p. 84). "All of these movements require hundreds of years to complete" (ibid., p. 101). In short, "geographical observation of long term movements guides us towards history's slowest processes" (ibid., p. 102).

[4] "The new element was the massive invasion by Northern Nordic ships, after the 1590's" (ibid., p. 119). Nor is it possible not to mention the war of Grenada.

[5] "These two different Mediterraneans were vehicles, one might almost say they were responsible for the twin empires" (ibid., p. 136).

[6] "Politics merely followed the outline of an underlying reality. These two Mediterraneans, commanded by warring rulers, were physically, economically, and culturally different from each other. Each was a separate historical zone" (ibid., p. 137).

[7] "These liaisons and partnerships, successively created and destroyed, summarize the history of the sea" (ibid., pp. 165–66).

[8] "The Mediterranean (and the accompanying Greater Mediterranean) is as man has made it. The wheel of human fortune has determined the destiny of the sea, expanding or contracting its area" (ibid., pp. 169–70).

[9] The city brings about, in the geographer-historian's discourse, a flood of dates (see, for example, ibid., pp. 332–34), so pregnant is the history of cities, as they confront the designs of territorial states, expanding or dying out in the wake of economic conditions. Yes, cities speak "of evolution and changing conditions" (ibid., p. 352) against the backdrop of constancies, permanence, and repetitions that are established on the first level of analysis.

[10] In the chapter on precious metals, money, and prices (ibid., pp. 462–542), the changes in commercial practices, the influx and outflow of metals cannot help but be dated: "The advance of the Portuguese along the Atlantic coast of Africa was an

event of major importance" (ibid., p. 469). And further on: "During the difficult war years, 1557–58, the arrival of the ships carrying bullion were the great events of the port of Antwerp" (ibid., p. 480). A profusion of dates accompanies the cycle of metals on the western routes. Royal bankruptcies are dated (1596, 1607). It is a question, of course, of grasping the stable factors in order to verify the explanatory schema. But this requires passing through the history of events with its dates, its proper names, naming Philip II and considering his decisions. In this way, level three casts a shadow on level two, due to the interferences between politics and war, on the one hand, and different economies, on the other.

[11] "The life-span of empires cannot be plotted by events, only by careful diagnosis and auscultation—and as in medicine there is always room for error" (ibid., p. 661).

[12] "Of all the possible solutions, Spain chose the most radical: deportation, the uprooting of a civilization from its native soil" (ibid., p. 796).

[13] It is in this way that Lepanto, which Voltaire ridiculed as being so unimportant, was, indeed, "the most spectacular military event in the Mediterranean during the sixteenth century. Daring triumph of courage and naval technique though it was, it is hard to place convincingly in a conventional historical perspective" (ibid., p. 1088). Lepanto would probably have had important consequences if Spain had been determined to pursue them. But, on the whole, "Lepanto had not accomplished anything." In this regard, we may note the fine pages devoted to Don John's calculations, that "instrument of destiny" (ibid., p. 1101)—the explanatory reflection corresponds exactly to William Dray's model of rational explanation, as well as to the Weberian model of explanation by means of contrary assumptions.

[14] In Braudel's article "History and the Social Sciences," we read: "A new kind of historical narrative has appeared, that of the conjuncture, of the cycle, and even of the 'intercycle,' covering a decade, a quarter of a century, and, at the outside, the half century of Kondratiev's classic cycle" (*On History,* trans. Sarah Matthews [Chicago: University of Chicago Press, 1980], p. 29) [the piece is excerpted here, pp. 115–145; the quoted passage is on p. 120]. In the *Cambridge Economic History of Europe,* vol. 4, Braudel defines the cycle in the following way: "Because the word cycle might be applied to a seasonal movement we should not be misled. The term designates a double movement, a rise and fall with a peak in between which, in the strictest sense of the term, is called a crisis" (ibid., p. 430). I am indebted to M. Reep, in an unpublished essay, for the reference to this text, as well as for the suggestion that the notion of cycle shares with the Aristotelian mythos the twofold feature of constituting a mimesis of economic life (in the sense of mimesis$_2$, of course) and of presenting a median structure, a reversal—that, precisely, which the notion of crisis introduces—between two intercycles.

[15] The title itself, *Le Temps du Monde,* promises more than it can deliver, as the author admits ("Avant-propos," p. 8). If it is his ambition to grasp the history of the world "in its chronological developments and its diverse temporalities" (ibid.), he has the modesty not to hide the fact that this world time does not cover the totality of human history. "This exceptional time governs, depending on the place and the age, certain spaces and certain realities. But other realities, other spaces escape it and remain foreign to it. . . . even in advanced countries, economically and socially speaking, world time does not include everything" (ibid). The reason is that the book follows a particular line that privileges a certain sector of material and economic history. Within these avowed limits, the historian strives "to study by means of comparisons on a world-wide scale, the sole variable" (ibid., p. 9). From such a height, the historian can attempt "to dominate time, henceforth our principal, or even our only, adversary" (ibid., p. 10). It is again the long time span that permits us to link together the successive experiences in Europe which deserve to be considered as world economies (1) in a space that varies only slowly, (2) around a few dominant capital cities (Venice, Amsterdam, and so on) that one after the other come to

predominate, and (3), finally, according to a principle of hierarchization concerning the zones of contact. The subject matter is therefore the division of time (and space) as a function of conjunctural rhythms, among which the secular trend—"the most neglected of all the cycles" (ibid., p. 61)—proves to be the most fruitful. For my own reflection on time, I take note that "the trend is a *cumulative* process. It adds on to itself; everything happens as if it raised the mass of prices and economic activities little by little until the moment when, in the opposite direction, with the same stubbornness, it began to work to lower them through a general, imperceptible, slow, and prolonged reduction. Year by year, it is barely noticeable; century by century, it proves to be an important actor" (ibid.). The image of a tide, with wave upon wave, intrigues us more than it explains anything to us: "the final word escapes us and, along with it, the exact meaning of these long cycles that seem to obey certain laws or rules governing tendencies unknown to us" (ibid., p. 65). Must we then say that what seems to explain the most is at the same time what helps us understand the least? In volume two, I shall take up the problem of giving a real meaning to what is here no more than an admission, even a truism, that "short time and long time exist together and are inseparable . . . for we live all at once in short time and in long time" (ibid., p. 68).

[16] "For it was the interaction of such pressing need, such disturbances and restorations of economic balance, such necessary exchanges, which guided and indirectly determined the course of Mediterranean History" (ibid., p. 138). Further on, Braudel speaks of the "general outline" (ibid., p. 230), the retreat of the Mediterranean from general history, a retreat delayed until the middle of the seventeenth century. Referring once more to the gradual replacement of city-states by capital cities, he writes: "Their message is one of evolution and changing conditions which hints at their approaching destiny: that decline proclaimed by so many signs at the end of the sixteenth century and accentuated in the seventeenth century" (ibid., p. 352).

[17] Discussing forms of war, especially of foreign wars (the Crusades, jihads), Braudel mentions once again the role of civilizations, those "major participants" (ibid., p. 842). These "characters," like the events in question, are defined in classical terms by their contribution to the main plot.

[18] I wonder if Braudel did not think he had avoided the problem of the overall unity of his work by letting the problem of reuniting the pieces of fragmented duration be taken care of by physical time. In *On History* we read: "These fragments are reunited at the end of all our labors. The *longue durée,* the conjuncture, the event all fit into each other neatly and without difficulty, for they are all measured on the same scale" (*On History,* p. 77). What scale, if not that of physical time? "For the historian everything begins and ends with time, a mathematical, godlike time, a notion easily mocked, time external to men, 'exogenous,' as economists would say, pushing men, forcing them, and painting their own individual times the same color: it is, indeed, the imperious time of the world" (ibid., p. 78). But then the long time span becomes one of the paths by which historical time is led back to cosmic time, rather than one way of increasing the number of time spans and speeds. Of course, historical time builds its constructions against the backdrop of cosmic time. But it is within physical time that the unifying principle of "the diverse colors of individual times" is to be sought.

[19] The polyphony comes from dozens of measures of time, each of them attached to a particular history. "Only the sum of these measures, brought together by the human sciences (turned retrospectively to account on the historian's behalf) can give us that total history whose image is so difficult to reconstitute in its rich entirety" (*The Mediterranean,* p. 1238). This total image would require the historian to have at once the geographer's, the traveler's, and the novelist's eye. The following are mentioned at this point by Braudel: Gabriel Audisio, Jean Giono, Carlo Levi, Lawrence Durrell, and André Chamson (ibid., p. 1234).

[20] His frank statement on structure and structuralism should be taken into consideration: "I am by temperament a 'structuralist,' little tempted by the event, or even by the short-term conjuncture which is after all merely a grouping of events in the same area. But the historian's 'structuralism' has nothing to do with the approach which under the same name is at present causing some confusion in the other human sciences. It does not tend toward the mathematical abstraction of relations expressed as functions, but instead toward the very sources of life in its most concrete, everyday, indestructible and anonymously human expression" (ibid., p. 1244).

Reformulations and New Proposals

────

FRANÇOIS FURET

Interpreting the French Revolution

1978

Even while criticism of unexamined assumptions and unintended consequences in social history developed apace, many historians worked to reformulate their methods in new ways. In particular, they began to disaggregate the notion itself of "the social." They did not presume that society and social relations had fixed meanings over time which could serve as neutral measuring points; instead, they investigated the changing constructions of the social both in terms of mental conceptions and in terms of behaviors and practices.

The pioneer of such reformulation was François Furet. In his 1978 book Penser la Révolution française *(Interpreting the French Revolution), which not only broke with the dominant historiography but also deviated from his own previous positions, he claimed that the false presumption that social relations determined the content of political life had distorted the historiography of the French Revolution. Arguing that the Revolution created a new mode of political action that aimed to transcend the given social structure, Furet both revitalized political history and demonstrated that history could be fruitfully rewritten in a political-philosophical vein.*

─────────────────────────────────────

From *Interpreting the French Revolution,* trans. Elborg Forster (Cambridge, Eng.: Cambridge University Press, 1981), pp. 48–53. First published as *Penser la Révolution française* (Paris: Gallimard, 1978).

If the Revolution thus experienced, in its political practices, the theoretical contradictions of democracy, it was because it ushered in a world where mental representations of power governed all actions, and where a network of signs completely dominated political life. Politics was a matter of establishing just *who* represented the people, or equality, or the nation: victory was in the hands of those who were capable of occupying and keeping that symbolic position. The history of the Revolution between 1789 and 1794, in its period of development, can therefore be seen as the rapid drift from a compromise with the principle of representation toward the unconditional triumph of rule by opinion. It was a logical evolution, considering that the Revolution had from the outset made power out of opinion.

Most histories of the Revolution fail to assess the implications of that transformation; yet none of the leaders who successively dominated the revolutionary scene wielded power in the normal sense, by giving orders to an army of underlings and commanding a machinery set up to implement laws and regulations. Indeed, the regime set up between 1789 and 1791 made every effort to keep the members of the Assembly away from executive power, and even to protect them from any such contamination. The suspicion of ministerial ambitions under which Mirabeau had to labor until the very end and the parliamentary debate about the incompatibility between the functions of representative and minister are telling illustrations of that attitude.[1] It was related to more than political circumstance and the Assembly's distrust of Louis XVI. It was inherent in a specific idea of power, for the Revolution held that executive power was by its very nature corrupt and corrupting, being separate from the people, out of touch with it and, hence, without legitimacy.

In actual fact, however, that ideological disqualification simply led to a *displacement of power*. Since the people alone had the right to govern—or at least, when it could not do so, to reassert public authority continually—power was in the hands of those who spoke for the people. Therefore, not only did that power reside in the word, for the word, being public, was the means of unmasking forces that hoped to remain hidden and were thus nefarious; but also power was always at stake in the conflict between words, for power could only be appropriated through them, and so they had to compete for the conquest of that evanescent yet primordial entity, the people's will. The Revolution replaced the conflict of interests for power with a competition of discourses for the appropriation of legitimacy. Its leaders' "job" was not to act; they were there to interpret action. The French Revolution was the set of new practices that added a new layer of symbolic meanings to politics.

Hence the spoken word, which occupied center stage, was constantly under suspicion, for it was by nature ambiguous. It strove for power yet denounced the corruption power inevitably entailed. It continued to obey the Machiavellian rationality of politics yet identified only with the ends to be achieved: that contradiction lay at the very root of democracy, from which it was inseparable, but the Revolution brought it to the highest degree of intensity, as if in a laboratory experiment.

Revolutionary activity par excellence was the production of a maximalist language through the intermediary of unanimous assemblies mythically endowed with the general will. In that respect, the history of the Revolution is marked throughout by a fundamental dichotomy. The deputies made laws in the name of the people, whom they were presumed *to represent;* but the members of the *sections* and of the clubs acted as the *embodiment* of the people, as vigilant sentinels, duty-bound to track down and denounce any discrepancy between action and values and to reinstate the body politic at every moment. As regards domestic politics, the salient feature of the period between May–June 1789 and 9 Thermidor 1794 was not the conflict between Revolution and counter-revolution but the struggle between the representatives of the successive Assemblies and the club militants for the dominant symbolic position, the people's will. For the conflict between Revolution and counterrevolution extended, with nearly unchanged features, far beyond 9 Thermidor, while the fall of Robespierre marked the end of a politico-ideological system characterized by the dichotomy I am trying to analyze here.

One of the most frequent misunderstandings of the historiography of the French Revolution is its attempt to reduce that dichotomy to a social cleavage by granting in advance to one of the rival powers a status that was precisely the undefined and quite literally elusive stake in the conflict, namely, the privilege of being the people's will. In substituting the opposition between the bourgeoisie and the people for the one between aristocratic plot and the people's will, that misunderstanding turns the "public safety" period into the culminating though temporary episode in which the bourgeoisie and the people marched hand in hand in a kind of Popular Front.[2] That rationalization of the political dynamic of the French Revolution has one major flaw, for in reifying revolutionary symbolism and in reducing political motivation to social concerns, it makes "normal" and obliterates what calls for explanation: the fact that the Revolution placed that symbolic system at the center of political action, and that it was that system, rather than class interest, that, for a time at least, was decisive in the struggle for power.

There is little need, therefore, to launch into a critique of that type of interpretation and to point out its incoherences with respect to the strictly social aspects of the problem. Not only has that critique already been made, notably by the late Alfred Cobban,[3] but, more important, that type of interpretation is *irrelevant to the problem at hand.* Even if it were possible to show—and that is not the case—that, for instance, the conflict between the Girondins and the Montagnards had its roots in the contradictory class interests of the antagonists or, on the contrary, that the period dominated by the Committee of Public Safety was character- ized by a compromise between "bourgeois" and "popular" interests, such a demonstration would still be altogether beside the point. The "people" was not a datum or a concept that reflected existing society. Rather, it was the Revolution's claim to legitimacy, its very definition as it were; for henceforth all power, all political endeavor revolved around that founding principle, which it was nonetheless impossible to embody.

That is why the history of the French Revolution, in the narrow sense, is characterized throughout by violent clashes between the different ver- sions of that legitimacy and by the struggle between the men and the groups who found ways to march under its banner. The successive as- semblies embodied the legitimacy of representation, which, however, was from the very outset fought against by direct democracy, as suppos- edly expressed in the revolutionary *journées.* Moreover, in between *jour- nées,* a vast range of organizations—newspapers, clubs, and assemblies of all kinds—were contending for the right to express direct democracy, and so for power. That double system gradually came to be institutional- ized in the Jacobin Club, which, as early as 1790, functioned as the sym- bolic image of the people controlling the Constituent Assembly and pre- paring its decisions. Its structure may have remained very diffuse—as diffuse, by definition, as direct democracy, since every *section,* every meeting, indeed every citizen was in a position to produce the people's will—but the fact remains that Jacobinism laid down the model and the working of direct democracy by dictating opinion in the first organized group to appropriate the Revolution's discourse on itself.

Augustin Cochin's fundamental contribution to the history of the French Revolution was to examine how that new phenomenon came into being through the production and manipulation of revolutionary ideology. Yet because his study sets out to show that the phenomenon worked in a nearly mechanical manner—as soon as the discourse of pure democracy, concealing an oligarchic power, had appropriated the consensus—it underestimates the cultural links that were also vitally necessary for that system. Although the exact congruity between revolu- tionary democracy—as proclaimed and practiced by the club militants— and the "people" was a fundamental and mythical image of the Revolu- tion, it is nonetheless true that this notion gave rise to a special relation- ship between politics and a section of the popular masses: the tangible "people"—a minority of the population to be sure, but very numerous compared to "normal" times—who attended revolutionary meetings, took to the streets on important *journées*, and provided visible evidence for the abstraction called "the people."

The birth of democratic politics, which is the only real "advent" of those years, could not have occurred without a common cultural environment in which the world of action and the world of conflicting values overlapped. Such a congruity is not unprecedented: that was how the religious wars of the sixteenth century, for example, had mustered most of their recruits. What is new in the laicized version of revolutionary ideology—the foundation of modern politics—is that action totally encompassed the world of values, and thus became the very meaning of life. Not only was man conscious of the history he was making but he also knew that he was saved or condemned in and by that history. That lay eschatology, which was destined to so great a future, was the most powerful driving force of the French Revolution. We have already noted its integrating function for a society in search of a new collective identity, as well as the extraordinary fascination it exerted by promoting the simple and powerful idea that the Revolution had no objective limits, only enemies. Those premises gave rise to an entire system of interpretation, which, strengthened by the first victories of the Revolution, became a credo whose acceptance or rejection separated the good from the wicked.

TRANSLATED BY ELBORG FORSTER

NOTES

[1] Debate of Nov. 1789.

[2] The expression "public safety" was used by Georges Lefebvre.

[3] Alfred Cobban's most important articles were collected in *Aspects of the French Revolution* (London: Jonathan Cape, 1968).

ROGER CHARTIER

The World as Representation

1989

A specialist in the cultural history of early modern France, Roger Chartier provides a global overview of the "crisis" of history at the end of the 1980s, even while contesting the accuracy of some diagnoses of its nature. Combining the perspectives of Norbert Elias and Pierre Bourdieu, he argues for attention to the collective representations of the social as a way of avoiding both social reductionism (assuming that everything cultural and political can be explained in terms of social origins) and the mirror-image view that political and intellectual life are entirely autonomous and separate from the social. Chartier suggests that we see in social representations and, more broadly, in cultural configurations, not the transcription of preexisting social relations but rather, on the contrary, one of the sites where social differentiation is constructed. This is expressed by way of practices (objects and their forms of appropriation, shared or specific codes, and symbolic deployments).

The editorial in the spring 1988 issue of the *Annales* calls upon historians to think about their work in the light of two presumed facts. The editors maintain, on the one hand, that there is a "general crisis of the social sciences," apparent in the collapse of global systems of interpretation, of the "dominant paradigms" that structuralism and Marxism once provided, as well as in the alleged repudiation of the ideologies responsible for their success (which I take to mean a belief in the possibility of radical, socialist transformation of liberal, capitalist, Western societies). On the other hand, the text to some extent excludes history from that diagnosis, for it concludes, "We do not believe, as some are only too willing to accept, that history is in crisis." History is thus seen as a discipline that is still healthy and vigorous, though burdened by uncertainties stemming from the weakening of its traditional alli-

Roger Chartier, "Le Monde comme représentation," *Annales* 44 (Nov.–Dec. 1989), pp. 1505–20.

ances (with geography, ethnology, and sociology) and its failure to achieve a unified set of principles around which objects and methods can be defined. The uncertainty that afflicts the profession today is thus presented as the obverse of a vitality which, in unfettered if chaotic fashion, is opening up new fields of research, experimentation, and collaboration.

Doubts About the Diagnosis

Why start by assuming a general crisis of the social sciences but continued vitality in history, albeit at the price of a rather anarchic eclecticism? The strategy at work in the text—and here I use the term "strategy" in the sense not of a conscious, rational calculation but, rather, of a more or less automatic adjustment to a given situation—seems to me dictated by a desire to preserve the discipline in a time perceived to be one of radical decline of the theories and doctrines on which history based its advances of the 1960s and 1970s. The challenge to history came initially from the most recently institutionalized and intellectually expansive disciplines, such as linguistics, sociology, and ethnology. The assault took many forms, some structuralist and some not, but all questioned the discipline's choice of objects (specifically, the primacy given to the study of economic and demographic conjunctures and social structures) and methodological certainties (which were measured against new theoretical requirements and found wanting).

The social sciences undermined history's dominant position in the universities by proposing new objects of study until then largely outside the domain of a discipline chiefly devoted to the exploration of the economic and social, and by developing new criteria of scientificity and new methods distinct from the criteria and methods of the exact sciences (including modeling, the hypothetico-deductive method, and collaborative research). New principles of legitimation imported from "literary" disciplines discredited history's empiricism and sought to convert the new disciplines' institutional fragility into intellectual hegemony.[1]

Historians responded in two ways. They rushed to fronts opened up by others in a strategy aimed at capturing new territory. This gave rise to new questions—about attitudes toward life and death, rituals and beliefs, kinship structures, forms of sociability, education, and so on. Historians claimed new territory for themselves by annexing the territory of others (ethnologists, sociologists, and demographers). A corollary of this was a massive return to one of the fundamental inspirations of the early *Annales,* the *Annales* of the 1930s: the study of "mental tools" that had been relegated to the second rank by the predominance of social history. Referred to variously as the *histoire des mentalités* or *psychologie historique,* a new field of research was carved out, distinct from both the old history of ideas and the history of structures and conjunctures. These new (or rediscovered) objects could be used to test new methods borrowed from adjacent disciplines, such as linguistic and semantic analysis, statistical tools borrowed from sociology, and various anthropological models.

However, this appropriation (of territories, methods, and criteria of scientificity) was not likely to yield real benefits unless the discipline retained its fundamental source of strength, which was the quantitative treatment of large volumes of serial data (such as parish registers, price reports, notarized documents, and so on). For the most part, the history of *mentalités* was therefore developed by applying the proven methods of economic and social history to new objects. This accounts for many of its distinctive features: the preference for large samples, hence for the investigation of so-called popular culture; reliance on numerical and serial data; a predilection for the *longue durée*; and a tendency to emphasize socioprofessional classifications. The distinctive features of the cultural history thus defined, which opened up new fields of research while keeping faith with the postulates of social history, reflected the strategy of the discipline, which gave itself a new scientific legitimacy—guaranteeing its continued institutional centrality—by turning to its own advantage the weapons that were supposed to bring it down. The operation was of course a brilliant success, establishing a close and trusting alliance between history and those disciplines that, for a time, seemed its most dangerous rivals.

The challenge that history faces in the late 1980s is the inverse of that just described: it is no longer rooted in a critique of the habits of the discipline in the name of innovations stemming from the social sciences but, rather, in a critique of the postulates of the social sciences themselves. The intellectual foundations of the attack are clear: on the one hand, the return to the philosophy of the subject, which denies the power of collective determinations and social conditionings, and seeks to rehabilitate "the explicit, deliberate component of action"; and on the other, the primacy accorded to the political, which is supposed to constitute "the most comprehensive level" of social organization and therefore to provide "a new key to the architecture of the totality." History is therefore summoned to reformulate its objects (in response to an inquiry into the very nature of the political), its partners (emphasizing new dialogues with political science and legal theory), and, still more fundamentally, its principle of intelligibility, divorced from the "critical paradigm" and redefined by a philosophy of consciousness. From this perspective, the most urgent need is therefore to make a clean break between the historical discipline (which can be saved only at the cost of "wrenching revisions") from the once-dominant social sciences (sociology and ethnology), which are condemned for their primary attachment to an obsolete paradigm.[2]

In its discreet, euphemistic manner, the diagnosis given in the *Annales* editorial, with its different treatment of history, said to stand at a "critical turning point," and the social sciences, said to be in a state of "general crisis," seems to me to share something of this position. This brings up a preliminary question: Can the diagnosis be accepted without reservations? To proclaim, after so many others, that the social sciences are in crisis is no proof that they actually are. The waning of Marxism and structuralism does not in itself indicate a crisis of sociology and ethnology; in France, at any rate, while those two doctrines were often invoked as theoretical references, their objectivist representations were largely ignored by those doing the most basic research, who were at pains to emphasize the innovative capacities of social actors rather than direct structural determinants and practical strategies rather than mechanical subservience to rules. This remark holds true a fortiori for history, which (but for a few important exceptions) remained uneasy about Marxist and structuralist models. Furthermore, the "back from China" syndrome that the editors cite to explain the ideological disillusionments and renunciations of the past decade appears to have had little to do with the anxieties or changing practices of historians, very few of whom made the journey to Beijing. It was undoubtedly a different story in the 1960s, however, when another generation of historians, just "back from Moscow," proposed replacing the dogmatic approach of orthodox Marxism with the then new (but today rejected) approach of quantitative social history.

CHANGING PRACTICES: THREE RENUNCIATIONS

I would suggest, therefore, that the real mutations in the historical work of the past few years stem not from a "general crisis of the social sciences" (which needs to be demonstrated rather than proclaimed) or from a "paradigm change" (which has not become a reality simply because some historians devoutly wish it to be so); instead, it stems from a change in the perspective of practical research itself, which has tended to abandon certain of the key principles that had governed historical methodology over the previous twenty or thirty years. Three of these principles deserve to be singled out: the aim to do global history, that is, a history capable of embracing the various levels of the social totality in a single, comprehensive vision; the definition of research objects in geographical terms, generally understood as involving the description of a society occupying a particular space (a city, "country," or region), as a necessary condition for the collection and treatment of the data required by total history; and the primacy accorded to social categorization, which was seen as a suitable way of organizing understanding of cultural differentiations and commonalities. This set of certainties gradually crumbled, however, opening the way to a variety of new approaches and understandings.

In giving up, for all practical purposes, the hope of describing the social totality in terms of the now-intimidating Braudelian model, historians searched for new ways to conceptualize social functions without assuming any rigid hierarchy of practices or time frames (economic, social, cultural, or political) and without giving priority to any one set of factors (technological, economic, or demographic). This led to attempts to decipher societies in new ways by delving into the complex defining networks of relations and tensions by way of some singular point of entry (an event, no matter how prominent or obscure, an account of a life, or a set of specific practices)—with the assumption, moreover, that there is no practice or structure that is not the product of the contradictory, competing representations in terms of which individuals and groups make sense of their world.

In giving up the idea that all research must be delimited in terms of territorial boundaries, French historians abandoned the "inventory" methodology they had inherited from *la géographie humaine*. Instead of mapping singularities, the explanation for which was to be sought in the diversity of geographical conditions, they began searching for regularities, thus harking back to the tradition of Durkheimian sociology, which was rejected by the *Annales* of the 1930s; instead of describing regional singularities, historians now sought to establish general laws, as required by social morphology.[3] This raised an urgent question: How do we obtain knowledge of the general if the accumulation of numerous individual observations is no longer sufficient? Answers have been proposed by a great many people, ranging from those who continue to believe in statistical measurement of correlations and constants to those who argue for the exemplarity of the atypical case and who use the paradoxical notion of the "normal exceptional" to search for what is most common in what is least ordinary.[4]

Finally, by refusing to grant tyrannical priority to social categorization for the explanation of cultural differences, recent work in history has shown that it is impossible to characterize cultural themes, objects, and practices in immediately sociological terms and, furthermore, that the distribution and uses of those themes, objects, and practices in a given society are not necessarily compatible with preexisting social divisions established on the basis of differences of status and wealth. This work has opened up new ways of thinking about the relation between cultural products and practices, on the one hand, and the social world, on the other, new correspondences sensitive to the multiplicity of divisions that exist within any society as well as to the diverse ways in which materials are used and the variety of shared cultural codes.

From the Social History of Culture to a Cultural History of the Social

The new approach requires us to move away from the basic principles of the traditional social history of culture. The first step is to abandon the narrowly sociographic conception according to which cultural differences necessarily reflect some previously constructed set of social categories. Any attempt to relate differences in cultural habits to social distinctions defined a priori must, I think, be rejected, regardless of whether those distinctions are defined macroscopically (between elites and people, say, or rulers and ruled) or in terms of finer differentiations (for example, between social groups arranged in a hierarchy on the basis of wealth and occupation).

In fact, cultural differences cannot necessarily be ordered in terms of any single social decomposition (where social category is assumed to determine differences in behavior as well as access to cultural artifacts). One must proceed instead in the opposite direction, first defining the (frequently composite) social zone in which a given corpus of texts circulates, or a given class of printed materials, or a given cultural product or norm. Starting with objects, forms, and codes rather than groups leads to the discovery that the social history of culture relied for too long on a mutilated conception of the social. By focusing exclusively on socio-professional classification, it ignored other factors of differentiation that were no less social and could be used more effectively to explain cultural differences. Among these factors we may include sex, generation, religion, child-rearing methods, territorial solidarities, and occupational habits.

Furthermore, the method of characterizing cultural configurations in terms of materials supposedly associated with them (to take a classic example, the identification of literature sold by hawkers with popular culture) can be seen as reductive in two senses. For one thing, it reduces the recognition of differences to the identification of inequalities of distribution; for another, it neglects the processes by which texts, formulas, and norms acquire meaning in the eyes of those who take them up or receive them.

Consider, for example, the circulation of printed texts in Ancien Régime societies. To understand this circulation we must modify the old approaches in two ways. First, in order to appreciate the mostly deeply socially embedded differences, we must examine how shared materials are used in contrasting ways. Contrary to what scholars have long argued, the same texts were appropriated by readers of different social stations, low and high. On the one hand, relatively humble readers came into possession of works not specifically intended for them (as in the case of Menocchio, the Friulian miller, who read Mandeville's *Voyages,* the *Decameron,* and *Fioretto della Bibbia,* and Jacques Ménétra, the Parisian glazier who was a fervent admirer of Rousseau).[5] On the other hand, shrewd, innovative printer-booksellers made available to a fairly broad spectrum of readers texts that had once circulated only in the circumscribed world of letters (as in the case of the collection known generically as the "Bibliothèque bleue," with which the printers of Troyes attempted from the late sixteenth century on to reach a humble readership). Hence, the crucial thing is to understand how the same texts (possibly in different printed forms) could be apprehended, handled, and understood in different ways.

This led to the need for a second change in historical practice: historians discovered the need to focus on the historically and socially various ways in which readers relate to texts. Reading is not simply an abstract intellectual operation: it is a matter of physical involvement, an inscription in space of one's relation to self and others. Thus, we need to find out how each community of readers—each "interpretive community," to borrow a term from Stanley Fish—went about reading.[6] A history of reading must be more than a genealogy of our own way of reading (silently, with the eyes): it must uncover forgotten gestures and vanished habits. This is important not merely because it reveals how remote once-common reading practices have become but also because it helps us to understand the distinctive structure of texts composed for uses unfamiliar to today's readers. In the sixteenth and seventeenth centuries, for example, it was still common for literary and nonliterary texts to be written implicitly in order to be read aloud by readers addressing an audience. Intended for the ear as well as the eye, such works relied on forms and procedures suited to the distinctive requirements of oral "performance." Any number of examples of this long-maintained link between text and voice can be adduced, from the themes of *Don Quixote* to the structures of books in the Bibliothèque bleue.

"Whatever they may do, authors do not write books. Books are not written at all. They are manufactured by scribes and other artisans, by mechanics and other engineers, and by printing presses and other machines."[7] This remark will serve to introduce another methodological revision. As against the representation developed by literature itself, according to which the text exists in itself, distinct from any material embodiment, it must be pointed out that there is no text apart from the material support that makes it available to the reader (or listener), and there is no reading of any written text that does not depend on the form in which it reaches the reader. A methodological distinction is therefore necessary between that which has to do with the author's textual strategies and intentions, on the one hand, and that which is the result of a publisher's decision or production constraint, on the other.[8]

Authors do not write books—they write texts that others transform into printed objects. This difference, which is precisely the space within which the meaning (or meanings) of a text is (are) constructed, has all too often been forgotten, not only in classical literary history—which conceives of the work as a thing in itself, an abstract text whose typographical forms do not matter—but also by *Rezeptionsästhetik,* which assumes, despite its desire to historicize the experience that readers have of works, a pure and immediate relation between the "signals" emitted by the text (which plays with accepted literary conventions) and the "horizon of expectation" of the audience to which it is addressed. Thus, the "effect produced" is said to be independent of the material forms in which the text is embodied.[9] Yet those forms not only shape the reader's anticipations of the text in important ways but also attract new audiences and inspire new uses.

Collective Representations and Social Identities

Drawing upon experience of research in this field, one can formulate a number of propositions relating social decompositions to cultural practices in a new way. The first of these propositions is offered in the hope of ending false debates around the supposedly universal distinction between objective structures (in the study of which history is presumed to be on the firmest ground, working to reconstruct societies as they really were by processing large numbers of serial, quantifiable documents) and subjective representations (presumed to be the subject of a different kind of history, focused on discourse and situated at some distance from the real). This distinction has left a profound stamp not only on history but also on other social sciences, such as sociology and ethnology, in which structuralist and phenomenological approaches have diverged, the former working at large scale to map the positions of and relations among various groups, often identified with classes, while the latter emphasize the study of the values and behavior of smaller communities, frequently taken to be homogeneous.[10]

In order to overcome this division, we must first treat the patterns from which classificatory and perceptual systems arise as veritable "social institutions," which incorporate the divisions of social organization in the form of collective representations: "The first logical categories were social categories; the first classes of things were classes of men in which those things were integrated."[11] As a corollary, we must look upon collective representations as matrices that shape the practices out of which the social world itself is constructed: "Even the highest collective representations truly exist as such only to the extent that they govern actions."[12]

This return to Marcel Mauss and Emile Durkheim as well as the notion of "collective representation" is perhaps more useful than the concept of *mentalité* in that it allows us to formulate three types of relation to the social world: first, the work of classification and decomposition that gives rise to the various intellectual patterns out of which reality is constructed in contradictory ways by the various groups that make up a society; second, practices that aim to win recognition of a social identity, to exhibit a proper way of being in the world, to signify symbolically a status and a rank; and finally, the institutionalized, objectified forms by means of which "representatives" (collective or individual) mark the existence of the group, community, or class in a visible and permanent manner.

Two avenues are thus opened up. One is to conceive of the construction of social identities as invariably being the outcome of a struggle between the representations imposed by those who have the power to classify and name and the definitions that each community then produces of itself, whether docile or resistant to the imposed representations.[13] The other is to look upon the objectified social decomposition as a reflection of the credence placed in the representation that each group gives of itself, based on its ability to win recognition of its existence through an exhibition of unity.[14] By working on struggles of representation in which the stakes are ultimately the organization and therefore the hierarchization of the social structure itself, cultural history may be able to free itself from an overly strict dependence on the kind of social history that is devoted exclusively to the study of economic conflicts. At the same time, it casts a fresh eye on the social itself by focusing on the symbolic strategies that determine positions and relations and construct for each class, group, or milieu a perceived-being constitutive of its identity.

For the historian of Ancien Régime societies, to construe the notion of representation as a crucial instrument of cultural analysis is to bestow operational pertinence on a concept that those societies themselves treated as central. Cognitive operations were part of the notional apparatus that contemporaries used to make their own societies less opaque to their understanding. Take, for example, the definitions of the word "représentation" in Antoine Furetière's 1727 *Dictionnaire universel*.[15] We find two different and apparently contradictory families of meanings:

on the one hand, a "representation" reveals an absence, which implies a clear distinction between that which represents and that which is represented; on the other, a "representation" is the exhibition of a presence, the public presentation of a thing or person. In the first sense, the representation is an instrument of mediated knowledge, which makes an absent object visible by substituting an "image" capable of restoring it to memory and "depicting" it as it is. Some such images are quite material, replacing the absent body with an object that may or may not resemble it: for example, the mannequins of wax, wood, or leather that were placed above the royal coffin during the funerals of French and English sovereigns: "When one goes to see dead princes lying in state, one sees only the *representation,* the effigy." Going back to an even earlier time, we find, more generally, the practice of covering the empty funeral litter with a winding cloth to "represent" the deceased: "Representation is also the word used in church to describe a mock coffin of wood covered with a mourning cloth, around which one lights candles when performing a service for the deceased."[16] Other images are pitched in a different register—that of symbolic relations, or, as Antoine Furetière puts it, "the representation of something moral by the images or properties of natural things. . . . The lion symbolizes valor, the ball, constancy, the pelican, maternal love." A decipherable relation is thus assumed to exist between the visible sign and the signified referent (although this does not mean, of course, that the sign is necessarily deciphered as it is intended to be).

The relation of representation—thus understood as a connection between a present image and an absent object, the one standing for the other because it is homologous to it—structures the whole theory of the sign in classical thought, which was most fully elaborated by the logicians of Port-Royal.[17] The various modalities of signs make it possible to discriminate between categories (certain or probable, natural or conventional, adherent to or separate from what is represented, and so forth) and to distinguish between symbols and other signs.[18] Furthermore, by identifying two necessary conditions for such a relation to be intelligible (namely, knowledge of the sign qua sign as distinct from the thing signified, and the existence of conventions regulating the relation of the sign to the thing), the *Logique* of Port-Royal framed a basic issue: the possibility of misunderstandings of a representation, whether from lack of "preparation" on the part of the reader (which raises the further issue of the form and manner in which conventions are imparted) or from "extravagance" in the arbitrary relation between sign and signified (which raises the question of the conditions under which accepted and shared equivalences are produced).[19]

The most obvious example of perversion of the relation of representation can be seen in the various forms in terms of which social life in the

Ancien Régime was theatricalized. In general, these forms of theatricalization were intended to ensure that the thing represented had no other existence but in the image that exhibited it, that the representation masked its referent rather than provide an adequate depiction of it. Pascal laid bare the mechanism of "display" by which signs were manipulated in order to mislead rather than to reveal things as they are:

> Our magistrates are quite familiar with this mystery, with their red robes and ermine collars, the thick furs in which they wrap themselves, the palaces in which they render judgment, the fleurs de lis—all this august apparatus is most essential. And if physicians had no cassocks and slippers and learned doctors did not wear mortarboards and overample four-piece gowns, they would never have fooled people who are helpless in the face of such authentic display. If the magistrates were in possession of true justice and if physicians truly knew the art of healing, they would have nothing to do with mortarboards. The majesty of their sciences would be venerable enough in itself. Yet, possessing only imaginary sciences, they must use these pointless instruments to impress the imaginations with which they must deal, and in that way they win respect for themselves.

The relation of representation is thus confused by the weakness of the imagination, which mistakes the decoy for the truth and takes visible signs to be reliable indices to a reality that does not exist. Diverted in this way, representation turns into a machine for producing respect and obedience, an instrument that produces an internalized constraint, which is necessary where the recourse to brute force is impossible: "Only men of war are not disguised in this way, because their role is in fact most essential; they establish themselves by force, the others by putting on airs."[20]

This framework provides a general context for thinking about Ancien Régime societies. It is useful for two reasons. First, it takes the "objective" position of each individual to be a function of the credence attached to that individual's self-representation by those from whom he or she hopes to receive recognition. Second, it includes forms of symbolic domination by "pomp and circumstance" (*appareil* and *attirail* in the words of Jean de La Bruyère) as a corollary of the absence or diminution of direct violence.[21] Thus it is within the context of a long-term process of eradication of violence, which became a monopoly of the absolutist state,[22] that we must situate the growing importance of conflicts of representation, the stakes of which were the organization and hence the hierarchization of the social structure itself.

THE MEANING OF FORMS

This observation leads to a second proposal, which is to use formal differences as a way of identifying deeply rooted social disparities. There are two possibly contradictory reasons for this. First, formal devices (textual or material) reflect in their very structures the expectations and competences of the audience at which they are aimed; and second, works and objects produce the social regions in which they are received far more than they are produced by preexisting, crystallized divisions. Recently, Lawrence W. Levine provided corroboration of this assertion by showing that the way in which Shakespeare's plays were produced in nineteenth-century America (in mixed spectacles that drew on farce, melodrama, ballet, and circus) created a very large, noisy, and active audience for them, an audience that extended far beyond the bourgeois literate elite.[23] These devices for the performance of Shakespearean drama can be compared with the "typographical" changes that the publishers of the Bibliothèque bleue introduced in the works they included in their catalogue: both devices were aimed at placing texts in a cultural matrix that was different from that of the audience for which it was originally intended, thereby allowing for more than one kind of appropriation.

The two examples lead to a consideration of cultural differentiations not as reflections of static, frozen divisions but, instead, as effects of dynamic processes. For one thing, a change in the form in which a text is made available allows it to be received in new ways, thereby creating new audiences and new uses for it. For another, sharing of the same cultural properties by different groups within a society spurs a search for new distinctions capable of marking continuing disparities. The history of printing in Ancien Régime France offers a good example of this: it appears that different manners of reading proliferated and distinctions became more subtle as printed texts became less rare, less subject to confiscation, and more ordinary. Whereas the mere possession of a book had long signified cultural superiority, that signifying function was gradually shifted to the uses to which books were put, whether sanctioned or ad hoc, and to the quality of printed objects, whether rare or commonplace.

What most impaired one classical way of writing the history of *mentalités* was no doubt the disproportionate attention paid to formal practices. This made it necessary to consider the devices of discourse itself, its rhetorical and narrative articulations, its persuasive and demonstrative strategies. Discursive structures and the categories on which they are based, such as systems of classification, distinguishing criteria, and modes of representation, cannot be reduced to the ideas they state or the themes they convey. They have their own internal logic—and it is a logic that may perfectly well be at odds with the letter of the text's message. Discontinuity and disharmony in discourse must also be taken into account. For a long time, it was taken for granted that there was a direct path from thematic analysis of a group of texts to the characterization of a "mentality" or "worldview" or "ideology," and from there to association with a unique social group. The difficulty of the task seems greater once one realizes that any series of discourses must be understood as a specific object with its own production sites (and milieus) and distinctive preconditions; it must be judged in the light of its own organizational and critical principles and questioned as to its modes of accreditation and truthfulness. To make Foucault's method for treating "discursive series" central to historical criticism is certainly to curtail the totalizing ambitions of a cultural history aimed at achieving global reconstructions. Yet it is also necessary, if the texts out of which the historian builds his archives are to be rescued from the kind of ideological and documentary reductionism that used to destroy them as "discontinuous practices."[24]

FIGURES OF POWER AND CULTURAL PRACTICES

My last proposal is aimed at relating cultural practices to the forms in which power is exercised. The approach I have in mind is skeptical about the "return to the political," which seems to have gripped a number of French historians. Their position gives priority to the freedom of the subject, conceived of as being independent of all determinations; it emphasizes the availability of ideas and the deliberate component of action. It has two major weaknesses, however. First, it ignores constraints of which the individual actors themselves are unaware, constraints that do not rise to the level of clear thoughts and may even be at odds with clearly articulated ideas; yet these constraints control representations and actions. Second, it assumes that ideas and discourses have an efficacy of their own, independent of the forms in which they are conveyed and divorced from the practices that, in seizing on them, invest them with multiple, concurrent meanings.

Instead, I propose using changes in the forms of power (which generate novel social formations) in order to understand changes in the structure of both the personalities and the institutions or rules that govern the production of works and the organization of practices. The link that Norbert Elias has established between court rationality (understood as a specific psychic economy produced by the requirements of a new social form, necessary to absolutism) and the distinctive features of classical literature (hierarchy of genres, stylistic characteristics, aesthetic conventions) clearly maps out one possible area of research.[25] Nevertheless, divisions established by power (between *raison d'état* and moral conscience, for example, in the sixteenth through eighteenth centuries, or between state patronage and inner freedom) can also serve as a starting point for appreciating the emergence of an autonomous literary sphere as well as for the constitution of a market of symbolic goods and intellectual or aesthetic judgments.[26] The space of free criticism thus established was gradually politicized against the Ancien Régime monarchy by cultural practices that the state had once monopolized to its own benefit or that grew up in the private sphere in reaction to state control.

At a time when the relevance of social interpretation is frequently being challenged, I hope that readers will not take these remarks and proposals as indicating support for that position. Offered instead in critical fidelity to the *Annales* tradition, they are intended to assist in reformulating the way in which historians relate the comprehension of works, representations, and practices to the social divisions that they both signal and construct.

TRANSLATED BY ARTHUR GOLDHAMMER

NOTES

[1] Data on morphological changes (measured by numbers of teachers and their levels of educational and social capital) in the university-level academic disciplines in the 1960s are collected in Pierre Bourdieu, Luc Boltanski, and P. Maldidier, "La Défense du corps," *Informations sur les sciences sociales* 10.4 (1971), pp. 45–86. These figures provide the statistical underpinning for Bourdieu's *Homo academicus* (Paris: Minuit, 1984).

[2] For a radical, logical statement of this case, couched in the form of a factual observation, see Marcel Gauchet, "Changement de paradigme en sciences sociales?" *Le Débat* 50 (May–Aug. 1988), pp. 165–70.

[3] Roger Chartier, "Science sociale et découpage régional: Note sur deux débats 1820–1920," *Actes de la recherche en sciences sociales* 35 (Nov. 1980), pp. 27–36.

[4] E. Grendi, "Micro-analisi e storia sociale," *Quaderni storici* 35 (1972), pp. 506–20.

[5] Carlo Ginzburg, *Il Formaggio e i vermi: Il Cosmo di un mugnaio del'500* (Turin: Einaudi, 1976); Jacques-Louis Ménétra, *Journal de ma vie: Jacques-Louis Ménétra, compagnon vitrier au 18ᵉ siècle*, with an introduction by Daniel Roche (Paris: Montalba, 1982).

[6] Stanley Fish, *Is There a Text in This Class? The Authority of Interpretive Communities* (Cambridge, Mass.: Harvard University Press, 1980), pp. 1–17.

[7] R. Stoddard, "Morphology and the Book from an American Perspective," *Printing History* 17 (1987), pp. 2–14.

[8] Roger Chartier, "Texts, Printing, Readings," in Lynn Hunt, ed., *The New Cultural History* (Berkeley, 1989), pp. 2–14.

[9] H. R. Jauss, *Literaturgeschichte als Provokation* (Frankfurt: Suhrkamp, 1970), pp. 144–207.

[10] Pierre Bourdieu, *Choses dites* (Paris: Minuit, 1987), pp. 47–71.

[11] Emile Durkheim and Marcel Mauss, "De Quelques formes primitives de classification. Contribution à l'étude des représentations collectives," *Année sociologique* (1903), reprinted in Marcel Mauss, *Oeuvres complètes,* vol. 2: *Représentations collectives et diversité des civilisations* (Paris: Minuit, 1969), pp. 13–89 (the quote is from p. 83).

[12] Marcel Mauss, "Divisions et proportions de la sociologie," *Année sociologique* (1927), reprinted in Marcel Mauss, *Oeuvres complètes,* vol. 3: *Cohésion sociale et divisions de la sociologie* (Paris: Minuit, 1982).

[13] For example, Carlo Ginzburg, *I Benandanti: Stregoneria e culti agrari tra cinquecento e seicento* (Turin: Einaudi, 1966).

[14] For example, Luc Boltanski, *Les Cadres: La Formation d'un groupe social* (Paris: Minuit, 1982).

[15] Antoine Furetière, *Dictionnaire universel, contenant généralement tous les mots français tant vieux que modernes et les termes des sciences et des arts,* corrected by M. Basnage de Bauval and revised by M. Brutel de la Rivière (The Hague, 1727), articles "Représentation" and "Symbole" (all quotes in this paragraph are from these two entries).

[16] R. E. Giesey, *The Royal Funeral Ceremony in Renaissance France* (Geneva: Droz, 1960), pp. 85–91.

[17] Antoine Arnauld and Pierre Nicole, *La Logique ou l'art de penser* (Paris: P.U.F., 1965). On Port-Royal's theory of the sign, see Louis Marin, *La Critique du discours: Étude sur la logique de Port-Royal et les* Pensées *de Pascal* (Paris: Minuit, 1975).

[18] Arnauld and Nicole, *La Logique,* bk. 1, ch. 4, pp. 52–54. For a discussion of the definition of the "symbolic," see the series of articles published in the *Journal of Modern History* following the publication of Robert Darnton, *The Great Cat Massacre and Other Episodes in French Cultural History* (New York: Basic, 1984), including Roger Chartier, "Texts, Symbols, and Frenchness," *Journal of Modern History* 57 (1985), pp. 682–85; Robert Darnton, "The Symbolic Element in History," *Journal of Modern History* 58 (1986), pp. 218–34; Dominique LaCapra, "Chartier, Darnton, and the Great Symbol Massacre," *Journal of Modern History* 60 (1988), pp. 95–112; and J. Fernandez, "Historians Tell Tales: Of Cartesian Cats and Gallic Cockfights," *Journal of Modern History* 60 (1988), pp. 113–27.

[19] Arnauld and Nicole, *La Logique,* bk. 2, ch. 14, pp. 155–60.

[20] Pascal, *Pensées* 104, in *Oeuvres complètes* (Paris: Gallimard, 1954), p. 1,118.

[21] Jean de la Bruyère, *Les Caractères* (Paris: Garnier-Flammarion), "Du Mérite personnel," 27, pp. 107–108.

[22] Norbert Elias, *Über den Prozess der Zivilisation: Soziogenetische und psychogenetische Untersuchungen* (Bern: Francke, 1969, and Frankfurt: Suhrkamp, 1979), vol. 2: *Entwurf zur einer Theorie der Zivilisation.*

[23] Lawrence W. Levine, *Highbrow-Lowbrow: The Emergence of Cultural Hierarchy in America* (Cambridge, Mass.: Harvard University Press, 1988), pp. 11–81.

[24] Michel Foucault, *L'Ordre du discours* (Paris: Gallimard, 1971), p. 54.

[25] Norbert Elias, *Die höfische Gesellschaft: Untersuchungen zur Soziologie des Königtums und der höfischen Aristokratie mit einer Einleitung: Soziologie und Geschichtswissenschaft* (Darmstadt, 1969).

[26] Reinhart Koselleck, *Kritik und Krise: Eine Studie zur Pathogenese der bürgerlichen Welt* (Freiburg: Karl Albert, 1959, and Frankfurt: Surhkamp, 1976).

BERNARD LEPETIT

Urban History in France:
Twenty Years of Research

1993

Urban history is not a novelty. It is practically as old as scholarly historiography. Of course, this does not mean that it has always enjoyed equal importance. Bernard Lepetit's provisional assessment of the field encourages us to ask why and how urban history became, once again, an active field of inquiry in the 1970s. He suggests two reasons: the transformation of contemporary French society, which reflected the belated but rapid urbanization of the country after World War II, and the very diverse social problems to which these spectacular changes gave rise, changes that demanded both the attention of the government and the expertise of social scientists. This led to the sustained growth of so-called urban studies, often financed by the government, out of which came a unique encounter of history, social science, geography, economics, sociology, and city planning around problems that brought together "social relations, urban policies, and economic planning." The very opacity of the city ensured that it "subsumed all the questions raised by the evolution of civilization over several centuries," in the words of Daniel Roche, and it did so within a compass narrow enough that researchers could identify, analyze, and explain the various interactions involved. Cities are complex places that lend themselves well to the kinds of approaches that are at the center of current debate, approaches aimed at explaining the complexity of social phenomena in terms of process. We can thus understand why urban history (especially in the wake of Jean-Claude Perrot's work, whose importance Lepetit emphasizes) has played a key role in efforts to rethink the aims and purposes of social history.

From *European Urban History: Prospect and Retrospect*, Richard Rodgers, ed. (Leicester, Eng.: Leicester University Press, 1993), pp. 84–93.

THE SIXTEENTH, SEVENTEENTH, AND EIGHTEENTH CENTURIES

A New Urban History: The Invention of the "Urban"

In order to illustrate the qualitative change that accompanied the quantitative development of urban history, extracts from two texts published fifteen years apart are reproduced. Their particularly revealing character justifies lengthy quotation. First, Pierre Deyon in 1967 explained the rationale behind one of the early urban history monographs in France as follows:

> The local framework imposed limits, but only it could allow us to measure, to count, and to proceed to a continuous comparison between the various levels of historical reality and perhaps to discover new relationships that other studies could build on and verify. In Amiens, a provincial capital, it was the state of the sources that, to a very large extent, guided this geographical choice. An important center for commerce and textile production, Amiens constituted, from an economic point of view, an observatory. In any case, it offered a framework for a study of bourgeois advancement and differentiation.[1]

At this point, urban history was clearly a means, not an end. Finding its justification outside itself, it had not acquired genuine autonomy. It was written into a social history that embraced it, and its aim was to contribute to the debates that stimulated it. Why focus on the town, then? Essentially because it constituted "a useful framework," a privileged observatory, a world of social contrasts where hierarchies were defined in a manner that was both more structured and more subtle. So towns offered a rich theater of operations for the discussions of social historians. Ultimately, because all levels of reality met in the city, it was the microcosm where explanatory variables that elsewhere remained indistinct or passed unnoticed could be observed.

In the second extract, published in 1983, Jean-Pierre Bardet's thesis allowed the shift in questioning to be measured. In response to the view stating that the existence of a town constitutes a phenomenon that is practically inexplicable, because, in Europe, the urban has been present for so long, Bardet argued that:

> on the contrary, the true dynamics of a city can be understood. Decoding urbanization does not consist solely in grasping the mechanism of urban development, which is inextricably linked to the means of production; it also involves qualifying and understanding its effects and the transformation of urban life. The town is both object and subject. Constructed by men, it is the platform of their activities. At the same time, the men and women who fashion the town are subject to its laws. It determines the thought, behavior, and ecology, which in their turn participate in the modes of urban renewal.[2]

The town thus acquired a dual autonomy. It found itself the focal point of questions: What is the mechanism of urbanization, what capacity has the urban to transform? It also became the object of history. Furthermore, urban perception and reality overlapped.

Both as an object of history, constructed by men and analyzed by historians, and as the subject of history, the town was more than a framework, more than the simple sum of its parts. By its very existence, it was the creator of innovations that affected its own evolution.

It is a straightforward matter to date the mutation that changed the status of the town from the by-product of research to that of the central character. In 1974, a wide-ranging article that went beyond its historiographical intent, and Perrot's thesis, completed in 1973 and published in 1975, represented the turning points by identifying the dynamic and interacting nature of urban phenomena.[3]

A Turning Point

A more detailed study of Perrot's book enables characteristics and difficulties to be more clearly defined. On first consulting the chapter headings, the book appears to be located within the mainstream of French historiography, which, from the 1950s, was heavily influenced by Ernest Labrousse. This historical tradition was based on a quantitative approach that was careful to differentiate between fluctuations in economic growth and long-run social and economic structures. However, unlike other urban history monographs, Perrot did not include any particular study of "social structures." The critique on the nature of Ancien Régime society, the debate to which Perrot had contributed earlier, obliged him to abandon such an approach. But the solution adopted in 1975 was different to that advanced seven years earlier. In 1968, believing that the analysis of structures was necessarily tautological, Perrot recommended the study of social relations. Public ceremonies, associations, meeting places, displays of violence constituted dimensions of town sociability, the description of which would enable past societies to be understood. The district, the street, the workshop, the tavern were all places where different forms of assembly were revealed, particularly those of a plebeian rather than bourgeois or aristocratic nature.[4] But these places were new observatories, offering both a framework for research, and a window on meetings and social control to the urban historian.

By 1975, Perrot regarded as reductionist the view that a society could be understood through descriptions of its constituent groups and their behavioral relations: "A discerning reader must feel that the behavior of the population, medical practice, processes which regulate production and exchange, the development of districts, effectively describe the foundations of social history."[5] Perrot's revisionism claimed that the town had no essence of its own. Towns were determined entirely by their social nature, which were likened to a *scoria* or cooling lava flow. This had a methodological consequence: the simple juxtaposition of studies—demographic, economic, social, cultural—would compartmentalize urban history and lead it into ruin. "The first action, therefore, consisted of combining sources since it was admitted that they were talking about the same thing"—the modern town.[6] Historians, therefore, had to identify their objectives, since sources did not themselves suggest interpretations. The book, in this sense, was a model, a "theoretical copy"; it was a simplified and abstract representation of the reality, constructed on the basis of a system of internally coherent relationships, and it was consistent with the empirical data. The first imperative of research is, therefore, to establish that its object exists at the point at which it is studied. In the eighteenth century, Caen became a "modern town," that is, it belongs to the same era as the writer, the twentieth-century historian. Two traits define urban modernity: the passage from a static to a dynamic economy, on the one hand, and the invention of functionalism, on the other. The first trait means that change is no longer reduced simply to a quantitative measure: "The size of Caen and its overall output . . . would cast no light upon the silent revolution that raised it to a degree of urbanization which only Paris, four large ports and a few places in the interior could equal."[7] The second trait, the development of functionalism, illuminates the ideas and actions of city dwellers in the second half of the eighteenth century. Three principles defined functionalist approaches: first, to understand the socioeconomic system, it was essential to distinguish between discrete activities, as for example, those associated with production, trade, and consumption; second, there were direct relationships and covariations between each of these functions—for example, the wealth of the population had an effect on agricultural development, or poverty on mortality; third, there were direct relationships between functions and space, and to increase economic activity or improve social relations, space would have to be distributed differently—for example, road construction expanded commerce, and quartering soldiers in barracks reduced disorderly conduct in towns. These two traits led Perrot to deny the bond previously established between industrialization (and proletarianization) and the origins of an awareness of the urban problem in the nineteenth century: "the invention of the urban question preceded that of the social question by a century."[8]

Associated particularly with the modern town are two characteristics with methodological implications for urban historians. First, representations by earlier societies made about themselves and their values, ideas, and perceptions may be suspect because of their subjectivity; but they are nonetheless revealing. Second, twentieth-century experience and perspectives enables present-day researchers into eighteenth- and nine-teenth-century towns to pose germane questions. Yet this, too, is a trap since temporal proximity makes it difficult if not impossible to question critically the way the urban analysis is attempted. In an effort to compre-hend the historical functioning of towns and cities, there is an inherent tension within and between the categories that brings them into focus.

Perrot gave urban historians a particularly intimidating objective when he affirmed that "all the meaning is in the relationship between the different levels of social organization."[9] If understanding the differ-ent levels of reality seems only to bring together traditional problems, linked to insufficient sources, how can the relationship between these levels be understood? Given this circularity, how can sociocultural phe-nomena be analyzed?

The very degree of complexity in which this historiographical ambi-tion was located was accompanied by risks. Two phrases, which define the character of the new urban history, are revealing: "The town be-comes the central character of a whole generation of works"[10] and "many fields of research have one great common factor: a refusal to consider the city as merely inert, lifeless."[11] The aim of the new urban history was not to endow towns and cities with intentions of their own but, rather, to emphasize both the autonomy of the urban space and its extraordinary complexity. Though the collection of threads that form the urban fabric do not fit comfortably within conventional disciplinary boundaries, the dangers of overgeneralization and of exaggeratedly claiming everything as urban are evident.

In France, as elsewhere, there is a risk that a shallow discourse on the nature of urban history will infinitely distend the research area and artificially maintain academic unity. Conversely, if the urban area is only the simple projection of society onto a map, the simple translation of social inequalities onto the ground, then the town is merely a shadow in the cave of social history. If the analysis of social relations is reduced to understanding the way in which people meet in towns, then urban his-tory is only a veil destined to cover the temporary incapacity of social history to provide explanations of solidarity and conflict inherent in soci-ety, and the town once more is merely a theater.

Changes in Scale

Focusing on the *urban variable* aims to delimit the specificity of the ur-ban. It also aims to avoid diffuseness and overcomplication by retaining the urban dimensions as the principal realm of study. To borrow the title of an article, it assumes an understanding of "cities as systems in a system of cities."[12] According to the meaning that one attributes to the word "system," research can be turned in various directions. If one defines the urban system as a collection of towns in a spatial and hierarchical configuration, then the study is that of networks and frameworks, studies in relation to space. If the town is defined as "a tangible construct upon a particular topography which is imprinted in the social structure of the town and expressed through its institutions, and translates itself into a way of life and culture,"[13] then the research develops into a systematic analysis of the "formation" under consideration. In both cases, a change of scale is required.

Two examples should illustrate this point. Since the mid-1960s, Fernand Braudel has stressed that a town was unable to exist without other towns, smaller or larger, close or distant, with satellites or rivals.[14] In a preindustrial context, the existence of an urban system was not a convincing hypothesis, since a town could not develop independently of its hinterland, on which its subsistence, much of its population, and its revenues depended. Even if towns were insulated from one another, they were still dependent upon one another. This set of relationships changed only in the nineteenth century, when agrarian and transport changes altered the nature of urban interdependence. Yet in the preindustrial setting, the size and general growth rate of each town depended on that of others.

If one considers France in the 1830s, that is, prior to industrialization, numerous signs such as geographical variations in prices or the diffusion of innovations showed a regional functioning at variance with an urban system.[15] In the north, the unification of economic activities, the intensity of interurban links, the receptiveness of city-based societies characterized the functioning of the urban system as a network. In the south, the persistence of economic compartmentalization, the slowness to innovate, the less pronounced changes in relations, and more inward-looking urban societies showed the functioning of the urban system as a framework that juxtaposed cells, each made up of a modest local metropolis and its surroundings, with few links between them.

An initial explanation attributes this north-south difference in the French urban system to the establishment of the road network, which began in the 1740s and was of greater benefit to the northern half of the country than to the southern.[16] Everything to do with the construction of roads proves the influence of the urban system. Under the Ancien Régime the roads that were built reinforced the established urban framework, accentuating the influence of Paris and of the Parisian basin, and serving as a matter of priority those towns with either important administrative responsibilities or those with an income from landownership. The reproduction of one structure by another was present again after the Revolution. In 1811, the administration of the Ponts et Chaussées (the Department of Civil Engineering) established the classification of imperial roads. The categories were also an installation program, since the network was not complete at that date and the classification of a road determined the financing it received. The network of roads was in turn superimposed on the new administrative framework for the country: equally sized, the new chief towns in the *départements* benefited from a better transport service than other towns.

Can it be said that the urban system of the 1830s originated from the creation of the *départements*, then in the choice of *préfectures* and *sous-préfectures* which formed the center? The reality is more complex. Despite redistribution of towns at the time of the reform in which many urban centers experienced promotion or demotion in the urban hierarchy, the balance continued to favor small- and medium-sized towns to the detriment of regional centers. To a considerable degree, this fossilized the situation that existed on the eve of the Revolution and ensured that France remained a country of small towns until World War II.[17] In the spatial order, the framework of a chief town in each *département* laid a standardizing, ossifying grid across the whole country. Yet in the occupational and social order, the administrative reform generalized urban functions. Each principal town became a point of concentration for landowners and members of the professions—lawyers, barristers, and doctors—who developed their living styles and consumer habits according to patterns more in keeping with eighteenth-century privileged social groups such as the high clergy, and in doing so provided these towns with some of their most durable economic functions by making them centers of consumer activity.[18]

These two new forms of regional development, roads and administration, illustrate how the urban system influenced its own evolution; the emergence of the urban system was both cause and effect. This complex interaction with spatial development resulted from the fact that physical structures and economic functions never coincided exactly. The new road system reinforced former geographical patterns by serving the most important towns. Simultaneously, though, it subverted vested interests by introducing new geographical relations and contesting existing arrangements, and in so doing allowed a more dynamic urban economic system to develop. The introduction of a revised administrative map during the Revolution also redefined structural relations and urban hierarchies. However, these perpetuated former economic functions, albeit diffusing them to a multiplicity of local capitals. Thus, the juxtaposition of new and old in economic, social, administrative, and cultural relations produced an urban system both permanently in disequilibrium and constantly engaged in its own transformation.

Since the urban mutation was ongoing, the evolution of space was neither mechanistic nor predictable. Diverse and subtle forms emerged over differing time periods according to local combinations of economic, social, and other factors, and depending upon historical circumstances. For example, the unequal density of the French administrative web and the dominance of Paris during the Ancien Régime were the product of the development of the state since the Middle Ages. The form of commercial networks, the relative density of occasional fairs, weekly markets, and permanent shops were the cumulative result of historical precedents. As Braudel's later books have suggested, "these realities piled up on top of one another," are constantly reformulated in the reconstruction of space.[19]

Changes of scale are not confined to geographical or physical space, but also relate to social relations. In-migration and emigration involved an almost permanent state of urban flux, though the importance of the number of newcomers and the power of the migratory magnet depended on the size and character of the town under consideration, its function and economic climate. Towns were crossroads where stable and mobile populations met with varying objectives and intentions. This pluralism, the product of differing urban scales and motives, was the hallmark of an urban society where the issue of identity and identification was posed differently than it was in more deeply rooted village societies. Historians, typically, tackled the question in two ways. On the one hand, they used the grids, terminology, and classification systems of sociology;[20] or alternatively, they interpreted the actors' language in a hermeneutic approach taken from the cultural anthropology inspired by Clifford Geertz, in which classes, orders, or socioprofessional categories were used as an explanatory framework for society.[21] The categorization employed by both approaches, however, predetermined the question of a social identity. Equally restrictive was the more traditional historical approach that viewed stable populations as the legitimate bearers of a "town identity" defended by a strict control of immigration and a policy of acculturation toward migrant populations.[22] This approach took account neither of the various trajectories of individual and family aspirations, nor of the diverse identities of urban populations.[23] As with E. P. Thompson's *The Making of the English Working Class*[24] where the term *making* captures the gradual yet dynamic nature of the process, so a new social history of towns needs to consider relationships as both more fluid and operating on multiple levels.[25]

The list of possible components of an urban identity is a long one. It might include sex, age group, family, "country" (for migrants), district, trade, brotherhood, order, institutions of urban power (civil, religious, sometimes military), religion, and so on. There is no question of choosing between these various elements in order to claim that a single element or a combination of them has particular force. It is a question of seeing them as a collation that uniquely identified the character of a town at a given time and place, and defined the activities of its inhabitants, be they individuals, families, or groups. To take a specific example, a silk merchant at the beginning of the eighteenth century could be a member of a trade guild, of a religious brotherhood, of the municipal administration, or he could fill a number of these roles at the same time. His networks of family alliances could expand these initial links or, alternatively, could establish others on the basis of complementary economic activities, place of origin, or even of residence. The combination of his choices, imposed or chosen, determined the importance of his economic standing and social identity; the degree of social cohesion and homogeneity determined the extent of social stratification.

Contrary to an approach that made social groups into "natural" categories, urban history developed a more subjective, a more individualized approach interested in networks, strategies, situations, and processes. Rather than relying on static relationships, the study of French towns centered on an urban society undergoing constant redefinition.

From this iterative urban process was born a new "local" history of politics. Municipal institutions were not accessible on an equal footing to all residents, yet the history of a town cannot be written without taking into account the social history of its institutions. The institutional organization of towns in the north of France and in the south of the Spanish Netherlands, for example, was above all a sociocultural construct—government by elites, local autonomy, and conscious social welfare elements fully impregnated with Catholic values, which, taken together, defined a "hispano-tridentin model of a good town."[26] Urban institutions at the end of the Ancien Régime were part of a secular history, and violent disputes about public order in towns need to be considered not only as indicative of behavior, relationships, and values but also as an opportunity to reconstruct a sociopolitical context that gives the town meaning and contributes to its unique identity.[27]

NOTES

[1] Pierre Deyon, *Amiens capitale provinciale*, p. viii–ix.

[2] Jean-Pierre Bardet, *Rouen aux XVIIᵉ et XVIIIᵉ siècles: Les Mutations d'un espace social* (Paris: SEDES, 1983), pp. 18–19.

[3] L. Bergeron and M. Roncayolo, "De la ille pré-industrielle à la ville industrielle: Essai sur l'historiographie française," *Quaderni storici* (1974), pp. 827–76; Jean-Claude Perrot, *Genèse d'une ville moderne*.

[4] A. Farge and A. Zysberg, "Les Théâtres de la violence à Paris au XVIIIᵉ siècle," *Annales ESC* (1979), pp. 984–1015; D. Roche, *Le Peuple de Paris: Essai sur la culture populaire au XVIIIᵉ siècle* (Paris, 1986).

[5] Perrot, *Genèse d'une ville moderne*, p. 944.

[6] Ibid., p. 947.

[7] Ibid., p. 951.

[8] Ibid., p. 9.

[9] Ibid., p. 947.

[10] Bergeron and Roncayolo, "De la Ville pré-industrielle," p. 827.

[11] F. Bedarida, "The French Approach to Urban History: An Assessment of Recent Methodological Trends," in D. Fraser and A. Sutcliffe, eds., *The Pursuit of Urban History* (London, 1983), pp. 395–406.

[12] B. Berry, "Cities as Systems Within Systems of Cities," *Papers of the Regional Science Association* 13 (1964), pp. 147–63.

[13] B. Chevalier, *Les Bonnes villes de France du XIVe siècle au XVIe siècle* (Paris, 1982), p. 11.

[14] F. Braudel, *Civilisation materielle: Economie et capitalisme XVe–XVIIIe siècle,* 3 vols. (Paris, 1979).

[15] B. Lepetit, *Les Villes dans la France moderne (1740–1840)* (Paris, 1988).

[16] G. Arbellot, "La Grande mutation des routes de France milieu du XVIIIe siècle," *Annales ESC* 31 (1973), pp. 765–91; B. Lepetit, *Chemins de terre et voies d'eau: Resaux de transport et organisation de l'espace en France, 1740–1780* (Paris, 1984); G. Arbellot, B. Lepetit, and J. Bertrand, *Atlas de la Révolution française,* vol. 1: *Routes et communications* (Paris, 1987).

[17] M.-V. Ozouf-Marignier, *La Formation des départements: La Représentation du territoire français à la fin du XVIIIe siècle* (Paris, 1989).

[18] B. Lepetit, "Event and Structure: The Revolution and the French Urban System," *Journal of Historical Geography* 16 (1990), pp. 17–37.

[19] F. Braudel, *L'Identité de la France,* 3 vols. (Paris, 1986).

[20] See, for example, W. H. Sewell, *Structure and Mobility: The Men and Women in Marseilles, 1820–1870* (Cambridge, Eng., 1982). For criticism, see M. Gribaudi and A. Blum, "Des Catégories aux liens individuels: l'analyse statistique de l'espace social," *Annales ESC* 45 (1990), pp. 1365–1402, and more generally the entire edition of the *Annales* entitled "Mobilités" (Nov.-Dec. 1990).

[21] For example, R. Darnton, *The Great Cat Massacre and Other Episodes in French Cultural History* (New York, 1984). For a critique, see R. Chartier, "Text, Symbol, and Frenchness," *Journal of Modern History* (1985), pp. 682–95, and G. Levi, "I Pericolo del geertzismo," *Quaderni storici* (1985), pp. 269–77.

[22] For an example of a swing in the balance of power to the detriment of the settled urban population, see L. Chevalier, *Classes laborieuses et classes dangereuses à Paris pendant la première moitié du XIXe siècle* (Paris, 1958).

[23] For a particularly successful demonstration, see M. Gribaudi, *Itinéraires ouvriers: Espaces et groupes sociaux à Turin au début du XIXe siècle* (Paris, 1987).

[24] E. P. Thompson, *The Making of the English Working Class* (London, 1963). Significantly, the first French translation of this book dates from 1988.

[25] S. Cerutti, *La Ville et les metiérs: Naissance d'un langage corporatif (Turin XVIIe–XVIIIe)* (Paris, 1990), p. 14.

[26] P. Guignet, *Le Pouvoir dans le ville au XVIIIe siècle: Pratiques politiques, mobilité et ethique sociale de part et d'autre de la frontière franco-belge* (Paris, 1990).

[27] A. Farge and J. Revel, *Logiques de la foule: L'Affaire des enlèvements d'enfants, Paris, 1750* (Paris, 1988); R. Descimon, "Les Barricades de la fronde parisienne: Une lecture sociologique," *Annales ESC* 45 (1990), pp. 397–422.

ROBERT BOYER

Economy and History: Toward New Alliances

1989

In the critical reflection that has gone on over the past few years around the journal Annales *and its agenda in social history, the problem of interdisciplinary relations and the status of interdisciplinarity has occupied a discreet but significant place. One can argue that what has distinguished the French program, from the very beginning, has been the conviction that history could rejuvenate itself and expand its horizons only by engaging in deliberate, open dialogue with other social disciplines. This fundamental alliance has been reinterpreted several times over the course of the twentieth century, both inside and outside France. Has it become problematic today? In one way or another, all the social sciences are going through a period of questioning and are seeking new definitions. The forms and modalities of interdisciplinary exchange no longer seem as obvious as, rightly or wrongly, they once did, if only because the grand integrating paradigms that once dominated the scientific scene have lost much of their force over the past twenty years.*

In the French historiographic experiment, historians looked first to geography, then to economics, and finally to anthropology as history's primary partners. These dialogues were often difficult (although the difficulties tended to be forgotten after the fact), and they had to reckon with internal changes within each discipline. Economics, with which Fernand Braudel attempted to carve out a terrain for mutual discussion (in his extended debate with François Perroux in the 1950s and 1960s), has changed profoundly, as the economist Robert Boyer points out in the introduction to the following piece, which he published in Annales *in 1989: "Economists and historians seem to have adopted different strategies for dealing with economic history: axiomatization, mathematization, and sophisticated econometric tools for*

Robert Boyer, "Economie et histoire: Vers de nouvelles alliances?" *Annales ESC* 44 (1989), pp. 1397–1426.

the former, conquest of a range of territories for the latter." In an effort to halt this divergence, Boyer attempts to set forth the conditions of what he calls "new alliances." These are to be based on respect for the internal logic of each discipline in the hope of achieving "a less fragmentary view of the logic of social behavior." Again, the goal is clearly to move toward greater complexity in the definition and interpretation of social objects.

A MULTIPLICITY OF LOGICS

And so it should be, too, with the analysis of the behavior, values, and objectives of individuals in society. Recent research appears to have made it more and more difficult to pursue a research program based on the assumption that there exists only one form of rationality, whose principles and modalities are valid in all times and places. Such an assumption meets with numerous objections. Epistemologically, the hypothesis of substantive rationality assumes that every social actor possesses an extraordinary capacity to gather all relevant information and to calculate the consequences of that information. The cognitive sciences teach us that practical as well as intellectual problem-solving abilities cannot be understood in terms of such a narrow definition of rationality. The concept of procedural rationality conforms better to both experimental data and the results of research in human and artificial intelligence.[1] From a strictly empirical point of view, observations of the actual behavior of consumers and firms by psychologists and the few economists who have attempted to make their discipline an experimental science show that consumers do not in fact maximize expected utility, nor do firms maximize profits. Significantly, variant behaviors have been noted even in the realm of finance, where the principles of economic efficiency and rationality ought to operate most readily.[2]

The weakened rationality principle takes on various forms, depending on the context in which actors are placed. Take the area of wages and employment, for example. Depending on various factors (such as the observability of work intensity and the availability to workers of credit and insurance), the maximization principle will imply different types of behavior for firms as well as for employees. The institutional features of the society are important: experts in law and industrial relations must be called upon to describe the context in which actors make their optimizations. In extreme cases, social norms may be so restrictive that the actors' autonomy is virtually nil.[3]

Yet sociology, political science, and history suggest an even greater relativization of the logic of behavior. There may exist, a priori, as many action principles as there are fields, although transfers from one field to another may occur. This relativization of the rationality principle is particularly clear if one looks at history in the long run. Indeed, the maximization of monetary income coincides with a distinct stage of history, that in which mercantile, industrial, and ultimately finance capitalism slowly extended their dominion. Yet even in contemporary societies, it would be misleading to suggest that the only legitimate actions are those that maximize profit, wealth, or social status.[4] Conflicts are continually erupting between the employee and the citizen, the taxpayer and the beneficiary of the welfare state, the producer and the family member or resident of a particular region. In short, the *homo oeconomicus* of theory is still evolving: he represents a tendency of contemporary society, not a reality.

The economist is therefore obliged to take account of logics other than the strictly economic. What economists are sometimes apt to interpret as irrationality is often a result of their failure to comprehend the variety of objectives, values, and beliefs that are themselves consequences of different social allegiances. By studying the work of historians, economists can thus broaden their horizons[5] and work toward a less blinkered vision of the logic of social behavior.[6] They can also develop a wider range of economic models than "pure" economic theory alone provides.

THE VARIETY OF SOCIAL BONDS AND MODES OF REGULATION

Indeed, if one were to take an intermediate object and collect the various related hypotheses concerning the actors' strategic logic and the nature of their interactions, it would be quite surprising if the results of historical research, international comparison, and numerous case studies defined a single, unique model of social and economic interaction. It would take all of an economic theorist's powers of imagination and abstraction to imagine that feudal society, court society, Indian society, and so on were all simply variants of the capitalist market model exhibiting greater or lesser degrees of perfection. The major objective of this research program is therefore to develop and elaborate models of social interaction turned up by historical and comparative research.

Although this program has by no means been the dominant practice in relations between historians and economists up to now, many of them have already acknowledged its pertinence. Norbert Elias, for example, describes the project of which his analysis of court society forms a part in the following terms: "Human relations are so manifold that, in the present state of our knowledge, it is practically impossible to imagine a scientific study of the evolution of any yet-to-be-examined human entity that would not contribute new knowledge to our understanding of ourselves and our world."[7] And Robert Solow has proposed the following program: "All specifically economic activity forms part of a network of social institutions, customs, beliefs, and attitudes. The economic consequences are undoubtedly affected by these factors.... The fact is that various social contexts call for different basic assumptions and therefore different models.... Economic history is useful for broadening the range of observations on which theorists can draw."[8]

The principal criticism that one can make of the "new economic history" is surely that it commits what for a historian is the worst of errors—anachronism. It would be absurd to treat economics as the dominant factor in a caste, court, or feudal society, for it is ultimately a property only of the most developed capitalist societies. What is more, Karl Polanyi has questioned the viability of a pure market society. Economic relations are always part of a system in which other kinds of relations are also present. Except in today's capitalist world, economic analysis must generally take a backseat to religious and political analysis. Even in the most advanced societies, moreover, the political and the economic are never separate, because the principles of citizenship and the market introduce permanent tensions in both spheres.[9]

One would not want to create a different model for every historical period, though. The goal should be to develop as few models as possible, each general enough to apply to many cases. Later, it might be appropriate to describe how the models relate to one another and develop a general theory of models. In no sense is the goal to contrast the thickness of description with the thinness of pure economic models; it is, rather, to develop a range of models or ideal types covering a broad spectrum of societies in various times and places. Then "the final product of economic analysis might be a series of models, contingent on social characteristics and historical circumstances rather than a single monolithic model for each period."[10]

Historians have long developed models of this type for societies of the past, demonstrating the possibility and value of the exercise. In general, the social, technological, and political context determines different modes of regulation in different times and places. For example, analyses of the feudal economy show that while it is based in part on a market economy, it is governed by principles quite different from those implicit in idealized models of pure and perfect competition.[11] Proving the existence of such historical modes of regulation was an important contribution to economic history, which required relating structural analysis to various assumptions about agriculture, industry, and demographics so as to submit conjunctural data to proper statistical interpretation.[12]

This leads to a key lesson for economists: over the long run, modes of regulation are transformed in various ways, yielding a range of different configurations. This was true in the 1930s, and a similar process may be at work today.[13] Maybe economists don't have to look for a unique model capable of perfectly describing everything that has happened over the past two centuries. Instead, they can try to detect the emergence of new models associated with changes in the international system, in social relations, in technology and organization. This ambition applies not only to the traditional domain of macroeconomics, which perhaps receives an undue share of the emphasis in the present paper, but also to much of the subject matter of economic and social history. For example, one recent study points out how different early modern urban economies were from the economies of cities at the time of the Industrial Revolution, despite the persistence of certain common features.[14]

Furthermore, looking back at the past may help to resolve certain debates about the evolution of modes of regulation. For example, some economists have suggested that the crisis of mass production ("Fordism") has reopened an avenue of economic development that was temporarily closed off at the end of the nineteenth century. The variability and uncertainty of markets, coupled with consumer demands for a range of products better suited to their needs and workers' aspirations for greater autonomy on the shop floor, have supposedly encouraged the development of a new model of "flexible specialization."[15] The argument for this is based on a reexamination of various historical studies in conjunction with comparative international research. This work also has bearing on the protoindustrialization debate that has raged among economic historians for the past twenty years. Information gathered by economic researchers may be useful for evaluating how relevant the model is to contemporary society.[16] The historian of technology can also contribute to this debate: it may be relevant, for example, to note that "Fordism" in its original form was beset as early as the 1920s by a crisis due to its excessive rigidity in the face of fluctuating demand and limitations inherent in totally standardized production.[17]

Finally, history shows that certain problems of economic organization have met with a variety of solutions. For instance, contemporary international comparisons show a very broad range of national reactions to the challenges of renewed international competition. In certain sectors of the economy, increased uncertainty, macroeconomic fluctuations, and heightened competition have triggered divergent reactions. Increased investment and training as well as more rapid innovation have been tried in countries with skilled and educated workforces and the financial wherewithal to make ambitious but calculated wagers on the future: this appears to have been the case in Japan and Sweden. By contrast, in the United States and to a lesser degree in the United Kingdom, the strategy has largely been one of deinvestment and defensive rationalization, with lower wages being paid to less well trained, nonunionized workers; investment strategies have mainly favored the short term over the long term.[18] Early research on corporatism suggests that these contrasting national reactions are rooted in each country's postwar (or even interwar) compromise between labor and management.[19]

To sum up, collaboration among political scientists, sociologists, and historians may help to transform the thinking of economists about even the most contemporary problems, including theoretical issues as well as matters of economic policy. Historicizing economic analysis is thus a promising avenue of research, one that a small community of economists is already exploring.[20]

PINPOINTING THE EMERGENCE OF RADICALLY NEW CONFIGURATIONS

The variability of modes of regulation in time and space raises a new set of questions. How do new institutions emerge to coordinate decentralized strategies? What factors are responsible when a mode of regulation moves from a phase of expansion into a phase of crisis? These questions introduce a new element into the historical description of economic dynamics. In recent years, the natural sciences, especially thermodynamics, have developed new models for dealing with phenomena such as irreversibility, self-organization,[21] and the dependency of a system's final state on initial conditions and/or stochastic perturbations affecting its trajectory.[22]

Eliminating the hypothesis of complete reversibility in the neighborhood of an essentially static equilibrium may very well be of benefit to historians. In the neoclassical theory of growth, for example, the growth rate was exogenously determined, and no matter what perturbations affected the working population, the savings rate compensated so as to bring about a gradual return to the path of balanced growth. Certain long-term growth models developed a more satisfactory view of the growth process as a result of increasing returns to scale: these allowed the population to increase, leading to new infrastructural development, thereby opening the way to additional increasing returns.[23] This gave rise to the chain reactions that constitute development. This long-term model revealed a much richer range of dynamics than did earlier models. Growth involved crossing certain thresholds and allowed for cycles in moving from one regime to another as the population-infrastructure relation was gradually altered. Historians can surely pick up some interesting ideas here for formalizing their growth models, particularly since certain models of the feudal economy already explicitly incorporated dynamics of this type.[24]

Similarly, the replacement of static equilibrium models by research on nonlinear dynamic systems offers a second area of major interest for the social sciences, namely, a focus on formal analysis—that is, on the qualitative properties of systems rather than just their quantitative evolutions. Physicists are today discovering how to deal with such important but previously neglected phenomena as turbulence, crystal formation, and phase transitions. The development over the past decade of research in economics on institutional logics, conventions, and norms governing the economic sphere suggests a certain parallelism between the natural and the social sciences.[25]

Nevertheless, the two research programs are independent, as historians can attest: the history of social systems cannot be reduced to that of the underlying biological and physical models.[26] The analysis of historical processes will never attain the same degree of determinism as that of physical systems: given certain initial conditions and nonlinear relations governing the interactions between individuals, can one describe economic history solely in terms of the dynamics of the resulting system? If, for example, the analyst succumbs to the logic of his instrument, he might be tempted to describe the Industrial Revolution as a totally deterministic process initiated by a "big bang" in the sixteenth century, the long-term consequences of which are still being felt today.[27] Is it an accident, moreover, that the mathematics of nonlinear dynamic systems may provide a better description of the movement of stock prices than do more deterministic formalisms? [28]

Beyond the technical difficulties of recognizing deterministic chaos in apparently stochastic processes, we can begin to measure the heroic character of the epistemological hypothesis essential to the validity of the stock market model—that no innovation or new information affects prospects for future returns! In short, observation of the stock market, that echo chamber for good and bad news, contradicts the view that history is nothing more than pure kinematics. Similarly, new technologies and increased productivity do not reflect the solution of dynamic programs written long ago; they are, rather, the result of a series of inventions and innovations, which (as etymology suggests) were by nature unpredictable, and which bring into play radically new factors whose consequences could not all be predicted *ex-ante*. As Joseph Schumpeter reminds us, the locomotive and the automobile were not the result of steady, easily predictable improvements to the stagecoach. The same is true of most radical innovations.[29] In what area have economists been able to prove the existence of the kinds of stable, long-term, highly nonlinear relations capable of giving rise to chaotic dynamic systems? Probably none. For the time being, models of this kind remain largely speculative; their interest is conceptual, not empirical.

Historical research offers numerous antidotes to the temptation to explain the present as totally determined by the past as well as to the opposite, teleological temptation to derive the past from observation of the present. It was by no means inscribed in the immanent laws of capitalism that the theologians of the Middle Ages should invent Purgatory.[30] The fact that the logic of early modern cities was different from that of industrial cities suggests that the latter were not an automatic consequence of the former.[31] Similarly, the invention of the "American system" marked a sharp break with the English system of manufacturing, and the emergence of the Fordian wage compromise was in no way implicit in the development of the assembly line.[32] In this area, the two world wars appear to have played an important though neglected role.[33] In the financial area, the institution of the Bretton Woods system was truly an innovation, not just a mechanical formalization of long-discernable tendencies.[34] A similar argument could be made with respect to social Darwinist theories of historical processes.[35]

History, then, along with sociology and anthropology, has a major role to play in economics—reminding economists that the economic sphere that is their subject matter is embedded in political, social, and religious structures created in and by history, and not as the result of any deterministic process. Readers may recognize here one of the major tenets of the "regulative" approach to economic theory. Indeed, one regulative research program involves the study of processes by which crises are overcome, along with possible factors for explaining why crises occur in a given mode of development.[36]

TRANSLATED BY ARTHUR GOLDHAMMER

NOTES

[1] F. E. Varela, *Connaître les sciences cognitives* (Paris: Seuil, 1988). For an exploration of the consequences on economic behavior and institutions, see O. Favereau, "Marchés internes, marchés externes," and A. Orléan, "Pour une Approche cognitive des conventions économiques," *Revue économique* 40.2 (Mar. 1989), pp. 241–328. "Hyperlogicism" was vigorously attacked by Marc Bloch in *Apologie pour l'histoire* (Paris: A. Colin, 1974), p. 142.

[2] R. Hogarth and W. Reder, eds., *Rational Choice: The Contrast Between Economics and Psychology* (Chicago: University of Chicago Press, 1987), especially the contributions by M. H. Miller and A. W. Kleidon.

[3] This idea can be found in many of Pierre Bourdieu's works, especially *La Distinction* (Paris: Minuit, 1979).

[4] Luc Boltanski and Laurent Thévenot, *Les Economies de la grandeur* (Paris: P.U.F., 1987).

[5] For John Hicks, "a major function of economic history, as I see it, is to be a forum where economists and political scientists, lawyers, sociologists, and historians—historians of events and of ideas and of technologies—can meet and talk to one an-

other." See *A Theory of Economic History* (Oxford: Oxford University Press, 1969), p. 2.

[6] The founders of the *Annales* stressed the role of historians in integrating visions of man stemming from different disciplines. See for example, N. Bloch, *Apologie pour l'histoire*. Karl Polanyi, *The Great Transformation* (Boston: Beacon, 1957), offers a vigorous argument against the possibility of explaining society in terms of the logic of the generalized market alone.

[7] Norbert Elias, "Sociologie et histoire," foreword to *La Société de cour* (Paris: Calmann-Lévy, 1974), p. xli.

[8] Robert Solow, "Economics: Is Something Missing?" in W. N. Parker, ed., *Economic History and the Modern Economist* (London: Basil Blackwell, 1986), p. 22.

[9] Samuel Bowles and Herbert Gintis, *Democracy and Capitalism: Property, Community, and the Contradictions of Modern Social Thought* (New York: Basic, 1986).

[10] Solow, "Economics," p. 23.

[11] Witold Kula, *Théorie économique du système féodal* (Paris: Mouton, 1970). Guy Bois, *Crise du féodalisme* (Paris: Presses de la Fondation Nationale des Sciences Politiques, 1976).

[12] Ernest Labrousse, *Esquisse du mouvement des prix et des revenus en France au XVIIIe siècle* (Paris, 1933), and *La Crise de l'économie française à la fin de l'Ancien Régime et au début de la Révolution* (Paris, 1934).

[13] Michel Aglietta, *Régulation et crises du capitalisme* (Paris: Calmann-Lévy, 1976); A. Lipietz, *Crise et inflation, pourquoi?* (Paris: Maspero, 1979); Robert Boyer and J. Mistral, "Le Temps présent: la crise (I): d'une analyse historique à une vue prospective," and "La crise (II): pesanteur et potentialité des années quatre-vingt," *Annales ESC* 3 (May–June 1983), pp. 483–506, and 38 (July–Aug. 1983), pp. 773–89; Robert Boyer, ed., *La Seconde transformation* (Paris: Economica, 1990); Michel Aglietta and A. Brender, *Les Métamorphoses de la société salariale* (Paris: Calmann-Lévy, 1984); J. Mazier, M. Basle and J.-F. Vidal, *Quand les crises durent* (Paris: Economica, 1984).

[14] Bernard Lepetit, *Les Villes dans la France moderne, 1740–1840* (Paris: A. Michel, 1988).

[15] Michael J. Piore and Charles Sabel, *The Second Industrial Divide* (New York: Basic Books, 1984).

[16] For an overview see P. Deyon, "Fécondité et limites du modèle protoindustriel: premier bilan," *Annales ESC* 39 (Sept.–Oct. 1984), pp. 868–81.

[17] It is a pity that economic research on technological and organizational flexibility does not make greater use of the wealth of historical research on industrial organization, especially in the United States. For example, D. A. Hounshell, *From the American System to Mass Production, 1800–1932* (Baltimore: Johns Hopkins University Press, 1984), refutes the notion that contemporary strategies of flexibility and product diversification are radically new.

[18] See R. Hollingsworth, P. Schmitter, and W. Streeck, *The Economic Governance of Sectors* (forthcoming). For a fuller development of themes in this paper, see Robert Boyer, "Transformations of Modern Capitalism," in this volume.

[19] B. Lutz, *Der kurze Traum immerwährender Properität* (Frankfurt: Campus, 1984).

[20] Pierre Dockès and B. Rosier, *L'Histoire ambiguë* (Paris: P.U.F., 1988); I. Joshua, *La Face cachée du Moyen Age* (Paris: La Breche, 1988).

[21] Some social scientists tend to use the insights of nonlinear thermodynamics in a rather mechanical way. Fortunately, Ilya Prigogine and Isabelle Stengers, *Entre le Temps et l'éternité* (Paris: Fayard, 1988), warn against this practice, correcting the misimpression that may have been left by their previous work, *La Nouvelle alliance* (Paris: Gallimard, 1979). For a discussion of this theme from a social scientific point of view, see Kryzstof Pomian, *L'Ordre du temps* (Paris: Gallimard, 1984).

[22] For a remarkable overview of the emerging new paradigm in the natural sciences, see James Gleick, *Chaos: Making a New Science* (New York: Viking, 1987), and I. Ekeland, *Le Calcul, l'imprévu: Les Figure du temps de Kepler à Thom* (Paris: Seuil, 1984).

[23] R. H. Day, "Economic Development in the Very Long Run: On the Multiple Phase Interaction of Population, Technology and Social Infrastructure," Working Paper 8732, Los Angeles, University of Southern California, Sept. 1987.

[24] See Kula, *Théorie économique du système féodal,* and Labrousse, *Esquisse.*

[25] See the models proposed in the special issue of *Revue économique* 40.2, "L'Economie des conventions" (March 1989), and the formalizations of nonlinear thermodynamics in Prigogine and Stengers, *Entre le temps et l'éternité.*

[26] This point is fully developed in N. Elias, *La Société de cour,* pp. xlv–xlix.

[27] Although the various nonlinear thermodynamic models used by R. H. Day are interesting, it is difficult to accept his epistemological assumption. Sophistication of the dynamic argument is not the same thing as historical richness. For more details, see Robert Boyer, "Les Théories macroéconomique face à l'irréversibilité," paper read to the Ecole des Hautes Etudes en Sciences Sociales colloquium on "Reversibilités," mimeographed (Paris, June 1989).

[28] Statistical tests in the case of the United States do not for the moment justify an affirmative response: see W. A. Brock, "Nonlinearity and Complex Dynamics in Economics and Finance," in D. Pines, ed., *The Economy as an Evolving Complex System* (New York: Addison-Wesley, 1988).

[29] Schumpeter, *Business Cycles: A Theoretical, Historical and Statistical Analysis of Capitalist Process* (New York: McGraw Hill, 1939), uses the term "serendipity" to describe the complex process that leads to invention, a product of both necessity and chance.

[30] Jacques Le Goff, *La Naissance du purgatoire* (Paris: Gallimard, 1981), and *La Bourse et la vie* (Paris: Hachette, 1986).

[31] Lepetit, *Les Villes dans la France moderne,* p. 401.

[32] This point is clearly made in histories of technical organization in the United States such as Hounshell, *From the American System to Mass Production;* see Robert Boyer, "L'Introduction du taylorisme en France à la lumière de recherches récentes," *Travail et emploi* 18 (Oct.–Dec. 1983), and, in *Annales ESC* 42 (Sept.–Oct. 1987), articles by P. Fridenson ("Un Tournant taylorien de la société française"), and A. Moutet, ("L'Industrie française des années trente: Une rationalisation de crise").

[33] P. Fridenson, *1914–1918: L'Autre front,* Cahiers du *Mouvement social* 2 (Paris: Ouvrières, 1977).

[34] Michel Aglietta, "Stabilité dynamique et transformations des régimes monétaires internationaux," paper read to EHESS colloquium on "Reversibilités," Paris, June 1989; Robert O. Keohane, *After Hegemony: Cooperation and Discord in the World Political Economy* (Princeton: Princeton University Press, 1984); S. D. Krasner, ed., *International Regimes* (Ithaca, N.Y.: Cornell University Press, 1983).

[35] N. Elias, *La Société de cour,* p. xlv; Lepetit, *Les Villes,* p. 17.

[36] Robert Boyer, *La Théorie de la régulation: Une analyse critique* (Paris: Découverte, 1986), pp. 111–35.

GÉRARD NOIRIEL

For a Subjectivist Approach to the Social

1989

"History and the social sciences," "history and sociology": these were recurrent themes in the French debate even before the Annales, *in fact since the turn of the century. The terms of this debate were for a long time set by François Simiand's 1903 paper on "Méthode historique et science sociale," which became an object of almost obsessive interest on the part of historians. As the introduction to this volume points out, Simiand in a somewhat imperious manner proposed that historians adopt the criteria of scientificity set forth by Durkheimian sociology. He offered an objectivist conception of the knowledge of social phenomena, modeled on the natural sciences.*

This, at any rate, is the most commonly accepted interpretation of Simiand's remarks. Has the time come for revision of this received view? Gérard Noiriel thinks so. Noiriel, along with others, points out that historians, and not least those associated with the Annales, *did not always abide by Simiand's prescriptions, protests to the contrary notwithstanding. For Noiriel, it was the growth of quantitative history in the 1950s and 1960s that really established the objectivist paradigm. His analysis is of more than just historiographical interest, however: a historian and sociologist of immigration, Noiriel argues for the development of a "subjectivist" paradigm, invoking both Wilhelm Dilthey and Max Weber, two thinkers whose work was long neglected in France (both have recently enjoyed a belated success). He proposes various ways of redirecting and rejuvenating social history, including taking the lived experience of social actors into account (a recommendation with which many historians today would agree) and historicizing the analytic categories that historians use and the objects they construct with those categories.*

Gérard Noiriel, "Pour une approche subjectiviste du social," *Annales* 44 (Nov.– Dec. 1989), pp. 1449–55.

I f social history is to constitute itself along the lines of economic and demographic history, it must first invent new forms of dialogue between history and sociology. Here I shall limit myself to discussing what historians can bring to this project of redefinition, focusing on two key problems.

THE DEBATE ABOUT SCIENTIFICITY

When today's historians say that history is not really a science because it enunciates no laws, they are merely echoing Charles Seignobos's objections to a certain nineteenth-century philosophical view of science, vaguely derived from Claude Bernard. By the 1930s, Lucien Febvre was already taking an ironic attitude toward Seignobos's claims, which reflected a certain false modesty and served as justification for all sorts of intellectual laziness. Today, we no longer believe in the nineteenth-century hypothetico-deductive model of science, and not only because Einstein's theory of relativity has pointed up its inadequacy. Since 1950, historians and philosophers of science have developed a new epistemology based on the actual practice of scientists: their research shows that the norms actually governing scientific research are developed by researchers themselves rather than imposed by outsiders. Paul Feyerabend, extending the work of Thomas Kuhn, has given the most radical formulation of this new epistemology. His famous slogan, "anything goes," suggests that real progress in science never comes from following preestablished recipes, and that there is usually a gap between scientific innovation and its theoretical justification, "which begins only after the real discoveries have been made."[1] Feyerabend's call for a materialistic analysis of the production of scientific facts, either by the producers themselves or by people with direct experience of scientific research, is perfectly compatible with the broad epistemological principles that Lucien Febvre repeatedly embraced, principles that are put to the test in much of the most interesting recent work in the sociology of science.[2] One important benefit of such epistemological relativism is that it creates a vast common ground on which historians and sociologists can reflect jointly on their research practices. Indeed, Kuhn's definition of a scientific paradigm[3] emphasizes the importance of the scientific community, defined as a group of individuals working in the same field, sharing similar training, invoking a common set of references, and therefore possessing a "tacit knowledge"[4] of their profession which is acquired more through practice than through written rules. From the standpoint of the new epistemology, what matters is not the philosophy of history but, instead, the sociology of historians. Similarly, if one begins with the principle that disciplines are communities of individuals with distinctive community traditions, then the question of interdisciplinary dialogue becomes largely a matter of translating from one language to another. Kuhn suggests a way of reviving the dialogue between historians and sociologists by calling upon people who do not understand each other to become translators. In so doing, "each will learn to translate the other's theory and its consequences into his own language and to describe simultaneously the world to which that theory applies."[5] These two requirements (concrete knowledge of the historical community and of the process of translating innovations in other fields into the language of the historian) were central tenets of Febvre's practical epistemology. Here, however, I will not discuss the question of translation, which has made little progress since Febvre, probably because of the belief that after World War II a pluridisciplinary utopia had been achieved. As for the sociology of scientific practice, recall that as long ago as 1950 Febvre remarked that "the theory of history has been done, but not the sociology." He added, moreover, that any assessment of the discipline would be "seriously incomplete if we did not look, without prejudice or indulgence, beyond the neat frameworks of our methodological statements at this perhaps somewhat troubling aspect of our historical labors."[6]

A number of recent historical works provide the first empirical material for attempting a social history of history. The "ego-histories" collected by Pierre Nora hint at the actual world of historians, touching on such topics as how historians learn their craft, what career strategies were available to fledgling historians, and what underlying factors influenced their choice of research specialty. One sees immediately how concrete conditions affected the questions that historians asked and the content of their research. It becomes apparent, for example, that young doctoral candidates chose to work on regional monographs less because of the influence of Vidal de la Blache than because of the perverse effects of the French educational system (after passing the agrégation, candidates were usually assigned to a provincial teaching post and chose the place to which they had happened to be assigned as the framework for their thesis work). Moreover, even the most ambitious joint research programs, such as the one initiated by Ernest Labrousse, depended on considerable division of labor and the accumulation of numerous regional monographs, hence they were vulnerable to what Maurice Agulhon calls "authorial vanity," as each young historian who completed his thesis sought to signal his originality by abandoning the monographic framework in order to broach more general issues, which were generally considered "nobler."[7] This brings us to that "somewhat troubling aspect" of historical work (or indeed of any scientific work) that Febvre alluded to—the search for social recognition, which is one of the principal motivations of intellectual effort. Without a social history of this phenomenon, we have no way of understanding what shape it took at different times, where and how it was expressed, what was at stake, and what distortions it may have introduced. It is a good bet that research in this area would plainly show that conceptual innovation, methodological progress, and the like cannot be explained solely by means of textual analysis, as the present-day "history of history" tends to do. Research on historical citations would be extremely illuminating in this regard, not only for the standard epistemological reasons already adduced by Simiand (the problem of citation as proof) but also at a more general level, as an indicator of the social existence of the community with its "shared traditions"[8] and permissible forms of "self-presentation," as reflected in "paratexts" and implicit in the range of reference and homages.[9]

THE SUBJECTIVIST PARADIGM

A second way of making the dialogue between historians and sociologists more fruitful is to extend the problem-framing of social history to the whole gamut of questions treated by sociology. If we adopt the concept of a paradigm, which Thomas Kuhn used to explain the structure of scientific revolutions,[10] it is possible to argue that French history's leap forward in the 1950s under the leadership of Fernand Braudel and Ernest Labrousse was the consequence of a sweeping revision of the existing idea of "normal historical science" in the light of the new paradigm of quantitative history. Why has this paradigm fallen flat in recent years? Partly because it proved incapable of generating answers to many questions that arose in the course of historical research, but equally, if not more, because the average age of university historians has increased as the flow of young history students dried up. As Simiand insisted, all vestiges of the subjective approach had to be sacrificed in order to make the quantitative approach operational—not only at the documentary level but at the problem-framing and methodological levels as well. Surely, the major challenge facing social history today is to bring historical imagination to bear on what has already been achieved in order to construct a subjectivist paradigm equal to what the historians of the 1950s and 1960s achieved in quantitative history. This is essential if we are to approach such subjects as the state, biography, and the political without reverting, as Jacques Le Goff fears we may,[11] to traditional ways of doing history and, instead, draw on the rich tradition of sociological research in these areas.

If the social sciences are to achieve maturity, however, social scientists must disprove the law that the only way for a new generation of investigators to do innovative work is by discrediting the previous generation. Unlike Febvre and Braudel, who denied that the work of their predecessors had any value the better to persuade their readers of their own genius, we need to emphasize the cumulative nature of historical research. Without the immense effort of cataloging and criticizing sources that distinguished historical work in the nineteenth century, which defined its goal as "knowledge through traces,"[12] subsequent historians would not have been able to expand their territory. I cannot agree, moreover, with the restrictive definition of social history and science that François Furet and Adeline Daumard proposed thirty years ago, when they stated that "scientifically speaking, the only social history is quantitative."[13] Yet no one can deny that the methods of quantitative history that were developed in the 1950s and 1960s are far from having exhausted all their possibilities.

Developing a subjectivist paradigm simply means applying historical analysis to everything that quantitative history was obliged to leave out. It also means drawing on areas of sociology that historians have hitherto ignored. Doing so will give rise to new fields of research, new questions, and new explanations that can only enrich our knowledge of the past. To make these assertions more concrete, I want to discuss a concept that is essential to the subjectivist tradition, that of lived experience (*Erlebnis*). This has been a central idea in sociology from Max Weber to today's interactionists, and it is worth considering what its interest for history might be. Most social historians remain deeply suspicious of the idea of experience, which they tend to associate with the idea of "authorial intentions" which Simiand criticized in Seignobos. In order to show that there is a problem here that deserves more than a facile ironic dismissal, I shall look at Maurice Halbwachs's book on collective memory, which has the virtues of being part of the French intellectual tradition and close to the preoccupations of historians.[14] Historians who have studied the problem of collective memory generally adopt Jules Michelet's metaphor of the nation as a thinking, remembering being. Consequently, an essential problem—how does one go from the multitude of individual memories to a collective national memory?—is never posed. Halbwachs, in distinguishing between souvenirs, collective memory, and tradition, notes that a subjectivist approach may proceed on several levels, and he discusses how the passage from the individual to the collective takes place, thus addressing a problem that quantitative history invariably skirts or ignores. Halbwachs uses the first-person singular constantly because memories are, in the first place, realities associated with the lived experience of an individual. Yet he is quick to add (and I think he was the only scholar to attempt to link the subjectivist approach to Durkheimian sociology prior to World War II) that recollections persist in our personal memory only if they are shared by a social group (family, classmates, co-workers, fellow citizens), that is, a collection of individuals who have lived through the same events. Many collective memories thus intersect in each of us, reminding us of the groups of which we were briefly or more permanently a part. The crucial point, however, is that these collective memories are a product of lived experience. They are significant only for those who not only know of the events they recall but also participated in them. The example of memorials to fallen soldiers, which Halbwachs singles out for special attention, is particularly illuminating: as individuals with direct experience of wartime suffering die out, the intensity of commemoration ceremonies at such monuments diminishes until commemoration becomes a faintly comical exercise or even an onerous burden for later generations. Tradition therefore does not begin to develop until living memory is wiped out. No one worries about preserving memories until those who participated in the events begin to die. Gradually, memory moves on to another plane: that of the written trace, the history that is taught through books and other pedagogical techniques—objective means of communication which are the only way of transmitting a neutral, universal message but at the cost of blunting the emotional charge borne by those familiar with the events in question. The scholar who studies the trace of an event after the fact can no longer understand (in Dilthey's sense) the event itself; instead, he will give it a new meaning, conditioned by the age he himself lives in.[15] What is perhaps most important in this concept of lived experience is the process it reveals, which sociologists call "objectification." In this perspective, the present is nothing but the crystallized past, fixed in material forms, rules of law, words, and mental structures. We are therefore living in the midst of the dead history produced by past battles that today lie buried in the apparent neutrality of the material forms to which they have given rise.[16]

The subjectivist approach thus encourages critical labor aimed at raising questions about what we take for granted in everyday life, at seeing things that seem natural to us as arbitrary products of social history. Here again, we see the revival of concerns that obsessed late-nineteenth-century France, accurately summed up in Maurice Barrès's phrase "the dead embrace the living," which we find reflected in the work not only of Paul Vidal de la Blache and Ernest Lavisse but also of Lucien Febvre.[17] Yet French historians looked for traces of the past mainly in rural society, as a sign of the rootedness and permanence of French traditions, whereas sociology has shown that what is most important for the contemporary world took place elsewhere: it was in legal codes, official classifications, and institutions—in short, at the level of the state—that the essential process of objectification occurred. That is where the past weighs upon the present. Why has it been so difficult to revise civil service hierarchies or to bring the legal codes of different European countries into conformity under the aegis of the expanded European Community, if not because such reforms run up against the weight of history, or, in other words, the habits, established interests, and ever-increasing interdependence of modern individuals. To understand this history, to penetrate its disguises, is therefore one of today's crucial tasks.

Now, the logic of *longue durée* quantitative history is incompatible with this approach. In order to quantify, one must first unify the sources, take them out of their context, eliminate all heterogeneous data, irregularities, and exceptions, and confine one's attention to that which repeats itself. Seignobos's critique of Durkheim's use of suicide statistics pointed out the limits of the statistical approach. Indeed, the term "suicide" refers to different things in different societies. Before drawing any conclusions, therefore, one must recover the meaning of individual actions. This is precisely what statisticians who work with artificially homogenized formal data do not do. The same type of criticism can also be applied to quantitative history. The oft-repeated assertion that quantitative history is the only scientific history because it treats the sources not as a given but as something to be constructed in light of a specific research project ignores the whole homogenization process to which the sources must be subjected before quantification is attempted. For example, by using nineteenth-century government occupational classifications without asking how they related to reality, economic historians have helped to distort the image of the lower classes by underestimating the number of workers holding multiple jobs or belonging to "mixed" categories such as worker-peasants, which were not included in official classifications.[18]

The second criticism that one can make of quantitative history, again from the subjectivist point of view, involves its refusal to historicize its material and instruments, thereby contributing to the naturalization of social objects. Take historical demography, for example. Much progress has been made in this area, all of it based on one assumption—that, unlike traditional historical evidence, records of vital statistics are objective sources, essentially natural objects without a history. In fact, though, birth, marriage, and death certificates were the object of a lengthy struggle to impose state control over individual identity, hence to inculcate certain social norms, a struggle that is still going on today, as any "undocumented alien" can tell you. It took centuries before the average citizen looked upon this official "paper" identity as something natural and obvious. The author of the 1849 *Dictionnaire de l'administration* still felt the need to point out to registrars of vital statistics that such official data were better recorded in registers than on loose sheets of paper; that mayors should not let days or months go by before signing documents; that public officials would do well to refrain from adding personal comments to official documents; and that relatives and friends who were not official witnesses to a marriage had no right to embellish official documents with their signatures. Thus, historical demography is guilty, in a sense, of accepting the view of the winning side in a long struggle, the side whose victory was so complete that it eradicated every vestige of opposing views.

If city hall employees today routinely abide by the official rules for recording vital statistics, it is because they have internalized those rules. Internalization, along with lived experience and objectification, is the third key element in the theoretical framework of subjectivist sociology: it is the equivalent at the individual level of objectification at the material level. As Stephen Lukes, among others, has shown, the concept of internalization was a fundamental discovery of Durkheimian sociology in the 1890s: using this concept, sociologists explained how preexisting norms and values became an integral part of individual personalities.[19] Later, Norbert Elias introduced the term into historical sociology. By relating it to the concept of interdependence, he was able to explain the "civilizing process" in Western societies.[20]

With the three concepts of lived experience, objectification, and internalization, the subjectivist paradigm opens up the possibility of deep new insights into social dynamics and the cumulative aspect of human history. Human beings die, but the traces they leave of their time on earth—including not just material traces but technologies, affective behaviors, and the forms of interdependence that link one to another—remain. Later generations discover the traces left by their predecessors, traces present from birth and therefore a familiar, almost natural part of their world. We successors make these traces our own without even noticing what we are doing, yet in fact we devote much of our lives to developing their consequences.

TRANSLATED BY ARTHUR GOLDHAMMER

NOTES

[1] Paul Feyerabend, *Against Method* (rev. ed., London: Verso, 1988).

[2] See, for example, Bruno Latour and S. Wooglar, *La Vie de laboratoire* (Paris: La Découverte, 1988), and E. Brian and M. Jaisson, "Unités et identités: Notes sur l'accumulation scientifique," *Actes de la Recherche en Sciences sociales* (Sept. 1988).

[3] Thomas Kuhn, *The Structure of Scientific Revolutions* (2d ed., Chicago: University of Chicago Press, 1962).

[4] Michael Polanyi, *Personal Knowledge* (Chicago: University of Chicago Press, 1958).

[5] Norbert Elias also insists on the need for sociology to free itself from heteronomous models and to invent its own language by jettisoning concepts borrowed from the

natural sciences and replacing them with others more directly derived from the social realities being studied. This may account for the simplicity of Elias's language compared to that of French sociologists, most of whom are steeped in philosophical abstraction. See Norbert Elias, *Qu'est-ce que la sociologie?* (Paris: Pandora, 1981), pp. 13–14.

[6] Lucien Febvre *Combats pour l'histoire* (Paris, 1956), p. 438; on this question, see also Pierre Bourdieu, *Homo academicus* (Paris: Minuit, 1986), and Daniel Roche, "Les Historiens aujourd'hui, remarques pour un débat," *XXe Siècle* (1986).

[7] Pierre Nora, ed., *Essais d'égo-histoire* (Paris: Gallimard, 1987).

[8] The expression is from Pierre Besnard, *L'Anomie* (Paris: P.U.F., 1987).

[9] Gérard Genette, *Seuils* (Paris: Seuil, 1987). To engage in a critical analysis of jacket copy, prefaces, footnotes, and the like is in a sense to look behind the scenes of history.

[10] Kuhn, *The Structure of Scientific Revolutions.*

[11] Jacques Le Goff, *Histoire et mémoire* (Paris: Gallimard, 1988).

[12] The expression is from Langlois and Seignobos and not Simiand, as Marc Bloch maintains in a significant slip in his *Apologie,* p. 56.

[13] François Furet and Adeline Daumard, "Méthode d'histoire sociale: Les Archives notariales et la mécanographie," *Annales ESC* 14 (Oct. 1959).

[14] Maurice Halbwachs, *La Mémoire collective* (Paris: P.U.F., 1964).

[15] On the subjectivist approach to history, see Paul Ricoeur, *Histoire et vérité* (Paris: Seuil, 1955), and Henri-Irénée Marrou, *De la Connaissance historique* (Paris: Seuil, 1975).

[16] This is the problem of hermeneutics, explored by Hans-Georg Gadamer in *Truth and Method,* trans. revised by Joel Weinsheimer and Donald G. Marshall (New York: Crossroad, 1989).

[17] Febvre even held that the principal social function of history was to "organize the past in such a way as to prevent it from being too much of a burden on the present." He regretted the absence of any systematic study of the problem of tradition. See *Combats,* p. 437.

[18] See Ernest Labrousse, ed., *Histoire sociale: Sources et méthode* (Paris: P.U.F., 1967).

[19] Stephen Lukes, *Emile Durkheim, His Life and Work: A Historical and Critical Study* (London: Penguin, 1973), p. 131.

[20] Elias's work must be taken into account by anyone working toward a new dialogue between history and sociology. As André Burguière observes, Elias, "by understanding reality as a process, combined the viewpoint of the sociologist with that of the historian": "Norbert Elias," in Andrè Burguière, ed., *Dictionnaire sciences historiques* (Paris: P.U.F., 1986). See also Roger Chartier's preface to Norbert Elias, *La Société de cour* (Paris: Flammarion, 1985).

New Sites of Experimentation

———

SIMONA CERUTTI

The City and the Trades

1991

In recent revisionist approaches to social history, new thinking about the analytical categories in terms of which historians construct the societies they study has occupied a central place. This is hardly unprecedented: debate about these categories has been crucial from Durkheim to Simiand, Labrousse, and Mousnier, to speak only of the French sociological and historiographical tradition. The same is true of other national historiographies: think, for example, of the contributions of Jürgen Kocka and Hans-Ulrich Wehler in Germany or of the debate that the Italian "microhistorians" Edoardo Grendi and Giovanni Levi initiated around the idea of "polythetic classifications," which they borrowed from the theoretical work of the British anthropologist Rodney Needham.

In France, this discussion has taken the form of a critical revision of the dominant forms of sociohistorical analysis, for the most part derived from Labrousse's model (at times at the cost of making that model unnecessarily rigid). The following text is a good example of this revisionist effort. Its author, Simona Cerutti (b. 1954), was trained in Italy under Giovanni Levi before coming to France to do her doctoral work. Her work thus brings together two very different perspectives, and the confrontation between them serves as a point of departure for her critique. Her study of trade guilds in Turin in the seventeenth and eighteenth centuries provided an opportunity for

———

Simona Cerutti, *La Ville et les métiers* (Paris: Editions de l'Ecole des Hautes Etudes en Sciences Sociales, 1991), pp. 7–14.

a much broader examination of fundamental questions: How do groups construct their social identities, if we reject the all too common assumption that such identities are self-evident (generally taken for granted in the highly "organicist" history of guilds)? Once we move away from simplistic "objective" distributions based on occupation, wealth, and income, what classifications allow us to take the social experience of the actors into account? Cerutti's work, with its emphasis on individual itineraries within social groups, points toward an analysis in terms of process, in which classification is one of the prizes at stake in social interaction. Hers is therefore a microhistorical approach, yet it pays heed to broader social contexts as well.

In one classical approach to urban history, the historian was expected to begin with a concise description of a city's inhabitants and their social and productive physiognomy before going on to give a detailed analysis of various aspects of the city's life. Two modes of exposition were frequently adopted, not necessarily mutually exclusive: one could give a portrait of the "social types" representing different orders of society (noble, bourgeois, merchant), or one could break the society down by occupation. The second approach in particular was once widely regarded as both useful and necessary, for it was supposed to provide an overall picture of the fundamental character of an urban space. By grouping the city's residents into various sectors of the economy, the historian was supposed to be painting a picture of the city's economic vocation (industry, manufacturing, services) as well as giving an implicit outline of its social stratification, based on the assumption that occupational classification reflected the social hierarchy.

The criteria of social classification have been the subject of a lengthy debate, the stages of which are well known. The strictly occupational criteria proposed by earlier researchers were eventually enriched by the addition of socioeconomic variables—such as sector of employment, wealth and income, and relations of dependence within certain trades— thus yielding increasingly refined social portraits. Nevertheless, some of the occupational classifications turned out to have defects that were difficult to overcome, particularly in areas where this type of approach should have yielded real benefits, especially in comparative research. Occupational categories came under fire for failing to take account of local realities, which proved too complex to reduce to a simple, uniform set of criteria. Imposing a single socioprofessional structure on diverse contexts often seemed a rather forced and fruitless exercise. Individuals from Paris, Grenoble, and Lyon who were placed in the same occupational categories did not necessarily enjoy the same social status or fulfill the same productive roles: for example, Parisian master craftsmen were skilled artisans who had little in common with the master craftsmen of Lyon, whose chief role was in commerce. Or, looking at Lyon again, many categories between master and journeyman simply vanish if one adopts a classification by sector rather than by trade. Similar problems arise in comparative research, where categories have to be chosen to permit comparison of different social entities. Because these kinds of problems often proved insuperable, certain major works of quantitative history, as well as many valuable regional and urban monographs, proved to be hard to generalize and thus failed to fulfill their promise.

The limited usefulness of occupational classifications for dealing with multiple realities may represent a sort of revenge of the local on the global, or perhaps it reflects a certain resistance of history to formalization. Ultimately, however, I feel that the real issue lies elsewhere, particularly since many of the most thoughtful criticisms of occupational classifications (such as Garden's) were formulated at a time when enthusiasm for quantitative history was at its height and there was unanimous agreement that all genuine social history had to be quantitative.

If we take a closer look, we see that the issue was not formalization itself but, instead, formalization in a sense that was completely foreign to the experience of the social actors. The first interventions in the debate over the social status ascribed to different occupations and social groups (a debate that has gone on uninterrupted now for twenty years) already envisaged the need to individualize descriptive criteria in a way that comes closer to the experience of contemporaries. To ask about the functions and social status of masters or the social utility of each trade, or about the social esteem ascribed to various occupations, was to ask—if not always in an explicit way—about how the social actors themselves viewed the social world. The possibility of describing social stratification with due attention to the language of contemporaries thus began to emerge.

During the 1970s and 1980s, several decisive advances were made along these lines, and some of this work proved essential in my own research. First there was the publication of Jean-Claude Perrot's monograph on eighteenth-century Caen. This was the first work to attempt explicitly to reconstruct contemporary interpretations of a city's social stratification and classifications. Perrot constructed a taxonomy of the trades in terms of the vocabulary used by residents of Caen in the seventeenth and eighteenth centuries: by comparing the lexicons and attributes ascribed to different trades at various times, he was able to reveal shifts in meaning as well as in the social hierarchy. These findings led to new questions about changes in the social fabric and of the actors' perceptions of those changes.

At the same time, although in a very different area of research having nothing to do with the concerns of quantitative historians, Natalie Zemon Davis published an important series of essays on the social stratification of sixteenth-century Lyon. Here, an in-depth interpretation of the sources resulted in a proliferation of new social actors. Age and sex were no longer merely variables within a scheme shaped by economic activity. In Lyon, these were factors that defined social groups acknowledged to occupy a specific place within an urban stratification.

A few years later, Edoardo Grendi also dealt with these themes. The protagonists in his work were women and youths, these being important social categories in late medieval statutes, which took account of criteria other than social functions and orders. Legally, distinctions of sex and age were fundamental: judicial archives referred to women and youths as frequently as to the nobility or the "little people." Civil and criminal statutes were thus read as "a cultural map of social relations, a source able to shed a unique light on the interaction between social values and realities."

The representation and analysis of urban social stratifications through the language of the social actors themselves (rather than through schemes imposed from without) thus turned out to be in one way or another central to all these works. It was not simply a matter of replacing a classification created by historians with another created by contemporaries; rather, it was a question of reconceptualizing both. In the case of Caen, the analysis of contemporary vocabulary proved insufficient in itself, but it did open the way to research into the systems of meaning underlying the contemporary classification. "The study of words is important only insofar as words themselves question realities." Together, the several levels of the analysis revealed the difference between the contemporary "vocabulary and the technical division" of labor, between the effort of classification and the objects classified. It showed, in particular, how "sectors of productive activity that contemporaries regularly lumped together owed this 'magnetic' quality to the agents' implicit social hierarchy."

What is more, the categories of sex and age discovered by Davis and Grendi could not simply be juxtaposed with categories of order and occupation but, instead, cut across them in such a way as to define new relations and to create new groups that fell between the cracks of existing systems of classification, of contemporaries as well as historians. In order to take the vocabulary of the social actors as a starting point, the principles of social classification had to be reformulated and the ways in which both historians and contemporaries described occupational and status hierarchies reconceptualized. How individuals were distributed among the sectors of the productive economy could thus be seen as a *possible* representation of the city but not necessarily the *only* one. The focus of attention accordingly shifted from the classification to the relations that produced it. It then became possible to see the variety of systems of representation that the inhabitants of the city expressed simultaneously. Seizing upon the language of the social actors marked the beginning of the search but certainly not its conclusion.

In this respect, the work mentioned thus far is to be distinguished from a more recent avenue of research that also claims to avail itself of the categories of the social actors themselves. I have in mind various works of history, relatively numerous in recent years, that invoke American cultural anthropology—more specifically, the work of Clifford Geertz—as their point of departure. Interpretive anthropology assumes, among other things, the "otherness" of its object of study. The historian can "capture" this otherness by deciphering systems of meaning reflected in behavior, texts, and other forms of social experience. In much of this work, attention is focused, obviously, on contemporary language and modes of designation. While the theory underlying the work of the social historians mentioned above has much in common with the theory behind the work inspired by interpretive anthropology, it would not be correct to say that the two are directly related. In fact, certain methodological differences give rise to important theoretical differences as well.

Analyses of "representations" tend to become closed systems. The assumption that every expression of the social gives access to a cultural totality whose logic the researcher aims to reconstruct leads, surprisingly, to a narrow reading of the sources. More precisely, the sources are analyzed in depth but in isolation from the processes that engendered them. This analysis is carried out, moreover, in the conviction that the sources can yield direct knowledge of the experience of the social actors. Take, for example, Robert Darnton's description of Montpellier in 1768, based on what is said to be an autonomous, isolated text by a bourgeois of that city. To be sure, the reader is warned that the narrative is incomplete: it does not express the reality of Montpellier or reflect the interpretations of other individuals or social groups. Yet Darnton does not offer any other source or contemporary reading; he considers it unnecessary, in other words, to ask about the modes of production that underlie this particular image, its relation to the space in question, or the individuals who created it. That is, he has failed to question the relation between interpretation and reality, where by "reality" I mean the range of convergent or divergent interpretations of the city that may have existed in Montpellier in 1768. Many of the historians who take their inspiration from cultural anthropology adopt a similar procedure. There is something paradoxical in the fact that the concept of representation, which underlies the social and cultural construction of each reality and therefore calls for in-depth, multidimensional analyses, is used to justify an attitude of passivity toward the sources: instead of an instrument for deconstructing reality, the concept becomes a way of reifying "discourse."

Language is central to all the works mentioned. In the works of social history, however, it serves to point up relations, conflicts, and alliances, whereas in the text on Montpellier these things are simply suggested by an uninvolved voice. What the reader is left with, in other words, is an impression of solid consensus.

Thus, adopting the language of the social actors is not sufficient in itself to bring us closer to the society we wish to study. The categories used by contemporaries, like those used by historians, arise out of an interpretation of the ambient society that, at some point in time, held sway over other, probably different interpretations. If we do not reconstruct the labor that underlies the social classification, we help to perpetuate a rigid image of urban society. More than that, our approach will be hindered, in my view, by what was also the chief limitation of external occupational classifications, namely, the assumption that occupational and social groups can be described before the relations that created them have been analyzed. The very definition of the urban context is at issue, and the problem cannot be resolved simply by adopting contemporary classifications. The city must be seen as an arena that shapes what happens within it, a social actor in itself. The change is methodological as well as theoretical. Different ideas of the urban context lead to different orientations in research: one approach requires constant cross-correlation of the sources, while the other leads to a two-stage analysis, of the context *first* and of behavior *second*.

When I say that we must look upon the city as a social actor, I mean that we must ask ourselves how its residents constructed their social categories in the past and how we construct our categories today. Instead of assuming that the relationship of individuals to social groups is self-evident (which leads us to define social actors a priori and study their relations on that basis), we must ask ourselves how social relations give rise to certain solidarities and alliances that eventually lead to the formation of social groups. What is important, then, is not to deny that occupational categories are ever useful but, rather, to insist that they can only be understood in terms of the social relations out of which they arise, in the present as well as the past.

In beginning my research, I felt that it was important to reconstruct social groups in terms of individual relations. There was nothing essentially new about this approach: the very earliest critiques of social classifications based on criteria of wealth and income were based on the need to look at intergroup alliances, particularly matrimonial alliances. Since then, history has benefited from new work in sociology and anthropology. Methodologically, for example, network analysis was an important research tool in my work. By reconstructing the networks of relations that various individuals were able to establish, I was able to understand how they saw the world in ways that went beyond their belonging to certain social orders or occupational groups. In short, I was able to understand the nature of urban groups.

Still, network analysis could not answer all my questions about the formation and consolidation of social groups. "Cities create inequality unmistakably and equality furtively." Furtively created equality can later solidify, transforming bonds of communication into stable networks and durable groups. Historians and sociologists have tended to focus on the formation of social groups more than on their consolidation or on the development of solidarities within them. Interpretations of these processes tend to be partial and partisan. The normative view, influenced by Emile Durkheim, sees solidarity as a function of a deep community of thought among group members who have internalized group norms. Individualist interpretations, by contrast, stress the instrumental aspect of personal strategies and, therefore, the ephemeral nature of collective commitments. In this light, the formation of solidarities and collective identities is a process that calls for explanation.

What the inadequacy of these approaches demonstrates, I think, is that neither network analysis nor Erving Goffman–inspired interactionist analysis has been able to overcome certain limitations in their basic conceptualization. Both arose as critiques of the concept of a "social role" as something attributed to an individual in virtue of his or her position in the social and productive hierarchy. For Goffman, a person is defined more by situations than by membership in a social group or groups. Yet the process whereby individuals with different histories and strategies can form a social group and share loyalties remains unexplored; instead of the group cohesiveness assumed by the Durkheimians, one has a collection of momentarily compatible personal strategies, but since those strategies are instrumental there is no real group cohesion. No new interpretive possibilities are opened up.

The success of cultural anthropology with many historians is at least partly a consequence, I think, of the inadequacy of both network analysis and the interactionist approach. Given the variety of individual strategies and behaviors, the interpretive approach seems to provide theoretical instruments for reconciling differences within a single cultural matrix. This idea of coherence and cohesiveness (which I believe to be a reductionist interpretation of Geertz's thinking) is responsible for the revival of the notion of a consensus of social actors in regard to social stratification. The belief that all forms of expression (including behavior and ideology) can be fitted into a single cultural matrix tends to minimize the role of conflict and discord in this type of social analysis. Although the analyst may allude to conflict, it is never explored as an integral component of the common discourse. What emerges in the end is an image of unanimous participation in a shared culture. At bottom, we are not very far from Roland Mousnier's image of a consensual social hierarchy.

In my view, however, the real problem is, rather, to understand how individuals with different experiences and histories can decide to come together and indeed create a common social identity. In other words, the problem is to explore how individual rationality relates to collective identity.

To sum up, then, let me list a few of the problems that gave rise to the present work: the relation between the descriptive and analytical categories developed by historians and the social organization of an Ancien Régime city as understood by its inhabitants; the relation of the social and productive classifications constructed by social actors to their own experiences (in other words, the identification of individuals with occupational and status categories); and finally, the relation between modes of alliance- and solidarity-formation and modes of institutionalization in urban groups.

TRANSLATED BY ARTHUR GOLDHAMMER

MAURIZIO GRIBAUDI AND ALAIN BLUM

The Statistical Analysis of Social Space

1990

This is another attempt to rethink the terms of sociohistorical analysis. Starting with a very different problem and different kinds of empirical data, this text raises questions and suggests solutions that have much in common with Simona Cerutti's work. One of the authors, Maurizio Gribaudi, also has a background similar to Cerutti's, having been trained in both Italy and France; Alain Blum is a demographer and statistician. Their text, published in a special issue of Annales (45, 1990) devoted to various kinds of "mobility" (social, geographic, occupational, and so on) can be read in two ways. It is, first of all, a critique of the classical (by which we mean the most widely accepted) approaches to the problem of social mobility. These have generally been macrosocial in orientation, aggregating the data as much as possible in terms of a hierarchical class structure: "deviant" and "erratic" cases are eliminated in favor of statistical modes and means. What happens if one attempts to construct a model to account for the actual diversity of social experience? This question brings us to the second aspect of the text: it takes a large volume of data collected for a collaborative study and puts it to various experimental uses under carefully controlled conditions.

The reader will note that the authors are once again calling for a microsocial analysis—in this case, of a large number of observations usually treated in macrosocial terms. Here the crucial element is not the size of the object but, rather, a specific conception of the construction of the social. The authors' conclusion is clear: "If we hope to account for the complexity of the social terrain and the movements that affect it, we must totally change our point of view and look at social space not in terms of group solidarities and movements but in terms of individual relationships and trajectories as they actually exist in practice."

Maurizio Gribaudi and Alain Blum, "Des Catégories aux liens individuels: L'Analyse statistique de l'espace social," *Annales* 45 (Nov.–Dec. 1990), pp. 1365–1402.

For decades, social historians tried to reconstruct the spaces and mechanisms that generate and shape individual and social physiognomies. After studying the many complex factors involved, scholars became aware of a certain distance between the phenomenon and its representations. They then developed an interest in the forms and categories of discourse as a way of understanding that distance and gauging what was at stake in any particular historical context. Paradoxically, however, the hermeneutic analysis of source documents and analytical categories has apparently induced neglect of the concrete social landscapes that initially gave rise to the very questions the hermeneutic approach was designed to answer.

This paradox is particularly apparent in contemporary history, a discipline that developed as an effort to understand contemporary social processes without the usual political and ideological preconceptions. Three phases stand out. In the first of these, which might be called the "illustrative" phase, historians were interested mainly in staking out the limits of various phenomena implicit in ideological interpretations of contemporary developments. They attempted, for example, to measure the pace and forms of industrialization and urbanization, as well as of the formation of groups traditionally presented as the chief protagonists in these transformations—the middle class, big merchants and entrepreneurs, government bureaucrats, workers' organizations, and so on.[1] The primary sources (which were taken at face value and treated in a synchronic setting) were the doctrinal statements of political movements and parties together with administrative statistics generated by government bureaucracies during the period under study.

These approaches imposed unduly restrictive models on complex patterns of behavior, and their limits soon became apparent. Thus, in a second phase, scholars tried to understand the same phenomena by studying the formation and evolution of social groups. Longitudinal methods coupled with source data that identified individuals by name made it possible to construct and describe a social space in the throes of change. The "new social history" sought to understand the origins and logic of social solidarities and distances by reconstructing the bonds between various social strata and groups at the local level, paying heed to both space and time.[2] Ultimately, however, the analysis never went beyond the descriptive level. Hampered by its reliance on various typologies, this approach basically adopted definitions of social and occupational categories that appeared to be implicit in the statistical sources used.[3]

The discovery of these methodological limitations led to widespread, and justifiable, distrust of quantitative methods in general, which brings us to the third phase, the one in which we find ourselves at the present time. Although research is still focused on the analysis of social practices, historians are now obliged to take a critical attitude toward their objects and tools if they are to overcome the constraints inherent in traditional statistical categories and classifications. Thus, the categories of statistical discourse have become an object of analysis in themselves, along with texts reflecting the ideological considerations that influenced the development of those categories.[4] For the time being, though, it appears to be impossible to look directly at the objects that led to the change in our point of view, for when we analyze those texts we tend to look mainly at those who produced them: the bureaucrats, entrepreneurs, and scholars who held the keys to understanding. As a result, other social groups vanish from the scene, once again made opaque by a history that passes over them.

There are reasons to worry that this temporary detour may become permanent. By focusing on the form of "statistical texts" and the manner of their production, we circumvent the issue of the relation between the statistical data and the tools used to analyze them (an issue that cannot be avoided on the practical level). For example, the chief tool of social history in the 1960s and 1970s was cross-tabulation, and its usefulness was never questioned.

The history of cross-tabulation is well known. Cross-tabulations of two or more dimensions have been in common use since Pitirim Sorokin,[5] and it is interesting to note that they incorporate techniques perfected by nineteenth-century administrative statisticians—the aggregation of data by categories, in some cases with hierarchization (not always explicit), normalization of difficult cases, and so on.[6] Although econometric modeling and factorial analysis have added powerful analytical tools to the arsenal, they have not changed the fundamental logic of the procedure.[7]

Clearly, then, the doubts that have arisen in the third phase of contemporary historiography's evolution grew out of an increasing disparity between the questions historians were asking and the tools they had for answering them. For if we have come to conceive of social systems as products of interdependencies governed by several different types of logic, always partial and contextual, we often study those systems with a statistical syntax that allows for the formulation of a macrosocial discourse and no other. Hence, it is no accident that the only possibility for answering the kinds of questions arising out of our new vision of society has come from prosopography.[8] By examining the lives of one or more concrete individuals, historians have been able to refine their accounts of the mechanisms that shape social physiognomies and to construct less schematic models of the processes of social stratification and mobility.

Has prosopography revealed terrains, itineraries, and mechanisms different from those disclosed by quantitative methods? Do the laws and causal mechanisms that have been discovered at the microscopic level cease to be operational at the macroscopic level? This is an old debate, and it may not be possible to give a definitive answer. There can be no doubt, however, that in our specialty at least the alleged discontinuity between the micro and macro levels often seems to be more a rhetorical by-product of different methodologies than a reflection of social reality.

What we want to do, then, is to examine all of these questions empirically. Using a sample of some fifty thousand marriage certificates,[9] we shall first apply a variety of traditional statistical techniques and then, abandoning those methods, attempt a new approach derived from the theory of graphs.[10]

Approaches that attempt to grasp the cleavages in a society by reconstituting large groups of individual physiognomies invariably run afoul of the same fundamental contradictions. Individual behaviors that are apparent in the sources cannot be understood in terms of the structures and dynamics that emerge from statistical studies of the data. In the current debate on these issues, attention has rightly been focused on the influence of ideological and political biases on the images put forth by nineteenth-century social and administrative statistics. Yet no one has asked whether those same biases are also implicit in the very methods by which today's statisticians proceed from individual records to aggregate categories to cross-tabulations of social mobility and, finally, to explanatory models.

The practical exercises that we have attempted show the importance of implicit methodological models in defining the phenomena under study. Each new grid reveals a different social landscape, apparently characterized by different dynamic processes and social divisions. Beyond this preliminary, and largely predictable, result, we were also surprised to discover that each methodological choice yielded macrostructural models that failed to reflect the social logics implicit in the original data. The drastic reduction of the data that statistical treatment required, the series of transformations imposed on the original information, and the translation of that information into global terms combined to make a return to the point of departure impossible. The logic of aggregation means that the value of the category is substituted for that of the individual datum—a procedure that is particularly dangerous, since many subsidiary occupations are clustered around each central one. Every feature that we were able to individualize raised important questions that demand satisfactory answers. Recognizing this sheds critical light not only on statistical tools and methods but also on the very concept of a structural phenomenon. The image of a society dynamically determined by such phenomena as industrialization, urbanization, and proletarianization is not supported by the detailed source data but created ex nihilo by a particular statistical method.

If we hope to account for the complexity of the social terrain and the movements that affect it, we must totally change our point of view and look at social space in terms not of group solidarities and movements but, instead, in terms of individual relationships and trajectories as they actually exist in practice. By starting with less commonly cited occupations and using an approach based on graph theory, we were able to shed detailed light on a number of occupational groups joined by strong mutual bonds. The resulting landscape is new, at once familiar and strange: familiar because it is filled with images known to us from the writings of novelists yet for the most part not reflected in the categories used by contemporary administrators and scholars; strange because the particularly vivid images that result from taking account of multiple occupational groups and the relations among them compels us to revise our traditional historiographic models. Occupations that the old methods forced us to group together turn out to have had connections with remote social terrains and contexts. Conversely, important links exist between occupations that used to be classified in totally different spheres. Above all, the graph theory approach enables us to give a precise measure of the number of social spaces to which a given occupational denomination is connected, as well as to analyze the contours and relations of each group. We can also appreciate the various social meanings implicit in a single occupational denomination. We can thus move beyond categories and taxonomies that place each occupation in a single group.

There can be no doubt that it is important to uncover the ideological models that lurk behind statistical categories. Yet something more is needed if we hope to avoid the pitfalls associated with traditional statistical methods and gain genuine insight into the kinds of behavior that we find in the sources. Traditional methods led to an impasse in which macrostructural and (essentially prosopographic) microstructural approaches were inevitably in conflict. Yet this impasse was, in fact, an artifact of the reliance on categories, aggregation, and statistical techniques unsuited to the study of social mobility. Things become much clearer if we reject rigid categories in favor of something more closely resembling the "polythetic categories" developed in other classificatory disciplines such as logic, social anthropology, and the natural sciences. With polythetic categories, "a simple characteristic is neither necessary nor sufficient for group membership."[11] The search for tools better suited to the treatment of detailed data sets and the analysis of social dynamics thus leads ineluctably to a lessening of the contradictions between the macrostructural and qualitative, prosopographic approaches.

Translated by Arthur Goldhammer

Notes

[1] Fernand Braudel and Ernest Labrousse, *Histoire économique et sociale de la France*, vol. 3: *1789–1880* (Paris, 1976); P. Léon, *Histoire économique et sociale du monde*, vol. 4: *La domination du capitalisme, 1840–1914* (Paris, 1978); and even, for the construction of the social framework of his analysis, Louis Chevalier, *Classes laborieuses et classes dangereuses à Paris pendant la première moitié du XIXe siècle* (Paris, 1958).

[2] T. Hershberg, *Philadelphia: Work, Space, Family, and Group Experience in the Nineteenth century* (Philadelphia, 1981); Joan Scott, *The Glassworkers of Carmaux: French Craftsmen and Political Action in a Nineteenth-Century City* (Cambridge, Mass.: Harvard University Press, 1974); Edward Shorter and Charles Tilly, *Strikes in France, 1830–1968* (Cambridge, Mass.: Harvard University Press, 1974); Stephen Thernstrom, *Poverty and Progress: Social Mobility in a Nineteenth-Century City* (Cambridge, Mass.: Harvard University Press, 1964); Louise Tilly and Joan Scott, *Women, Work, and the Family* (New York, 1981); Y. Lequin, *Les Ouvriers de la région lyonnaise, 1848–1914* (Paris, 1977); Michelle Perrot, *Les ouvriers en grève, France 1871–1890* (Paris: Mouton, 1974).

[3] Social dynamics were almost always studied in terms of classifications that largely reproduced contemporary occupational categories, themselves the product of the long history of the development of administrative statistics and its relation to sociology.

[4] Joan Scott, "Statistical Representation of Work: The Politics of the Chamber of Commerce's Statistique de l'Industrie à Paris, 1847–1848," in S. Kaplan and C. Koepp, eds., *Work in France: Representations, Meaning, Organization, and Practice* (Ithaca, N.Y.: Cornell University Press, 1986).

[5] Pitirin Sorokin, "Social Mobility" (1927), reprinted in *Social and Cultural Mobility* (Glencoe, Ill.: Free Press, 1959).

[6] These methods were developed in light of a mechanistic, macrosocial view of history based on large numbers and typical individuals, the product of a long tradition going all the way back to Q Quetelet and Emile Durkheim.

[7] J. H. Goldthorpe, *Social Mobility and Class Structure in Modern Britain* (Oxford: Clarendon Press, 1970) was an important milestone. See also R. M. Hauser, "Some Exploratory Methods for Modeling Mobility Tables and Other Cross-classified Data," in K. F. Schuessler, ed., *Sociological Methodology* (1980), pp. 413–58; C. Thélot, "L'Evolution de la mobilité sociale dans chaque génération," *Economie et statistique* 161 (Dec. 1983), pp. 3–21.

[8] D. Bertaux, ed., *Biography and Society: The Life History Approach in the Social Sciences* (Beverly Hills, 1981); Tamara Hareven, ed., *The Family and the Life-Course in Historical Perspective* (New York, 1978); Maurizio Gribaudi, "Itinéraires personnels et stratégies familiales: Les ouvriers de Renault dans l'entre-deux-guerres," *Population* 6 (Nov.–Dec. 1989); Louise Tilly, "Individual Lives and Family Strategies in the French Proletariat," in Wheaton and Tamara Hareven, eds., *Family and Sexuality in French History* (Philadelphia: University of Pennsylvania Press, 1980).

[9] The data are taken from the "three thousand family" project direct by J. Dupâquier. The set is composed of nineteenth-century marriage certificates in which one spouse had a family name beginning with the letters "TRA." For more details on

this data set, see *Bulletin des 3000 familles*, the project's biennial information bulleten published by the Laboratoire de Démographie Historique.

[10] C. Berge, *Théorie des graphes* (Paris: Dunod, 1967).

[11] Rodney Needham, "Polythetic Classification: Convergence and Consequences," *Man* (Sept. 1975), pp. 349–69.

PATRICK FRIDENSON

Organizations: A New Object

1989

Patrick Fridenson comes clean right from the start: "There is no obvious connection between 'organizational science' and 'historical analysis.'" This is all the more true because French social history has largely ignored both organizations and the decision-making process, problems that have received far greater attention in other historiographical traditions (especially the American) and other disciplines (including economics and some branches of sociology). Fridenson is a historian of modern industrial economies and the author of a pioneering and now-classic book on the automobile manufacturer Renault (1972), thus his remarks should be taken first of all as symptomatic of something that has been missing in French economic history. Yet they are also an invitation to think about what organizations do and how they operate, to investigate a particular type of social relation that has received too little attention, and to consider some of the inconsistencies of certain functionalist approaches to the subject. The essay that follows takes up these issues by examining the relation of strategies to structures.

The Relations Between Strategy and Structure

Strategy can be defined in game-theoretic terms as a set of decisions (to cooperate or compete) made in response to hypotheses about the behavior of other parties in a specified situation. Recent work in organizational analysis can help historians in three ways: by demystifying the concept of strategy, which social science has done so much to debase; by restoring its complex relations to structure; and by suggesting new approaches to decision-making and social change.

Patrick Fridenson, "Les Organisations, un nouvel objet," *Annales* 44 (Nov.–Dec. 1989), pp. 1470–75.

The Demystification of Strategy

Organizational science relies on two distinct approaches to strategy. The first is external: the investigator determines after the fact what was done and then attempts to reconstitute the meaning of a series of actions by relating them to external variables. The second is internal: the investigator analyzes the decision-making process and reconstitutes the rationalities and interactions involved. The two most ambitious examples of this second approach are analyses of the death of the *Saturday Evening Post* in 1969 and of the resurrection of the English chemical firm ICI in 1983.[1] Historians will recognize this methodological distinction: they, too, differentiate between cases in which internal archives are available and cases in which they are not. They know that the danger of the external approach is after-the-fact rationalization, while the internal approach offers the advantage of revealing what possibilities other than the chosen strategy were explored, what principles were applied, how the options were evaluated, and, if there was disagreement over the ultimate choice, what sorts of bargaining took place.

Eventually, however, historians are forced to admit that organization theory yields a new picture of the decision-making process. The organizational approach explodes the rational concept of strategy according to which a strategy is first elaborated by decision-makers and then implemented. The empirical realities do not bear out this view. The Canadian management theorist Henry Mintzberg, whose work should be of great interest to historians, proposes discarding the idea of rational strategies and replacing it with three new concepts. Mintzberg applies the term "deliberate strategies" to intentions that are first explicitly formulated and then implemented. Sometimes, however, intentions fail to be implemented because expectations are unrealistic, judgments about the environment are erroneous, or changes are made along the way: Mintzberg calls these "unrealized strategies." Finally, some strategies are carried out without being rationally formulated at the outset, and in many cases these are formalized after the fact; Mintzberg calls these "emergent strategies." As an example, he cites the United States' decision to enter the Vietnam War in 1965.[2] Mintzberg's approach has countless potential applications in history. Indeed, organization theorists have reason to be critical of historians who treat strategy as something explicit, consciously elaborated, deliberately applied, and fully worked out before any specific decisions are made. Mintzberg, for example, rejects Alfred Chandler's celebrated definition of business strategy as "the determination of the firm's fundamental, long-term goals and the adoption of policies and allocation of resources necessary for the realization of those goals." For Mintzberg, this definition fails to capture reality from the standpoint of both the organization and the historian.[3]

The study of organizations can also serve as a warning against another traditional temptation of historians, which is to see strategy in military terms, that is, solely in terms of confrontation. True, organization theorists are often deeply interested in military strategy, whether from ancient China or modern Sweden, and often apply its ideas to present-day organizations. However, most of them see possibilities for combining confrontation and cooperation even in military strategy. They often cite the pioneering work of Graham Allison on the peaceful resolution of the Cuban missile crisis in 1962 as well as the ensuing détente.[4] Combining confrontation with cooperation amounts to viewing one's adversary as a partner to whom one holds out the prospect of a reduced level of violence. Theories of dissuasion are relevant here: organizations that cannot destroy themselves are condemned to engage in dialogue, just as individual actors are. Strategy thus leads to bargaining based on relative strength. One American economist has theorized the goals of such bargaining, the explicit attitudes, the types of behavior that the partners hope to achieve, and the resulting image.[5] This concept of implicit bargaining has recently been applied to the problem of analyzing organizations in the Soviet economy. The central authorities in Moscow want to tighten their control and to enforce national priorities, whereas local production units want to minimize central control and secure guarantees of flexibility at the local level. The interests of the parties are contradictory. Subordinate units try to undermine the legitimacy of central controls by persuading the dominant authorities that they cannot meet their commitments and that quotas must be reduced.[6]

From Strategy to Structure

Why and under what conditions will an organization change strategy? On this point, organizational science is indebted to history, and especially to the work of the American economic historian Alfred Chandler. Chandler worked with an explicitly behaviorist model: organizations are governed by inertia; they change strategy only when the environment changes or when crises occur; changes in strategy will succeed only if accompanied by changes in structure.[7]

In France, Chandler's work has influenced mainly business historians, but it has the potential to bring about a revolution in institutional history by treating organizational structure and internal relations as important objects, as well as by focusing attention on structural change. In organizational science, by contrast, the impact of Chandler's work has been enormous. Moreover, some of the research it has stimulated has provided new subjects and new tools for historians.

It has been shown, for example, that strategic change need not always precede structural change. Chandler has recently reformulated his position as follows: "Structure has as much impact on strategy as strategy on structure. . . . From the outset, moreover, my goal has been to study the complex interaction among structure, strategy, and the perpetually changing external environment in modern industrial firms."[8]

Furthermore, by interpreting Chandler's problem as a competitive selection process that results in changes in the way in which actors coordinate their activities, organizational analysts have developed two new theories about how maximally efficient solutions are adopted.

Economic analysts of property rights "analyze the impact of the extent of property rights (*usus, fructus, abusus*) on the behavior of individualistic actors. The use and allocation of resources by a community depend on the distribution of property rights. Institutional performance therefore depends on the distribution of rights."[9]

The theory of transaction costs, developed by the American economist Oliver Williamson, starts with the hypothesis that in exchanges between agents (or organizations), all parties involved share a common interest in minimizing transaction costs, including costs of negotiation as well as implementation. Agents will choose the institutional form best suited to that purpose. In an economic context, for example, they may choose the market and commercial contracts, or a hierarchical organization, or some intermediate form. Historians may find several suggestions in this theory: trade can be studied in terms of costs, for example, and one can model choice in terms of the costs of alternative solutions. The theory is thus applicable to any number of historical situations.[10] Two possible objections come to mind, however. The "basic assumption that the institutional can always be reduced to the contractual" is tenuous, as one economist has noted.[11] Furthermore, even if we acknowledge the importance of transactions, it does not follow that all organizational knowledge production can be explained in terms of the conditions of the transactions that constitute the life of the organization. The question of innovation arises here. Historians who look at the economics and sociology of innovation (or even of knowledge) may well be thankful for new insights into the conditions under which knowledge is produced, the strategic stakes of knowledge production, and the transactions on which it is based, and yet they still feel that intellectual activity has real content and therefore cannot be reduced to the conditions under which it takes place. Basically, they share the economist's objections to the dangers of reductionism inherent in careless application of the nevertheless very suggestive theory of transactions.

Finally, Chandler's work has also given rise to a third line of research in contingency theory. Here the idea is that organizations must change their internal attributes (structures, strategies, and processes) in order to cope with changes in their environment.[12] Historians will note yet another influence of Darwinian biology, but with two important differences: the environmental pressure for adaptation is long term, and organizations have to change themselves.

Another Look at Change

Organizational analysts who study strategies and structures can contribute to historical work in two complementary ways. First, they focus attention not on events but on flows. Instead of viewing a decision as the isolated formulation of a strategy, Mintzberg looks at strategy as "a model embedded in a stream of decisions."[13] Organizational research also gives historians new ways to think about social change.

For organization theorists, change is a creative process. Existing schemes and beliefs are called into question by tensions and inconsistencies in the relations of various organizational actors with each other and the environment. The effects of this questioning are unpredictable: success is not guaranteed. Change is often triggered by individuals who do not stand at the top of the organizational hierarchy. The management theorist Armand Hatchuel, for example, interprets Du Pont's decision to change its corporate structure to one of independent divisions differently than does Chandler, who was the first to consider the question. Hatchuel sees a "bloody brawl" between two coalitions of actors with different visions of the organization. Top executives believed that the crisis could be resolved by simple changes in the decision-making process and management techniques; others, whom Chandler describes as "relatively young but experienced" managers, felt a need to restructure individual and unit relations within the firm. They worked out a new organizational structure, which the top executives rejected; but the innovators did not take no for an answer, and in 1921 put their ideas to work in the form of a "de facto division."[14] After two years of internecine warfare, they won: their model emerged as the solution to the crisis because it was based on thorough knowledge of the organization's problems, and because it promoted creative transformation of the corporate structure. Change, in other words, taught lessons that led to the emergence of new actors.

I have not attempted here to provide a comprehensive overview of organizational science or to discuss what historians might contribute to it. I simply wanted to show how organizations could be a worthy object of historical research, and to explore, from a historian's point of view, a few of the ways in which a dialogue between the two disciplines might be useful.

The theories, concepts, models, and methods of organizational science are diverse, perhaps unsettlingly so for historians. Dynamic models may prove to be the most useful. In these, one focuses on an organization within a limited time frame, which itself consists of a number of interrelated subsidiary time frames. The organizations studied tend to be limited in size, and much attention is paid to concrete examples and deviations from the basic model.

Historians should also be on their guard against the optimism inherent in much organizational research, which may bias their results. They must also be careful to avoid the kinds of errors that one management researcher has rightly criticized: it is easy for the investigator to become a mere sounding board for the actors' own rationalizations (as reflected in documents, interviews, and explanations), that is, to wear the same blinders as the actors themselves. He must therefore weigh what the actors say in light of his own detailed knowledge of their activities, taking their interpretations with a grain of salt and allowing for the variety of their personal outlooks. In some cases, he must go beyond their work to construct alternatives to the decisions they reached and to understand the implicit consequences of other choices. However, these are things that historians have been learning how to do for the past three decades, even without formal study of systems analysis.[15]

With these indispensable precautions in mind, however, it would be difficult to overstate the importance of what organizational science has to offer historical analysis. Once one gets over the shock of dealing with such an alien world, organization theory can help historians overcome their habits of thinking in terms of an opposition between structure and conjuncture, and of distinguishing too sharply between the economic, social, and cultural levels of analysis. It also demonstrates the value of "constructive" models in which learning and transformative processes are of central importance.

TRANSLATED BY ARTHUR GOLDHAMMER

NOTES

[1] R. I. Hall, "The Natural Logic of Management Policy Making: Its Implication for the Survival of an Organization," *Management Science* (Aug. 1984), and A. Pettigrew, *The Awakening Giant: Continuity and Change in ICI* (Oxford: Basil Blackwell, 1985).

[2] Henry Mintzberg, "Patterns in Strategy Formation," *Management Science* (May 1978), p. 945. See also his *The Structuring of Organizations: A Synthesis of Research* (Englewood Cliffs, N.J.: Prentice Hall, 1979), and the very stimulating collection of essays in J. B. Quinn, Henry Mintzberg, and R. M. James, *The Strategy Process: Concepts, Contexts, and Cases* (Englewood Cliffs, N.J.: Prentice Hall, 1988).

[3] Mintzberg, "Patterns in Strategy Formation," p. 935.

[4] Graham T. Allison, *Essence of Decision: Explaining the Cuban Missile Crisis* (Boston:

Little, Brown, 1971), and "Conceptual Models and the Cuban Missile Crisis," *American Political Science Review* (Sept. 1969).

[5] Thomas C. Schelling, *Micromotives and Macrobehavior* (New York: W. W. Norton, 1978)

[6] J. Sapir, *L'Economie soviétique,* manuscript cited.

[7] T. McCraw, *The Essential Alfred Chandler* (Boston: Harvard Business School Press, 1988), p. 13. See also L. Galambos, "What Have CEOs Been Doing?" *Journal of Economic History* (June 1988), pp. 248–50.

[8] Alfred Chandler, *Strategy and Structure: Chapters in the History of Industrial Enterprise* (Cambridge, Mass.: MIT Press, 1962).

[9] E. G. Furubotn and S. Pejovich, eds., *The Economics of Property Rights* (Cambridge, Mass.: Ballinger, 1974): see E. Brousseau, "De Nouvelles approches," p. 87.

[10] See, most recently, O. E. Williamson, *The Economic Institutions of Capitalism* (New York: Free Press, 1985), and *Economic Organization* (Brighton: Wheatsheaf Books, 1985).

[11] O. Favereau, "Organisation et marché," p. 82.

[12] P. R. Lawrence and J. W. Lorsch, *Adopter les structures de l'entreprise* (2d ed., Paris: Editions d'Organisation, 1989).

[13] Mintzberg, "Patterns," p. 935.

[14] Private communication, A. Hatchuel to author. See also A. Hatchuel, "L'Entreprise sur longue périod: incohérence et intelligibilité," in *ISEOR, Méthodologies fondamentales en gestion* (Paris: FNEGE, 1986), pp. 238–51.

[15] H. Dumez, "Petit organon à l'usage des sociologues, historiens et autres théoriciens des pratiques de gestion," *Economies et sociétés* (Aug. 1988).

ALAIN COTTEREAU

"Public Spirit" and the Capacity to Judge

1992

In the 1980s, historians in France as in many other Western countries began to write about the "public sphere," a term that reflected the influence of the German philosopher Jürgen Habermas, who argued that the history of the West could be written largely in terms of its emergence and subsequent decline. Habermas's work, like that of his predecessor Hannah Arendt, encouraged historians to rethink their political categories. Alain Cottereau demonstrates the fruitfulness of such an approach but provides it with a richly suggestive social and historical contextualization. Rather than study the biographies or lifestyles of local elites, for example, he shows how the "notables" learned to function in a new intermediary public space. The most productive unit of analysis turns out to be neither state institutions nor individual political actors but, rather, conceptions of space and distance that encourage the development of new forms of political behavior.

In 1789–90, certain markers of public visibility vanished with the collapse of the old authorities, and with them went the signs by which people identified *honnêtes gens* (decent folk) and *recommandables* (commendable) fellow citizens. If we are to understand the politics of public virtue, we must bear in mind the magnitude of the void left by the abolition of the old system of notables. In the late Ancien Régime, the moment an individual moved beyond the local sphere in which he was well known, beyond his commune, parish, corporation, guild, market, or what have you, he could do nothing until he had established his credibility not only with certain private individuals but also with guild officials, religious authorities, police, bureaucrats, magistrates, and military officials. To do this, he needed the recommendation of a notable,

Alain Cottereau, " 'Esprit public' et capacité de juger: La stabilisation d'un espace public en France aux lendemains de la Révolution," *Raisons pratiques* 3 (1992), pp. 240–72.

which took various forms, ranging from a parish priest's note vouching for a humble migrant laborer to a recommendation from a courtier enmeshed in political intrigue, and including letters from merchants, *billets de confession* (offering proof of religious practice), the secret correspondence of *compagnonnages* (journeymen's organizations), certificates issued by *commissaires de police,* and character references delivered by itinerant merchants. Recommendations of this sort played a part in the formation of patronage networks in much the same way as the extrajudicial arbitration discussed earlier: the importance and credibility of notables depended on these things, which were also signs of just that importance and credibility.

Conceptually, this space defined by patronage networks was antithetical to large-scale public space. Instead of engaging in open, public relations, one trafficked in recommendations. Nevertheless, elements of modern "publicness" were at work in the eighteenth century. One of the achievements of Jürgen Habermas's early work was to give substance to the idea of public space: this involved the creation of a sphere of public opinion, associated with bourgeois sociability and the Enlightenment, as well as a redrawing of the boundaries between public and private space. Yves Castan has also provided an excellent account of how an ideal of civility took hold in the eighteenth century. This allowed the notion of private virtue to be extended to the nation as a whole, a notion that was the obverse of a public liberty available to all, regardless of station, and out of which developed an art of expressing "opinions" with no authorization other than that of one's fellow citizens.

When the system of recommendation by notables collapsed, the municipal revolution of 1789–91 naturally moved in to fill the void—though not for political reasons, apparently, so much as to meet a pressing need. It naturally fell to mayors and municipal sections to certify residences and honorable reputations, just as they were also required to certify births, marriages, and deaths when the clergy failed or was denied the right to do so. The democratic implications of such initiatives emerged in hindsight, after royal treason, constitutional crisis, and war sowed suspicion and enshrined it in law. It was then that the Jacobin clubs most intent on unmasking internal enemies denounced the old practices of recommendation as well as earlier procedures for granting *certificats de civisme*: they charged municipalities and sections with awarding certificates in the absence of solid information, without inquiry, simply because no serious complaints were known to have been lodged against an individual in their *quartier* or city. This was a negative way of identifying the fundamental liberal revolution of the previous few years: the citizen in anonymous public space no longer bore the burden of having to establish his moral worth. Municipal assemblies had revolutionized the old patronage system and set a clear example of what they meant by "public spirit." Just as, according to the Declaration of the Rights of Man and after the great judicial reforms, every citizen was presumed innocent until proven guilty, so, too, was every citizen in the anonymity of a great fraternal nation presumed to be *recommandable,* that is, worthy of trust and credit and worth listening to. Yet this principle was untenable without subsidiary measures of verification, which were established only in the wake of terrorist suspicion and its condemnation.

As every French schoolchild knows, the Consulate and Empire raised multiple obstacles to citizenship: they abolished freedom of the press and eliminated aspects of representative government in favor of an authoritarian regime limited by civil liberties, advised by consultative councils, and supported by a network of notables kept under close government surveillance. While all this is true, it is nevertheless worth calling attention to the positive elements of citizenship which remained. Broadly speaking, the postrevolutionary compromises succeeded, at the national level, only in establishing and consolidating a negative public space; citizen initiatives were possible only at the local level. Citizens could communicate with the central government only through the mediation of local authorities. Local government thus became a crucial point of intersection between local public space and a new sphere of authority encompassing local notables and the central government. Although this new sphere was not public per se, it did occupy the critical interstices of public authority.

The polysemic evolution of the idea of public *spirit* can help us to locate the links between government and notables. In one of its senses, "public spirit" became a common bureaucratic phrase, the subject of periodic reports to the central government, first by its *commissaires* and later by its *préfets* and their staffs. Over time, these reports grew more and more detailed, eventually defining a genre, examples of which can still be consulted in the National Archives. Many works of history have drawn on this source. These reports gauged the people's state of mind in regard to various public matters, relying on such indices as political activity, attitudes toward authority, and notes of conversations in public and private places. The public spirit was judged to be good or not so good, bad or not so bad; but the criterion of "goodness" was no longer the universalistic orientation of citizen judgments. It was based, instead, on two related judgments—of the credibility of authority and the governability of its subjects.

Collective action could henceforth avail itself of certain national points of reference, but these were not meant for use by citizens. They possessed a certain technical usefulness as indicators of governmental feasibility. The rules of the literary genre defined by the reports on public spirit dictated that they had to be written from a fictitious point of view, which was neither that of the head of government (personal reports had their own distinct set of rules) nor that of a national community, but, rather, totally detached: an ideal point of view identified with the "general interest," or, in plain language, the point of view of the state, which posed as the source of the laws that guaranteed the security of civil society.

This historic shift symbolizes a possible antinomy between the meaning of the word "public" to citizens and to the state (even if it is a state of laws), once responsibility for promoting the general interest is reserved to specialists; ordinary citizens are, presumably, left to look after the private interests of "civil society." "Statocentrism" (by analogy with ethnocentrism) then takes the place of democratic public space. The birth of state statistics in the same period is another manifestation of the same phenomenon: these, too, were measures of governmental feasibility intended not to ascertain the citizens' state of mind but, rather, to provide a broad overview of their activities and projects, ultimately in quantitative form. The reasons they acted as they did were hidden from view, the better to map out potential actions by the state and its servants—to be based of course on general assessments and purposes.

Statocentrism slowly infiltrated the sphere of notable-government relations between the Directory and the Empire. If the invasion had been complete, democratic public space would have vanished. In the period of postrevolutionary stabilization, however, the relations of citizens to notables and of notables to the central government were profoundly "regenerated." The word "notable," common to the lexicons of the Ancien Régime and the nineteenth century, may be misleading. Patronage networks and power based on private influence did not revive, any more than did the *esprit de corps* of the old corporate institutions of the Ancien Régime. One can, of course, find instances of "patronage" and clientelism, but these were perceived as scandalous rather than legitimate, as in decades past. They were deviations that confirmed the norm, much as exceptions confirm the rules of grammar.

This achievement of the Revolution has become so familiar in France that few historical works remark on it or pause to analyze it. Today, when one thinks of the insuperable difficulties of clientelism and corruption in most Third World countries, one is inclined to view it as a miracle that the old habits of the Ancien Régime were not revived, even though notables once again became obligatory mediators. The object of mediation was reversed, however: instead of *incorporating* members of local communities into networks of influence, allegiance, and patronage, local functionaries, mayors, and judges were now obliged to use their *proxim-*

ity in order to achieve a *public distantiation* from local antagonisms, local norms, and corporate existences. This practice of proximate distantiation in the absence of a national public space is the distinguishing feature of local, postrevolutionary public space in France.

INTERMEDIATE PUBLICS

The practice described above was complex and discreet. It was not the communal autonomy that Tocqueville praised in Britain and the United States, nor was it "Napoleonic" bureaucratic centralism, which has all too often been caricatured by looking at only one side of the equation. Institutional historians point to the proliferation of measures opposed to communal universal suffrage, the free election of mayors, and the direct election of city councillors from the Directory to the beginning of the July Monarchy, when communes were granted a modest degree of *affranchissement*; all these measures reflect a fear of popular judgment at the national level. Yet this historiographic tradition has failed to take note of an essential constraint imposed on local magistrates by the combined demands of citizens and the central bureaucracy. There is little explicit evidence of this constraint in official reports. We find traces of it in an insistence on local hearings and local authority in citizen complaints, to which the supervisory authorities scrupulously attended. The constraint of local legitimacy has thus left negative traces in the mass of documents in the départemental and national archives that are filled with the denunciations of the unsatisfied and with complaints of all sorts about perceived irregularities in the performance of local magistrates.

When we look into the daily details of local government activities, we are struck by the scrupulous concern with excluding notables from the process if there was even the slightest suspicion of partiality, favoritism, or influence by special interests. When prefects used their authority to appoint mayors and other local officials, they were careful to avoid any appearance of clientelism. While public denunciations of private individuals were no longer permissible, denunciations of notables were still taken very seriously—not only by the accused but also by the local citizenry and higher authorities.

Local hearings could take a variety of forms, which can be conveniently summarized as ranging between two extremes. The first amounted to a kind of local assembly, embodying local democracy through consensus without oversight by higher authorities. At the other extreme, the local hearing was, in effect, a symbolic confrontation, in some cases accompanied by provocative acts of violence—a forum for individuals or groups who felt their rights had been unjustly infringed upon but who had no institutional recourse. Magistrates challenged in this way were seen as successful if they could come up with solutions acceptable to the interested parties, whereas the recourse to repressive violence, which supervisory authorities often deemed necessary for reasons of state, was clearly perceived by everyone as a failure, an *impuissance* of the local magistrate.

A prefectoral report from 1803, paraphrased in a local monograph by Fernand L'Huillier, illustrates the first case. "Many communes have no endowment income, and the supplemental tax established by law yields much less than is needed for urgent expenses. Usually, during the early years of the consulate, the residents imposed additional assessments on themselves voluntarily to make up the shortfall." Later, on the subject of denunciations for poor fiscal management, L'Huillier states that "on the whole, municipal institutions do not yet appear to have the maturity necessary for independence." Here, in the eyes of both the prefect and the historian, state criteria of feasibility make it appear that local authorities are in need of oversight, whereas from the standpoint of communal citizenship the self-assessment reflects a substantial capacity for collective action: if rural communes could voluntarily come to agreement on how to distribute the tax burden without legal forms of deliberation, they were obviously quite capable of discussion and compromise. In the context of the time, tax payments would never have been made unless informal debate had resulted in some kind of consensus, for if there had been any hint of local despotism or patronage then denunciations would surely have followed.

A more common form of legitimation operated according to a local jurisprudential model, it, too, semiclandestine and safe from national legicentrism. Whenever a dispute or difficulty arose in a local community, the mayor, constable, justice of the peace, or *conseil de prud'hommes* would intervene. When untoward events occurred, notables were called upon to demonstrate their ability to arbitrate by forestalling disputes, squelching unfounded rumors, and stopping violent attacks on scapegoats. In more difficult cases, the *prud'hommes* or justice of the peace might be called in to deal with a matter that required more formal debate and the consent of the community. In reports to the supervisory authorities, these situations were portrayed as fires that needed to be put out before they got out of hand. When we follow the history of specific decisions in the judicial archives, however, and read the justifications offered by the various parties, we find a whole jurisprudential system of enforcing local norms in which village residents took the initiative: their actions sometimes served as exemplary cases establishing something like a local law, a precedent or custom, which would then be enforced by justices of the peace, commercial courts, and *conseils de prud'hommes*.

The possible connection between local validity and normative universalism, which seems paradoxical at first sight, appears less so when we look from the inside at how judgments were made. Borrowing terms from topology, we can say that the local space in question may be "open," with no external border, rather than opposed to some extralocal entity deemed invalid. In other words, the local is specified in terms of certain peculiar features of local life as seen from within. The criteria of judgment may then be tested in terms of their acceptability to those affected, without prejudicing others more remote, or there may perhaps be two degrees of acceptability—a sort of normative livability for the affected community and a simple standard of causing no harm outside that community.

Conceptually, understanding these dynamics raises a number of issues, among them a rather more theoretical problem of democratic citizenship. Generally, we conceive of the lives of citizens on two levels, in terms either of immediate social contacts or of large, anonymous political entities. It might be more useful to add an intermediate level that is not reducible to either of the two others—not *corps intermédiaires* (intermediate bodies) but *public intermédiaires* (intermediate publics). By this I mean proximate public spaces in which collective action extending beyond the circle of immediate acquaintances can be tested through face-to-face interactions, with recourse if necessary to accessible authorities. Such testing involves a degree of distantiation from a community that may be too familiar or close.[1] This distantiation may come about through deliberation in regard to actions to be taken, but it can also be introduced as a narrative integrally connected with action itself from the original initiative to normative discussion of its possible outcomes to depicting the course of events, the reception of the initiative, and various tests of its acceptability.[2] The notion of a proximate or intermediate public space is interesting only as a way of introducing a distinction between the local community and local public space. The relation between them is one of the administration of a legacy, a concerted revival of outmoded forms, a tentative return to traditional ways of life. In this way, it is possible to experiment simultaneously with negative and positive liberty, with promotion and preservation of capacities for collective action, with forgetting and recognition.

In the ideal case, the proximate public space becomes an obligatory intermediary. It helps citizens to cope with the uncertainties inherent in collective government when possibilities of clarification through direct experience become increasingly difficult to obtain. It enables individuals to take some distance from the groups to which they belong, try out the idea of anonymous citizenship, and experiment with collective government in anonymous spaces on a human scale. This can provide experiential references useful for imagining large-scale power as *a capacity for concerted action* without causing the individual to succumb to the anxiety of the strange and without aiming to compensate for the uncertainty of public action by imposing allegiance or subjugation.

TRANSLATED BY ARTHUR GOLDHAMMER

NOTES

[1] For a historical example, see Elisabeth Claverie and Pierre Lamaison, *L'Impossible marriage* (Paris: Hachette, 1982).

[2] See Paul Ricoeur, *Soi-même comme une autre* (Paris: Seuil, 1990).

CÉCILE DAUPHIN, ARLETTE FARGE,
GENEVIÈVE FRAISSE, CHRISTIANE KLAPISCH-
ZUBER, ROSE-MARIE LAGRAVE, MICHELLE
PERROT, PIERRETTE PÉZERAT, YANNICK RIPA,
PAULINE SCHMITT-PANTEL,
AND DANIÈLE VOLDMAN

Women's Culture and Power

1986

In comparison to the United States, women's history made a relatively late entry into historical circles in France. The foremost proponent of women's history came not from the circle around the Annales *but from the university: Michelle Perrot, who, after beginning her career as a historian of the working class (see the excerpt "Workers on Strike," pp. 413–422) and collaborating briefly with Michel Foucault, turned progressively toward the history of women, eventually collaborating with Georges Duby in directing a multivolume foundational work on the history of women from ancient times to the present (Georges Duby and Michelle Perrot, eds.,* Histoires des femmes en occident, *5 vols. [Paris: Plon, 1991–92];* A History of Women in the West *[Cambridge, Mass.: Harvard University Press, 1992–94]). The article excerpted here was first written as part of the collective work of the seminar that preceded the collaborative project on the history of women, a project that eventually involved scores of historians. The article, which was published in* Annales, *provides a brief overview of the entire field and a set of questions for future consideration. Although the body of work referred to in the article is considerable, the rhetoric is still somewhat hortatory—as if the claim that the history of women should be incorporated into the mainstream of historical research were still less than unanimously endorsed not among historians of women but among those mainstream historians themselves.*

Cécile Dauphin, Arlette Farge, Geneviève Fraisse, et al., "Culture et pouvoir des femmes: Essai d'historiographie," *Annales* 41 (Mar.–Apr. 1986), pp. 271–94.

Much can be learned about the place of women's history in the historical discipline, about its choice of objects and its methods for dealing with them, by looking at the "years in the desert" as well as at recent work in the field. Over the past ten years, there have been important changes in the way we select and analyze historical objects. Within this broad transformation of the discipline, which has thus far received less attention than it deserves, the women's history has gone from exclusion to toleration to, most recently, normalization. There are two good reasons for explicit discussion of these changes: to ensure that women's history preserves a critical attitude toward its own practice and to raise new questions about how this field relates to historical research in general. This is an ambitious project, and we are well aware of the difficulties involved. It is always easier to ask questions than to answer them. History, though, is not just production of knowledge; it is also a form of questioning. The questions that history inspires or that are put to it also constitute a distinct area of research, one that we think is in urgent need of open discussion. It is no accident that we have chosen the *Annales* for that discussion. Our purpose is not, however, to stake out territory in a journal that, while not exactly ignoring the history of women, has not welcomed it with open arms.[1] Rather, we want to raise explicit questions about ways of analyzing sexual roles that have appeared in *Annales* and ask about the treatment of the masculine and feminine in certain recent historical work.

We begin with a brief overview of women's history, the details of whose development may not be familiar to all our readers. Women's history, which developed initially out of a conviction that women had been banished and forgotten, found its voice around 1970, impelled by the explosion of feminism and associated with the burgeoning of anthropology and of the history of *mentalités* as well as with various achievements of social history and work on popular memory. In this crucial period, militant feminists were doing women's history even before women's historians were. With this impetus, the universities created new research groups, offered courses in women's history, encouraged research, and suggested research topics. All this intellectual effervescence tended to gravitate toward two poles: on the one hand, to explore the central role of women in history (thus overcoming the absence of any concern with sexual differentiation from most work in the field), and, on the other, to bring to light instances of the oppression, exploitation, and domination of women by men. In this particular context, during which ideology and identification were integral parts of the object of study, the history of women was a supplement to general history, an extra. It was not uncommon for theses written by men to contain a supplemental chapter on women, a symbolic token to a suddenly obtrusive feminism. Feminism, though, not the history of feminism: confusion between the two has been deliberately perpetuated, so that a clear distinction has to be made, because the history of feminism and the history of women are two distinct objects. Is one a subset of the other, a subset of a subset for which recognition within the historical discipline is already hard enough to obtain? Or perhaps the relation between the two is more complex, insofar as the interrogation of historical feminism extends beyond the history of women? In any case, the fact remains that women's history is for the most part done by women, and it is tolerated on the fringes of a discipline on which it exerts no direct influence.

As the new field of research developed, broadened, and acquired a certain structure, some women historians sensed a serious danger of intellectual isolation, which could only lead to work of a depressingly tautological character; these historians wanted to speak to the whole discipline, not just to their sisters. In order to do so, they had to refine their concepts and take a critical look at what they had produced. This was the time of the first assessments, which saw the formation of study groups,[2] the organization (with government assistance) of a women's history colloquium,[3] and the creation within the Centre National de Recherche Scientifique of an "Action Thématique Programmée" around the theme of women.[4] This official recognition of the "woman question" only intensified doubts that had already arisen about some of the concepts that historians of women were using. It revived fears that, owing to certain deficiencies of women's history, it might fail to become a spearhead of historical research or even a thorn in the discipline's side. Among those deficiencies were:

· a persistent predilection for the study of the body, sexuality, maternity, female physiology, and professions supposedly feminine by "nature"

· the persistent recourse to a dialectic of domination and oppression, which verges on tautology so long as no effort is made to analyze the specific mediations through which that domination is exercised in different places and times

· too much emphasis on the study of normative discourses, which take little account of social practice or resistance, leading at times to a kind of self-induced fascination with woe

· a misunderstanding of the history of feminism and its relation to political and social history

· a lack of methodological and, above all, theoretical reflection.

Even as these doubts were being raised, the appearance of history itself was changing in ways not always evident at the moment. One phenomenon that deserves separate treatment was the sudden surge of interest on the part of male ethnologists and historians in sex-role differentiation: the work of Maurice Godelier and Georges Duby is emblematic of a broad new outlook.[5] This change came about as a result of broader changes in historical research: the history of *mentalités* and the exploration of new areas such as sexuality, criminality, death, diet, and deviance had apparently fallen out of favor. Work that had been prized only a short while before suddenly seemed less attractive and was sometimes abandoned, even though the problems it had raised had hardly been resolved. Other broad themes emerged, all with a certain tendency to minimize the interpretive importance of social differences—fear, sin, the relations between public and private life. Along the way a new field of research was called into being: the history of social and cultural representations (and to a lesser extent political representations). In this framework, the new notion of "women's culture" found its place, and women's behavior and practices were analyzed in themselves.

Without a doubt, the success of cultural history and of the history of representations, coupled with the growing contribution of ethnological and anthropological approaches, have allowed studies of sex roles to take on a new look. That new look calls for close scrutiny, however, particularly since it is gaining support and, what is more, the endorsement of an innovative and brilliant new school of historians. In seeking to describe women's roles, researchers have uncovered a number of specific practices which, through a complex interplay of compensations, interferences, and symbolic interpretations, ultimately define a women's culture that is crucial to maintaining social meanings.[6] Furthermore, study of the symbolic opposition of masculine and feminine, whose forms and meanings change constantly from period to period and motif to motif, shows that sex roles are intricately constructed so as to oppose all forms of sexual nondifferentiation as a lethal danger to society. While we do not mean to mount a systematic challenge to this way of looking at things, we do wish to point out some of its limitations and unintended consequences. By casting a critical eye on methodology, we hope to say what the approach has achieved and what its blind spots are.

HAVING POWER?

The Cultural Approach to Gender

It is correct to say that, in a given society, a person's sex determines certain attitudes, beliefs, and codes. It is also correct to note that such gender differentiation also differentiates between societies. Attention to this dimension has opened up new areas of research and produced some stimulating results. Two, in particular, are worth mentioning: the identification of feminine objects, spaces, and behaviors, and inflection of the dichotomy between male domination and female oppression which previously shaped all study of gender roles.

It was an essential step to identify and measure the presence of women in specifically female places, institutions, and roles. Doing so highlighted the categories masculine and feminine, which had previously been buried beneath a gender neutrality that in fact benefited only men in a man's world. After studying modes of male sociability in places such as youth hostels, barracks, cafés, cabarets, garrets, and hunting parties, historians could legitimately turn their attention to female sociability defined by the same criterion—the absence of gender-mixing. This led to fruitful studies of washhouses, bakehouses, markets, and the home and yielded a variety of insights into these "female" sites, all more or less connected with productive activity, whereas the male sites had mostly been associated with leisure. Work was also done on important life stages such as birth, marriage, and death. Here we are thinking of the work of the ethnologist Yvonne Verdier, who deciphered the social and symbolic meaning of the actions of seamstresses, washerwomen, and cooks.[7] She was able to reveal the common thread linking the speech, acts, know-how, and roles of women in a Burgundian village. At the heart of feminine culture was the singular power of the female body, articulated as a series of taboos and temporal symbolisms.

Other work was hampered, however, by a narrow framing of the issues exclusively in terms of the dialectic of domination and oppression, with no attention to frequent and complex variations or to exclusively female forms of power. One constant and universal factor summed up all relations between the sexes—male supremacy. The numerous components of male supremacy that so-called cultural studies usefully highlighted were forgotten. Indeed, if women have their own version of social meaning, if they are involved in a variety of practices intended to help the entire community on its way through life and on to death, then clearly they have power, which can be analyzed in such a way as to reorient debate and open up new avenues of interpretation. In this way, women's studies can hope to free itself from the straitjacket of tautology in order to explain the ever-changing realities of the past and present.

Take, for example, Martine Segalen's work on rural society in the nineteenth century. Segalen clearly shows how male authority and female powers, inscribed in various rituals and representations, were the two vectors that determined the structure of sexual life, work, space, and relations between couples and the community.

Nevertheless, such emphasis on women's powers can be a slippery slope, leading to distorted, ideological results. To point out that women have cultural power may yield too rosy a picture, in which pluralistic, complementary cultures are juxtaposed with no notice of the fact that relations between the sexes can also be violent and inegalitarian. A little theoretical rigor might help to prevent old stereotypes from emerging beneath the cover of modern formulations.

Dead Ends

Complementarity, a theme that figures in a number of studies of rural society, works so well that it has given rise to an image of social life in which men and women divide space and time and each sex has its own specific gestures and rituals; roles and tasks are neither antagonistic nor competitive; and social life seems to be organized around two apparently equivalent poles—masculine authority and female powers. Although it is sometimes shown that the sexual division of labor is not static, and that areas of overlap and exchange develop in such a way as to break down the opposition between female domestic labor and male productive labor, there are still numerous ambiguities in the notion of complementarity. Domestic work, for example, is never gender mixed: the activities of fetching water, tending fire, and preparing food are feminine, and men cannot engage in them without losing face. This is not an area that men are interested in conquering either materially or symbolically. Conversely, some normally male chores cannot be completed without the assistance of women. When this happens, however, women derive no additional prestige from their participation, since the female "quality" inherently destroys the value of any acquired skill (a process whose effects can be discerned in contemporary job classifications). In short, women are not "deskilled" because they can never become "skilled."

The very reassuring idea of complementarity has the effect of warding off the specter of confrontation. Because the threat is eliminated from the outset, there is no need to interpret its specific forms and features. Inversion of the male-female opposition is possible, but the terms remain the same. Sweetness and light are the rule, and the study of the masculine/feminine lapses into a profound silence concerning the possibilities of tension and conflict, of rivalry and alternation in power. In some of its forms, the history of *mentalités* lends support to these attitudes. Starting from a cultural definition of masculine and feminine spaces, one proceeds to construct a real and symbolic equilibrium between two worlds from which confrontation and violence are banished—hence social phenomena such as compensation, consent, and opposition are blunted by the fact that each symbolic and practical position is supposedly in constant need of the other within an equivalent system of values. In this formulation, the jarring contrasts of everyday reality are hidden from view, and one slips from a notion of gender difference to that of an imposed binary social structure from which sharp conflict is excluded. The resulting portrait is tempting but reductive.

This shift of the problematic toward recognition of a "female culture" drew on research that focused on historical periods in which that culture was still present and observable. Its primary locale, rural society, is described in this work with little or no reference to the historical context, the crucial changes that took place in the nineteenth and twentieth centuries (railroads, postal service, schools, "universal" suffrage, migrations, wars, urbanization), or such internal factors as technological innovation and fluctuating land prices. What emerges from these analyses is a static, harmonious, ahistorical society, which leaves a strange impression of atemporality. Attention is focused exclusively on a culture that is actually disappearing.

For decades now, historians have worked with a dialectic of long versus short periods. In general, distinct objects are associated with each time frame. In the area that interests us, however, the dialectic develops within a single domain, that of gender relations. How, then, are we to relate a largely static "gender symbolism" to practical changes in gender relations? According to the theory of representations, which focuses on the way in which social and political structures are represented in the imagination, we cannot do any such thing. Either nothing changes (that is, both the place of women in society and thinking about gender division remain the same) or everything does. Methodologically speaking, it is not satisfactory to distinguish between a "real time" subject to history and a "mental time" more or less outside history. The distinction between two "levels of analysis" remains entirely formal, with the main interest being the situation of "female culture" in the *longue durée*.

In other words, our doubts about the *longue durée* problematic stem from the observation that none of the work in anthropological history on gender difference—indeed, more precisely, none of the work focusing on women—has been able to use the *longue durée* perspective to pose the question of gender relations in fresh historical terms.

Other Ways of Thinking About Women's Culture

The goal is no longer to reconstruct what women specifically said and knew, or what forgotten powers they may have possessed; it is, rather, to understand how a women's culture was constructed within a system of inegalitarian relations and how it concealed the flaws of that system. We must bring old conflicts back to life, map the use of time and space, and show how women conceived of their place in the larger society.

Cultures are based on the consensus of a certain community. In this sense, women's culture is, in fact, a culture of interest to the entire community. Yet every element of a culture must be conceptualized in terms of relations and dependencies—relations to and dependencies on the other sex, the social group, the political and economic context, and the entire cultural domain. Divisions are never neutral: the important thing is to characterize the positions of both sexes, since a value system based on division need not imply equivalence of the parts. Acknowledging the importance of women in certain aspects of social life need not lead to repression of the central problem of male domination. In the modern Greek village studied by Marie-Elisabeth Handmann as well as among the nineteenth-century bourgeois women of northern France studied by Bonnie Smith, unavowed male resistance focused on inegalitarian gender relations. Women, torn between their aspirations and their assigned roles, both attacked the inequality of the system and, in contradictory fashion, offered justifications and alibis for it.

Clearly, the history of female culture cannot relegate conflicts and contradictions to the margins. These are central issues. Like other cultures, women's culture develops amid tensions that shape certain more or less temporary symbolic equilibria, contracts, and compromises. These conflicts can be seen in certain silences or in the absence of certain specific practices. They can justify, modify, or limit the power of the strong over the weak.[8] The history of such conflicts needs to be written.

Having Power?

"*Les femmes, quelle puissance!*"[9] This quasi aphorism is not just a tactical maneuver, a sort of consolation prize offered to women. It is also a conviction widely shared by ordinary people of the past and by historians today, persuaded that "customs," that is, private life and civil society, ultimately count more than the political and the state. People today are daunted by the failure of deliberate efforts to bring about political change and impressed by the power of social inertia; contemporary ideology therefore emphasizes the social as opposed to "the illusion of the political." Out of the protests of the 1960s came the idea that outsiders, minorities, and women are the driving force behind social change, and that everyday life is a source of boundless innovation. Yet this outlook, whose heuristic value is considerable—and which, moreover, is perfectly in tune with *longue durée* social and cultural history—has the drawback of effacing conflict and tension: both the class struggle and the gender struggle. This so-called return to political history, or, more precisely, to the history of political theory, is not a return to the narrative of events but, rather, a reflection on political issues, actors, and forms of mobilization as well as on the ideas of consent, enticement, and resistance. The gender dimension of this analysis is not obvious, however. One participant in a recent colloquium was moved to shout that "a political relation exists only between social groups."[10] How can we introduce gender into this kind of history while at the same time bringing the benefits of the new approach to women's history?

Forms of Male Domination

One might answer the colloquium participant mentioned above by pointing out that gender relations are also social relations. They are social constructs rather than natural givens, and they can be studied in the same way as other relations, egalitarian or inegalitarian, between social groups. Thus, "male domination" is one of many possible types of unequal social relations. It is a form of inequality found in many societies, regardless of their level of development. It is not unique to Western societies, and to uncover its existence in many places is not an instance of unjustifiable ethnocentrism.[11] With all due respect to the mythical Amazons, "there is at present no conclusive proof of the existence of societies exempt from male domination."[12] To speak of "male domination" is to make a scientific judgment, not a moral one. The truth of this is widely known yet repeatedly called into question.

In precapitalist as well as in industrialized societies, male domination is inseparable from a mode of production in which women are denied the fruits of their labor. In domestic production, women are exploited for both their work and their reproductive capacities: the fruits of their labor go to their legal guardian, while their procreation is subject to community controls. Women thus become "useful property," a situation not found in archaic systems. This domestic mode of production is in effect perpetuated in other forms in the capitalist system through family relations of production (artisanal, commercial, or agricultural). Whether in baking[13] or farming, domination is exercised through monopoly control of trades, status, knowhow, and inherited property.[14] The history of dowries is perhaps another example of a dispossession of women that is structurally related to gender inequality and to a mode of social reproduction. Finally, it goes without saying that among wage earners the social division of labor is also a sexual division of labor.[15]

Compensation and Resistance

Through the effects of male domination, women, especially as agents of reproduction, are targeted for special manipulation by government. The discourse and practices associated with the interests of the family, civil society, and the state change over time. The degree of constraint to which women are subjected varies from one period to the next. Women also receive various kinds of compensation, including certain powers, which can help us to understand why they consent to the system, for it could not function without their tacit agreement.

In modern industrial societies, for example, the "weakness" of women (as well as their maternal "capital") entitles them to certain special protections, in the workplace for example, thanks to special legislation. In France, women stopped working in mineshafts in the mid-nineteenth century. They were banned from night work, and limits were placed on the length of their working day—limits so severe that they were in fact excluded from many factory jobs. During World War I, the large-scale employment of women in wartime industries led to certain health improvements and to closer supervision of workplace conditions (by *surintendantes d'usine*). These protections had unintended consequences, leading in some cases to sexist discrimination and, ultimately, to a temporary relegation of women to sectors of the economy said to be less harmful to their health and more compatible with their "nature," such as home-based work. Women were nevertheless exempt from the brutality of big industry, as they were from military service and war.

Owing more to these formal and informal precautions than to their biological resistance (which in any case diminishes when females have access to a masculine way of life), women enjoyed unusual longevity. The gap between male and female death rates has continued to widen in developed societies. In France, the death rate for women of all walks of life is eight points lower than for men. Might it be that French women are "more modern" than French men? "Why, in today's world and especially in France, is the weaker sex the one that has traditionally been characterized as the stronger?" one demographer has asked.[16] Women, who frequently survive their spouses and are left in charge of jointly owned property are the guardians of memory during long years of widowhood, which in some cases are the years of a woman's greatest power; others, however, must endure an extended period of growing loneliness and impoverishment.

The history of seduction and of the forms of male and female desire, which can be found, for example, in works on the history of appearance,[17] makeup, clothing, cooking, housing, and even advertising, should show men and women caught up in a complex game. Neither sex has the keys to this game, whose explicit and identifiable codes change rapidly over time, revealing not only the state of male-female relations but also society's image of sexual conquest and attraction. Hence, these things can be treated as historical objects in the same way as taste, intimacy, and private life.

The nineteenth century saw a change in the relation of the public to the private sphere, with new emphasis being placed on "social power," which was at first largely masculine but gradually conceded in part to women, who were urged to move beyond the gentle pleasures of home and hearth and go out into the world.[18] Both religious and government leaders hailed "the social power of women," which is said to have played a key role in the development of the welfare state.[19] In Germany, this took the form of a veritable "social maternity."[20] Middle-class women aided, educated, and controlled poor and working-class women. Encouraged by the associations to which they belonged, they transformed themselves from "poor visitors" (Joseph-Marie Gérando's old philanthropic phrase) into volunteer investigators, from patrons into "social assistants," the forerunners of today's social workers. During the war, the *surintendantes d'usine* sent by socialist war minister Albert Thomas to monitor wartime factory work were recruited among the well-to-do, and this practice continued after the war was over.[21] Similarly, doctors enlisted women as allies in the battle for public health improvements, which was also a way of making a moral issue of the poverty hidden beneath the filth. Many women found in this battle an outlet for their energies, as well as for the uneasiness they felt because they did no work in a society increasingly governed by the values of utility and labor.

How did women use the powers they were granted and the flaws in the system? What advantage did they take of what was left to them and of the missions with which they were entrusted? What role did these things play in breaking up a potential gender identity? How did women know how to circumvent the taboo and use cunning, that weapon of the oppressed with which they are so readily credited—a weapon that, as Marie-Elisabeth Handmann and Susan Rogers have shown, ultimately drained male domination of its real content? What needs to be looked at is the subtle interaction of powers and counterpowers, the hidden texture of the social fabric. We need to add gender relations as a new dimension in an approach largely inspired by the work of Michel Foucault. This will, of course, require breaking new ground, and the work will be difficult, but it may be possible to break down simplistic dichotomies in order to write a history of familial, social, and political power from the inside.

The Political Stakes

When we make use of an idea such as domination, and assert that it is universal and that it invariably results in the exclusion of women from the political sphere, we are stating a conviction, not making an analysis. It may be that emphasizing the study of domination (whether from the standpoint of oppression or that of rebellion) prevents perceiving it as a dialectical relation. Most of the time, we are content to juxtapose dominator and dominated in a way that tells us little about the operation and nothing about the causes of the domination in question. When we affirm that gender relations are social relations, however, we introduce a distinction between the social and the political, which may help us to refine the concept of domination. Although the political originates in the social, it has its own specific function, namely, to determine the common rules that are to govern collective life. While it is possible to identify political power, it is more difficult to understand how the political, as an agency of social structuration, regulation, coordination, and control, defines what we perceive historically as the public-private distinction. Is it enough to observe that men have been assigned to the public and women to the private, and then to state that the private sphere is not exempt from the political game? No. We must, rather, ask how the definition and separation of powers arose out of transformations of the political itself. The opposition between the social and the political does not coincide with that between the private and the public: it may be possible to see both dualities as aspects of a larger unity. To treat this theoretical problem as an issue of particular significance for women's history is already a methodological proposition. When we bring the political dimension back into our thinking about the masculine/feminine dichotomy, we focus attention on the public (and therefore on the civil, economic, and political as well) without denying the importance of the private. The opposite approach, which would deduce the public from the private, is hardly possible. The feminist Jeanne Deroin told Proudhon, who was well known as a champion of the confinement of women within the home, that since men already had both the city *and* the family, women could also combine the two.[22] She pointed out that the presence of women in civic life denied nothing of the reality of the family, whereas the exclusion of women inevitably turned on an unrealistically rosy representation of women's lives.

Instead of simply accepting the alleged absence of women from the political sphere and swallowing accounts that systematically minimize their participation in political life, we can try to gauge the political significance of events in which they did participate. By "reevaluate" we mean thinking of what is generally interpreted as a social fact in terms of political intervention; we mean looking at women in historical moments during which the singularity of the event was as important as the repetition of cultural facts. For example, we can take a fresh look at the role of women in eighteenth-century riots, in nineteenth-century social struggles, and in contemporary feminist practices. One immediate result of this would be to put an end to the view that women's history is simply an account of the gradual evolution of a supposed "female condition."

Is the concept of power the only useful way of thinking about politics? Here, again, a question of method is involved: What would happen if, rather than ask about women's power, we framed the question instead in terms of freedom? Very likely, we would be obliged to change our representation of the situation and jettison the categories of hierarchy and compensation. In the history of feminism, for example, we encounter the problem of how power is exercised, but we also encounter the issues of enfranchisement, emancipation, and liberation. Might this lead to reevaluation of the concepts of the public and the political?

TRANSLATED BY ARTHUR GOLDHAMMER

NOTES

[1] A systematic review of articles published in *Annales* between 1970 and 1982 on women and on the masculine/feminine dichotomy can be found in Arlette Farge, "Pratique et effets de l'histoire des femmes," in Michelle Perrot, ed., *Une Histoire des femmes est-elle possible?* (Paris: Rivages, 1984), pp. 18–35.

[2] Various study groups formed both in Paris and in the provinces, either as adjuncts to academic institutions or as independent entities.

[3] The colloquium entitled "Femme, féminisme, recherche" was held in Toulouse in 1983.

[4] "Action thématique programmée: Recherches sur les femmes, recherches féministes, 1984–1988."

[5] Maurice Godelier, *La Production des grands hommes* (Paris: Fayard, 1982); Georges Duby, *Le Chevalier, la femme et le prêtre* (Paris: Hachette, 1981).

[6] Jacques Revel, "Masculin/féminin: Sur l'usage historiographique des rôles sexuels," in M. Perrot, ed., *Une Histoire des femmes est-elle possible?* pp. 122–40.

[7] Yvonne Verdier, *Façons de dire, façons de faire: La Laveuse, la couturière, la cuisinière* (Paris: Gallimard, 1979).

[8] Michel de Certeau, *L'Invention du quotidien*, vol. 1: *Arts de faire* (Paris: 10/18, 1980), pp. 18ff.

[9] The phrase is Jules Michelet's.

[10] Quoted in N. Mathieu, "L'Arraisonnement des femmes," *Cahiers de l'homme* (1985), p. 171.

[11] Ibid.

[12] Eleni Varikas, "Genèse d'une conscience féministe dans la Grèce du XIXᵉ siècle, 1887–1907," thesis in progress, University of Paris VII.

[13] I. Bertaux-Wiame, "L'Installation dans la boulangerie artisanale," *Sociologie du travail* 34 (1982).

[14] D. Barthélemey, A. Barthez, P. Labat, "Patrimoine foncier et exploitation agricole," Paris, SCEES, Collection de statistiques agricoles, *Etude* 235, Oct. 1984); R. M. Lagrave, "Egalité de droit, inégalité de fait entre hommes et femmes en agriculture," *Connexions* 45 (1985), pp. 93–107.

[15] Renaud Sainsaulieu, *L'Identité au travail* (Paris: Presses de la Fondation Nationale des Sciences Politiques, 1977).

[16] M. L. Levy, "Modernité, mortalité," *Population et sociétés* 192 (June 1985).

[17] Philippe Perrot, *Le Travail des apparences* (Paris: Seuil, 1984).

[18] Pierre Rosanvallon, *Le Moment Guizot* (Paris: Gallimard, 1984).

[19] "The Social Power of Women" was the title of a book by George Deherme, a disciple of Auguste Comte, which appeared in 1912.

[20] Paper read at Princeton in March 1985 by Piestov Sachsse, professor at Kassel, Germany.

[21] A. Fourcaut, *Femmes à l'usine* (Paris: Maspero, 1982).

[22] This polemic took place in 1849 in the pages of two newspapers, *Le Peuple* and the *Opinion des femmes*.

PIERRE NORA

Between Memory and History:
Les Lieux de Mémoire

1984

Among the problematic objects that historians are reinventing today, memory occupies a place of exceptional importance and significance. This phenomenon, of course, is not unique to France. In many developed societies, the collective investment in memory is a response to the acceleration of history, to rapid social change, and to the problems of identity that such changes are pressing home with growing urgency. In "new" countries, the recourse to memory is often a way of decolonizing history. It is likely that every society worries about the traces it will leave in history, yet few have been as assiduous as modern Western societies in preserving the historical record and storing it in archives. It appears that our relation to the past is changing, that we are experiencing a transformation of the nature of historicity. Naturally, this has consequences for historians and their approach to the past.

This reevaluation of memory makes it possible to propose a new kind of history, a very contemporary history, deeply imbued with the valences of the past as they are capitalized upon and made vital in the present. Very different ways of going about this have been attempted—from the British "history workshops" to oral history and, more generally, what is sometimes called "history from the bottom up." It should come as no surprise that the French have come up with their own distinctive approaches to memory, for France is a country blessed with, if not overwhelmed by, a long and glorious past—yet it is also a country that has, over the past half century, moved from the front ranks to the status of a middling power. The rise of memory is thus contemporary with a cruel twist in the nation's history.

In this vein, the project to which Pierre Nora here provides an

From "Between Memory and History: *Les Lieux de mémoire*," trans. Marc Roudebush, *Representations* 26 (Spring 1989), pp. 7–25. First published "Entre mémoire et histoire," in Pierre Nora, ed., *Les Lieux de mémoire*, vol. 1 (Paris, 1984), pp. xvii–xlii.

introduction is particularly noteworthy, not only for its scope and the rigor of its analyses but also for its success in establishing the untranslatable phrase lieu de mémoire, *which is on its way to becoming a permanent fixture of the French vocabulary. Inaugurated in 1984 with a volume on republican memory, the* Lieux de mémoire *series continued with three more volumes on the nation in 1986 and another three on the diversity of France in 1993. This collective work, to which a large number of French historians contributed, has been widely praised but also criticized. There can be no doubt, in any case, that it is an important symptom of the rethinking of history currently in progress.*

Our interest in *lieux de mémoire* where memory crystallizes and secretes itself has occurred at a particular historical moment, a turning point where consciousness of a break with the past is bound up with the sense that memory has been torn—but torn in such a way as to pose the problem of the embodiment of memory in certain sites where a sense of historical continuity persists. There are *lieux de mémoire,* sites of memory, because there are no longer *milieux de mémoire,* real environments of memory.

Consider, for example, the irrevocable break marked by the disappearance of peasant culture, that quintessential repository of collective memory whose recent vogue as an object of historical study coincided with the apogee of industrial growth. Such a fundamental collapse of memory is but one familiar example of a movement toward democratization and mass culture on a global scale. Among the new nations, independence has swept into history societies newly awakened from their ethnological slumbers by colonial violation. Similarly, a process of interior decolonization has affected ethnic minorities, families, and groups that until now have possessed reserves of memory but little or no historical capital. We have seen the end of societies that had long assured the transmission and conservation of collectively remembered values, whether through churches or schools, the family or the state; the end too of ideologies that prepared a smooth passage from the past to the future, or that had indicated what the future should keep from the past— whether for reaction, progress, or even revolution. Indeed, we have seen the tremendous dilation of our very mode of historical perception, which, with the help of the media, has substituted for a memory entwined in the intimacy of a collective heritage the ephemeral film of current events.

This conquest and eradication of memory by history has had the effect of a revelation, as if an ancient bond of identity had been broken and something had ended that we had experienced as self-evident—the equation of memory and history. The fact that only one word exists in French to designate both lived history and the intellectual operation that renders it intelligible (distinguished in German by *Geschichte* and *Historie*) is a weakness of the language that has often been remarked; still, it delivers a profound truth: the process that is carrying us forward and our representation of that process are of the same kind. If we were able to live within memory, we would not have needed to consecrate *lieux de mémoire* in its name. Each gesture, down to the most everyday, would be experienced as the ritual repetition of a timeless practice in a primordial identification of act and meaning. With the appearance of the trace, of mediation, of distance, we are not in the realm of true memory but of history. We can think, for an example, of the Jews of the diaspora, bound in daily devotion to the rituals of tradition, who as "peoples of memory" found little use for historians until their forced exposure to the modern world.

Memory and history, far from being synonymous, appear now to be in fundamental opposition. Memory is life, borne by living societies founded in its name. It remains in permanent evolution, open to the dialectic of remembering and forgetting, unconscious of its successive deformations, vulnerable to manipulation and appropriation, susceptible to being long dormant and periodically revived. History, on the other hand, is the reconstruction, always problematic and incomplete, of what is no longer. Memory is a perpetually actual phenomenon, a bond tying us to the eternal present; history is a representation of the past. Memory, insofar as it is affective and magical, only accommodates those facts that suit it; it nourishes recollections that may be out of focus or telescopic, global or detached, particular or symbolic—responsive to each avenue of conveyance or phenomenal screen, to every censorship or projection. History, because it is an intellectual and secular production, calls for analysis and criticism. Memory installs remembrance within the sacred; history, always prosaic, releases it again. Memory is blind to all but the group it binds—which is to say, as Maurice Halbwachs has said, that there are as many memories as there are groups, that memory is by nature multiple and yet specific; collective, plural, and yet individual. History, on the other hand, belongs to everyone and to no one, whence its claim to universal authority. Memory takes root in the concrete, in spaces, gestures, images, and objects; history binds itself strictly to temporal continuities, to progressions and to relations between things. Memory is absolute, while history can only conceive the relative.

At the heart of history is a critical discourse that is antithetical to spontaneous memory. History is perpetually suspicious of memory, and its true mission is to suppress and destroy it. At the horizon of historical societies, at the limits of the completely historicized world, there would occur a permanent secularization. History's goal and ambition is not to exalt but to annihilate what has in reality taken place. A generalized critical history would no doubt preserve some museums, some medallions and monuments—that is to say, the materials necessary for its work—but it would empty them of what, to us, would make them *lieux de mémoire.* In the end, a society living wholly under the sign of history could not, any more than could a traditional society, conceive such sites for anchoring its memory.

It once seemed as though a tradition of memory, through the concepts of history and the nation, had crystallized in the synthesis of the Third Republic. Adopting a broad chronology, between Augustin Thierry's *Lettres sur l'histoire de France* (1827) and Charles Seignobos's *Histoire sincère de la nation française* (1933), the relationships between history, memory, and the nation were characterized as more than natural currency: they were shown to involve a reciprocal circularity, a symbiosis at every level—scientific and pedagogical, theoretical and practical. This national definition of the present imperiously demanded justification through the illumination of the past. It was, however, a present that had been weakened by revolutionary trauma and the call for a general reevaluation of the monarchic past, and it was weakened further by the defeat of 1870, which rendered only more urgent, in the belated competition with German science and pedagogy—the real victors at Sadowa—the development of a severe documentary erudition for the scholarly transmission of memory. The tone of national responsibility assigned to the historian—half preacher, half soldier—is unequaled, for example, in the first editorial of the *Revue historique* (1876) in which Gabriel Monod foresaw a "slow scientific, methodical, and collective investigation" conducted in a "secret and secure manner for the greatness of the fatherland as well as for mankind." Reading this text, and a hundred others like it, one wonders how the notion that positivist history was not cumulative could ever have gained credibility. On the contrary, in the teleological perspective of the nation the political, the military, the biographical, and the diplomatic all were to be considered pillars of continuity. The defeat of Agincourt, the dagger of Ravaillac, the day of the Dupes, the additional clauses of the treaty of Westphalia—each required scrupulous accounting. The most incisive erudition thus served to add or take away some detail from the monumental edifice that was the nation. The nation's memory was held to be powerfully unified; no more discontinuity existed between our Greco-Roman cradle and the colonies of the Third Republic than between the high erudition that annexed new territories to the nation's heritage and the schoolbooks that professed its dogma. The holy nation thus acquired a holy history;

through the nation our memory continued to rest upon a sacred foundation.

To see how this particular synthesis came apart under the pressure of a new secularizing force would be to show how, during the crisis of the 1930s in France, the coupling of state and nation was gradually replaced by the coupling of state and society—and how, at the same time and for the same reasons, history was transformed, spectacularly, from the tradition of memory it had become into the self-knowledge of society. As such, history was able to highlight many kinds of memory, even turn itself into a laboratory of past mentalities; but in disclaiming its national identity, it also abandoned its claim to bearing coherent meaning and consequently lost its pedagogical authority to transmit values. The definition of the nation was no longer the issue, and peace, prosperity, and the reduction of its power have since accomplished the rest. With the advent of society in place of the nation, legitimation by the past and therefore by history yields to legitimation by the future. One can only acknowledge and venerate the past and serve the nation; the future, however, can be prepared for: thus the three terms regain their autonomy. No longer a cause, the nation has become a given; history is now a social science, memory a purely private phenomenon. The memory-nation was thus the last incarnation of the unification of memory and history.

The study of *lieux de mémoires,* then, lies at the intersection of two developments that in France today give it meaning: one a purely historiographical movement, the reflexive turning of history upon itself, the other a movement that is, properly speaking, historical: the end of a tradition of memory. The moment of *lieux de mémoire* occurs at the same time that an immense and intimate fund of memory disappears, surviving only as a reconstituted object beneath the gaze of critical history. This period sees, on the one hand, the decisive deepening of historical study and, on the other, a heritage consolidated. The critical principle follows an internal dynamic: our intellectual, political, historical frameworks are exhausted but remain powerful enough not to leave us indifferent; whatever vitality they retain impresses us only in their most spectacular symbols. Combined, these two movements send us at once to history's most elementary tools and to the most symbolic objects of our memory: to the archives as well as to the tricolor; to the libraries, dictionaries, and museums as well as to commemorations, celebrations, the Pantheon, and the Arc de Triomphe; to the *Dictionnaire Larousse* as well as to the Wall of the Fédérés, where the last defenders of the Paris Commune were massacred in 1870.

These *lieux de mémoire* are fundamentally remains, the ultimate embodiments of a memorial consciousness that has barely survived in a historical age that calls out for memory because it has abandoned it. They make their appearance by virtue of the deritualization of our world—producing, manifesting, establishing, constructing, decreeing, and maintaining by artifice and by will a society deeply absorbed in its own transformation and renewal, one that inherently values the new over the ancient, the young over the old, the future over the past. Museums, archives, cemeteries, festivals, anniversaries, treaties, depositions, monuments, sanctuaries, fraternal orders—these are the boundary stones of another age, illusions of eternity. It is the nostalgic dimension of these devotional institutions that makes them seem beleaguered and cold—they mark the rituals of a society without ritual; integral particularities in a society that levels particularity; signs of distinction and of group membership in a society that tends to recognize individuals only as identical and equal.

Memory Seized by History

Modern memory is, above all, archival. It relies entirely on the materiality of the trace, the immediacy of the recording, the visibility of the image. What began as writing ends as high fidelity and tape recording. The less memory is experienced from the inside the more it exists only through its exterior scaffolding and outward signs—hence the obsession with the archive that marks our age, attempting at once the complete conservation of the present as well as the total preservation of the past. Fear of a rapid and final disappearance combines with anxiety about the meaning of the present and uncertainty about the future to give even the most humble testimony, the most modest vestige, the potential dignity of the memorable. Have we not sufficiently regretted and deplored the loss or destruction, by our predecessors, of potentially informative sources to avoid opening ourselves to the same reproach from our successors? Memory has been wholly absorbed by its meticulous reconstitution. Its new vocation is to record; delegating to the archive the responsibility of remembering, it sheds its signs upon depositing them there, as a snake sheds its skin.

What we call memory is in fact the gigantic and breathtaking storehouse of a material stock of what it would be impossible for us to remember, an unlimited repertoire of what might need to be recalled. Leibnitz's "paper memory" has become an autonomous institution of museums, libraries, depositories, centers of documentation, and data bases. Specialists estimate that in the public archives alone, in just a few decades, the quantitative revolution has multiplied the number of records by one thousand. No society has ever produced archives as deliberately as our own, not only by volume, not only by new technical means of reproduction and preservation, but also by its superstitious esteem, by its veneration of the trace. Even as traditional memory disappears, we feel obliged assiduously to collect remains, testimonies, documents, images, speeches, any visible signs of what has been, as if this burgeoning dossier were to be called upon to furnish some proof to who knows what tribunal of history. The sacred is invested in the trace that is at the same time its negation. It becomes impossible to predict what should be remembered—whence the disinclination to destroy anything that leads to the corresponding reinforcement of all the institutions of memory. A strange role reversal has occurred between the professional, once reproached for an obsession with conservation, and the amateur producer of archives. Today, private enterprise and public administration keep everything, while professional archivists have learned that the essence of their trade is the art of controlled destruction.

In just a few years, then, the materialization of memory has been tremendously dilated, multiplied, decentralized, democratized. In the classical period, the three main producers of archives were the great families, the church, and the state. Yet who today does not feel compelled to record his feelings, to write his memoirs—not only the most minor historical actor but also his witnesses, his spouse, and his doctor. The less extraordinary the testimony, the more aptly it seems to illustrate the average mentality.

The imperative of our epoch is not only to keep everything, to preserve every indicator of memory—even when we are not sure which memory is being indicated—but also to produce archives. The French Social Security archives are a troubling example: an unparalleled quantity of documents, they represent today three hundred linear kilometers. Ideally, the computerized evaluation of this mass of raw memory would provide a reading of the sum total of the normal and the pathological in society, from diets to lifestyles, by region and by profession; yet even its preservation and plausible implementation call for drastic and impossible choices. Record as much as you can, something will remain. This is, to take another telling example, the conclusion implied by the proliferation of oral histories. There are currently in France more than three hundred teams employed in gathering "the voices that come to us from the past" (Philippe Joutard). Yet these are not ordinary archives, if we consider that to produce them requires thirty-six hours for each hour of recording time and that they can never be used piecemeal, because they only have meaning when heard in their entirety. Whose will to remember do they ultimately reflect, that of the interviewer or that of the interviewed? No longer living memory's more or less intended remainder, the archive has become the deliberate and calculated secretion of lost memory. It adds to life—itself often a function of its own recording—a secondary memory, a prosthesis-memory. The indiscriminate production of archives is the acute effect of a new consciousness, the clearest expression of the terrorism of historicized memory.

This form of memory comes to us from the outside; because it is no longer a social practice, we interiorize it as an individual constraint.

The passage from memory to history has required every social group to redefine its identity through the revitalization of its own history. The task of remembering makes everyone his own historian. The demand for history has thus largely overflowed the circle of professional historians. Those who have long been marginalized in traditional history are not the only ones haunted by the need to recover their buried pasts. Following the example of ethnic groups and social minorities, every established group, intellectual or not, learned or not, has felt the need to go in search of its own origins and identity. Indeed, there is hardly a family today in which some member has not recently sought to document as accurately as possible his or her ancestors' furtive existences. The increase in genealogical research is a massive new phenomenon: the national archives reports that 43 percent of those doing archival research in 1982 were working on genealogical history, as compared with the 38 percent who were university researchers. It is striking that we owe the most significant histories of biology, physics, medicine, and music not to professional historians but to biologists, physicists, doctors, and musicians. Educators themselves have taken charge of the history of education, from physical education to instruction in educational philosophy. In the wake of attacks on established domains of knowledge, each discipline has sought validation in the retrospective perusal of its own origins. Sociology goes in search of its founding fathers; anthropology undertakes to explore its own past, from the sixteenth-century chroniclers to the colonial administrators. Even literary criticism occupies itself in retracing the genesis of its categories and tradition. As for history, positivism, long since abandoned by professional historians, has found in this urgent need a popularity and necessity it never knew before. The decomposition of memory-history has multiplied the number of private memories demanding their individual histories.

Les Lieux de Mémoire: ANOTHER HISTORY

Lieux de mémoire are simple and ambiguous, natural and artificial, at once immediately available in concrete sensual experience and susceptible to the most abstract elaboration. Indeed, they are *lieux* in three senses of the word—material, symbolic, and functional. Even an apparently purely material site, like an archive, becomes a *lieu de mémoire* only if the imagination invests it with a symbolic aura. A purely functional site, like a classroom manual, a testament, or a veterans' reunion belongs to the category only inasmuch as it is also the object of a ritual. And the observance of a commemorative minute of silence, an extreme example of a strictly symbolic action, serves as a concentrated appeal to memory by literally breaking a temporal continuity. Moreover, the three aspects always coexist. Take, for example, the notion of a historical generation: it is material by its demographic content and supposedly functional— since memories are crystallized and transmitted from one generation to the next—but it is also symbolic, since it characterizes, by referring to events or experiences shared by a small minority, a larger group that may not have participated in them.

Lieux de mémoire are created by a play of memory and history, an interaction of two factors that results in their reciprocal overdetermination. To begin with, there must be a will to remember. If we were to abandon this criterion, we would quickly drift into admitting virtually everything as worthy of remembrance. One is reminded of the prudent rules of old-fashioned historical criticism, which distinguished between "direct sources," intentionally produced by society with a view to their future reproduction—a law or a work of art, for example—and the indiscriminate mass of "indirect sources," comprising all the testimony an epoch inadvertently leaves to historians. Without the intention to remember, *lieux de mémoire* would be indistinguishable from *lieux d'histoire*.

On the other hand, it is clear that without the intervention of history, time, and change, we would content ourselves with simply a schematic outline of the objects of memory. The *lieux* we speak of, then, are mixed, hybrid, mutant, bound intimately with life and death, with time and eternity; enveloped in a Möbius strip of the collective and the individual, the sacred and the profane, the immutable and the mobile. For if we accept that the most fundamental purpose of the *lieu de mémoire* is to stop time, to block the work of forgetting, to establish a state of things, to immortalize death, to materialize the immaterial—just as if gold were the only memory of money—all of this in order to capture a maximum of meaning in the fewest of signs, it is also clear that *lieux de mémoire* only exist because of their capacity for metamorphosis, an endless recycling of their meaning and an unpredictable proliferation of their ramifications.

Let us take two very different examples. First, the Revolutionary calendar, which was very much a *lieu de mémoire* since, as a calendar, it was designed to provide the a priori frame of reference for all possible memory while, as a revolutionary document, through its nomenclature and symbolism, it was supposed to "open a new book to history," as its principal author ambitiously put it, or to "return Frenchmen entirely to themselves," according to another of its advocates. The function of the calendar, it was thought, would be to halt history at the hour of the Revolution by indexing future months, days, centuries, and years to the Revolutionary epic. Yet to our eyes, what further qualifies the revolutionary calendar as a *lieu de mémoire* is its apparently inevitable failure to have become what its founders hoped. If we still lived today according to its rhythm, it would have become as familiar to us as the Gregorian calendar and would, consequently, have lost its interest as a *lieu de mémoire*. It would have melted into our memorial landscape, serving only to date every other conceivable memorial site. As it turns out, its failure has not been complete; key dates still emerge from it to which it will always remain attached: Vendémiaire, Thermidor, Brumaire. Just so, the *lieu de mémoire* turns in on itself—an arabesque in the deforming mirror that is its truth.

Let us consider too the celebrated *Tour de la France par deux enfants*, also incontestably a *lieu de mémoire;* like the *Petit Lavisse,* it trained the memory of millions of French boys and girls. Thanks to it, the Minister of Public Instruction could draw his pocket watch at 8:05 A.M. and declare, "All of our children are crossing the Alps." Moreover, the *Tour* was an inventory of what one ought to know about France, an exercise in identification and a voyage of initiation. Yet here things get more complicated: a close reading shows that as of its publication in 1877, the *Tour* portrayed a France that no longer existed, and that in this year, when May 16 saw the consolidation of the Third Republic, it drew its seductive power from a subtle enchantment with the past. As is so often the case with books for children, the *Tour* owed its initial success to the memory of adults. And later? Thirty-five years after publication, on the eve of the war of 1914 when it was still a sovereign text, it seemed already a nostalgic institution: despite revisions, the older edition sold more than the new. Then the *Tour* became rare, employed only in marginal areas in the remote countryside. Slipping out of collective memory, it entered historical memory, then pedagogical memory. For its centennial, in 1977, however, just as the sales of an autobiography from the provinces, Pierre Hélias's *Le Cheval d'orgueil,* reached a million copies and when an industrial France stricken by economic crisis discovered its oral memory and peasant roots, the *Tour* was reprinted, and once again entered the collective memory, a different one this time, but still subject to being forgotten and revived in the future. What is the essence of this quintessential *lieu de mémoire*—its original intention or its return in the cycles of memory? Clearly both: all *lieux de mémoire* are objects *mises en abîme.*

It is this principle of double identity that enables us to map, within the indefinite multiplicity of sites, a hierarchy, a set of limits, a repertoire of ranges. This principle is crucial because, if one keeps in mind the broad categories of the genre—anything pertaining to the cult of the dead, anything relating to the patrimony, anything administering the presence of the past within the present—it is clear that some seemingly improbable objects can be legitimately considered *lieux de mémoire* while, conversely, many that seem to fit by definition should in fact be excluded. What makes certain prehistoric, geographical, archaeological locations important as sites is often precisely what ought to exclude them from being *lieux de mémoire:* the absolute absence of a will to remember and, by way of compensation, the crushing weight imposed on them by time, science, and the dreams of men. On the other hand, not every border marking has the credentials of the Rhine or the Finistère, that "Land's End" at the tip of Brittany ennobled in the pages of Les Michelet. Every constitution, every diplomatic treaty is a *lieu de mémoire,* although the Constitution of 1793 lays a different claim than that of 1791, given the foundational status of the Declaration of the Rights of Man; and the peace of Nimwegen has a different status than, at both ends of the history of Europe, the Verdun compromise and the Yalta conference.

Amid these complexities, it is memory that dictates while history writes; this is why both history books and historical events merit special attention. As memory's ideal historical instruments, rather than as permutations of history and memory, they inscribe a neat border around a domain of memory. Are not every great historical work and the historical genre itself, every great event and the notion of event itself, in some sense by definition *lieux de mémoire?*

One simple but decisive trait of *lieux de mémoire* sets them apart from every type of history to which we have become accustomed, ancient or modern. Every previous historical or scientific approach to memory, whether national or social, has concerned itself with *realia,* with things in themselves and in their immediate reality. Contrary to historical objects, however, *lieux de mémoire* have no referent in reality; or, rather, they are their own referent: pure, exclusively self-referential signs. This is not to say that they are without content, physical presence, or history; it is to suggest that what makes them *lieux de mémoire* is precisely that by which they escape from history. In this sense, the *lieu de mémoire* is double: a site of excess closed upon itself, concentrated in its own name, but also forever open to the full range of its possible significations.

This is what makes the history of *lieux de mémoire* at once banal and extraordinary. Obvious topics, classic material, sources ready at hand, the least sophisticated methods: one would think we were returning to long outmoded historical methods. But such is not the case. Although these objects must be grasped in empirical detail, the issues at stake are ill suited to expression in the categories of traditional historiography.

Reflecting on *lieux de mémoire* transforms historical criticism into critical history—and not only in its methods; it allows history a secondary, purely transferential existence, even a kind of reawakening. Like war, the history of *lieux de mémoire* is an art of implementation, practiced in the fragile happiness derived from relating to rehabilitated objects and from the involvement of the historian in his or her subject. It is a history that, in the last analysis rests upon what it mobilizes: an impalpable, barely expressible, self-imposed bond; what remains of our ineradicable, carnal attachment to these faded symbols; the reincarnation of history as it was practiced by Michelet, irresistibly putting to mind the recovery from lost love of which Proust spoke so well—that moment when the obsessive grasp of passion finally loosens but whose true sadness is no longer to suffer from what one has so long suffered, henceforth to understand only with the mind's reason, no longer with the unreason of the heart.

This is a very literary reference. Should we regret it or, on the contrary, suggest its full justification? Once again, the answer derives from our present historical situation. In fact, memory has never known more than two forms of legitimacy—historical and literary. These have run parallel to each other but until now always separately. At present the boundary between the two is blurring; following closely upon the successive deaths of memory-history and memory-fiction, a new kind of history has been born, which owes its prestige and legitimacy to the new relation it maintains to the past. History has become our replaceable imagination—hence the last stand of faltering fiction in the renaissance of the historical novel, the vogue for personalized documents, the literary revitalization of historical drama, the success of the oral historical tale. Our interest in these *lieux de mémoire* that anchor, condense, and express the exhausted capital of our collective memory derives from this new sensibility. History has become the deep reference of a period that has been wrenched from its depths, a realistic novel in a period in which there are no real novels. Memory has been promoted to the center of history: such is the spectacular bereavement of literature.

TRANSLATED BY MARC ROUDEBUSH

NOTE

This text constitutes the theoretical introduction to a vast collaborative work on the national memory of France that I titled *Les Lieux de mémoire*. The work is divided into three parts: *La République* (1 vol., 1984), *La Nation* (3 vols., 1986), *Les France* (3 vols., forthcoming).

My intention was to substitute case studies for general historical developments. Thus, the method used consists of a concentrated analysis of the specific objects that codify, condense, anchor France's national memory. These can be monuments (the *château* of Versailles or the cathedral of Strasbourg); emblems, commemorations, and symbols (the tricolor of the French flag, the Fourteenth of July, the Marseillaise); rituals (the coronation of the kings at Reims) as well as monuments (such as the *monuments aux morts* in every French village or the Pantheon); manuals (a textbook used by all French children, a dictionary); basic texts (the Declaration of the Rights of Man or the *Code civil*); or mottos (for example, "Liberté, Egalité, Fraternité").

Each subject was given to a specialist. In order to show how the subjects, to all appearances diverse, could be brought together under the same category of analysis and interpretation, I used a term, *lieux de mémoire,* which did not exist in French. The entire work consists in the elaboration of this idea, its classification, hierarchy, and typology.

The term has no English equivalent. It owes its origin to the admirable book by Frances Yates, *The Art of Memory* (1966), which traces a long tradition of mnemotechnia. As codified by Cicero and Quintilian, the classical art of memory taught orators to remember their speeches by associating each topic to be covered with some part of a real or imagined building in which the oration was to be delivered—the atrium, columns, furniture, and so on. The art of memory was founded on an inventory of memory places, *loci memoriae.* The term *lieu de mémoire* has profound connotations in French: historical, intellectual, and emotional, often subconscious. These are due, on the one hand, to the specific role of memory in the construction of the idea of the nation as well as in recent changes in the attitude of the French people to their national past. It is this role the work in question attempts to shed light on; it is this change in attitude it attempts to illustrate; and it is precisely the term *lieu de mémoire* that this introduction attempts to explain, elaborate, and justify.

I therefore thank *Representations* and my excellent translator for conserving the term in French, while occasionally using *site* as an English equivalent.

HENRY ROUSSO

The Vichy Syndrome: History and Memory Since 1944

1987

*The title of Rousso's work is very significant: memories of Vichy—
the four years of occupation, collaboration, and defeat in France,
1940–1944—are like symptoms of a trauma that cannot be entirely
assimilated. The evolution of memories of Vichy provides a remarkable test case for the study of the relationship between history and
memory. The author's use of vaguely psychoanalytic categories (syndrome, neurosis, resistance, the return of the repressed) stands in stark
contrast to most historical practice in France, which, despite the attention to* mentalités *and the interests of some historians such as
Michel de Certeau, remained indifferent to the development of psychological categories of analysis. This is all the more surprising in
that psychoanalysis as a therapeutic practice and theoretical domain
is probably more influential in French social and intellectual life
than anywhere else in the world.*

THE FIELD OF MEMORY

For some years now, historians have been taking an increasing interest
in "phenomena of memory." At first glance, it would seem that history
and memory are two clearly different ways of looking at the past. The
difference has frequently been analyzed, most recently by Pierre Nora.[1]
Memory is a living phenomenon, something in perpetual evolution,
whereas history—as understood by historians—is a scholarly and theoretical reconstruction and as such is more apt to give rise to a substantial,
durable body of knowledge. Memory is plural, moreover, in that distinct
memories are generated by different social groups, political parties,
churches, communities, language groups, and so on. Thus "collective

From *The Vichy Syndrome: History and Memory Since 1944*, trans. Arthur Goldhammer (Cambridge, Mass.: Harvard University Press, 1991). First published as *Le Syndrome de Vichy de 1944 à nos jours* (2d ed., Paris: Gallimard, 1990).

memory" might seem to be a figment of the imagination, or at any rate little more than a misleading composite of disparate and heterogeneous memories. By contrast, history has a more universal, if not more ecumenical, purpose. For all that history may be controversial, it remains a fundamental instrument for the education of citizens. Memory at times lives on in a religious or sacred key; history is critical and secular. Memory is subject to repression, whereas nothing lies in principle outside the historian's territory.

Yet the distinction between history and memory is a characteristic trait of the twentieth century, first identified as such by Maurice Halbwachs, a disciple of Henri Bergson, and exemplified by the evolution of contemporary historiography, whose goal is no longer legitimation but the advancement of knowledge. In the nineteenth century, the difference was all but nonexistent, particularly in France. The function of history then, of what Nora has called "history as memory," was essentially to legitimate the nascent Third Republic and to forge a national feeling. Today, no such confusion is possible: the disintegration of rural society and of the ancestral traditions it embodied, the proliferation of sources of information and, concomitantly, new approaches to social reality, the weakening of nationalist sentiment in Western Europe since World War II, and the depth of internal divisions including those born of Vichy—all these have caused history and memory to evolve in different directions:

> Once society had supplanted the nation, legitimation via the past, hence via history, gave way to legitimation via the future. The past was something one could only study and venerate, and the nation something one could only serve, but the future is something for which the groundwork has to be laid. Thus, the three terms—nation, history, memory—regained their autonomy: the nation ceased to be a cause and became a given; history became a social science; and memory became a purely private phenomenon. The memory-nation was thus the last incarnation of memory-history."[2]

Thus, a new field of study has been opened up for historians—the history of memory, that is, the study of the evolution of various social practices and, more specifically, of the form and content of social practices whose purpose or effect is the representation of the past and the perpetuation of its memory within a particular group or the society as a whole.

This history is rooted in what Nora and his colleagues have called *lieux de mémoire,* or mnemonic sites, embodying concrete traces of the past, visible and durable signs of its celebration. The history of memory can arise out of the memory of a particular group: the Camisards, for example, as studied by Philippe Joutard,[3] or combat veterans, as studied by Antoine Prost.[4] But it may also be associated with certain key events, whose memory survives long after the last flames have been extinguished and whose influence extends over the whole of society: examples include the French Revolution, of course,[5] the wars in the Vendée that grew out of it and have attracted renewed attention,[6] and World War II.[7] Historians are interested not only in ascertaining the facts about such events but also in comprehending their persistence.

It is no accident that these events were all associated with times of deep crisis for France's national unity and identity. These are the times that have left the most lasting, most controversial, and most vivid memories—all the more so in that each new crisis has fed upon its predecessors: the Dreyfus Affair on the French Revolution, Vichy on the Dreyfus Affair, the Algerian war on Vichy, and so on. Memories of the past have themselves become components of the crisis, albeit at times of secondary importance.[8]

An "event-oriented" approach is useful in that it allows giving due weight to the tensions involved in any would-be collective representation of the past. Such tensions arise, first of all, among rival social groups, each jealous of its own reconstruction. An ex-POW will not share the same memories as a former partisan or a person deported to a concentration camp. There may also be tensions between such group memories and what might be called the "dominant memory," that is, a collective interpretation of the past that may even come to have official status; here, for example, I am thinking of Gaullist or communist memory. There may also be tension between, on the one hand, the "voluntarist" memory that builds monuments, decorates graves, and buries heroes and, on the other hand, latent or implicit memory, subject to repression and therefore to slips, lapses, or silences—manifestations of the return of the repressed. For study reveals that, even at the social level, memory is a structuring of forgetfulness.

These same tensions also exist in the writing of history. Whether professional or amateur, the historian is always a product of his own time and place. He stands at a crossroads in the byways of collective memory: on the one hand he, like any other citizen, is influenced by the dominant memory, which may subconsciously suggest interpretations and areas of research; on the other hand, he himself is a "vector of memory" and a carrier of fundamental importance, in that the vision he proposes of the past may, after some delay, exert an influence on contemporary representations.

As a result, the history of Revolution, Vichy, or the Algerian war cannot really be called universal. Now that history no longer has the purpose of forging a national identity, it has no therapeutic value, and in the short term, at least, it often has the effect of perpetuating old divisions, as a glance at the controversial nature of the so-called *guerre franco-*

française, or Franco-French internal war, will show. And of those wars none has been more divisive than the war over Vichy.

WHY VICHY?

Rather like the unconscious in Freudian theory, what is known as collective memory exists first of all in its *manifestations,* in the various ways by which it reveals its presence. The Vichy syndrome consists of a diverse set of symptoms whereby the trauma of the Occupation, and particularly that trauma resulting from internal divisions within France, reveals itself in political, social, and cultural life. Since the end of the war, moreover, that trauma has been perpetuated and at times exacerbated.

A chronological ordering of these symptoms brings into focus a four-stage process of evolution. Between 1944 and 1954, France had to deal directly with the aftermath of civil war, purge, and amnesty. I call this the "mourning phase," whose contradictions had a considerable impact on what came afterward. From 1954 to 1971, the subject of Vichy became less controversial, except for occasional eruptions in the period 1958–62. The French apparently had repressed memories of the civil war with the aid of what came to be a dominant myth: "resistancialism." This term, first coined after the Liberation by adversaries of the purge, is used here in a rather different sense. By resistancialism I mean, first, a process that sought to minimize the importance of the Vichy regime and its impact on French society, *including its most negative aspects;* second, the construction of an object of memory, the "Resistance," whose significance transcended by far the sum of its active parts (the small groups of guerrilla partisans who did the actual fighting) and whose existence was embodied chiefly in certain sites and groups, such as the Gaullists and communists, associated with fully elaborated ideologies; and, third, the identification of this "Resistance" with the nation as a whole, a characteristic feature of the Gaullist version of the myth.

Between 1971 and 1974, this carefully constructed myth was shattered; the mirror was broken. This was the third phase of the process, which is analyzed here as a "return of the repressed." In turn, this inaugurated a fourth phase, continuing to this day: a phase of obsession, characterized, on the one hand, by the reawakening of Jewish memory and, on the other, by the importance that reminiscences of the Occupation assumed in French political debate.

The first part of this book thus attempts to trace the contours of a "neurosis." What is borrowed from psychoanalysis is simply a metaphor, not an explanatory schema. No attempt is made to sort out different types of symptoms: an offhand remark by a French president is treated on the same level as the scandal triggered by a film or a notorious political trial. At this stage of the argument, all that matters is the patent topicality of a reference to the past, however insignificant it may be in itself.

In the second part, however, I attempt to establish a hierarchy of symptoms by investigating the vectors of the past, particularly those that played a decisive role in the history of the syndrome: commemorations, film, and historiography (including both historical research and teaching). I consider commemorations because of their apparent failure to construct an official memory of the past; film because visual images seem to have had a decisive impact on the formation of a common, if not a collective, memory; and historiography because historians and their books are a primary vector of memory.

Finally, after analyzing the vectors of memory and studying the formulation of the signs used to represent the past (or reveal its existence), I turn my attention to the recipients, to what might be called "diffuse memory" as opposed to the organized memory of groups and political parties and of scholarly re-creation. This is, indeed, the ultimate winner in the contest among representations because it cannot by itself formulate a coherent and operational vision of the past that is anything other than individual. The question here is: Were French people of various ages and outlooks influenced by the representations offered to them?

Based on the idea that the past survives in an active form in the present and on the assumption that such survival can be studied historically, this book is intended to be open-ended. So I make no claim to have said the last word on the subject. And one final remark: I have tried within the limits of my power not to become a prisoner of the syndrome I am describing.

TRANSLATED BY ARTHUR GOLDHAMMER

NOTES

[1] Pierre Nora, ed., *Les Lieux de mémoire,* vol. 1: *La République*; vol. 2: *La Nation* (Paris: Gallimard, 1984 and 1986).

[2] Ibid., vol. 1, p. xxv.

[3] Philippe Joutard, *La Légende des Camisards: Une Sensibilité au passé* (Paris: Gallimard, 1977).

[4] Antoine Prost, *Les Anciens combattants et la société française, 1914–1939* (Paris: Presses de la Fondation Nationale des Sciences Politiques, 1977).

[5] See, for example, Mona Ozouf, "Peut-on commémorer la Révolution française?" and François Furet, "La Révolution dans l'imaginaire politique français," *Le Débat* 26 (Sept. 1983); cf. Maurice Agulhon, "Faut-il avoir peur de 1789?" *Le Débat* 30 (May 1984).

[6] There was much debate surrounding Reynald Secher's *Le Génocide franco-français: la Vendée-Vengé* (Paris: P.U.F., 1986). See also Jean-Clément Martin, *La Vendée et la France* (Paris: Seuil, 1987), and *La Vendée de la mémoire, 1800–1980* (Paris: Seuil, 1989).

[7] See Alfred Wahl, ed., *Mémoire de la seconde guerre mondiale,* proceedings of a Metz colloquium, October 6–8, 1983 (Metz: Centre de Recherche Histoire et Civilisation de l'Université, 1984), and Institut d'Histoire du Temps Présent, *La Mémoire des français: Quarante ans de commémoration de la seconde guerre mondiale* (Paris: CNRS, 1986).

[8] Related issues are explored in "Les Guerres franco-françaises," *Vingtième siècle: Revue d'histoire* 5 (1985). For a comparison of crises, see Michel Winock, *La Fièvre hexagonale, les grandes crises politiques de 1871 à 1968* (Paris: Calmann-Lévy, 1986).

Bibliography

For the convenience of the reader, we have divided the bibliography into three major categories: general trends in French intellectual life in the twentieth century; the French historical "schools" and their development, including the *Annales;* and general issues in historical scholarship that have some bearing on the evolution of French historical writing. This bibliography is suggestive rather than exhaustive, and it includes some foreign-language works for the benefit of those who wish to pursue the issues further.

I. FRENCH INTELLECTUAL LIFE IN THE TWENTIETH CENTURY: GENERAL TRENDS

"A Propos de Durkheim," *Revue française de sociologie* 17.2, special issue (1976).

BESNARD, PHILIPPE, ed., *The Sociological Domain: The Durkheimians and the Founding of French Sociology* (Cambridge, Eng.: Cambridge University Press, and Paris: Maison des Sciences de l'Homme, 1983).

BOURDIEU, PIERRE, *Homo academicus* (Paris: Minuit, 1984). [English translation: *Homo academicus,* trans. Peter Collier (Stanford, Calif.: Stanford University Press, 1988)]

CLARK, TERRY N., *Prophets and Patrons: The French University and the Emergence of the Social Sciences* (Cambridge, Mass.: Harvard University Press, 1973).

DESCOMBES, VINCENT, *Le Même et l'autre: Quarante-cinq ans de philosophie contemporaine, 1933–1978* (Paris: Minuit, 1979). [English translation: *Modern French Philosophy,* trans. L. Scott-Fox and J. M. Harding (Cambridge, Eng.: Cambridge University Press, 1980)]

DESCOMBES, VINCENT, *Philosophie par gros temps* (Paris: Minuit, 1989). [English translation: *The Barometer of Modern Reason: On the Philosophies of Current Events,* trans. Stephen Adam Schwartz (New York: Oxford University Press, 1993)]

DIGEON, CLAUDE, *La Crise allemande de la pensée française (1870–1914)* (Paris: P.U.F., 1959).

———, "Les Durkheimiens," *Revue française de sociologie* 20.1, special issue (1979).

GARGANI, ALDO, ed., *Crisi della ragiona: Nuovi modelli nel rapporto tra sapere e attività umane* (Turin: Einaudi, 1979).

GUILLAUME, MARC, *L'Etat des sciences sociales en France* (Paris: Découverte, 1986).

HUGHES, H. STUART, *The Obstructed Path: French Social Thought in the Years of Desperation, 1930–1960* (New York: Harper, 1968).

———, *Les Idées en France, 1945–1948: une chronologie* (Paris: Gallimard, 1989).

KARADY, VICTOR, "Durkheim, les sciences sociales et l'université: Bilan d'un semi-échec," *Revue française de sociologie* 17.2 (1976), pp. 267–311.

KARADY, VICTOR, "Naissance de l'ethnologie universitaire," *L'Arc* 48: special issue on Marcel Mauss (1972), pp. 33–40.

LEFORT, ISABELLE, *Géographie savante—géographie scolaire (1870–1970): Éléments pour une histoire de la pensée géographique,* thèse de doctorat, University of Paris, First Section, 1989–90.

LEPENIES, WOLF, *Les Trois cultures: Entre science et littérature, l'avènement de la sociologie* (Paris: Editions de la Maison des Sciences de l'Homme, 1990). [English translation: *Between Literature and Science: The Rise of Sociology,* trans. R. J. Hollingdale (Cambridge, Eng.: Cambridge University Press, 1988)]

LÉVY-BRUHL, LUCIEN, *La Mentalité primitive* (Paris, 1922). [English translation: *Primitive Mentality,* trans. Lilian A. Clare (New York: Macmillan, 1923)]

———, *Les Fonctions mentales dans les sociétés inférieures* (Paris, 1910). [English translation: *How Natives Think,* trans. Lilian A. Clare (New York: Alfred A. Knopf, 1925)]

LINDENBERG, DANIEL, *Le Marxisme introuvable* (Paris: Calmann-Lévy, 1975).

MONGIN, OLIVIER, *Face au scepticisme: Les mutations du paysage intellectuel, ou l'invention de l'intellectual démocratique* (Paris: Découverte, 1994).

ORY, PASCAL, AND JEAN-FRANÇOIS SIRINELLI, *Les Intellectuels en France, de l'Affaire Dreyfus à nos jours* (Paris: Armand Colin, 1986; 2nd ed., 1992).

PAUL, HARRY W., *The Sorcerer's Apprentice: The French Scientist's Image of German Science, 1840–1919* (Gainsville: University of Florida Press, 1972).

PROST, ANTOINE, *L'Enseignement en France, 1800–1967* (Paris: Armand Colin, 1968).

RIEFFEL, RÉMY, *Le Tribu des clercs: Les intellectuels sous la Ve république, 1958–1990* (Paris: Calmann-Lévy, 1993).

RINGER, FRITZ R., *Education and Society in Modern Europe* (Bloomington: Indiana University Press, 1978).

———, *Fields of Knowledge: French Academic Culture in Comparative Perspective, 1890–1920* (Cambridge Eng.: Cambridge University Press, and Paris: Editions de la Maison des Sciences de l'Homme, 1992).

SIRINELLI, JEAN-FRANÇOIS, ed., *Histoire des droites en France,* vol 2: *Cultures* (Paris: Gallimard, 1992).

VERDÈS-LEROUX, JEANNINE, *Le Reveil des somnambules: Le parti communiste, les intellectuels et la culture, 1956–1985* (Paris: Fayard/Minuit, 1987).

VERDÈS-LEROUX, JEANNINE, *Au Service du parti: Le parti communiste, les intellectuels et la culture, 1944–56* (Paris: Fayard/Minuit, 1983).

WEISZ, GEORGE, *The Emergence of Modern Universities in France, 1863–1914* (Princeton, N.J.: Princeton University Press, 1983).

II. FRENCH HISTORICAL SCHOOLS

AFANAS'EV, I. N., *Istorizm protiv eklektiki: Frantsuzkaia istoricheskaia shkola Annalov'v sovremennoi [Historism Against Eclecticism: French "Annales" School in Contemporary Bourgeois Historiography]* (Moscow: Myse, 1980).

ALLEGRA, LUCIANO, AND ANGELO TORRE, *La Nascita della storia sociale in Francia* (Turin: Einaudi, 1977).

ARIÈS, PHILIPPE, WITH M. WINOCK, *Un Historien du dimanche* (Paris: Seuil, 1980).

ATSMA, HARTMUT AND ANDRÉ BURGUIÈRE, eds., *Marc Bloch aujourd'hui: Histoire comparée et sciences sociales* (Paris: Editions de l'Ecole des Hautes Etudes en Sciences Sociales, 1990).

AYMARD, MAURICE, "The 'Annales' and French Historiography," *The Journal of European Economic History* 1 (1972), pp. 491–511.

BLOCH, MARC, *Apologie pour l'histoire ou métier d'historien* (Paris: Armand Colin, 1949). [English translation: *The Historian's Craft,* trans. Peter Putnam (Manchester, Eng.: Manchester University Press, 1954)]

BOURDÉ, GUY, AND HERVÉ MARTIN, *Les Ecoles historiques* (Paris: Seuil, 1983).

BRAUDEL, FERNAND, *Ecrits sur l'histoire* (Paris: Flammarion, 1969). [English translation: *On History,* trans. Sarah Matthews (Chicago: University of Chicago Press, 1980)]

BURGUIÈRE, ANDRÉ, ed., *Dictionnaire des sciences historiques* (Paris: P.U.F., 1986).

————, "The Fate of the History of 'Mentalités' in the 'Annales'," *Comparative Studies in Society and History* 24 (1982), pp. 424–37.

BURKE, PETER, *The French Historical Revolution: The* Annales *School, 1929–89* (Oxford, Eng.: Polity, 1989).

CARBONELL, CHARLES OLIVIER, AND GEORGES LIVET, eds., *Au Berceau des Annales: Le milieu strasbourgeois. L'histoire en France au début du XXe siècle,* Actes du colloque de Strasbourg, October 11–13, 1979 (Toulouse: Presses de l'Institut d'Etudes Politiques de Toulouse, 1983).

CEDRONIO, M., F. DIAZ, AND C. RUSSO, *Storiografia francese di ieri e di oggi* (Naples: Guida, 1977).

CERTEAU, MICHEL DE, *L'Absent de l'histoire* (Tours: Mame, 1973).

————, *L'Ecriture de l'histoire* (Paris: Gallimard, 1975. [English trans: *The Writing of History,* trans. Tom Conley (New York: Columbia University Press, 1988)]

CHAUNU, PIERRE, *Histoire science sociale: La durée, l'espace et l'homme à l'époque moderne* (Paris: SEDES, 1973).

————, *Histoire quantitative, histoire sérielle,* "Cahiers des Annales" 37 (Paris: Armand Colin, 1978).

CHIROT, DANIEL, "The Social and Historical Landscape of Marc Bloch," in Theda Skocpol, ed., *Vision and Method in Historical Sociology* (Cambridge, Eng.: Cambridge University Press, 1984), pp. 22–46.

COMITÉ FRANÇAIS DE SCIENCES HISTORIQUES, ed., *La Recherche historique en France de 1940 à 1965* (Paris: CNRS, 1965).

COUTEAU-BÉGARIE, HERVÉ, *Le Phénomène "nouvelle histoire": stratégie et idéologie des nouveaux historiens* (Paris: Economica, 1983).

DI DONATO, RICCARDO, *Per una antropologia storica del mondo antico* (Florence: Nueva Italia, 1990).

DUMOULIN, OLIVIER, *"Profession historien," 1919–1939: Un métier en crise?,* thèse de 3e cycle, Ecole des Hautes Études en Sciences Sociales, Paris, 1983 (429 p.).

ERBE, M., *Zur neueren französischen Sozialgeschichtsforschung: Die Gruppe um die "Annales"* (Darmstadt: Wissenschaftliche Buchgesellschaft, 1979).

FEBVRE, LUCIEN, WITH L. BATAILLON, *La Terre et l'évolution humaine: Introduction géographique à l'histoire* (Paris: Renaissance du Livre, 1922). [English transation: *A Geographical Introduction to History,* trans. E. G. Mountford and J. H. Paxton (London: Kegan Paul, 1932)]

FINK, CAROLE, *Marc Bloch: A Life in History* (Cambridge, Eng.: Cambridge University Press, 1989).

FORSTER, ROBERT, "Achievements of the 'Annales' School," *Journal of Economic History* 38 (1978), pp. 58–76.

FURET, FRANÇOIS, *L'Atelier de l'histoire* (Paris: Flammarion, 1982). [English translation: *In the Workshop of History,* trans. Jonathan Mandelbaum (Chicago: University of Chicago Press, 1984)]

GEMELLI, GIULIANA, AND MARIA MALATESTA, eds., *Forme di sociabilità nella storiografia francese contemporanea* (Milan: Feltrinelli, 1982).

GILBERT, FELIX, "Three Twentieth Century Historians: Meinecke, Bloch, Chabot," in John Higham, Leonard Krieger, and Felix Gilbert, eds., *History* (London, 1965).

GLÉNISSON, JEAN, "L'Historiographie française contemporaine: Tendances et réalisations," in *La Recherche historique en France de 1940 à 1965* (Paris: CNRS, 1965), pp. ix–lxiv.

GUREVICH, ARON, "Medieval Culture and Mentality according to the New French Historiography,"*Archives européennes de sociologie* 24.1 (1983), pp. 167–95.

HILL, A. O., AND B. H. HILL, "Marc Bloch and Comparative History," *American Historical Review* 85 (1980), pp. 828–46.

"Histoire des sciences et mentalités," *Revue de synthèse* 111–12, special issue (1983).

Historiens et sociologues aujourd'hui, Journées d'études annuelles de la Société française de sociologie (Lille, June 14–15, 1984) (Paris: CNRS, 1986).

KEYLOR, WILLIAM R., *Academy and Community: The Foundation of the French Historical Profession* (Cambridge, Mass.: Harvard University Press, 1975).

KINSER, SAM, "Annales Paradigm: The Geo-Historical Structuralism of Fernand Braudel," *American Historical Review* 86 (1981), pp. 63–105.

LE GOFF, JACQUES, *Intervista sulla storia* (Bari: Laterza, 1982).

LE GOFF, JACQUES, AND PIERRE NORA, eds., *Faire de l'histoire* (Paris: Gallimard, 1974), 3 vols. [English translation: *Constructing the Past: Essays in Historical Methodology* (Cambridge, Eng.: Cambridge University Press, 1985)]

LE GOFF, JACQUES, ROGER CHARTIER, AND JACQUES REVEL, eds., *La Nouvelle histoire* (Paris: Retz, 1978).

Lendemains, Zeitschrift für Frankreichforschung und Französischstudium 2, special issue on the *Annales* (Nov. 1981)

MANN, HANS DIETER, *Lucien Febvre: La Pensée vivante d'un historien,* preface by Fernand Braudel (Paris: Armand Colin, 1971).

MASTROGREGORI, MASSIMO, *Il Genio dello storico: Le considerazioni sulla storia di Marc Bloch e Lucien Febvre e la tradizione metodologicà francese* (Naples: Edizioni Scientifiche Italiane, 1987).

MAZON, BRIGITTE, *Aux Origines de l'Ecole des Hautes Études en Sciences Sociales: Le rôle du mécénat américain (1920–1960)* (Paris: Cerf, 1988).

Mélanges en l'honneur de Fernand Braudel (Toulouse: Privat, 1973), 2 vols., with a bibliography on the writings of Braudel.

NORA, PIERRE, *Les Lieux de mémoire* (Paris: Gallimard, 1986), Vol. 2: *La Nation.*

POMIAN, KRZYSZTOF, "L'Heure des *Annales*: La terre—les hommes—le monde," in Pierre Nora, ed., *Les Lieux de mémoire,* vol. 2: *La Nation* (Paris: Gallimard, 1986), pp. 377–429.

REVEL, JACQUES, "Les Paradigmes des Annales," *Annales ESC* 6 (1979), pp. 1360–76.

Review 1. 3–4, special issue on the *Annales* school (1978).

RONCAYOLO, MARCEL, *La Ville et ses territoires* (Paris: Gallimard, 1990).

SIMIAND, FRANÇOIS, *Méthode historique et sciences sociales,* ed. Marina Cedronio (Paris: Archives contemporaines, 1987).

STOIANOVICH, TRAIAN, *French Historical Method: The* Annales *Paradigm* (Ithaca, N.Y.: Cornell University Press, 1976), preface by Fernand Braudel.

Y a-t-il une nouvelle histoire? Colloquium, Loches, 1980.

III. GENERAL ISSUES IN HISTORICAL SCHOLARSHIP

ARON, RAYMOND, *Introduction à la philosophie de l'histoire* (Paris: Gallimard, 1938); (nouvelle édition critique par S. Mesme, Paris, Gallimard, 1986). [English translation: *Introduction to the Philosophy of History: An Essay on the Limits of Historical Objectivity,* trans. George J. Irwin (Westport, Conn.: Greenwood, 1976)]

————, *Leçons sur l'histoire* (Paris: Fallois, 1989).

BURKE, PETER, ed., *New Perspectives on Historical Writing* (Oxford: Polity, 1991).

CANTIMORI, DELIO, *Storici e storia: Metodo, caratteristiche e significato del lavoro storiografico* (Turin: Einaudi, 1971).

FAURE, PIERRE, "La Constitution d'une science du politique, le déplacement des objets et l'irruption de l'histoire réelle," *Revue française de science politique* 33.2 (1983), pp. 181–219.

HEXTER, J. H., *On Historians: Reappraisals of Some of the Makers of Modern History* (Cambridge, Mass.: Harvard University Press, 1979).

HOBSBAWM, ERIC J., "From Social History to the History of Society," in F. Gilbert and S. S. Graubard, *Daedalus* 100, special issue: "Historical Studies Today" (1971), pp. 20–45.

IGGERS, GEORG G., AND PARKER, HAROLD T., eds., *International Handbook of Historical Studies, Contemporary Research and Theory* (Westport, Conn.: Methuen, 1980).

IGGERS, GEORG G., *New Directions in European Historiography* (Middletown, Conn.: Wesleyan University Press, 1975).

KUHN, THOMAS *The Structure of Scientific Revolutions* (2d ed., Chicago: University of Chicago Press, 1970).

MOMIGLIANO, ARNALDO, "Linee per una valutazione della storiografia nel quindicennio 1961–1976," *Rivista storica italiana* 3–4 (1977), pp. 596–609.

————, "Lo Storicismo nel pensiero contemporaneo," *Rivista storica italiana* 73 (1961), pp. 104–19.

POMIAN, KRZYSZTOF, *L'Ordre du temps* (Paris: Gallimard, 1984).

RABB, THEODORE K., AND ROBERT I. ROTBERG, eds., *The New History: The 1980s and Beyond: Studies in Interdisciplinary History* (Princeton, N.J.: Princeton University Press, 1982).

REDONDI, PIETRO, ed., "Science: The Renaissance of a History," *History and Technology* 4.1–4, special issue: Actes du colloque international Alexandre Koyré, Paris, 1986 (1987).

ROSSI, PIETRO, ed., *La Storia comparata: Approcci e prospettive* (Milan: Saggiatore, 1990).

STONE, LAWRENCE, *The Past and the Present* (London: Routledge and Kegan Paul, 1982).

VEYNE, PAUL, *Comment on écrit l'histoire: Essai d'épistémologie* (Paris: Seuil, 1971). [English translation: *Writing History: Essay on Epistemology,* trans. Mina Moore-Rinvolucri (Middletown, Conn.: Wesleyan University Press, 1984)].